THE CAMBRIDGE COMPANION TO

HEGEL AND NINETEENTH-CENTURY PHILOSOPHY

The Cambridge Companion to Hegel and Nineteenth-Century Philosophy examines Hegel within his broader historical and philosophical contexts. Covering all major aspects of Hegel's philosophy, the volume provides an introduction to his logic, epistemology, philosophy of mind, social and political philosophy, philosophy of nature, and aesthetics. It includes essays by an internationally recognized team of Hegel scholars. The volume begins with Terry Pinkard's article on Hegel's life – a conspectus of his biography on Hegel. It also explores some new topics much neglected in Hegel scholarship, such as Hegel's hermeneutics and relationship to mysticism. Aimed at students and scholars of Hegel, this volume will be essential reading for anyone interested in nineteenth-century philosophy. The up-to-date bibliography includes the most important English-language literature on Hegel written in the last fifteen years.

Frederick C. Beiser is Professor of Philosophy at Syracuse University. He is the author of *The Romantic Imperative, German Idealism*, and *Hegel* and is the editor of *The Cambridge Companion to Hegel*.

OTHER VOLUMES IN THE SERIES OF CAMBRIDGE COMPANIONS:

ABELARD *Edited by* JEFFREY E. BROWER *and* KEVIN GUILFOY
ADORNO *Edited by* THOMAS HUHN
ANSELM *Edited by* BRIAN DAVIES *and* BRIAN LEFTOW
AQUINAS *Edited by* NORMAN KRETZMANN *and* ELEONORE STUMP
ARABIC PHILOSOPHY *Edited by* PETER ADAMSON *and* RICHARD C. TAYLOR
HANNAH ARENDT *Edited by* DANA VILLA
ARISTOTLE *Edited by* JONATHAN BARNES
ATHEISM *Edited by* MICHAEL MARTIN
AUGUSTINE *Edited by* ELEONORE STUMP *and* NORMAN KRETZMANN
BACON *Edited by* MARKKU PELTONEN
BERKELEY *Edited by* KENNETH P. WINKLER
BRENTANO *Edited by* DALE JACQUETTE
CARNAP *Edited by* RICHARD CREATH *and* MICHAEL FRIEDMAN
CRITICAL THEORY *Edited by* FRED RUSH
DARWIN *Edited by* JONATHAN HODGE *and* GREGORY RADICK
SIMONE DE BEAUVOIR *Edited by* CLAUDIA CARD
PICO DELLA MIRANDOLA: NEW ESSAYS *Edited by* M. V. DOUGHERTY
DESCARTES *Edited by* JOHN COTTINGHAM
DUNS SCOTUS *Edited by* THOMAS WILLIAMS
EARLY GREEK PHILOSOPHY *Edited by* A. A. LONG
EARLY MODERN PHILOSOPHY *Edited by* MICHAEL RUTHERFORD
FEMINISM IN PHILOSOPHY *Edited by* MIRANDA FRICKER *and* JENNIFER HORNSBY
FOUCAULT 2nd edition *Edited by* GARY GUTTING
FREUD *Edited by* JEROME NEU
GADAMER *Edited by* ROBERT J. DOSTAL
GALEN *Edited by* R. J. HANKINSON
GALILEO *Edited by* PETER MACHAMER
GERMAN IDEALISM *Edited by* KARL AMERIKS
GREEK AND ROMAN PHILOSOPHY *Edited by* DAVID SEDLEY
HABERMAS *Edited by* STEPHEN K. WHITE
HAYEK *Edited by* EDWARD FESER

Continued after the Index

The Cambridge Companion to

HEGEL AND NINETEENTH-CENTURY PHILOSOPHY

Edited by
Frederick C. Beiser
Syracuse University

CAMBRIDGE
UNIVERSITY PRESS

CAMBRIDGE UNIVERSITY PRESS
Cambridge, New York, Melbourne, Madrid, Cape Town, Singapore, São Paulo, Delhi

Cambridge University Press
32 Avenue of the Americas, New York, NY 10013-2473, USA

www.cambridge.org
Information on this title: www.cambridge.org/9780521539388

First published 2008

Printed in the United States of America

A catalog record for this publication is available from the British Library.

Library of Congress Cataloging in Publication Data

The Cambridge companion to Hegel and nineteenth-century philosophy /
edited by Frederick C. Beiser.
    p.   cm. – (Cambridge companions)
Includes bibliographical references (p.   ) and index.
ISBN 978-0-521-83167-3 (hardback) – ISBN 978-0-521-53938-8 (pbk.)
    1. Hegel, Georg Wilhelm Friedrich, 1770–1831.   I. Beiser, Frederick C., 1949–
II. Title: Companion to Hegel and nineteenth-century philosophy.   III. Series.
B2948.C283   2008
193–dc22   2008021176

ISBN   978-0-521-83167-3 hardback
ISBN   978-0-521-53938-8 paperback

Contents

Preface   *page* ix

Contributors   xi

Introduction: The Puzzling Hegel Renaissance   1
FREDERICK BEISER

1   Hegel: A Life   15
    TERRY PINKARD

2   Ancient Skepticism, Modern Naturalism, and
    Nihilism in Hegel's Early Jena Writings   52
    PAUL FRANKS

3   Hegel's *Phenomenology* as a Systematic Fragment   74
    JON STEWART

4   The Independence and Dependence of
    Self-Consciousness: The Dialectic of Lord and
    Bondsman in Hegel's *Phenomenology of Spirit*   94
    PAUL REDDING

5   Hegel's Logic   111
    STEPHEN HOULGATE

6   Hegel's Idealism   135
    ROBERT STERN

7   Hegel and Hermeneutics   174
    MICHAEL N. FORSTER

8   Hegel's Social Philosophy   204
    FREDERICK NEUHOUSER

9   Hegel's Philosophy of Religion   230
    PETER C. HODGSON

10 Hegel and Mysticism   253
    GLENN ALEXANDER MAGEE

vii

viii   Contents

11   Philosophizing about Nature: Hegel's Philosophical Project   281
      KENNETH R. WESTPHAL

12   Hegel's Criticism of Newton   311
      EDWARD C. HALPER

13   The Logic of Life: Hegel's Philosophical Defense of
      Teleological Explanation of Living Beings   344
      JAMES KREINES

14   Hegel and Aesthetics: The Practice and "Pastness" of Art   378
      ALLEN SPEIGHT

15   The Absence of Aesthetics in Hegel's Aesthetics   394
      ROBERT PIPPIN

Bibliography   419
Index   423

Preface

In the spring of 2002, the late Terry Moore proposed that I produce a new edition of *The Cambridge Companion to Hegel*, the original of which had appeared in 1993. What precise form the new edition should take was left to my discretion. After discussion with Paul Guyer, who received a similar request around the same time regarding *The Cambridge Companion to Kant*, I decided to produce a completely new collection of essays rather than re-editing the older ones. Although I had no misgivings about the first edition, I thought that a new edition would be more fruitful for Hegel scholarship. It was one of the aims of the *Companion* series, as conceived by Terry Moore, that it should be in the vanguard of discussion in the field. In that spirit, it seemed that a completely new edition was better than just a revised version of the older one. This gave opportunity for older contributors to write on new topics as well as for new contributors to join in the discussion.

This new edition is not meant to replace the older one but to complement it. Like the older edition, this one strives to provide a broad introduction to Hegel's philosophy. But it also attempts to cover areas of Hegel's philosophy that were omitted or underrepresented in the older edition. The previous edition contained little about Hegel's philosophy of religion and *Naturphilosophie*, whereas this edition has two essays on Hegel's philosophy of religion (those by Magee and Hodgson) and three on Hegel's philosophy of nature (those by Westphal, Halper, and Kreines). This edition also focuses more on the aesthetics (the essays by Pippin and Speight) and the epistemological issues surrounding Hegel's philosophy (the essays by Franks and Forster).

I thank the many contributors to this volume for their patience for its slow and delayed production. Like all volumes in the *Companion* series, this one is a tribute to Terry Moore.

Frederick Beiser
Syracuse, May 2008

New York Press, 1998); "Hegel's Family Values," *Review of Metaphysics* 54 (2001), 815–858; "The Idealism of Hegel's System," *The Owl of Minerva* 34 (2002), 19–58; and "Positive and Negative Dialectics: Hegel's *Wissenschaft der Logik* and Plato's *Parmenides*," in *Platonismus im Idealismus: Die platonische Tradition in der klassischen deutschen Philosophie*, edited by B. Mojsisch and O. F. Summerell (Munich: K. G. Saur Verlag, 2003). He has been particularly interested in understanding the systematic dimension of Hegel's philosophy and in showing how Hegel uses categories from his *Logic* to treat other topics.

PETER C. HODGSON is Charles G. Finney Professor of Theology, Emeritus, Divinity School, Vanderbilt University. He coordinated a new edition and translation of Hegel's *Lectures on the Philosophy of Religion* (1984–1988), which was recently reprinted by Oxford University Press. His monograph, *Hegel and Christian Theology* (2005), and his edition/translation of *Hegel's Lectures on the Proofs of the Existence of God* (2007) have been published by Oxford University Press.

STEPHEN HOULGATE is a professor of philosophy at the University of Warwick. He is the author of *Hegel, Nietzsche and the Criticism of Metaphysics* (Cambridge University Press, 1986); *An Introduction to Hegel: Freedom, Truth and History* (2nd ed. Blackwell, 2005); and *The Opening of Hegel's Logic: From Being to Infinity* (Purdue University Press, 2006). He is also the editor of *Hegel and the Philosophy of Nature* (SUNY Press, 1998), *The Hegel Reader* (Blackwell, 1998), and *Hegel and the Arts* (Northwestern University Press, 2007). He has served as vice president and president of the Hegel Society of America and was editor of the *Bulletin of the Hegel Society of Great Britain* from 1998 to 2007.

JAMES KREINES is Assistant Professor of Philosophy at Claremont McKenna College. He has written articles on metaphysics, epistemology, and philosophy of science in Kant and Hegel, including "Between the Bounds of Experience and Divine Intuition" in *Inquiry* (2007); "The Inexplicability of Kant's Naturzweck" in *Archiv für Geschichte der Philosophie* (2005); and "Hegel's Critique of Pure Mechanism and the Philosophical Appeal of the Logic Project" in *European Journal of Philosophy* (2004). His current work aims to interpret the different forms of idealism defended by both Kant and Hegel and to uncover the different philosophical strengths of both views.

GLENN ALEXANDER MAGEE is Assistant Professor of Philosophy at the C.W. Post Campus of Long Island University. He is the author of *Hegel and the Hermetic Tradition* (Cornell University Press, 2001; revised paperback edition 2008) and *The Hegel Dictionary* (forthcoming from Continuum) and editor of *The Cambridge Handbook of Western Mysticism and Esotericism* (forthcoming from Cambridge University Press).

FREDERICK NEUHOUSER is Professor of Philosophy at Barnard College, Columbia University. He is the author of *Rousseau's Theodicy of Self-Love (Amour-propre): Evil, Rationality, and the Drive for Recognition* (Oxford University Press, 2008); *Foundations of Hegel's Social Theory* (Harvard University Press, 2000); and *Fichte's Theory of Subjectivity* (Cambridge University Press, 1990).

TERRY PINKARD is Professor of Philosophy at Georgetown University. He is the author of *Hegel* (Cambridge University Press, 2000) and *German Philosophy, 1760–1860: The Legacy of Idealism* (Cambridge University Press, 2002). He also edited and wrote the introduction for *Henrich Heine: On the History of Religion and Philosophy in Germany* (Cambridge Texts in the History of Philosophy, Cambridge University Press, 2007).

ROBERT PIPPIN is Evelyn Stefanson Nef Distinguished Service Professor in the Committee on Social Thought, University of Chicago. He is the author of many books on Kant and German Idealism, among them *Kant's Theory of Form* (Yale University Press, 1982); *Hegel's Idealism: The Satisfactions of Self-Consciousness* (Cambridge University Press, 1989); *Idealism as Modernism* (Cambridge University Press, 1997); and *The Persistence of Subjectivity: On the Kantian Aftermath* (Cambridge University Press, 2005).

PAUL REDDING is Professor of Philosophy at the University of Sydney. He is the author of *Hegel's Hermeneutics* (Cornell University Press, 1996), The *Logic of Affect* (Cornell University Press, 1999), *Analytic Philosophy and the Return of Hegelian Thought* (Cambridge University Press, 2007), and *Continental Idealism: Leibniz to Nietzsche*, to be published by Routledge in 2009.

ALLEN SPEIGHT is Associate Professor of Philosophy at Boston University. He is a recipient of Fulbright, DAAD, and NEH fellowships and is the author of *Hegel, Literature and the Problem of Agency* (Cambridge University Press, 2001) and *The Philosophy of Hegel* (Acumen/McGill-Queen's University Press, 2008). He is the editor and translator (with Brady Bowman) of *Hegel: Heidelberg Writings* (Cambridge University Press, 2009). He has published numerous journal articles on aesthetics and ethics in German Idealism and Romanticism.

ROBERT STERN is Professor of Philosophy at the University of Sheffield. He is the author of *Hegel, Kant and the Structure of the Object* (Routledge, 1990); *Hegel and the Phenomenology of Spirit* (Routledge, 2002); and *Hegelian Metaphysics* (Oxford University Press, forthcoming).

JON STEWART is Associate Research Professor at the Soren Kierkegaard Research Centre at the University of Copenhagen. He is the author of *The Unity of Hegel's Phenomenology of Spirit* (Northwestern University Press, 2000), *Kierkegaard's Relations to Hegel Reconsidered* (Cambridge University Press, 2003), and *A History of Hegelianism in Golden Age Denmark* (C. A. Reitzel, 2007). He is also the editor of *The Hegel Myths and Legends* (Northwestern University Press, 1996).

KENNETH R. WESTPHAL is Professor of Philosophy at the University of Kent, Canterbury. He has published widely on both Kant's and Hegel's theoretical and practical philosophies. His books on Hegel include *Hegel's Epistemological Realism* (Kluwer, 1989); *Hegel, Hume und die Identität wahrnembarer Dinge* (Klostermann, 1998); and *Hegel's Epistemology: A Philosophical Introduction to the Phenomenology of Spirit* (Hackett, 2003). He is editor of *The Blackwell Guide to Hegel's Phenomenology of Spirit* (Blackwell, 2008) and is completing a book titled *From Naive Realism to Understanding: Hegel's Critique of Cognitive Judgment*.

THE CAMBRIDGE COMPANION TO
HEGEL AND NINETEENTH-CENTURY PHILOSOPHY

Introduction: The Puzzling Hegel Renaissance

No one who looks at the bibliography to this new edition of *The Cambridge Companion to Hegel* will be unimpressed by the remarkable growth of interest in Hegel. The bibliography covers only the last fifteen years – roughly those since the appearance of the first edition of this book – and it deals with books in English alone. To prevent it from ballooning to twice, thrice, or four times its size, the editor had to exclude French, German, and Italian books on Hegel. Such a surge in interest is remarkable for any philosopher, but especially for one who, some fifty years earlier, would have been treated as a pariah.

How do we explain the great contemporary interest in Hegel? It is necessary to admit that it is rather puzzling. After the rise of analytic philosophy in the 1920s, and due to the growing influence of positivism in the 1930s, Hegel's reputation fell into steep decline in Britain. The patron saint of British Idealism had become the ogre of positivism and the very model of how *not* to do philosophy. Hegel's fortunes began to change in the 1960s as the result of the growth of interest in Marxism. For the student rebellion and trade union movements of the 1960s, Marx became the guiding spirit; but the Marx that inspired them was not so much the mature Marx of *Das Kapital* but the early Marx of the 1844 Paris manuscripts. The concepts and terminology of the early Marx – "alienation," "self-consciousness," "mediation" – made Marx's debts to his great forbear obvious. It was clear that one could understand the precise meaning of these important but strange concepts only if one made an intensive study of Hegel, who had not been studied in Britain since the early 1900s. Although Marx claimed that he broke with Hegel – that he stood Hegel on his head – it was obvious that one could appreciate this only with a good grasp of Hegel. And so Hegel was once again on the agenda, someone worth studying, talking, and writing about, even if he was treated only as a footstool for Marx. Not surprisingly, the study of Hegel was mainly focused on his more social and political works, especially the *Phenomenology of Spirit, Philosophy of Right,* and *Philosophy of World History.*[1] No one bothered with the study of Hegel's system as a whole, still less any of its integral parts: the *Philosophy of Nature, Philosophy of Spirit,* and, least of all, the *Science of Logic.*

Yet, what is so puzzling about the contemporary interest in Hegel is how much it has outlived the original source of its inspiration. With the fall of the Berlin Wall and the collapse of the Soviet Empire, Marxism has suffered – for better or worse – a steep decline in prestige. But as Marx's star fell, Hegel's only rose. Somehow, the servant to Marx became a master in his own right. Now every aspect of his philosophy became of interest. Hegel was restored to the pantheon of great philosophers, taking his place alongside Leibniz and Kant.

So our original question returns: Why the contemporary interest in Hegel? How has it managed to outlive its initial debt to Marxism? The mystery only deepens when we consider the subsequent course of the Hegel renaissance. The apex of the Anglophone Hegel revival was the publication in 1975 of Charles Taylor's *Hegel.*[2] With grace, precision, and remarkable erudition, Taylor surveyed the depth and breadth of Hegel's entire system and showed it to be an edifice of great intellectual subtlety and sophistication. Unlike earlier scholars, Taylor did not limit himself to Hegel's social and political thought; he treated every aspect of Hegel's system and examined in depth its central core and foundation: its metaphysics. The central theme of that metaphysics, Taylor argued, was the concept of self-positing spirit. What held every part of the system together, what made it into a unified whole, was the idea of an absolute spirit that posits itself in and through history and nature. Because of its remarkable clarity, Taylor's book proved to be a great success, going through several editions and translations. Yet, it is difficult to understand how Taylor's book could lead to a growth in interest in Hegel. The idea of self-positing spirit, which Taylor made the very heart of Hegel's philosophy, is so speculative, so metaphysical,

---

[1] The chief monographs were Shlomo Avineri, *Hegel's Theory of the Modern State* (Cambridge, UK: Cambridge University Press, 1972); G. D. O'Brian, *Hegel on Reason and History* (Chicago: University of Chicago Press, 1975); B. T. Wilkins, *Hegel's Philosophy of History* (Ithaca: Cornell University Press, 1974); Bernard Cullen, *Hegel's Social and Political Thought* (Dublin: Gill & Macmillan, 1979); and Raymond Plant, *Hegel* (London: George, Allen & Unwin, 1971). Also much discussed in the 1970s were George Armstrong Kelly, *Idealism, Politics and History: Sources of Hegelian Thought* (Cambridge, UK: Cambridge Univerity Press, 1969), John Plamenatz's two chapters on Hegel in *Man and Society* (London: Longman, 1963), II, pp. 129–268; and Z. A. Pelczynski's substantial "Introduction" to *Hegel's Political Writings* (Oxford: Oxford University Press, 1964), pp. 5–137.

[2] Charles Taylor, *Hegel* (Cambridge, UK: Cambridge University Press, 1975).

and so religious that it is hard to understand how it could convince modern readers of Hegel's intellectual merits. These readers had been raised in a much more secular and skeptical age, in a philosophical culture suffused with positivism, and so the idea of a self-positing spirit proved very problematic. When Taylor's book appeared, the academic establishment in Britain and the United States was already dominated by analytic philosophy, which never had much time for metaphysics. So, ironically, given the emphasis it placed on Hegel's metaphysics, and given the anti-metaphysical atmosphere in Anglophone academia, Taylor's book was more likely to bury than revive Hegel. Yet, interest in Hegel only grew. Why?

For all its merits, this had little to do, I believe, with Taylor's book. Instead, it had much more to do with the fact that scholars began to ignore or underplay that aspect of Hegel's philosophy that Taylor had placed center stage: metaphysics. Some scholars fully admitted the metaphysical dimension of Hegel's philosophy; nevertheless, they insisted it is not important for every aspect of his philosophy, especially his social and political thought. Since the early 1960s, many scholars of Hegel's social and political thought claimed that it could be understood without his metaphysics.[3] Hegel was appreciated for his critique of liberalism, his conception of freedom, and his theory of the state, all of which seemed to have point and meaning independent of the rest of his system. To see value in Hegel's critique of social atomism or contract theory, for example, one did not have to accept his theory of self-positing spirit. Other scholars, however, began to question the metaphysical

---

[3] The first of these scholars was Z. A. Pelczynski in "An Introductory Essay" to his edition of *Hegel's Political Writings*, trans. by T. M. Knox (Oxford: Clarendon Press, 1964). Since then, many other scholars have followed his lead and the nonmetaphysical approach has been the dominant one in the interpretation of Hegel's social and political thought. See Steven Smith, *Hegel's Critique of Liberalism* (Chicago: University of Chicago Press, 1989), p. xi; Allen Wood, *Hegel's Ethical Thought* (Cambridge, UK: Cambridge University Press, 1990), pp. 4–6; Mark Tunick, *Hegel's Political Phiosophy* (Princeton: Princeton University Press, 1992), pp. 14, 17, 86, 99; Michael Hardimon, *Hegel's Social Philosophy* (Cambridge, UK: Cambridge University Press, 1994), p. 8; and Alan Patten, *Hegel's Idea of Freedom* (Oxford: Oxford University Press, 1999), pp. 16–27; Paul Franco, *Hegel's Philosophy of Freedom* (New Haven, CT: Yale University Press, 1999), pp. 83–84, 126, 135–136, 140, 151–152, 360–361; John Rawls, *Lectures on the History of Moral Philosophy* (Cambridge, MA: Harvard University Press, 2000), p. 330. For some protests against this approach, see Yirmiahu Yovel, "Hegel's Dictum that the Rational is the Actual and the Actual is the Rational," in *The Hegel Myths and Legends*, ed. by Jon Stewart (Evanston, IL: Northwestern University Press, 1996), pp. 26–41; and Adrian Peperzak, *Modern Freedom: Hegel's Legal, Moral and Political Phiosophy* (Dordrecht, The Netherlands: Kluwer, 2001), pp. 5–19.

interpretation of Hegel's philosophy, claiming that his entire system is best understood apart from, or even as a reaction against, traditional metaphysics. Taylor's interpretation was rejected because it seemed to make Hegel's thought much too metaphysical. Since the 1970s there have been at least three kinds of nonmetaphysical interpretations. First among them was the *category theory* of Klaus Hartmann and his school.[4] According to Hartmann, Hegel's philosophy is not speculation about mysterious entities, such as the absolute or spirit, but an attempt to develop a system of categories, the most basic concepts by which we think about the world. It is only in a metaphorical sense that Hegel's *Science of Logic* is about "the essence of God before the creation of the world"; in the proper literal sense it is only about the structure of our most basic concepts, those necessary to think about being as such. Another nonmetaphysical interpretation was that developed by Robert Pippin in his *Hegel's Idealism*.[5] Pippin places Hegel's idealism essentially in the Kantian tradition, as a theory about the necessary conditions of possible experience. The subject that is at the heart of Hegel's idealism lies not in any conception of a self-positing spirit but in Kant's unity of *apperception*, the principle that self-consciousness is a necessary condition for all experience. Yet another nonmetaphysical approach has been worked out more recently by Robert Brandom.[6] "The master idea that animates and structures Hegel's metaphysics and logic," Brandom writes, is "his way of working out the Kant–Rousseau insight about a fundamental kind of normativity based on autonomy according to the model of reciprocal authority and responsibility whose paradigm is mutual recognition."[7] Brandom sees Hegel as fundamentally a theorist about the normative dimension of life, experience, and discourse, and claims that all his talk about spirit has to be understood in terms of the mutual recognition implicit in such norms.

So we now have something of an explanation for our mystery, for why the Hegel revival survived the decline of Marxism and Taylor's metaphysical interpretation. Interest in Hegel endured because the most difficult and troubling aspect of his philosophy – his metaphysics – was either ignored or read out of his system. The nonmetaphysical readings

---

[4] See Klaus Hartmann, "Hegel: A Non-Metaphysical View," in *Hegel*, ed. by A. MacIntyre. New York: Doubleday, 1972), pp. 101–124. See also the anthology of his students, *Hegel Reconsidered*, ed. by Terry Pinkard (Dordrecht, The Netherlands: Kluwer, 1994).
[5] Robert Pippin, *Hegel's Idealism: The Satisfactions of Self-Consciousness* (Cambridge, UK: Cambridge University Press, 1989).
[6] Robert Brandom, *Tales of the Mighty Dead* (Cambridge, MA: Harvard University Press, 2002).
[7] Ibid, p. 234.

of Hegel have been acts of enormous interpretative charity: they have interpreted Hegel in a way to make him acceptable to the standards of a more secular and positivistic age. They have worked so well because they have made Hegel conform to the image of what we think a philosopher should be.

Yet, despite their success, these interpretations have not been able to suppress a nagging doubt: Are we interested in Hegel only because we have made him reflect *our* interests? Do we find him acceptable now only because we have re-created him in our image? If that is so, it leaves us with an even more troubling question: Is the Hegel revival perhaps a mistake? Are we interested in Hegel only because we have a false image of him?

Although the nonmetaphysical interpretations are interesting and illuminating, they have never succeeded in convincing many Hegel scholars. The problem is that the metaphysical dimension of Hegel's thought has proven stubbornly irreducible. When push comes to shove, all those who advocate a nonmetaphysical reading have to admit that they have not revived the real historical Hegel but only some aspect of him that reflects our own contemporary interests and values. One respect where the nonmetaphysical interpretations are especially problematic concerns the religious dimension of Hegel's thought. There can be no doubt that, ever since his Frankfurt years, a crucial part of Hegel's program was to demonstrate the fundamental truths of Christianity.[8] We have to take Hegel at his word when he tells us in his lectures on the philosophy of religion that God is the alpha and omega, the end and centerpoint of philosophy.[9] Of course, Hegel's God is not the theistic God of orthodox Christianity, and still less the deistic God of the eighteenth-century philosophers. Nevertheless, whatever the precise nature of his God, he still answered to the general concept of the infinite or absolute, and still complied with the St. Anselms classical definition of God as "*id quo nihil maius cogitari possit*" (that of which nothing greater can be conceived). We cannot explain away the Hegelian absolute in terms of the completeness of a system of categories, the subject of the Kantian unity of apperception, or the structure of mutual recognition involved in norms. For all these interpretations give us only one half of the Hegelian equation: the manner in which we *think* about the universe; they do not give us the other half: the universe itself. The

---

[8] See my *Hegel* (London: Routledge, 2005), pp. 124–152.
[9] See Hegel, *Vorlesungen über die Philosophie der Religion*, in *Werke in zwanzig Bänden*, ed. by E. Moldenhauer and K. Michel (Franfurt: Suhrkamp, 1969), XVI, 28, 32–33, 94. For the role of religion in Hegel's philosophy, see the article by Peter Hodgson in Chapter 9 in this volume.

Hegelian absolute was always meant to be the universe as a whole, the identity of subject and object, not only how we think about the world but the world itself.

Another respect in which the nonmetaphysical interpretations have proven problematic is with regard to Hegel's *Naturphilosophie*. This was an integral part of Hegel's system, indeed, its very heart and center, the middle part of the three-part *Encyclopedia of philosophical Sciences*. But its very large presence has always been an embarrassment for his nonmetaphysical expositors. In his *Naturphilosophie*, Hegel speculates about the nature of the living and material universe, and he employs an a priori methodology very unlike the method of observation and experiment of contemporary natural science. Hegel's *Naturphilosophie* is explicitly and emphatically a metaphysics. It is implausible to interpret it as only a system of categories, for Hegel is patently and explicitly attempting to tell us about nature itself, not only how we should think about it or the normative structure for discourse about it. In sum, Hegel's *Naturphilosophie* scarcely fits into the modern conception of natural science, and it is far removed from any contemporary conception of what philosophy should be. Yet there it is, in the very heart of his system, all 538 pages of it in the *Werkausgabe* edition.

It might now seem as if the Hegel revival has been indeed a mistake. The premise behind that revival is that Hegel has something interesting to say to us now from the standpoint of our own philosophical culture, that he can somehow address our philosophical concerns in the early twenty-first century. But the more we examine the real historical Hegel, the more we can say that his chief interests and goals were far removed from our own. For Hegel was first and foremost a metaphysician, someone intent on proving the existence of God, someone eager to establish a priori the first principles of *Naturphilosophie*. Nothing better, it seems, shows him to be a typical early nineteenth-century thinker. So, unless we are interested in the nineteenth century for its own sake, it would seem we have no reason to study Hegel. A contemporary philosopher has no more reason to study Hegel, it would seem, than he has reason to study Napoleon's strategy at the battle of Jena or the costume of the early romantic age.

At this point Hegel scholarship confronts a dilemma. If our scholarship is historically accurate, we confront a Hegel with profound metaphysical concerns alien to the spirit of contemporary philosophical culture, which mistrusts metaphysics. But if we continue to interpret Hegel in a nonmetaphysical manner, we have to accept that our interpretation is more a construction of our contemporary interests than the real historical school. This is just one version of the classical dilemma that plagues all history of philosophy: that between anachronism and antiquarianism. The more we interpret historical figures from *our* standpoint and according to our interests, the more we commit anachronism, imposing the present upon the past; but the more we interpret them from *their* standpoint, the more we engage in antiquarianism, as if any historical facts were interesting for their own sake.

Is this dilemma inescapable? It is not so in principle. We can imagine a more religious, less positivistic culture for which the original Hegelian program would be an inspiration. For this culture, the more it delves into the real historical Hegel, the more its philosophical interest grows, because the past very much reflects its own interests. Such, indeed, was the scenario behind the Hegel renaissance in England and North America in the late nineteenth and early twentieth centuries. Hegel was then much more popular and pervasive than he is today;[10] indeed, it is only when we realize this that we can understand the deep aversion to Hegel that has persisted in English philosophy for decades; that aversion was the product of a profound reaction. Since that culture was much more religious than our own, philosophers had a much less anachronistic and antiquarian interest in the real historical Hegel. For thinkers in this epoch were still troubled by the conflict between reason and faith, the very conflict that had once troubled Hegel himself. The problem for the Hegel revival, of course, is that our culture is no longer so religious. For our own more secular, scientific, and skeptical age, the dilemma does appear utterly inescapable.

We might think that the dilemma is escapable after all if we resort to a strategy often used by some scholars.[11] Although they admit that their nonmetaphysical interpretation does not conform exactly to the "letter" or appear in the texts of Hegel, they still claim that it represents his "spirit" or intention. It is as if their interpretation were what Hegel really meant to say after all, even if he never did say it *expressis verbis*. If we talk about what Hegel "really meant" or what he "intended to say," it seems as if we get around the gulf between the real historical Hegel and our contemporary philosophical interests. But this strategy engages in a form of self-deception. It conflates the factual with the normative,

---

[10] To get a sense of just how popular Hegel was in late nineteenth century Britain, see William James 1908 Hibbert Lectures *A Pluralistic Universe* (New York: Longmans & Green, 1909), pp. 52–54.

[11] For more on this strategy and those who employ it, see my "Dark Days: Anglophone Scholarship since the 1960s," in *German Idealism: Contemporary Perspectives*, ed. by Espen Hammer (London: Routledge, 2007), pp. 77–80.

what Hegel really did say with what we think he *ought to have said* if he were reasonable like us. Ultimately, we have to admit: it is a hypostasis of our own contemporary philosophical interests that has little to do with actual historical reality.

While the dilemma between antiquarianism and anachronism does seem inescapable, at least for our nonmetaphysical age, it does not follow that the Hegel revival is a mistake. It will be a mistake only if we continue to delude ourselves, that is, to assume that the real historical Hegel is essentially the same as our contemporary philosophical interests. But there is no need to make this assumption. We can admit that Hegel's philosophical program was essentially metaphysical, and that much of the historical Hegel is of little interest to us today. Nevertheless, having made this admission, we do not have to accept the dilemma in every respect, as if it were true across the board or for every aspect of Hegel. There are still many other aspects of the real historical Hegel that are still of philosophical interest for us today, and that we can proceed to reconstruct without fear of either anachronism or antiquarianism. Historical research on Hegel is not doomed to philosophical irrelevance; and philosophical reconstruction of Hegel need not be condemned to anachronism. But to avoid these extremes, the philosophical historian has to be skillful; he has to work back and forth between the demands of history and philosophy; he must know enough history to avoid anachronism, enough philosophy to avoid antiquarianism. If he is successful in negotiating between the demands of history and philosophy, he can sometimes find that middle path where the real historical Hegel and our contemporary interests coincide. This has indeed sometimes happened with the nonmetaphysical interpretations. Although these interpretations have been slow to acknowledge the distance between the real historical Hegel and their own reconstructions of him, they have sometimes brought out aspects of the real historical Hegel that are philosophically important and interesting.

In negotiating between the demands of philosophy and history, the philosophical historian can proceed in two different ways. He can begin from his own contemporary philosophical interests and hope that there is something answering to these interests in the real historical Hegel; or he can start from the real historical Hegel and hope that something philosophically interesting derives from him, something which might or might not answer to contemporary philosophical interests.

While either approach works and has its advantages, they also both have their risks and disadvantages. The former brings with it the risk of anachronism, the latter that of antiquarianism. On the whole, scholars in the Anglophone world have preferred the former approach, and so they have often run the risk of imposing their own philosophical interests on the texts and confusing their philosophical reconstruction with the real historical Hegel. The coincidence between the real historical Hegel and our contemporary interests is then only forced and artificial. We think that Hegel answers to our interests only because we read these interests into him.

To avoid this common pitfall, and contrary to the direction of most Anglophone scholarship, I would like to say a word here in behalf of the latter approach, the path less travelled. There is a strong case to be made for bracketing our own contemporary philosophical interests and examining Hegel in his historical context. In this case, we reconstruct Hegel's position as a contribution to a past conversation. We will fully understand the point and meaning of Hegel's philosophy only when we see it in discussion with the positions of others. If we ignore its precise place in the past conversation, we run the risk of confusing Hegel's position with those of others or we fail to see his precise intentions. This approach has the advantage of being closer to the real historical Hegel; and it has real philosophical content insofar as it sees Hegel's position in a philosophical discussion. While there is no a priori guarantee that closer historical study will bring results answering to our contemporary interests, it does have a possible greater benefit: that we widen our philosophical horizons and discover issues that are interesting for their own sake even if they answer to no contemporary concern. In the next section, I will suggest some of the ways in which this approach might take Hegel scholarship in new and interesting directions.

Granted that the Hegel renaissance is not a mistake, or at least need not be one, the question remains where it should go? Prima facie, it would seem that there is nowhere further that it can go; such has been the sheer volume of writings on Hegel that it would seem that no stone has been unturned and no corner unexplored. Indeed, repetition has become the order of the day: the same ground is gone over again and again, often with little variation. There are so many commentaries on Hegel's *Phenomenology*, so many studies of the *Philosophy of Right*, that there seems no point in doing another. If there were ever a case to be made for too many scholars chasing too few texts, it would seem to apply to Hegel's body of work.

Nevertheless, despite all the work done on Hegel, I would like to suggest that there is still much to do; indeed, in some respects, work has been scarcely begun. Let me just briefly indicate here some of the few places where Hegel research needs to go if it is to make any progress in the near future.

One of the most spectacular developments in research on German idealism in the last decades has been the *Konstellationsforschung* initiated by Dieter Henrich.[12] Crudely, *Konstellationsforschung* means the detailed investigation into the network of intellectual relationships between writers during the famous *Wunderjahre* in Jena and Weimar (1790–1800). This research attempts to get beyond the usual narrow focus on a few major writings of a few famous canonical figures, which fails to provide an accurate picture of a period as a whole. Instead, it strives to acquire a broader perspective by reconstructing, as far as possible or as the sources permit, the discussions between all the thinkers in a period, whether major or minor, that took place in letters, articles, reports on conversations, and so on. After these lost conversations have been reconstructed, it is then possible to see major works in their precise historical and philosophical context, to understand their point and meaning through their specific place in a discussion. The problem with the older approach, which was oriented toward the analysis of a few texts, is that it often gave a false impression about the period as a whole. If, for example, one were to generalize from a study of the main writings of Reinhold, Fichte, and Schelling, one would think that this period is characterized by the predominance of foundationalism, by a search for the self-evident first principles of philosophy from which all the results of Kant's philosophy could be deduced. But a closer examination of the discussions between the many more "minor" thinkers of this period demonstrates something much more interesting: that most thinkers were highly critical of Reinhold, Fichte, and Schelling's foundationalist project, and that foundationalism was in fact a minority view on the defensive. This result is of the greatest importance for an understanding of the genesis of early romanticism, whose aesthetic grew out of the antifoundationalist epistemology of the period.

Although it is of the utmost importance for Hegel research, *Konstellationsforschung* on Hegel has scarcely begun. When Hegel arrived in Jena in 1801, the heady creative years were over; still, their effects were a fresh memory. Seen in context, Hegel's early Jena writings show themselves to be contributions to the recent conversations among his contemporaries. We need to reconstruct Hegel's philosophy in the Jena

---

[12] See Dieter Henrich, *Konstellationen: Probleme und Debatten am Ursprung der idealistischen Philosophie (1789–1795)* (Stuttgart: Klett-Cotta, 1991); *Der Grund im Bewußtsein: Unterscuhungen zu Hölderlins Denken (1794–1795)*, (Stuttgart: Klett-Cotta, 1992); and *Grundlegung aus dem Ich: Unterscuhungen zur Vorgeschichte des Idealismus, Tübingen-Jena, 1790–1794* (Frankfurt: Suhrkamp, 2004). See also Manfred Frank, *Unendliche Annäherung: Die Anfänge der philosophischen Frühromantik* (Frankfurt: Suhrkamp, 1997), and Violetta Waibel, *Hölderlin und Fichte 1794–1800* (Paderborn: Schöningh, 2000).

years – some of the most formative for his intellectual development – as parts of those conversations. Nowhere is this more evident than with regard to Hegel's *Phenomenology*, the crowning work of his Jena phase. The methodology outlined in its famous introduction should be seen as Hegel's response to the dispute about foundationalism in the 1790s. When placed in this context, we should have a much clearer and accurate understanding of Hegel's aims in the *Phenomenology*.[13]

Integration with *Konstellationsforschung* is only one of the unfulfilled desiderata of current Hegel research. There are other aspects of Hegel's philosophy that are in desperate need of further investigation. One of these is Hegel's *Naturphilosophie*, the darkest *terra incognita* of the Hegelian world. For decades, this realm remained shrouded in utter obscurity, because *Natrphilosophie* had become so discredited with the rise of the empirical sciences in the latter half of the nineteenth century. For the positivists, *Naturphilosophie* became the very model of how not to do science. It was speculative, used a priori reasoning rather than patient empirical investigation; and it seemed anthropocentric, reviving final causes, occult powers, and essences.[14] Yet the positivist conception of *Naturphilosophie* is scarcely tenable. The more we study the context of late eighteenth- and early nineteenth- century science in Germany, the more we find that *Naturphilosophie* was not a distinct discipline from the empirical sciences; it was rather "the normal science" of its day.[15] At the very least Schelling and Hegel did not violate the standard ways of pursuing science in their day. They did not scorn empirical research but went to pains to inform themselves about it and to make their thinking conform to the latest findings. Those who were more active empirical researchers – Goethe, Ritter, and Alexander von Humboldt – were no less philosophical than Schelling or Hegel. The distinction between *Naturphilosophie* and empirical science, which has been the cornerstone of the positivist interpretation, is not only anachronistic but deeply question-begging, because most *Naturphilosophen* would not have accepted the distinction between the a priori and the empirical that became so prevalent in nineteenth-century science and philosophy. Schelling and Hegel would have refused to distinguish philosophy from natural science because philosophy seemed essential to

---

13 See the article by Paul Franks in Chapter 2 in this volume, which takes an interesting step in this direction.

14 On these criticisms of *Naturphilosophie*, see the articles by Kenneth Westphal, Ed Halper, and James Kreines, Chapters 11–13 in this volume.

15 I have defended this argument elsewhere. See my "Kant and the *Naturphilosophen*," in *The Romantic Imperative* (Cambridge, MA: Harvard University Press, 1993), pp. 153–170.

make sense of the remarkable developments in physics, geology, and the life sciences. The final decades of the eighteenth century, when *Naturphilosophie* was born, were some of the most exciting and turbulent in the history of science. It was in these years that the mechanical world picture collapsed utterly, that the reigning preformation theory in biology was replaced with epigeneisis, that geology made its first steps toward a systematic investigation of the ages of the earth. One major result of the new dynamic conception of matter and the rise of epigenisis was the collapse of the Cartesian dualisms and the emergence of a new paradigm to explain mental–physical interaction. Rather than distinct substances, the mind and body could now be understood as different degrees of organization and development of living force. Like every *Naturphilosoph* of their generation, Schelling and Hegel struggled to make sense of these developments, to restore the lost unity that had disappeared after the demise of the mechanistic world view. Under these conditions, what could any thinker do than speculate and attempt to formulate new paradigms?

Once we admit that *Naturphilosophie* was the normal science of the late eighteenth century, and once we accept that *Naturphilosophie* was central to Hegel's philosophy, we find ourselves standing before a vast unexplored jungle. How do we understand the concepts of Hegel's *Naturphilosophie*, how do we relate them to the empirical research of his day, and how do we individuate them in the light of opposing theories – these are among some of the basic questions that cry out for answers. It should be obvious, however, that we can begin to answer them only if we have a good understanding of Hegel's philosophy as well as a detailed knowledge of the empirical sciences of his day. Since the 1970s, much progress has been made toward the study of Hegel's *Naturphilosophie*. The work of M. J. Petry, Gerd Buchdahl, Dietrich Engelhardt, Heinz Kimmerle, and Brigitte Falkenberg has helped to open this vast field of investigation.[16] They deserve no little credit for starting investigation into areas that have been made taboo by positivisit prejudices. Yet, all these scholars would be the first to insist that much remains to be done in this area, where even the most basic questions remain unanswered. The prevalence and popularity of nonmetaphysical

---

[16] See M. J. Petry, ed. by *Hegel und die Naturwissenschaften* (Stuttgart: Frommann-Holzboog, 1986) and *Hegel and Newtonianism* (Dordrecht, The Netherlands: Kluwer, 1993); Gerd Buchdahl, "Hegel's Philosophy of Nature and the Structure of Science," *Ratio* XV (1973), 1–27; Dietrich Engelhardt, *Hegel und die Chemie* (Wiesbaden: Pressler, 1976); Heinz Kimmerle, "Hegels Naturphilosophie in Jena," *Hegel-Studien* IV (1967), 125–167; Brigitte Falkenberg, *Die Form der Materie: Zur Metaphysik der Natur um 1800.* (Frankfurt: Athenäum, 1987).

interpretations of Hegel, unfortunately, has done nothing to encourage these investigations. The recent appearance of several new anthologies and monographs is, however, a welcome sign that the times are changing.[17]

Of all areas of Hegel's philosophy it would seem that his social and political doctrines are least in need of further investigation. Since they have been so controversial and least subject to positivist opprobrium, they have been the most intensively studied part of Hegel's philosophy. But here too some of the most basic issues remain to be explored and investigated. On the whole, the study of Hegel's social and political thought has been much too abstracted from its historical context. The works of Franz Rosenzweig and Jacques D'Hondt have been major steps in the right direction;[18] but much still needs to be done. One of the most basic – and least understood – aspects of Hegel's social and political is his theory of natural law. That it was fundamental to Hegel we know from the very subtitle of the *Philosophy of Right*: "Natural Law and Political Science in Outline." Despite this, Hegel has been constantly portrayed as a radical historicist who wants to make all right depend on historical development. Seen more closely, Hegel's theory of natural law was his attempt to rehabilitate the natural law tradition while taking into account the criticisms of the historical school. To appreciate his theory, we have to locate it in its precise historical context, seeing it as Hegel's contribution to several important controversies in his day. One of these was the famous theory–practice dispute in the 1790s concerning the role of reason in politics: the rationalists (Kant and Fichte) held that moral principles governed the political world, that practice must conform to theory; the empiricists (Burke, Gentz, Rehberg, Möser) claimed that moral principles have to adapt to particular circumstances, that theory must conform to theory. Another was the celebrated controversy between Friedrich Savigny and A. J. Thibaut in 1814 concerning the source of the law: whether it should be a rational plan imposed by the state or an historical legacy derived from the *Volksgeist*. Hegel's theory of natural law was his attempt to steer a middle path between the extremes in these debates. But exactly how Hegel does so, how the theory works and takes issue with them, has still been insufficiently explained in Hegel scholarship. Yet, without a sound interpretation of

---

[17] See the works cited in the bibliography under the heading Philosophy of Nature.
[18] See Franz Rosenzweig, *Hegel und der Staat* (Berlin: Oldenbourg, 1920); Jacques D'Hondt, *Hegel secret* (Paris: Presses Universitaires de France, 1968); and Jacques D'Hondt, *Hegel en son temps (Berlin 1818–1831)* (Paris: Editions Sociales, 1968). It is an enormous pity that Rosenzweig's book, still the most authoritative on its subject, has not been translated into English.

Hegel's theory of natural law, we have very little understanding of the very foundation of his social and political thought.

There are many other areas of Hegel's philosophy that stand in need of much further research. But these examples should suffice to convince even the most jaded and tired Hegel scholar that there still remains much to do. However questionable Hegel's philosophy might be, it remains of great significance for its vast historical influence in the past two centuries. All modern schools of thought – existentialism, Marxism, pragmatism, analytic philosophy, neo-Kantianism – have either built on him or reacted against him. Self-conscious and self-critical philosophers are those who know their place in history; and in finding that place they will – eventually but inevitably – bump up against Hegel, grandfather of all virtues and vices. Like a stage of consciousness in Hegel's *Phenomenology*, we will understand ourselves only when we know the story of our becoming; and an essential part of that story will be about Hegel. It is not easy to appropriate Hegel; but that we must do to understand ourselves. Of Hegel, the old Goethean dictum is especially true: *"Was du von deinem Vätern hast, erwerb es, um es zu besitzen."*

1   Hegel: A Life

Hegel's birthplace, Stuttgart, lay in the Duchy of Württemberg, the Swabian speaking area of south Germany.[1] In one sense, Württemberg looked like so many other *Länder* in Germany at the time. The use of the German term, *Land* and its plural, *Länder*, is here intentional; it was not a state, not a province, not a department, not even a political unity of elements that would be immediately recognizable today; instead, it was *sui generis*, a *Land*.[2] At the time of Hegel's birth in Württemberg, people did not speak of general "rights" (the common discourse of our contemporary politics); there were only *particular* rights, *particular* liberties, and the like, which were restricted to particular groups and almost none of which applied to the populace at large. (This or that guild had the right to use metal nails in its carpentry, this or that group had the right to be exempt from a certain tax that other groups had to pay, and so on.) All in all, Württemberg had virtually all the features of what the historian Mack Walker called the German "hometowns," the odd early modern entities kept alive by the singular oddness of the existence of the Holy Roman Empire: As a set of "hometowns," the Empire was governed by a mostly unwritten set of customs and mores that included a sense of various communities both having an obligation to take care of their own members and the right to police the mores of their members in fine grained ways (including the prohibition of marriage by a "hometowner" to an unseemly "foreign" spouse). It was, above all, structured by a strong sense of who did and did not belong to the local communities and by the nearly absolute right of the community to decide whom to admit and not to admit. The elaborate rituals and ceremonies of each "hometown" were centered on keeping that community intact; it was suspicious

---

[1] The material in this article is distilled from Terry Pinkard, *Hegel: A Biography* (Cambridge, UK: Cambridge University Press, 2000).

[2] See James Sheehan, *German History: 1770–1866* (Oxford: Oxford University Press, 1989).

of outsiders and quick to denounce those members who broke the rules.[3]

However, in another sense Württemberg was the odd duck among almost all the other German *Länder*. In terms of the Treaty of Augsburg of 1555, religious toleration was to be established in Germany under the doctrine that the local prince had the right to impose his own religion on the population he governed (impose, that is, the Catholic or Lutheran version of Christianity, with other Protestants, such as Anabaptists and Calvinists, being almost entirely excluded from such toleration). Yet for a long time, Württemberg, with its mostly Protestant population, had been governed by a set of Catholic dukes, who although certainly wanting to impose their religion on the population, had nonetheless at every stage been prevented from doing so by popular resistance, which included a reliance on what Württembergers called their constitution and the "good old law" that embodied their traditional rights and privileges. Moreover, because of the peculiarities of Württemberg's history, the nobility, instead of answering immediately to the duke himself, were almost all immediate to the emperor of the oxymoronically named Holy Roman Empire, and thus took no part in political life in Württemberg. Filling the vacuum, the Protestants had a estate called the *Ehrbarkeit*, the "non-noble notables," into which one had to be born (even though there were no titles that went that status, as was the case with the nobility), who mostly ran Württemberg affairs and and who reserved certain key positions in the Württemberg government and in important institutions for themselves.

In 1770, the year of Hegel's birth, there was in fact a "constitutional settlement" in Württemberg between the Protestant estates and the Catholic duke that reaffirmed the traditional rights of those estates (and which was enforced against the Catholic duke by the Catholic Holy Roman Emperor in light of pressure from the Protestant Prussian ruler, against whom the Württemberg duke had earlier allied himself in a war). In 1770, that is, it seemed that Württemberg had settled forever its odd status as what it had always been. That was soon to change, and the indications of that change were already present in Hegel's childhood.

STUTTGART: 1770–1788

Hegel's own family was an up-and-coming middle class family in Württemberg, although they were not part of the *Ehrbarkeit*. Hegel's

---

[3] Mack Walker, German Hometowns: Community, State, and General Estate 1648–1871 (Ithaca: Cornell University Press, 1971).

father, who had taken a degree in law from Tübingen, was a minor official at the Royal Treasury, and his mother came from a distinguished background of Swabian Protestant reformers. They seem to have been Württembergers proud of their Protestant tradition (and probably shared the widely held Württemberg view of their land as that of heroic Protestants defending their traditions and true faith against the predations of an absolutizing Catholic monarch), but they were also modernizers, subscribing to the Enlightenment-oriented journals of their day. As outsiders to the *Ehrbarkeit*, but nonetheless up-and-coming members of the middle class, they based their claims to rank and promotion on learning and ability, not on family connections. This had no small part in forming Hegel's own conception of himself and his place in the world.

From what we can tell, Hegel's father put a good deal of emphasis on practical matters and social uprightness, whereas Hegel's mother stressed learning. When Hegel was thirteen, both he and his mother were gravely ill, and she died on September 20, 1783. Hegel survived and seemed to carry some of that survivor's guilt with him. About a year after his mother's death, Hegel's father decided that the young Hegel would follow his mother's wishes and pursue studies to become a theologian and a pastor. However, instead of sending him off to one of the seminary preparatory schools ("cloister schools," as they were called) as was usually the case for young men, he was sent to the local university preparatory school, the *Gymnasium Illustre* (a very short walk from the family's house), which, although not exactly a hotbed of Enlightenment ideas, was nonetheless a forward-oriented school, mixing new Enlightenment ideals with an older German renaissance tradition in learning. (It is most likely that Hegel's father actually wanted to send him to some kind of more vocationally oriented school, such as the *Karlsschule* in Stuttgart, but compromised with Hegel's mother's desire that he become a man of learning, a theologian.) At the *Gymnasium Illustre*, Hegel received a good background in literature, ancient and modern languages, mathematics, and the natural sciences (the latter being his favorite subjects at the time), and he came into contact with some accomplished teachers who recognized his native talents and gave him the encouragement he needed. Hegel reciprocated, became the star student, and graduated first in his class. (Hegel's only surviving brother, born in 1776, was in fact sent to the *Karlsschule*.)

Like many young men of his day, Hegel kept a kind of diary in which he dutifully noted what he was thinking about. Like all such diarists, he kept not so much a factual record of his thoughts but tried to present a picture of himself as he wanted to imagine himself to his imaginary "dear reader." The adolescent Hegel that emerges in the entries is a rather earnest young fellow, a kind of self-described young fogy, although he is also a voracious reader, and someone dedicated to something like a noble career as an enlightened pastor and occasional writer, a "teacher of the people."

But despite his attempts at prescribing for himself a studiousness beyond his years, in those diaries, Hegel also gives himself away as a more typical adolescent, who succumbs to sentimentality, heaps praise on popular novels of no particular merit, and notes how he and friends like to pass the time looking at the pretty girls. He also reveals the alienation he surely felt at the time; for example, he notes how he likes to spend as much time as possible at the public library (which was quite rich in its holdings); this was obviously intended to show himself to "dear reader" as a budding young man of learning, but instead it more poignantly indicated how he took measures to get out of the house and out from under his father's discipline.

At the time, he was quite taken with the figure of Gotthold Ephraim Lessing, a writer and literary giant of the time, probably even daydreaming a bit about how his own career might follow that of Lessing's. (Lessing was also originally trained as a theologian.) The adolescent Hegel was particularly struck by Lessing's 1779 novel, *Nathan the Wise*, a tale of Enlightenment religious toleration, whose basic theme was that all people seek God in their own way and thus what makes Nathan a good Jew is what makes other characters good Christians: It is the character and commitment of a person that makes him worthy of admiration, not the doctrinal or cultural (or ethnic) background from which he comes. But most particularly, the character of Nathan seemed to show that one could combine a kind of Enlightenment commitment to universalism with an equally passionate commitment to one's own traditions. For a young Württemberger brought up to be proud of the traditions and the "good old law," *just because* it was the "Württemberg" tradition, and who was becoming equally caught up in the growing Enlightenment fever and commitment to a new, universalized vision of humanity, *Nathan the Wise* was heady stuff.

TÜBINGEN: 1788–1793

In 1788, Hegel was sent off to the Protestant Seminary attached to the university in Tübingen (just a few kilometers south of Stuttgart). The university at Tübingen had for some time been in a steep decline from its earlier glory years, and, by the time Hegel arrived, it was more of an appendage to the rather distinguished Protestant Seminary than the other way around. The students at the Seminary were required to wear long black coats resembling cassocks bordered with white cuffs and collars; in effect they were expected to live like Protestant monks. Most of the seminarians came from one of the cloister schools in Württemberg where similar restrictions had been in place; Hegel, who had lived with his family, who had experienced a fair amount of independence, and who was intent on following out his mother's image of himself as a man of learning, found the environment completely stifling. The star scholar and dutiful son quickly became a sullen and rebellious student. On his entry into the Seminary, he had been ranked the first in his class. In a relatively short period of time, Hegel combined some assiduous drinking with constant violations of all kinds of petty rules, and, together with his generally ignoring what he was supposed to be studying (and instead reading voraciously about other things), he managed to lower his class ranking rather steeply and rather rapidly.

Hegel seems to have decided almost immediately on arriving at Tübingen that he was not going to be a pastor. In his first year there, he managed to make some very good friends who were just as alienated from the requirements of the seminary as he was and felt just as passionately as he did about the big ideas circulating in Germany at the time. Among them was Friedrich Hölderlin, born the same year as Hegel, with whom Hegel shared a room. In 1789, the French Revolution brought to a boiling point what those young alienated seminarians found unacceptable. The influence of Pietism led many young Germans at the time to see the Revolution as the next step in that process, heralding a new spiritual reform of the world. (Pietism was a Protestant religious movement in Germany that stressed an immediate, emotional connection to God coupled with both a deep skepticism about the need for theologians to interpret that word for believers and an equally strong belief that although the Reformation had reformed the Church, the world remained as corrupt as ever and in even more need of reform.)

Some lands in Alsace belonged to the Württemberg duke, and that meant that in the conduit provided by the French students at the Seminary, news of the Revolution swept into the Seminary with even more speed and regularity than it did elsewhere. In 1790, Hegel and Hölderlin came to share a room with a newly admitted seminarian who was five years younger than them but who came with a reputation for being a young genius: Friedrich Schelling. The three shared a room at the Seminary, and they became the best of friends – reading, arguing, and discussing among themselves the new works in philosophy (particularly, Rousseau and Kant, although Hegel seemed not to have been so enamored of Kant as the other two were), with each reinforcing the other's antipathy to the staid ways of seminary life and with each sharing their joint enthusiasm for the Revolution and its progress. (Schelling even translated the Marseillaise at this time.) Hegel's own love of the local taverns during this period seems to have gained momentum, and he was not infrequently cited for disciplinary infractions during this period. His young-fogy personality, however, did not entirely desert him, and even with his rather jovial, pub-crawling personality, he acquired the nickname, "the old man," from his fellow students.

Amidst all the intellectual revelry (and the hijinks that have always been a part of student life), there was, however, a fundamental anxiety plaguing Hegel and his friends: All the students at the Seminary had their costs subsidized by a kind of "fellowship" from the Consistory in Stuttgart, and they were thus legally required to serve as pastors if a position for them opened up. The silver lining in that cloud was that there were far too many applicants for such positions than there were actual positions, so neither Hegel, nor Hölderlin, nor Schelling really had to worry too much about suddenly finding themselves assigned to minister to a small conservative congregation in Swabian Germany. Still, the threat was there, and it also meant that they had to receive permission from the Württemberg consistory to do anything else other than serve as a pastor (or to leave Württemberg to go someplace else for any employment). The path of studies at the Seminary required the students to study philosophy for the first two years (which was just fine with Hegel, even if he did find the quality of instruction to be a bit below the mark), followed by three years of theology and biblical instruction. (Philosophy was considered to be only a propaedeutic to the real object of study, theology.) However, to avoid even the chance of succumbing to the fate of being a pastor, Hegel tried to switch to the law faculty after his first two years, but his father refused to let him do it. (The decision probably had to do with his father's sense that Hegel had promised to study theology, he had to keep his word, and the fear that if Hegel switched, he might have to repay the full stipend his son had received from the Consistory.)

However, the next three years at the Seminary proved to be crucial for Hegel's development. The continued friendship and joint development of ideas among Hegel, Hölderlin, and Schelling were transformative for the three of them. Together they came under the influence of Carl Immanuel Diez, an older student at the Seminary who was responsible for assisting in the instruction of the younger students. Diez had been a theologian who had turned into something like an antireligious agnostic under the influence of Kant's writings; and, combining a commanding intellect with a personal charisma, Diez mixed together a heady sense of philosophical mission by using Kantian ideas to think through how to put an end to the dogmas and conformism strangling German life. Diez's inspiring use of Kant, and the way in which Kantian doctrines of autonomy (seen under Diez's light) seemed to merge cleanly into the calls for liberty, equality and fraternity emanating from France clearly captured the imagination of the three young Seminarian friends.[4] Nonetheless, Hegel himself at first had some trouble accepting Diez's radicalized Kantianism; ever the good Württemberger, he thought that the Kantian appeals to "pure practical reason" left no room for the "hometown" appeal to tradition and to the impulses coming not from reason but from the kind of embodied wisdom caught in tradition and the "good old law." That particular problem stayed with him the rest of his life.

The three friends also were deeply interested in what had been the very public dispute between F. H. Jacobi and Moses Mendelssohn over the status of Spinoza in contemporary thought. Spinoza's arguments to the effect that that there could only be one substance of which both the mental and the physical were merely different attributes struck them as exactly the right doctrine to combine with the Kantian idea of a sharp separation between the deterministic world of experience and the freedom we had to practically presuppose for ourselves (which Kant located in the "noumenal" world, that is, the world conceived apart from the conditions under which we could experience it). Their tendency in this direction was augmented by their negative reaction to what they were being taught by one of the leading theologians at the Seminary, Gottlob Storr, who argued, more or less, that Kant's arguments really pointed the way to a supernaturalist doctrine of the bible as the revelation of a truth that reason could not establish.

Their joint and growing interest in all things "ancient Greek" helped to flesh out this evolving common position. Together, they formed a rough idea of a new nondoctrinal form of religion that would resemble what they took be the ancient Greek religion. In their imaginations, they saw it as a religion of beauty, just like their idealized Greek religion, and as resting on a kind of insight into the one substance of the world – that is, as expressing the Spinozistic God. Moreover, it would be, as Kant was to put it in the 1790 *Critique of Judgment*, the supersensible basis of both nature and freedom which oriented aesthetic judgments in the experience of the beautiful. In Hegel's yearbook in 1791, in fact, Hölderlin entered the Greek phrase, "Hen kai pan," the "one and all" to indicate their emerging view of a kind of synthesis of Kantianism,

---

[4] Among the seminarians, Diez was known as a Kantian *enragé*, a kind of Kantian who also a Jacobin at heart. Diez ultimately left theology, studied medicine, had an important impact on the philosophical development of some of the post-Kantian philosophers at Jena, and died in 1796 in Vienna where he had been treating typhus victims. See Dieter Henrich, *Konstellationen: Probleme und Debatten am Ursprung der idealistischen Philosophie (1789–1795)* (Stuttgart: Klett-Cotta, 1991). See also Dieter Henrich, *Grundlegung aus dem Ich* (Frankfurt: Suhrkamp, 2004), vols. 1–2. (Henrich makes an especially strong case for Diez's influence in the latter book.)

Spinozism, and an (idealized) Greek view of the world. They began to throw about Kant's special use of the term "the invisible church" as a kind of code among themselves to indicate their joint commitment to a revolutionary new world based on virtue, not dogma, and understood by them to be part of a modern process of moral and spiritual renewal – a revival of the Greek democratic and religious ideals.

During his Seminary years, Hegel apparently had bouts of bad health, and he used one of them to finagle an extended return to Stuttgart for his last semester in order to "recover." Most likely by the end of his seminary studies, he had decided on some kind of vague career as a "man of letters"; the issue was only how to find the right format and theme to make his mark on the world. (At that point he had virtually no interest in becoming a professor; the universities, so it seemed, were about the last place in Germany at the time to try out new ideas.) He used his time in Stuttgart to write a long manuscript on the nature of religion (posthumously called, oddly enough, the "Tübingen Essay"), in which he divided religion into "subjective" and "objective" religion, the distinction roughly amounting to that between religion that meshes with the whole of human existence, which motivates people by appeal to their heart as much as head, and the "objective" religion taught in classes in Dogmatics that spells out the institutionalized conditions under which one can count as a Christian (or as Catholic or Protestant). The issue lying just below the surface of this youthful manuscript was the unsettling one as to whether Christianity had already played out its role on the historical stage and could no longer serve as a "modern" religion that could effectively play a role in the new world emerging out of the shock of the Revolution – this was an issue that continued to ferment in Hegel's mind for a good part of his adult life.

BERNE: 1793–1796

On taking his final exam (while still in Stuttgart) from the Consistory in 1793, Hegel managed to land a job as a house-tutor to a family in Berne (the von Steiger family). He was required to get permission from the Württemberg Consistory to take the job and to leave Württemberg, but the permission was quickly granted. The life of house-tutors was notoriously difficult, and it proved to be no less so for Hegel. However, the stay in Berne was intellectually fruitful even though his personal life suffered there. Berne, at the time, was an outmoded oligarchy run by a small set of patrician families, of which the von Steiger's were one. Captain von Steiger, the head of the family, was vehemently opposed to the French Revolution and advocated an alliance with Prussia and Austria that would go to war against France. Not unsurprisingly, Hegel and Captain von Steiger quickly had a falling out, and the rest of his time there was filled with tension. However, the family had one of the best private libraries in Europe, and that, together with the massive Bernese public library, gave Hegel his introductions to Scottish Enlightenment thought, in particular to the writings of Adam Smith. During this period, Hegel had become a kind of "applied Kantian" who wanted to work out the practical implications of Kantian moral and political philosophy; as he emphatically put it in one of his letters to Schelling: "From the Kantian philosophy and its highest completion I expect a revolution in Germany. It will proceed from principles that are present and that only need to be elaborated generally and applied to all hitherto existing knowledge."[5] If anything else, Hegel's Berne experience turned him forever against all so-called "aristocratic" constitutions.

Although in retrospect Hegel's sojourn in Berne turned out to be immensely intellectually fruitful, for him at the time it was simply depressing. As was the case with all house-tutors, he did not have much free time for himself, and he lamented in letters to Schelling how little time he had to work out his own ideas, how isolated he felt, and how little progress he was making. Even worse, he had Schelling's own example staring him in the face. After Schelling had left the Seminary, he had staged a meteoric rise in the German philosophical world, becoming an "Extraordinarius" professor – an "extra" professor on the faculty beyond what the normal funding allowed – at Jena in his early twenties and publishing tract after tract on his own ideas about the new post-Kantian idealism emerging at the time in Jena. The contrast between the absence of any published work by him and the spectacular career his old friend Schelling was carving out for himself could not have been starker. Nonetheless, it was during his stay in Berne that he consolidated his Kantianism, strengthened his distaste for ecclesiastical orthodoxy, was opened up to the ideas of the Scottish Enlightenment (particularly, Adam Smith's work), and he probably read Gibbon for the first time while there.

Hegel's own personal disdain for the Bernese aristocracy and for the von Steiger family in particular, did, however, lead to his first published book, even though it was years later that anybody really knew about it. He translated a revolutionary tract from French into German about the oppression of the French-speaking Vaud by the German-speaking Bernese; he also provided a commentary on the tract, drawing out the

---

[5] *Briefe von und an Hegel*, ed. by Johannes Hoffmeister (Hamburg: Felix Meiner Verlag, 1969), vol. I, no. 11; *Hegel: The Letters*, trans. by Clark Butler and Christiane Seiler (Bloomington: University of Indiana Press, 1984), p. 35. (hereafter cited as *Briefe*, volume number; and *Letters*, page number.)

themes of the absolute value of freedom versus economic gain. (Hegel praised the Americans for putting liberty before such prosaic economic matters.) He published it anonymously in 1798, after he had left Berne; at his death, even his own family did not know that it was his own book and thought it was only a youthful souvenir of his time in Berne.

Hegel's letters to Schelling bemoaning how little progress he was making only show how high Hegel had set the bar for what counted as progress. While in Berne, Hegel was also busy drafting some fragments for a proposed philosophical "system" and even wrote two book-length manuscripts that he never published. One was the "Life of Jesus," an insightful redescription of Jesus' life and teachings fairly much in line with Kant's views on "religion as morality." He also wrote out a long manuscript titled, "The Positivity of the Christian Religion" that both reprised his 1793 Tübingen essay about whether Christianity was the appropriate religion for modern life (especially in light of the Revolution) and extended Hegel's own attempt to mesh Kantianism with his admiration for Greek political and religious life. In it, Jesus is portrayed as a Kantian prophet striving to get his followers to be free and to achieve virtue by their own efforts; but the corruption of the time meant that instead of founding the religion of freedom that he sought to found, Jesus was instead taken by his followers to be a divine personality laying down something like positive law backed up divine authority (hence the title of the essay), and with that, Jesus' nonauthoritarian religion of freedom inevitably turned into an authoritarian religion of dogma. In the manuscript, clearly discernible Hegelian themes and problems began to appear, particularly the idea that it is the "spirit of the times" that moves great world revolutions, not failures of will or self-imposed tutelage, and the issue of whether a religion's beauty is incompatible with its truth. In the end, however, the manuscript was not sent off for publication because it did not answer the crucial question Hegel put to Christianity in it: Can Christianity become a free, modern religion? It failed to answer that question because, at that point, Hegel had simply not made up his mind.

Fortunately, his friend, Hölderlin, who at that time was living in Frankfurt as a house tutor, sensing his friend's depression and feelings of isolation, managed to maneuver an offer to Hegel for a position as a house-tutor for a wealthy wine merchant in Frankfurt. Hölderlin's letters to Hegel at this point give testament to just how much he valued their friendship, and Hegel even replied with a long poem written (sort of) in Hölderlin's own style. The idea of rejoining a center of intellectual life and of being together again with his best friend from Seminary days made Hegel's final days in Berne passable. For his part, Hölderlin told Hegel: "I would still have much to tell you, but your coming here must be the preface to a long, long, interesting, *un-highbrow* book by you and me."[6]

FRANKFURT: 1797–1800

In 1797, Hegel moved to Frankfurt, elated at his chance to escape Berne and the von Steiger's. (As always, he had to get permission from the Württemberg Consistory to make this move; but Hegel was so sure of receiving it that he began work in Frankfurt before he actually had received permission to do so.) On the way to Frankfurt, Hegel stopped off in Stuttgart to visit his family. While there, he had a brief flirtation with a young woman boarding with the Hegel family, Nanette Endel, who was living with them while she did her studies to become a milliner. Nanette Endel teased him endlessly about his seriousness (so out of place for a young man), even suggesting that he was choosing an ascetic life for himself, while he teased her about her devotion to Catholicism and its rigorous morality. (Nanette Endel had also become good friends with Hegel's sister, Christiane, who was not pleased with the attention the two were paying to each other.) While he was pursuing these erotic interests, though, the "old man" found himself increasingly preoccupied with the rather rapidly unfolding set of political events in Württemberg. After the Revolution had both fallen into the Jacobin Terror and then extricated itself from it, the French had begun to take more and more incursions into Germany to protect the new republic. Württemberg itself was invaded by French forces in 1796. In the tumult, Württemberg began to be more and more ungovernable, and the *Ehrbarkeit* saw their chance to finally wrest large parts of political power from the duke. (The struggle for supremacy between the duke and the estates was in fact to last many years; it ended when by virtue of Napoleon's power, the duke became a king and was thereby able to emaciate what remaining rights under the "good old law" the *Ehrbarkeit* had – but none of that was foreseeable at the time Hegel was there.) An explosion of political pamphlets on various subjects filled Stuttgart, and Hegel tried his best to get one of his own into the fray. His friends dissuaded him from this, claiming that his invocation of the French Revolution in his own projected pamphlet would only alienate the people of Württemberg, who, he was assured, had long since turned against the Revolution. Dismayed by this, Hegel published his translation of the pamphlet against the Bernese aristocracy instead.

---

[6] *Briefe*, I, 19; *Letters*, pp. 48–49 ("un-highbrow" translates *"ungelehrten"*).

Hegel's arrival in Frankfurt lifted him from his Bernese depression, and his letters to Nanette Endel (while full of the mutual teasing they both indulged in) showed him to be greatly enjoying the urban life of balls and concerts, and to have finally thrown off his rather youthful moralistic tone of wanting to reform the world. Hegel even told her (hoping, no doubt, for a little frisson on her part) that he didn't even go to church anymore. (It seems likely that Hegel's sons, who turned out to be much more moralistic than their father, destroyed Nanette Endel's letters to Hegel, along with the letters from some others; only his letters to her survive.)

Hegel entered into a rather intense philosophical circle of friends in Frankfurt and, true to his character, he continued to work on various manuscripts, although none of them were ever published. (There is no record of Hegel actually trying to get any of them published; he did not think any of them met the high standards for publication that he imposed on them.) His conversations, however, with Hölderlin, Isak von Sinclair, Jacob Zwilling, and a set of others, who formed a rather intense "Frankfurt intellectual circle," brought Hegel into contact with Fichte's writings and forced him to see that his own idea of being an "applied Kantian" depended on taking too many deeper issues for granted. The internal problems of Kant's own theory and the possibilities of working out a genuine version of Kantianism (or "idealism") began to seem more and more to the point, and this led Hegel to alter his program for his life considerably.

In 1799, another event intervened in Hegel's life that had just as much an impact. Hegel's father died, and, like all people suffering the loss of parent, Hegel was moved to think about his own life and his own future prospects. It had to be clear to him that he was almost thirty and had nothing really to show for himself. In 1799, Schelling, by contrast, had become, after Fichte's dismissal from Jena University on spurious charges of atheism, Fichte's successor as professor there. When Hegel arrived in Frankfurt, Hölderlin was entering one of his most productive periods, being on the verge of establishing himself as one of Europe's great poets, and at the same time was beginning a passionate and ulti-mately tragic affair with the beautiful, gifted wife (Susette Gontard) of the rather philistine banker for whose family he was the house-tutor. By 1799, however, Hölderlin's affair with Susette Gontard had become truly tragic, and Hölderlin was beginning to show the signs of the mad-ness that would eventually overtake him by around 1803; the closeness of the two friends was now under great strain, and it was clear that they, who had once been inseparable, were now going in different directions. After his father's estate was divided, Hegel came into a small inheri-tance on which he could (if he were frugal) live for a few years, and so, after a trip to Mainz in 1800 (which earlier had even briefly joined the French Republic), Hegel swallowed his pride and wrote to Schelling (with whom he had not been in contact for a while), asking him for recommendations on where he might go to get his philosophical affairs in order. Mentioning that he sincerely hoped they could be friends again, Hegel in effect confessed to Schelling that he (Hegel) had been wrong and Schelling been right all along about what was at stake in all the intellectual, literary, and political upheavals going on around them. He informed Schelling that "in my scientific development, which started from more subordinate needs of man, I was inevitably driven toward science, and the ideal of youth had to take the form of reflection and thus at once of a system."[7] Hegel's tone of seeking an invitation to Jena in the letter is not hard to miss, and, as he hoped, Schelling replied with just that, inviting Hegel to stay with him until he found his own place.

JENA: 1801–1807

In 1801, Hegel arrived in Jena. Jena was at that time a small town of about 4,500 people, whose only real claim to fame up until 1785 had been its university of no particular distinction. In the 1780s and 1790s, that changed. For a variety of contingent reasons – important among which was the appointment of Goethe as the minister to the prince in Weimar who had *de facto* oversight over the university – the university suddenly became famous. At the time, universities had a particularly low standing in Europe, being seen by many as outmoded institutions staffed by tenured professors teaching outmoded knowledge and populated by students who cared only about getting as drunk as they could. Better, it was thought, to abolish these medieval holdovers altogether and replace them both with more vocationally minded institutes to teach the students useful knowledge and to set up the equivalent of research institutes (like the various royal societies) for people to pursue new theoretical knowledge. The university at Jena changed all that. Offering intellectual freedom (although not much money) to intellectuals in Germany, it had by 1785 gathered a stellar crowd around itself. It became the center for the propagation of the Kantian philosophy, and the Jena *General Literary Newspaper* (*Allgemeine Literatur Zeitung*), a de facto organ of the Kantian movement, became one of the most successful and widely read journals in Germany. Fichte took Kantianism a step further in his lectures there, and the entire movement of early Romanticism formed around and in reaction to Fichte at that time in

---

[7] *Briefe* I, 29; *Letters*, p. 64.

Jena. The university's success changed the picture of the university and had a far-reaching influence on the development of other universities in the nineteenth century. It brought a new idea into the discussion of university education, that of the union of teaching and research, that is, of bringing the best young minds to study with the leading intellectual figures of the day, who would in turn teach them about the cutting edge developments in their fields. It also brought to preeminence the faculty of philosophy (which in American universities eventually split up into something like the contemporary form of the College of Arts and Sciences) vis-à-vis other faculties (such as theology, law, and medicine).

By the time Hegel arrived in 1801, however, the university's new flame was flickering out. The fallout from the nasty dustup over Fichte's alleged atheism, which had led to Fichte's resignation and dismissal from the university, had soured many of the faculty and led many of them to pack up and go elsewhere. Even the prestigious *Allgemeine Literatur Zeitung* departed from Jena. Nonetheless, Hegel assiduously set himself to work, having managed to get his *Magister* from Tübingen counted as a doctorate, and by the end of August, he had "habilitated" (the German requirement of something like a second dissertation, which officially gives one the right to teach at the university). By the next Winter Semester, he was offering courses in philosophy. As such a lecturer, Hegel was given no salary by the university, although he was allowed to charge admissions to his lectures (all professors did this) and to charge students for examining them (for their degree, as all professors did). This, of course, amounted to little more than pocket change, and Hegel was thus forced to live on his inheritance. Schelling suggested that he and Hegel found and edit a journal (*The Critical Journal of Philosophy*) more or less to propagate the emerging Schellingian turn in post-Kantian philosophy and to bring in some extra cash; in 1801, Hegel also published his first real book, *The Difference Between Fichte's and Schelling's Systems of Philosophy*, a defense of Schelling against Fichte but in which something more resembling the mature Hegelian set of ideas first made their appearance, even if only in the background.

There were obvious stresses in the relationship between Hegel and Schelling by this point; Schelling was famous, Hegel was at best known as Schelling's friend and defender, and Schelling seemed to have had no problem treating Hegel as a kind of hired hand to further the Schellingian cause (while still officially posing as making a common project with Hegel). Schelling scandalized Jena society when he first had an affair with an older and highly intellectual woman (Caroline Michaelis Böhmer Schlegel), who at the time was married to the great critic, aesthetician, and translator, August Schlegel, which led to her divorce and to her marriage to Schelling. (Caroline herself was an independent, free-thinking woman who caused controversy by simply terrifying some of the men around Jena with her wit, intellect, and independence; Schiller, for example, referred to her as "Dame Lucifer"; but others adored her.) Part of the scandal had to do with Schelling having been first engaged to Caroline's daughter by her first marriage; after the daughter had died of a mysterious illness, rumors immediately began to circulate that Caroline had killed her own daughter to win Schelling for herself. When the possibility arose for a position at the newly reformed university of Würzburg in 1803, Schelling departed, as did several other Jena luminaries. Hegel was left behind, the journal folded, he did not have a job, and the university was falling apart around him. Moreover, his reputation in German intellectual life at that point was that of being Schelling's spear carrier, so it was virtually impossible for him to get a job elsewhere.

With his inheritance dwindling (and being progressively devalued by the rising inflation all around him), Hegel became quite depressed. Still, in that period from 1803–1806, he managed to write several different drafts of several different "systems" of philosophy (each similar to the previous one but differing in many details), and by 1805, he began work on his epochal, *Phenomenology of Spirit*, finishing it in 1806.[8]

That Hegel was able to write so much and to refuse to submit it for publication (because in his mind it just was not good enough) is a testament both to Hegel's own self-confidence (which many of his detractors, not without some justification, always saw as arrogance) and to his stubbornness. (Hegel's philosophical development in Jena was in fact so startling and the amount he wrote and did not publish in that period so large that it has managed to sustain a kind of cottage industry in Hegel studies for almost one-hundred years.) As he was finishing up his *Phenomenology* in 1806, Napoleon (now the "Emperor of the French") took on the vaunted Prussian army in Jena and within thirty minutes had them in a full rout, a victory that put the final nail in the coffin of the old Holy Roman Empire. After the battle, Hegel's own apartment was ransacked by French soldiers. Even worse, for Hegel, his landlady, married to a man who had abandoned her, was then pregnant by Hegel. His illegitimate son, Ludwig, was born February 5, 1807.

---

[8] For the *Phenomenology of Spirit*, see this volume. I have given a lengthy commentary on the *Phenomenology of Spirit* in Terry Pinkard, *Hegel's Phenomenology: The Sociality of Reason* (Cambridge, UK: Cambridge University Press, 1994) and reprised it in shorter form (with some small changes of emphasis) in the relevant sections of *Hegel: A Biography*, and *German Philosophy 1760–1860: The Legacy of Idealism*.

BAMBERG: 1807–1808

The battle of Jena made what had been a very bad situation in Jena into something approaching a collapse. Needless to say, the students had all fled, and few of them returned for the next semester. Finances for the university continued to dry up, and Hegel was writing to just about everybody he knew in his last couple of years at Jena pleading for some kind of employment, especially university employment. (He even proposed to the officials in Jena that he would be an excellent professor of Botany and caretaker of the Botanical Garden.) Out of the blue, one of his old Swabian friends, Immanuel Niethammer (older than Hegel but a fellow graduate of the Seminary, who had also been at Jena but had since moved to Würzburg) found him a job editing a newspaper in Bamberg. With no other options, Hegel reluctantly accepted the offer (writing to Schelling that his new position was, although "not even completely respectable... at least not dishonest"[9]).

At this point, Hegel's conscience was still bothered by the fact of his new son, and he arranged to borrow money to help support the boy. However, he made the move to Bamberg with apparently few regrets as far as Ludwig and his mother were concerned, and there never seems to have been any intention to bring the two with him. The newspaper Hegel edited, the *Bamberger Zeitung*, was pro-Napoleonic in orientation, in part because Bavaria (where Bamberg was located) was officially allied with Napoleon and in part because that was the newspaper's short tradition. That orientation fit Hegel just fine. Hegel relished the idea of being a public personage, and he took to his duties with more fervor than could have been expected. He pledged to maintain a certain impartiality (and to a good extent, he succeeded), but he also made sure that the reportage included accounts of French victories, covered the establishment of the kingdom of Westphalia (with Napoleon's brother on the throne), and so forth. He also became a bit of the man about town, attending various balls and great events and consorting with society all around him. (He even attended a costume ball dressed as a valet, an ironic gesture from someone who had claimed in his *Phenomenology* that no man is a hero to his valet because the valet is, after all, only a valet, somebody focused on the here and now instead of on the greater meaning of the events surrounding him; the passage was well known.) As always, he also continued to write to anybody he knew about landing a post at a university so he could further his chosen career as a philosopher.

Hegel's stay in Bamberg was, however, more than a mere interlude for him. He was able to see up close how the reformers in Bavaria

---

[9] *Briefe*, I, 90; *Letters*, pp. 75–78.

were handling things (reform having been foisted on many German *Länder* as a result of the Napoleonic threat around them.) It became more and more clear that reform could not simply be mandated from above but required a corresponding institutional reform. The "Kantian" ideal of simply setting up laws of justice that abstracted away from the real, empirical interests that people had began to show itself more and more as ineffective; and Hegel's ideas about the necessity for a type of institutionalized mores to give a kind of substantiality to what would otherwise be merely generalized and ineffective morality began to be worked out in Hegel's thought more and more during this period. (This came to fruition in his reworking a few years later of the ancient Greek ideal of a harmonious *Sittlichkeit*, or such institutionalized mores, into a modern form of *Sittlichkeit*.)

Journalism, however, was not the place where Hegel wanted to be, even if it had been one of his youthful ideals. When in 1808, he found himself being investigated by the authorities for publishing information about French troop movements that had already been published in other newspapers, he was outraged. Not only did this throw his livelihood into question, it also threw the livelihood of the people who worked for him into danger. He began hammering away at Niethammer with his standard plea: Get me out of here and help me find a university post. In October, 1808, Niethammer wrote him to officially offer him part of what he wanted: He had found a post for Hegel in Nuremberg running and teaching at a university preparatory school (a *Gymnasium*, as the Germans call it), and he was to be in charge of philosophical examinations for the kingdom of Bavaria. Disappointed by not having managed to land a professorship at a university, Hegel nonetheless was delighted to be getting out of journalism, and he set off to assume his *Gymnasial* professorship in Nuremberg at the end of 1808.

NUREMBERG: 1808–1816

Niethammer was able to do this favor for Hegel because by 1808, he had become the commissioner in charge of educational reform in Bavaria. Niethammer also wanted an ally in his efforts to reform Bavarian education. He belonged to the "neohumanist" camp in Germany, which aimed at producing through education a certain ideal of a self-directing, learned individual possessing good taste and a sense of the "deeper" things in life. Their opponents fell into two camps: Those (misleadingly called "utilitarians" at the time) who wanted to focus on vocational skills in education; and conservatives, who wanted to use education to produce the types of individuals who would stay within their traditional roles and class boundaries. Hegel and Niethammer were on the same side of the issue, and their shared, curious Württemberg past gave them a leg up in the debate. Württemberg education had long had more unity to it than did other systems in Germany, and the persistence of the Protestant *Ehrbarkeit* allied against the Catholic duke had meant that a certain tradition of Renaissance humanism had never disappeared from the Württemberg curriculum; the neohumanists in turn had fused all of that with a sense of the superiority of ancient Greek culture. As former students of theology, both Hegel and Niethammer were schooled in ancient Greek, not a language one would normally learn at the university, and this too gave them a leg up in the debate.

Hegel was, however, stepping into a political minefield in Nuremberg. The city itself, which had been self-ruling for centuries, had recently lost its independence in the Napoleonic wars and had suffered under various occupations by different armies. It was given by the French to Bavaria in 1806 (with no input from the Nurembergers themselves), and the formerly free city, Protestant in population, now found itself subject to a Catholic king. Moreover, the particular *Gymnasium* to which Hegel was going had formerly been a prestigious, forward looking center of education but, like many such institutions in Germany, it had failed to keep up and had become yet one more pool of mediocrity. Niethammer was determined to use this Protestant institution as the centerpiece and showpiece of his educational reforms, and he thus put a lot of responsibility on Hegel's shoulders.

The beginning was not auspicious. The reformers in Bavaria, like many modern reformers, were more or less having to make up modern economic finance as they went along. Thus, at first and for quite a while, they actually had no real idea how much things cost and how the costs of many different things impacted on each other. As a result, they were forever issuing decrees that they failed to back up with monetary resources, leaving people like Hegel to pick up the pieces. Hegel's own salary would go for months without being paid, he found himself having to take out loans until he was paid, he had to pay school expenses out of his pocket, and the various promises about reconstructing the physical infrastructure went unfulfilled for long periods of time. When Hegel learned that after some rebuilding, the relevant authorities had then failed to put in toilets in a building housing all-day preteen to teenage boys, Hegel ruefully remarked to Niethammer that "this is a new dimension of public education, the importance of which I have just now discovered – so to speak, its hind side."[10]

---

[10] *Briefe,* I, 145; *Letters,* p. 190.

But he put himself to the task and brought order to the school. He managed to reorganize a demoralized teaching staff, shifting unproductive professors into other areas where they could do little harm (such as moving unproductive mathematics teachers into teaching religion), and he did this not only without antagonizing the faculty but in a way that earned him applause. (Anyone who has spent even a little time around educational institutions knows how improbable that is.) He instilled order and discipline in the school and earned both the respect and the affection of the students. In addition to teaching philosophy for sixteen hours a week, writing his *Science of Logic*, carrying out all his other administrative duties (without a copyist – the equivalent these days of having no secretary or wordprocessor), he also reviewed once a year all of the work of the students (including their homework), had a personal chat with each of them about their studies, what books they were reading outside of class, what their future plans were, giving them advice on how to do better, and the like.[11]

It was clear that Hegel was both dedicated to and more than up to the task, and the people of Nuremberg responded warmly. Hegel saw himself and his philosophy as part of the process of the emerging modern world, and he was firmly dedicated to the neo-humanist ideals of education; he quite clearly saw himself as an educator trying to instill the modern ideals of freedom into his students, and saw his philosophical works as part and parcel of that project. One of his most fervently held beliefs was his belief in the idea of "careers open to talent" (a slogan of the French Revolution); his Württemberg background and his family (who were not members of the *Ehrbarkeit* but were better educated) played more than just a small role. Hegel made it a point in his yearly addresses to the public as the rector that one of the key issues in such a program had to do with providing poor but gifted students the means to procure an education for themselves. It had been part of his program at Jena, and in Nuremberg, he had a chance to put it into practice; he continued to harp on this theme, even making it a point of pride when he became several years later the Rector of the Berlin University. (In Hegel's day, in fact, professors received some of their income by the fees students paid to attend lectures and to be examined for degrees; from his days in Jena to Berlin, Hegel always waived such fees for those students.)

It also seemed clear to Hegel by the time he reached Nuremberg that his predilection for the French Revolution and for Napoleon's modernizing tendencies had put him on the right side of history. The French

---

11 For the *Science of Logic*, see this volume. I have given a short account of the *Science of Logic* in the relevant sections of *Hegel: A Biography and German Philosophy 1760–1860: The Legacy of Idealism.*

seemed unstoppable, and Napoleonic Germany (those parts allied with and under the influence of the French regime) was in a process of modernizing itself in a way that the anti-Napoleonic part of Germany seemed to be lacking.

However, there continued to be strains within the Bavarian government among the devotees of the older order and the reformers. Since many of the opponents of the reforms were Catholic, the series of events they initiated (including almost shutting down the *Gymnasium* on a fabricated legal pretext to seize its money) reinforced within Hegel a view that modern freedom was possible only in Protestant regimes and that Catholicism, as a religion of authority and dogma, was incompatible with modern freedom. He never again abandoned that view, and it got him into trouble off and on in Berlin, where his anti-Catholic outbursts were not taken kindly. Frustrated with the prevarications of the Catholics in the Bavarian government, Hegel confided to Niethammer that he had come to see the difference between Protestantism and Catholicism as being crystallized in their attitudes to education: For Protestants, it is universities and all centers of instruction that are important, and "all Protestants look upon these institutions as their Rome and council of bishops .... The sole authority [for Protestants] is the intellectual and moral *Bildung* [education and cultural formation] of all, and the guarantors of such *Bildung* are these institutions ... To Catholics, however, it [*Bildung*] is something optional, since what is sacred is in the church, which is separated off in a clergy."[12]

Hegel's newly elevated status in Nuremberg life even led to his marriage to a daughter of one of the oldest aristocratic patrician families in Nuremberg: the von Tucher family. The courtship leading up to the marriage was not itself without all the usual ups and downs and twists and turns that always seemed to accompany Hegel's life, Marie was in fact twenty years younger than Hegel, and there was the fact that Hegel, a commoner with no "von" in his name, was marrying into a family much above his social estate. There was, of course, one hitch in Hegel's background that might have derailed this part of his social ascension: His illegitimate son back in Jena, about which Hegel seems not to have thought much about during his initial years in Nuremberg. (In fact, there is some, but not very trustworthy evidence, that the mother of the boy made a bit of a fuss about the wedding, claiming that Hegel had earlier promised to marry her when he got a settled position.) In any event, the matter was settled, and the marriage went forward. On September 15, 1811, he and Marie Helena Susanna von Tucher were married.

---

[12] *Briefe*, II, 309; *Letters*, p. 328.

The new arrangements were also not without their own bit of family romance. Marie's father died shortly thereafter, and her mother, who was only one year older than Hegel, took an obvious liking to him, making him in effect into the titular head of the family and expending lots of energy on projects to please her illustrious son-in-law (including a large yearly production of *Lebküchen* for Hegel's enjoyment). Hegel and Marie, moreover, had to deal not only with Marie's father's early death, they also had to deal with the tragedy of the death of their first child, a daughter, after only a few months; moreover, Hegel's only surviving brother was part of the Napoleonic army that invaded Russia, and he died during that campaign. (The Hegels did manage to have two more sons who both lived to ripe old ages.)

In 1814, Hegel did what was expected of a person in his position and invited his sister, Christiane, to come stay with them. Christiane, gifted and strong willed, who received no higher education (but might well have been as naturally gifted as her celebrated brother) had never married (although she had turned down some proposals of marriage), and had instead elected to stay home and care for her father. Since the great fear of any middle class woman was having to become a servant in somebody else's house, the mores of the time held that the only decent thing to do was to invite her to come to live with one's own family (after one had married), usually on the pretext of "helping out" around the house as the children arrived. Christiane also had a strong attachment to her brother, and when Hegel was away on a trip, he came back to find that his wife and Christiane were more or less at each other's throats. Christiane was "required" to leave, and she expressed intense feelings of hatred for Marie to one of her cousins after she left. The estrangement between Hegel and his sister was never really overcome; they never saw each other again, although they continued to correspond intermittently. (Her letters to him are another missing part of Hegel's letters and were probably among the stack of documents that one of Hegel's sons later destroyed.)

In addition to these personal difficulties, Hegel also had to deal with the shock of Napoleon's sudden fall after the disaster of the Russian campaign. It threw into question whether the Napoleonic reforms would continue, and Hegel watched with more than a little nervousness as the Congress of Vienna met. He was, of course, greatly relieved to see that virtually none of Napoleonic Germany was going to be changed (the newly established kings of Württemberg and Bavaria, although conservative, certainly did not want to turn the clock back and return all the lands they had received for earlier allying with Napoleon.)

Hegel continued to flourish as Rector. He in fact took on additional duties as the school inspector for Bavaria (with a substantial raise), and he managed not only to get a teacher's college established in Nuremberg, he also managed to get permission for the establishment of an educational schools for girls that functioned until 1831, when it was absorbed into the larger Nuremberg school system.

HEIDELBERG: 1816–1818

In 1816, Hegel's long held wish finally came true: The university at Heidelberg offered him a position as professor of philosophy. Berlin expressed interest too, but there were complications with the offer, and Hegel's wife made it clear that she did not want to move so far away from her family. Hegel accepted the offer from Heidelberg, and about six months after moving there, the family took Hegel's illegitimate son, Ludwig Fischer, into the family. (Why they had not done so earlier is a bit unclear, but it is clear that it had something to do with the standing of the von Tucher's in that city, and some evidence points to it being more of a matter of reluctance on Marie's part than reluctance on her family's part.) Ludwig had many problems fitting into the Hegel family. He had after all been abandoned by his mother, effectively abandoned by his father, and he clearly had some issues he needed to work out. It also seems clear that the Hegel family was not entirely sympathetic to the obvious stresses in his condition, and Hegel's two sons (Karl and Immanuel) also did not make much of a secret of seeing Ludwig as an interloper on their territory. On Ludwig's own account, Marie Hegel was less than kind toward him, and Ludwig seems to have been regarded more or less as a "foster child" by the Hegel family.

For Hegel, though, none of those stresses counted as much as finally settling down as a professor at a prestigious institution, happily married and with a family. It had taken Hegel until the age of forty-six to finally achieve his goal, and he settled down rapidly into a productive professional life and, more or less, a happy family life. He and Marie traveled in the area, entertained quite a bit, and Hegel made any number of new personal and professional friends, among them, the great legal theorist, A. F. J. Thibaut; he participated in "musical evenings" at Thibaut's house and often volunteered his own house for the occasion. (Thibaut was also an accomplished musicologist and was interested in early polyphonic music.) That and the acquaintance he made with the Boisserée brothers (and their vaunted collection of "old German" paintings and prints, which included many Dutch paintings) helped to form Hegel's aesthetic taste, which was to find fruition in his extremely popular and epochal lectures on aesthetics in his Berlin period. Hegel was able to renew his acquaintance with Goethe, this time more as an equal than as a poor supplicant begging for a position at Jena, and he made the acquaintance of other literary celebrities, such as Jean Paul. In all of that tumult, he also managed to finish and publish the first edition of his *Encyclopedia of the Philosophical Sciences* (1817), and he worked out in lectures the details of what was become his final book, the *Philosophy of Right*, published in Berlin in 1820.

The background to Hegel's lectures on political philosophy had to do with several disputes that were erupting in post-Napoleonic Germany, one of them being the dispute between Thibaut and Karl Friedrich von Savigny over the codification of German law. In effect, Thibaut argued that for such a codified law to be normatively binding, it had to be rational in a sense Kant would have recognized; Savigny, on the other hand, argued that whatever it is that *de facto* binds a people together is really binding for it. (Hegel took Thibaut's side.) Savigny's point about a norms being binding simply because they were the established norms of a people found expression in the growing movement of German nationalism and the appeal to being authentically German. Hegel would have none of it; as he was fond of saying, the appeal to *Deutschtum* (German-dom) is just being *Deutschdumm* (German-dumb).[13]

Hegel's own intense interest in shaping the modern world also led him to throw his hat into the ring around a bitter political dispute in Württemberg in 1817. In effect, the Württemberg King and the estates found themselves at odds over a proposed new constitution that would have effectively taken power away from the old *Ehrbarkeit* and the nobility (who, after the collapse of the Holy Roman Empire, had no emperor to whom they were "immediate"). Part of the dispute had to do with power grabs on both sides, and part of the dispute had to do with the forces of tradition versus a kind of rationalizing modernity. (The king's proposed constitution granted liberty of the press and full rights to Jews but kept the power and purse strings in his own hands.) In an article published while the dispute was still in full force, Hegel sided with the king, arguing that the views put forth by the proponents of the "good old law" were antiquated, too much like "social contract" views of state power (except that the contract was not between individuals but distinct social estates and classes), and that the so-called golden age to which the defenders of tradition appealed was a myth. He concluded that the *Ehrbarkeit* and their allies were like the deposed French aristocrats after the Revolution, for "*they have forgotten nothing and learnt nothing. [The Württemberg estates] seem to have slept through the last twenty-five years, possibly the richest that world history has had, and for us the most instructive, because it is to them that our world and our*

---

[13] *Briefe*, II, 241; *Letters*, p. 312.

ideas belong."[14] (Almost all of Hegel's friends took umbrage at his essay, since it seemed to them that he was siding with the rather autocratic inclinations of the king rather than taking a more nuanced view of the need for checks against the king, and it cost him certain long-standing friendships.)

In 1817, Berlin came through with a very attractive offer for Hegel to take over Fichte's long absent chair in philosophy. Marie's reluctance to move was overcome by her mother's intervention on Hegel's side of the argument, and on October 5, 1818, the Hegel family arrived in Berlin.

BERLIN: 1818–1831

Prussia, which had been in danger of vanishing as a great power (or perhaps vanishing altogether) during the Napoleonic period, had emerged as stronger than ever and substantially larger than it had been prior to that period. Pushed to reform by necessity and not any kind of forward thinking, the Prussian king had instituted a couple of different reform movements that had tried to put in place a more rational, "universalist" government and society (with "careers open to talent") to replace the antiquated "particularist" structures of the early modern Germany. However, the bureaucratically installed reformers were trying to put into place an enlightened system of bureaucratic government without having virtually any popular support for their cause. (Their constituency consisted of a handful of ministers and the king himself.)

By the time Hegel arrived in Berlin, the reform movement had slowed to a crawl, although many, including Hegel, thought that this was at best a temporary loss of momentum in what would be an inevitable coming to terms with the modern world. It was, in fact, during this period of reform that the new Berlin university was founded (in 1809), including within itself many of the ideals of the short-lived Jena experiment. Berlin's own version was, of course, destined to set the model for virtually all universities around the world as it established an institution oriented toward the unity of teaching and research, with its goal being to turn out the well-educated young men who would be necessary to staff the newly emerging professions within the institutions of the modern world.

---

[14] Hegel, "Proceedings of the Estates Assembly in the Kingdom of Württemberg 1815–1816," in *Hegel's Political Writings*, trans. by T. M. Knox (Oxford: Oxford at the Clarendon Press, 1964), p. 282; also in *Werke in zwanzig Bänden*, ed. by Eva Moldenhauer and Karl Markus Michel (Frankfurt am Main: Suhrkamp Verlag, 1971), vol. 4, p. 507.

Hegel's arrival in Berlin was accompanied by the curiosity among the educated elite as to how he would fare. By that time, Hegel had established himself as the leading voice of the new post-Kantian movement in philosophy, with his only real competitors to that title being Schelling and J. F. Fries.[15] Hegel was invited to join one of the exclusive clubs in Berlin, and he and Marie made the rounds at various social events and at the opera. That easy-going life, however, was quickly clouded over by more distressing events. The assassination of a conservative literary figure in August, 1819 fueled the overactive imaginations of the Prussian king and many of the conservative figures around him, all of whom began to see Jacobin plots everywhere. This in turn led them into a hunt for these supposed "demagogues" (or "subversives"), and by the end of August in 1820, the "Karlsbad decrees" had been promulgated for the German Confederation which codified the hunt for demagogues and made it impossible, for example, for any professor dismissed as a demagogue from a teaching post in one university to attain a teaching post at another university in the German confederation of states.

Hegel found himself quickly embroiled in these disputes when one of his Heidelberg students, Gustav Asverus (who was the son of Hegel's lawyer in Jena and who handled Hegel's negotiations with Ludwig Fischer's mother about his marriage to Marie von Tucher) was arrested and held incommunicado as a "demagogue." Hegel intervened, wrote to the ministry without avail, and ended up hiring a lawyer to intervene for Asverus; as a condition of Asverus's release, Hegel was required to purchase a state bond (costing roughly one-third of his annual salary).

The persecution of the "demagogues" picked up its pace, and soon a Berlin professor, Wilhelm de Wette (a theologian), lost his position because of it. (J. F. Fries, who was a friend of the Berlin theologian and who detested Hegel and whom Hegel detested in return, also lost his position in Jena – an event in which Hegel took with no small measure of *Schadenfreude*). At this time, Hegel tried to have one of his gifted students, Friedrich Wilhelm Carové, accepted as his teaching assistant, but Carové lacked the *Habilitation*, and the faculty denied the request. As Carové was working on the *Habilitation*, he was brought under suspicion of being a "demagogue" and investigated. Although Carové

---

[15] I examine Kant and the post-Kantian movement up to and beyond Hegel in Terry Pinkard, *German Philosophy 1760–1860: The Legacy of Idealism* (Cambridge, UK: Cambridge University Press, 2002). The movement from Kant up to but not including Hegel is admirably treated in Frederick Beiser, *German Idealism: The Struggle against Subjectivism 1781–1801* (Cambridge, MA: Harvard University Press, 2002). For the complement to that volume, see also Frederick Beiser, *Hegel* (London: Routledge, 2005).

was initially cleared of the charges, he remained under suspicion. By 1820, however, the die was cast, and Carové was officially banned as a demagogue from all teaching in the German confederation.

Hegel confided to friends that although he still believed in progress, one had to admit that things seemed only to be getting worse, and he expressed great anxiety about the current trends. His second choice for his assistant, an aristocrat who had fought in the wars against Napoleon, L. D. von Henning, also came under suspicion, as did some other students of Hegel's. Henning was arrested and put into jail in a cell facing the Spree River. Hegel and some other students went out at midnight in a skiff on the river and facing the window of his cell, they spoke with him and tried to cheer him up; from the skiff, Hegel conducted a conversation with von Henning in Latin (so that if the guards overheard, they could not understand). After seven weeks, von Henning was released, but the authorities required him to take the assistantship for one year at no pay in order to prove his worthiness.

In 1820, in the midst of all of this, with Hegel's students being arrested all around him, he met with some students in Dresden, and at dinner on July 14, he turned down the local wine, purchasing instead for himself and students a bottle of the most expensive champagne in Europe. On filling their glasses and downing the champagne with them (and with the students rather astounded that the old fellow was doing this for them and having no idea why he was doing this), he explained the reason for his generosity: Hegel turned to them in mock astonishment and with raised voice declared, "This glass is for the 14th of July, 1789 – to the storming of the Bastille."[16]

The tensions in the worsening political situation in fact brought out many of the competing qualities in Hegel's personality. On the one hand, he had an angry public argument with Schleiermacher over the propriety of the government's banning professors from teaching in 1819, in which Hegel defended the principle, provided that the government continued to pay the professor's salary; he and Schleiermacher became thereafter somewhat bitter antagonists. Hegel nonetheless paid into the secret fund to support the banned theologian (whose ideas he found close to nonsense) when no such salary was forthcoming. As previously mentioned, he risked going out in a skiff at night to talk with an imprisoned student; but he also led a rather unpretentious, Biedermeier life; yet, he also did things like attend *Fasching* balls in a Venetian cape and mask (looking no doubt like some figure out of the musical, *Amadeus*). Hegel had been brought up as a proud Stuttgarter who was not a member of

---

[16] Günther Nicolin, ed., *Hegel in Berichten seiner Zeitgenossen* (Hamburg: Felix Meiner Verlag, 1970), no. 323, p. 214.

the *Ehrbarkeit*, and, like the rest of his family, he remained a bit prickly about alleged affronts to his status. Many contemporaries described him as simple, unpretentious, and gregarious; many others described him as arrogant, wooden, and stuffy. In fact, he was all those things at once. He loved playing cards with nonacademic types (such as the royal stable-master), and he maintained friendships with both the artistic and the more bohemian elements of Berlin society. One of his best friends was the head of the Berlin musical choral academy (the *Singakademie*), K. F. Zelter, who was the son of a mason; together he and Hegel had a clear sense that they were both the products of the idea of a "career open to talent," and both enjoyed each other's rather down to earth ways.

In fact, the kind of supreme self-confidence that had taken him through the years of depression and bleakness in Jena and had led to his *Phenomenology of Spirit* often tended to get played out in Berlin as a kind of arrogance. Hegel had a fearsome anger when he thought some kind of line had been crossed (particularly when it concerned his status as a professor), and his irony and sarcasm (usually more of the latter) expressed itself not always in the most flattering ways. That same self-confidence, however, also allowed him to maintain a kind of equanimity and light-heartedness in many of his dealings with people, and to be a jovial and witty companion on many social occasions.

Hegel finally published his *Philosophy of Right* in 1820.[17] Although the book reconstructed and defended what Hegel took to be the rational underpinnings of the kind of social and political order sought by the reformers, along with ideas of his own that incorporated other ideals arising out of the British and French models, it was virtually immediately taken by reviewers to be an apology for the existing, repressive Prussian regime. Hegel had only himself to blame: He included in the preface a bitter attack on J. F. Fries, which was taken by many as an uncalled for piece of aggression against a leading thinker who had just lost his job because he was declared to be a demagogue; he also inserted an indirect attack on de Wette, the Berlin theologian who had also lost his position for being convicted of being a demagogue, and he concluded with the infamous Hegelian "double proposition" that what is rational is actual, and what is actual is rational, which many reviewers took at face value to be saying that what is, is right, and what is right is what happens to be the case; or in other words, the Prussian regime is in power, and that makes it right and rational. Hegel was taken aback at this interpretation, and he even played a role in having a later "Brockhaus Encyclopedia" entry about him specifically deny that he ever meant such a thing at

[17] For the Philosophy of Right, see my own account in *German Philosophy 1760–1860: The Legacy of Idealism*.

all; under Hegel's guidance, the writer of the entry on Hegel even went so far as to say "to the extent that Hegel's view on the state are known to us through his writings, [that phrase] was in no way employed *later on* for the benefit of the ruling classes but arose out of the foundations of his philosophy, which everywhere combats *empty* ideals and seeks to reconcile thoughts and actuality in the absolute Idea through, as it were, the Idea itself."[18] Hegel's own ongoing disputes with the liberal reformer, Schleiermacher, and his friendship with some of the few remaining reformers in the government gave him the undeserved reputation that he was a lackey of the existing regime (despite the fact that leading members of the government found him suspicious and actually advised students against going to his now famous lectures).

By 1821–1822, Hegel had come under a lot of stress. The arrest of his students, his wife's on again, off again state of health – Marie suffered from several miscarriages during their marriage – his workload (he had taken on some extra duties), together with his normal activities (researching for his lectures and trying to write more for publication while doing his part in university service) put a strain on his health and his mood. Moreover, a membership in the Berlin Academy of the Sciences was consistently denied him, almost entirely due to the bad blood between him and Schleiermacher, who blackballed Hegel every time his name was proposed for inclusion; his exclusion from the group was not only a wound to his pride, it also meant a not inconsiderable loss of income for him. The attacks on the *Philosophy of Right* accusing him of obsequiousness vis-à-vis the ruling powers did not help things. Hegel was stung by Schleiermacher's antipathy to him, and in 1822 in a preface to a book on the philosophy of religion by one of his former students, Hegel inserted a phrase to the effect that if the views of some theologians (Schleiermacher, although not specifically named) were taken seriously, namely, that "if religion grounds itself in a person only on the basis of feeling, then such a feeling would have no other determination than that of a *feeling of his dependence,* and so a dog would be the best Christian, for it carries this feeling most intensely within itself and lives principally in this feeling. A dog even has feelings of salvation when its hunger is satisfied by a bone."[19]

For Schleiermacher and his allies, this was the last straw; the attacks on Hegel increased. However, it did nothing to stop his growing

---

[18] Cited and discussed by Friedhelm Nicolin, "Der erste Lexicon-Artikel über Hegel (1824)," in Friedhelm Nicolin, *Auf Hegels Spuren: Beiträge zur Hegel-Forschung,* p. 212.

[19] G. W. F. Hegel, "Vorrede zu Hinrichs Religionsphilosophie," *Werke,* vol. 11, pp. 43, 58.

celebrity. By the mid-1820s, he had become perhaps *the* dominant intellectual figure in Berlin. One participant in the Berlin scene put it this way: "Whether a new and famous picture emerged from the workplaces of a famous painter or whether a new, very promising invention had directed the attention of the industrialists to it, whether some thought of genius in the sciences made its way into the learned world, or Miss Sontag sang in a concert, in all cases Berlin asked: What does Hegel think about it?"[20]

Some of the reform-minded figures in the government managed to get Hegel an extra stipend to compensate partially for his exclusion from the Academy of the Sciences. Hegel used some of the money to take three major trips. Hegel's travels were always for self-improvement; as a middle class Württemberger who prized *Bildung* above all and as someone who had never had the opportunity to travel much, Hegel valued seeing the various museums, architectural features, and daily life of the places he visited. In 1822, he went to Holland, a rich and "modernizing" country. On the way to Holland, he managed to stop off in Magdeburg to visit with one of his youthful heroes, the French mathematician-engineer-politician, Carnot, who had played such a big role in the Revolution and the Napoleonic period and who had been living under house arrest in Magdeburg after the fall of Napoleon. Holland itself proved to be a real eye opener for Hegel; cosmopolitan, tolerant, and rich, it gave him an idea of what Germany could and should turn out to be.

In 1824, he took another trip to Vienna. It is safe to say that he simply loved the place; he attended opera after opera, visited picture gallery after picture gallery, took in the wonderful Viennese cuisine, took in even more Viennese wine, and, in general, reflected on the differences between the two great German powers: Protestant Prussia and Catholic Austria. Hegel clearly valued the cultural richness of Vienna over the more staid and less vibrant Berlin; but he also saw Austria as a land of the past; the future belonged, he thought, to the great Protestant powers, Britain and Prussia.

When Hegel arrived back home from the Vienna trip, he found out that an old friend (and a former student of sorts), Victor Cousin, had been arrested by the Prussians for being a "demagogue." Cousin was a liberal reformer in France and a friend of Hegel since his Heidelberg days; the charges were also clearly fraudulent. (It later turned out the Prussian government was in effect doing a favor for the restoration French police.) Even worse, Cousin's alleged coconspirators included a friend of Ludwig Fischer Hegel and Julius Niethammer (the son of Hegel's

---

[20] Hegel in Berichten seiner Zeitgenossen, no. 558, p. 378.

friend, Immanuel Niethammer). Hegel courageously wrote a letter to the Prussian interior ministry testifying to Cousin's innocence and requesting an audience with Cousin (which was denied). Hegel was joined in the protest by people like Schleiermacher (for once they were on the same side), and Hegel's celebrity and continuing pressure for Cousin's release was instrumental in obtaining his release some months afterward. Cousin was forever grateful to Hegel afterward.

This raised Hegel's celebrity, but it did not tamp down the attacks on him; and, if nothing else, it raised Hegel's own somewhat aggressive and sarcastic attacks against his opponents up another notch. (He managed to get himself into trouble again when he repeated in his lectures an old Protestant canard about Catholic beliefs in the Eucharist requiring Catholics to worship a mouse who had eaten a consecrated wafer; the Catholic community was, simply put, outraged over that remark.)

It was at this time that Hegel also became very good friends with the very gifted young Jewish jurist, Eduard Gans, who himself became a convert to Hegelianism. The two became quite close; in August, 1826, Hegel wrote to Marie (who was with the children visiting family in Nuremberg) that "I'm living very quietly; I see virtually only Gans, my true friend and companion."[21] Hegel supported Gans's application to become a professor of law; but many in the law faculty, led by von Savigny, objected to a Jew obtaining such a position even though the Emancipation Edict of 1812 clearly opened up such possibilities for Jews. The debate over whether to appoint Gans became quite heated, but Gans's opponents managed to get the ear of the king, who, in order to stop Gans from becoming a professor, revoked the entire Edict in 1822. Thus, in order to stop a Jewish Hegelian from becoming a professor, Jewish emancipation in Prussia was effectively abolished.

In 1825, while in Paris, Gans quite cynically converted to Christianity. (Gans was said to have claimed about his conversion that "if the state is so stupid as to forbid me to serve it in a capacity which suits my particular talents unless I profess something I do not believe – and something which the responsible minister knows I do not believe; all right then, it shall have its wish."[22]) The ploy worked, and Gans became a professor over Savigny's objections; he also immediately became one of the most popular professors with the students and was instrumental in furthering the Hegelian line of thought. (Gans himself later had a very famous student: Karl Marx.)

[21] *Briefe*, III, 520, *Letters*, p. 506.
[22] Cited in S. S. Prawer, *Heine's Jewish Comedy: A Study of His Portraits of Jews and Judaism* (Oxford: Clarendon Press, 1983), p. 12.

It was also almost certainly the close friendship between Gans and Hegel that led Hegel in Berlin to reverse his views on Judaism that he had held all his adult life. From at least Tübingen onward, Hegel had viewed Judaism as a religion of egoism and servility, but after becoming friends with Gans, Hegel completely changed his view, claiming in his lectures that Judaism was the first religion of freedom, a religion that put goodness and wisdom into the concept of divinity and which stood on a higher plane even than the religion of the Greeks. (Prior to his conversion, Gans had also been the president of the short lived but historically influential Society for Jewish Culture and Science.)[23]

With Gans's help, Hegel founded a new journal that brought together various luminaries to write on "scientific" subjects (in the sense of German *Wissenschaft*). The journal was never the success Hegel hoped it would be, but it reflected his commitment to be more than just a university professor; he wanted to establish a public forum that the graduates of the new Berlin-style universities (with their ideal of the "unity of teaching and research") could stay abreast of the trends in thought in various fields, ranging from literature to theology and the natural sciences.

Hegel himself continued to consort with people of all levels of society, once even having to intervene in a purported duel between a friend, the Jewish satirist, Moritz Saphir, and another acquaintance, a nouveau-riche lottery winner who had felt himself grievously insulted by one of Saphir's witticisms. (Hegel was supposed to have been Saphir's "second" at the duel, and his comical presence at such an otherwise dire occasion led both parties to call off the feud.)

In 1826, Hegel's friends had a surprise birthday party for him that went on all night. The event was reported in the newspapers, and the king, whose birthday was a couple of weeks earlier, became quite peeved that Hegel's birthday got more attention in the press than did his own. However, he had a solution: He simply banned the reporting of such private birthday celebrations in the newspapers. It did not take much effort for Hegel (or anyone else) to read between the lines and see the threat contained therein. Around the same time, Victor Cousin praised Hegel in the preface to a translation of Plato's *Gorgias*, citing Hegel's "noble conduct" during the "Cousin affair" and his courage in running such a risk; when the director of police in Berlin learned of Cousin's book, he was, to put it simply, outraged. Realizing that being on the bad

---

[23] Eduard Gans has undeservedly languished in some obscurity as a kind of footnote to the Hegelian movement. Fortunately, that is beginning to change. See especially the crucial work by Norbert Waszek, *Eduard Gans (1797–1839): Hegelianer-Jude-Europäer. Texte und Dokumente* (Frankfurt am Main: Peter Lang, 1991).

side of both the king and the director of police was not exactly the ideal situation to be in, Hegel laid low for a while.

To make matters worse for Hegel, the long-standing friction between Ludwig Fischer Hegel and the other members of the Hegel family finally came to a head. Hegel told Ludwig that Karl and Immanuel were going to university but that he was not; there wereas simply not enough family finances for that. (That Hegel might have cut back on other things to provide for Ludwig's education was apparently not up for discussion.) Ludwig, who was certainly qualified for university education, was instead apprenticed for a career in business. Ludwig rebelled, and, on one account, ran away. (On another account, he was thrown out of the house.) He joined the Dutch army, but Hegel did try to find out how to do something for him by speaking with Dutch friends. (Ludwig later died of a fever in Batavia in 1831.; Hegel, who also died in 1831, never learned of Ludwig's death and, nor did Ludwig ever learn of his father's death.) After Hegel's death, his sons apparently tried very diligently to erase Ludwig's memory; for example, all of the letters Hegel wrote to his friend, F. Frommann, in Jena about Ludwig (Frommann and his sister were in charge of caring for Ludwig) survived, whereas all of Frommann's responses (apparently containing references to Ludwig) vanished.

In 1827, Victor Cousin invited Hegel to visit him in Paris. This was not only something Hegel had long wanted to do; it also offered him a convenient excuse to be out of town for his birthday and avoid any complications on that day that might irritate the king again. More than any of his other trips, the visit to Paris was an eye-opener. Paris, the seat of the Revolution, to which Hegel drank a toast every July 14, was all that Hegel could have hoped for a modern city. He wrote to Marie, exclaiming about the cultural riches, the cosmopolitan atmosphere, and the wealth and vibrancy of the city; he was, he told her, in the "capital of the civilized world."[24] He met various leading political figures and intellectuals, he got to travel to a Rousseau site (which required him to ride on a donkey in the sun on a hot day but which, he noted, was well worth the trip), he took in the theater, the opera, and the museums. Hegel, a life-long Francophile who until then had never been to France, was entranced by the French way of life. "When I return," he wrote to Marie, "we shall speak nothing but French."[25] Unfortunately, the French cuisine proved too much for Hegel's more pedestrian German stomach; after only a little while, he contracted a severe case of indigestion

[24] *Briefe*, III, 559; *Letters*, p. 649.
[25] *Briefe*, III, 562; *Letters*, p. 656.

and had to find a table d'hôte that served German food for the rest of his stay.

Hegel's life gradually settled down into the routine of being attacked by all kinds of detractors, being nominated for a position at the Academy of Sciences, and being immediately blackballed by Schleiermacher, all the while being a leading intellectual celebrity in Berlin, besieged by admirers, asked for favors, even asked for the equivalent of celebrity endorsements for products. He continued his card games with his less-exalted friends and his continued associations with the Bohemian element of Berlin. Hegel had become by then a Berlin fixture; the picture of Hegel finishing his lectures early in the evening (around 5:00 pm) and walking across the street to the Royal Opera House to catch that evening's performance was part of Berlin life. His students, such as Heinrich Heine and Felix Mendelssohn-Bartholdy, were themselves becoming celebrities, and the attendance at his lectures continued to rise, with people coming from all around to hear him expound his views on the nature of art and the philosophy of history. Hegel published very little after 1820; indeed, part of the most influential set of his writings were his Berlin lectures, compiled by his students and published after his death.

In a trip to the Karlsbad spa in 1829 (for health reasons having to do with chest pains), Hegel unexpectedly encountered Schelling. There had certainly been a falling out between the two over the years; Schelling had not taken kindly to Hegel's reference in the 1807 *Phenomenology* to Schelling's "identity philosophy" as the "night in which all cows are black." (In a letter, Hegel had denied it was a reference to Schelling, insisting that it referred only to his misguided followers, but Schelling did not, with some right, believe it.) Schelling was somewhat bitter over how his old friend had eclipsed him in fame, and he was convinced that Hegel had borrowed far more from him than Hegel had ever admitted in print or in private. They both reported back on their encounter to their wives; Hegel said it was just like old times, but Schelling was far more circumspect and cold about the meeting. It was clear that Hegel, who now thought of himself as an old man in fact and not just in nickname, and who was not in the best of health, felt an emotional hole in his life that had followed the breakup of himself, Schelling and Hölderlin as each had gone their separate ways. He was ready for a reconciliation; Schelling was not (or at least not yet).

In recognition of his status, he was made Rector of the university for 1829 to 1830. In 1830 at a lunch with the royal family, Hegel was reminded by the wife of the king's brother that her father was the prince of Homburg vor der Höhe, a postage- stamp principality outside of Frankfurt where Isak von Sinclair had employed Hölderlin after

Hölderlin's dismissal from the Gontard household. She and Hegel drifted off into reminiscences of those days, especially of Hölderlin, now living in Tübingen in a state of non-violent but nonetheless complete madness. Hegel, caught up again in his memories as he had been with Schelling, began to speak at length about his old friend (as the princess noted in her diary, taking on an almost Proustian voice *avant la lettre,*: "At that point, he began to speak of Hölderlin, whom the world has forgotten – of his book, *Hyperion* – all of which had constituted an *époque* for me on account of my sister Auguste's relation to them – and I found by the sounding of this name a true joy – a whole lost past went through me ... it was a remembrance awakened as otherwise would be done through a smell or melody or sound."[26])

Hegel's health continued to deteriorate; the gastrointestinal ailment that eventually killed him in 1831 was acting up throughout the year of 1830; he had to confine himself to bland foods and abandon many of the things he liked, such as drinking tea; his wife noticed how his normally cheery temperament was not so much in evidence, and Hegel rarely felt good enough to go out in the evening, even to his beloved opera. As his health deteriorated, his outbursts of temper, which could take on a kind of gale force at times, began to accelerate. He became more dogmatic about his own views, quick to take offense, and more likely both to start an argument and refuse to back down even when it was clear that he was wrong. But even Hegel himself knew something was wrong with him; he confessed to his friend, Zelter, that he had become too caught up in dealing with his opponents, and after one violent argument with a good friend, Varnhagen von Ense, Hegel responded to Varnhagen's offer of a handshake with an embrace, tears in his eyes. Hegel himself seemed not to like the person his illness and stresses were making him into.

When the French in 1830 staged a new revolution, driving out the restoration king and installing Louis Philippe, the "bourgeois king," Hegel's students were ecstatic, and they thought he would be too. Instead, they found him with a grumpy response, a kind of dismissal of the new Revolution's seriousness, and even a dislike of it as some kind of adolescent, Romantic replay of the first Revolution, only this time with a great danger to the European peace and the movement of European reform than had been the hard won prize of the first Revolution and the Napoleonic wars. To his baffled students, Hegel, the gregarious man who each year toasted the storming of the Bastille, seemed to be fading into an old man, fearful of the future.

[26] Cited in Otto Pöggeler, "Einleitung," in Christoph Jamme and Otto Pöggeler, eds., *Homburg vor der Höhe in der deutschen Geistesgeschichte: Studien zum Freundeskreis um Hegel und Hölderlin* (Stuttgart: Klett-Cotta, 1986), p. 15.

This was, however, not quite true. For the first time, Hegel took up the meaning of modern events in his lectures on the philosophy of history, and when he came to the Revolution, he virtually echoed Wordsworth's lines (about which he did not know) of the glory of being young at that time when he told the students, "The principle of the freedom of the will therefore vindicated itself against existing right ... This was accordingly a glorious dawn. All thinking beings jointly celebrated this epoch. Sublime emotion ruled at that time, a spiritual enthusiasm peered into the heart of the world, as if the reconciliation between the divine with the secular were now first accomplished."[27] In addition to these lectures, he also embarked on a lengthy critique of the upcoming English Reform Bill then being debated in the English parliament and which was being followed with intense interest across Europe, particularly among the reform minded in Germany. He bitterly attacked the English system of awarding office on the basis of aristocratic family connections (claiming that in England, instead of valuing university education and science, they value the "crass ignorance of fox-hunters"[28]), and he gave an eloquent description and moral denunciation of the English treatment of the conquered Irish. What was at work in England, he thought, was the darker side of modern life, the tendency for property and monetary interests to take over, such that only individual "rights" (that is, property rights) come to count. Indeed, the English constitution, rather than being the model for all European development (as many German reformers seemed to think) was in fact a system flawed in its core. The proposals of the reform bill, he argued, will only accelerate the weakening of communal ties and the thick structure of mediating institutions needed to keep the forces of modern commercial society in check and present England with what it ought to fear most: Violent revolution. (That England, the other great Protestant power, besides Prussia, was apparently heading down this path was, of course, immensely troubling to Hegel.)

The outbreak of a cholera epidemic in Eastern Europe that spread to Germany by the summer of 1831 led the Hegel family to retreat to the countryside outside of Berlin (in Kreuzberg, today as much a part of the inner city as anywhere else). Hegel had his birthday celebration there, and all seemed to be well. The family moved back into their quarters in the city as the new term began, and Hegel began lecturing on the philosophy of right. By now, however, Hegel's star had begun to set with the

---

[27] Hegel, *Philosophie der Geschichte*, *Werke*, 12, p. 529; *Philosophy of History* (New York: Dover Publications, 1956), p. 447.

[28] Hegel, "Über die englische Reformbill," *Werke*, 11, p. 103; "The English Reform Bill," in *Hegel's Political Writings*, p. 310.

students; his dismissal of the July Revolution of 1830, and his increasing frailty led them to other younger more popular teachers. (Hegel resented this.) On Sunday, November 13, 1831, Hegel and Marie were looking forward to having some friends over for dinner; during the day, however, Hegel took ill and got progressively worse. The next day, his condition worsened, and the doctors thought it might be cholera. Hegel, who was very fearful of contracting the disease (thinking that with his bad digestive system, he was particularly at risk), must have suspected the worst when he saw the next day that not one but two doctors were attending to him (two doctors being required by Prussian law if cholera was suspected in a patient). Not wishing to distress his family, he retained a sangfroid about the matter. Around 5:00 in the afternoon, Marie sent for Hegel's next-door neighbor and good friend, Johannes Schulze. By the time Schulze arrived at the Hegel house a few minutes later, Hegel was dead.

Hegel's sudden death came as a great shock to the Berlin community. His funeral on November 16 was attended by a massive audience. The funeral orations by the theologian, F. Marheineke, and his friend, Friedrich Förster, likened him to a modern savior who had come to explain the modern world to itself.

Even though Hegel and his sister, Christiane, had not seen each other since early in Hegel's Nuremberg days, Christiane took the news of his death very badly; after a short correspondence with Marie, Christiane went to the Nagold River a month after Hegel's death and drowned herself. The Hegelian school that immediately formed (and immediately dedicated itself to putting out a complete edition of his works, including the unpublished lectures) began also almost immediately to fight among themselves as to who was the true bearer of the Hegelian philosophy. Before the 1840s had even begun, the Hegelian school had split into several different factions, and the wing known as the "left" Hegelians (a phrase originally made as a jest by David Friedrich Strauss) began to take Hegel's thought in an unanticipated revolutionary direction, much to the alarm of the Prussian government (and later to the alarm of all the reigning powers). The most gifted of them, Karl Marx, claimed to have transformed Hegel's "idealism" into a scientific materialism that was supposed to provide both the critique of the old order and the blueprint for a new socialist order.

In the late 1830s, Schelling introduced himself to one of Hegel's sons who was attending his lectures in Munich; never having reconciled with Hegel while both were still alive, Schelling sought his reconciliation with Hegel's son, and the two became friends. A few years later, in the ensuing uproar over the "left" Hegelians, the government offered a special chair to Schelling, specifying that among other things he had a duty to "stamp out the dragon seed of Hegelianism in Berlin." On November 15, 1841 – almost ten years to the day after Hegel's death – Schelling gave his inaugural lecture in Berlin. Sitting in his audience that day were Søren Kierkegaard, Michael Bakunin, and Friedrich Engels – the early exponents of what would later be called existentialism, anarchism, and Marxism. The long march of Hegel's posthumous influence on European history had begun. Hölderlin, thinking of Hegel, died in 1843. Schelling died in 1854.

2 Ancient Skepticism, Modern Naturalism, and Nihilism in Hegel's Early Jena Writings

I. INTRODUCTION

Hegel has often been portrayed as a dogmatic metaphysician, uninterested in epistemological issues and in defending his philosophy against epistemic challenges. Indeed, the very idea of epistemology as a distinct philosophical focus or discipline was framed in part by those who opposed Hegelianism.[1]

But the portrayal is a caricature. Hegel is interested in epistemological issues and, as several interpreters have recently observed, has a sophisticated view of the epistemic status of his philosophy.[2]

Central here is Hegel's relation to skepticism, a recurring theme throughout his career. This chapter is concerned with the view of skepticism expressed in Hegel's early Jena writings – not only in his essay on ancient and modern skepticism, the topic of recent discussion, but also in his writings about Jacobi. Others have explored, to great effect, Hegel's preference for ancient over modern scepticism. I will argue that the modern skepticism disparaged by Hegel should be understood as a kind of *naturalism*, and that, notwithstanding his view

---

All Hegel references are cited from *Gesammelte Werke* (*GW*), ed. by Rhenisch-Westfälische Akademie der Wissenschaften (Hamburg: Meiner, 1968-); *Theorie Werk-Ausgabe* (*TW-A*), ed. by Eva Moldenhauer and Karl-Markus Michel (Frankfurt: Suhrkamp, 1970); and the pertinent English translation. Unascribed translations are my own.

[1] See Klaus Christian Köhnke, *Entstehung und Aufstieg des Neukantianismus: Die deutsche Universitätsphilosophie zwischen Idealismus und Positivismus* (Frankfurt am Main: Suhrkamp, 1986), partially trans. by R. J. Hollingdale as *The Rise of Neokantianism. German Academic Philosophy between Idealism and Positivism* (Cambridge: Cambridge University Press, 1991).

[2] See Michael Forster, *Hegel and Skepticism* (Cambridge, MA: Harvard University Press, 1989) and *Hegel's Idea of a Phenomenology of Spirit* (Chicago, IL: University of Chicago Press, 1998); also, Kenneth Westphal, *Hegel's Epistemological Realism* (Dordrecht: Kluwer, 1989) and *Hegel's Epistemology* (Indianapolis, IN: Hackett, 2003). It should be noted that having epistemological interests does not of itself render one's philosophy nonmetaphysical.

of its philosophical merits, it remains in competition with his own philosophical project. I will also argue that the ancient skepticism taken by Hegel to be of philosophical importance is not merely retrieved from the pages of ancient books, for Hegel views it as intimately connected to modern philosophy's *nihilism*, thematized by Jacobi. While Hegel's views about skepticism and other important matters shifts significantly after Schelling's departure from Jena in 1803, his early views constitute the indispensable backdrop against which to understand the *Phenomenology* and his later writings. Nowhere is this more true than in the case of skepticism.

II. MODERN SKEPTICISM AND POST-KANTIAN NATURALISM

Three questions can help us to examine a philosopher's interest in skepticism. First, which *element* of knowledge does the pertinent skepticism *target*? Recalling Plato's account of knowledge as true belief plus *logos*, we might ask, for example, whether aspersion is cast upon truth, belief, or reason. Second, what does the philosopher want to *do* to this skepticism? Does she want, for example, to *refute* it, or to use it as a *filter*, taking her stand on what survives? Does she want to change the question from "Do we know anything at all?" to "*How* do we know what we know?" Or does she want, say, to *preempt* skepticism, by avoiding ways of thinking that let skeptical doubts arise? Third, what does the philosopher take the *upshot* of skepticism to be? For Descartes, our power to doubt reveals human freedom: the infinity of the will outruns the finitude of our knowledge. For Kant, our skepticism about synthetic *a priori* principles shows that we constitute the empirical world through *a priori* synthesis. What does Hegel take skepticism's upshot to be?

Here, we must ask these questions twice, since Hegel distinguishes two kinds of skepticism, in which he takes different interests. I will consider first the modern skepticism that Hegel disparages, and then the ancient skepticism he valorizes.

Hegel's explicit target is Gottlob Ernst Schulze. Already famous for his pseudepigraphic criticism of the first German idealist project in 1792,[3] Schulze is taken by Hegel to represent modern skepticism. This, however, is in fact, according to Hegel, not scepticism at all, but rather

---

3 See Schulze, *Aenesidemus, oder Über die Fundamente der von dem Herrn Professor Reinhold in Jena gelieferten Elementar-Philosophie, nebst einer Verteidigung des Skeptizismus gegen die Anmassungen der Vernunftkritik*, ed. by Manfred Frank (Hamburg: Meiner, 1996). A selection is translated in *Between Kant and Hegel: Texts in the Development of Post-Kantian Idealism*, trans. and ed. by George di Giovanni and H. S. Harris (Indianapolis, IN: Hackett, 2000), hereafter *BKH*.

a version of *dogmatism* that takes specific aim at *the speculative* – that is, at what Hegel considers genuinely philosophical.

In characterizing this pseudo-skepticism, Hegel does not have Schulze alone in view. In the *Encyclopedia* of 1827 and 1830, he refers readers to the earlier essay for a comparison with ancient skepticism of modern skepticism and Humean skepticism in particular.[4] Accordingly, Michael Forster seeks to generalize Hegel's target. First, Forster argues that, whereas ancient skepticism is based on a *method*, modern skepticism in contrast:

> is founded on a cluster of *specific problems* – in the correlative threefold sense of problems which arise for some kinds of claims or beliefs but not for others, which are raised not in the service of any positive goal but simply because they seem to demand solutions, and which essentially rely on the presupposition of the correctness of certain *other* claims or beliefs. Typically the modern skeptic's specific problems concern the legitimacy of proceeding from claims about a certain kind of subject matter, the knowledge of which is assumed to be absolutely or relatively unproblematic, to claims about a second kind of subject matter, the knowledge of which is not felt to be unproblematic in the same way. At one time, the unproblematic subject matter might be one's own (current) mental states, and the unproblematic subject matter might be the external physical world, and the problematic subject matter the objects of religious belief. Schulze, the modern skeptic with whom Hegel is directly concerned in *The Relation of Skepticism to Philosophy*, is understood by Hegel to emphasize the latter kind of skeptical problem, while Hume's writings contain examples of both kinds of examples.[5]

Forster then proceeds to "focus on one of those problems, the problem of our knowledge of the external world, or what Berkeley called the problem of a "veil of perception."[6]

Forster is right to generalize Hegel's target. However, to characterize Hegel's target in this particular way is problematic. First, Schulze is not himself a "veil of perception" skeptic. In fact, he is a *direct realist*. In his *Kritik der theoretischen Philosophie* – the work discussed by Hegel – Schulze follows Thomas Reid in rejecting what he calls "the groundless hypothesis that all our knowledge of objects is mediated by representations".[7]

---

[4] Hegel, *GW*, 19:57, 20:77; *TW-A*, 8:112; *The Encyclopedia Logic*, trans. by T. F. Geraets, W. A. Suchting and H. S. Harris (Indianapolis, IN: Hackett Publishing, 1991), p. 80, §39A.

[5] Michael Forster, *Hegel and Skepticism* (Cambridge, MA: Harvard University Press, 1989), p. 11.

[6] Forster, *Hegel and Skepticism*, p. 13.

[7] Schulze, *Kritik der theoretischen Philosophie* (Hamburg: Bohn, 1801), 2:7. Forster is aware that Schulze is not a "veil of perception" skeptic. See Footnote 6 above and Forster, *Hegel and Skepticism*, 188, note 10, where he notes that Schulze exempts

Second, if we pay more attention to the specific details of Schulze and his allies, we will find that modern skepticism is indeed, contrary to Forster, based on a *method*. To be sure, this method is quite different from that of ancient skepticism, and its use in philosophy is virulently opposed by Hegel. It is *the method of the natural sciences*.

Schulze is in fact a representative of a larger tendency that may be characterized as sharing two commitments: *post-Kantian naturalism* and *post-Jacobian foundationalism*.[8] Others include Carl Christian Erhard Schmid – the target of Fichte's infamous annihilation – Johann Friedrich Fries – Hegel's academic rival and philosophical/political enemy – and Friedrich Eduard Beneke – whom Hegel helped to push out of the University of Berlin and against whom the accusation of "psychologism" was first levelled.[9]

Post-Kantian naturalism is the view that what is most valuable in Kant's revolution is the continuation of Hume's demolition of rationalist metaphysics. Kant's transcendental method, however, is regarded as an unfortunate residue of Kant's own rationalist metaphysics. On this view, what philosophy requires, if it is to be set on the sure path of a science, is the method of the natural sciences, which is alone capable of attaining knowledge. Philosophy should therefore become, in Fries' words, "psychological or, better, anthropological cognition."[10]

Post-Kantian naturalism is, then, a *methodological* naturalism. Some versions are, however, *substantively nonnaturalist*. For example, Fries maintains that, although we cannot *know* things in themselves, we can and should have *faith* in the noumenal realm. In contrast, Schulze is not only a methodological but also a *substantive naturalist*. He argues that we should be wholly *agnostic* about things in themselves, and even about whether human knowledge is in principle limited to appearances. This is Schulze's version of skepticism: we can know objects given by

from skepticism the modern natural sciences, specifically physics and astronomy. Yet, for most of his discussion, Forster sets this point aside.

8 See Franks, "Serpentine Naturalism and Protean Nihilism: Transcendental Philosophy in Anthropological Neo-Kantianism, German Idealism, and Neo-Kantianism," in *Oxford Handbook of Continental Philosophy*, ed. by Brian Leiter and Michael Rosen, (Oxford: Oxford University Press, 2007), pp. 252–256.

9 Johann Eduard Erdmann, *Grundriss der Geschichte der Philosophie*, 2nd ed., (Berlin: Hertz, 1870), 2:646, seems to have used the term first, to criticise Beneke, in whose forced departure from the University of Berlin Hegel had apparently been involved. Wilhelm Windelband, *Geschichte der neueren Philosophie* (Leipzig: Breitkopf & Härtel, 1880), pp. 386–397 extends the term to others whose method is not transcendental, for example, Fries.

10 Fries, *Neue oder anthropologische Kritik*, text of the 1828–1831, 2nd edition, which revised the 1807 edition, reprinted in *Sämtliche schriften*, ed. by Gert König and Lutz Geldsetzer (Aalen: Scientia Verlag, 1967), 1:29.

means of the senses, but we cannot know anything about things in themselves, and so we cannot know whether the objects we know are appearances of things in themselves. Though hardly Kantian, it is certainly *post*-Kantian.

The second feature of the broader tendency represented by Schulze is what I call post-Jacobian foundationalism. This is a version – or, rather, a family of versions – of the thesis *that any body of genuine knowledge has foundational elements that either cannot or should not be doubted*. These foundational elements are termed "matters of fact" (*Tatsachen*).[11]

Nobody is more identified with this approach than Jacobi, whom Hegel characterizes as possessed by "holy zeal for the good cause of actual things".[12] Jacobi argues forcefully that the philosophical tradition since Aristotle, with its assumption that justification consists in demonstration from first principles, can never refute skepticism – and indeed cannot avoid nihilism, to which I will return later. The only escape is to preempt scepticism by insisting on the foundational status of indemonstrable matters of fact. Now, Jacobi is neither a

---

[11] This neologism was coined by Joachim Johann Spalding in his partial translation of Bishop Butler's *The Analogy of Religion, Natural and Revealed to the Constitution and Course of Nature* (London: Knapton, 1736), as an equivalent to the English "matters of fact", itself a translation of the Latin "*res facti*". See *Bestätigung der natürlichen und geoffenbarten Religion aus ihrer Gleichförmigkeit*, trans. by Spalding, in *Abriß von dem neuesten Zustand der Gelehrsamkeit und einigen wichtigen Streitigkeiten in der Politischen Welt* (Göttingen: Schmid, 1739), 8:176–200. The English phrase has its original home in legal discourse, where it is used to designate an act or event accepted by the court as having occurred, on the basis of stipulation or of evidence supplied by witnesses. Robert Boyle had deployed this notion of a fact – that is, an event verified by witnesses – in his defence of the epistemic status of experimental reports, which were crucial to the new natural science but which did not fit the model of demonstration from first principles still championed by, for example, Thomas Hobbes. See Rose-Mary Sargent, *The Diffident Naturalist: Robert Boyle and the Philosophy of Experiment* (Chicago, IL: University of Chicago Press, 1995), pp. 49–50, 131–138. Later, Butler had used the very same notion to argue that, if natural science could rely on the evidence of witnesses, then so could Christianity. In its new German setting, cut off from its origins in common law, the term "*Tatsache*" spread quickly, coming to signify that which any reasonable person should acknowledge, even if it originates in an epistemic source unrecognized by philosophical tradition.

[12] Hegel, *GW*, 4:378; *T-WA*, 2:380; *Faith and Knowledge* (hereafter, *FK*), trans. by Walter Cerf and H. S. Harris, (Albany, NY: SUNY Press, 1988), p. 140. I have modified the Cerf and Harris translation, since Hegel does not use the term "*Tatsachen*" in the original. But Cerf and Harris have understood Hegel's intention. See *GW*, 4:371; *T-WA*, 2:370; *FK*, 131: "Köppen ... expresses Jacobi's conception of knowledge in an easily intelligible way: we human beings receive the things as matters of fact [*Thatsachen*] through sense and through the supernatural revelation of seeing, perceiving and feeling."

methodological nor a substantive naturalist. As we shall see, he tends to see modern natural science as part of modern philosophy, hence as potentially nihilistic. He also thinks that we have the ability to perceive not only sensible but also supersensible objects. But, as Hegel notes, Jacobi begins around 1800 to moderate his anti-philosophical talk, calling for philosophy to be renewed rather than abandoned.[13] After 1805, Jacobi allies himself with Fries, hence with post-Kantian methodological naturalism, which is not to say that he adopts this position.[14]

We can now make sense of Schulze's specific position as targeted by Hegel in 1802. According to Schulze:

the existence of that which is given as present within the domain of our consciousness has entirely undeniable certainty. For since it is present in consciousness, we could doubt its existence just as little as consciousness itself; to want to doubt consciousness however is absolutely impossible, because such a doubt, since it cannot occur without consciousness, would therefore be nothing. Now one calls that which is given in and with consciousness a fact of consciousness. Consequently the facts of consciousness are the undeniable actuality to which all philosophical speculation must relate itself, and which is to be explained or made graspable through these speculations.[15]

What is the *content* of the facts of consciousness appealed to by Schulze? Forster supplies the following gloss:

Modern skeptics suppose that no skeptical difficulties can arise about their own (current) mental contents, and so feel themselves justified in retaining beliefs about them as part of the basis of their skeptical attack on beliefs about the external world.[16]

But, as I have mentioned, Forster himself would admit that Schulze's facts of consciousness are not beliefs about my current mental contents. In Schulze's words, cited by Hegel:

Those facts are either *cognitions of objects,* or *expressions of volitions,* or *feelings of pleasure and displeasure* . . . .[17]

---

[13] Jacobi, "Über eine Weissagung Lichtenbergs", in *Taschenbuch für das Jahr 1802,* ed. by J. G. Jacobi (Hamburg: Perthes, 1802), p. 40n, cited by Hegel, *GW,* 4:374n; *T-WA,* 2:374n; *FK,* 135n.

[14] See, for example, Jacobi's many citations of Fries in his 1815 preface to the reprint of *David Hume* in vol. 2 of *Friedrich Heinrich Jacobi's Werke,* ed. by J. F. Köppen and C. J. F. Roth (Leipzig, Fleischer, 1812–1825); *MPW,* 537–590.

[15] Schulze, *Kritik,* 1:51.

[16] Forster, *Hegel and Skepticism,* p. 14.

[17] Schulze, *Kritik,* 1:52, cited by Hegel, *GW,* 4:200; *T-WA,* 2:218; "On the Relationship of Skepticism to Philosophy, Exposition of its Different Modifications and Comparison of the Latest Form with the Ancient One" (hereafter *RSP*), trans. by H. S. Harris, in di Giovanni and Harris, *BKH,* 317.

Note that facts of the first kind, which underlie theoretical philosophy, are cognitions *of objects*, not *of mental representations of objects*.
Specifically, they are what Schulze calls "immediate (intuitive) cognitions", that is, states or episodes in which

the known object is itself present to the knowing I, and that object
comes into the domain of consciousness, or is that in which consciousness
extends to the object without the mediation of something distinct from the
object.[18]

In other words, the *immediacy* of facts of consciousness consists neither
in their mental character nor in the nonconceptuality of their content.
It consists rather in their being *direct* presentations of external objects.
Facts of consciousness, in *this* sense, ground modern natural sciences
such as physics and astronomy, which are well-grounded insofar as they
explain the sensible data in terms of natural laws. Similarly, the task of
theoretical philosophy is to explain how the human mind is capable of
these immediate cognitions.

I turn now to the three questions announced earlier. First, post-
Kantian naturalism is skeptical about *justification* or *logos* – more
specifically, what Hegel calls "the rational" or the Absolute, the theme
of true or speculative philosophy. In this respect, it is a descendant of
the naturalistic skepticism that awoke Kant from his dogmatic slumber,
which could find no room for reason in what it took to be the natural world. And it differs from external world skepticism, which questions whether knowledge-claims meet the *truth* condition – whether,
for example, mental representations correspond to external things.
Second, as we shall see, what Hegel wants to *do* to the modern skepticism he disparages is to subject it to the ancient skepticism he valorises,
so discussion is premature. However, third, we can already anticipate
the *upshot* of Hegel's discussion of Schulze's so-called skepticism. It is
that the method of speculative philosophy *must not* be the method of
natural science.

III. ANCIENT SKEPTICISM

In 1802, Hegel is not yet in a position to make the positive claim that the
nonnaturalistic method of speculative philosophy is intimately related
to ancient skepticism. For this development, the *Phenomenology* must
be consulted. But he is already in a position to say that the method
of ancient skepticism is indispensable to speculative philosophy – as a

[18] Schulze, *Kritik*, 1:56.

weapon in the struggle with unphilosophy, including Schulze's pseudo-skepticism.

Hegel distinguishes three kinds or moments of ancient skepticism: Pyrrhonian, Platonic, and Agrippan. On what he calls their negative sides, all are directed against some version of what Hegel terms dogmatism. Their positive sides – in my terminology, their upshots – are, however, quite different. What concerns me, once again, is in the first place, the question of identification. However, whereas in Part II of this chapter, we had the contemporaneous instance and needed to formulate the general kind of scepticism, we have here the general kind and need to identify the contemporaneous instance.

Hegel's focus on the method of Agrippan skepticism, along with his definition of dogmatism, gives us a specification of ancient skepticism as an attack on *logos* or the justificatory element of knowledge. The Agrippan method is encapsulated in the five Agrippan tropes: 1. diversity/discrepancy, 2. infinite regress, 3. relativity, 4. arbitrary presupposition/hypothesis, and 5. circularity. Robert Fogelin gives the following, helpful characterization of how the tropes operate:

Two of Agrippa's modes, discrepancy and relativity, trigger a demand for justification by revealing that there are competing claims concerning the nature of the world we perceive ... Thus the modes of discrepancy and relativity force anyone who makes claims beyond the modest expression of opinion to give reasons in support of these claims ... The task of the remaining three modes – those based on regress *ad infinitum*, circularity and (arbitrary) hypothesis – is to show that it is impossible to complete this reason-giving process in a satisfactory way. If the Pyrrhonists are right, no argument, once started, can avoid falling into one of the traps of circularity, infinite regress, or arbitrary assumption.[19]

These three traps have come to be known collectively as *the Agrippan trilemma*. The picture is that the dogmatist makes a claim; the skeptic then triggers a demand for justification by showing the claim either to be one among many, or else to be relative to some context or other; in response, the dogmatist attempts to provide a *logos* or justificatory account of the claim, an account that the skeptic tries to impale on one of the three horns of infinite regress, circularity and arbitrary hypothesis; and the skeptic concludes that the dogmatist's claim amounts not even to justified belief, let alone knowledge.

[19] Robert Fogelin, *Pyrrhonian Reflections on Knowledge and Justification* (Oxford: Oxford University Press, 1994), p. 116. Hegel agrees with Fogelin in distinguishing the trilemma from the other two tropes. He differs only insofar as he takes discrepancy and relativity, not only as possible triggers, but also as possible skeptical conclusions.

Hegel defines the target of ancient skepticism as follows:

The essence of dogmatism consists in this that it posits something finite, some-thing burdened with an opposition (e.g., pure Subject, or pure Object, or in dual-ism the duality as opposed to the identity) as the Absolute".[20]

"To posit something as the Absolute" means here, I suggest, to treat a ground as escaping the Agrippan trilemma. What Hegel adds is a diagno-sis: no ground can escape the trilemma if it is "finite" or "burdened with opposition". Conversely, he thinks, unlike an Agrippan skeptic, that a properly "infinite" ground *does* escape the Agrippan trilemma. The con-temporaneous significance of Hegel's parenthesis is clear: Fichte's abso-lute I ("pure subject"), Spinoza's substance ("pure object") and Kant's transcendental unity of apperception ("duality" of subject and object) are all finite and hence vulnerable to Agrippan skepticism. In contrast, the speculative principle of Schelling's and Hegel's identity philosophy is infinite and hence absolute.

Also implicit here is Hegel's view that any attempt to posit something as the Absolute *by means of concepts of the understanding* is bound to posit something *finite* as the Absolute, even if the posited something can make *some* claim to be infinite – as is the case with Fichte, Spinoza and Kant. This is because all concepts of the understanding operate according to a law for which it is hard to find a better formulation – though Hegel does not cite it – than Bishop Butler's well-known statement that "Every thing is what it is, and not another thing."[21] This means that every thing is the determinate thing that it is in virtue of 1. its positive aspect or identity, typically spelled out in terms of intrinsic properties, and 2. its negative aspect or difference from other things, typically spelled out in terms of relational properties, where 3. there is between identity and difference an unqualified difference and in no sense an identity. Any determination of a ground by means of a concept governed by this law will *ipso facto* burden the ground in question with opposition, since the ground is in part determined by means of a difference that is in no sense an identity.

For present purposes, we need not determine precisely what, in 1802, Hegel means by "infinite". We may also pass quickly over Pyrrhonian skepticism. This first kind or moment of ancient skepticism is "directed, like all philosophy generally, against the dogmatism of ordinary con-sciousness itself", while its positive side lies "wholly and only in char-acter" – that is, in a way of life characterized by "neutrality towards

[20] Hegel, *GW*, 4:219; *T-WA*, 2:245; *RSP*, in *BKH*, 335.
[21] Joseph Butler, "Preface to the Second Edition," *Fifteen Sermons Preached at the Rolls Chapel* (London: Knapton, 1729), p. 39.

the necessity of nature."[22] After the discovery of the New World, we moderns are well aware that our particular ways of life are not the only ones, and so we need no particular contemporaneous equivalent.

For "Platonic skepticism", on the other hand, Hegel evidently thinks that there is a contemporaneous equivalent whose identification presents no challenge. In a striking passage, he writes:

> What more perfect and self-sustaining document and system of genuine skepticism could we find than the *Parmenides* in the Platonic philosophy? It embraces the whole domain of knowledge through concepts of understanding, and destroys it. This Platonic skepticism is not concerned with doubting these truths of the understanding...; rather it is intent on the complete denial of all truth to this sort of cognition. This skepticism does not constitute a particular thing in a system, but is itself the negative side of the cognition of the Absolute, and directly presupposes Reason as the positive side ... if in any one proposition that expresses a cognition of Reason, its reflected aspect – the concepts that are contained in it – is isolated, and the way that they are bound together is considered, it must become evident that these concepts are together sublated, or in other words they are united in such a way that they contradict themselves; otherwise it would not be a proposition of Reason but only of understanding.[23]

The contemporaneous equivalent is clearly Hegel's early version of logic. Like Platonic skepticism, it is intended to be 1. not merely doubtful but destructive of knowledge through concepts of the understanding, 2. and comprehensive insofar as 3. it presupposes a systematic account of the categories and the syllogism, an account taken from a speculative metaphysics that employs the method, not of skeptical destruction, but rather of construction in intuition.[24] Closely related to the early Jena logic is the project of *critique*, undertaken in the *Critical Journal* in which Hegel's early writings, including the essay on skepticism, appear. Critique is also destructive and it also assumes "the Idea of philosophy" as "the precondition and presupposition without which it would only be able to set one subjective view against another for ever and ever, and never set the Absolute against the conditioned."[25] Unlike Platonic skepticism and logic, however, critique merely responds to contemporaneous cases of unphilosophy, making no pretension to comprehensiveness.

[22] Hegel, *GW*, 4:214; *T-WA*, 2:238–239; *RSP*, in *BKH*, 331.
[23] Hegel, *GW*, 4:207-208; *T-WA*, 2:228-229; *RSP*, in *BKH*, 323-324.
[24] For a helpful account, see Forster, *Hegel's Idea*, pp. 110–114, 167–177.
[25] Hegel, *GW* 4:117; *T-WA* 2:171; "Introduction on the Essence of Philosophical Criticism Generally, and its Relationship to the Present State of Philosophy in Particular", trans. H. S. Harris, in *BKH*, 275. On critique in Hegel's early Jena thinking, see William Bristow, *Hegel and the Transformation of Philosophical Critique* (Oxford: Oxford University Press, 2007).

For my purposes, the interesting and challenging question of identi-fication is: what is the contemporaneous equivalent of Agrippan skepti-cism? Like Platonic skepticism, Agrippan skepticism is *comprehensive* in its destructiveness. But it does not attain comprehensiveness because it is *systematic*, in virtue of presupposing the speculative principle of identity. Rather, it attains comprehensiveness because it *has* no presup-positions of its own. It subjects dogmatism to an immanent critique that provisionally assumes only the presuppositions of the dogmatists themselves. Of Agrippan skepticism Hegel writes:

The *five later* tropes of skepticism, which make up the genuine arsenal of its weapons against philosophical cognition, are wholly and exclusively related to this complete separation of philosophies, and the complete fixation of their dogmas and dividing lines, and likewise related to the contemporary orientation of skepticism against dogmatism on one side, and against philosophy itself on the other.[26]

The phrase "the contemporary orientation of skepticism" [*nunmehrige Richtung*] could refer only to the role of skepticism within late ancient philosophy, with its competing schools. But it could also refer to the role of skepticism in Hegel's day, with its competing systems. I have already noted Hegel's parenthetical reference to Fichte, Spinoza and Kant as examples of dogmatism. Now I want to propose that Agrippan skep-ticism has not only contemporaneous targets, but a contemporaneous equivalent, which should be identified with what Jacobi calls *nihilism*, or something very close to it.

IV. MODERN NIHILISM

First, an objection must be preempted. Far from being a modern tendency corresponding to Agrippan skepticism, what Jacobi calls nihilism is, according to Beiser, a radical version of external world skepticism – exactly the modern skepticism that, on Forster's view, Hegel disparages:

The most important point to note about Jacobi's use of the term ['nihilism'] is that he uses it to designate a specifically epistemological position. The term is virtually synonymous with, although slightly broader than, another term of Jacobi's: 'egoism' (*Egoismus*). According to the early Jacobi, the egoist is a radical idealist who denies the existence of all reality independent of his own sensations. He is indeed a solipsist, but a solipsist who disputes the permanent reality of his own self as much as the external world and other minds. In his later writings, however, Jacobi tends to replace the term 'egoist' with 'nihilist'. Like the egoist, the nihilist is someone who denies the existence of everything independent of the

[26] Hegel, *GW*, 4:218; *T-WA*, 2:243; *RSP*, in *BKH*, 334.

immediate contents of his own consciousness, whether external objects, other minds, God, or even his own self. All that exists for the nihilist is therefore his own momentary conscious states, his fleeting impressions or representations; but these representations represent, it is necessary to add, nothing.[27]

Though nihilism is "a specifically epistemological position" according to Beiser, it nevertheless has *ethical* ramifications:

The ethical element of Jacobi's usage becomes perfectly explicit when he says that the nihilist denies the existence not only of things, but also of values. Since he denies the existence of an external world, other minds, a soul, and God, the nihilist discharges himself from all obligations to such pseudo-entities.[28]

Now, Beiser is certainly correct about *one* strand of Jacobi's thinking. Jacobi explicitly connects nihilism – of which he speaks first in his 1799 open letter to Fichte (519) – with what he had earlier called *egoism*; and what he had earlier called "egoism" seems to be a radicalized, external world skepticism.[29]

However, there is also *another* strand of Jacobi's thinking that gives rise to a *different* conception of nihilism. What I want to identify as the contemporaneous version of Agrippan skepticism is this *other* conception – quite different from Beiser's, but equally grounded in Jacobi's thinking.

Early in his 1799 open letter to Fichte, Jacobi says that he "first found entry into the *Wissenschaftslehre* through the representation of an *inverted* Spinozism."[30] He also refers explicitly to a passage from the second edition (1789) of his Spinoza book, a passage that he actually reprints as Supplement I to the letter. I will comment on this important passage shortly. For now, my point is just that, whereas Beiser mentions only the connection between what Jacobi calls nihilism and his criticism of Kant's idealism as egoism, there is also a connection between what Jacobi calls nihilism and his criticism of *Spinozism*. Whatever else Jacobi may find to criticize in Spinoza, he does *not* regard him as an egoist.

---

[27] Beiser, *Fate of Reason* (Cambridge, MA: Harvard University Press, 1987), p. 82.

[28] Beiser, *Fate of Reason*, p. 82. See also Beiser, *Hegel* (London: Routledge, 2005), pp. 27–29, 175, for the view that Hegel is deeply concerned with nihilism in this sense.

[29] For Jacobi's earlier reference to "speculative egoism" in the context of his criticism of Kant, see his "Supplement on Transcendental Idealism", *David Hume über den Glauben, oder Idealismus und Realismus. Ein Gespräch* (Breslau: Löwe, 1787), p. 228; Jacobi, *The Main Philosophical Writings and the Novel Allwill*, trans. and ed. by George di Giovanni (Montreal and Kingston, ON: McGill-Queen's University Press, 1994) (henceforth *MPW*), p. 338. Jacobi first uses the term "nihilism" in *Jacobi an Fichte* (Hamburg: Perthes, 1799), p. 39; *MPW*, 519. Earlier in the letter, he uses the term "egoism." See *Jacobi an Fichte*, 3; *MPW*, 502.

[30] Jacobi, *Jacobi an Fichte*, 4; *MPW*, 502.

Instead, Jacobi comments on Spinoza's realism and even claims to have learned something from Spinoza about how to be a realist![31]

How, then, is Agrippan skepticism connected to both Spinozism and nihilism? First, I note that Jacobi seems to have been deeply troubled by Agrippan skepticism in his youth. He claims to have been afflicted, from the age of eight or nine, by two horrifying visions: the thought of eternity *a parte ante* made him cry out loud and fall "into a kind of swoon"; while the thought of annihilation, which had always been dreadful, now became even more dreadful, nor could he bear the vision of an *eternal forward duration* any better."[32] Although he managed to free himself from the associated "state of unspeakable despair", he claimed in 1789 that he still took constant care to avoid it, and wrote:

I have reason to suspect that I can arbitrarily evoke it in me any time I want; and I believe that it is in my power, were I to do so repeatedly a few times, to take my life within minutes by this means.[33]

According to Jacobi's own analysis – which Hegel mocks – temporality and causality are intimately connected, and the cause-effect relationship is almost always conflated with the ground-consequence relationship.[34] So it is plausible to interpret Jacobi's despair as arising from two of the tropes that constitute the Agrippan trilemma: infinite regress and arbitrary presupposition or hypothesis. He despairs, in short, because he

---

[31] For Jacobi on Spinoza's realism, see, for example, *Über die Lehre des Spinoza in Briefen an den Herrn Moses Mendelssohn* (Breslau: Löwe, 1785), p. 142; *MPW*, 223: "XXVII. An immediate concept, considered in and for itself alone, is without representation. [As di Giovanni notes, "In the second edition Jacobi adds: "– is a feeling!"] XXVIII: Representations arise from mediated concepts, and require mediated objects, that is, where there are representations, there must also be several individual things that refer to one another; with something 'inner' there must also be something 'outer.'" Jacobi credits Spinoza with "the seminal ideas" for his realistic deduction of causality in a footnote added to *David Hume* in 1815. See *David Hume*, pp. 215–216n; *MPW*, 297, note 25. On Jacobi's deduction, see Hegel, *GW* 4:349–350; *T-WA* 2:339–340; *FK*, 101.

[32] Jacobi, *Über die Lehre des Spinoza. Neue vermehrte Ausgabe* (Breslau: Löwe, 1789), 328; *MPW*, 362–363.

[33] Ibid.

[34] In *Über die Lehre des Spinoza* (1785), p. 17; *MPW*, 188, Jacobi claims that a consistent rationalism must treat time as illusory; and in *David Hume*, pp. 93–102; *MPW*, 287–290, he argues for the need to distinguish the cause-effect relationship, which can be grasped conceptually, from temporal succession, which cannot be grasped conceptually, but which can be known through the living experience of action. This is a distinction that, in Jacobi's view, the rationalist philosophical tradition cannot make. See Hegel, *GW*, 4:348–350, 352–357, 359; *T-WA*, 2:335–339, 341–349, 353; *FK*, 98–101, 104–110, 114.

lacks an absolute principle that would serve as a satisfying response to the Agrippan skeptic.

What about circularity, the trilemma's third horn? I have argued elsewhere that, in his seminal Spinoza book of 1785, Jacobi reconstructs the first book of Spinoza's *Ethics* as an argument that only a specific kind of system can escape the Agrippan trilemma: what I have called a Holistic Monist system.[35] Such a system is (a) *holistic*, insofar as every finite element is what it is only in virtue of its role within the whole. And (b) it is *monistic* in the sense that the whole is constituted as a whole – as opposed to a mere aggregate – by a single, immanent, absolute, and infinite first principle. I have constructed the argument elsewhere and will not go over it now. For present purposes, what matters is that a Holistic Monist system is intended to be *virtuously circular*: the totality of the finite requires the infinite first principle as its ground, but the immanence of the infinite first principle means that it cannot be without the totality of the finite. As Jacobi puts it, "the sum of all finite things . . . is one and the same as the infinite thing itself."[36] All the German idealists, from Reinhold to Hegel, accept in effect Jacobi's Spinozistic argument that Holistic Monist systematicity alone offers the hope of escaping Agrippan skepticism.

Jacobi, however, thinks that Holistic Monism is *tantamount to nihilism*. The fundamental point can be put in terms of the law governing concepts of the understanding discussed earlier. Finite things whose determinacy consists solely in negation, lacking positive identities altogether, are "nonentia". This might suggest that the infinite "is the one single true *ens reale*".[37] But, since this infinite is, in Lessing's favourite phrase, *hen kai pan*, one and all, it lacks any contrast by virtue of which it could be determinate, so it is *ouden kai panta*, nothing and all things.[38] As Jacobi remarks, parenthetically but pithily, in a footnote to his 1785 Spinoza book:

(. . . an absolute individual is just as impossible as an individual Absolute. *Determinatio est negatio, Op. Posth.*, p. 558)[39]

---

[35] Franks, *All or Nothing: Systematicity, Transcendental Arguments, and Nihilism in German Idealism* (Cambridge, MA: Harvard University Press, 2005), pp. 85–86.
[36] Jacobi, *Über die Lehre des Spinoza* (1785), pp. 121–123; *MPW*, 217.
[37] Jacobi, *Über die Lehre des Spinoza* (1785), p. 131; *MPW*, 220.
[38] Jacobi, *Eduard Allwills Briefsammlung* (Königsberg: Nicolovius, 1792), p. 295; *MPW*, 488.
[39] Jacobi, *Über die Lehre des Spinoza* (1785), p. 20n; *MPW*, 190. Jacobi is referring to Spinoza's Letter 50, to Jarig Jelles, 2 June 1674, *Opera Posthuma*, ed. by Jarig Jelles (Amsterdam: Riewertsz, 1677), p. 558; *Complete Works*, trans. by Samuel Shirley, ed. by Michael Morgan (Indianapolis, IN: Hackett, 2002), p. 892: "it is obvious that matter in its totality, considered without limitation, can have no figure, and

Hence, no matter what Spinoza says about God, his system is atheistic. And, no matter what he says about human freedom, his system is
fatalistic. Moreover, the same is true of *any* Holistic Monist system: no
matter how it differs in detail from Spinoza's, it cannot make room for
individuality, whether divine, human, or natural.[40]

In 1789, Jacobi locates his interpretation of Spinozism within a
broader view of the method of modern natural science. It becomes clear
that, according to Jacobi, Spinoza is providing a metaphysical foundation for modern natural science by employing the method of natural
science, and that nihilism is accordingly a consequence of the philosophical employment of that method.

Here is the passage that Jacobi repeats ten years later, in his open
letter to Fichte:

We comprehend a thing whenever we can derive it from its proximate causes, or
whenever we have insight into the order of its immediate conditions. What we
see or derive in this way presents us with a mechanistic context. For instance, we
comprehend a circle whenever we clearly know how to represent the mechanics
of its formation, or its physics; we comprehend the syllogistic formulas, whenever we have really cognized the laws to which the human understanding is
subject in judgment and inference, its physics, its mechanics; or the principle
of sufficient reason, whenever we are clear about the becoming or *construction
of a concept in general*, about its physics and mechanics. The construction *of
a concept as such* is the *a priori* of every construction; and at the same time
our insight into its construction allows us to cognize with full certainty that
it is not possible for us to comprehend whatever we are not in a position to
construct. For this reason we have no concept of qualities as such, but only
intuitions or feelings. Even of our own existence, we have only a feeling and no
concept. Concepts proper we only have of figure, number, position, movement,
and the forms of thought. Whenever we say that we have researched a quality,
we mean nothing else by that, save that we have reduced it to figure, number,
position, and movement. We have resolved it into these, hence we have *objectively* annihilated the quality. From this we can easily perceive, without further
argument, what must in each case be the outcome of the efforts on the part of

that figure applies only to finite and determinate bodies. For he who says that he
apprehends a figure, thereby means to indicate simply this, that he apprehends
a determinate thing, and the manner of its determination. This determination
therefore does not pertain to the thing in regard to its being; on the contrary, it is
its nonbeing. So since figure is nothing but determination, and determination is
negation, figure can be nothing other than negation, as has been said." The passage
is of importance for Hegel's later account of determinate negation.

[40] It is important to note that this argument can be made independently of Jacobi's
own positive views, notably his version of foundationalism.

reason to generate a distinct concept of the *possibility* of the existence of our world.[41]

By "mechanism", Jacobi later explains, he means any concatenation of necessary conditions, whether physical or not.[42] To comprehend something – *zu begreifen*, to conceptualize – is thus to represent the necessary conditions for the thing's formation or construction. Comprehension, so understood, involves abstracting from qualitative features – or, rather "objectively annihilating" them – and focusing solely on constructible or quantitative features: "figure, position, number and movement." As Jacobi sees it, the conceptualizing method of modern natural science is essentially *instrumental*. It should be subordinated, either to practical ends, or to the scientist's end – which is not to explain, but rather "to unveil existence, and to reveal it."[43]

The error lies, then, not in natural scientific method itself, but in the confusion of the conceptualized mechanism with *nature itself*. Not only does modern rationalism commit just this mistake, but also, in its zeal to escape Agrippan skepticism, it employs exactly the same method in the metaphysics by means of which it seeks to ground modern natural science. Thus Spinozism is "speculative materialism": it contextualizes modern natural science within a Holistic Monist system, construed materialistically. Consequently, it annihilates not only the qualitative features of nature, but also the individuality of the human mind and of God.

This sheds light on Jacobi's suggestion that we think of Fichte's *Wissenschaftslehre* as "an *inverted* Spinozism".[44] Like Spinozism, Fichtean idealism aspires to a Holistic Monist system, and it consequently annihilates individuality. However, Fichtean idealism is deeper than Spinoza's materialism:

Speculative materialism, or the materialism that develops a metaphysics, must ultimately transfigure itself into idealism of its own accord; since apart from dualism there is only egoism, as beginning or end, for *a power of thought that will think to the end.*[45]

One might think that a materialistic metaphysics would provide an appropriate foundation for physics, among whose fundamental notions is that of matter. But Jacobi appears to think that, since the method

---

[41] Jacobi, *Über die Lehre des Spinoza* (1789), pp. 419–420n; *MPW*, 373–374, note 28. See also *Jacobi an Fichte*, pp. 62–64; *MPW*, 528.
[42] Jacobi, *Jacobi an Fichte*, pp. 62–63n; *MPW*, 528.
[43] Jacobi, *Über die Lehre des Spinoza* (1785), p. 31; *MPW*, 194.
[44] Jacobi, *Jacobi an Fichte*, p. 4; *MPW*, 502.
[45] Jacobi, *Jacobi an Fichte*, p. 3; *MPW*, 503.

consists in idealization, it is better understood in idealistic rather than in materialistic terms. At the heart of the project of Holistic Monist systematization lies what Jacobi calls *"the will that wills nothing"*.[46] Fichte's system exposes this will more transparently than Spinoza's.

Observe, first, that this conception of nihilism pertains, not only to epistemology, but also to ontology and ethics. Any Holistic Monist system is nihilistic, on this conception, whether the finite elements in question are beliefs, things, or, say, ethical judgments. Indeed, Jacobi makes his case in all three arenas. Thus, we can see his criticism of Kant's transcendental idealism as arguing, in effect, that it contains a conflict between, on the one hand, the demand for an Holistic Monist system of beliefs with the transcendental unity of apperception as absolute and immanent principle, and, on the other hand, the demand for what we might call *epistemic individuality* – that is, for immediate, perceptual beliefs formed independently of the subject's system of beliefs.[47] Jacobi's criticism of Spinoza can be seen as making an ontological version of the case that Holistic Monism is tantamount to nihilism. And an ethical version of the thesis can be found in Jacobi's novel, *Allwill*. There Jacobi is concerned about the nonrelational *character* without which no virtuous dispositions can be acquired. Edward Allwill, the novel's suitably named protagonist has a will that is entirely relational, and that flows constantly into passions that are relative to given situations. Thus Allwill lacks any genuine individual character. Without any restricting conditions, his passions are highly seductive. But the impassioned subject is all will, and therefore, ethically speaking, nothing – just as Spinoza's God is all being, and therefore, ontologically speaking, nothing. The subject who is all reason is no better:

As little as infinite space can determine the particular nature of any one body, so little can the *pure* reason *of man* constitute with its will (which is evenly good everywhere since it is *one and the same* in all men) the foundation of a particular, *differentiated* life, or impart to the *actual person* its proper individual value.[48]

Someone who achieved Kantian autonomy would, in Jacobi's view, be just as incapable of ethical agency as the protoromantic Allwill.

Note also that, to say that Holistic Monist systems are nihilistic is *at least* to say that they leave no *theoretical* room for individuality, but it *may* be to say more than that. It may be to say that, *if* someone were

---

[46] Jacobi, *Jacobi an Fichte*, p. 32; MPW, 515.
[47] I have argued elsewhere that Jacobi's criticism misfires, but this can be set aside for present purposes. See *All or Nothing*, pp. 154–158.
[48] Jacobi, *Eduard Allwills Briefsammlung*, p. 295; MPW, 488.

to *live* in accordance with a Holistic Monistic system, individuality of the pertinent kind would actually be *annihilated* for that person. This seems most plausible in the ethical case: Allwill lacks ethical character, a necessary condition for the development of virtuous dispositions. He differs radically from two moral heroes taken by Jacobi from Herodotus: the unreflective but virtuous Spartans, Sperchis and Bulis, who willingly sacrificed themselves for their land, laws and fellow-Spartans:

> They did not appeal to their understanding, to their fine judgment, but only to *things* and their desire for them. Nor did they boast of any virtue; they only professed their heart's sentiment, their affection. They had no philosophy, or rather, their philosophy was just history.[49]

If the point seems less clear in the epistemological and ontological cases, it is because it seems more plausible that the nihilist can live his ethical views than that he can live his epistemological or ontological views. This is subject to debate in the 1790s. Schelling argues that Spinoza could and did live his ontological nihilism, insofar as it gave rise to an ethics of the annihilation of individuality. Fichte responds, on the contrary, that only the true idealist – that is, the adherent of the *Wissenschaftslehre* – can live her philosophy. But, of course, Fichte rejects the charge that the *Wissenschaftslehre* is nihilistic.[50]

V. HEGEL ON NIHILISM

I now return to the claim that, in his 1802 essay, Hegel considers nihilism – as just characterized – to be the contemporary equivalent of Agrippan skepticism. Note first that the targets of contemporary Agrippan skepticism implicitly identified by Hegel in the skepticism

[49] Jacobi, *Über die Lehre des Spinoza* (1785), pp. 181–183; *MPW*, 238. As di Giovanni observes (*MPW*, 637, note 38) Jacobi gives the wrong reference, but must mean Herodotus, *The Persian Wars III: Books V–VII*, trans. by A. D. Godley (Cambridge, MA: Loeb Classical Library, 1922), 7:133–136. For Hegel's criticism of Jacobi's subjectivization of this episode and of ethical life in general, see *GW*, 4: 381–382; *T-WA*, 2:385–386; *FK*, 145–146.

[50] See Schelling, Philosophische Briefe über Dogmatismus und Kriticismus (1795), in Schelling, *Sämmtliche Werke*, ed. by K. F. A. Schelling (Stuttgart: Cotta, 1856–1861), 1:29–244, trans. by Fritz Marti as "Philosophical Letters on Dogmatism and Criticism," in Schelling The Unconditional in Human Knowledge: Four early essays 1794–6 (Lewisburg, PA: Bucknell University Press, 1980), pp. 155–196; and Fichte's two introductions to the *Versuch einer neuen Darstellung der Wissenschaftslehre* (1797), in Fichte, *Sämmtliche Werke*, ed. by I. H. Fichte (Berlin: Veit, 1845), 1:419–520, trans. by Daniel Breazeale, in Fichte, *Introductions to the Wissenschaftslehre and Other Writings* (Indianapolis, IN: Hackett, 1994), pp. 2–105.

essay – Fichte, Spinoza, and Kant – are exactly identical with the explicit targets of Jacobi in his writings about nihilism. Moreover, Hegel also refers explicitly to Jacobi, noting his superiority to Schulze. Thus he cites with approval Leibniz's attitude towards philosophical controversy, and notes that this passage is an epigraph to Jacobi's Spinoza book.[51] He also cites Jacobi's open letter to Fichte, saying that:

Jacobi's opinion about knowledge in general, comes true here [i.e., in the case of Schulze's so-called skepticism]: the Nuremberg caprice-game is played over and over, 'so that we get sick of it, once all the moves and turns are known and thoroughly familiar to us.'[52]

In short, Jacobi's criticism is exactly what Schulze needs.

Jacobi plays a distinctive role in Hegel's writings from 1801 to 1803. Whereas Hegel regards Kant and Fichte as achieving *positive* insight into the speculative which, however, they betray in the development of their positions, Hegel portrays Jacobi as attaining a primarily *negative* insight into the speculative.[53] This is expressed in Jacobi's negative response to the nihilism he finds in philosophy:

---

[51] Hegel, *GW*, 4:199; *T-WA*, 2:216; *RSP*, *BKH*, 315.

[52] Hegel, *GW*, 4:224; *T-WA*, 2:253; *RSP*, *BKH*, 341, referring to Jacobi, *Jacobi an Fichte*, p. 24; *MPW*, 511–512: "Taken *simply as such*, our sciences are games that the human spirit devises to pass the time. In devising these games, *it only organizes its non-knowledge* without coming a single hair's breadth closer to a cognition of *the true*. In a sense it rather moves from it thereby, for in thus busying itself it distracts itself from its non-knowledge, ceases to feel its pressure, even grows fond of it, since the non-knowledge is *infinite*, and the game that it plays with the human spirit becomes ever more varied, engrossing, extended, and intoxicating. If the game thus played with our non-knowledge were not infinite, and not so constituted that at its every turn a new game arose, we would fare with science just as with the so-called caprice game of Nüremberg: we would be sick of it once all its moves and possible turns are known and familiar to us. The game is spoiled for us because we understand it entirely, because we *know* it." As Harris notes in *BKH*, 360, note 85, "The *Nürenberger Grillenspiel* is a form of solitaire." According to the *Deutsches Wörterbuch*, ed. by Jakob and Wilhelm Grimm (Leipzig: Hirzel, 1854–1960), 9:332, the game involves thirty three cones, which must be removed from a board in a rule-governed manner. I have modified the translation of di Giovanni, who opts for "tic-tac-toe", which is a two-player game, albeit a predictable one.

[53] Whatever positive insight into the speculative Jacobi attains, he can express only in what Hegel considers the inappropriately subjective form of an aphorism. See *GW*, 4:361–362; *T-WA*, 2:356; *FK*, 117: "Presented as aphoristic esprit, Reason guards itself against lifting itself up into the infinity of the concept, against becoming a common good, and science. Instead, it remains affected by subjectivity, it remains something personal and particular. Attached to the ring, which it offers as a symbol of reason, there is a piece of the skin from the hand that offers it; and if Reason is scientific connection, and has to do with concepts, we can very well do without that piece of skin."

His abhorrence of the nullification [*Vernichtung*] of the finite is as fixed as his correspondingly absolute certainty of the finite; and this abhorrence will everywhere show itself to be the basic character of Jacobi's philosophy.[54]

Hegel clearly thinks that Jacobi's ascription of nihilism to the philosophies of Kant and Spinoza is correct. What he rejects is only Jacobi's *negative attitude* to nihilism:

According to Kant, all these concepts of cause and effect, succession, etc., are strictly limited to appearance; the things in which these forms are objective as well as any cognition of them are simply nothing at all *in themselves*. This is the very result which gives Kant the immoral merit of having really made the beginning of a philosophy. Yet it is precisely in this nothingness of finitude that Jacobi sees an absolute-in-itself. With this dream as his weapon he fights Spinoza wide awake.[55]

Here nihilism is at once both ontological and epistemological: both *things* and *cognitions* of the things are said to be nothing in themselves. And Jacobi's abhorrence of nihilism – of the nullification of the finite – is said to result from his absolutization of the finite: from what, in the skepticism essay, Hegel calls *dogmatism*.

Hegel contrasts the false faiths of Kant, Jacobi and Fichte with what he calls:

… true faith [in which] the whole sphere of finitude, of being-something-on-one's-[own]-account, the sphere of sensibility sinks into nothing before the thinking and intuiting of the eternal. The thinking here becomes one with the intuiting, and all the midges of subjectivity are burned to death in this consuming fire, and *the very consciousness* of this surrender and nullification is nullified.[56]

What true faith and speculative philosophy have in common, then, is the annihilation of the whole sphere of finitude, *including subjectivity*. Indeed, far from defending Fichte against Jacobi's charge of nihilism, Hegel argues that Jacobi is right! The problem with the *Wissenschaftslehre* is only that it is *not nihilistic enough*, as the following passages show:

We have already shown why Jacobi so violently abhors the nihilism he finds in Fichte's philosophy. As far as Fichte's system itself is concerned, nihilism is certainly implicit in pure thought as a task. But this pure thought cannot reach it because it stays on one side, so that this infinite possibility has an infinite actuality over against it and at the same time with it … The first step

---

54 Hegel, *GW*, 4:351; *T-WA*, 2:340; *FK*, 103.
55 Hegel, *GW*, 4:350; *T-WA*, 2: 338–339; *FK*, 101.
56 Hegel, *GW*, 4:379; *T-WA*, 2:382; *FK*, 141.

in philosophy is to recognize the absolute nothing. Fichte's philosophy does not achieve this, however much Jacobi may despise it for having done so.[57]

Thus Fichte's system of knowledge is as little able to transcend dualism as Jacobi could possibly want. The reality that is not dualistic exists for Fichte only in faith, and the Third that is truly the First and the Only One is not to be found in his system; nor can the negativity which is not dualistic, infinity, the nothing, be pure in it. It ought to be pure, but it does not become pure. Rather, it gets fixed again, so that it becomes absolute subjectivity. Jacobi, who focused his attention on one side of the antithesis, on infinity, on formal identity, felt that this nihilism of transcendental philosophy would tear the heart out of his breast. But he only needed to reflect on the other side of the antithesis, which is present with the same absoluteness.[58]

In other words, Jacobi would not have been so horrified, had he only realized that Fichte fails to ground philosophy in "pure nothingness", and that, because Fichte employs the reflective concept of the I, what Fichte posits as Absolute fails to escape finitude.

If a genuine Absolute is to be posited, then, what is needed is a more radical nihilism, a more thoroughgoing annihilation of just the individuality that Jacobi holds sacred. This would reduce the opinions of Schulze and other unphilosophers to nothingness, and it would radicalize the legacy of Kant and Fichte, eliminating the residual subjectivity.

It follows that what Hegel wants to do with Agrippan skepticism, and with its contemporary descendant, nihilism is not to *refute* them, but to *survive* them. Put another way, he wants to use them to filter out all the unphilosophies and philosophical dogmatisms, letting through only the one true philosophy. As noted earlier, in Schulze's view, "to doubt consciousness ... is absolutely impossible, because such a doubt, since it cannot occur without consciousness, would therefore be nothing."[59] Hegel considers such a self-annihilation of consciousness, or of reflective-dogmatic un-philosophy, to be not only possible but required.

What does Hegel think is the *upshot* of Agrippan skepticism and of contemporary nihilism? A rigorous answer would be: *nothing at all*. That is to say, seen from the reflective standpoint, nihilism shows only that philosophy's best effort to escape the Agrippan trilemma is no better than falling into the skeptic's trap. A further step is required if we are to reach Jacobi's conclusion that we should return to prephilosophical common sense and refuse the Agrippan skeptic's demand for justification. A further step is also required if we are to reach Hegel's conclusion

---

[57] Hegel, *GW*, 4:398; *T-WA*, 2:410; *FK*, 168.
[58] Hegel, *GW*, 4:399; *T-WA*, 2:412; *FK*, 170.
[59] Schulze, *Kritik*, 1:51.

that we should adopt the speculative standpoint. Nihilism alone leaves us precisely *nowhere*.

However, one of the major developments that separates Hegel's thinking in 1801–1803 from his thinking in 1804–1806 is the realization that nihilism has a positive upshot after all. In addition to a presuppositionless nihilism that can effect upon reflective philosophy an operation of *abstract* negation that leads precisely nowhere; and in addition also to a Platonic skepticism that derives speculative logic from the destruction of reflective philosophy by *presupposing* speculative metaphysics; Hegel comes to think that there is another version of skepticism that can *both* annihilate reflective philosophy *and* anticipate speculative logic – not by means of any presupposition, but rather by the *determinate* negation of reflective philosophy.[60] What Hegel comes to call phenomenology is the offspring of this marriage between nihilism and Platonic skepticism. From Hegel's later perspective, then, the upshot of nihilism consists not only in the annihilation of naturalism, but also in the fulfillment of philosophy's need for a nonnaturalistic method.

In 1802, this view of nihilism's upshot still lies in Hegel's future. But his early consideration of the comparative merits of modern and ancient skepticism has an enduring consequence nevertheless. For Hegel has already realized that, if his own philosophical project is to succeed, methodological naturalism must be overcome, and that it can be overcome only with the help of nihilism.[61]

---

[60] See Forster, *Hegel's Idea*, pp. 152–160, 177–184, 285–287; Bristow, *Hegel and the Transformation*, pp. 105–168.

[61] I gratefully acknowledge the helpful conversation and comments of Jay Bernstein, Fred Beiser, Stephen Houlgate, Fred Rush, Hindy Najman, and audiences at the 2006 Annual Meeting of the Hegel Society of Great Britain, the New School, and the Joint Initiative for German and European Studies at the University of Toronto.

3   Hegel's *Phenomenology* as a Systematic Fragment

The inherent problem with any philosophy which claims to be systematic is as easy to pose as it is troublesome to solve; namely, how do the parts of the system hang together? Of all the great systems in the history of philosophy, perhaps none has been subject to as much criticism as Hegel's. One author baldly claims that it makes sense to dismiss Hegel entirely "if one emphasizes the *Logic* and Hegel's rhetoric about 'system' and *'Wissenschaft.'*"[1] Likewise, as John Dewey, a great admirer of Hegel, writes, "The form, the schematism, of his [sc. Hegel's] system now seems to me artificial to the last degree."[2] The tendency to shy away from Hegel's own statements about the systematic nature of his philosophy is doubtless due to the complexity and opacity of the Hegelian system which have baffled scholars since Hegel's own time. A common reaction to these problems has been simply to abandon any attempt to understand Hegel's philosophy as a systematic whole.

Due to these problems and despite Hegel's own statements to the contrary, the *Phenomenology of Spirit* has often been criticized as an unsystematic text. In the words of one scholar:

The *Phenomenology* is indeed a movement, or rather a set of movements, an odyssey, as Hegel later said it was, a wandering, like Faust, with skips and jumps and slow meanderings. Those who take Hegel at his word and look for a "ladder" or a path or yellow brick road to the Absolute are bound to be disappointed. The *Phenomenology* is a conceptual landscape, through which Hegel leads us somewhat at his whim.[3]

---

[1] Richard Rorty, "Philosophy in America Today," in his *Consequences of Pragmatism* (Minneapolis: University of Minnesota Press, 1982), p. 224.

[2] John Dewey, "From Absolutism to Experimentalism," in *Contemporary American Philosophy*, vols. 1–2, ed. by George P. Adams and W. P. Montague (New York: Macmillan Co., 1930), vol. 2, p. 21.

[3] Robert C. Solomon, *In the Spirit of Hegel* (New York and Oxford: Oxford University Press, 1983), p. 236.

Another commentator echoes this view: "The *Phenomenology of Spirit* is a profoundly incongruous book."[4] Finally, the suggestion has been made that the *Phenomenology* be read not as a "single-minded argument" but rather as a disconnected "panoramic painting,"[5] which has no bona fide sense of unity or coherence. The work is thus seen simply as an odd collection of atomic analyses on sundry topics. This view has been dubbed the "poetic" conception of the work by some commentators, and its basic presupposition is as follows: "The *Phenomenology* is a loose series of imaginative and suggestive reflections on the life of the Spirit."[6] This view, however, disregards Hegel's own stated intent and reflects a failure to understand the general conception of the work.

Scholars holding this view have been able to satisfy themselves by trying to understand individual sections of the *Phenomenology* in which Hegel analyzes issues, such as alienation, religion, Greek tragedy, and the Enlightenment, while ignoring the schematic connections between these issues that his philosophical system seeks to demonstrate. The result is analyses and interpretations of individual sections of Hegel's text taken out of their larger systematic context. This method seems to offer a convenient way to present Hegel's thoughts on specific issues, but its use necessarily misrepresents his positions, which can only be fully understood within the framework of his system.

A good example of this distortion of Hegel's systematic intent in the *Phenomenology* is provided by Alexandre Kojève's Marxist reading, which almost entirely ignores the "Consciousness" chapter[7] and interprets the goal not only of the "Self-Consciousness" chapter but, indeed, of the entire *Phenomenology* as overcoming the various lordship and bondage relations that he sees mirrored in class structures. Kojève simply ignores sections which fail to accord with his Marxist agenda. One can say without exaggeration that, for Kojève, the importance of the entire *Phenomenology* is limited to the "Self-Consciousness" or "Spirit"

---

4 Walter Kaufmann, *Hegel: A Reinterpretation* (Notre Dame: University of Notre Dame Press, 1978), p. 142. Cf. "I should prefer to speak of charades: now a tableau, now a skit, now a brief oration" (ibid., p. 127). In "Hegel's Conception of Phenomenology," (in *Phenomenology and Philosophical Understanding*, ed. by Edo Pivcevic (Cambridge, UK: Cambridge University Press, 1975), p. 229), Kaufmann writes in a similar vein, "One really has to put on blinkers and immerse oneself in carefully selected microscopic details to avoid the discovery that the *Phenomenology* is in fact an utterly unscientific and unrigorous work."
5 Robert C. Solomon, *In the Spirit of Hegel*, op. cit., p. 221.
6 Walter Kaufmann, "Hegel's Conception of Phenomenology," op. cit., p. 220.
7 He gives it only the following short pages: pp. 43–48. See Alexandre Kojève, *Introduction à la lecture de Hegel* (Paris: Gallimard, 1947). Cf. Philip T. Grier, "The End of History and the Return of History," *The Owl of Minerva*, vol. 21 (1990), p. 133.

chapters, while the "Consciousness," "Reason," and "Religion" chapters are more or less irrelevant to what he perceives as the desired goal of the text.

In order to save Hegel, according to this strategy, one must first apologize for his excessive systematic pretensions, which amounts, in most cases, to forsaking the system altogether. Clearly, one cannot do away with the systematic structure of Hegel's *Phenomenology* in such an offhanded manner and still hope to understand the text as Hegel intended it to be understood. Hegel is firmly committed to a systematic conception of philosophy, and thus if one is to attempt to interpret him by wholly abandoning his expressly stated intentions in this regard, then one must have very compelling reasons for doing so.

I. HEGEL'S VIEW OF SYSTEMATIC PHILOSOPHY

From the passages cited earlier, it is clear that often no distinction is made between the notion of "systematic" in the everyday sense of "orderly" or "well-organized" and in the technical sense in which it is used in German idealism. This confusion evinces the fact that many scholars are not even aware of the technical use of this concept in this philosophical tradition and thus are not sensitive to Hegel's appropriation of it.

With respect to the question of systematic philosophy, Hegel is a typical representative of the entire German idealist tradition, which aimed at offering a systematic and exhaustive account of the cognitive faculties. Kant, for instance, says of his own philosophy, "it is nothing but the *inventory* of all our possessions through *pure* reason, systematically arranged."[8] Kant's transcendental philosophy can thus be seen as a catalogue of the various functions of the intellect by means of which we come to *know* and *understand*. This inventory, he claims, is ordered in a necessary, systematic fashion: "As a systematic unity is what first raises ordinary knowledge to the rank of science, that is, makes a system out of a mere aggregate of knowledge," he explains, "architectonic is the doctrine of the scientific in our knowledge and therefore necessarily forms part of the doctrine of method."[9] For Kant, it is the ensemble or organic unity of knowledge that makes it a true science, and what does not belong to this systematic unity is a "mere aggregate" or collection of facts. One might be able to make specific observations about the operation of the intellect, but, to adequately account for it, one must consider

---

[8] Kant, *Critique of Pure Reason*, trans. by N. Kemp Smith (New York: St. Martin's Press, 1929), p. 14, Axx.

[9] Kant, ibid., p. 653, A832–B860.

all of the cognitive faculties and their interconnections, or otherwise the observations remain incomplete. In the Preface to the second edition of the *Critique of Pure Reason*, Kant writes, "For pure speculative reason has a structure wherein everything is an organ, the whole being for the sake of all others.... Any attempt to change even the smallest part at once gives rise to contradictions, not merely in the system, but in human reason in general."[10] To change or remove the account of one individual cognitive faculty would destroy the system since there would then be something open-ended about our cognitive functions which the system could not explain with the remaining faculties. It is thus reason itself, for Kant, which demands this systematic unity.[11]

Kant's successors accepted, without serious qualification, his insistence on system as an organic unity. Fichte, for instance, in the "First Introduction" of the *Science of Knowledge* claims, "As surely as they are to be grounded in the unitary being of the intellect, the intellect's assumed laws of operation themselves constitute a system."[12] Likewise, Schelling, in his *System of Transcendental Idealism*, states that his goal in philosophy is not to add anything to what has already been said but to rearrange the information (already provided by Kant and Fichte) into a genuine system. "Now the purpose of the present work is simply this," he writes, "to enlarge transcendental idealism into what it really should be, namely a system of all knowledge."[13] Given this unanimous insistence among the German idealists on the systematicity of philosophy, Hegel can hardly be regarded as a maverick on this point. If one assumes a dismissive stance toward him on this issue, then one might just as well dismiss the entire tradition of German idealism. He simply inherits this approach from his predecessors and expands it in his own way. One can, of course, still raise the question of how successful Hegel was at carrying out his systematic program, but there can be no doubt that this was a key element in his general approach.

Like his forerunners, Hegel believed that the very notion of truth was necessarily bound up with its systematic form.[14] In some ways it is

---

[10] Kant, ibid., Bxxxvii–xxxviii.

[11] See Kant, ibid., p. 33, A840/B869.

[12] Fichte, "First Introduction to the Science of Knowledge," in *The Science of Knowledge*, trans. by Peter Heath and John Lachs (Cambridge, UK: Cambridge University Press, 1982), p. 22.

[13] Schelling, *System of Transcendental Idealism*, trans. by Peter Heath (Charlottesville: University Press of Virginia, 1978), p. 1. Cf. p. 15: "It will be assumed as a hypothesis, that there is a *system* in our knowledge, that is that it is a whole which is self-supporting and internally consistent with itself."

[14] See, for example, *EL*, §14; *Jub.*, vol. 8, p. 60. *PhS*, p. 11; *Jub.*, vol. 2, p. 24. Cf. *EL*, §16; *Jub.*, vol. 8, pp. 61–63. *PhS*, p. 3; *Jub.*, vol. 2, p. 14. *PhS*, 13; *Jub.*, vol. 2, p. 27.

odd that anglophone philosophers have been so quick to dismiss Hegel's conception of systematic philosophy given the fact that in contemporary thought, his conception, albeit under names, such as the "network theory of truth," "a scientific paradigm," or "holism," remains quite popular. While the names used today to designate this way of thinking differ from Hegel's designation of "speculative philosophy," the idea underlying them is fundamentally the same: individual parts of the system have their meaning only in their necessary relation to the other parts and thus as parts of a larger whole.

Hegel's methodological investment in this view is demonstrated in the *Phenomenology*. He portrays the notion of a systematic philosophy by means of an organic analogy. The development of a plant at its different stages is necessary for the plant as a whole, and no single stage represents the plant's entire history. He writes,

> The bud disappears in the bursting-forth of the blossom, and one might say that the former is refuted by the latter; similarly, when the fruit appears, the blossom is shown up in its turn as a false manifestation of the plant, and the fruit now emerges as the truth of it instead. These forms are not just distinguished from one another, they also supplant one another as mutually incompatible. Yet at the same time their fluid nature makes them moments of an organic unity in which they not only do not conflict, but in which each is as necessary as the other; and this mutual necessity alone constitutes the life of the whole.[15]

Just as when a plant grows and develops, each of its individual stages is necessary for the succeeding stages, individual concepts in a philosophical system have their meaning in the context of other concepts from which they were developed. Just as the different stages of its development change the plant's appearance so radically that it appears to become another "contradictory" species – contradictory concepts can contribute to the development of a single philosophical system. What this simile makes clear is that the system, for Hegel, involves the sum total of the individual parts as they develop themselves organically. Thus, just as the plant is not merely the sum total of its parts at a

---

(*EL: The Encyclopaedia Logic. Part One of the Encyclopaedia of the Philosophical Sciences*, trans. by T. F. Gerats, W. A. Suchting, and H. S. Harris (Indianapolis: Hackett, 1991). *Jub.* : *Sämtliche Werke.* Jubiläumsausgabe in 20 Bänden, ed. by Hermann Glockner (Stuttgart: Friedrich Frommann Verlag, 1928–41). *PhS: Hegel's Phenomenology of Spirit*, trans. by A. V. Miller (Oxford: Clarendon Press, 1977).

[15] Hegel, *PhS*, p. 2; *Jub.*, vol. 2, p. 12. Hegel uses the same metaphor in his lectures on the philosophy of history: "And as the germ bears in itself the whole nature of the tree, and the taste and form of its fruits, so do the first traces of Spirit virtually contain the whole of that history." *Phil. of Hist*, p. 18; *Jub.*, vol. 11, p. 45. *Phil. of Hist: The Philosophy of History*, trans. by J. Sibree (New York: Wiley Book Co., 1944).

given moment in its development, but rather the organic whole of its developmental stages, so also a philosophical system is the complete development or unfolding of individual concepts.

In the Preface of the *Phenomenology*, Hegel flatly claims, "The true shape in which truth exists can only be the scientific system of such truth."[16] A little later, he says, "knowledge is only actual, and can only be expounded, as Science or as *system*."[17] Surely, one could ask for no clearer statement of the relation of truth to a system; hence, however opaque Hegel may be about the *details* of the system, he is crystal clear that a systematic approach is necessary to reach the truth. To understand Hegel's systematic pretensions merely as a simple matter of the orderly presentation of ideas is to miss his philosophical point.[18] The systematic whole is essentially bound up with the notion of truth itself and cannot be sundered from it.

This conception of a network of interrelated beliefs implies a certain kind of philosophy, namely, one that examines the totality of beliefs, concepts, institutions, and so forth, instead of concentrating only on certain individual isolated ones. The kind of philosophy that examines the whole is what Hegel, following tradition, calls "speculative philosophy." He contrasts it to what he calls "dogmatism," which treats concepts individually and thus abstracted from their organic unity:

But in the narrower sense dogmatism consists in adhering to one-sided determinations of the understanding whilst excluding their opposites. This is just the strict "either-or," according to which (for instance) the world is *either* finite *or* infinite, but *not both*. On the contrary, what is genuine and speculative is precisely what does not have any such one-sided determination in it and is therefore not exhausted by it; on the contrary, being a totality, it contains the determinations that dogmatism holds to be fixed and true in a state of separation from one another united within itself.[19]

Here Hegel refers to Kant's "First Antinomy," which presents the universe as both finite and infinite.[20] By choosing this example, Hegel thereby implicitly praises Kant's speculative treatment of the issue. The

---

[16] Hegel, *PhS*, p. 3; *Jub.*, vol. 2, p. 14.
[17] Hegel, *PhS*, p. 13; *Jub.*, vol. 2, p. 27.
[18] See, for example, Walter Kaufmann, *Hegel: A Reinterpretation*, op. cit., p. 243: "The central point of our philological excursus is, of course, to show how Hegel himself handled his system: not as so much a necessary truth, deduced once and for all in its inexorable sequence, but rather as very neat and sensible way of arranging the parts of philosophy – not even the neatest and most sensible possible, but only the best he could do in time to meet the printer's deadline."
[19] Hegel, *EL*, §32, Addition; *Jub.*, vol. 8, p. 106.
[20] Kant, *Critique of Pure Reason*, op. cit., pp. 399–402, A426/B454-A433/B461.

key point for our purposes is that speculative philosophy removes concepts from the isolation of abstraction and puts them in their appropriate systematic context where they can be properly analyzed. "The *speculative* or *positively rational*," says Hegel, "apprehends the unity of determinations in their opposition, the *affirmative* that is contained in their dissolution and in their transition."[21] In a similar passage from the introduction to the *Science of Logic*, he writes, "It is in this dialectic as it is here understood, that is, in the grasping of opposites in their unity or of the positive in the negative, that speculative thought consists."[22] Speculative philosophy involves examining the whole universe of thought, which invariably involves contradictions. Instead of insisting on one side of a contradiction or the other or stopping once a contradiction has been reached, it observes the dynamic movement in pairs of opposites and looks beyond the immediate contradictory terms toward a higher truth that arises from the dialectical development of the contradiction.

One can, of course, continue for the sake of pedagogical expedience to cut and splice Hegel to make him fit into the customary undergraduate course, but in so doing one must recognize that such a procedure is entirely contrary to his own methodology and thoroughly goes against the grain of his conception of philosophy. Hegel conceived of his philosophy as a system, and it is in this context that his thought must be understood. Even if one no longer finds systematic philosophy plausible, one is nonetheless obliged to attempt to understand Hegel in this way in order to be able to grasp his philosophical motivations and intuitions. If one chooses instead to simply purge Hegel's work of its systematic elements, then one in effect loses Hegel in the process.[23]

II. THE AMBIGUOUS ROLE OF THE PHENOMENOLOGY

One of the earliest commentators to point out the ambiguous nature of the argumentation in the *Phenomenology* was Rudolf Haym in his

---

[21] Hegel, *EL*, §82; *Jub.*, vol. 8, p. 195.

[22] Hegel, *SL*, p. 56; *Jub.*, vol. 4, p. 54.

[23] Other commentators have, of course, also attempted to understand Hegel in a systematic fashion, for example, L. Bruno Puntel, *Darstellung, Methode und Struktur. Untersuchung zur Einheit der systematischen Philosophie G. W. F. Hegels* (Bonn: Bouvier, 1973); Gerd Kimmerle, *Sein und Selbst. Untersuchung zur kategorialen Einheit von Vernunft und Geist in Hegels Phänomenologie des Geistes* (Bonn: Bouvier, 1978); David Lamb, *Hegel: From Foundation to System* (The Hague: Martinus Nijhoff, 1980); Pierre-Jean Labarrière, *Structures et mouvement dialectique dans la Phénoménologie de l'esprit de Hegel* (Paris: Aubier, 1968); and Merold Westphal, *History and Truth in Hegel's Phenomenology* (Atlantic Highlands, NJ: Humanities Press, 1979).

Hegel und seine Zeit from 1857. Haym pointed out that the work contains two kinds of argument. The first is what he designates as "transcendental-psychological."[24] This is characteristic of the analyses in the first part of the work, which traces the forms of the individual consciousness on its road of discovery and self-knowledge. By contrast, there is also a "historical"[25] form of argumentation, in which the individual forms of consciousness are suddenly transformed into historical epochs. Thus, apparently without explanation, the development of consciousness becomes the development of historical peoples. Haym argues that these two different forms of argumentation make the work disunified. Using a metaphor from classical philology, he claims that the work is a palimpsest, on which one text was originally written only to be eclipsed by another text with a different conception, which was subsequently written over the first text.[26] These two different texts reflect different conceptions of the work itself.

In a celebrated paper delivered at the 1933 Hegel Congress in Rome,[27] Theodor Haering took up this view, arguing that the *Phenomenology* was a disunified work due to the fact that Hegel changed his mind about the conception of its philosophical task during the composition of the text itself. The change concerns specifically what philosophical work the *Phenomenology* is intended to do. According to Haering's account, the *Phenomenology* was originally conceived as an introduction to a philosophical system and as the "experience of consciousness." Through the beginning of the "Reason" chapter, so the argument goes, the work proceeded as planned. But then the chapters became much longer and much less unified and departed from the original argumentative structure of the work established in the "Consciousness" and "Self-Consciousness" chapters. In the middle of the "Reason" chapter, the account of the development of the forms of individual consciousness grew into an account of the forms of "Spirit" or group consciousness. At this point, the work could no longer be considered a mere introduction but rather had grown into a substantive part of the system in its own right. This view is purportedly confirmed by, among other things, Hegel's own ambiguous statements about the role of the

---

[24] Rudolf Haym, *Hegel und seine Zeit. Vorlesungen über Enstehung und Entwickelung, Wesen und Werth der Hegel'schen Philosophie* (Berlin: Verlag von Rudolph Gaertner, 1857), pp. 235–236.

[25] Rudolf Haym, *Hegel und seine Zeit*, ibid., pp. 236–238.

[26] Rudolf Haym, *Hegel und seine Zeit*, ibid., p. 238.

[27] Theodor Haering, "Entstehungsgeschichte der *Phänomenologie des Geistes*," in *Verhandlungen des III. Internationalen Hegel Kongresses 1933*, ed. by B. Wigersma (Haarlem: N/VH.D. Tjeenk Willink & Zn. and Tübingen: J. C. B. Mohr, 1934), pp. 118–136.

Phenomenology and various bits of biographical information surrounding its composition.

In his Preface, Hegel indicates that the *Phenomenology* is to be understood as the first part of the system: "Further, an exposition of this kind constitutes the *first* part of Science, because the existence of Spirit *qua* primary is nothing but the immediate or the beginning – but not yet its return into itself."[28] Moreover, the *Encyclopaedia Logic*, written ten years later, still refers to the *Phenomenology* as "the first part of the system of science."[29] Thus, Hegel appears at this later date still to consider the *Phenomenology* to be the first part of a system. However, in a letter to Schelling shortly after the publication of the work, he writes, "I am curious as to what you will say to the idea of this first part, which is really the introduction – for I have not yet got beyond the introducing right into the heart of the matter."[30] This seems to indicate that the *Phenomenology* is a mere introduction and the actual subject matter of the system has not yet been broached. This ambiguity has been interpreted as evidence of Hegel's own confusion about the status and philosophical task of the text.

In addition to the arguments offered by Haym and Haering concerning the ambiguous role of the *Phenomenology*, there has been confusion concerning an intermediate title page that appeared after the preface in the work's first edition.[31] The original title was *The Science of the Experience of Consciousness*, which was apparently replaced at the last minute, indeed after some copies had already been printed, by the title *Science of the Phenomenology of Spirit*. This amendment has been interpreted as evidence that Hegel originally intended to give an account of the experience of *consciousness* but, during the course of the work, changed his mind and added social and historical forms which went beyond individual consciousness; he then accordingly altered the title

---

[28] Hegel, *PhS*, p. 20; *Jub.*, vol. 2, p. 36. Cf. also *PhS*, p. 15; *Jub.*, vol. 2, p. 30: "It is this coming-to-be of *Science as such* or of *knowledge*, that is described in this *Phenomenology of Spirit*. Knowledge in its first phase, or *immediate Spirit*, is the non-spiritual, i.e. *sense-consciousness*." Cf. Hegel, *Phil. Prop.*, p. 56; *Jub.*, vol. 3, p. 102: "The Science of consciousness is, therefore, called *The Phenomenology of Mind* [or *Spirit*]." [*Phil. Prop.*: *The Philosophical Propaedeutic*, trans. by A. V. Miller, ed. by Michael George and Andrew Vincent (Oxford: Basil Blackwell, 1986).]

[29] Hegel, *EL*, §25; *Jub.*, vol. 8, p. 98.

[30] Hegel to Schelling [95], Bamberg, May 1, 1807, *Letters*, p. 80; *Briefe*, vol. 1, pp. 159–162. [*Letters*: *Hegel: The Letters*, trans. by Clark Butler and Christine Seiler (Bloomington: Indiana University Press, 1984). *Briefe I–III* = *Briefe von und an Hegel*, vols. 1–3, ed. by Johannes Hoffmeister (Hamburg: Meiner, 1951–54; 3rd ed., 1969).]

[31] See Friedhelm Nicolin, "Zum Titelproblem der *Phänomenologie des Geistes*," *Hegel-Studien*, vol. 4 (1967), pp. 113–123.

to reflect the change in content. The new title then refers not merely to consciousness but rather to *Spirit*.

Although these arguments offer evidence that the *Phenomenology* serves at least two distinct philosophical agendas, they are not sufficient to justify the conclusion that it is a disunified text. Many works of philosophy and literature have changed direction during the course of their composition, without necessarily being disunified. It depends, of course, on the individual text and the nature of the changes. In one case, the author may be so overpowered by the discontinuous strands of the work that the final product is indeed chaotic, but in another the author may succeed in incorporating the new conception into the material which had been written up until that point. The new element may then be seen as an improvement, an expansion, or a supplement and need not necessarily imply that the final product is disunified. It cannot be assumed that a change in the conception of a work during its composition always results in a disunified text.

Hegel appears to have realized that his transcendental argument, which gives an exhaustive account of the necessary conditions of the possibility of objective thought, would be incomplete without an account of the social interactions and historical influences which constitute the medium in which truth claims are determined. He was able to incorporate these analyses into his overall plan for a transcendental argument without damaging the unity of the work as a whole. To be sure, these analyses differed from those given in the "Consciousness" and "Self-Consciousness" chapters with respect to content, but the aim of the analyses and their dialectical form remained the same. Thus, the conception of the *Phenomenology* as a transcendental argument never changed, although, during the composition of the text, Hegel discovered new aspects and elements of this argument that he had not considered when he started on the work.

III. THE COHERENCE PROBLEM IN GENERAL

Haym's thesis about the disunity of the *Phenomenology* has been reworked with more philological detail by subsequent authors. Most notably, Otto Pöggeler in his influential essay on the composition of the work confirms the main points of Haym's and Haering's discontinuity thesis although differing from it in some details.[32] Other commentators

---

[32] Otto Pöggeler, "Die Komposition der *Phänomenologie des Geistes*," in *Hegel-Tage Royaumont 1964. Beiträge zur Phänomenologie des Geistes*, ed. by Hans-Georg Gadamer. *Hegel-Studien*, Beiheft 3 (Bonn: Bouvier, 1966), pp. 27–74. Cited from the reprint in *Materialien zu Hegels Phänomenologie des Geistes*, ed. by Hans

use this thesis as a point of departure or presupposition for their own interpretation of individual parts of the text as atomic units. The question of the *Phenomenology* as an introduction or as a first part of a system has fallen somewhat into the background, while the thesis that it is disunified remains as strong as ever.

The main arguments used by Pöggeler and later commentators can be broken into two interrelated groups. The first line of argumentation is external to the text itself and uses as evidence biographical information about Hegel during the period of the composition of the *Phenomenology*. This sort of argument begins with some fact about Hegel's life or the circumstances of the composition of the work and then proceeds to a claim about the patchwork nature of the text. The second line of argumentation is internal to the text. In this view, the text of the *Phenomenology* on its own terms cannot be made sense of as a systematic work. The transitions between the individual chapters are seen as unclear, and the radical diversity of themes treated is seen to undermine any continuity.

A. The Arguments Based on Hegel's Biography

There are, above all, biographical reasons to believe that the *Phenomenology* could not be a carefully organized and unified argument. Hegel purportedly wrote the work, or at least a large part of it, during an extremely short period of time. Although he had already sent off the first half of the text shortly after Easter of 1806, he was under tremendous pressure to complete the manuscript by October 18 of that year. This was the deadline set by his publisher, Goebhardt, who was appeased only after Hegel's friend Niethammer offered to personally pay the printing costs if Hegel failed to deliver the rest of the manuscript on time.[33] On October 8, Hegel sent a part of the second half of the manuscript and had to finish the rest of the work in great haste to meet the deadline.

Yet even if the composition of the final part of the text was quite hurried, it does not necessarily follow that the text is disunified. There is evidence that Hegel used much of the subject matter found in the *Phenomenology* in his lecture courses throughout the Jena period,[34]

Friedrich Fulda and Dieter Henrich (Frankfurt a. M.: Suhrkamp, 1973), pp. 329–390.

[33] For Hegel's problems with his publisher, see his letters to Niethammer [67], [68], [70], [72], [73], [76]; *Briefe*, vol. 1, pp. 112ff.

[34] For example, Hegel's "System of Ethical Life" (1802–1803), "First Philosophy of Spirit" (1803–1804), and his "The Philosophy of Spirit" (1805–1806). These texts are available in English in Hegel, *System of Ethical Life and First Philosophy of Spirit*, ed. and trans. by H. S. Harris and T. M. Knox (Albany: SUNY Press, 1979) and *Hegel and the Human Spirit. A Translation of the Jena Lectures on the Philosophy*

which suggests that he had been working with the same material for some years. A work which he had already thought out and worked through in his lectures would presumably have required much less time to compose than a work that had to be constructed from the ground up.

A related biographical argument is that the threatening approach of the French army and the confusion and disorder surrounding the Battle of Jena distracted and distressed Hegel during the composition of the *Phenomenology*.[35] First, the Battle of Jena compelled him to finish the work quickly, thus providing yet another external pressure that magnified the difficulties he was already having with his publisher. Second, he had to fear for his personal safety. French soldiers who came to his house had to be appeased with food and wine, and Hegel, then completely destitute, ultimately had to seek refuge in the home of a friend.

Again, however, the fact that a work is composed in chaotic circumstances does not necessarily mean that the finished product must be disunified. A number of philosophical masterpieces were written under similarly trying circumstances. Boethius wrote the *Consolation of Philosophy* while awaiting the death sentence to be carried out; Condorcet wrote his systematic masterpiece, *Sketch of a Historical Description of the Progress of the Human Spirit*, under similar circumstances. The Golden Age of Roman literature corresponds to the period of the bloody Civil Wars. Examples of writers and philosophers who were active during the World Wars in the twentieth century are too numerous to list. Therefore, this sort of argument against the unity of the *Phenomenology* seems to be simply a non sequitur.

A final version of the argument relies on Hegel's own remarks that suggest that he had his own doubts about the unity of the text. In a letter to Schelling, he laments, "Working into the detail has, I feel, damaged the overview of the whole. This whole, however, is itself by nature such an interlacing of cross-references back and forth that even were it set in better relief, it would still cost me much time before it would stand out more clearly and in more finished form."[36] This passage is often cited as evidence that Hegel's text is disunified.[37] However, a closer reading of it shows that Hegel's frustration arises not because his work

---

of Spirit (1805–6), by Leo Rauch (Detroit: Wayne State University Press, 1983). See also Hegel, *The Jena System, 1804–5: Logic and Metaphysics*, ed. and trans. by John W. Burbidge and George di Giovanni (Kingston and Montreal: McGill-Queen's University Press, 1986).

35 See, Hegel to Niethammer [74], *Letters*, pp. 114–115; *Briefe*, vol. 1, pp. 119–122.

36 Hegel to Schelling [95], Bamberg, May 1, 1807, *Letters*, p. 80; *Briefe*, vol. 1, pp. 159–162.

37 See Otto Pöggeler, "Die Komposition der *Phänomenologie des Geistes*," in *Materialien zu Hegels Phänomenologie des Geistes*, op. cit., pp. 330, 373.

is disunified but because time constraints precluded him from making its unity more explicit. Here, Hegel clearly indicates that, in fact, his text does have a unified structure and a developed plan, but, since he had so busied himself with the details of the individual arguments, he simply neglected to give his readers sufficient instruction about the overall structure. Further evidence that he believed the book to be unified may be found in his advertisement for the work which appeared in October 1807. There he writes, "The wealth of the appearances of Spirit, which at first glance seems chaotic, is brought into a scientific order which presents them according to their necessity."[38]

Another passage which has been cited in support of arguments that the *Phenomenology* is a disunified text comes from a letter written long after the original publication of the work. Hegel's old publisher Goebhardt had been bought out, and his successor Wesche had obtained the remaining copies of the first edition of the *Phenomenology* and was putting into motion plans to print a second edition without securing Hegel's approval or soliciting his suggestions for corrections or other changes. Hegel, upset by this effrontery, wrote to von Meyer, "His [sc. Wesche's] attitude here seemed to be that he considers my consent and agreement to conditions for a new edition to be strictly unnecessary. He does not even take into account that I regard revision of the work to be necessary."[39] This comment appears at first glance to imply that Hegel regarded the *Phenomenology* as a confused work since it required revision, and this seems to support the disunity thesis. The passage, however, fails to support the lack of unity argument because it offers no insight whatsoever into the nature of the revisions Hegel deems necessary. He might have wished to make the book's systematic connections more explicit or, for that matter, to simply correct some grammatical or typographical errors. The biographical and text-external arguments as a whole thus remain unpersuasive.

B. The Text-Internal Arguments

Many arguments against the unity of the work are based on the apparent heterogeneity of the themes and analyses it contains. Hegel treats traditional epistemological issues and historical figures, and he also gives accounts of scientific communities, various forms of social life, and historical time periods. The challenge is to try to bring all the arguments of the *Phenomenology*, many of which appear to have little in common

---

[38] *Miscellaneous Writings of G. W. F. Hegel*, ed. by Jon Stewart (Evanston: Northwestern University Press, 2002), p. 282.

[39] Hegel to von Meyer [605a], Berlin, August 9, 1829, *Letters*, p. 121; *Briefe*, vol. 4, pp. 30–32.

with one another, under the same roof. Most such arguments concern themselves with the transitions between the individual chapters, which seem to contain disparate analyses.

One celebrated tension concerns the continuity problem of the first two chapters: "Consciousness" and "Self-Consciousness." One commentator succinctly writes, "there appears to be little connection between the topics of chapter four [sc. Self-Consciousness] and the theoretical issues addressed in the first three chapters [sc. Consciousness]."[40] Another writes, "One of the more mysterious transitions in the *Phenomenology* is the transition from the purely epistemic chapter on 'understanding' in which the topic under discussion is Newtonian forces and various problems in the philosophies of Leibniz and Kant, to a discussion of 'life' and 'desire.' "[41] In the "Consciousness" chapter Hegel seems to concern himself with what are usually considered to be standard epistemological issues. He considers objects viewed as pure undifferentiated being, as substances with properties and finally as appearances caused by unseen forces. But then, by contrast, in the "Self-Consciousness" chapter, we find the lordship and bondage dialectic and Hegel's account of alienation, followed by discussions of Stoicism, Skepticism, and the unhappy consciousness.[42] The traditional epistemological inquiry of the previous chapter appears to have been abandoned altogether.[43] Findlay writes that with the transition to the "Self-Consciousness" chapter, "the dialectic suddenly swings over into the social sphere."[44] He further claims that the movement is "from the epistemological to the practical, social level."[45] As a result of this view,

---

[40] Robert Pippin, *Hegel's Idealism: The Satisfactions of Self-Consciousness* (Cambridge, UK: Cambridge University Press, 1989), p. 143.

[41] Robert C. Solomon, "Truth and Self-Satisfaction," *Review of Metaphysics*, 28 (1975), p. 723.

[42] See Ivan Soll, *An Introduction to Hegel's Metaphysics* (Chicago: University of Chicago Press, 1983), p. 4: "The magnificently ambitious, if quixotic and unfulfilled, program of the *Phenomenology of Spirit* required ordering all forms of consciousness into a single ascending series.... But also included in the series are such apparently non-epistemological and only partially epistemological forms as the master-servant relation, the conflict between human and divine law as exemplified in Sophocles' *Antigone*, the moral view of Kant's ethics, and various forms of art and religion."

[43] Preuss, for instance, argues that the "Self-Consciousness" chapter betrays the true goals of the *Phenomenology* with a radical break from the "Consciousness" chapter. P. Preuss, "Selfhood and the Battle: The Second Beginning of the *Phenomenology*," in *Method and Speculation in Hegel's Philosophy*, ed. by Merold Westphal (Atlantic Highlands, NJ: Humanities Press, 1982), pp. 71–83.

[44] John Findlay, *The Philosophy of Hegel: An Introduction and Re-Examination* (London: George Allen and Unwin, 1958), p. 93.

[45] Ibid., p. 94.

most commentators take this change of topic for granted and argue about the specifics of the content of the two sections without much concern for their coherence as a common philosophical project. Most of the dis-agreement is about the internal continuity of the two sections taken individually and not about what their relation to one another might be. Hegel's unambiguous claims about the systematic connections in his philosophy are simply cast aside.

Another transition which has been considered problematic is the one from "Self-Consciousness" to "Reason." With respect to this transition, one commentator writes,

The reader forgets the image of the ladder and wonders which of the many fea-tures of this tableau are in any sense necessary and essential to this stage; and the author too, has plainly lost sight of the idea and plan of his book, and far from compressing his exposition severely, dwells at unnecessary length on irrelevan-cies. . . . Hegel obviously was unable to continue the development that he had traced so brilliantly through several stages, beyond this point, to another stage.[46]

In the literature it has been extremely difficult to make out any sort of meaningful connection between the analysis of religious consciousness in "Unhappy Consciousness" and the natural scientific understanding of the world in "Observing Reason" that would serve as a bridge or connecting link between these two chapters.

The original controversies about the unity of the work focused on the "Reason" chapter, the length of which appears entirely disproportionate to the "Consciousness" and "Self-Consciousness" chapters.[47] This was interpreted as evidence that Hegel changed his agenda in the course of composing the "Reason" chapter. One commentator writes, "The table of contents bears out that the work was not planned painstakingly before it was written, that parts V and VI (Reason and Spirit) grew far beyond the bounds originally contemplated and that Hegel himself was a little confused about what he had actually got when he was finished."[48] In the "Reason" chapter the epistemological analyses of "Consciousness" are apparently absent, and the confrontation of the two self-conscious subjects from the "Self-Consciousness" chapter is nowhere to be found. Instead, we find an analysis of Hegel's philosophy of nature and various conceptions of virtuous and moral living. Thus, with respect to con-tent, the earlier chapters seem to have little in common with "Reason,"

---

[46] Walter Kaufmann, *Hegel: A Reinterpretation*, op. cit., p. 141.

[47] See Johannes Hoffmeister, "Einleiting des Herausgebers," in *Georg Wilhelm Friedrich Hegel, Sämtliche Werke, Kritische Ausgabe*, vol. 11, *Phänomenologie des Geistes* (Leipzig: Felix Meiner, 1937), p. xxxv. Cf. also Theodor Haering, "Entstehungsgeschichte der *Phänomenologie des Geistes*," op. cit., pp. 129ff.

[48] Walter Kaufmann, *Hegel: A Reinterpretation*, op. cit., p. 135.

and, moreover, there seems to be little continuity among the individual analyses found within the chapter.

Yet another problematic transition is that between the "Reason" and the "Spirit" chapters. "Reason" ends with a criticism of morality conceived as an empty set of formal laws, while "Spirit" begins with a discussion of Sophocles' tragedy *Antigone,* used to illustrate the shortcomings of the form of social life resulting from individuals who immediately and unreflectively identify themselves with larger institutions. Needless to say, this transition raises many questions. Is this analysis of the Greek *polis* supposed to be historical? If so, then why does it start here with *Antigone* and not earlier, for example, with Homer?[49] What is the relation between this seemingly historical account and the analysis of the moral laws in the previous chapter ("Reason")? Is the "Spirit" chapter itself meant to be historical? If so, why does it pass over certain periods and key events?

The transition from "Spirit" to "Religion"[50] and the content of "Religion" itself are no less problematic. Is the "Religion" chapter also a historical account? If so, then why is it not simply incorporated into the historical account of the "Spirit" chapter? However, if it is a complete account of religious consciousness from beginning to end, then why are forms of religious consciousness treated in earlier chapters, for example, in the "Unhappy Consciousness" section? Is it, as one author says, "eccentric"[51] to treat forms of art in the "Religion" chapter? Why does Hegel here treat non-European religions, whereas in "Spirit" he gave no account of non-European history, but rather started, as is traditionally done, with the Greeks?

IV. THE SOLUTION: THE PARALLELISMS IN THE TEXT

Although these transitions may seem abrupt, the key to understanding them is to grasp the complicated series of corresponding analyses in the individual sections of the work. It would, of course, require a full-length commentary to explore all of these in detail,[52] but the point can be illustrated in a very general way by means of a brief overview.

---

[49] See Rudolf Haym, *Hegel und seine Zeit. Vorlesungen über Entstehung und Entwicklung, Wesen und Werth der hegel'schen Philosophie* (Berlin: Rudolf Gaertner, 1857; reprint, Hildesheim: Olms, 1962), p. 242: "The selection [sc. of historical forms] is absolutely arbitrary."

[50] See Joseph C. Flay, "Religion and the Absolute Standpoint," *Thought,* 56 (1981), pp. 316–327.

[51] Walter Kaufmann, "Hegel's Conception of Phenomenology," op. cit, p. 214.

[52] I have attempted such a commentary in my *The Unity of Hegel's Phenomenology of Spirit* (Evanston: Northwestern University Press, 2000).

In each of the subordinate levels of the *Phenomenology* consciousness seeks a criterion for truth in an "other" which it believes to exist independently of itself. In "Sense Certainty," the initial analysis of the "Consciousness" chapter, natural consciousness has yet to progress beyond the level of common sense realism. As subject, it seeks a criterion for truth in the given object which it perceives. This analysis parallels the analysis given in the section, "The Observation of Nature," in the "Reason" chapter. There the various objects of perception have been consolidated into the more abstract concept of nature, which, nonetheless, is still conceived as existing independently from and offering a truth criterion for the scientific observer. They are taken to be objectively true in themselves apart from the interference or observation of the scientific observer. This is taken to an even higher level in "The Ethical World" analysis in the "Spirit" chapter. Reason has now progressed to viewing itself in the context of a historical and moral world. Its other is now morality which is to society what nature and its laws are to unconscious objects. Moral laws are assumed to be pre-existent facts about the world. In the *Antigone*, one reads of the ethical laws: "They are not of yesterday or today, but everlasting. / Though where they came from, none of us can tell."[53] The final parallel analysis in this series is the first discussion of "Religion," namely, "God as Light." Although the object in question has changed, the general conception of it remains the same. Here the other has progressed to a conception of the divine understood as fire or light, which combines elements of the object, nature, and morality. It too is conceived as a straightforwardly existing other of nature, with no conscious element. This is conceived as immediately given and true, independent of any human influence.

A parallel movement to this one takes place on the side of the subject, beginning with "The Truth of Self-Certainty" in the "Self-Consciousness" chapter. According to this conception, self-consciousness takes itself to be the criterion for truth and thus denies the truth and validity of the object sphere. At the simplest level of self-consciousness, this means destroying and appropriating objects of nature for its own satisfaction. This is further developed in "Pleasure and Necessity" in the "Reason" chapter, where the subject is no longer an atomic agent but rather enters the moral sphere. Here the self-conscious subject reduces the external world, including other human beings, to objects of its own pleasure. They have truth and value only insofar at they can serve the hedonistic ends of the pleasure-seeking subject. The historical manifestation of this is treated in "The World of

---

[53] Hegel, *PhS*, p. 261; *Jub.*, vol. 2, p. 333.

Self-Alienated Spirit" in the "Spirit" chapter. In contrast to the world of Antigone, where moral laws were eternally given facts about the external world, the self-alienated spirit denies the validity of all such positive laws, regarding them as irrational, arbitrary, and oppressive. Again the truth is sought on the side of the subject, which by means of reason alone can determine new laws that can pass the strict test of rational scrutiny. Finally, this account appears again in the "Religion" chapter in "The Abstract Work of Art." Instead of the divinity being conceived as an object of nature such as fire, now the divine, in Greek polytheism, is conceived as a self-conscious subject. The gods have a human form as is seen in various portrayals in Greek art, such as sculpture. What all of these views have in common is the positing of the criterion for truth on the side of the subject. Hegel exhausts this concept, running through all its forms from the most abstract form of a single self-conscious agent confronted with the world of nature to the subject conceived as a self-conscious, anthropomorphic god.

Parallels of this kind run through the entire text and constitute its intended systematic unity. Increasingly complex object models are systematically applied to increasingly complex kinds of subject matter. The systematic structure consists in the dialectical movement, which posits the truth first on the side of the object, in its many different forms, and then on the side of the subject, in its many different forms, and then finally in the unity of the two. This dialectical movement is traced with unflagging consistency through ever more sophisticated contexts. This is the systematic structure that Hegel intended to make apparent in the different analyses. Once the reader grasps these parallels and this dialectical movement, the seemingly heterogeneous discussions within the text are seen to be organized in a regular and systematic manner.

V. THE PHENOMENOLOGY AS FRAGMENTARY

It has often been noted that some of Hegel's analyses in the latter part of the *Phenomenology* seem perfunctory. In particular it has been argued that "Religion," the final chapter before "Absolute Knowing," shows clear signs of a hurried composition. Hegel's analyses of natural religion are only a few pages long and do not seem fully developed. (The same has been said of the short "Absolute Knowing" chapter.) In conjunction with the biographical information about the stressful circumstances of the composition of the latter part of the text, this position has often led to the claim that the *Phenomenology* is fragmentary rather than systematic.

This argument, like those cited above, is simply a non sequitur. In the letter to Schelling mentioned above, Hegel states he was not able to work out all of the analyses and their parallel discussions to his satisfaction. It is thus no surprise to find that some of his chapters or sections are rather cursory. However, it by no means follows that there is no systematic concept behind the work as a whole or behind these specific analyses. The systematic structure is there, even if Hegel did not fill out all of the individual analyses in satisfactory detail.

The idea that Hegel had a clear view of the systematic whole of the "Religion" chapter can be seen from the fact that his extensive *Lectures on the Philosophy of Religion* retains the same basic structure from the *Phenomenology*. Since he gave these lectures over several semesters, he was able to work out the individual analyses in much more detail than he had been able to do in his early book. But the key point is that the analyses given in his lectures, which he explicitly claims represent a systematic account of religion, correspond fairly straightforwardly to those of the *Phenomenology*.

In his lectures, Hegel begins with a purely conceptual account of what religion is. In the second part he moves on to a historical account of the development of different forms of religion, which corresponds to the analyses in the *Phenomenology*. The first main section in both works is "Natural Religion." In the *Phenomenology* this constitutes the series of Zoroastrianism ("God as Light"), Hinduism ("Plant and Animal"), and Egyptian polytheism ("The Artificer"). The *Lectures on the Philosophy of Religion* explores these same topics in far greater detail. Hegel tinkers with some aspects of the analysis, for example, reversing the order of his treatment of Zoroastrianism and Hinduism, but these changes are less important than the overall structural continuities. The second section of "Religion" in the *Phenomenology* is "Religion in the Form of Art," which is an analysis of Greek polytheism. This corresponds to the second division in Hegel's lectures, which he calls "The Religion of Spiritual Individuality." Finally, the third and final section of "Religion" in the *Phenomenology* is Christianity or "The Revealed Religion." This corresponds straightforwardly to what is called "The Absolute Religion" in the lectures.

To be sure, new analyses and examples are added in the lectures, but the basic triad of "Natural Religion," and "The Religion of Beauty" and "The Revealed Religion," established in the *Phenomenology*, continues to serve as the guiding paradigm. This means that Hegel knew the systematic structure that he was to follow but simply had insufficient time to execute every analysis in its details. Thus, the systematic structure of the *Phenomenology* does exist, at least in outline form in the "Religion" chapter.

This conclusion, that the *Phenomenology* is a fragment but yet also a system, will doubtless strike some as paradoxical and untenable. However, there is no intrinsic contradiction in the notion of a systematic fragment. The idea is simply that there is a systematic structure present behind the scenes. To be sure, this structure is at times skeletal, but that does not undermine Hegel's systematic intent. It merely makes it more difficult to perceive and understand. The work is a fragment with regard, not to the structure itself, but to the development of the individual analyses and dialectical arguments. Due presumably to the hasty composition of the second half of the work, some of the analyses that appear there are not fully worked out and thus remain in fragmentary form. They only receive their full analysis years later in Hegel's lectures. This understanding of the *Phenomenology* as a systematic fragment helps to do justice, on the one hand, to the belief that the text does not always work out all the details and, on the other hand, to Hegel's explicit claims for a system, which are usually cast aside as a result of that intuition.

4 The Independence and Dependence of Self-Consciousness: The Dialectic of Lord and Bondsman in Hegel's *Phenomenology of Spirit*

"Self-consciousness exists in and for itself when, and by the fact that, it so exists for another; that is, it exists only as something acknowledged."[1]

This sentence commences, and anticipates the key lesson from, what is perhaps the most-read section of any of Hegel's texts: the eight or nine pages titled, "Independence and Dependence of Self-Consciousness: Lordship and Bondage," which is embedded within chapter 4 of the *Phenomenology of Spirit*. The chapter itself, which is titled "The Truth of Self-Certainty," is the only chapter of a section that is labeled "B: Self-Consciousness" and that follows the three-chaptered "A: Consciousness" and precedes "C: Reason."

The general idea summarily introduced here – that we are the sorts of beings we are with our characteristic "self-consciousness" only on account of the fact that we exist "for" each other or, more specifically, are *recognized* or *acknowledged* (*anerkannt*) *by* each other, an idea we might refer to as the "acknowledgment condition" for self-consciousness – constitutes one of Hegel's central claims in the *Phenomenology*. This is a substantial claim indeed, and is at the heart of the thesis of "the sociality of reason".[2] It is, however, introduced in a seemingly arbitrarily way in the paragraph prior to the "Independence and Dependence" section, and at the conclusion of a discussion examining "desire" as a model for self-consciousness. Exactly *why* we are meant to accept the acknowledgment condition is, to say the least, far

---

[1] G. W. F. Hegel, *Phänomenologie des Geistes* (*Werke in zwanzig Bänden*, ed. by Eva Moldenhauer and Karl Markus Michel (Frankfurt: Suhrkamp, 1969), vol. 3), p. 145; English translation by A. V. Miller *Hegel's Philosophy of Spirit* (Oxford: Oxford University Press, 1977), § 178. (Occasionally the translation has been modified as here.) Henceforth, references to Hegel's *Phenomenology* will be given parenthetically, the page number of the German edition following the paragraph number of the English translation.

[2] Cf., Terry Pinkard, *Hegel's Phenomenology: The Sociality of Reason*, (Cambridge, UK: Cambridge University Press, 1994).

94

from clear, and while even a cursory reading of the famous lord and bondsman "dialectic" that follows enables one to get the general picture, the philosophical significance we are meant to extract from it is not obvious. In Hegel's exploration of the nature and conditions of self-consciousness in these pages, much hangs on his use of the terms "being in itself," "being for itself," and "being for another," but as with so many of Hegel's characteristic expressions, while it is easy enough to get an impression of what he means to convey with these expressions, it is far from easy to make that impression explicit. This is an effort that really cannot be avoided, however, if we are to appreciate both the nature and grounds of Hegel's claims.

"BEING IN ITSELF," "BEING FOR ITSELF," AND "BEING FOR ANOTHER"

In our everyday unreflective experience of the world we often seem to presuppose that the objects we are experiencing are presented to us just as they "really" are "in themselves." That is, we assume that were they *not* being experienced they would still be *just as* they for us *in* our experience. This everyday attitude is the attitude of "consciousness," the experience of which had been traced in section "A: Consciousness"; and in the opening paragraph of "B: Self-Consciousness," Hegel reiterates what has been learnt *from* consciousness's earlier experience. While the initial orientation of consciousness had been to take something *other than itself*, the seemingly independent "in itself" presented *to* it, to be reality, what had been revealed within the course of its experience was that this supposedly independent in-itself is in fact "a manner [Weise] in which the object is only for an other" (§166, p. 137).

Perhaps the easiest way to get a grip on consciousness's terminating attitude is to describe it as a type of radicalized Kantianism. Kant had conceived of the objects existing for consciousness – "appearances" – as having a form contributed by the conscious subject itself, and had distinguished such appearances from that thing as it was "in itself." But while Kant had retained the idea of such an unknowable "thing in itself" to contrast with the subjectively constituted appearance known, *here* consciousness has arrived at the position that what is presented to it (Kant's "appearance") is the real, but has now equated that with *itself* as that which constitutes it *as* known.[3] That is, what it had originally taken to be an independent thing "in-itself," is now grasped as something *entirely* of its own making, an "appearance" wholly dependent upon *it*.

---

[3] The claim that this more radical view was implied by Kant's more moderate position was first made by Jacobi.

As Hegel cryptically puts it, now "the *in-itself* is consciousness" (ibid.). In being conscious of its *object*, consciousness is thus conscious of *itself*.

But how are we to think of this *self*-consciousness? One tempting way might be to think of self-consciousness as some type of immediate self-reflection along the lines found in Descartes's *cogito*, and this can seem to be essentially how Fichte construed the "for-itself" in his "First Introduction to the *Wissenschaftslehre*": "A thing ... may possess a variety of different features; but if we ask, *"For whom* is it what it is?"* no one who understands our question will answer that "it exists for itself." Instead, an intellect also has to be thought of in this case, an intellect *for* which the thing in question exists. The intellect, in contrast, necessarily is for itself whatever it is, and nothing else needs to be thought of in conjunction with the thought of an intellect."[4] But the Cartesian conception is not sufficient to capture the initial orientation of self-consciousness; neither is Fichte's conception. In a departure from Descartes's notion of the mind as a thinking *thing* or *substance*, Fichte categorized the self with the neologism *"Tathandlung"* – a "fact-act" – in contrast with *"Tatsache"* – a *mere* thing or fact. Thus on Fichte's account, it was important that the self be conscious of itself *as it actually is*, that is, *as* activity. The *I* is "for it-self *whatever* it is." It is, we might say, conscious of itself, or for itself, *as it is in-itself*. Thus Fichte characterised the self-conscious intellect as an *"immediate* unity of being and seeing,"[5] suggesting, an immediate unity of a way of being (as activity) and awareness *of* this way of being.

This Fichtean characterization of self-consciousness seems clearly relevant to the orientation from which Chapter 4 starts, "Self-certainty,"[6] but when Hegel, in §178, speaks of the conditions of a self-consciousness being *both* "for itself" *and* "in itself" we might see a hint of there being something other than an *"immediate* unity" involved. That is, Hegel's "and" might be taken to suggest that self-consciousness must somehow combine these two aspects against the background of the possibility of its being considered in terms of one mode or the other. Indeed, as we will see, in the story of the lord and his bondsman, both lord and bondsman will be portrayed as realizing each of these one-sided

---

[4] J. G. Fichte, *Introductions to the Wissenschaftslehre and Other Writings*, trans. and ed. by Daniel Breazeale, (Indianapolis: Hackett, 1994), p. 21.

[5] Ibid.

[6] Although it is true that Hegel is here not concerned with particular philosophical theories as he is in later sections of the *Phenomenology*, it seems clear that with "the truth of self-certainty," Hegel intends a model of self-consciousness that finds its most explicit and developed philosophical account in Fichte.

modes. Moreover, this "and" will be important *methodologically* for Hegel, because, while there is still a Cartesian element in the immediacy of Self-certainty's knowledge, it is crucial for Hegel's epistemology that we progress by learning from our *failures*. The form of self-consciousness manifesting this initial certainty of being in itself *as it is immediately* for itself will come to a more developed conception of itself by way of passing through a conception of itself in which its complementary *in-itself* character is brought to the fore. Moreover, we have already seen something of how this "both" is to be achieved, as the experience of consciousness itself had revealed that to *have* the character of an "in-itself" was really to be "for-another." With the dialectic between lord and bondsman Hegel will try to bring out how crucial this existence "for-another" is.

SELF-CONSCIOUSNESS AS DESIRE

By the end of section "A," *consciousness* (that attitude that had taken the status of something's *givenness* to it as indicating its independent existence) had learned that what was apparently given was really constituted by its mode of *constructing*, and had had thereby become *self-consciousness*. But constructing is an activity, and so the transition from consciousness to self-consciousness has also been a change from a primarily *contemplative* form of thought to one that is essentially *practical*. It should not then be too surprising that the shape of self-consciousness first encountered in this section is an overtly practical orientation – desire. In fact, desire seems to provide a good instantiation of the idea of a self grasping *itself* as the essence of its apparently given object. While we tend to think of desires as world-directed mental attitudes, on reflection it might be thought that since the desired object is picked out exclusively by the fact *that one desires it*, it can equally be considered as a projection or construction of one's own state. Hegel seems to have something like this in mind when he says at §167 that consciousness "as self-consciousness ... has a double object: one is the immediate object ... which ... has the character of a *negative*; and the second, namely, viz. *itself*, which is the true *essence* and is present in the first instance only as opposed to the first object" (§167, p. 139).

I have suggested that Hegel portrays the initial orientation of self-consciousness in generally "Fichtean" terms, but this needs qualification: Hegel's word for desire here, *Begierde*, suggests "appetite," and Fichte's essentially Kantian conception of *moral* self-consciousness was anything but a practical orientation based on *appetite*. Fichte had appealed to the idea of the mind's basic orientation to the world as a type of *striving* or *endeavouring* rather than a *passively contemplative knowing*, but such "striving" is clearly far from reducible to any naturalistic "appetite-driven" process. For Fichte as for Kant, it was the independence or autonomy of *moral* action that had been the key concern, thus Fichte considered the finite ego as striving against all that which *limits and determines it*, including its own apparently given inclinations and appetites. As such, the primacy of *practical* reason was for Fichte the primacy of the practical or moral *faculty* that, following Kant, he called the faculty of *Begehrung*, also translated as "desire," but used in this sense without the corporeal connotations of "*Begierde*." We might start to see, however, how from Hegel's perspective such moral intentionality still has an underlying structure most obviously manifested in *Begierde*. *Begierde* is fundamentally a negating attitude to anything that is given to it, and this is the attitude of the Fichtean moral subject to whatever threatens to determine it from without. Moral desire, it might be said, is a desire to be freed from any first-order desires or natural inclinations, and it treats *them* in the way that *they* treat their objects. In the next section, I will further suggest that Hegel's use of *Begierde* is bound up with his introduction of the topic of appetite's natural context, the realm of *life*, but what should be noted here is the way that for Hegel the inadequacy of desire as a model for self-consciousness is connected to its *immediacy*.

It had been Fichte's assumption of the *immediate* unity of the ego's in-itselfness and for-selfness that precluded the possibility of Self-certainty being *mistaken* about its view of itself. In contrast, from Hegel's perspective, it is the difference between the way that the ego is *immediately for itself* and the way that it is *in-itself* that creates the space that it can traverse in its experiential journey to the *truth* of its self-understanding – its being *in-and-for-itself*. But there are other consequences of this initial gap which are crucial to Hegel's approach, as the fact that we can always counter the question of how self-consciousness is *immediately* for-itself with that concerning how it is *in-itself* introduces the issue of how a self-consciousness can be *for-another*. One consequence of this concerns the place it provides for the consciousness or viewpoint shared by "we" observers of the journey of consciousness, the so-called phenomenological we.[7] Another is that it introduces a place for a certain "nature-philosophical" inflection into the "Fichtean" dimension of Hegel's account.

---

[7] As with many components of Hegel's account this too seems to have its origin in Fichte's philosophy, as Fichte distinguished philosophical consciousness as a type of higher-order consciousness aware of the activity of first-level consciousness. See Fichte, *Introductions to the Wissenschaftslehre*, pp. 48–49.

DESIRE IN THE CONTEXT OF LIFE

In his earlier *"Differenzschrift"* of 1801, written in a more Schellingian idiom,[8] Hegel had criticized Fichte for being limited in his account to a "subjective," and as lacking a complementary "objective" – there a type of nature-philosophical – conception of the autonomous self-conscious subject, the so-called subject-object. That Fichte had been restricted to a "subjective" conception of the "subject-object" (or what Hegel was later to label "Idea" as "what is true *in and for itself, the absolute unity of Concept and objectivity"*)[9] was to remain Hegel's basic complaint against him.[10] In the *Phenomenology*, this charge effectively had become the idea that in the *desire* model of self-consciousness, the "for-self" (subjective and independent) aspect of self-consciousness predominates over or eclipses the "in-itself" (objective and dependent) aspect. Moreover, the nature-philosophical viewpoint to which Hegel had appealed in the *Differenzschrift* had provided a new sense to the notion of what it is to be "for oneself," a sense freed from the more Cartesian aspects of Fichte's usage with which we started. Self-maintaining and self-directing organisms manifest a form of "for-selfness" in those very activities. But an organism is, of course, an objectively existing thing – an "in-itself" which, in contrast to a Cartesian mind, can exist as something *for another.*[11]

Throughout section "A," because we had taken a consciousness that was *for us* as an "in-itself," we phenomenological observers had been able to grasp something about the nature of consciousness that eluded consciousness itself: its *active* role in constituting its object. Now, in

---

8 G. W. F. Hegel, *Differenz des Fichte'schen und Schelling'schen Systems der Philosophie*, (Werke, 2), translated as *Difference between Fichte's and Schelling's Systems of Philosophy*, trans. by H. S. Harris and Walter Cerf, (Albany: State University of New York Press, 1973). Hegel's complaint against Fichte outlived his allegiance to Schelling. In fact, even in the *Differenzschrift*, Hegel had departed from Schelling in crucial ways.

9 *Enzyklopädie der philosophischen Wissenschaften im Grundrisse 1830, Erster Teil: Die Wissenschaft der Logik Mit den mündlichen Zusätzen*, (Werke, 8), translated as *The Encyclopaedia Logic*, trans. by T. F. Geraets, W. A. Suchting, and H. S. Harris, (Indianapolis: Hackett, 1991), §213. Hegel further characterizes the idea as *"the Subject–Object"* on §214.

10 Such an analysis of the failings of Fichte's system is fully apparent, for example, in Hegel's comments in the *Lectures on the History of Philosophy: Volume 3, Medieval and Modern Philosophy*, trans. by E. S. Haldane and Frances H. Simson, (Lincoln: University of Nebraska Press, 1995), ((Werke, 20): §3, C1).

11 Thus as Schelling had asserted: "Every organic product exists *for itself*; its being is dependent on no other being." F. W. J. Schelling, *Ideas for a Philosophy of Nature*, trans. by Errol E. Harris and Peter Heath, (Cambridge, UK: Cambridge University Press, 1995), p. 30.

the chapter on self-consciousness, where Self-certainty grasps itself as subjective activity and its object as dependent on it and so a "nothing," the situation is in some sense reversed. We observe a self-consciousness that is immediately for-itself as a type of active self-moving object, and we grasp it as acting on objects that, although *it* regards as *nothings*, must *for us* essentially belong to the same objective order as this self-consciousness itself. To be *observed* to act, one needs, as it were, something *upon* which to act. That is, *we* understand how the objects with which it interacts have more to them than what self-consciousness itself *intends* for them – *we* can see how self-consciousness's activity is itself *dependent* on these objects, and this is what self-consciousness must itself learn through its practical experience.[12] *It* too must learn that they possess a necessary *independence* (§168, p. 139).

It is in this way, then, that Hegel introduces the theme of *life* in §168 when he notes: "But *for us*, or *in itself*, the object which for self-consciousness is the negative element has, on its side, returned into itself, just as on the other side consciousness has done. Through this reflection into itself, the object has become Life" (ibid.). From the subjective or first-person point of view, desire might be experienced immediately as the desire to negate some object; but from an external, objective point of view (that of "we" phenomenological observers), desire is the sort of thing that is expressed in the teleological action of an organism interacting with others in order to preserve itself or take for itself, as it were, *the life* that they possess. But while we may see such desire as aimed at a universal life itself, this universal aspect must be presentable to the desiring subject itself *as* a distinct object; its desire must be directed at the "*living thing*" whose life it will attempt to appropriate. And with this we see how self-consciousness must incorporate the multifaceted development characteristic of consciousness, such that its mediating object has the characteristics of objects of those shapes of consciousness explored in chapters 1–3: Sense-certainty (*die sinnliche Gewissheit*), Perception (*die Wahrnehmung*), and Understanding (*der Verstand*). "What self-consciousness distinguishes from itself as having *being*" notes Hegel, "also has in it, in so far as it is posited as being, not merely the character of sense-certainty and perception, but it is being that is reflected into itself, and the object of immediate desire is a *living thing* [ein *Lebendiges*]" (ibid.).

It can seem as if Hegel simply *presupposes* this "nature-philosophical" account that is introduced here, but on closer inspection it is clear that Hegel believes he is entitled to so locating desire in

---

[12] As desire "self-consciousness, by its negative relation to the object, is unable to supersede [aufzuheben] it" (§175, p. 143).

the living realm from what has been learned throughout chapters 1–3.[13] Consciousness had started out taking the immediate qualitatively determined "this" of Sense-certainty as the *truth* of its object and had come to learn that such immediately perceivable quality is just an aspect of the more complex object of *Perception*. In contrast to the simplicity of the "this" of sense certainty, the perceived object has an internal structure such that an underlying substance has changeable phenomenal properties. But, in turn, Perception learns too that that *its* object is in truth more complicated again, the distinction between it and the Understanding roughly enacting the distinction between the everyday commonsensical and scientific or "nomological" views of the world. While from the point of view of Perception we might think of the world as simply an assemblage of propertied objects, from the point of view of the Understanding, such objects will be integrated as interacting components of a single, unified, law-governed world.

"*Self*-certainty," the immediate form of self-consciousness, is the practical analogue of *Sense*-certainty. Here a felt appetite is directed to some particular sensuously presented "this" in which desiring self-consciousness is aware of itself. At its most basic, my desire is directed to *this* sensuous thing before me – a succulent ripe pineapple, say – but presented to me *as* this bare singular thing known only in terms of an appealing sensuous quality that determines it as something to be, literally, negated as an independent existence. But this is only the immediate form in which the mediating desired object is presented; and it must in fact be far more complex, as it is a fundamental principle of Hegel's method that each subsequent phase of consciousness or self-consciousness retains in negated, or "*aufgehoben*," form all aspects revealed in previous stages. Self-certainty must learn that the immediate "this" is not the *truth* of its object, but *we* phenomenological observers, who know that its object is *not* a mere nothing, know this object as also having the aspects revealed to Perception (the desired object must have the property of being *living*) and, crucially, the Understanding. A little

---

[13] Ludwig Siep (*Der Weg der Phänomenologie des Geistes*, (Frankfurt am Main: Suhrkamp, 2000), p. 100) raises the question as to whether Hegel simply assumes metaphysical nature-philosophical notions here. Jon Stewart (*The Unity of Hegel's Phenomenology of Spirit: A Systematic Interpretation*, (Evanston: Northwestern University Press, 2000), p. 117)) defends Hegel against any such "vitalist" interpretation by construing "life" as a purely *logical* category, while Robert Williams, (*Hegel's Ethics of Recognition*, (Berkeley: University of California Press, 1997), p. 48)) interprets "life" here in essentially *practical* terms. H. S. Harris (*Hegel's Ladder 1: The Pilgrimage of Reason*, (Indianapolis: Hackett, 1997), ch. 7) has an extensive account of Hegel's use of this notion here, grounding its introduction in the earlier account of "Understanding."

background is needed in order to appreciate what Hegel thinks grasping objects in this third way entails.

First, in relation to the Understanding, we must note the particular *dynamicist* interpretation that Hegel, essentially following in the tradition of Leibniz and Kant, had given to the Newtonian view of the world. In contrast to the prevalent mechanistic interpretations, the dynamicists conceived of Newton's laws as not holding of moving lumps of inert matter but of "moving forces" which interact via attraction or repulsion. These moving forces will effectively form the templates for the *self*-moving, that is, *organic* elements of the nature-philosophical account in chapter 4. Indeed, Fichte himself had developed such a conception of the organic realm based on a dynamic account of physics in his 1794–1795 *Foundations of the Entire Wissenschaftslehre*,[14] but it was as part of his foundation for *practical*, not *theoretical* knowledge, and so, in Hegel's terms, conceived *negatively* as a realm to be *striven against*. Next, for Hegel "the Understanding" represents a form of epistemic relation to the world which is locked into the finite cognitive forms that Kant had opposed to "reason" (*"die Vernunft"*), and which is restricted to the realm of "appearance." Thus for Kant (and also for Fichte) explanatory posits such as forces could never represent the *ultimate* constituents of the world "in-itself," but only the world as it is *for a subject.* In scientific explanation a force might be posited to *explain* some empirical, law-governed regularity, the posited *explanans* thus being distinguished from the phenomena being explained. But the Kantian idea of the unknowability of reality as it is in itself implies for Hegel that "this difference is no difference" and that the explaining force and explained law are, rather, "constituted exactly the same" (§154, p. 125). Thus Hegel describes the Understanding as positing a difference only to withdraw it: to its initial claim to know the *world* it then adds the metaclaim that what is known is an appearance that it-itself constitutes (§163, p. 133). The Understanding is so constituted to *posit a difference* and then *deny* it, but *we* can see that this activity in which a difference is posited only to be then somehow reabsorbed within a subsequent identity is characteristic of this form of conceptually articulated consciousness itself. (We see this explicitly, for example, in what "desire" does in positing the desired object that mediates it *qua* self-consciousness.) "What is, for the Understanding, an object in a

---

[14] *Grundlagen der gesamten Wissenschaftslehre,* translated as "Foundations of the Entire Science of Knowledge," in J. G. Fichte, *The Science of Knowledge,* trans. by Peter Heath and John Lachs (Cambridge, UK: Cambridge University Press, 1982), part III, p. 7.

sensuous covering, is *for us* in its essential form as a pure concept" (§164, p. 134).

With this we might now start to glimpse how Hegel at least *believes* that he has purchased the nature-philosophical position (and much else besides) that seems to be presupposed in Chapter 4. The "*Aufheben* principle" implies that the essential object that mediates self-consciousness must, despite self-consciousness's initial way of conceiving it, behave something like those reciprocally interacting forces posited by the Understanding. The action of a desiring organism on another will be met by a reciprocal action of another, opposed, desiring organism. Furthermore, we know these dynamic and self-moving objects to have a structure exhibited by the Understanding itself. This movement (which is implicitly self-consciousness) involves the positing of differences which are then overcome or superseded. But this is just the type of "movement" can be *seen in* the interactions of those self-moving forces or powers of the *organic* world.

The natural world, understood in this way, will thus provide a model for the dynamic context within which self-consciousness is possible. However, self-consciousness cannot be understood as possible within the *merely* living world. *We* can see how that which is expressed in an organism's behaviour might be regarded as a "desire" not only for the particular thing with which it interacts, but for the "living" property that it bears (*qua* object of Perception), and how this might be extended to desire *to be* a participant in the round of "life" itself, *qua concrete* universal, the implicit object of the systematic Understanding. However, the mere organism cannot learn this because the merely living system is unable to produce the point of view from which the universal *could* be recognized as an end: the dynamic genus of life "does not exist for itself" but "points to something other than itself, namely, to consciousness, for which life exists as a unity, or as genus [Gattung]" (§172, p. 143).[15] And with this inability to grasp the universal, *natural* desire cannot be an adequate model for self-consciousness: caught in the problem of a contradictory relation to its immediate object, desire *is dependent upon* its object in order to *show its independence* in its act of negating it. This conceptual problem will equally afflict Fichtean moral self-consciousness, conceived as it is as a *metadesire*. Moral self-consciousness strives to free itself from dependence on objects by negating its own inclinations; but here "satisfaction" will deprive self-consciousness of the resources necessary for its existence.

---

[15] Effectively here Hegel follows Aristotle: merely living, nonhuman animals can recognize only particulars.

Neither desire nor the moral self-consciousness modeled on it can therefore be regarded as self-sufficient. Self-consciousness can, Hegel says, achieve satisfaction, not by negating the object, but "only when the object itself effects the negation within itself." But of course self-negation is, as we have seen, just what Fichtean self-consciousness as metadesire itself *does*. Thus the new model is one in which "*self-consciousness achieves satisfaction only in another self-consciousness*" and with this Hegel has introduced the theme of recognition/acknowledgement (*Anerkennung*). Self-consciousness exists in-and-for-itself "only as something acknowledged" by another self-consciousness. Now the realm of *mere life* will be replaced by another concrete universal, which Hegel calls "spirit" (*Geist*), the universal within which distinctively human lives are lived out within patterns of intersubjective and conceptually mediated recognition, a realm of *self-conscious life*.

LIFE, RECOGNITION, AND SPIRIT

Far from being original to Hegel, the notion of *Anerkennung* is again taken over from Fichte, specifically from his theory of *rights* in the 1796–1797 *Foundations of Natural Rights*.[16] Indeed, in treating the subject's recognition of rights of others as a necessary condition for self-consciousness, Fichte had made recognition central to his model of self-consciousness. Hegel was to employ Fichte's recognitive conception of rights in his later *Philosophy of Right* where the relation of contract was to be treated as a matter of the mutual recognition by the contractors of each other's abstract rights as proprietors.[17] But for Hegel this legalistic approach to recognition does not get at its essence: in fact, in its *formal* character Fichte's conception of recognition testified to the fact of its still being in the thralls of the *desire model* of self-consciousness. In the formal recognition of the other's right, recognition is just *the other side* of an act of negation or annihilation of one's own desire. To acknowledge another's right to an object is just to limit one's own interested actions toward that object.

Just as in the realm of life, the concrete universal or "genus" of life itself pointed to a consciousness "for which life exists as a unity, or as a genus" (§172, p. 143), in the realm of abstract right as Hegel treats it in

---

[16] J. G. Fichte, *Foundations of Natural Right*, ed. by Frederick Neuhouser, trans. by Michael Baur (Cambridge, UK: Cambridge University Press, 2000).

[17] G. W. F. Hegel, *Grundlinien der Philosophie des Rechts*, (*Werke*, 7), translated as *Elements of the Philosophy of Right*, ed. by Allen W. Wood, trans. by H. B. Nisbet, (Cambridge, UK: Cambridge 1991), p. 71, *Zusatz*.

the *Philosophy of Right*, the abstract, legalistic sphere of the recognition of rights found in "civil society" is dependent on another realm within which the circle of recognition itself can be grasped as a genus – the family. In the family, members are conscious of the genus as their essence (there the participants grasp themselves primarily *as* family members), and recognition is not *opposed* to felt impulses or affections but is in immediate identity with them.[18] And, of course, the family, as a more *immediate* form of objectified spirit, is closer to the realm of *natural life*. In this way, then, the opposed recognitive realms of family and civil society in Hegel's later philosophy instantiate the categories of the "in itself" and the "for itself," with both being incorporated into the more self-sufficient expression of spirit objectified in nature (objective spirit), the state, which in contrast to the family and civil society, is "in-and-for-itself." But the roots of this later treatment are already discernable in the *Phenomenology*'s treatment of recognition.[19]

The protagonists of a *merely* living sphere, as we have seen, cannot grasp their desired object in terms of the universal that we can see it to be: this capacity is available only to a genuinely or fully self-conscious being. And if we now reflect on this we can quickly grasp the type of consequences that *could* flow from the possession of the capacity to recognize the universal by a self-conscious member of a realm of struggle. If one *could* grasp that beyond the desired annihilation of the other's independence lies the desire for a universal, such as *life* itself, one could then grasp the possibility of there being *alternate ways* of realizing that desire. And this is indeed what is grasped by one antagonist of the sort of struggle that Hegel describes among *self-consciously* living beings. Struggle in this realm can end in the *submission* of one antagonist to the other, thereby establishing a relation of lord to bondsman.[20]

Hegel's actual *story* itself is reasonably clear, at least in its broad outlines. Against the contrasting background of the struggling organic world, the realm of nature "red in tooth and claw" – perhaps Hobbes's "state of nature" – we see another type of struggle with a possible resolution other than that of annihilation of one of the antagonists. The movement in this sphere, Hegel says, "repeats the process which presented itself as the play of Forces," but the process obtaining within the

---

[18] Hegel, *Philosophy of Right*, pp. 158–180.
[19] On the unity of Hegel's early and later approaches to recognition see Robert R. Pippin, "What is the Question for which Hegel's Theory of Recognition is the Answer?" *European Journal of Philosophy*, 8, 2 (2000), pp. 155–172.
[20] "In this experience, self-consciousness learns that life is as essential to it as pure self-consciousness" (§150, p. 189).

concrete universal of life is "repeated now in consciousness," that is, the elements in their full logical articulation (*qua* objects of Sense-certainty, Perception, and Understanding) are now available *for* the protagonists themselves. In contrast to the sphere of mere life, the protagonists thus have a more complexly negating attitude to each other, for each has the other before it not "merely as it exists primarily for desire, but as something that has an independent existence of its own, which, therefore, it cannot use for its own purposes, if that object does not, of its own accord do what the first does to it" (§182, p. 146).

The minimal protosociety of lord and bondsman that resolves such self-conscious struggles is a conventional form of life in which two individuals live out distinctive existences *via* the differentiated and coordinated social roles of victor and vanquished – lord and bondsman. "They exist as two opposed shapes of consciousness; one is the independent consciousness whose essential nature is to be for itself, the other is the dependent consciousness whose essential nature is simply to live or to be for another. The former is lord, the latter is bondsman" (§189, p. 150).

THE DYNAMICS OF LORDSHIP AND BONDAGE

In this model each member has taken on one side of the "in-and-for-itself" structure which is the essence of self-consciousness: the lord maintains the orientation of an independent desiring "for-self" while the bondsman, by having abandoned its own desire and accepted the role of a mere object or instrument of the other's will, opts for the status of a dependent "in itself," an object used by the lord for the satisfaction of his desire. But it is important that the bondsman's role has been *chosen*, rather than simply accepted as "given." His existence is *implicitly independent* – the lord cannot use the bondsman "for his own purposes" unless the bondsman does "of its own accord what [the lord] does to it" (§182, p. 146). The bondsman has, we might say, *committed* himself to this identity in exchange for his life and he *holds himself to* this commitment in his continual acknowledgement of the other as *his* lord by treating him as such.[21] This structure of holding and being held to such commitments is constitutive of such social roles and is, for Hegel, fundamentally *conceptual* or rule-governed, the interactions of lord and bondsman being mediated by the linked pair of action-guiding concepts, "lord" and "bondsman." Because of this participation of conceptuality,

---

[21] Thus the bondsman "sets aside its own being-for-self, and in so doing itself does what the first does to it," the act which Hegel describes as the first "moment of recognition" (§152, p. 191).

this primitive form of sociality is an instantiation of reason within the realm of life, albeit a primitive one.

The society of lord and bondsman thus instantiates, although in an immediate and inadequate way, the type of structure whose essential shape Hegel has posited as that which responds to the inadequacies of the model of self-consciousness as desire. "*Self-consciousness achieves its satisfaction only in another self-consciousness*" (§175, p. 144), and this is what the lord has found in his bondsman, a self-consciousness that in renouncing his desire "effects the negation within itself". And so with this sphere "we already have before us the concept of *Spirit*" (§177, p. 144–145), a realm not abstractly opposed to *mere* life but one in which life's dynamic has been integrated (*aufgehoben*) within it: a realm of *self-conscious* life. In fact, to ignore this fact and think of spirit and life as *simply* opposed would be to remain, like Fichte, in the grip of the desire model.[22] But while such truths about spirit can at this point be recognized by "we" phenomenological observers, "the experience of what spirit is – this absolute substance which is the unity of the different independent self-consciousnesses which, in their opposition, enjoy perfect freedom and independence: "I" that is "We" and "We" that is "I," as yet "lies ahead *for consciousness*" (ibid.).

In the ensuing pages we learn how this embryonic society of lord and bondman is unstable and how each member actually comes to take on the characteristics of the other. This dialectical development follows from the initial *nonreciprocal* distribution of independence and dependence, "one being only *recognized*, the other only *recognizing*" (§185, p. 147); as condition of self-conscious life, this social arrangement does not live up to its essence. As we have seen, the bondsman, by his self-denial, effects negation within himself, but the same cannot be said for the lord. The lord, as victor, has not had his immediately "for-self" character shaken. His self-consciousness still remains modeled on *desire*, and this means that as a structure of recognition, that obtaining between lord and bondsman will be rent by contradiction. The lord cannot become adequately conscious of *himself* as a self-conscious individual in the recognition of the bondsman, because, treating him as a thing, he doesn't explicitly *recognize* the bondsman *as* a self-consciousness. And so *qua* object for the lord, the bondsman "does not correspond to its concept" (§192, p. 152), and in failing to recognize the bondsman as

---

[22] This tendency that may, in fact, be manifest in the popular interpretation that sees at the centre of Hegel's account a "struggle for recognition," which is abstractly opposed to the more naturalistic Hobbesian accounts of an original struggle over survival.

a self-consciousness, the lord negates the very conditions for his own self-consciousness.

As for the bondsman, "just as lordship showed that its essential nature is the reverse of what it wants to be, so too servitude in its consummation will really turn into the opposite of what it immediately is" (§193, p. 152). In the work performed for the lord, the bondsman himself, by working on and transforming the objects of the world, learns to *master* it. He attains the *negating* orientation to the objective world that goes beyond the more primitive "for-self" orientation of the lord whose negations essentially are tied to the satisfactions of immediate desire. It is thus the bondsman who "through his service ... rids himself of his attachment to natural existence in every single detail; and gets rid of it by working on it" (§194, p. 153). Moreover, in the transformations of natural objects brought about by his work, the bondsman has the chance to recognize his own *negating* activity: "Through his work ... the bondsman encounters himself [kommt ... zu sich selbst]" (§195, p. 153). With this then, we can see the beginnings of a *dynamic* process internal to this protosociety that puts it on a developmental path. It will be the servile consciousness marked by formative activity and "*inhibited* desire [gehemmte Begierde]" (§195, p. 153), and not the lord, who will inherit the earth.

With this we see the beginnings of *history* as a process in which the conditions of *reciprocal* recognition essential to the development of self-consciousness are gradually brought about; but Hegel's final paragraph of this section signals a warning concerning how to understand the laboring self-consciousness' final victory. "In fashioning the thing" Hegel remarks, "the bondsman's own negativity, his being-for-self, becomes an object for him only though his negating the existing *shape* confronting him" (§196, p. 154). That is, ultimately, it would seem, as a vehicle for or model of self-consciousness "fashioning" self-consciousness suffers from the same limitations as desire. The bondsman's initial orientation was that of fear – fear of the lord, but also fear of something more general that had been represented by the lord, "the fear of death, the absolute Lord" (§194, p. 153). This was the attitude of the bondsman as it initially had been "in itself," but its concluding attitude, its explicitly "for-self" moment, is that the shapes of the external realm confronting him are negated. Again, the truth of self-consciousness can only be understood as the *unity* of these two moments. "If consciousness fashions the thing without that initial absolute fear, it is only an empty self-centred attitude; for its form or negativity is not negativity *per se*, and therefore its formative activity cannot give it a consciousness of itself as essential being" (§196, p. 154).

THE PLACE OF RECOGNITION IN HEGEL'S
PHENOMENOLOGY OF SPIRIT

Hegel's comments concerning the limits of the bondsman's "fashioning" self-consciousness may be taken as a warning against readily accepting as Hegel's own view the reading (or perhaps "creative misreading") given by Alexandre Kojève in his influential *Introduction to the Reading of Hegel*.[23] In Kojève's account, which projects into Hegel's story concepts derived from the early Marx as well as from Heidegger, the lord–bondsman episode, and the "struggle for recognition" which it exemplifies, are taken as the interpretative key to a reading of Hegel's *Phenomenology* as a type of philosophical anthropology describing the bondsman's – effectively *humanity's* – historical self-liberation through the collectively achieved conscious fashioning of the world. Regardless of the value of Kojève's work as an original piece of political philosophy, it is questionable as an accurate rendering of Hegel's own account. In the *Phenomenology* the lord–bondsman dialectic is just one of a series of similar dialectics within which the notion of "recognition" plays a central role. Moreover, neither would it seem that the concept of recognition is a fundamentally *practical* notion restricted to a constitutive role in the *institutional* realm of "objective spirit." As H. S. Harris has pointed out,[24] Hegel's first use of the idea of "reciprocal recognition" had appeared in his early "critical" treatment of the conflicts between antithetical *philosophical* views.[25] "Recognition," this would seem to suggest, would thus play a role in the realm of *absolute* spirit – the realms of art, religion, and philosophy – and not only those of *objective* spirit.

---

[23] Alexandre Kojève, *Introduction to the Reading of Hegel*, ed. by Allan Bloom, trans. by J. H. Nichols, Jr., (New York: Basic Books, 1969). Kojève's reading was crucial in shaping the "Hegel" that was first embraced in France in the 1940s and 1950s and popularised by Sartre, but later denounced by structuralists and poststructuralists.

[24] In "Skepticism, Dogmatism and Speculation in the Critical Journal," in George di Giovanni and H. S. Harris, eds., *Between Kant and Hegel* (Albany, NY: State University of New York Press, 1985), pp. 253–254.

[25] In the "Introduction" to *The Critical Journal of Philosophy*, 1, 1, (1802), "Über das Wesen der philosophischen Kritik überhaupt und ihr Verhältnis zum gegenwärtigen Zustand der Philosophie insbesondere" (*Werke*, 2, p. 173), translated in di Giovanni and Harris, *Between Kant and Hegel*, p. 276. Hegel describes the polemical situation between a philosophy and an "*unphilosophy*" that does not self-consciously grasp its views *as* philosophical. Because they no longer share the "Idea" of philosophy, reciprocal recognition here has been "suspended [aufgehoben]."

With this in mind, it might be conjectured that the concept of reciprocal recognition is implicit within the very fabric of Hegel's *Phenomenology*. As we have seen, Hegel relies on the existence of a distinct philosophical point of view, that of the "phenomenological we"
at which the reader is located and for which each shape of consciousness or self-consciousness can be presented as an "in-itself." It might
be asked, however, how one is to stop a threatening infinite regress
of *meta*consciousnesses here? Is not a *further* consciousness required
for which *our* consciousness could be described objectively as an "in
itself"? Hegel's solution to this problem seems bound up with the central insight of chapter 4 – *recognition*. Towards the conclusion of the
Phenomenology and on the threshold of "Absolute Knowledge" – the
standpoint of "science" itself – Hegel briefly reviews the development
that has unfolded in the book to that point. With this he seems to
be inviting us, as philosophical readers, to recognize *ourselves* in the
history of developing forms of consciousness: it is *our history*, and in
grasping this we return from this "meta" position to the world itself.
With this, the circle of spirit as self-conscious life is finally closed. *Qua*
readers of the *Phenomenology* we supposedly have now been brought to
the standpoint of science – philosophy – itself.[26]

---

[26] I would like to thank Frederick Beiser, Jean-Philippe Deranty, Simon Lumsden,
George Markus, Emmanuel Renault, and Robert Sinnerbrink for very helpful comments on an earlier version of this essay.

5   Hegel's Logic

Hegel's *Science of Logic* does not enjoy the best of reputations. It is invariably criticized for being obscure and impenetrable, or it is simply ignored altogether, as if it had never been written in the first place. Allen Wood speaks for many who have read some of Hegel's dense and difficult text when he maintains that the philosophical paradoxes explored in it are frequently based on "shallow sophistries" and that the resolution to such paradoxes supplied by Hegel's system is often "artificial and unilluminating". With even friends of Hegel, such as Wood, dismissing the *Logic* in this way, it is hardly surprising that (as Wood notes) "Hegel's system of dialectical logic has never won acceptance outside an isolated and dwindling tradition of incorrigible enthusiasts".[1]

In the eyes of such enthusiasts, however – who include, for example, Hans-Georg Gadamer, Dieter Henrich, Jean Hyppolite, and John Burbidge – Hegel's *Logic* is by no means shallow or sophistical, but is one of the most subtle and profound works of philosophy ever produced. My aim in this chapter is to shed light on the distinctive purpose and method of Hegelian logic in the hope of enabling many more readers than hitherto to discover that subtlety and profundity for themselves.

THE CATEGORIES OF THOUGHT

Hegel's speculative, dialectical logic is set out in two texts – the monumental *Science of Logic* (or the so-called Greater Logic)[2] and the more

---

[1] Allen W. Wood, *Hegel's Ethical Thought* (Cambridge, UK: Cambridge University Press, 1990), pp. 4–5.

[2] See *Hegel's Science of Logic*, trans. by A. V. Miller (Amherst, NY: Humanity Books, 1999) (hereafter *SL*); G. W. F. Hegel, *Wissenschaft der Logik*, ed. by E. Moldenhauer and K. M. Michel, 2 vols., *Werke in zwanzig Bänden*, vols. 5, 6 (Frankfurt am Main: Suhrkamp Verlag, 1969) (hereafter *Werke*, 5 or 6). The *Science of Logic* was first published between 1812 and 1816. The first part of the text, "the doctrine of

truncated *Encyclopaedia Logic* (or the so-called Lesser Logic)[3] – but its purpose is in each case the same: to derive and clarify the basic categories of thought.

Following Kant (and in contrast to Locke), Hegel argues that our fundamental categories are not drawn from sensory experience through a process of abstraction, but are generated a priori by the understanding and are then employed to comprehend and make sense of what we perceive. Such categories are distinguished by Hegel from mere words: categories are "forms of thought" (*Denkformen*) with a logical structure of their own, whereas words are sounds (or written signs) by means of which such forms of thought (as well as other representations) are given expression. Hegel insists, however, that the use of categories is inseparable from the use of language: "we *think* in names".[4] Conversely, language is itself shot through with a priori categories: "everything that [the human being] has transformed into language and expresses in it contains a category [*Kategorie*] – concealed, mixed with other forms or clearly determined as such, so much is logic his natural element".[5] Since language informs and conditions all our conscious perceptions, what we perceive is thus always understood in terms of categories. In Hegel's view, human beings have no unconceptualized perceptions (or at least none of which we can be aware).[6]

Like Kant, Hegel distinguishes between fundamental categories and empirical concepts, such as "dog" or "chair". Categories are much more general and abstract than empirical concepts and contain no perceptual element. Yet categories are not abstruse or esoteric concepts known only

---

being", was revised towards the end of Hegel's life and was reissued posthumously in 1832.

[3] See G. W. F. Hegel, *The Encyclopaedia Logic*, trans. by T. F. Geraets, W. A. Suchting, and H. S. Harris (Indianapolis: Hackett, 1991) (hereafter *EL*); G. W. F. Hegel, *Enzyklopädie der philosophischen Wissenschaften im Grundrisse (1830). Erster Teil: Die Wissenschaft der Logik*, ed. by E. Moldenhauer and K. M. Michel, *Werke in zwanzig Bänden*, vol. 8 (hereafter *Werke, 8*). Hegel's *Encyclopaedia* was first published in 1817 and then revised and reissued in 1827 and 1830. On the limitations of the *Encyclopadia Logic*, see *EL*, 1, 39, Preface to first edition and §16; *Werke*, 8:11, 60.

[4] *Hegel's Philosophy of Mind*, trans. by W. Wallace, together with the *Zusätze* in Boumann's text, trans. by A. V. Miller (Oxford: Clarendon Press, 1971) (hereafter *EPM*), p. 220, §462 remark; G. W. F. Hegel, *Enzyklopädie der philosophischen Wissenschaften im Grundrisse (1830). Dritter Teil: Die Philosophie des Geistes*, ed. by E. Moldenhauer and K. M. Michel, *Werke in zwanzig Bänden*, vol. 10 (hereafter *Werke, 10*), p. 278.

[5] Hegel, *SL*, 31; *Werke*, 5:20.

[6] See Hegel, *EL*, 57, §24 addition 1; *Werke*, 8:82: "in all human intuiting there is thinking".

to philosophers; categories are the general concepts through which all of us – all of the time – make sense of our world. Indeed, Hegel writes, they are "what we are *most familiar* with [*das Bekannteste*]: being, nothing, etc.; determinacy, magnitude, etc.; [...] one, many, and so on".[7] As we learn in the course of Hegel's logic, other categories include "something", "other", "form", "content", "whole", "part", "substance", "cause", and "object". Categories are thus the basic, everyday concepts that allow us to say the simplest things, such as "there is *something* on the floor", "the dog *caused* the child to cry" or "this leaf *is* green".[8]

The fact that categories "pass our lips in every sentence we speak", and so are deeply familiar to us, does not, however, mean that we always use them appropriately or fully understand their logical structure or meaning. As Hegel reminds us, "what is *familiar* [*bekannt*] is not for that reason *known* or *understood* [*erkannt*]".[9] Indeed, Hegel thinks that for the most part we employ categories without a clear consciousness of all that they entail. Furthermore, precisely because the categories are so familiar to us, we do not see the need to examine them directly and thereby ensure that we understand their logical structure properly. As Hegel notes, "*being*, for example, is a pure thought-determination; but it never occurs to us to make 'is' [*das Ist*] the subject matter of our inquiry".[10] Categories permeate all our everyday experience; in Hegel's view, however, our very familiarity with them blinds us to the possibility that we may not actually understand them as well as we think we do.

The task of Hegel's logic is to discover the right way to understand the categories by determining their intrinsic and necessary structure. In this way, Hegel's logic aims to correct any misunderstanding of them to which everyday consciousness falls prey:

At first [categories] enter consciousness separately and so are variable and mutually confusing; consequently they afford to mind only a fragmentary and uncertain actuality; the loftier business of logic therefore is to clarify [*reinigen*] these categories and in them to raise mind to freedom and truth.[11]

This process of conceptual "clarification" is undertaken partly for its own sake – simply to allow us to contemplate in peace and freedom the true character of our own fundamental concepts – but also to train us to think properly in everyday life. Hegel believes that philosophical

---

[7] Hegel, *EL*, 45, §19 remark; *Werke*, 8:67.
[8] Hegel, *EL*, 27, §3 remark; *Werke*, 8:45.
[9] Hegel, *SL*, 33; *Werke*, 5:22, translation altered.
[10] Hegel, *EL*, 59, §24 addition 2; *Werke*, 8:85. A similar concern is later expressed by Heidegger; see Martin Heidegger, *Being and Time*; trans. by J. Macquarrie and E. Robinson (Oxford: Blackwell, 1962), p. 23.
[11] Hegel, *SL*, 37; *Werke*, 5:27.

comprehension does not have to remain cut off from, but can penetrate, everyday life.[12] Philosophy can, therefore, perform a practical function by transforming the way we think in our personal, social, or religious activity. As Hegel writes in the *Science of Logic*, "the study of this science [i.e. speculative logic], to dwell and labour in this shadowy realm, is [thus] the absolute education and discipline [*Bildung und Zucht*] of consciousness".[13]

Hegel points out that the categories do not just inform our everyday consciousness, but have also been employed by previous philosophers to comprehend the world. Metaphysicians such as Spinoza, Leibniz, and Wolff made self-conscious use of categories to understand the world in terms of "substance and attributes", "causality", or "force". The problem, in Hegel's view, is that such philosophers did not first undertake a thorough examination of these categories in order to establish precisely how they are to be conceived. They simply assumed that the categories had a certain logical structure and then used them to interpret the world. Hegel does not deny that different philosophers have conceived categories such as "substance" in subtly different ways; but he believes that since the categories were first rendered explicit by Plato and Aristotle they have never been subjected to truly radical, critical scrutiny. What Hegel calls "former metaphysics" thus "incurred the just reproach of having employed these forms *uncritically* [*ohne Kritik*]".[14] The aim of Hegel's logic, therefore, will be not only to clarify the categories that inform everyday consciousness but at the same time to provide a critical "reconstruction" of the categories of metaphysics.

Ordinary consciousness and previous metaphysics have often – though not always – presupposed that certain fundamental categories are clearly distinct from or opposed to one another, that is, "that infinity is different from finitude, that content is other than form, that the inner is other than the outer, also that mediation is not immediacy". According to Hegel, however, the task of logic is to consider whether such distinctions and oppositions are in fact sustainable – without assuming in advance that they are or that they are not. That is to say,

it is the requirement and the business of logical thinking to enquire into just this, whether such a finite without infinity is something true, or whether such an abstract infinity, also a content without form and a form without content, an inner by itself which has no outer expression, an externality without an inwardness, whether any of these is *something true* or *something actual*.[15]

[12] Hegel, *EL*, 48, §19 addition 3; *Werke*, 8:71.
[13] Hegel, *SL*, 58; *Werke*, 5:55, translation altered.
[14] Hegel, *SL*, 64; *Werke*, 5:61.
[15] Hegel, *SL*, 41–42; *Werke*, 5:33.

KANT'S CONTRIBUTION

What prompts Hegel to undertake this critical investigation of the basic categories of thought is, on the one hand, a simple interest in truth and a concern that we not be misled by what is most familiar to us. On the other hand, he is also influenced by the modern spirit of critical freedom. In Hegel's view, we moderns live in a world in which the authority of tradition should no longer be taken for granted, but everything – including our most cherished beliefs and the concepts and principles with which we are most intimately familiar – should be examined with a free and critical eye. This does not mean that our everyday and traditional philosophical assumptions should necessarily be abandoned; but it does mean that they should no longer be taken on trust as *givens* that govern our lives.

Hegel credits Kant in particular with focussing critical attention on the categories employed in philosophy, science, and everyday life. Yet despite inaugurating the "critical turn" in philosophy, Kant is not as critical as he should be, in Hegel's view, for he confines himself to considering the *epistemic status* of the categories – that is, their range of validity – but does not examine their internal *logical structure* and seek to determine whether that structure has been properly understood by previous philosophers. As Hegel puts it in the *Encyclopaedia Logic*, Kant's critical philosophy "does not involve itself with the *content* [. . .] or with the determinate mutual relationship of these thought-determinations to each other; instead, it considers them according to the antithesis of *subjectivity* and *objectivity* in general".[16] Kant argues that the categories yield knowledge only within the realm of empirical experience – only within the realm of what Hegel here calls "subjectivity" – and should not be held to disclose anything about what lies beyond such experience. Yet Kant did not challenge the way the categories have traditionally been conceived. Aristotle understood substance, for example, to be "that which is neither said of a subject nor in a subject", and Kant defined it in a similar way as "something that can be thought as a subject (without being a predicate of something else)".[17] The difference between the "precritical" Aristotle and the "critical" Kant thus does not lie in the way they conceive the categories but merely in the fact that Kant restricted the categories' range of legitimate application.

---

[16] Hegel, *EL*, 81, §41; *Werke*, 8:113. See also *SL*, 47; *Werke*, 5:40.

[17] See *The Complete Works of Aristotle*, ed. by J. Barnes, 2 vols. (Princeton, NJ: Princeton University Press, 1984), vol. 1, p. 4; I. Kant, *Critique of Pure Reason*, trans. by P. Guyer and A. W. Wood (Cambridge, UK: Cambridge University Press, 1997) (hereafter *CPR*), p. 277 [B 186].

Kant further belies his critical intentions by simply *assuming* that all acts of understanding are acts of judgment and that all concepts, including our basic categories, are "predicates of possible judgments".[18] For Kant, the purpose of the concept of "substance" is not to stand alone as an independent object of contemplation but to be *applied* to something in a judgment such as "X is a substance". (It should be remembered, however, that when X is judged in this way to be a "substance", it is judged to be an irreducible *subject* and not a quality or "predicate" of anything else). Having assumed that thought is minimally judgment, Kant then proceeds to derive the basic categories of thought from the various forms of judgments with which we are familiar from formal logic. The affirmative judgment, "S *is* P", yields the category of "reality", the negative judgment, "S *is not* P", yields the category of "negation", the problematic judgment, "S *might be* P", yields the category of possibility, and so on. The categories can, of course, serve as *predicates* in any form of judgment: one can equally well say that "S is possible", or "S is not possible", or that "S might be a substance". Each category, however, has its *origin* in a particular form of judgment (or, more precisely, in the specific way in which the subject and predicate are united in a particular form of judgment).[19] Each judgment form thus gives rise to a specific category that can then serve as a predicate in several different forms of judgment.

Kant's deduction of the categories is clear and logical. In Hegel's view, however, that deduction is problematic because the categories are derived not from the very nature of thought as such but from what Kant simply *assumes* to be thought's fundamental activity, namely, *judgment*. Since Kant never proves that judgment is essential to thought, or that judgment must take certain forms, but just takes all of this for granted uncritically, he cannot prove – at least to Hegel's satisfaction – that he has discovered all the basic categories of thought or that he has conceived of them properly.

Hegel sees more merit in Fichte's approach, since Fichte derived the categories sequentially and necessarily from what appears more obviously to be an irreducible feature of thought: the fact that the I thinks or "posits" a distinction between itself and what is not itself. Yet Fichte's way of proceeding remains problematic, because – like Descartes – he simply assumes from the start that thought is the activity of an "I". He thus begins from what Hegel considers to be "a subjective standpoint" whose legitimacy is never properly established.[20]

---

[18] Kant, *CPR*, 205 [B 94].
[19] Kant, *CPR*, 211 [B 104–105].
[20] See Hegel, *EL*, 84, §42 remark; *Werke*, 8:117, and *SL*, 47; *Werke*, 5:41.

Both Kant and Fichte, therefore, take too much for granted in their derivation of the categories and start from unwarranted assumptions about thought. The aim of Hegel's logic will be to make up for the deficiencies of Kant and Fichte by endeavouring to "deduce [the categories] from thinking itself" *without* making unwarranted assumptions about thought or the categories.[21] If this deduction is successful, it will, in Hegel's view, be the first genuinely critical and self-critical study of the categories. As such, it will reveal not only which categories are made necessary by the very nature of thought but also how those categories are properly to be understood.

Hegel's logic may be dismissed by some as obscure and impenetrable. It is important to remember, however, that it was intended by Hegel himself to be the rigorous, unprejudiced derivation and clarification of the basic categories of thought. It was intended to be a modern, post-Kantian science that would transform for the better both philosophy and our everyday practices.

LOGIC AND METAPHYSICS

Speculative logic is conceived by Hegel as the discipline in which human thought is to achieve full self-understanding and self-consciousness. Yet is that all that is going on in Hegel's logic? Is this logic simply thought's account of its *own* basic categories? For the advocates of the "nonmetaphysical" interpretation of Hegelian logic – inspired by Klaus Hartmann – the answer is "yes".[22] Terry Pinkard, for example, insists that "the *Science of Logic* is a reconstruction not of the movement of things in the cosmos but is instead one of *conceptions*". It explains "how these conceptions relate to each other and what principles underlie them".[23]

Robert Pippin's interpretation of Hegel's logic is subtly different from Pinkard's. Pippin maintains that Hegel gives an account not just of our basic conceptions and the relations between them but of the "conditions necessary for objects to be objects at all".[24] That is to say, Hegel describes not merely how *we* must think if we are to think coherently, but how *objects* in the world are to be conceived if they are to be regarded as

[21] Hegel, *EL*, 59, §24 addition 2; *Werke*, 8:85.

[22] See Klaus Hartmann, "Hegel: A Non-Metaphysical View", in *Hegel: A Collection of Critical Essays*, ed. by A. MacIntyre (1972) (Notre Dame: University of Notre Dame Press, 1976), pp. 101–124.

[23] Terry Pinkard, *Hegel's Dialectic. The Explanation of Possibility* (Philadelphia, PA: Temple University Press, 1988), pp. 12, 14, my emphasis.

[24] Robert B. Pippin, *Hegel's Idealism. The Satisfactions of Self-Consciousness* (Cambridge, UK: Cambridge University Press, 1989), p. 176.

genuine objects. It becomes clear in the course of Pippin's discussion, however, that his interpretation of Hegel's logic remains firmly lodged in the nonmetaphysical camp. For Pippin's Hegel does not set out the logical conditions required for objects to *exist* or to *be* objects in their own right, but rather articulates the conceptual conditions required for something to be an "object of cognition" or an "object of a possibly self-conscious judgment".[25] That is to say, Hegel's logic analyses "what is required in order for a subject to judge self-consciously about objects".[26] Hegel's proof that the categories of "negation" and "opposition" are necessary does not, therefore, establish that "*beings* actually oppose and negate each other and [...] could not be what they are outside such a relation". It shows only that they have to be "characterized 'contrastively'" *by potentially self-conscious thought* if they are to be conceived by such thought as determinate objects.[27]

On Pippin's reading, therefore, Hegel's logic is merely a transcendental philosophy that shows the conditions needed for objects to be determinate objects of *thought*. It is not a metaphysics or ontology that discloses the intrinsic structure of *things themselves* (or the "conditions" required for them to *be* the things they are).

In my view, however, the "nonmetaphysical" interpretation of Hegel's logic – as presented by Pinkard or Pippin – tells only half the story: for Hegel makes it clear that the categories set out in his logic are both the necessary concepts of thought *and* the intrinsic determinations of beings themselves. That is to say, Hegel's logic, by his own admission, is both a logic and a metaphysics or an ontology. This is stated in both versions of Hegel's logic. In the *Science of Logic* Hegel describes the "logical science" as "metaphysics proper [*die eigentliche Metaphysik*] or purely speculative philosophy"; and in the *Encyclopaedia Logic* he writes that "*logic* coincides with *metaphysics*, with the science of *things* grasped in *thoughts* that were taken to express the essentialities of the things".[28]

Hegel conceives of his logic as both a logic and a metaphysics or an ontology because he understands the fundamental concepts of thought to be *identical* in logical structure to the fundamental determinations of being itself. This is true of all the categories analysed in the *Science of Logic*. The logical structure of the concept of "something" – a concept that *we* must employ – is at the same time the logical structure of whatever *is* something in the world. The concept of "something" is

[25] Pippin, *Hegel's Idealism*, pp. 176, 250.
[26] Pippin, *Hegel's Idealism*, p. 248.
[27] Pippin, *Hegel's Idealism*, p. 188.
[28] Hegel, *SL*, 27; *Werke*, 5:16, and *EL*, 56, §24; *Werke*, 8:81, translation altered.

inseparably linked to that of "other", "being-in-itself", and "being-for-other" and, correspondingly, whatever *is* something in the world is also inseparably related to what is other than it. (*Pace* Pippin, Hegel's claim is thus that beings *do* "actually oppose and negate each other [. . .] and could not be what they are outside such a relation".)

Similarly, the logical structure of the concepts of quantity, measure, causality, objectivity, and life *is* the logical structure of those aspects of being themselves. This is even true of "judgment" and "syllogism", which Hegel, unlike Kant, proves to be immanent in – and thereby necessary to – thought. These are not only forms of human thought, for Hegel, but also logical structures in the world. The "syllogistic form [*Form des Schließens*] is a universal form of all things", Hegel writes; "all of them are particulars that unite themselves [*sich zusammenschließen*] as something universal with the singular".[29] In Hegel's view, therefore, every category analyzed in his logic, however "subjective" it might appear, is both a necessary concept of thought *and* a fundamental determination of being.

Nonmetaphysical interpreters of Hegel, such as Pinkard and Pippin, have done much to illuminate the complexities of Hegel's logic and to demonstrate that it is a rigorous, modern discipline. In my view, however, Jean Hyppolite is right to maintain that philosophical knowledge, for Hegel, is just as much "knowledge of being" as it is "self-knowledge".[30] Hegel's logic is not only a post-Kantian discipline that undertakes a fully critical study of the categories of thought; it also continues the metaphysical labours of Parmenides, Plato, and Spinoza by endeavouring to understand the true nature of being itself.

Hegel notes in the *Science of Logic* that "ancient metaphysics had [. . .] a higher conception of thinking than is current today". He explains:

this metaphysics believed that [. . .] things and the thinking of them [. . .] are explicitly in full agreement, thinking in its immanent determinations and the true nature of things forming one and the same content.[31]

In both the *Science of Logic* and the *Encyclopaedia Logic* it is made clear that this metaphysical understanding of thought is one that Hegel – even after Kant – continues to share.

[29] Hegel, *EL*, 59, §24 addition 2; *Werke*, 8:84, translation altered. See also *SL*, 586; *Werke*, 6:257.

[30] Jean Hyppolite, *Logic and Existence*, trans. by L. Lawlor and A. Sen (Albany, NY: SUNY Press, 1997), p. 71.

[31] Hegel, *SL*, 45; *Werke*, 5:38. See also Alfredo Ferrarin, *Hegel and Aristotle* (Cambridge, UK: Cambridge University Press, 2001), p. 131.

Yet how is it possible for Hegel, as a committed post-Kantian, to adopt this stance? Didn't Kant argue that the categories yield knowledge only of the objects of possible empirical experience, and that they grant us no knowledge of things as they are in themselves? Is not the very idea of a post-Kantian metaphysics or ontology in the strong, Spinozan sense simply an oxymoron?

Hegel thinks not, because he considers the recognition that thought is immediately aware of *being* to be the direct consequence of the modern demand that philosophy be radically self-critical. By contrast, he considers Kant's idea that thought's proper cognitive function is merely to understand what is given in empirical experience, and that by itself, without the aid of empirical intuition, thought can conceive only of what is *possible*, rather than what *is*, to be an uncritical assumption of "*reflective* understanding".[32]

Hegel believes that a modern science of logic that seeks to derive and clarify the basic categories of thought without making unwarranted assumptions about thought must abstract from all that thought and its categories have traditionally been held to be and must consider thought at its simplest and most minimal. A radically self-critical science of logic, he argues, "should be preceded by *universal doubt*, i.e., by total *presuppositionlessness* [*Voraussetzungslosigkeit*]". This requirement is fulfilled "by the freedom that abstracts from everything, and grasps [...] the simplicity of thinking [*die Einfachheit des Denkens*]".[33] At its simplest and most minimal, however, thought is not the thought of what is possible, necessary, substantial, or objective, but simply the thought of being; it is the simple awareness that "there *is* ... ". Feeling and imagination do not assert that what they bring to mind *is there* or is *real*; but thought is distinguished precisely by its understanding that "what is *thought*, *is*, and that what *is*, only is in so far as it is thought [*Gedanke*]".[34] Therefore, a fully self-critical philosophy that seeks to take as little as possible for granted about thought must start out by recognizing that thought is minimally the awareness of being.

Furthermore, a fully self-critical philosophy cannot assume at the outset that *being* is anything beyond what thought is minimally aware of. It cannot assume that being is in truth nature or spirit; nor can it assume that being in any way exceeds the reach of thought. If it is to make no unwarranted assumptions about being, such a philosophy

---

[32] Hegel, *SL*, 45; *Werke*, 5:38.

[33] Hegel, *EL*, 124, §78 remark; *Werke*, 8:168. See also *SL*, 70; *Werke*, 5:68–69.

[34] Hegel, *EPM*, 224, §465; *Werke*, 10:283, translation slightly altered.

must begin with the idea that being is simply what thought is minimally aware of – no more and no less.

A fully self-critical philosophy must thus start from the twofold idea that (a) thought is the awareness of being and (b) being is itself simply what thought discloses. This means that the science of logic cannot be anything other than *ontology*: because the study of thought must be, at the same time, the study of *being*. In this ontology the structure of being will be found not through sense perception or observation of nature but simply by analysing the structure of the *thought* of being. The structures of being and thought thus cannot but be identical.

The argument above clearly conflicts with Kant's conception of the matter. From Kant's point of view, a properly cautious and critical philosophy should recognise that human thought by itself entertains no more than the *possibility* of things.[35] Accordingly, the claim that our thought by itself discloses the nature of *being* or of "things in themselves" is an uncritical and unjustified assumption that attributes to our thought a capacity for "intellectual intuition" it can never enjoy.

From Hegel's point of view, however, "possibility" is itself a highly complex concept that stands in relation to the equally complex concepts of "actuality" and "necessity".[36] Significantly, for Hegel, there is much *more* complexity – not *less* – in the thought of "mere" possibility than in the thought of being. Possibility is not, therefore, the least that thought can think. It is that which we come to think when we *reflect* on the being of which we are initially aware. Thought that takes itself to be aware only of possibility thus actually (though unwittingly) claims more for itself than does thought that takes itself to be aware of simple being, even though the latter, from the Kantian perspective, appears to be more presumptuous.

Hegel insists that a fully self-critical science of logic must begin with the least that thought can be. At its simplest and most minimal, he believes, thought is not the thought of "mere" possibility but the thought of simple being. It is thus with this idea that thought is the awareness of *being* – of what *is* – that Hegel's science of logic must begin.

For Hegel, therefore, there is no contradiction in the idea of a post-Kantian ontology, because the post-Kantian demand that philosophy

---

35 I. Kant, *Critique of Judgment*, trans. by W. S. Pluhar (Indianapolis, IN: Hackett, 1987), p. 284, §76.
36 For Hegel's extended discussion of possibility, actuality and necessity in the *Logic*, see *SL*, 542–550; *Werke*, 6:202–213. See also Stephen Houlgate, "Necessity and Contingency in Hegel's *Science of Logic*", *The Owl of Minerva* 27, 1 (Fall 1995), pp. 37–49.

be fully critical and self-critical requires that we take thought at the start of logic to be the awareness of being. Hegel thus rejects Kant's understanding of thought and its limitations, and he retains the ancient conviction that thought discloses the character of being, because he wishes to be *more* self-critical and to take *less* for granted about thought than Kant himself. It is precisely because he embraces the "critical turn" more consistently than Kant that Hegel continues in the wake of Kant to be a metaphysician in the strong Aristotelian and Spinozan sense.

Hegel also believes that the standpoint of speculative logic – in which thought is understood to disclose the nature of being, and being in turn is understood to be identical in structure to thought – is justified by the analyses he carries out in his *Phenomenology of Spirit*. Contrary to some commentators, I do not think that Hegel regards phenomenology as the indispensable precondition of speculative logic. As we saw above, Hegel states in the *Encyclopaedia Logic* that such logic presupposes nothing but the willingness freely to suspend one's favoured assumptions about thought and to consider only "the simplicity of thought". A similar claim is made in the *Science of Logic*. All that is required to begin speculative logic, Hegel writes, is "the resolve [*Entschluss*], which can also be regarded as arbitrary, that we propose to consider thought as such". Acting on this resolve and actually setting all presuppositions to one side leads directly to the thought of pure *being* with which speculative logic starts. "To enter into philosophy, therefore, calls for no other preparations, no further reflections or points of connection".[37]

There are those, however, who are not quite so ready to set aside their inherited beliefs and who are especially wedded to the assumptions of ordinary, everyday consciousness. Such consciousness does not deny that the world is knowable, but it understands the world to be something clearly distinct from itself: "consciousness [...] knows objects in their antithesis [*Gegensatz*] to itself, and itself in antithesis to them".[38] It thus believes that it gains knowledge of the world through perception and observation of, or practical engagement with, that which is *other* than it. As a consequence, everyday consciousness cannot but consider the standpoint of speculative logic, in which the structure of being is discovered simply by examining the structure of thought, to be "perverse" [*verkehrt*].

The role of Hegel's *Phenomenology* is to persuade readers who are reluctant to let go of the assumptions of everyday consciousness that

---

[37] Hegel, *EL*, 124, §78 remark; *Werke*, 8:168, and *SL*, 70, 72; *Werke*, 5:68, 72.

[38] G. W. F. Hegel, *Phenomenology of Spirit*, trans. by A. V. Miller (Oxford: Oxford University Press, 1977), p. 15; G. W. F. Hegel, *Phänomenologie des Geistes*, ed. by E. Moldenhauer and K. M. Michel, *Werke in zwanzig Bänden*, vol. 3, p. 30.

the standpoint of speculative logic is in fact by no means as perverse as they think it is. The *Phenomenology* carries out its prolonged act of persuasion by demonstrating that the different conceptions of the world adopted by consciousness themselves lead logically to the standpoint of speculative logic. Consciousness may hold to its everyday beliefs as strongly as it likes; Hegel shows, however, that when the implications of those beliefs are fully worked out and taken to their logical conclusion, the standpoint to which consciousness finds itself committed is precisely that of speculative logic. Everyday consciousness itself makes speculative logic necessary, therefore, despite its own best intentions.[39]

Phenomenology examines "every form of the *relation of consciousness to the object* and has the concept of science [i.e. speculative logic] for its result".[40] Speculative logic or "pure science" in turn presupposes the "liberation from the opposition of consciousness" that is brought about by phenomenology (or, alternatively, by the free act of suspending one's familiar assumptions). Such logic understands, therefore, that thought by itself discloses the true nature of being and, conversely, that the logical structure of being is identical to that of thought (properly conceived). In Hegel's own words, it understands that "the absolute truth of being is the known concept [*Begriff*] and the concept as such is the absolute truth of being".[41]

Hegel clearly takes his speculative logic to be not just a logic or a transcendental philosophy, but a metaphysics and an ontology in the strong, Spinozan sense. At the same time, however, his logic is *nonmetaphysical* in so far as it is a self-critical discipline that accepts none of the determinate assumptions about being made by pre-Kantian metaphysicians. Speculative logic does not begin with the idea that being is "substance", "nature", "actuality" or "form", but starts from the simple idea of being as such, of being "without any further determination".[42] Similarly, such logic does not retain the traditional metaphysical presupposition that being is an "object" (or realm of objects) *about which* the philosopher has thoughts: "what we are dealing with in logic", Hegel writes, "is not a thinking *about* something which exists independently as a base for our thinking".[43] The fully self-critical speculative philosopher has no

---

[39] For a more detailed study of the role of Hegel's *Phenomenology*, see Stephen Houlgate, "G. W. F. Hegel (1770–1831)", in *The Blackwell Guide to the Modern Philosophers From Descartes to Nietzsche*, ed. by S. Emmanuel (Oxford: Blackwell, 2001), pp. 278–305.

[40] Hegel, *SL*, 48; *Werke*, 5:42. Miller translates *Begriff* as "notion" rather than "concept".

[41] Hegel, *SL*, 49; *Werke*, 5:43.

[42] Hegel, *SL*, 82; *Werke*, 5:82.

[43] Hegel, *SL*, 50; *Werke*, 5:44.

warrant at the outset to assume that being is such an "object", any more than he can assume being to be substance or nature. All he can claim at the beginning of logic is (a) that there *is* being and (b) that the structure of being itself can be discovered in the structure of the *categories* of thought. The fully self-critical speculative philosopher does not, therefore, look out into the world in order to discover the nature of being, but sets out to derive and clarify the categories of thought in order to discover the nature of being in them. For such a philosopher, "the necessary forms and self-determinations of *thought* are [thus] the content and the ultimate truth itself".[44] Since this is the case, speculative metaphysics or ontology is necessarily equivalent to *logic*.

This last point is crucial, in my view, and is worth repeating. Hegel's speculative metaphysics is a modern, post-Kantian, and therefore fully self-critical discipline that suspends the determinate assumptions about being and thought that are found in pre-Kantian metaphysics. Consequently, it does not take being at the outset to be an "object" outside or over against thought. All it is entitled to claim to start with is that the intrinsic character of being – whatever that will turn out to be – will be disclosed in the categories of thought itself. Since it looks to the categories of *thought* in order to discover the nature of being, Hegel's post-Kantian metaphysics necessarily takes the form of logic. *Pace* Pinkard and Pippin, Hegel's logic is, indeed, a metaphysics; but it is a metaphysics in the form of *logic* because it is a modern, "nonmetaphysical" metaphysics that assumes nothing about being except that its true nature will be discovered in the structure of thought itself.

THE METHOD OF HEGEL'S LOGIC

Hegel insists that a free and fully self-critical logic should start by suspending all presuppositions (apart from the conviction that thought discloses the nature of being): "all [. . .] presuppositions or assumptions must equally be given up when we enter into the Science, whether they are taken from representation or from thinking".[45] Speculative logic should thus be *presuppositionless*. This claim, however, is easy to misunderstand.

Hegel does not deny that speculative logic presupposes an *interest* on the part of the philosopher in discovering the true character of thought or being.[46] Equally, such logic presupposes an interest in ensuring that

---

[44] Hegel, *SL*, 50; *Werke*, 5:44, my emphasis.
[45] Hegel, *EL*, 124, §78; *Werke*, 8:167.
[46] Hegel, *EL*, 24, §1; *Werke*, 8:41. For a more detailed study of the presuppositions of Hegel's presuppositionless philosophy, see Stephen Houlgate, *The Opening of*

philosophical thought be free and unencumbered and a corresponding readiness to set to one side the governing assumptions of traditional metaphysics and everyday consciousness (or, at least, a willingness to read the *Phenomenology* and possibly be persuaded by it). Speculative logic also presupposes the ability to use language – since, as we have already seen, "we *think* in names"[47] – and the ability to abstract and hold in mind pure and often highly complex concepts. (In this latter respect, Hegel maintains, "[Aristotelian] formal logic undoubtedly has its use. Through it [. . .] we sharpen our wits; we learn to collect our thoughts, and to abstract".)[48] Finally, Hegel's logic presupposes a certain familiarity on our part with the basic concepts of thought:[49] for if we lacked this familiarity, we could not recognise that the concepts developed in that logic are in fact revised and "clarified" versions of the concepts we use in everyday life. In all these respects, therefore, speculative logic is clearly *not* presuppositionless.

In two other respects, however, speculative logic is to be presuppositionless. First, the philosopher should not assume at the outset of such logic that the categories of thought are to be understood in a specific way, or indeed that thought entails any particular categories at all. He should keep in the back of his mind the familiar senses of the categories, but in the science of logic itself he should start from scratch by considering the sheer "simplicity of thinking" as such and wait to discover which categories, if any, are inherent in thinking and how they are to be conceived. As new categories are derived in the course of speculative logic, the logician can compare them with the categories with which he is familiar and so determine to what extent our everyday understanding of the categories is adequate.[50] That everyday understanding should not, however, play any role in the logical derivation of the categories themselves. In speculative logic itself the categories must be derived purely immanently – without presuppositions – from the sheer "simplicity" of thought. The aim of logic, as Hegel puts it, is "to exhibit the realm of thought [. . .] in its own immanent activity or what is the same, in its necessary development".[51]

Second, the philosopher may not take for granted at the outset any specific rules or laws of thought. He may not presuppose that thought

Hegel's Logic. From Being to Infinity (West Lafayette, IN: Purdue University Press, 2006), pp. 54–71.
[47] Hegel, *EPM*, 220, §462 remark; *Werke*, 10:278
[48] Hegel, *EL*, 52, §20 addition; *Werke*, 8:76, translation slightly altered.
[49] Hegel, *EL*, 24, §1; *Werke*, 8:41.
[50] See Hegel, *SL*, 708–709; *Werke*, 6:406–407.
[51] Hegel, *SL*, 31; *Werke*, 5:19.

should abide by the rules of syllogistic inference or that it should be governed by the law of noncontradiction, and so may not find thought wanting if it fails to respect these principles. Nor, indeed, may he presuppose that thought should be "dialectical" (and certainly not that it should develop according to the pattern of "thesis–antithesis–synthesis"). The speculative logician may not presuppose such rules and laws because it is the task of logic itself to discover whether any rules or laws are actually made necessary by the "simplicity" of thought. In Hegel's own words, the "forms of reflection and laws of thinking [. . .] constitute part of [logic's] own content and have first to be established within the science".[52] Until this has been achieved, no rules or laws of thought can be assumed to be valid.

How then is the speculative logician to proceed? Is there any *method* that such a logician must follow? Yes, indeed. The method he must follow is simply to *let* the "simplicity" of thought unfold and determine itself before our very eyes according to whatever principles prove to be immanent in it. Heidegger is the philosopher with whom the idea of "letting be" is usually associated.[53] Many years before Heidegger, however, Hegel argued that "letting" lies at the heart of genuinely free, modern philosophizing. "When I think", Hegel explains, "I give up my subjective particularity, sink myself in the matter, let thought follow its own course [*lasse das Denken für sich gewähren*]; and I think badly whenever I add something of my own". My role as philosopher is thus not to pass judgment on this or that proposition or argument according to certain presupposed rules and criteria, but simply to "let the inherently living determinations [of thought] take their own course [*für sich gewähren lassen*]".[54] If one does this, Hegel claims, one will discover what thought (and being) prove logically to be *of their own accord*. The understanding of the categories that emerges in this way may or may not agree with that of traditional metaphysics or everyday consciousness; but it is the *true* understanding of the categories, because it is the understanding that is made necessary by the very nature and movement of thought.

Our role as philosophers, therefore, is predominantly passive. As W. T. Stace puts it, "it is, in fact, not *we* who deduce the categories at all. They deduce themselves".[55] We simply look on as the categories emerge immanently from the very "simplicity" of thought. Yet we are

[52] Hegel, *SL*, 43; *Werke*, 5:35.
[53] See, for example, Heidegger, *Being and Time*, p. 405.
[54] Hegel, *EL*, 58–59, §24 addition 2; *Werke*, 8:84–85.
[55] W. T. Stace, *The Philosophy of Hegel. A Systematic Exposition* (1924) (New York: Dover, 1955), p. 85.

not completely passive observers of this process. First of all, *we* are the ones who think through thought's immanent development: that development does not occur outside of us, like a film or a play, but takes place *in our thinking of it.* Second, although each category is made necessary by the one that precedes it and is not simply dreamt up by us, *we* nonetheless have to render explicit the categories that are implicit in thought at any particular point in its logical development. The deduction of the categories, Hegel maintains, is analytic in that it involves nothing more than the *"positing [Setzen]* of what is already contained in a concept";[56] but *we* are the ones who actually have to carry out this act of "positing" or rendering-explicit.

The speculative logician who *lets* thought determine itself is thus both passive and active: he allows his own thinking to be guided and determined by what is immanent in thought *and* plays an active role in bringing what is immanent in thought out into the open. Indeed, Hegel notes, there is a degree of activity in our very passivity itself: for we can allow our thought to be guided by the matter at hand only if we actively focus on that matter and hold our own bright ideas at bay. Hegel makes this point in these important, but rarely noted, lines:

Philosophical thinking proceeds analytically in that it simply takes up its object, the Idea, and lets it go its own way [*dieselbe gewähren läßt*], while it simply watches, so to speak [*gleichsam nur zusieht*], the movement and development of it. To this extent philosophising is wholly passive [*passiv*]. [...] But this requires the effort to beware of our own inventions and particular opinions which are forever wanting to push themselves forward.[57]

One might be forgiven for suspecting that Hegel's method of simply "letting" thought determine itself is a recipe for lazy, vague, and undisciplined thinking. This, however, is far from the truth. Hegel's method demands "that each thought should be grasped in its full precision [*Präzision*] and that nothing should remain vague and indeterminate".[58] It also demands that one pay close and subtle attention to the logical structure of categories and render explicit only what is implicit in each category. Indeed, in my view, Hegel's method requires greater mental discipline than any other philosophical method in history. It also requires greater mental flexibility: for the speculative philosopher has not only to achieve a high degree of precision in his understanding

---

[56] Hegel, *EL*, 141, §88 remark; *Werke*, 8:188.
[57] Hegel, *EL*, 305, §238 addition; *Werke*, 8:390–391, translation slightly altered.
[58] Hegel, *EL*, 128, §80 addition; *Werke*, 8:171. See also John Burbidge, *On Hegel's Logic. Fragments of a Commentary* (Atlantic Highlands, NJ: Humanities Press, 1981), p. 42.

of categories but also to allow those categories to mutate into new ones before his very eyes as he renders their necessary implications explicit.

BEING, NOTHING, BECOMING

A fully self-critical logic that suspends all inherited assumptions about thought must begin with thought at its most minimal, that is, with thought as the simple awareness of being.[59] The first category to be considered in Hegel's logic is thus that of "being" itself (*das Sein*). Such being is conceived not as substance or nature but as sheer, indeterminate being as such: "*being, pure being*, without any further determination".[60] The task of the speculative logician is thus to think this category and discover any other categories that may be implicit in it. The language used to conceive of pure being is, of course, replete with terms, such as "without", "any", and "further", that have a familiar, determinate meaning. Yet these terms are employed to hold at bay all determinate thoughts and allow us to focus on a category that is itself wholly indeterminate.[61]

As we consider that initial, indeterminate category, however, something strange and surprising happens: for, due to its sheer and utter indeterminacy, pure, featureless being actually vanishes before our very eyes into *nothing*. Pure being is "pure indeterminateness and emptiness". Accordingly, Hegel writes,

> there is *nothing* to be intuited in it, if one can speak here of intuiting [...]. Just as little is anything to be thought in it, or it is equally only this empty thinking. Being, the indeterminate immediate, is in fact *nothing*, and neither more nor less than *nothing*.[62]

There is an immediate and obvious difference between *being* and *nothing*; but when being is thought in its purity as sheer, indeterminate being, that difference immediately disappears and being evaporates into nothing whatsoever.

Yet this does not bring speculative logic to an end, because the thought of *nothing* immediately turns back into the thought of being. This is because sheer and utter nothing has an irreducible *immediacy*

---

[59] Hegel, *SL*, 70; *Werke*, 5:68–69.
[60] Hegel, *SL*, 82; *Werke*, 5:82.
[61] See Dieter Henrich, "Anfang und Methode der Logik", in Henrich, *Hegel im Kontext* (Frankfurt am Main: Suhrkamp Verlag, 1971), p. 85.
[62] Hegel, *SL*, 82; *Werke*, 5:82–83.

of its own. Nothing, in its utter purity, *is* precisely nothing and cannot be thought except as *being* the nothing that it is. Nothing thus immediately slips back into being as soon as it is thought. This is not just a trick of language. Pure nothing proves *logically* to be indeterminate being because its very purity as *nothing* paradoxically gives it an immediacy and *being* of its own. Logically, nothing thus turns out to be "the same determination, or rather absence of determination, and thus altogether the same as, pure *being*".[63]

According to Hegel, therefore, the thought of *pure, indeterminate being* vanishes immediately into that of nothing, and the thought of *pure nothing* vanishes immediately into that of *pure being*. Each proves to be logically unstable and to disappear into the opposite of itself. Indeed, Hegel points out, each proves to be nothing but the *process* of its own disappearance. What we discover at the start of Hegel's logic is thus not only that being and nothing vanish into one another, but that each simply *is* its own *vanishing*. As such, each is immediately the coming-to-be of the other. With this insight we reach a new category: neither being nor nothing is purely itself because each is nothing but the *becoming* of the other. In Hegel's own words:

their truth is [...] this movement of the immediate vanishing of the one in the other: *becoming*, a movement in which both are distinguished, but by a difference which has equally immediately dissolved itself [*sich aufgelöst*].[64]

This is the first major lesson of Hegel's logic: *pace* Parmenides, being is not just pure and simple being after all, but *becoming*. The concept of "becoming" does not, however, simply replace that of "being", and the latter is not revealed to be a mere fiction (as Nietzsche will later argue).[65] Hegel's point is that there *is* being, but that such being itself proves logically to be becoming. This is a metaphysical claim about what there is, but one that is established solely by considering the *category* of "being".

Several distinctive features of Hegel's logic become evident in these opening moves. First, although Hegel does not presuppose that speculative thought should be dialectical, such thought does in fact prove to be dialectical of its own accord. Dialectic, for Hegel, is not a relation *between* different things (for example, between an individual and

[63] Hegel, *SL*, 82; *Werke*, 5:83.
[64] Hegel, *SL*, 83; *Werke*, 5:83, translation altered.
[65] See Friedrich Nietzsche, *Twilight of the Idols/The Antichrist*, trans. by R. J. Hollingdale (Harmondsworth: Penguin Books, 1968), p. 36 (in *Twilight of the Idols*, "'Reason' in Philosophy", §2).

society), but is the process whereby one category or phenomenon *turns into* its own opposite: "the *dialectical* moment is the self-sublation [*Sichaufheben*] of these finite determinations on their own part, and their passing into their opposites".[66] The categories of being and nothing prove to be dialectical by vanishing into one another, and all subsequent categories will turn out to exhibit a similar dialectic of their own. Dialectic is thus not a method devised by Hegel and brought to bear on categories from the outside, but belongs to those categories (and corresponding aspects of being) themselves. It is "the inwardness of the content, *the dialectic which it possesses within itself*".[67]

Second, Hegel's logic progresses by simply thinking through the process whereby categories transform themselves logically and dialectically into new categories. This process is wholly immanent in that it is driven by nothing but the logical character of the categories themselves. New categories are not introduced by the *philosopher* in order to avoid contradictions in the categories under consideration (as Pinkard argues) or to move us on from less adequate to more adequate concepts (as Schelling appears to suggest).[68] They are generated autonomously by the categories that precede them. It is thus "the *nature of the content* alone which *moves itself* [*sich bewegt*] in scientific cognition".[69]

Third, the development of the categories is *nonteleological* in that it is not propelled forward by any desire on the part of the individual philosopher or thought in general to reach some goal (such as "the Idea" or "spirit"). Nor (as Schelling claims) are the categories judged to be inadequate by comparison with the projected goal of concrete knowledge of the world "at which science finally is to arrive".[70] The speculative logician is not aiming to reach any particular endpoint, but simply seeks to understand the specific category that is in view. Equally, the categories themselves are not secretly "striving" to become moments of a greater whole, but transform themselves into new categories simply by *being* – and, as it were, "trying to remain" – what they are.

Fourth, Hegel describes a process of "sublation" or *Aufheben* in which the opposed categories of "being" and "nothing" lose their independence and become mere "moments" of a unity, "becoming".[71] That

---

[66] Hegel, *EL*, 128, §81; *Werke*, 8:172.

[67] Hegel, *SL*, 54; *Werke*, 5:50.

[68] See Pinkard, *Hegel's Dialectic*, pp. 26, 29, and F. W. J. von Schelling, *On the History of Modern Philosophy*, trans. by A. Bowie (Cambridge, UK: Cambridge University Press, 1994), p. 143.

[69] Hegel, *SL*, 27; *Werke*, 5:16, translation altered.

[70] Schelling, *On the History of Modern Philosophy*, p. 138.

[71] Hegel, *SL*, 105–107; *Werke*, 5:112–114.

unity, however, is not in any way separate from or "prior" to the categories that come to be its moments. It is the unity that those categories constitute through their own dialectic. Categories, such as being and nothing, are thus *themselves* responsible for generating the very unity of which they are moments. The process of sublation is not, therefore – as is sometimes suggested by Hegel's deconstructive critics – comparable to the process of eating and digesting in which independent elements are assimilated or absorbed into, and thereby subordinated to, a greater whole that is tacitly or explicitly presupposed. Nor does this process have any sinister, "totalitarian" political connotations.[72] It is the autonomous process whereby categories unite together *of their own accord.*

It is clear, then, that much can be learned about speculative logic from Hegel's initial account of the categories of *being*, *nothing*, and *becoming*. It should be borne in mind, however, that the further development of the category of becoming, and of the subsequent categories that emerge from it, will not take precisely the same form as the development of pure, indeterminate being. All further development will remain immanent, nonteleological, and dialectical; but precisely because it will be *immanent* and thus rooted in the *specific* logical structures of the categories to come, it will take a subtly different form in each case.

FROM BEING TO THE IDEA

In the remainder of Hegel's logic there emerge numerous categories that fall into three overall groups: the categories of "being", "essence", and "concept". The categories of "being" include "determinate being" (*Dasein*) – which arises directly from "becoming" – "something", "other", "being-in-itself", "being-for-another", "finitude", "infinity", "quantity", and "measure" (*Maß*). Each of these categories proves to be dialectical in its own distinctive way and thereby discloses the dialectical structure of the corresponding aspect of being itself. Determinate being, for example, turns out to entail both *reality* and *negation*; so things are determinate, for Hegel, not only through being what they are, but also through *not* being what they are not. Similarly, something proves to be not only something in its own right but also *other* than something else. Every something is thus necessarily related to other things and vulnerable to their effects on it. As Hegel puts it, "it is the

---

[72] One such critic is Christina Howells who speaks both of "the all-devouring rigour of Hegel's search for *Savoir Absolu*" and of "Hegelian totalitarianism" in her (otherwise excellent) book, *Derrida. Deconstruction from Phenomenology to Ethics* (Oxford: Polity Press, 1998), pp. 85, 90.

quality of something to be open to external influences".[73] Hegel's analysis of the category of "something" thus leads him to a metaphysical position that directly contradicts Leibniz's doctrine that the world is made up of "windowless" monads.

The categories of "being" turn dialectically into one another, but they nonetheless retain a degree of independence.[74] Thus, even though something is always *other* than – and so related to – something else, it remains something in its own right with its own intrinsic character. (This, indeed, is what enables philosophers such as Leibniz to overlook the inherent vulnerability of things to external influence.) Similarly, quality and quantity remain to a certain extent independent of one another, although a thing may well undergo qualitative change if it gets too big, too small, too hot, or too cold (as occurs, for example, when water reaches a certain temperature and turns into steam or ice). By contrast, the categories of "essence" – and the aspects of being itself to which they correspond – enjoy no independence at all, because each comes to be what it is only through the mediation of its opposite. Identity, for example, emerges only through difference; force comes to be force only in its expression; and the cause becomes the cause only in producing its effect. None of these determinations has a separate character of its own, but each is constituted at its core by its relation to its opposite. The logical distinction drawn by Hegel between the categories of "being" and "essence" thus leads to a significant metaphysical claim: a thing's *qualities* are related to and partly determined by, but also separate from, those of other things; by contrast, a thing's *identity* is established *solely through* its differences from, relations to, and causal interaction with other things and so is utterly inseparable from them.[75]

Note that, in Hegel's understanding, "essential" determinations that are logically prior to others do not simply and unambiguously *precede* those to which they give rise. The cause produces the effect and in that sense is "prior" to it. Yet the cause comes to be a cause only with the emergence *of* its effect. It is thus only a cause *thanks to its effect*. It cannot, therefore, be a cause on its own and exist as such before its effect. It is, rather, that to which its effect – once the latter has emerged – necessarily *points back*. Like the ground and force, the cause is that which only turns out *at the end* to come first.[76] The evidently

[73] Hegel, *SL*, 124; *Werke*, 5:133.

[74] Hegel, *SL*, 123; *Werke*, 5:133.

[75] On the general difference between the doctrines of being and essence, see Hegel, *EL*, 237, 306, §161, 240; *Werke*, 8:308, 391.

[76] For a more detailed study of Hegel's account of causality, see Stephen Houlgate, "Substance, Causality, and the Question of Method in Hegel's *Science of Logic*",

paradoxical character of determinations such as cause and force does not, however, render them any less real. Together with all the determinations analysed in Hegel's logic, they constitute necessary aspects of *being*.[77]

By Hegel's own admission the doctrine of essence is the most difficult section of speculative logic.[78] Things get a little easier in the doctrine of "the concept", in which categories are no longer held to be the prior *ground* of others and at the same time to be mediated by those they ground. The "universal", for example, is not the ground or cause to which the "particular" and "individual" *point back*, but rather that which develops into and *continues itself in* the particular and individual.[79] Like all categories, the universal turns dialectically into new ones. In so doing, however, it preserves its own identity. The particular and individual are thus not simply "other" than the universal, nor are they merely its "effects"; they are the *universal itself* in the form of particular, individual things. Subsequent categories, such as mechanism, chemism, and life, preserve this interpenetration of universal, particular, and individual. Living beings are thus not simply individuals, but individuals of a certain *species* and *genus*.

The final category of Hegel's logic is that of the "absolute Idea". This is the conception of being as a self-determining totality.[80] This totality includes all the determinations that have been analysed in the course of speculative logic: quality, quantity, identity, difference, causality, mechanism, chemism, and life. The final lesson of Hegel's logic is thus that being is not to be equated with any one of its constituent determinations but unites all of them into one self-determining whole. On the last page of the *Science of Logic* (and in the last paragraph of the *Encyclopaedia Logic*), Hegel then considers one last dialectical move: he shows that the self-determining totality or "absolute Idea" that being proves to be actually exists in the form of *nature*. At this point, speculative logic ends and the second part of Hegel's philosophy, the philosophy of nature, begins.

CONCLUSION

What Hegel shows in his logic is that being necessarily entails a whole range of different ways of being: being something, being finite, being

in *The Reception of Kant's Critical Philosophy. Fichte, Schelling and Hegel*, ed. by S. Sedgwick (Cambridge, UK: Cambridge University Press, 2000), pp. 232–252.

[77] Hegel, *SL*, 440; *Werke*, 6:75: "an absolute determination of essence must be present in every experience, in everything actual".

[78] Hegel, *EL*, 179, §114 remark; *Werke*, 8:236.

[79] Hegel, *SL*, 602; *Werke*, 6:276.

[80] Hegel, *SL*, 825, 843; *Werke*, 6:550, 573.

causal, being mechanical, being alive, and so on. Not every object in the universe will exhibit each way of being (as Stace claims),[81] since not every object is, for example, *alive*; but every object will incorporate some of the ways of being discussed in each of the three parts of Hegel's logic: the logics of "being", "essence", and "concept". For example, the pen with which I write – or Herr Krug's rather more famous one – is *something* and so is intrinsically related to *other* things that can affect it in various ways. It has a certain *identity* of its own and *causes* marks to appear on paper. It is also an *individual* of a certain kind, namely, a *mechanical* object. What Hegel's logic shows is that each of these different ways of being has its own specific logical structure, and that an object such as a pen cannot be properly understood except by understanding those logical structures. Of course, such structures alone do not suffice to explain everything about a pen: one also needs to understand its physical characteristics (such as its colour and texture), its mode of construction, and the social and personal uses to which it is put. Nevertheless, the pen is what it is at least in part because it exhibits some of the ways of being that are analysed in speculative logic. One can, therefore, deduce a priori certain fundamental ontological features of a pen, if not – as Hegel famously insists – every aspect of its make-up.[82]

Hegel demonstrates the necessity of the fundamental ways of being by proving that the *thought* or *category* of being turns dialectically into all the other categories he analyses. His ontology is thus established through *logic*. As we have seen, Hegel's logic is a fully self-critical science that presupposes nothing about thought (or being), except that thought by itself can disclose the inherent logical structure of being. This science is, as Hegel himself acknowledges, difficult and complex.[83] In my view, however, it contains the most profound and subtle insights and is well worth prolonged and careful study. Indeed, I would argue that Hegel's detailed presentation of that science – the *Science of Logic* – should be counted together with Kant's *Critique of Pure Reason* as one of the two greatest works of modern philosophy.

---

[81] Stace, *The Philosophy of Hegel*, p. 128.
[82] See *Hegel's Philosophy of Nature*, trans. by A. V. Miller (Oxford: Clarendon Press, 1970), p. 23, note to §250 remark; G. W. F. Hegel, *Enzyklopädie der philosophischen Wissenschaften im Grundrisse (1830). Zweiter Teil: Die Naturphilosophie*, ed. by E. Moldenhauer and K. M. Michel, *Werke in zwanzig Bänden*, vol. 9, p. 35.
[83] Hegel, *SL*, 31, 42; *Werke*, 5:19, 33.

6   Hegel's Idealism

In an influential article on this topic, Karl Ameriks posed the question: "But can an interesting form of Hegelian idealism be found that is true to the text, that is not clearly extravagant, and that is not subject to the [charge] of triviality . . . ?",[1] and concluded by answering the question in the negative: "In sum, we have yet to find a simultaneously accurate, substantive, and appealing sense in which Hegel should be regarded as an idealist".[2] Other commentators on this issue have tended to be more positive; but then the fact that these commentators have differed sharply between themselves may suggest that another concern is over the coherence of Hegel's position, and whether a consistent account is possible of it at all.

In this article, I will consider the charges of inaccuracy, triviality, and extravagance that Ameriks and others have raised. Of these charges, the first two are obviously damaging; but it might reasonably be felt that that last is less clearly so (why shouldn't a philosophical theory be extravagant?), and also that it is open to different readings (for example, does it mean "not consistent with 'common sense' ", or "not consistent with the findings of the sciences" – but what do these include?). The context for a concern of this sort, however, might well be whether Hegel's position can be made consistent with Kantian objections against the pretensions of metaphysics, either by respecting those objections, or at least by satisfactorily addressing them. The interpretative issue here is thus one of charity: Hegel's position will seem reactionary and ill-informed if it appears to be conceived in ignorance of the work of his great predecessor. One prominent recent interpreter has put the worry as follows:

More to the general and more obvious point, however, much of the standard view of how Hegel passes beyond Kant into speculative philosophy makes very puzzling, to the point of unintelligibility, how Hegel could have been the

---

[1] Karl Ameriks, "Hegel and Idealism", *The Monist*, 74 (1991), pp. 386–402, at p. 397.
[2] Ibid., p. 398.

post-Kantian philosopher he understood himself to be; that is, how he could
have accepted, as he did, Kant's revelations about the fundamental inadequacies
of the metaphysical tradition, could have enthusiastically agreed with Kant that
the metaphysics of the "beyond," of substance, and of traditional views of God
and infinity were forever discredited, and then could have promptly created a
systematic metaphysics as if he had never heard of Kant's critical epistemology. Just attributing moderate philosophic intelligence to Hegel should at least
make one hesitate before construing him as a post-Kantian philosopher with a
precritical metaphysics.[3]

In considering the issue of extravagance, then, I shall conceive it primarily in this manner, as concerning the relation between Hegel's position
and Kant's "critical turn" in metaphysics. I will argue that a view of
Hegel's idealism emerges from Ameriks' criticisms, which is defensible against his three charges; however, to make sense of it we have to
see that Hegel's conception of idealism has aspects that are unusual in
terms of the contemporary debate, while nonetheless his position still
has a direct bearing on it.

I. HEGEL AS A KANTIAN IDEALIST

The account of Hegel's idealism which Ameriks charges with textual
inaccuracy is the one put forward by Robert Pippin in his book on this
topic,[4] which has been widely discussed.[5]

---

[3] Robert B. Pippin, *Hegel's Idealism: The Satisfactions of Self-Consciousness*
(Cambridge, UK: Cambridge University Press, 1989), p. 7.

[4] Pippin, *Hegel's Idealism*.

[5] As well as the paper by Ameriks mentioned in Footnote 1 above, see also: Terry
Pinkard, "The Categorial Satisfaction of Self-Reflexive Reason", *Bulletin of the
Hegel Society of Great Britain*, 19 (1989), pp. 5–17; H. S. Harris, "The Problem
of Kant", *Bulletin of the Hegel Society of Great Britain*, 19 (1989), pp. 18–27;
Terry Pinkard, "How Kantian Was Hegel?", *Review of Metaphysics*, 43 (1990),
pp. 831–838; Ludwig Siep, "Hegel's Idea of a Conceptual Scheme", *Inquiry*, 34
(1991), pp. 63–76; Karl Ameriks, "Recent Work on Hegel: The Rehabilitation
of an Epistemologist?", *Philosophy and Phenomenological Research*, 52 (1992),
pp. 177–202; Kenneth R. Westphal, "Hegel, Idealism, and Robert Pippin", *International Philosophical Quarterly*, 33 (1993), pp. 263–272; Sally Sedgwick, "Pippin
on Hegel's Critique of Kant", *International Philosophical Quarterly*, 33 (1993),
pp. 273–283; Frank B. Farrell, *Subjectivity, Realism and Post-modernism: The
Recovery of the World* (Cambridge, UK: Cambridge University Press, 1994),
pp. 20–29. Replies by Robert Pippin to some of these pieces can be found in "Hegel's
Idealism: Prospects", *Bulletin of the Hegel Society of Great Britain*, 19 (1989),
pp. 28–41 and "Hegel's Original Insight", *International Philosophical Quarterly*,
33 (1993), pp. 285–295.

Pippin argues that Hegel's idealism should be seen in the light of Kant's turn from traditional metaphysics to critical metaphysics, a turn which Hegel followed and which led both him and Kant towards idealism. Simply put, Kant believed that metaphysics could not be carried out in the traditional rationalist manner, of claiming insight into the fundamental features of reality on the basis of a priori speculation; rather, we must direct our inquiry to the concepts we use to think about the world and which are necessary for us to have experience of it as self-conscious subjects, so that (as Pippin puts it) "[t]hereafter, instead of an *a priori* science of substance, a science of 'how the world must be'...a putative philosophical science was directed to the topic of how any subject must 'for itself' take or construe or *judge the world to be*".[6] The hope was that this critical turn would make metaphysics more tractable and less vainglorious: we would now be proceeding by investigating the necessary conditions of our experience, rather than things in general.[7] However, an obvious difficulty with this enterprise is the scope it leaves open for scepticism: why should we think that the concepts which are necessary to enable us to have experience actually correspond to the world? Surely, it might be objected, "[a]n inquiry into the structure of human thought is...something quite different from an inquiry into the structure of the world thought is about",[8] so how can the Kantian approach claim to be doing metaphysics in any sense at all? Now, one Kantian response to this worry is to reject the realist assumption on which it is based, namely, that such a gap between mind and world could arise, and thus that there is any coherent notion of "world" on the basis of which the problem could be posed; rather, it is argued, notions like "object", "representation", "truth", "knowledge", and so on only apply *within* the conceptual scheme we are considering. This outlook is often characterised as "antirealism" or "internal

---

[6] Robert B. Pippin, "Hegel and Category Theory", *Review of Metaphysics*, 43 (1990), pp. 839–848, at p. 839.

[7] Cf. Pippin, "Hegel's Original Insight", p. 286. Cf. also P. M. S. Hacker's characterization of the motivation of P. F. Strawson's turn from metaphysics as "limning the ultimate structure of the world" to "sketching the structure of our conceptual scheme": "The conception of a form of necessity that is not logical, but no less adamantine than logical necessity, that is an objective, language-independent form of necessity that can nevertheless be apprehended a priori by reason alone is, surely rightly, dismissed as a fiction" (P. M. S. Hacker, "On Strawson's Rehabilitation of Metaphysics", in Hans-Johann Glock, ed., *Strawson and Kant* (Oxford: Oxford University Press, 2003), pp. 43–66, at p. 55).

[8] Michael J. Loux, *Metaphysics: A Contemporary Introduction* (London: Routledge, 1998), p. 9.

realism", in so far as it rejects the realist "external" standpoint that appears to make scepticism about conceptual schemes of genuine concern, but without the more strongly idealist commitment to the claim that things in the world are "mental" or "mind dependent" in any phenomenalist sense.[9]

Now, according to Pippin, Hegel followed Kant in taking this critical turn, and thus in attempting to determine the categories necessary for a conceptual scheme, based on the conditions for unified self-consciousness (what Kant called "apperception"). However, where Kant had undermined his own position by allowing room for the realist notion of "things-in-themselves" as possibly lying outside our conceptual framework, Pippin takes Hegel's project to be that of developing a more thorough-going antirealism, which would close off any such possibility. Thus, for Pippin, Hegel follows Kant in so far as "the issue of the 'determinations of any possible object' (the classical Aristotelian category issue) has been critically transformed into the issue of 'the determinations of any object of a possibly self-conscious judgment'"; but he goes beyond Kant in so far as "he has, contra Kant, his own reasons for arguing that any skepticism about such results (about their holding only for 'our' world, for self-conscious judgers 'like us') is, although logically coherent, epistemically idle".[10] Pippin thus gives Hegel's idealism a strikingly Kantian interpretation and rationale: accepting the lesson of Kant's critical turn that "contrary to the rationalist tradition, human reason can attain nonempirical knowledge only *about itself*, about what has come to be called recently our 'conceptual scheme'".[11] Hegel nonetheless claims also to be investigating the nature of reality itself in so far as no content can be given to the realist or sceptical thought that reality might, in fact, lie "outside" of the scheme altogether, by showing that there can be no such "external" standpoint: "[W]hat Hegel is after is a way of demonstrating the 'ultimate' or absolute objectivity of the Notion not by some demonstration that being as it is in itself can be known to be as we conceive it to be, but that a Notionally conditional actuality is all that 'being' could intelligibly be, even for the most committed realist skeptic. Or, if you like, Hegel's skeptic is co-opted into the idealist program, not simply 'refuted'".[12]

---

[9] Pippin characterises Hegel's position as a form of antirealism at several places, for example, *Hegel's Idealism* p. 99, p. 262 note 15, and p. 267 note 23.

[10] Ibid., p. 250.

[11] Ibid., p. 8.

[12] Ibid., p. 98.

There are undoubtedly many aspects of Pippin's account of Hegel's idealism that make it profound and attractive. By placing such emphasis on its Kantian background, and how much Hegel shared in the Kantian critique of traditional metaphysics, Pippin offers a reading that shows Hegel to be in tune with the progressive intellectual forces of his time, rather than the reactionary philosophical figure of some standard interpretations. Pippin also argues that Hegel's position follows "immanently" from Kant's own, suggesting that in the second edition version of the transcendental deduction in the *Critique of Pure Reason*, Kant himself took back his earlier strict distinction between intuition and understanding, so that he now argues that no representation could be given to us in sensuous intuition unless it were subject to the categories.[13] This, according to Pippin, opens up the way for Hegel's own radicalization of Kant's transcendental approach, so that "it is with the denial that a firm distinction can ever be usefully drawn between intuitional and conceptual elements in knowledge that distinctly Hegelian idealism begins, and Hegel begins to take his peculiar flight, with language about the complete autonomy, even freedom of 'thought's self-determination' and 'self-acutalization'".[14] By linking Hegel to Kant in this way, Pippin shows how contemporary developments from Kant have every reason to take Hegel seriously. Pippin's reading also casts fresh light on many of the darker aspects of Hegel's texts, particularly his introductory remarks to Book III of the *Science of Logic*, where Hegel identifies his own account of the Concept or Notion [*Begriff*] with Kant's doctrine of apperception, and in terms that seem to fit Pippin's transcendental interpretation.[15] Moreover, Pippin is able to offer a challenging

---

[13] Cf. ibid., pp. 29–32. For doubts about Pippin's reading of Kant, see Sedgwick, "Pippin on Hegel's Critique of Kant", with a reply from Pippin in his "Hegel's Original Insight".

[14] Pippin, *Hegel's Idealism*, p. 9.

[15] Pippin, *Hegel's Idealism*, pp. 18, 232. Pippin has the following sort of remark from Hegel in mind: "It is one of the profoundest and truest insights to be found in the *Critique of Pure Reason* that the *unity* which constitutes the nature of the *Notion* is recognized as the *original synthetic* unity of *apperception*, as unity of the *I think*, or of self-consciousness" (G. W. F. Hegel, *Science of Logic*, trans. by A. V. Miller (London: George Allen & Unwin, 1969), p. 584; *Werke in zwanzig Bänden*, ed. by Eva Moldenhauer and Karl Markus Michel, 20 vols. and index (Frankfurt: Suhrkamp, 1969–1971), VI, p. 254). However, Pinkard has argued that comments such as these should not be taken to imply that Hegel is taking the transcendental turn, but rather that he is drawing attention to the way in which the structure of the Notion resembles the structure of the unity of apperception, so that it is the structural similarity between the Notion and the "I think" that is here being highlighted: "Thus, in Hegel's eyes, what is important in the Kantian philosophy is *not* its attempt to derive everything from the conditions of self-consciousness, but its

account of how Hegel's system works in general, particularly how the *Phenomenology* relates to the *Logic*.

Nonetheless, Pippin's reading remains controversial with Hegel scholars, where Ameriks and others have questioned its textual accuracy, and how far it does justice to Hegel's actual position and procedures. It is not possible to go into all the details here, but one issue is fundamental, namely, whether Pippin is right to claim that Hegel followed Kant in attempting to deduce the categories from the conditions of self-consciousness, to "'ground' them in the 'I'".[16] For Pippin, as we have seen, such "grounding" is essential to the critical turn in metaphysics, as no other basis for metaphysics as the nonempirical inquiry into "how the world must be" can be taken seriously after Kant. Nonetheless, as Pippin recognizes, in presenting his account of the categories in the *Logic*, Hegel seems to go further than this, in framing his argument in more straightforwardly ontological terms, and so "slips frequently from a 'logical' to a material mode, going far beyond a claim about thought or thinkability, and making a *direct* claim about the necessary nature of things, direct in the sense that no reference is made to a 'deduced' relation between thought and thing".[17] Now, Pippin argues that these "slips" are merely apparent.[18] However, critics of

---

attempt to construct a self-subsuming, self-reflexive explanation of the categories. Self-consciousness is only an *instance* of such a reflexive structure"(Pinkard, "The Categorial Satisfaction of Self-Reflexive Reason", p. 8). Cf. Hegel, *Science of Logic*, p. 583 (*Werke*, VI, p. 253), where Hegel says that "the *I* is the pure Notion itself which, as Notion, has come into *existence*" because the I is like the Notion, in combining the moments of universality and individuality, and thus of being a unity that contains difference within it: "This absolute *universality* which is also immediately an absolute *individualization*, and an absolutely determined being, which is a pure positedness and is this *absolutely determined* being only through its unity with the *positedness*, this constitutes the nature of the *I* as well as of the Notion; neither the one nor the other [i.e. the I and the Notion] can be truly comprehended unless the two indicated moments [of universality and individuality] are grasped at the same time both in their abstraction and also in their perfect unity". Henrich explains what Hegel is getting at here as follows: "By saying 'I think,' the self asserts its distinctive existence; but the self also knows, with respect to the structure of this act, that it does not differ from other selves.... For reasons that now may well be evident, Hegel says that the ontological constitution of the self is the structure of the Notion". (Dieter Henrich, *Between Kant and Hegel: Lectures on German Idealism*, ed. by David S. Pacini (Cambridge, MA: Harvard University Press, 2003), p. 323).

[16] Pippin, *Hegel's Idealism*, p. 33.

[17] Ibid., p. 187.

[18] See, for example, ibid., p. 193: "Thus, if there is a logical problem in Hegel's introduction of finitude, it does not lie in carelessly confusing the conceptual with the real order. I have tried to show that the issues are conceptual throughout and determined by the overall conceptual strategy of the *Logic*".

Pippin's approach are unconvinced and argue instead that Hegel's position is *non*transcendental, in that he rejects any Kantian restriction of metaphysics to a method based around the conditions of self-consciousness rather than of "being as such".[19]

Of course, Pippin might well reply that from a properly Kantian perspective, the whole idea is that there is no such distinction, which is why Hegel could be happy conducting his metaphysics in a transcendental manner, by arguing from the necessary conditions of self-consciousness. But, it would seem that Pippin's critics could respond by saying that if there really is no sense to a radical mind-world dichotomy, why think of an investigation into the categories as an investigation into the conditions of *self-consciousness* at all, and so why treat the "I" (rather than "being") as the "ground" of the inquiry? According to Pippin, as we have seen, Kant himself made his critical turn to the "I" because he believed he had reason to think that here we could establish genuinely necessary claims: but why is this so obviously so? Why is there any reason to think that the necessary conditions for apperception are any easier to establish than the necessary conditions for reality as such? Or even, if one has naturalistic or sceptical doubts about the intelligibility of necessary conditions for the latter, that these doubts can be removed concerning necessary conditions for the former? In fact, doesn't any such expectation reveal a Cartesian privileging of the "inner" over the "outer", or "self-knowledge" over "worldly knowledge", of the kind that Hegel himself seems to have rejected as suspect.[20] Thus, critics of Pippin's transcendental reading of Hegel can agree that Hegel is a post-Kantian in accepting important elements of Kant's critique of traditional metaphysics, particularly as a *metaphysica specialis* with its focus on transcendent entities like God and the soul, while still arguing that Hegel is closer to Aristotle than Kant in conducting his inquiry ontologically, as a *metaphysica generalis*, for which "[t]he categories

---

[19] Cf. Pinkard, "The Categorial Satisfaction of Self-Reflexive Reason", pp. 7–10; Pinkard, "How Kantian Was Hegel?", pp. 832–834; Ameriks, "Hegel and Idealism", p. 391; Siep, "Hegel's Idea of a Conceptual Scheme", pp. 71–72; Stephen Houlgate, "G. W. F. Hegel (1770–1831)", in Steven M. Emmanuel, ed., *The Blackwell Guide to the Modern Philosophers: From Descartes to Nietzsche* (Oxford: Blackwell, 2001), pp. 278–305, at p. 282; Stephen Houlgate, *The Opening of Hegel's* Logic (West Lafayette: Purdue University Press, 2006), esp. pp. 137–143.

[20] Cf. G. W. F. Hegel, *Lectures on the History of Philosophy*, trans. by E. S. Haldane and Frances H. Simson, 3 vols. (London: K. Paul, Trench , Trübner, 1892–1896; reissued Lincoln and London: University of Nebraska Press, 1995), III, p. 486 (*Werke*, XX, p. 392): "[For Descartes and Fichte] The ego is certain, it cannot be doubted; but Philosophy desires to reach the truth. The certainty is subjective, and because it is made to remain the basis, all else remains subjective also without there being any possibility of this form being removed".

analysed in the *Logic* are all forms or ways of being . . . ; they are not merely concepts in terms of which we have to understand what is".[21]

Nonetheless, even if it is accepted that Pippin is wrong to claim that Hegel followed Kant in attempting to "ground" the categories in the "I" as conditions for self-consciousness, it is still possible that he is right to treat Hegel's idealism as a form of antirealism, for the two positions are logically distinct. However, much of the *motivation* for the latter comes from the former, as it is antirealism that gives the transcendental inquiry metaphysical teeth. And yet, without antirealism as a block to realist scepticism, how can Hegel claim that his *Logic* is a metaphysics?[22] On what basis can he show that he is establishing the fundamental nature of being, in a way that will silence sceptical doubts? Here it might be tempting to reintroduce a form of antirealism, and thus to return to something like Pippin's view of Hegel's idealism, as a way of enabling Hegel to see off the sceptic.

It is of course the case that Hegel had every confidence in his inquiries and that the *Logic* shows that it is possible to arrive at a metaphysical picture of the world that has a legitimate claim to truth. But is that confidence based on a commitment to antirealism, or the more traditional grounds that this picture has been thoroughly tested against all alternatives and shown to be the most comprehensive, cohesive, and coherent? Of course, the antirealist strategy is more radical than this because it makes (or tries to make) sceptical doubt *senseless* or *unassertible*, by closing any *possible* gap between how we think about the world and how it is.[23] But what is wrong with the less radical, but

---

[21] Houlgate, "G. W. F. Hegel", p. 282. On the move from a *metaphysic specialis* to a *metaphysica generalis*, cf. Hegel, *Science of Logic*, pp. 63–64 (*Werke*, V, p. 61), where Hegel notes that the *Logic* will not concern itself with "particular substrata taken primarily from figurate conception [*aus der Vorstellung genommenen Substrate*], namely the soul, the world and God", but consider the "forms of pure thought" (i.e. the categories) "free from those substrata, from the subjects of figurate conception".

[22] Cf. Hegel, *Science of Logic*, pp. 27, 63 (*Werke*, V, pp. 16, 61); G. W. F. Hegel, *The Encyclopaedia Logic: Part I of the Encyclopaedia of Philosophical Sciences*, trans. by T. F. Geraets, W. A. Suchting, and H. S. Harris (Indianapolis: Hackett, 1991), §24, p. 56 (*Werke*, VIII, pp. 80–81).

[23] Cf. Pippin, *Hegel's Idealism*, pp. 98–99: " . . . what Hegel is after is a way of demonstrating the 'ultimate' or absolute objectivity of the Notion not by some demonstration that being as it is in itself can be known as we conceive it to be, but that a Notionally conditional actuality is all that 'being' could intelligibly be, even for the most committed realist skeptics. . . . Hegel's resolution of the objectivity and skepticism problems raised by his idealism must involve a way of arguing *that* such a self-knowledge by Spirit, although not 'metaphysically identical' with 'what there is, in truth,' nevertheless in some way defines or transcendentally constitutes the possibility of 'objects'" .

also less demanding strategy of asking the sceptic to come up with some *grounds* for thinking that the gap really exists, by showing that we have reason to think our world-view is flawed in some way, where the aim would be to show the sceptic that no such flaw can be found, so that in this more modest sense the sceptic has no place to stand? Wouldn't this render scepticism "epistemically idle", but without any commitment to antirealism, as the view that any such "external" questioning is unintelligible simply *because* it is "external"? On this view, Hegel has no conceptual argument to rule out scepticism *in advance*, but, on the other hand, the sceptic must do more than raise just the abstract *possibility* of error: grounds for doubt must be given by showing how the picture being put forward of reality is mistaken, where the inquiry is successfully concluded if and when any such grounds have been dealt with and excluded. Seen from this perspective, both antirealism and sceptical realism make the same mistake, as both attempt to establish the necessity or impossibility of knowledge too *early*, by claiming to show prior to starting that we can or cannot succeed in coming to know how things are: in the face of a priori realist scepticism, the antirealist provides a priori reassurance. It might be argued, however, that Hegel simply sets out on the path of inquiry aiming to establish how things are (for why should we believe in advance that we cannot?) but without seeking any sort of guarantee (for why is this needed, unless we have some reason for such a doubt?).

I would therefore question Pippin's claim that Hegel could not possibly be a realist, but must be committed to some form of antirealism, because he is a "modern philosopher" who feels compelled to make the "critical turn" as a response to scepticism: "This all leads Hegel into a wholly new way of resolving the great problem of post-Cartesian philosophy – how can we reassure ourselves that what initially can only be *our* way of taking up, discriminating, categorizing the world, and our criteria for evaluating deeds, can also ultimately be critically and reflectively transformed, secured from realist skepticism, and somehow pass from 'ours' to 'Absolute' status".[24] What Pippin ignores, I believe, is Hegel's insight that it is fatal (and quite uncalled for) to *begin* with anything like the Kantian "instrument" model of cognition, and thus with the presupposition that the categories are "only *our* way of taking things up, discriminating, categorizing the world": for this approach "presupposes that the Absolute stands on one side and cognition on the other",[25] while vainly struggling to close the gap. To make this

[24] Pippin, 'Hegel's Original Insight', p. 287.
[25] G. W. F. Hegel, *Hegel's Phenomenology of Spirit*, trans. by A. V. Miller (Oxford: Oxford University Press, 1977), p. 47 (*Werke*, III, p. 70).

anything *more* than a presupposition, we must be shown where it is that there is something wrong with our way of thinking, which raises the real (and not just abstract) doubt that it is merely "ours", and so not related to the world; but to do that, we need to be shown a genuine case where that thinking breaks down, otherwise scepticism is just a form of paranoia, "whereby what calls itself fear of error reveals itself rather as fear of the truth".[26] The *Phenomenology* thus justifies the project of the *Logic* by showing that a series of *particular* arguments a sceptic might give to suggest that the world is unknowable are based on questionable epistemological and metaphysical assumptions – from the "supersensible beyond" of the Understanding to the transcendent God of certain forms of religious consciousness – so that in removing these sceptical grounds for doubt, "pure science [i.e. the *Logic*] presupposes liberation from the opposition of consciousness",[27] and thus liberation from the worry that if for example we find "pure being" incoherent as an idea (because it seems indistinguishable from nothing) this just tells us something about *us*, and not the nature of the world (namely, that if anything *is*, it must be determinate): but there is nothing in this "liberation" that commits Hegel to antirealism.

But, it might be said, even if Hegel sees no need to turn to antirealism at the *outset* of his inquiry, surely the nature of that inquiry shows that we need to be antirealists *at the end*, because how do we otherwise explain the success of our metaphysical investigations into the fundamental nature of reality? After all, hadn't Kant been brought to see that there was something deeply mysterious about metaphysical knowledge, a mystery he encapsulated in the question "how is synthetic a priori knowledge possible"? Kant's concern was that when we reach a metaphysical conclusion (such as "every event must have a cause"), we cannot do so either by knowing the meaning of the concepts in question (because these metaphysical propositions are not analytic), or "by reading it off" the world in any direct sense (because our only direct confrontation with the world is in sensible experience: and this experience tells us just that things are thus and so, but not that they could not be otherwise).[28] The metaphysical rationalist might argue that we reach our metaphysical conclusions by finding that we cannot contemplate how things could be any other way (e.g. an event occurring without a cause). But, if our metaphysical conclusions are reached on the basis of what *we* find conceivable, what *we* can envisage, what account can we give of how these conclusions come to conform to *the world*? Kant

---

[26] Ibid.
[27] Hegel, *Science of Logic*, p. 49 (*Werke*, V, p. 43).
[28] Cf. Kant, *Critique of Pure Reason*, B3.

argued that it is unsatisfactory to offer as an explanation some sort of preestablished harmony between the limits of what we find conceivable and the limits of how things can be, as if God or some "third thing" ensured that the former correspond to the latter, because this leaves open the question of why God should have arranged things this way, and why we should expect him to continue to do so.[29] Rather, Kant argued, we must make the "Copernican turn", and accept that it is because things must conform to our conceptual structures that the limits of the latter can tell us about the limits of the former (although this knowledge only extends as far as things as they appear within those structures, not to things as they are in themselves). So, if Hegel is to claim that his *Logic* is a metaphysics, doesn't he have to explain this in antirealist terms?

However, it is not clear that the metaphysician need feel obliged to accept this Kantian way out, because he may not feel compelled to accept the terms in which the problem is posed in the first place. For, this rests on the assumption that when we accept a metaphysical proposition on the basis of our inability to conceive of its negation, there is some *special* difficulty, which is that we are moving from the limits of our thought to the limits of the world. But this assumes, Hegel would argue, that in metaphysical thinking we are limning the limits of what we can conceive rather than what is conceivable *as such*. But can we accept this restriction, unless we can make more sense of there being *other* ways of conceiving things than Kant can properly allow? For, there is a dilemma here for the Kantian: Either he argues that it is because of the limits on what we can conceive that we find some ways of being to be unthinkable, where he convinces us that this is really down to some fact about us – but then why would we stick to the modal claim and not rather abandon it? Or he convinces us to stay with the modal claim, by arguing that it is impossible, *in general* (not just *for us*), to conceive of things any other way: but then if all minds must think in

[29] The seeds of this dissatisfaction can be found in the famous letter to Marcus Herz of 21 February 1772; and for later expressions of the point see, for example, *Critique of Pure Reason*, B167 and *Prolegomena to Any Future Metaphysics*, §36. Cf. also John Stuart Mill, *Collected Works of John Stuart Mill*, edited by John M. Robson (London and Toronto: University of Toronto Press, 1963), IX, p. 68: "even assuming that inconceivability is not solely the result of limited experience, but that some incapacities of conceiving are inherent in the mind, and inseparable from it; this would not entitle us to infer, that what we are thus incapable of conceiving cannot exist. Such an inference would only be warrantable, if we could know *a priori* that we must have been created capable of conceiving whatever is capable of existing: that the universe of thought and that of reality, the Microcosm and the Macrocosm (as once they were called) must have been framed in complete correspondence with one another.... "

this way, and there is no way of conceiving the world differently, isn't *this* now an extraordinary fact, the best explanation for which lies in the impossibility of things being any other way, thereby providing an argument for realism rather than antirealism? As a result, we can now see why Hegel might say that *"logic"*, as "the science of *things* grasped in *thought"*, coincides with *"metaphysics"*, which has been "taken to express the *essentialities* of the *things".*[30]

We have found, therefore, that there are interpretative and philosophical reasons to be doubtful about Pippin's account of Hegel's idealism: Hegel's texts suggest he did not feel compelled by Kant's arguments to take an antirealist turn in metaphysics, and the arguments that the Kantian might give to make this seem necessary can be reasonably resisted. We can now proceed by looking at other ways of understanding Hegel's idealism.

II. HEGEL AS A MENTALISTIC IDEALIST

As we have seen, Pippin's treatment of Hegel's idealism was in part a reaction against other accounts that he takes to raise Ameriks' concern of "extravagance", which treat Hegel as an idealist in the sense of a "spirit monist", "who believed that finite objects did not 'really' exist (only the Absolute Idea exists), [and] that this One was not a 'substance' but a 'subject,' or mental".[31] To Pippin and others, this kind of idealism appears to be a return to the "metaphysics of the 'beyond'", which treats the absolute mind as the transcendent cause or ground of the world, in a thoroughly precritical manner; they argue we should therefore hesitate before attributing this position to Hegel.

Now, one way to respond to this charge of precritical "extravagance" might be to try to license Hegel's position as a natural extension of Kant's, and thus to claim that this interpretation (like Pippin's) also builds on Hegel's Kantian heritage, but in a way that is closer to full-blooded mentalistic or Berkeleyan idealism than antirealism. Thus, according to these interpretations of Hegel's idealism, Kant held that the empirical world – everything in space and time – is mind-dependent, so that the world as we know it is nothing but an appearance. However, Kant retained a residual element of realism in his conception of things-in-themselves [*noumena*], which exist independent of our minds and outside the boundaries of our knowledge. It is argued that Hegel then came to reject this realism as incoherent, and so radicalized Kant's mentalistic idealism, thereby arriving at the doctrine of an *absolute*

---

[30] Hegel, *Encyclopaedia Logic*, §24, p. 56 (*Werke*, VIII, p. 81).
[31] Pippin, *Hegel's Idealism*, p. 4.

mind, in which all reality is contained as the experience of a supra-individual subject. On this account, then, Hegel is an idealist in the sense that he treats the world as thoroughly mind-dependent, a transformation of Kant's merely "subjective" idealism into a form of *absolute idealism*.[32]

However, one difficulty with this approach, is that in order to claim that this kind of Hegelian idealism is an extension of Kant's, it is necessary to begin with a mentalistic account of Kant's idealism, which is itself problematic because it ignores the full complexity of Kant's talk of "appearances" and "things-in-themselves" and his distinction between empirical realism and transcendental idealism. Thus, if it is claimed that Hegel derived his idealism from a Berkeleyan reading of Kant, it will seem, to many, that this position is founded on a simplistic misunderstanding of Kantianism, and one that we no longer have any reason to take seriously.[33]

[32] For interpretations of Hegel along these lines, see the following: Robert C. Solomon, *Continental Philosophy since 1750* (Oxford: Oxford University Press, 1988), p. 57: "The dialectic is not so much a method as it is the central idea of Hegel's philosophy, and its purpose, in each of his works, is to demonstrate the ultimate necessity of an all-encompassing acceptance of the self as absolute – which Hegel calls 'Spirit' (*Geist*)s . . . [Hegel] accepted the general move of Kant's first Critique, regarding objects as being constituted by consciousness, but he also saw the manifest absurdity of making this an individual matter, as if each of us creates his or her own world; it is consciousness in general that does this, collectively and not individually, through the shared aspects of a culture, a society, and above all through a shared language"; Peter Singer, *Hegel* (Oxford: Oxford University Press, 1983), pp. 72–73: "Hegel rejects the view that there are countless different 'realities' corresponding to the countless different minds that exist. He calls this form of idealism *absolute idealism* to distinguish it from subjective idealism. For Hegel there is only one reality, because, ultimately, there is only one minds . . . [Hegel] needs the conception of a collective or universal mind not only to avoid a subjective form of idealism, but also to make good his vision of mind coming to see all of reality as its own creation"; William H. Walsh, "Subjective and Objective Idealism", in Dieter Henrich, ed., *Kant oder Hegel* (Stuttgart: Klett-Cotta, 1983), pp. 83–98, at p. 95: "[Hegel] wanted to argue that things are not just coloured or informed by mind, but penetrated and constituted by it . . . To put it crudely, mind could know the world because the world was mind writ large".

[33] Cf. Arthur W. Collins, *Possible Experience: Understanding Kant's* Critique of Pure Reason (Berkeley: University of California Press, 1999), p. 25: "The things that Kant says prominently and repeatedly about space and time and appearances . . . make it easy to understand how his principal German successors could have taken his transcendental idealism to be an idealist philosophy like their own. But they are nonetheless mistaken. Thus the German idealists are among those who, in an essentially Cartesian spirit, equate Kant's subjectivism with idealism and imagine that he ascribes a mental status to objects in so far as he says that they are, as appearances, irreducibly subjective".

As well as the issue of "extravagance", there are, moreover, textual reasons to resist this account as a reading of Hegel. For, this account seems to misunderstand Hegel's notion of "absolute mind", which is mind that is able to "free *itself* from the connection with something which is for it an Other", where "[t]o attain this, mind must liberate the intrinsically rational object from the form of contingency, singleness, and externality which at first clings to it".[34] Thus, mind for Hegel becomes absolute when it finds itself "at home in the world", and thus is able to make the world intelligible to itself; but this conception in no way entails that as absolute, mind somehow "contains" or constitutes the world, and so involves treating the latter as dependent on the former in any mentalistic sense. Hegel would seem to reject just this position, when at one point in his lectures he characterizes as "spiritualism" the view which holds that "spirit is what is independent, true, that nature is only an appearance of spirit, not in and for itself, not truly real", and comments of this view that it would be "utter foolishness to deny its [nature's] reality".[35] And of course, in systematic terms, the fact that Nature comes before Spirit creates difficulties for the mentalistic reading.

But surely, it might be argued, how can Hegel be so confident that the Kantian (or the sceptical realist) is wrong to talk of things-in-themselves as outside our cognitive capacities, unless he has brought the world "within" the mind and so collapsed the distinction? To exclude talk of "things-in-themselves", doesn't Hegel have to believe he has some sort of guarantee that the mind will conform to the world, and isn't the only way to provide that guarantee some sort of mentalistic idealism?[36]

It is not clear, however, that this kind of guarantee is something that Hegel needed or sought, and thus that he felt this kind of motivation towards mentalistic idealism. For, Hegel's objection to Kant's

[34] G. W. F. Hegel, *Hegel's Philosophy of Mind: Part Three of the Encyclopaedia of the Philosophical Sciences*, trans. by William Wallace and A. V. Miller (Oxford: Oxford University Press, 1971), §441 addition, p. 182 (*Werke*, X, p. 233).

[35] G. W. F. Hegel, *Vorlesungen über die Philosophie des Geistes. Berlin 1827/1828, Nachgeschrieben von Johann Eduard Erdmann und Ferdinand Walter*, ed. by Franz Hespe and Burkhard Tuschling (Hamburg: Felix Meiner, 1994), p. 17. It should be said, however, that passages can be found which are closer to the traditional reading: cf. Hegel, *Philosophy of Mind*, §448 addition, p. 198 (*Werke*, X, p. 253): "But when we said that what is sensed receives from the intuiting mind the form of the spatial and temporal, this statement must not be understood to mean that space and time are only subjective forms. This is what Kant wanted to make them. But things are in truth themselves spatial and temporal; this double form of assunderness is not one-sidedly given them by our intuition, but has been originally imparted to them by the intrinsically infinite mind, by the creative eternal Idea".

[36] Cf. Singer, *Hegel*, pp. 70–71.

conception of "things-in-themselves" is that it sets up an absolute limit to our cognitive capacities, telling us that the gap between mind and world cannot be bridged; but how can such a positive claim be made, unless something is already known about the world on the other side of the gap? The difficulty is that this looks like a form of skepticism that is nonetheless based on a metaphysical claim about what is supposed to be unknowable, and which can be answered by pointing out this incoherence. Or, if Kant refuses to make any such metaphysical claim, how can his block on our inquiries be motivated, as nothing can now be said about what it is we do not know?[37] However, in removing the skeptical worry here, Hegel is *not* thereby committing himself to the opposite view, that knowledge of the world is guaranteed, and that before we set out in our inquiries, we can be sure they will succeed; he is just objecting to any attempt to set an absolute barrier to that inquiry at the outset.[38] Our response here thus parallels the response we offered to the similar worry in the previous section: just as we found there no reason to think Hegel's epistemic optimism requires a commitment to antirealism, so here we have found it also doesn't require any commitment to mentalistic idealism.

We have thus found reason to accept Ameriks' critical claims regarding this kind of idealism as a reading of Hegel: not only is it "extravagant" and so objectionable on that score, but it is also textually unwarranted, as Ameriks also recognizes.[39]

---

[37] Cf. Hegel, *Science of Logic*, p. 36 (*Werke*, V, pp. 25–26): "The way in which the critical philosophy understands the relationship of these three terms is that we place our thoughts as a medium between ourselves and the objects, and that this medium instead of connecting us with the objects rather cuts us off from them. But this view can be countered by the simple observation that these very things which are supposed to stand beyond us and, at the other extreme, beyond the thoughts referring to them, are themselves figments of subjective thought, and as wholly indeterminate they are only a single thought-thing – the so-called thing-in-itself of empty abstraction." Cf. also Hegel, *The Encyclopaedia Logic*, §44, p. 87 (*Werke*, VIII, pp. 120–121), and Hegel, *Phenomenology of Spirit*, pp. 46–48 (*Werke*, III, 68–70).

[38] It might be argued on Kant's behalf that it mischaracterize the Kantian position to describe it in these terms, as the limits Kant claims to discern are not set in advance, but through a recognition of the intractable difficulties faced by our inquiries into certain metaphysical questions; but here, of course, Hegel is more optimistic than Kant over our capacity to resolve these questions, and so would also reject this Kantian motivation for scepticism as ungrounded and premature. For further discussion of this issue, see Robert Stern, *Hegel and the* Phenomenology of Spirit (London: Routledge, 2002), pp. 36–41.

[39] Karl Ameriks, "Introduction: Interpreting German Idealism", in Karl Ameriks, ed., *The Cambridge Companion to German Idealism* (Cambridge, UK: Cambridge University Press, 2000), pp. 1–17, esp. pp. 7–10. For a more detailed discussion that

III. HEGEL AND THE IDEALISM OF THE FINITE

In the face of these exegetical difficulties, it is tempting to return to Hegel's own writings, and look there at what Hegel says about idealism as a philosophical doctrine, and see how this relates to his own position. This is a strategy Ameriks also tries, but he thinks it either leads us back into "extravagance", or into the third of his interpretative vices, namely, "triviality".

If one looks at the way in which Hegel himself characterizes idealism, the results are certainly striking. Here is one passage where the characterization seems clear:[40]

> The proposition that the finite is ideal [*ideell*] constitutes idealism. The idealism of philosophy consists in nothing else than in recognizing that the finite has no veritable being [*wahrhaft Seiendes*]. Every philosophy is essentially an idealism, or at least has idealism for its principle, and the question then is how far this principle is actually carried out. This is as true of philosophy as of religion; for religion equally does not recognize finitude as a veritable being [*ein wahrhaftes Sein*], as something ultimate and absolute or as something underived, uncreated, eternal. Consequently the opposition of idealistic and realistic philosophy has no significance. A philosophy which ascribed veritable, ultimate, absolute being to finite existences as such, would not deserve the name of philosophy; the principles of ancient or modern philosophies, water, or matter, or atoms are *thoughts*, universals, ideal entities, not things as they immediately present themselves to us, that is, in their sensuous individuality – not even the water of Thales. For although this is also empirical water, it is at the same time also the *in-itself* or *essence* of all other things, too, and these other things are not self-subsistent or grounded in themselves, but are *posited* by, are *derived* from, an *other*, from water, that is they are ideal entities.[41]

counters any mentalistic conception of German Idealism generally, but which does not include any extended discussion of Hegel himself, see Frederick C. Beiser, *German Idealism: The Struggle Against Subjectivism 1781–1801* (Cambridge, MA: Harvard University Press, 2002).

[40] Pippin has argued that we should not read too much into this passage, because its context is a limited one, in so far as here "Hegel is ... quite self-consciously appropriating the language of a pre-critical metaphysics and making his point in passing within the assumptions of such a framework ... In general, dipping onto Book One of the *Logic* for 'definitions' of what Hegel means by 'idealism' ... and so forth is very unwise" (Pippin, "Hegel's Original Insight", p. 289, note 6). However, as we shall see, this is by no means the only place within the system where Hegel uses "idealism", "ideal", and so on in the way suggested in this passage, and in fact this use turns out to be fairly typical throughout Hegel's works; so Pippin's warning seems misplaced.

[41] Hegel, *Science of Logic*, pp. 154–155 (*Werke*, V, p. 172). For an equivalent passage in the *Encyclopaedia Logic*, see §95, p. 152 (*Werke*, VIII, p. 203): "[F]initude ... is under the determination of reality at first. But the truth of the finite is rather

Can anything be gained in our understanding of Hegel's idealism by considering passages such as these?

Ameriks cautions against optimism here, because he think that by taking this passage at face value, we will end up making Hegel's idealism merely trivial, as Hegel seems to be saying only that "immediate appearances point to something else, some non-immediate things or relations": "The alternative to idealism [in this sense] is such a straw man that here the real issue becomes simply what specific variety of idealism one should develop".[42] The charge of triviality arises if by idealism Hegel merely means that the world as it presents itself immediately to the senses is not how the world actually is, so that the former cannot be ascribed any ultimate truth – the "booming, buzzing confusion" of mere sensible experience is not a veridical representation of reality (assuming, indeed, that this notion of experience is even coherent).

Now, it would certainly seem right that if this is all that Hegel is saying here, Ameriks can justifiably argue that he is not saying very much. But, in claiming that "finite existences" lack "veritable, ultimate, absolute being", Hegel would appear to be talking not about the ephemeral phenomena presented to us in sensation, but ordinary concrete objects, such as this table, this tree, and so on;[43] Ameriks is therefore wrong to identify "immediate appearances" with the former and not the latter. There is thus enough in Hegel's position here to overcome the charge of triviality, if we take his "finite existences" to be concrete individual objects and not just sensory appearances.

However, Ameriks argues that if we try to escape triviality in this way, we expose Hegel to the opposite danger, which is extravagance. It is the threat of this danger that I now wish to explore, as it arises from different readings of this passage.

One reading of the passage, which would return us to the kind of extravagant position discussed in the previous section, would be to take Hegel here to be characterizing idealism in mentalistic terms, as claiming that "the finite has no veritable being" because finite existences qua

---

its *ideality*... This ideality of the finite is the most important proposition of philosophy, and for that reason every genuine philosophy is *Idealism*".

[42] Ameriks, "Hegel and Idealism", pp. 387–388.

[43] Cf. G. W. F. Hegel, *Element of the Philosophy of Right*, trans. by H. B. Nisbet (Cambridge, UK: Cambridge University Press, 1991), §44 addition, p. 76 (*Werke*, VIII, p. 107): "The free will is consequently that idealism which does not consider things [*Dinge*], as they are, to be in and for themselves, whereas realism declares them to be absolute, even if they are found only in the form of finitude. Even the animal has gone beyond this realist philosophy, for it consumes things [*Dinge*] and thereby proves that they are not absolutely self-sufficient". Cf. also Hegel, *Phenomenology of Spirit*, p. 65 (*Werke*, III, p. 91).

individual objects are dependent on an absolute mind. But, in fact this charge of extravagance is obviously misplaced, as in reality this passage counts *against* a mentalistic conception of Hegel's idealism. For, we can see here that Hegel did not mean anything mentalistic by idealism, because if he did, it would surely have been an absurd exaggeration to say that "[e]very philosophy is essentially an idealism", as mentalistic idealism is a position held by few philosophers, and not by those classical philosophers directly and indirectly referred to here, such as Thales, Leucippus, Democritus and Empedocles, not to mention Plato and Aristotle. Hegel clearly recognized this,[44] and so is hardly likely to have claimed that "[e]very philosophy is essentially an idealism" if this is what he meant by the position.

Another reading of the passage sees Hegel as offering a picture of idealism here not as mentalistic, but as *holistic*.[45] On this account, Hegel claims that finite entities do not have "veritable, ultimate, absolute being" because they are dependent on other entities for their existence in the way that parts are dependent on other parts within a whole; and idealism consists in recognizing this relatedness between things, in a way that ordinary consciousness fails to do.[46] The idealist thus sees the

---

[44] Hegel, *Lectures on the History of Philosophy*, II, pp. 43–44 (*Werke*, XIX, pp. 54–55): "[T]he idealism of Plato must not be thought of as being subjective idealism, and as that false idealism which has made its appearance in modern times, and which maintains that we do not learn anything, are not influenced from without, but that all conceptions are derived from out of the subject. It is often said that idealism means that the individual produces from himself all his ideas, even the most immediate. But this is an unhistoric, and quite false conception; if we take this rude definition of idealism, there have been no idealists amongst the philosophers, and Platonic idealism is certainly far removed from anything of this kind".

[45] Cf. Kenneth R. Westphal, *Hegel's Epistemological Realism* (Dordrecht, The Netherlands: Kluwer, 1989), p. 143: "Hegel's idealism is thus an ontological thesis, a thesis concerning the interdependence of everything there is, and thus is quite rightly contrasted with epistemologically based subjective idealism", and his "Hegel's Attitude toward Jacobi" in "The Third Attitude of Thought Toward Objectivity", *Southern Journal of Philosophy*, 27 (1989), pp. 135–156, at p. 146: "The basic model of Hegel's ontology is a radical ontological holism". Cf. also Thomas E. Wartenberg, "Hegel's Idealism: The Logic of Conceptuality", in Frederick C. Beiser, ed., *The Cambridge Companion to Hegel*. (Cambridge, UK: Cambridge University Press, 1993), pp. 102–29 at p. 107: "[Hegel's] manner of characterizing his idealism emphasizes that it is a form of holism. According to this view, individuals are mere parts and thus are not fully real or independent".

[46] Cf. Hegel, *Encyclopaedia Logic*, §45 addition, p. 88 (*Werke*, VIII, p. 122): "For our ordinary consciousness (i.e., the consciousness at the level of sense-perception and understanding) the objects that it knows count as self-standing and as self-founded in their isolation from one another; and when they prove to be related to each other, and conditioned by one another, their mutual dependence upon one another is regarded as something external to the object, and not as belonging

world differently from the realist, not as a plurality of separate entities that are "self-subsistent or grounded in themselves", but as parts of an interconnected totality in which these entities are dependent on their place within the whole. It turns out, then, that idealism for Hegel is primarily an ontological position, which holds that the things of ordinary experience are ideal in the sense that they have no being in their own right, and so lack the self-sufficiency and self-subsistence required to be fully real.

Now, this is an account of Hegel's idealism that Ameriks also considers, but dismisses on the grounds of extravagance. For, if Hegel is taken to be suggesting that finite existences lack "veritable, ultimate, absolute being", it may seem he is basing this on the claim to have found a candidate for absolute status elsewhere – in the "world-whole", which as "a self-standing, self-realizing structure" constitutes a limit to explanation in the way no finite entity can, because as a totality "there is nothing else it could depend on".[47] But if it involves theorizing about the world-whole in this way, it may appear that Hegel's idealism is guilty of just the kind of pre-Kantian metaphysical irresponsibility that Pippin and others have sought to escape.[48] As contemporary philosophers, it could be argued, we should treat this project with caution.[49]

It is not clear, however, that this account of Hegel's idealism should be dismissed on these grounds, because not all forms of holism of this kind need be seen as extravagant, at least from a Kantian perspective. For, while such a theory will require the abandonment of a purely

---

to their nature. It must certainly be maintained against this that the objects of which we have immediate knowledge are mere appearances, i.e., they do not have the ground of their being within themselves, but within something else." Cf. also *Philosophy of Mind*, §420 addition, pp. 161–162 (*Werke*, X, p. 209); translation modified: "Although perception starts from the observation of sensuous materials it does not stop at these, does not confine itself simply to smelling, tasting, seeing, hearing, and feeling (touching), but necessarily goes on to relate the sensuous to the universal which is not observable in an immediate manner, to cognize each thing as in itself a connectedness: in force, for example, to comprehend all its manifestations; and to seek out the connections and mediations that exist between separate individual things. While therefore the merely sensuous consciousness merely *shows* things, that is to say, exhibits them in their immediacy, perception, on the other hand, apprehends the connectedness of things, demonstrates that when such and such circumstances are present such and such a thing follows, and thus begins to demonstrate the truth of things".

47 Willem A. deVries, *Hegel's Theory of Mental Activity* (Ithaca and London: Cornell University Press, 1988), pp. 13, 15.

48 Cf. Ameriks, "Hegel and Idealism", p. 397.

49 Cf. deVries, *Hegel's Theory of Mental Acitivity*, p. 13: "We have to be extremely suspicious of Hegel's rather dogmatic belief that the world-whole does form a unitary totality".

naturalistic explanatory framework, which is suspicious of explanations which have global scope and have a reflexive or "free-standing" structure, this abandonment is arguably already a feature of Kant's transcendental turn, where the aim is (as David Bell has put it), to provide a "genuinely self-subsistent, self-warranting framework of explanation".[50] Where the theory would become objectionable in Kantian terms, would be if it led to a *transcendent* claim, and so to a form of explanation based on appeal to some metaphysical ground *outside* or *beyond* the empirical world – for example, a self-positing infinite Absolute that gives rise to finite existents as their creator. But it seems clear that a proponent of Hegel as an holistic, absolute-theorist could plausibly claim that Hegel's aim was to *avoid* any transcendence of this kind,[51] while nonetheless holding that the world-whole constitutes a satisfactory limit to explanation; so proponents of this reading will characteristically argue that Hegel's position was designed to show that the world is a kind of totality that makes notions of "cause" and "ground" inapplicable at this level, rather than to bring the regress of explanation to an end by positing a transcendent starting-point.[52] Thus, the holistic strategy is arguably to claim that the pressure towards transcendence only arises because we are operating with an incomplete picture of the world which drives us into a regress of explanations which this transcendent first cause is then designed to block; but once we see the world as a totality in itself, no such transcendent answer to the question of explanation will be needed. The aim of this approach, then, is "to articulate an alternative vision of reality – and not a vision of some alternative

---

[50] David Bell, "Transcendental Arguments and Non-Naturalistic Anti-Realism", in Robert Stern, ed., *Transcendental Arguments: Problems and Prospects* (Oxford: Oxford University Press, 1999), pp. 189–210, at p. 199; see also David Bell, "Is Empirical Realism Compatible With Transcendental Idealism?", in Ralph Schumacher, ed., *Idealismus als Theorie der Repräsentation?* (Paderborn: Mentis, 2001), pp. 167–180.

[51] Cf. Hegel, *Encyclopaedia Logic*, §94 addition, p. 150 (*Werke*, VIII, p. 200): "Philosophy does not waste time with such empty and otherworldly stuff. What philosophy has to do with is always something concrete and strictly present".

[52] Cf. G. W. F. Hegel, *Hegel's Philosophy of Nature: Part Two of the Encyclopaedia of the Philosophical Sciences*, trans. by Michael John Petry, 3 vols. (London: George Allen & Unwin, 1970), §247 addition, I, p. 208 (*Werke*, IX, pp. 26–27), translation modified: "To our ordinary thinking [*Vorstellung*], the world is merely a collection of finitudes [*Endlichkeiten*], but if grasped as universal, as a totality, the question of a beginning at once disappears". For further discussion of this "negative" strategy, which (I claim) can also be found in the work of some of the British Idealists who commented on Hegel, see Robert Stern, "British Hegelianism: A Non-Metaphysical View?", *European Journal of Philosophy*, 2 (1994), pp. 293–321.

reality",[53] so that far from being a form of pre-Kantian metaphysics that tries to claim access to some extramundane absolute, Hegel's idealism is a form of absolute-theory that can be treated as in line with the transcendental turn, of giving us a conception of the world that will show how the need for explanation can be satisfied without going *beyond* it.

However, even if it is right to say that holism can be thought of as an option that follows not just from metaphysical extravagance on Hegel's part, but from a concern with the limits of naturalistic explanation that was also shared by Kant, the suspicion may nonetheless be raised that Hegel goes further here than Kant would allow, in that Kant did not want his "alternative vision of reality" to undercut our ordinary, "empirical", conception of the world,[54] while Hegel's form of holism by contrast threatens to undermine it completely. For, it is often held that Hegel's holism is Spinozistic, and based around the principle that *"omnis determinatio est negatio"* ["all determination is negation"],[55] understood as the idea that everything depends on its difference from other things to be itself. If this is so, it may appear that the status of individuals within this holism is lost: for a consequence seems to be that nothing has any *intrinsic* properties as each is what it is through its relation to others, so there are only relational properties, and in such a purely relational system, how can the relata be said to be entities in their own right, even to the extent of being parts – so that in the end, the whole becomes the One.[56] By posing a threat to the status of

---

[53] Bell, "Is Empirical Realism Compatible With Transcendental Idealism?", p. 177.

[54] Cf. ibid, p. 177: "If the goal of a transcendental theory is to articulate an alternative vision of reality – and not a vision of some alternative reality – then clearly it is a condition of success that there must be some sense in which the notion of reality remains constant throughout. There must, that is, be a sense in which 'philosophy leaves everything as it is,' in which it 'leaves the world alone' and refrains, say, from contesting the findings of natural science as if those findings were simply *false"*.

[55] Cf. Hegel, *Encyclopaedia Logic*, §91 addition, p. 147 (*Werke*, VIII, pp. 196–197). As was his wont, Hegel was slightly misquoting Spinoza here; in his Letter 50 (to Jarig Jelles, 2 June 1674), Spinoza writes "determinatio negatio est". See *On The Improvement of the Understanding, The Ethics, Correspondence*, trans by R. H. M. Elwes (New York: Dover Publications, 1955), p. 370: "This determination [i.e. figure] therefore does not appertain to the thing according to its being, but, on the contrary, is its nonbeing. As then figure is nothing else than determination, and determination is negation, figure, as has been said, can be nothing but negation". Whether Hegel is right to interpret Spinoza's remarks in the way he does can be questioned: see Pierre Macherey, *Hegel ou Spinoza*, 2nd edn. (Paris: Éditions La Découverte, 1990), ch. 4.

[56] This concern was raised by Jacobi, in his critical discussion of Spinoza that (inadvertently) did so much to introduce Spinoza into the thinking of the period. See F. H. Jacobi, *Concerning the Doctrine of Spinoza in Letters to Herr Moses Mendelssohn*,

individuals in this manner, Hegel's holism may appear to be revisionary in a way that Kant claimed his idealism was not (as well as having troubling ethical consequences, of the sort also sometimes attributed to him, concerning the low moral value of individuality within Hegel's system).

Now, there are possible replies that might be given to this kind of concern from the perspective of a holistic reading of Hegel, such as questioning whether this can indeed be derived from the idea of determination through negation, or the assumption that even if this means there are relations "all the way down", this leaves no room for individuals. However, another response is to question the holistic reading as an accurate account of Hegel's position. For, in fact, this reading suffers from a textual difficulty, which can be explained as follows. The passage we are discussing comes as part of a "Remark" appended to the second chapter of Book I of the *Science of Logic*, where this chapter is divided into an account of "Determinate Being (*Dasein*) as such", "Finitude" and "Infinity", so that the passage forms part of a sequel to Hegel's discussion of the relation between the finite and the infinite. This is important, because it strongly suggests that when Hegel writes that finite things lack "veritable being" and so are ideal because not "self-sufficient or grounded in themselves", he does not mean that they are related to other finite things (as on the holistic reading), but rather that they are related to the *infinite*, which is the conclusion he has been trying to establish in the part of the chapter to which this Remark is appended. Immediately before the Remark, Hegel makes this clear by saying: "ideal being [*das Ideelle*] is the finite as it is in the true infinite – as a determination, a content, which is distinct but is not an *independent, self-subsistent* being, but only a *moment*".[57]

---

in *The Main Philosophical Writings*, trans. by George di Giovanni (Montreal and Kingston: McGill-Queen's University Press, 1994), p. 220, where Jacobi glosses Spinoza's remark in Letter 50 as follows: "Individual things, therefore, so far as they only exist in a certain determinate mode, are *non-entia* [non-entities]; the indeterminate infinite being is the one single true *ens reale, hoc est, est omne esse, & praeter quod nullum datur esse* [real being; it is the all of being, and apart from it there is no being]". The quotation in the last part of Jacobi's remark comes from Spinoza's *On The Improvement of the Understanding*, p. 29.

[57] Hegel, *Science of Logic*, pp. 149–150 (*Werke*, V, p. 165). Cf. also ibid., pp. 151–152 (*Werke*, V, p. 168): "The resolution of this contradiction [that finite and infinite are both the same and different] is not the recognition of the equal correctness and equal uncorrectness of the two assertions – this is only another form of the abiding contradiction – but the *ideality* of both, in which as distinct, reciprocal negations, they are only *moments*... In this being which is thus the *ideality* of the distinct moments [of finite and infinite], the contradiction has not vanished abstractly, but

That this context is important to understanding Hegel's conception
of idealism is equally clear in the equivalent discussion in the *Encyclopaedia Logic*, where again Hegel's striking claim that "every genuine philosophy is *idealism*" is made in the course of his discussion
of the connection between the finite and the infinite. Here he argues
that while "finitude...is under the determination of reality at first"
because finite things are seen to have the reality of "being-there" or
Dasein, it now becomes clear that they are not merely self-related but
contain their "other", where this other is the infinite, which is likewise
essentially related to the finite in a relation Hegel calls "being-for-itself"
[*Fürsichsein*], whereby the one is "sublated" [*aufgehoben*] in the other:

> In being-for-itself the determination of *ideality* has entered. *Being-there*, taken
> at first only according to its being or its affirmation, has *reality* (§91); and hence
> finitude, too, is under the determination of reality at first. But the truth of the
> finite is rather its *ideality*... This ideality of the finite is the most important
> proposition of philosophy, and for that reason every genuine philosophy is *Ideal-
> ism*. Everything depends on not mistaking for the Infinite that which is at once
> reduced in its determination to what is particular and finite.[58]

The details of Hegel's position and terminology here are difficult, but the
basic idea is fairly straightforward: the infinite cannot be "beyond" the
finite as something external to it, as this would be to limit the infinite
and thus make it finite; the infinite must therefore be incorporated
within the finite in some way, so that the finite is not to be viewed as
simply "being-there", but as related to its "other" while preserving its
difference from its other and remaining finite, so that the distinction
between the one side and the other is "sublated", in Hegel's sense of
being both "cancelled" and "preserved".[59] It would appear from this,
then, that what Hegel means by claiming that the finite is ideal, is not
that finite things depend on one another as parts of a whole (as on the
holistic reading), but that these things stand in a complex dialectical
relation to the infinite.

Now, at first sight, none of this may appear to help us much with the
worry that Hegel's idealism poses a threat to the status of individuals and
so does not "leave the world alone" in a properly Kantian manner; for it
may now seem that we are obliged to move from holism to *monism* as an
account of Hegel's system, and while the former can at least in principle
allow for the status of individuals (even if in Hegel's hands it seems it

is resolved and reconciled, and the thoughts are not only complete, but they are
also *brought together*".
[58] Hegel, *Encyclopaedia Logic*, §95, p. 152 (*Werke*, VIII, pp. 202–203).
[59] Cf. Hegel, *Encyclopaedia Logic*, §96 addition, p. 154 (*Werke*, VIII, pp. 204–205) and
Science of Logic, pp. 106–107 (*Werke*, V, pp. 113–114).

might not), monism cannot do so even in principle. For, while holism stresses the dependence of finite things on one another, in its *modest* form it can still respect the individuality of finite things in so far as parts can be individuals, to the extent of having identity conditions that make it intelligible to treat a part as the *same*, and so as persisting over time; but monism denies the individuality of finite things in these respects, treating them as "accidents" or "modifications" or "appearances" of a unified substance or ground or underlying reality that takes on these forms, in the way that a single piece of paper may have many wrinkles, or a face may have many expressions, where the paper or the face constitute individuals of which the wrinkles and the expressions are modifications, lacking in any of the continuity or identity conditions that make them individuals (e.g. it doesn't make sense to ask "is the smile you have got today the same as the one you had yesterday?", whereas it does make sense to ask of a limb that has been sown back onto a body "is that the arm you had before, or someone else's?").[60] While of course monism has had its philosophical defenders, it is clearly more revisionary of our common-sense ontology than a modest holism, and so would make Hegel's idealism problematic in the same was as it was on the earlier holistic reading, if this is what it has turned out to involve.

The question is, then, if we take Hegel's idealism to amount to the claim that the finite and infinite are dialectically related, does this commit us to giving a monistic reading of this position? In fact, I do not believe this is so, for this would be to overlook the complexity of Hegel's thinking here. As Hegel's discussion later in the *Logic* shows, he holds that categories like substance and accident or ground and existence can be misleading in the kind of metaphysical picture they give rise to: but this is what happens on the monistic reading, where the infinite is treated as if it itself must be a self-standing individual or substance, and because it cannot be one individual amongst others, this means that the individuality of finite existents is thereby lost. Hegel's preferred model, by contrast, is to think of finite existents as embodiments of the infinite, but not in a way that robs them of their individuality[61] – just as Thales took the principle of everything to be water, which is permanent and

[60] This way of characterising monism is to treat it as an answer to the question of how many individuals there are (sometimes called "substance monism"), rather than as an answer to the question of how many types or varieties of things there are (sometimes called "kind monism").

[61] Thus, while commenting that "to be a follower of Spinoza is the essential commencement of all Philosophy" (Hegel, *Lectures on the History of Philosophy*, III, p. 257 (*Werke*, XX, p. 165)), Hegel makes it very clear that he could not accept the monism he found in Spinoza: "As all differences and determinations of things and of consciousness simply go back into the One substance, one may say that in the

eternal, but which has its existence in *individual* things, while Democritus thought the same of atoms and Empedocles of the four material elements. From Hegel's perspective, therefore, the picture of the infinite/finite relation that might lead to a monistic worry is really based on a simplistic model of that relation, and one that he believed we ought not to take up.[62]

We can now see why for Hegel, a position like Thales' is idealistic in his sense, with his doctrine that "the principle of all is water". On the one hand (at least following Aristotle's account), Thales treated the world as containing ordinary finite objects, while on the other hand, he recognized in these objects an eternal and imperishable material substance – water – which constitutes these objects through a process of change, as it takes on new forms. Objects are thus transient and perishable, but in this transience water remains as permanent and unchanging, so that the finite contains the infinite within it. At the same time, water is required to take on these changing manifestations as part of its nature: it has no being simply as water, so that in this sense the infinite also requires the finite. Similarly, atoms or matter are the infinite contained within the finite, as is a law within its instances, or a universal within its instantiations. All such positions are idealistic in Hegel's sense; and once we see this, we can also see that Hegel's idealism is neither straightforwardly a form of monism or holism, though it is related to both. His idealism is not monistic in the sense we have discussed, because the finite entities retain their status as individuals, and are not mere attributes of a single substance. And his idealism is not holistic, because the fact that a finite thing is constituted by something "ultimate and absolute", like water or atoms, does not make it a part of a whole with other such things, any more than two houses that are both made from bricks are so related. However, while this shows that idealism for Hegel does not entail holism, it is no accident that Hegel will talk of the parts of a whole as "ideal":[63] for Hegel believed that a

system of Spinoza all things are merely cast down into this abyss of annihilation. But from this abyss nothing comes out" (ibid., p. 288 (*Werke*, XX, p. 166)).

[62] Another route from holism to monism, adopted after Hegel by F. H. Bradley, is to argue from the unreality of relations to the nonexistence of any kind of plurality of individual things, even as parts within a whole: but there is no reason to think that Hegel would have endorsed this argument either. For further discussion, see Rolf-Peter Horstmann, *Ontologie und Relationen: Hegel, Bradley, Russell und die Kontroverse über interne und externe Beziehungen* (Königstein: Athenäum, 1984).

[63] See, for example, G. W. F. Hegel, *Hegel's Aesthetics: Lectures on Fine Art*, trans. by T. M. Knox, 2 vols. (Oxford: Oxford University Press, 1975), I, p. 120 (*Werke*, XIII, pp. 162–163): "The process of life comprises a double activity: on the one hand, that of bringing steadily into existence perceptibly the real differences of all the

proper part must be seen as a limited reflection of the totality to which it belongs, where this relation makes the whole "infinite" in relation to the parts as "finite". Thus, for example, Hegel describes the state as "infinite within itself" because it can be viewed holistically in this way: "this divided whole exhibits a fixed and enduring determinacy which is not dead and unchanging but continues to produce itself in its dissolution".[64] We can therefore see that while idealism in Hegel's sense may not entail holism (cf. Thales and the ancient atomists), nonetheless holism may entail idealism for Hegel, in that to be a part is to be a limited aspect of a totality, as when the parts of a body manifest the life of the whole, or the state as a unity is manifested in its different constitutional elements, much in the way matter is realized through different finite individuals.

Of course, a metaphysical position of this kind is not without its difficulties; and Hegel does not attempt to work them through here, at the stage of the *Logic* which we have been discussing: rather, he goes on to do so in the third book of the *Logic*, in his "Doctrine of the Concept". There, we are introduced to the dialectically interrelated structure of universality, particularity and individuality, whereby each category is seen to imply the others, so that the Concept as such forms a self-contained system that abolishes the problem of an external "ground": for, an individual is no more than a particularized universal (I [individual] am a human being [universal] of such and such a height, weight, and so on [particular]); particularization is no more than the individualization of the universal (my height, weight etc pertain to me as an individual human being, and not as a "bare individual"); and the universal is distinguished from other universals by the way it is particularized into individuals ("human being" differs from "lion" qua universal, by the way in which it belongs to one group of determinate individuals,

members and specific characteristics of the organism, but, on the other hand, that of asserting in them their universal ideality (which is their animation) if they try to persist in independent severance from one another and isolate themselves in fixed differences from one another. This is the idealism of life. For philosophy is not at all the only example of idealism; nature, as life, already makes a matter of fact what idealist philosophy brings to completion in its own spiritual field"; and Hegel, *Philosophy of Right*, §276 addition, p. 314 (*Werke*, VII, pp. 441–442): "This ideality of the moments [in the state] is like life in an organic body: it is present at every point, there is only one life in all of them, and there is no resistance to it. Separated from it, each point must die. The same applies to the ideality of all the individual estates, powers, and corporations, however much their impulse may be to subsist and have being for themselves. In this respect, they resemble the stomach of an organism which also posits itself as independent [*für sich*] but is at the same time superseded and sacrificed and passes over into the whole".

[64] Hegel, *Philosophy of Right*, §270 addition, pp. 302–303 (*Werke*, VII, p. 429).

and not others). This can be seen as Hegel's own attempt to complete the project which he thought began with Thales and which he takes to be distinctive of philosophy itself, of finding a way of thinking that will articulate the kind of self-reflexive structure needed to understand the relationship between the conditioned and the unconditioned, which recognizes the limited nature of the former without making the latter transcendent – just as each of the categories of the Concept require the others in order to be explained and understood, without any having priority *over* the others as an "external" ground.[65]

IV. HEGEL'S IDEALISM AS A CONCEPTUAL REALISM

We have seen, then, that an account of Hegel's idealism which treats it primarily as a metaphysical position – as the claim that finite existents should not be treated as "ultimate and absolute" – need not necessarily lead into absurd extravagance while it can also avoid triviality and have some claim to textual accuracy. However, this account may seem to suffer from a fourth vice, namely, a kind of *irrelevance*, because to be told that this is what Hegel's idealism amounts to is to be presented with a form of idealism that is rather *sui generis* and hard to connect to contemporary debates that surround the idealism/realism issue, which essentially concern how the mind relates to things outside the mind, and what these things (if any) are. Of course, it would be wrong to criticize Hegel himself on this score alone; but it would nonetheless suggest that there is less to be gained from considering Hegel's idealism than we might at first have hoped. Hegel may seem merely to be claiming the following: Finite things are not themselves infinite, but are limited forms in which the infinite is realized; they therefore lack "veritable being", because they are not in themselves "ultimate and absolute or ... underived, uncreated, eternal"; they are therefore ideal, while "it is not the finite which is real but the infinite".[66] Even if we grant Hegel this conclusion, it is hard to see how this would establish "idealism" in a way that relates to current concerns.

However, though I think we should take the way Hegel characterizes "idealism" seriously, and take note of the ontological use he gives it, it is

---

[65] It is of course profoundly difficult to assess whether this distinctive Hegelian conception of the Absolute is ultimately cogent, as it forms the basis for the critique of Hegel from late Schelling onwards: it is impossible to consider this debate in any further detail here, but in different ways the work of Dieter Henrich, Michael Theunissen, Manfred Frank, Rolf-Peter Horstmann, and Vittorio Hösle would all be relevant. Among authors working in English, the contributions of J. N. Findlay, Stanley Rosen, and Andrew Bowie also bear on this issue.

[66] Hegel, *Science of Logic*, p. 149 (*Werke*, V, p. 164).

also clear that Hegel takes his position here to have wider implications, which may make what he says of greater contemporary relevance and interest. To see what these implications might be, we should focus on Hegel's claim that "[e]very philosophy is essentially an idealism", where here Hegel is suggesting that any properly philosophical position must endorse idealism as he conceives it. His implied contrast here, I think, is not just with "common sense" or "ordinary consciousness", which recognizes that objects are "not self-subsistent or grounded in themselves", but cannot reconcile this with its stronger sense that objects are individuals and thus (it supposes) "self-standing and self-founded", and so this form of consciousness cannot grasp the complex philosophical outlook Hegel is proposing which is supposed to accommodate both insights;[67] an additional contrast, I believe, is also with *non*philosophy, which for Hegel is a position associated with the empiricist tradition as it existed in Germany, particularly in the work of F. H. Jacobi.[68] For Hegel, Jacobi counts as a follower of "those radical arch-empiricists, Hume and Locke" because like them, he has "posited the particular as such as the Absolute",[69] rather than seeing that finite particulars lack "veritable being" in Hegel's sense, that is, that they are "not self-subsistent or grounded in themselves"; Jacobi has thus ended up with a position in which "the *finite* is posited as absolute",[70] and so with a position that counts as an example of *realism*, in Hegel's use of this term. Thus, while Hegel believes that as far as *philosophy* is concerned, "the opposition of idealistic and realistic philosophy has no significance", he does not expect it to have no significance for ordinary consciousness or (more importantly) *non*philosophy of the sort propounded (Hegel thinks) by Jacobi. In tracing out this issue further, we will see that Hegel's idealism is relevant to contemporary issues after all, because of the wider questions this raises.

[67] Cf. Hegel, *Encyclopaedia Logic*, §45 addition, p. 88 (*Werke*, VIII, p. 122). Hegel of course believed that this kind of difficulty is characteristic of "ordinary consciousness", which oscillates between 'one-sided' views that it is unable to reconcile.

[68] Jacobi himself characterised his own position as a "nonphilosophy": see Jacobi, *Jacobi to Fichte*, in the *Main Philosophical Writings*, p. 501, p. 505, p. 519. Cf. Hegel's remark that 'the only philosophy acknowledged [by Jacobi and his followers] is not a philosophy at all!' (Hegel, *Lectures on the History of Philosophy*, III, p. 477 (*Werke*, XX, p. 384)).

[69] G. W. F. Hegel, *Faith and Knowledge*, trans. by Walter Cerf and H. S. Harris (Albany: SUNY Press, 1977), p. 137 (*Werke*, II, pp. 376–377).

[70] Hegel, *Encyclopaedia Logic*, §74, pp. 120–121 (*Werke*, VIII, p. 163): "The form of immediacy gives to the *particular* the determination of *being*, or of relating *itself* to *itself*. But the particular is precisely the relating of itself to *another* outside it; [but] through that form [of immediacy] the *finite* is posited as absolute".

What this dispute with Jacobi brings out, is that for Hegel his idealism requires a repudiation of empiricism, and thus a richer conception of the relation between thought and world. Idealism for Hegel, as we have seen, is a position that does not treat finite things as "ultimate and absolute" in themselves but relates them to an enduring and infinite "ground" of some kind, of which these finite things are limited realizations; but what idealism in this sense requires, Hegel thinks, is that we move beyond "empirical cognition". This is because this infinite ground is not something that is apparent to us in experience, but can only be something we arrive at through reflection.[71] The idealist must therefore be prepared to treat this nonobservable form of being as *real* in the way that the empiricist refuses to do, because the empiricist cannot allow such "ideal entities" into his ontology. Now, Hegel takes it to be characteristic of the philosopher that he *is* prepared to take this step and to take such "ideal entities" to be real, because he is prepared to trust in those capacities of thought that go beyond the direct evidence of our senses through a process of theorizing and intellectual reflection that arrives at a deeper level of explanation and understanding. This is why, then, Hegel believes he can claim that "[e]very philosophy is essentially an idealism" in his sense: for in his view the philosopher is characteristically driven to seek more satisfactory forms of explanation than can be given at the level of the observable phenomena, while being a realist about the entities such explanations require, whether these are Thales' water, Democritus' atoms, or the laws and genera of natural science, in which "things as they immediately present themselves to us" have a more stable grounding:

Nature offers us an infinite mass of singular shapes and appearances. We feel the need to bring unity into this manifold; therefore, we compare them and seek to [re]cognise what is universal in each of them. Individuals are born and pass away; in them their kind is what abides, what recurs in all of them; and it is only present for us when we think about them. This is where laws, e.g., the laws of the motion of the heavenly bodies, belong too. We see the stars in one place today and in another tomorrow; this disorder is for the spirit something incongruous, and not to be trusted, since the spirit believes in an order, a simple, constant, and universal determination [of things]. This is the faith in which the spirit has directed its [reflective] thinking upon phenomena, and has come to know their laws, establishing the motion of the heavenly bodies in a universal

---

[71] Cf. Hegel, *Lectures on the History of Philosophy*, III, p. 445 (*Werke*, XX, pp. 352–353): "It is certainly correct to say that the infinite is not given in the world of sensuous perception; and supposing that what we know is experience, a synthesis of what is thought and what is felt, the infinite certainly cannot be known in the sense that we have a sensuous perception if it. But no one wishes to demand a sensuous proof in verification of the infinite; spirit is for spirit alone".

manner, so that every change of position can be determined and [re]cognised on the basis of this law . . . From all these examples we may gather how, in thinking about things, we always seek what is fixed, persisting, and inwardly determined, and what governs the particular. This universal cannot be grasped by means of the senses, and it counts as what is essential and true.[72]

This, then, explains Hegel's incongruous-looking claim in the main passage we have been considering, that "the principles of ancient or modern philosophies, water, or matter, or atoms are *thoughts*, universals, ideal entities", when this may seem hard to square with the sort of *materialism* that Hegel is here referring to. The explanation for this claim, we can now see, is that even a materialist like Thales as well as a more modern materialist must agree that their conception of matter is not matter as it is given to us in experience (not just *empirical* water), and thus that "there is no truth in the sensible as such",[73] because "matter is itself already something abstract, something which cannot be perceived as such".[74] It is for this reason that Hegel believes that "[w]ith Thales we, properly speaking, first begin the history of Philosophy",[75] because Thales starts the process of looking for an explanation for the nature of finite existents while at the same time seeing that this explanation must go further than our "sensuous perception" in whatever "first principle" it comes up with, as nothing revealed to us by the senses can be "ultimate and absolute" in a way that is required to make this explanation satisfactory: "The simple proposition of Thales [that the principle of all things is water] therefore, is Philosophy, because in it water, though sensuous, is not looked at in its particularity as opposed to other natural things, but as Thought in which everything is resolved and comprehended".[76] Thales is therefore responsible for allowing "the world of

---

[72] Hegel, *Encyclopaedia Logic*, §21 addition, p. 53 (*Werke*, VIII, pp. 77–78). Cf. Hegel, *Lectures on the History of Philosophy*, III, p. 440 (cf. *Werke*, XX, p. 347): "The question of whether a completed sensuousness or the Notion is the higher may . . . be easily decided. For the laws of the heavens are not immediately perceived, but merely the change in position on the part of the stars. It is only when this object of immediate perception is laid hold of and brought under universal thought determinations that experience arises therefrom, which has a claim to validity for all time. The category which brings the unity of thought into the content of feeling is thus the objective element in experience, which receives thereby universality and necessity, while that which is perceived is rather the subjective and contingent".

[73] Hegel, *Encyclopaedia Logic*, §76, p. 122 (*Werke*, VIII, p. 166).

[74] Ibid., §38, p. 79 (*Werke*, VIII, p. 111).

[75] Hegel, *Lectures on the History of Philosophy*, I, p. 171 (*Werke*, XVIII, p. 195).

[76] Ibid., p. 179 (*Werke*, XVIII, p. 202).

Thought [*die Gedankenwelt*]" to be found, without which "there is as yet no pure unity".[77]

Now, while Hegel takes it to be characteristic of a classical philosopher like Thales to accept that his nonempirical conception of water is valid on purely theoretical grounds (because it provides a unifying form of explanation), he recognizes that in modern philosophy "the presupposition of the older metaphysics, namely, that what is true in things lies in thought"[78] has been radically questioned; in its place has come a kind of empiricist positivism, which trusts only experience to tell us about the world, and so treats as real only what is observable:

Ancient metaphysics had in this respect a higher conception of thinking than is current today. For it based itself on the fact that the knowledge of things obtained through thinking is alone what is really true in them, that is, things not in their immediacy but as first raised into the form of thought, as things *thought*. Thus this metaphysics believed that thinking (and its determinations) is not anything alien to the object, but rather is its essential nature, or that things and the thinking of them – our language too expresses their kinship – are explicitly in full agreement, thinking in its immanent determinations and the true nature of things forming one and the same content.

But *reflective* understanding took possession of philosophy.... Directed against reason, it behaves as ordinary common sense and imposes its view that truth rests on sensuous reality, that thoughts are *only* thoughts, meaning that it is sense perception which first gives them filling and reality and that reason left to its own resources engenders only figments of the brain. In this self-renunciation on the part of reason, the Notion of truth is lost; it is limited to knowing only subjective truth, phenomena, appearances, only something to which the nature of the object itself does not correspond: knowing has lapsed into opinion.[79]

[77] Ibid., p. 178 (*Werke*, XVIII, p. 203). Adorno may have had this passage from Hegel in mind when he wrote: "[I]n the thought of such early so-called anti-metaphysicians and materialists as Leucippus and Democritus, the *structure* of the metaphysical, of the absolute and final ground of explanation, is nevertheless preserved within their materialistic thought. If one calls these materialists *metaphysical* materialists, because matter for them is the ultimate ground of being, one does not entirely miss the mark" (Theodore W. Adorno, *Metaphysics: Concepts and Problems*, edited by Rolf Tiedemann, translated by Edmund Jephcott (Cambridge: Polity Press, 2000), p. 9).

[78] Hegel, *Encyclopaedia Logic*, §38 addition, p. 79 (*Werke*, VIII, p. 110); translation modified.

[79] Hegel, *Science of Logic*, pp. 45–66 (*Werke*, V, p. 38). Cf. also ibid., p. 160 (*Werke*, V, p. 178): "However, to call thought, spirit, God, *only* an ideal being, presupposes the standpoint from which finite being counts as real, and the ideal being of being-for-one has only a one-sided meaning"; ibid., p. 590 (*Werke* VI, p. 262): "Would one ever have thought that philosophy would deny truth to intelligible entities because they lack the spatial and temporal material of the sensuous world?"; ibid.,

In his work, Hegel treats Jacobi as a typical product of this modern turn, and uses him to illustrate its consequences. The basis on which Jacobi takes this turn is a hostility to any search for explanation of the sort that philosophy goes in for, which he fears leads into empty abstractions: as Jacobi famously puts it, "In my judgment the greatest service of the scientist is to unveil *existence*, and to reveal it.... Obsession with explanation makes us seek what is common to all things so passionately that we pay no attention to diversity in the process; we only want always to join together, whereas it would often be much more to our advantage to separate.... Moreover, in *joining* and *hanging* together only what is explainable in things, there also arises in the soul a certain lustre that blinds us more than it illuminates".[80] As a result of this fear of abstractionism, Hegel argues, Jacobi no longer treats our intellectual capacities as a source of knowledge, and instead prioritizes the "*faculty*

---

p. 707 (*Werke*, VI, p. 404): "A philosophizing that in its view of being does not rise above sense, naturally stops short at merely abstract thought, too, in its view of the Notion; such thought stands opposed to being"; *Encyclopaedia Logic*, §21, p. 52 (*Werke*, VIII, p. 76): "In §5 we mentioned the old belief that what is genuine in objects, [their] constitutions, or what happens to them, [i.e.,] what is inner, what is essential, and the matter that counts, is not to be found in consciousness immediately; that it cannot be what the first look or impression already offers us, but that we must first *think it over* in order to arrive at the genuine constitution of the object, and that by thinking it over this [goal] is indeed achieved"; ibid., §22 addition, p. 54 (*Werke*, VIII, p. 79): "...it has been the conviction of every age that what is substantial is only reached through the reworking of the immediate by our thinking about it. It has most notably been only in modern times, on the other hand, that doubts have been raised and the distinction between the products of our thinking and what things are in themselves has been insisted on... The sickness of our time, which has arrived at the point of despair, is the assumption that that our cognition is only subjective and that this is the last word about it"; Hegel, *Philosophy of Mind*, §465 addition, p. 224 (*Werke*, X, p. 286): "Those who have no conception of philosophy become speechless, it is true, when they hear the proposition that *Thought is Being*. None the less, underlying all our actions is the presupposition of the unity of Thought and Being. It is as rational, thinking beings that we make this presupposition... Pure thinking knows that it alone, and not feeling or representation, is capable of grasping the truth in things, and that the assertion of Epicurus that the true is what is sensed, must be pronounced a complete perversion of the nature of mind"; Hegel, "Aphorisms from the Wastebook", in Jon Stewart, ed., *Miscellaneous Writings of G. W. F. Hegel* (Evanston, IL: Northwestern University Press, 2002), p. 246 (*Werke*, II, p. 542): "The peasant woman lives within the circle of her Lisa, who is her best cow; then the black one, then the spotted one, and so on; also of Martin, her boy, and Ursula, her girl, etc. To the philosopher, infinity, knowledge, movement, empirical laws, etc. are things just as familiar".

[80] F. H. Jacobi, *Concerning the Doctrine of Spinoza in Letters to Herr Moses Mendelssohn*, in *The Main Philosophical Writings*, pp. 194–195.

of perception" over the *"faculty of reflection"*.[81] The consequence of this position, Hegel claims, is that Jacobi cannot do anything other than treat finite entities as "self-subsistent and grounded in themselves", because to offer any deeper explanation of them would require violating the "immediacy" of perception and going beyond "sensuous reality". Hegel therefore writes: "In this declaration ... Jacobi explicitly restricts faith and eternal verities to what is temporal and corporeal".[82] We can see, then, how Hegel might reasonably associate philosophy as he conceives it with idealism in his sense, and why he might think of Jacobi as illustrating the link between the abandonment of this idealism and the turn to nonphilosophy.[83]

Now, as a matter of interpretation, it might be said that Hegel's view of Jacobi here is rather curious: for, if one considers the *theological* side of Jacobi's position, Jacobi was no straightforward empiricist, as he recognized a *higher* faculty that gives us access to God as a supernatural entity – a faculty which Jacobi came to call "reason".[84] His claim was

---

[81] F. H. Jacobi, *Preface to David Hume on Faith*, in *The Main Philosophical Writings*, p. 541. Cf. also *David Hume on Faith*, in *The Main Philosophical Writings*, p. 303: "It follows that, with respect to all created beings, their rational cognition would have to be tested, ultimately, against their sensible one; the former must borrow its *validity* from the latter".

[82] Hegel, *Faith and Knowledge*, p. 139 (*Werke*, II, p. 379). Cf. also ibid., p. 169 (*Werke*, II, p. 410): "Jacobi reproaches the Kantian system for being a mishmash of idealism and empiricism. Of these two ingredients, however, it is not the empiricism, but the idealistic side, the side of infinity, which incurs his reproach. Although the side of infinity cannot win through to the perfection of the true nothing, still Jacobi cannot bear it because it endangers the absoluteness of the empirical ... "; and ibid., p. 125 (*Werke*, II, p. 363): "Jacobi becomes as abusive about the nullification of this empirical truth and of faith in sense-cognition [by Kant] as if it were an act of sacrilege or a temple robbery".

[83] A related diagnosis informs Hegel's discussion of scepticism, and in particular his contrast between ancient and modern scepticism: for whereas he saw the former as a prelude to philosophy in its *questioning* of experience as a source for knowledge, he saw the latter as a form of nonphilosophy, because it leaves experience *unquestioned*, and so abandons all attempts to go beyond it. See G. W. F. Hegel, "Relationship of Skepticism to Philosophy: Exposition of its Different Modifications and Comparison to the Latest Form with the Ancient One", trans. by H. S. Harris, in George di Giovanni and H. S. Harris, eds., *Between Kant and Hegel* (Albany: SUNY Press, 1985) (*Werke*, II, pp. 213–272). Cf. also Hegel, *Encyclopaedia Logic*, §39, p. 80 (*Werke*, VIII, p. 112): "In Humean scepticism, the *truth* of the empirical, the truth of feeling and intuition, is taken as basic; and, on that basis, he attacks all universal determinations and laws, precisely because they have no justification by way of sense-perception. The old scepticism was so far removed from making feeling, or intuition, into the principle of truth that it turned itself against the sensible in the very first place instead."

[84] Jacobi, *Preface to David Hume on Faith*, *Main Philosophical Writings*, p. 569.

that to get to an awareness of God, we could not use the *understanding*, which merely "hovers above the intuitions of the senses"[85] by looking for causal explanations in a way that cannot lead us to the unconditioned but only to an infinite regress: so while reason is akin to the senses in being immediate, it gives us access to a very different kind of being, one that is infinite rather than finite; and, in view of this, how can Hegel's characterisation of Jacobi as positing "the *finite* . . . as absolute" be considered appropriate?

It could be replied, however, that if there is a difficulty here, it is Jacobi's and not Hegel's. For, of course, Hegel was fully aware of this theological side to Jacobi's thinking, and was critical of it in its turn, in ways that need not concern us here. But the fact that this side of Jacobi's position is in tension with his attempt to give experience of ordinary objects priority over the "abstractions" of philosophy (for doesn't Jacobi's "reason" also threaten the store we set by that experience?)[86] does not show that Hegel is wrong to identify elements of empiricist "commonsensism" in Jacobi's thinking, even if these may seem to conflict with aspects of his theological position.[87]

We can now also understand the way in which Hegel compares his idealism to Kant's. On the one hand, Kant is an idealist in Hegel's sense, because he treats "things . . . in their sensuous individuality" as less than the full story about reality, and so goes beyond empiricism, which takes these things to be all that is real: "Critical Philosophy has in common with Empiricism that it accepts experience as the *only* basis for our cognitions; but it will not let them count as truths, but only as cognitions of appearances".[88] While this goes against "ordinary consciousness", which holds that what exists "can be perceived by the senses (e.g., this

---

[85] Ibid., p. 568.
[86] Cf. ibid., p. 569, where Jacobi talks of reason as a "different faculty of perception" from ordinary experience, which is a "spiritual eye" that gives us access to "spiritual objects"; but this does not tell us how it is these "spiritual objects" stand in relation to the "visible and tangible" ones, and thus how our faith in the latter can remain "immediate", once our "spiritual eye" is opened.
[87] Hegel himself seems to remark on this conflict when he notes that Jacobi speaks of faith (*Glaube*) in relation to God, but also in relation to our awareness of our bodies and outer objects (cf. Jacobi, *Concerning the Doctrine of Spinoza*, in *Main Philosophical Writings*, p. 231), and comments: "Hence the expression faith, which had a deep significance in religion, is made use of for different contents of every kind; this in our time is the point of view most commonly adopted" (Hegel, *Lectures on the History of Philosophy*, III, p. 419 (*Werke*, XX, p. 324)).
[88] Hegel, *Encyclopaedia Logic*, §40, p. 80 (*Werke*, VIII, p. 112). Cf. also Hegel, *Faith and Knowledge*, p. 103 (*Werke*, II, p. 341): " . . . Kant's most important result [as against Jacobi] will always remain this: these relations of the finite (whether they are relations within the sphere of the subject alone, or relations of things as well) are

animal, this star)" because "this appears to it as what subsists on its own account, or as what is independent", Hegel endorses Kant's position here, agreeing with what he takes to be the Kantian point, that "what can be perceived by the senses is really secondary and not self-standing". Now, against this view held by "ordinary consciousness", as we have seen, Hegel wants to argue that reality does not fully reveal itself to us in perception, but also requires us to use thought, which is able to arrive at a grasp of the "ideal entities" which constitute the "enduring and inwardly stable" basis of reality. According to Hegel, Kant was unable to take this second step of granting objective truth to such "ideal entities", because he held that "thoughts, although they are universal and necessary determinations, are still only *our* thoughts, and are cut off from what the thing is *in-itself* by an impassable gulf". Thus, while Kant recognized that thought was required in order to grasp the world as more than the "fleeting and transient" objects of experience, he did not accept that this thought gave us access to the world as such; he therefore did not recognize "the true objectivity of thinking . . . : that thoughts are not merely our thoughts, but at the same time the *In-itself* of things and of whatever else is objective".[89] To Hegel, therefore, Kant

nothing in themselves, and cognition in accordance with them is only a cognition of appearances, (even though it becomes absolute because it is not to be transcended)."

[89] Hegel, *Encyclopaedia Logic*, §41 addition, pp. 82–83 (*Werke*, VIII, pp. 115–116). Cf. also Hegel, *Philosophy of Nature*, §246 addition, I, pp. 200–201 (*Werke*, IX, p. 19), translation modified: "Intelligence does not of course familiarize itself with things in their sensuous existence. In that it thinks them, it sets their content within itself, and to practical ideality, which for itself is mere negativity, it adds form, universality so to speak, and so gives affirmative determination to the negative of particularity. This universality of things is not something subjective and belonging to us; it is, rather, the noumenon as opposed to the transient phenomenon, the truth, objectivity, and actual being of the things themselves. It resembles the platonic ideas, which do not have their being somewhere in the beyond, but which exist in individual things as substantial genera. Proteus will only be compelled into telling the truth if he is roughly handled, and we are not content with sensuous appearance. The inscription on the veil of Isis, 'I am what was, is, and shall be, and my veil has been lifted by no mortal', melts before thought"; G. W. F. Hegel, *Introduction to the Lectures on the History of Philosophy*, trans. by T. M. Knox and A. V. Miller (Oxford: Oxford University Press, 1985), p. 90 (*Einleitung in die Geschichte der Philosophie*, ed. by Johannes Hoffmeister (Hamberg: Meiner, 1940), p. 121): "A thought is the universal as such; even in nature we find thoughts present as its species and laws, and thus they are not merely present in the form of consciousness, but absolutely and therefore objectively. The reason of the world is not subjective reason. Thought is what is substantive and true, in comparison with the singular which is momentary, passing, and transient. Knowledge of the nature of thought removes the subjective mode of its appearance, and then this means that thought is not something particular, subjective, belonging to our consciousness merely, but is the universal, objective absolutely".

remains a merely subjective idealist, in contrast to his own objective idealism, because Kant is not prepared to treat "what is universal and necessary" as really anything more than "what is only thought by us", and so not as ultimately real.

If this is the view that Hegel's idealism leads to, however, isn't it still guilty of precritical extravagance, when set against the kind of epistemological and metaphysical outlook (of which Kant is part) which abandons "the presupposition of the older metaphysics, namely, that what is true in things lies in thought",[90] and so tries to go no further than the empirical phenomena?[91] In fact, however, Hegel would claim that in finding something in the classical tradition that still needs to be taken seriously, he was building on the real lesson to be learned from Kant (even if it was not learned by Kant himself). This is that there can be no workable distinction between "immediate" experience and "mediated" thought, as conceptualisation runs through *all* cognitively relevant levels, making it impossible for the empiricist to question our faith in thinking without ending up in total scepticism:[92] for to claim that we should not

---

[90] Cf. Pippin, "Hegel's Original Insight", p. 288, note 5: ". . . such an interpretation [of Hegel as a concept realist] still makes Hegel a fundamentally pre-critical philosopher, committed to the basic rationalist dream shattered by Kant. Hegel's many remarks about 'completing' the Kantian revolution, or celebrating the modern 'principles of subjectivity,' are very hard to understand on such a reading. It is as if Hegel simply missed the point, the massive, unavoidable point, of the *Critique of Pure Reason*".

[91] There is little indication that Hegel had any patience for appeals to modesty of this kind. Cf. Hegel, *Lectures on the History of Philosophy*, I, p. 277 (*Werke*, XVIII, p. 318): "It shows excessive humility of mind to believe that knowledge [*das Erkennen*] has no value; but Christ says, 'Are ye not better than the sparrows?', and we are so inasmuch as we are thinking; as sensuous we are as good or bad as sparrows"; and *Lectures on the History of Philosophy*, I, p. xliii (*Werke*, XVIII, pp. 13–14): "The love of truth, faith in the power of mind, is the first condition in Philosophy. Man, because he is Mind, should and must deem himself worthy of the highest; he cannot think too highly of the greatness and the power of his mind, and, with this belief, nothing will be so difficult and hard that it will not reveal itself to him. The Being of the universe, at first hidden and concealed, has no power which can offer resistance to the search for knowledge; it has to lay itself open before the seeker – to set before his eyes and give for his enjoyment, its riches and its depths".

[92] Cf. Hegel's claim against Jacobi, that the latter sets up an unworkable antithesis between immediacy and mediation: cf. *Encyclopaedia Logic*, §§65–67, pp. 114–116 (*Werke*, VIII, pp. 155–158), and *Lectures on the History of Philosophy*, III, p. 421 (*Werke*, XX, p. 328): "This opposition between immediacy and mediacy is thus a very barren and quite empty determination; it is a platitude of the extremest type to consider anything like this to be a true opposition; it proceeds from a most wooden understanding, which thinks that an immediacy can be something on its own account, without a mediation within itself".

trust our conceptual capacities when it comes to theorizing about the world is to imply that we should not trust our experience of it either, as Kant showed that these capacities are involved in the latter as much as in the former.[93] This interpretation, then, draws on the same line of argument as Pippin's Kantian one, which also recognizes (as we have seen) that "it is with the denial that a firm distinction can ever be usefully drawn between intuitional and conceptual elements in knowledge that distinctively Hegelian idealism begins"; but it takes this argument in a different direction, that attempts to do greater justice to the other important influence on Hegel, which is the classical tradition. Insofar as Kant himself points *beyond* empiricism, therefore, Hegel can claim not to have made a merely regressive move.[94]

Ameriks himself offers two objections to the kind of account of Hegel's idealism that I have offered. The first is that the implied difference from Kant is misleading,[95] a point that we cannot consider in the detail it requires here; and the second it that "[this] notion of idealism does not mark a contrast with traditional realism",[96] for while it holds that "what is true in things lies in thought", this does not

---

[93] Cf. *Encyclopaedia Logic*, §47, p. 90: " ... Kant himself makes cognition in general, and even *experience*, consist in the fact that our *perceptions* are thought, i.e. that the determinations which first belong to perception are *transformed* into thought-determinations" (*Werke*, VIII, p. 125). Cf. also *Encyclopaedia Logic*, §20 and §24 addition, pp. 51, 57–58 (*Werke*, VIII, p. 74, p. 83): "Kant employed the awkward expression, that I 'accompany' all my representations – and my sensations, desires, actions, etc., too... 'I' is the existence of the entirely *abstract* universality, the abstractly *free*. Therefore 'I' is *thinking* as the *subject*, and since at the same time I am in all my sensations, notions, states, etc., thought is present everywhere and pervades all these determinations as [their] category.... / In the 'I' there is a manifold inner and outer content, and, according to the way in which this content is constituted, we behave as sensing, representing, remembering, [beings], etc. But the 'I' is there in all of these, or, in other words, thinking is present everywhere. Thus man is always thinking, even when he simply intuits". This is arguably also the moral of Hegel's discussion of sense-certainty in the *Phenomenology*, where once again the target may plausibly be taken to be Jacobi's empiricism, which *per impossibile* tries to avoid all *comprehension* in favour of sheer *apprehension*: see Hegel, *Phenomenology of Spirit*, pp. 58–66 (*Werke*, III, pp. 82–92).

[94] Cf. Hegel, *Lectures on the History of Philosophy* III, p. 176 (*Werke*, XX, p. 79); translation modified: "The empirical is not merely an observing, hearing, feeling, etc., a perception of the individual; for it really sets to work to find the species, the universal, to discover laws. Now because it does this, it comes within the territory of the Notion – it begets what pertains to the region of the Idea.... The demand of *a priori* knowledge, which seems to imply that the Idea should construct from itself, is thus a reconstruction only".

[95] Ameriks, "Hegel and Idealism", pp. 394–395.

[96] Ibid., p. 395.

mean that things are mind-dependent, but that they are fundamentally constituted in a way that is accessible to thought rather than sense, by "universals, ideal entities, not things as they immediately present themselves to us". I do not see this second point as a difficulty, however: for why should any contrast be expected or required? To think that there must be a contrast between idealism and realism is to see idealism as having only its modern sense, according to which the former treats things as mind-dependent and the latter as mind-independent. But once it is recognized that idealism can also be understood in a more classical manner, where the disagreement is whether the world contains "ideal entities" (and thus with positivism and nominalism) and not whether the subject constitutes the world (and thus not with realism), we can see how Hegel could have quite properly called himself an idealist whilst remaining a realist, so no contrast need to be drawn here to make sense of his position in the way we have done.[97]

We have thus found two (related) senses in which Hegel is an idealist, and one in which he is a realist, and shown how these positions are compatible: he is an idealist in his special sense, of holding that the "finite is ideal", and (therefore) an idealist in the more classical (antinominalist) sense of holding that taken as mere finite individuals, things in the world cannot provide a satisfactory terminus for explanation, but only when they are seen to exemplify "universals, ideal entities" (in the manner of Thales' water onwards) which are not given in immediate experience, but only in "[reflective] thinking upon phenomena". Hegel's idealism, in other words, amounts to a form of *conceptual realism*, understood as "the belief that concepts are part of the structure of reality".[98] However, none of this implies that Hegel is an idealist in the modern (subjectivist) sense of claiming that the world is mind-dependent, for individuals can be understood as instantiations of such "universals, ideal entities", which then in turn explains how such

---

[97] In his later article, "Introduction: Interpreting German Idealism", p. 8, Ameriks himself seems to recognize the legitimacy of thinking of idealism in this way. For further discussion, see my *Hegel, Kant and the Structure of the Object* (London: Routledge, 1990), ch. 5.

[98] Michael Rosen, "From *Vorstellung* to Thought: Is a 'Non-Metaphysical' View of Hegel Possible?', in Dieter Henrich and Rolf-Peter Horstmann (eds), *Metaphysik nach Kant?* (Stuttgart: Klett-Cotta, 1988), pp. 248–262, at p. 262; reprinted in Robert Stern (ed.), *G. W. F. Hegel: Critical Assessments*, 4 vols. (London: Routledge, 1993), III, pp. 329–344, at p. 343. For further discussion of this way of taking Hegel's idealism, see Robert Stern, *Hegel, Kant and the Structure of the Object*, esp. ch. V, and the other papers collected in Robert Stern, *Hegelian Metaphysics* (Oxford: Oxford University Press, 2009).

individuals are accessible to minds, without the need for this subjectivist turn.[99] And I have also tried to suggest that this can be presented as more than just a reversion to a precritical outlook, in so far as the Kantian objection to the cogency of empiricism plays a vital role at a crucial point, albeit it in a way that Kant did not envisage and would no doubt have tried to resist – so this is a case of *"reculer pour mieux sauter"*, where the intention is not *just* to go back, but to go back *in order* also to get further, and go "beyond Kant" as well. In the end, therefore, we have arguably reached an account of Hegel's idealism that meets Ameriks' original desiderata, of being textually accurate, philosophically interesting, and not dubiously extravagant.[100]

[99] Cf. Hegel, *Science of Logic*, p. 51 (*Werke*, V, p. 45): "*Thought* is an expression which attributes the determinations contained therein primarily to consciousness. But inasmuch as it is said that understanding, reason, is in the objective world, that mind and nature have universal laws to which their life and changes conform, then it is conceded that the determinations of thought equally have objective value and existence"; Hegel, *Encyclopaedia Logic*, §24 addition, p. 57 (*Werke*, VIII, p. 82): "Just as thinking constitutes the substance of external things, so it is also the universal substance of what is spiritual... If we regard thinking as what is genuinely universal in everything natural and everything spiritual, too, then it overgrasps all of them and is the foundation of them all".

[100] I am grateful to David Bell, Fred Beiser, Paul Franks, Sebastian Gardner, Rolf-Peter Horstmann and James Kreines for very helpful comments on earlier versions of this paper. I would also like to acknowledge the support of the Arts and Humanities Research Council, for funding the research leave during which this paper was written.

7   Hegel and Hermeneutics

Hegel played a large role in the development of modern hermeneutics (or interpretation-theory), inheriting richly from its past (especially from Herder) and bequeathing copiously to its future (especially to Dilthey and Gadamer).

Certain of Hegel's contributions in this area concern what one might call the *scope and significance* of hermeneutics, and are, I think, of unquestionable validity and importance. In this connection, he in particular championed several ideas which were to some extent already in the air, but to which he lent a new force and influence. Among these ideas are the following: First, he plausibly identified as expressions of mind or meaning requiring interpretation not only linguistic texts and utterances, but also nonlinguistic arts (especially architecture, sculpture, painting, and instrumental music),[1] a broad set of social institutions and activities which he calls "objective mind," and individual actions. For these positions, see, for example, respectively, Hegel's *Aesthetics*, his *Encyclopaedia of the Philosophical Sciences*, and his *Lectures on the Philosophy of World History*. Subsequent hermeneutics has largely taken over this broadening of focus. For example, the mature Dilthey and Gadamer take the meaningfulness, and hence interpretability, of nonlinguistic art for granteds; Dilthey adopts a version of Hegel's conception of "objective mind" (explicitly singling this out as

---

[1] Much of the hermeneutical tradition before and even contemporaneous with Hegel tended to deny this: in particular, one side of Herder, who in the earlier parts of his *Critical Forests* had treated such arts as merely sensuous rather than meaningful; Kant, with his famous theory of the nonconceptual nature of beauty; and one side of Schleiermacher, who, despite his explicit project of developing hermeneutics into a universal discipline, generally excluded the nonlinguistic arts, instead treating them in a central strand of his *Aesthetics* lectures as merely sensuous rather than meaningful (just as Herder had done). On the other hand, Herder's mature position, which he began to develop in the later parts of his *Critical Forests*, Hamann's *Metacritique*, and a later strand in Schleiermacher's *Aesthetics* lectures did accord meaning to the nonlinguistic arts. So Hegel's position was by no means entirely without precedent here.

one of Hegel's most important contributions;[2] and Dilthey stresses that in addition to intentional expressions of mind and meaning (such as linguistic texts and utterances, artworks, and social institutions), there are also unintentional ones, especially people's actions, which consequently stand just as much in need of interpretation in order to be understood.[3]

Second, Hegel recognized that *history* is therefore a process which centrally involves expressions of mind and meaning, and that the historian must consequently deploy interpretation as his main tool.[4] Dilthey subsequently takes over this position of Hegel's. Accordingly, he praises Hegel in his *Die Jugendgeschichte Hegels* as a "founder of the history of the innerness of the human spirit,"[5] and he himself makes mind and its expressions the central subject matter of history, consequently identifying (psychology or later on) hermeneutics as the central method of the historian.[6]

Third, Hegel also recognized that the interpretation of historical others is essential for a proper *self*-understanding.[7] One reason for this is that it is only by comparing one's own outlook with the different outlooks of (historical) others that one can become fully cognizant of its character.[8] Another reason is that perceiving how one's own outlook has developed out of other outlooks which were its historical antecedents

---

[2] See, especially, W. Dilthey, *The Formation of the Historical World in the Human Sciences* (Princeton: Princeton University Press, 2002), p. 170 ff.

[3] See, especially, ibid., p. 226. Concerning some important later incarnations of this idea in Gadamer and in the anthropologist Geertz, see G. B. Madison, "Hermeneutics' Claim to Universality," in *The Philosophy of Hans-Georg Gadamer*, ed. by L. E. Hahn (Chicago, Open Court, 1997), p. 353.

[4] This position of Hegel's was not entirely without precedent, however. Voltaire and especially Herder had already argued for shifting the historian's focus away from traditional political–military history and toward the history of culture, and hence for according interpretation a central role in the discipline of history.

[5] W. Dilthey, *Gesammelte Schriften* (Leipzig/Berlin, Vandenhoeck and Ruprecht, 1914–), vol. 4, p. 157.

[6] See, for example, Dilthey, *The Formation of the Historical World in the Human Sciences*, esp. p. 299.

[7] This idea was again by no means entirely without precedent, but had its roots in Herder's "genetic method."

[8] See, for example, Hegel's 1808 speech "On Classical Studies," in G. W. F. Hegel, *Early Theological Writings* (Philadelphia, University of Pennsylvania Press, 1981), esp. pp. 327–328. For a helpful discussion of this idea, and of its centrality to Hegel's conception of culture [Bildung], see H.-G. Gadamer, *Truth and Method* (New York, Continuum, 1982), p. 13 ff.; cf. A. Berman, *L'épreuve de l'étranger* (Paris, Gallimard, 1984), ch. 3.

enables one to comprehend it more fully.[9] In one variant or another, this whole conception has remained central to hermeneutical thought since Hegel. For example, it reappears in Nietzsche's project of a "genealogy of morals" and in Foucault's of an "archaeology of knowledge."

In this chapter, I will not pursue these important Hegelian contributions concerning the scope and significance of hermeneutics any further, however. Instead, I would like to consider his ideas concerning the very nature of interpretation itself. For in this connection too he had ideas which exercised a very strong influence on the subsequent development of hermeneutics – though whether for good or ill in this case is a question which we will need to consider.

I

Two positions which were central to pre-Hegelian hermeneutics – by which I mean primarily the hermeneutics of Herder, as substantially continued by Hegel's famous contemporary Schleiermacher –[10] were the following:

> Position (1). Interpretation of a linguistic text or utterance is a matter of recovering an author's original meaning – which is something that had the character it did independently of whatever history, and, in particular, history of interpretation, may have taken place since. Because concepts, beliefs, and so forth vary from age to age, culture to culture, and even individual to individual in both subtle and not-so-subtle ways, this requires that the interpreter resist a constant temptation to assimilate the concepts and beliefs expressed by a text or utterance to his own (or to others with which he happens to be especially familiar). In particular, he should not assume that what is expressed will turn out to be true by his own lights. Instead, he normally

---

[9] This idea is especially prominent in Hegel's *Phenomenology of Spirit*. For a fuller discussion of both ideas as they appear in that work, see my *Hegel's Idea of a Phenomenology of Spirit* (Chicago, University of Chicago Press, 1998), pp. 430–446.

[10] I am here presupposing a somewhat unorthodox conception of Herder's leading role in developing hermeneutics in this period for which I have argued elsewhere. See especially my "Friedrich Daniel Ernst Schleiermacher," in *The Stanford Encyclopedia of Philosophy* (available online: http://plato.stanford.edu/entries/schleiermacher/); *J. G. Herder: Philosophical Writings* (Cambridge, Cambridge University Press, 2002), "Introduction"; and "Schleiermacher's Hermeneutics: Some Problems and Solutions," *Harvard Review of Philosophy*, 13 (2005).

needs to use a set of careful interpretive methods in order to arrive at an accurate understanding (e.g., careful scrutiny of the passages in which a particular word is used aimed at discerning the rule governing its use and hence its meaning).[11]

Position (2). Meaning consists in word-usage, and accordingly, thought essentially depends on (Schleiermacher would even say, albeit too strongly: is identical with) language. Therefore, to the extent that apparently nonlinguistic arts such as architecture, sculpture, painting, or instrumental music express meanings and thoughts, they must in fact do so in virtue of a prior *linguistic* articulation or articulability of those meanings and thoughts by the artist – so that interpretation of the meanings and thoughts in question must proceed via interpretation of the artist's language.[12]

A prominent strand of Hegel's thought rejected these two positions, however, and in doing so exercised an enormous influence on the subsequent course of hermeneutics – especially in Gadamer and Dilthey. Thus, as Gadamer points out and takes as his model in *Truth and Method*, a prominent strand in Hegel rejects position (1) in favor of a form of interpretation which (like that advocated by Gadamer himself) involves a significant measure of assimilation to the interpreter's own

---

[11] It should be mentioned that this fairly conventional picture of what interpretation is like for Herder and Schleiermacher has been subjected to certain challenges since Gadamer's ascription of such a picture to them, and attack upon it. In particular, Irmischer has attempted to retrieve a contrary, proto-Gadamerian picture of interpretation from some of Herder's texts (see H. D. Irmischer, "Grundzüge der Hermeneutik Herders," in *Bückeburger Gespräche über J.G. Herder 1971* (Bückeburg, Grimme, 1973)), and Frank has attempted to do something similar for Schleiermacher (see M. Frank, *Das individuelle Allgemeine* (Frankfurt am Main, Suhrkamp, 1985), especially later parts of the book). These attempts seem to me relatively implausible in exegetical terms (especially where Schleiermacher is concerned). But more importantly, their potential interest mainly derives from an assumption of the validity of Gadamer's own position which, as will become clear in this article, seems to me to be ill-grounded.

[12] This is the position at which Herder arrived in his maturest and best reflections on the subject, beginning in the later parts of the *Critical Forests*. It is also a position to which Schleiermacher was strongly attracted in his final reflections on the subject in his *Aesthetics* lectures. For a more detailed account of Herder's and Schleiermacher's (somewhat unstable) positions in this area, see my "Gods, Animals, and Artists: Some Problem Cases in Herder's Philosophy of Language," *Inquiry*, 46 (2003); "Hegel and Some (Near) Contemporaries: Narrow or Broad Expressivism?" in W. Welsch and K. Vieweg, eds., *Das Interesse des Denkens* (Munich, Wilhelm Fink Verlag, 2003); and "Schleiermacher's Hermeneutics: Some Problems and Solutions."

viewpoint, including the interpreter's own concepts and convictions.[13] For example, as Gadamer emphasizes,[14] Hegel supports such an alternative approach to interpretation when he writes in the "Religion" chapter of the *Phenomenology of Spirit* of 1807 concerning the transition from polytheistic Greek and Roman culture to the more modern standpoint of monotheistic Christianity:

The works of the Muse now lack the power of the Spirit, for the Spirit has gained its certainty of itself from the crushing of gods and men. They have become what they are for us now – beautiful fruit already picked from the tree, which a friendly Fate has offered us, as a girl might set the fruit before us. It cannot give us the actual life in which they existed, not the tree that bore them, not the earth and the elements which constituted their substance, not the climate which gave them their peculiar character, nor the cycle of the changing seasons that governed the process of their growth. So Fate does not restore their world to us along with the works of antique Art, it gives not the spring and summer of the ethical life in which they blossomed and ripened, but only the veiled recollection of that actual world. Our active enjoyment of them is therefore not an act of divine worship through which our consciousness might come to its perfect truth and fulfillment; it is an external activity – the wiping-off of some drops of rain or specks of dust from these fruits, so to speak – one which erects an intricate scaffolding of the dead elements of their outward existence – the language, the historical circumstances, etc. in the place of the inner elements of the ethical life which environed, created, and inspired them. And all this we do, not in order to enter into their very life but only to possess an idea of them in our imagination. But, just as the girl who offers us the plucked fruits is more than the Nature which directly provides them – the Nature diversified into their conditions and elements, the tree, air, light, and so on – because she sums all this up in a higher mode, in the gleam of her self-conscious eye and in the gesture with which she offers them, so, too, the Spirit of the Fate that presents us with those works of art is more than the ethical life and the actual world of that nation, for it is the *inwardizing* in us of the Spirit which in them was still [only] *outwardly* manifested; it is the Spirit of the tragic Fate which gathers all those individual gods and attributes of the [divine] substance

---

[13] Gadamer, *Truth and Method*, pp. 147–150. For Gadamer Hegel is thus an important forerunner and inspiration of such central principles of his own as that in interpretation the interpreter must effect a "fusion of horizons" (ibid., p. 273ff.), accept (a measure of) his own distinctive "prejudices" (ibid., p. 245ff.), and in particular assume that the interpreted text or utterance is true by his own lights (ibid., pp. 259–260, 264, 270–271). (Gadamer also believes there to be some important differences between his own position and Hegel's – for a helpful discussion of which, see P. Redding, *Hegel's Hermeneutics* (Cornell, Cornell University Press, 1996), esp. pp. 48–49.)

[14] *Truth and Method*, pp. 149–150.

into one pantheon, into the Spirit that is itself conscious of itself as Spirit.[15] (para. 753)

Moreover, as I have argued elsewhere,[16] the "Religion" chapter of the *Phenomenology of Spirit* is also striking for actually *implementing* an approach to interpretation which assimilates the interpreted material to Hegel's own standpoint. For example, in sharp contrast to the earlier "Unhappy Consciousness" section of the work, which had interpreted Christianity in a scrupulously non-assimilating way as a position that *failed* to recognize what Hegel believes to be God's identity with mankind, the "Religion" chapter instead interprets Christianity as a position that *expressed* the insight that God and mankind are identical.

Nor is such an alternative approach to interpretation by any means confined to later parts of the *Phenomenology of Spirit*: it is either theoretically espoused or implemented or both in many other Hegelian texts as well, including some of Hegel's earliest and some of his latest. For example, already in *The Life of Jesus* of early 1795, we find Hegel assuming that the standpoint of Kantian moral philosophy is basically correct,[17] and interpreting the Jesus of the gospels as expressing that standpoint as well. Again, in his 1802 essay *On the Nature of Philosophical Critique* Hegel advocates interpreting past philosophy in such a way as to maximize in the interpretation the recovery of what is correct or true by his own lights, and in other essays from the same period such as *Faith and Knowledge* he actually implements that interpretive approach. Finally, and most famously, Hegel's later lecture series on art, religion, and philosophy self-consciously employ such an approach as well.[18]

---

[15] G. W. F. Hegel, *Phenomenology of Spirit*, trans. by A. V. Miller (Oxford, Oxford University Press, 1979). I cite passages by means of Miller's helpful paragraph numbers.

[16] See my *Hegel's Idea of a Phenomenology of Spirit*, pp. 417–418.

[17] Hegel would of course soon afterwards give up this assumption.

[18] Some relevant methodological statements from the *Lectures on the Philosophy of Religion*: "These definite religions ... are included in ours as essential ... moments, which cannot miss having in them absolute truth. Therefore in them we have to do not with what is foreign to us, but with what is our own ... The thought of incarnation, for example, pervades every religion"; in interpreting the definite religions we must "recognize the meaning, the truth ... ; in short get to know what is *rational* in them ... We must do them this justice, for what is human, rational in them, is *our own*, too, although it exists in our higher consciousness as a moment only ... We look at these definite religions in accordance with the Concept [i.e., the principle of Hegel's own philosophy]" (*On Art, Religion, Philosophy*, ed. by J.G. Gray (New York, Harper Torchbooks, 1970), pp. 198–200).

Likewise, especially in his mature *Aesthetics* lectures, Hegel rejects position (2) in favor of a position according to which, while meaning and thought do indeed essentially depend on the possession of some suitable material-perceptible medium of expression or other,[19] this need not be language but, in certain cases, may be a different expressive medium, such as architecture (as in the case of the ancient Egyptians) or sculpture (as in the case of the ancient Greeks).[20] (To be a little more specific, Hegel's move to this position takes the less radical of two possible forms: he believes that in certain cases a person can, by using such alternative expressive media, express meanings and thoughts which *the person himself* cannot express linguistically, but he does not believe that the person can thereby express meanings and thoughts which are inexpressible by language *tout court*.[21])

This move has again had a major impact on the subsequent development of hermeneutics, especially in Dilthey. Until around 1900 Dilthey was strongly attracted to position (2). For example, he favors this position in "The Development of Hermeneutics" (1900), where he associates it with such predecessors as Schleiermacher and Preller.[22] However, in 1905 he wrote his classic study of the early Hegel, *Die Jugendgeschichte Hegels*, and apparently in the course of doing so fell under the influence of the alternative Hegelian position just described. For he henceforth treated not merely language but a broader class of "expressions" as fundamental to meaning and thought,[23] in particular, for example, arguing in his little essay *Musical Understanding* that instrumental music, while it does sometimes express linguistically articulable thoughts, in its highest forms also expresses thoughts which are *not* linguistically articulable.[24] Similarly, Gadamer generally seems inclined to reject position (2), and to accept instead a version of Hegel's alternative position.[25]

[19] See my "Hegel and Some (Near) Contemporaries: Narrow or Broad Expressivism?" pp. 168–170.
[20] See ibid., pp. 168–171.
[21] See ibid., p. 174 note 53.
[22] See "The Development of Hermeneutics," in *Dilthey's Selected Writings*, ed. by H. P. Rickman (Cambridge, Cambridge University Press, 1979), esp. pp. 248–249.
[23] See, for example, *The Formation of the Historical World in the Human Sciences*, pp. 168, 173, 230–231.
[24] See ibid., p. 245. Dilthey's position here is not a straightforward borrowing of Hegel's, however. For one thing, unlike Hegel, Dilthey seems attracted to the more radical version of the alternative position (that according to which the content expressed by a nonlinguistic medium is sometimes inexpressible by language *tout court*). For another thing, as we will see below, Hegel did not himself consider instrumental music a counterexample to principle (2).
[25] See especially Gadamer, *Truth and Method*, pp. 360–363; *Gesammelte Werke* (Tübingen, J.C.B. Mohr, 1993), vol. 8, pp. 4–5. Like much of the German tradition, however, Gadamer seems to vacillate on this question (concerning such

In short, a prominent strand of Hegel's thought rejected positions (1) and (2), and by doing so prepared the ground for the subsequent hermeneutical positions of Gadamer and Dilthey.

II

But are these two Hegelian turns in hermeneutics progress? As a prelude to addressing that question, it is worth noting that Hegel himself actually seems quite torn about them, that much of the time he himself instead seems inclined to stay *faithful* to positions (1) and (2).

Thus, counterbalancing the passages from later parts of the *Phenomenology of Spirit* which bespeak a rejection of position (1), there are earlier parts of the text which seem rather to bespeak its *acceptance*. For example, in a passage from the introduction which echoes Herder both conceptually and verbally, Hegel writes concerning the work's investigation into the history of shapes of consciousness: "We do not need to import standards [Maßstäbe], or to make use of our own bright ideas and thoughts during the course of the inquiry; it is precisely when we leave these aside that we succeed in contemplating the matter in hand as it is *in and for itself*" (para. 84).[26] And as I have already mentioned, while the work's late "Religion" chapter interprets Christianity in an assimilationist manner as expressing the Hegelian insight of God's identity with mankind, the earlier "Unhappy Consciousness" chapter on the contrary interprets Christianity in the spirit of position (1) as *failing* to recognize God's identity with mankind.[27]

Likewise, the other writings of Hegel's cited earlier which seem to bespeak a rejection of position (1) are counterbalanced by writings which seem rather to bespeak its acceptance. For example, as early as 1788 we find Hegel arguing that the ancients, and in particular the Greeks, had concepts different from ours, and that it is consequently one of

---

vacillations elsewhere in the German tradition, see my "Hegel and Some (Near) Contemporaries: Narrow or Broad Expressivism?" pp. 169–175). For example, in some passages he seems on the contrary to *favor* position (2) (e.g., *Truth and Method*, pp. 72–73, 360, 433), and indeed his frequent emphasis on the linguisticality of all understanding seems to commit him to doing so as well. Moreover, while the passages cited at the beginning of this note seem to support Hegel's moderate version of his alternative position, other passages seem to support the more radical alternative, namely that nonlinguistic art can sometimes express meanings and thoughts which are not linguistically expressible *at all* (e.g., ibid., pp. xii–xiii; *Gesammelte Werke*, vol. 8, p. 388).

[26] Cf. Redding, *Hegel's Hermeneutics*, pp. 81–82. Concerning the echoes of Herder in this passage, see my *Hegel's Idea of a Phenomenology of Spirit*, p. 414.

[27] See ibid., pp. 417–418.

the main advantages of learning their languages that we can thereby enrich our conceptual resources.[28] Again, unlike *The Life of Jesus*, the later parts of *The Positivity of the Christian Religion* from just shortly afterward are written very much in the spirit of position (1). For example, they emphasize the sharp *differences* between ancient Judeo-Christian moral and religious thought and what Hegel takes to be the correct moral-religious outlook, and they go to considerable interpretive pains to depict the former as it actually was. Again, the 1808 speech "On Classical Studies" stresses the importance of penetrating ancient Greek and Roman thought in its alienness to our own by means of a scrupulous study of the relevant languages and texts. Finally (and perhaps most strikingly), in a long and thoughtful review article from as late as 1826 on a work by Wilhelm von Humboldt,[29] Hegel shows great respect for two associates of the Herder–Schleiermacher tradition in hermeneutics, namely, von Humboldt himself and August Wilhelm Schlegel; Hegel strongly praises von Humboldt's approach of scrupulously going back to the ancient Indians' original texts and language in order to discover their outlook in its "distinctiveness [Eigentümlichkeit]," and of refusing to go beyond the strict sense of the original;[30] and Hegel himself mercilessly hunts down and rejects a series of false assimilations of ancient Indian concepts and beliefs to modern European ones.[31]

Similarly, counterbalancing Hegel's prominent rejection of position (2) in his *Aesthetics* lectures, there are several features of various Hegelian texts which seem rather to bespeak a *commitment* to position (2). For one thing, his earlier treatment of aesthetic matters in the *Phenomenology of Spirit* seems much more strongly *in favor* of position (2) than opposed to it. It is no doubt possible to read the short, cryptic statements concerning ancient architecture and sculpture near the start of the "Religion" chapter as already implying Hegel's later position concerning these artforms (namely, insofar as they seem to treat ancient architecture and sculpture as artforms which were nonlinguistic but which nonetheless at least in *some* way expressed religious facts not yet expressed or expressible in any other fashion). But the main

---

[28] See ibid., p. 360 note 2.
[29] *Rezension der Schrift "Über die unter dem Namen Bhagavad-Gita bekannte Episode des Mahabharata. Von Wilhelm von Humboldt,"* in G. W. F. Hegel, *Werke* (Frankfurt am Main, Suhrkamp, 1986), vol. 11.
[30] Ibid., pp. 132–133.
[31] Ibid., pp. 141, 184, 203, and so forth. There is, however, another side of Hegel's article which somewhat qualifies this whole strong identification with the existing hermeneutical tradition: a thesis to the effect that there is nonetheless *something* which all human minds share in common, namely our most general concepts (ibid., pp. 149, 184, 203).

thrust of the text is instead supportive of position (2).[32] Thus, to begin with some earlier parts of the text, Hegel's strategy of argument in the "Sense-certainty" chapter presupposes that thought essentially requires articulability in language (or by pointing). And in the "Physiognomy and Phrenology" section he writes even more explicitly that "although it is commonly said that reasonable men pay attention not to the word but to the thing itself, . . . this is at once incompetence and deceit, to fancy and to pretend that one merely has not the right *word*, and to hide from oneself that really one has failed to get hold of the thing itself, i.e. the concept. *If one had the concept, then one would also have the right word*" (para. 328; emphasis added).[33] Accordingly, when we reach the treatment of ancient Egyptian architecture and sculpture in the "Religion" chapter, Hegel seems to want to say that because these artforms lacked language, they were *not* really meaningful:

On account of the merely *abstract* intelligibleness of the form, the significance of the work is not in the work itself, is not the spiritual self. Thus either the works receive Spirit into them only as an alien, departed spirit that has forsaken its living saturation with reality and, being itself dead, takes up its abode in this lifeless crystal [i.e. the pyramid]; or they have an external relation to Spirit as something which is itself there externally and not as Spirit – they are related to it as to the dawning light, which casts its significance on them [i.e. the sun / Amun Ra] . . . But the work still lacks the shape and outer reality in which the self exists as self; it still does not in its own self proclaim that it includes within it an inner meaning, it lacks speech, the element in which the meaning filling it is itself present. Therefore the work, even when it is wholly purged of the animal element and wears only the shape of self-consciousness, is still the soundless shape which needs the rays of the rising sun in order to have sound which, generated by light, is even then merely noise and not speech, and reveals only an outer, not the inner, self . . . The soul of the statue in human shape does not yet come forth from the inner being, is not yet speech, the outer existence that is in its own self inward. (paras. 692–697; cf. paras. 697–698, 709–710, 713)

Nor is this tension merely one between the early Hegel and the late Hegel, for even the late Hegel is still at points strongly attracted to position (2). One symptom of this is the fact that within the *Aesthetics* lectures, although, as we have seen, he interprets certain nonlinguistic arts, namely, ancient architecture and sculpture, as counterexamples

---

[32] I am here modestly revising what now seems to me a hasty implication at "Hegel and Some (Near) Contemporaries: Narrow or Broad Expressivism?" pp. 172–173 that Hegel's position on this matter in the *Phenomenology of Spirit* is the same as his position in the *Aesthetics* lectures.

[33] Cf. "Hegel and Some (Near) Contemporaries: Narrow or Broad Expressivism?" p. 173.

to position (2), he instead interprets other nonlinguistic arts, namely, Christian-era painting and instrumental music, as *conforming* to position (2): to the extent that they express meaning or thought at all, this has a prior linguistic articulation or articulability.[34] To be a little more precise, sometimes in the *Aesthetics* lectures he commits himself to the naïve and untenable view that these two nonlinguistic arts simply do not express meanings or thoughts at all, but in more considered remarks he rather suggests that they do so (at least in some cases), but that the meanings and thoughts in question are parasitic on a prior linguistic articulation or articulability. This whole position can be seen from the text in two main ways: First, for Hegel, whereas ancient architecture and sculpture are paradigmatically "symbolic" and "classical" arts, respectively, Christian-era painting and music (along with poetry) are paradigmatically "romantic" arts. But according to Hegel "romantic" arts are grounded in, and express, the outlook of the Christian religion, i.e. an outlook whose primary expression is *linguistic*.[35] Second, Hegel's specific interpretive comments on Christian-era painting and instrumental music reinforce the moral that he understands whatever meanings and thoughts they express to have a prior linguistic articulation or articulability. To take painting first, that is certainly true of his interpretations of Christian religious painting. For example, when he interprets Raphael's controversial painting the *Transfiguration* he does so in terms of ideas from the bible, and indeed actually quotes from Matthew's gospel what he takes to be the central biblical text expressed in the painting: "Where two or three are gathered in my name, there am I in the midst of them."[36] But the same is also true of Hegel's interpretation of the other main category of painting on which he focuses: Dutch genre painting. Occasionally he treats this naively as lacking meanings and thoughts altogether, as *merely* imitative of the Dutch landscapes and other aspects of life which it depicts. However, in his more considered remarks he instead treats it as indeed expressing

---

[34] I do not mean to suggest that this striking asymmetry in Hegel's treatment of different nonlinguistic arts in the *Aesthetics* lectures in itself amounts to an inconsistency or that it is merely inadvertent. To say that *certain* nonlinguistic arts express content in an original way whereas *other* nonlinguistic arts only do so in a way that is parasitic on language is not inconsistent. Moreover, far from being inadvertent, this asymmetry plays an important systematic role for Hegel, constituting the foundation for his famous thesis of the end of art, that is, his famous thesis that art loses its importance in the modern period.

[35] See, for example, *Hegel's Aesthetics* (Oxford, Oxford University Press, 1998), p. 526.

[36] Ibid., p. 860.

meanings and thoughts but in such a way that they were ones which had a prior linguistic articulation or articulability, pointing out – very perceptively, I think – that Dutch genre painting does not in fact merely imitate, but also expresses such thought-imbued sentiments as the Dutch's pride in their hard-won political autonomy, in their hard-won religious autonomy (Protestantism), and in a landscape which is largely their own creation.[37] Similarly: Hegel sometimes naively thinks of instrumental music as not expressing meanings or thoughts at all but only contentless subjectivity or feeling[38] – whatever meanings or thoughts it may cause to occur being caused to occur only accidentally.[39] But in more considered remarks he instead implies that it sometimes does, and moreover ought to, convey meanings and thoughts (albeit vaguely), and he evidently understands the meanings and thoughts in question to be ones which were already linguistically expressed or expressible by the composer rather than a monopoly of the instrumental music in question.[40]

Moreover, in an even stronger late commitment to position (2), Hegel in his *Encyclopaedia* repeats the claim of thought's essential dependence on language which we recently saw him committed to in the *Phenomenology of Spirit*:

It is in names that we *think* ... We ... only have determinate, genuine thoughts when we give them the form of objectivity, of being distinguished from inwardness, i.e. the form of externality, and indeed of such an externality as at the same time bears the imprint of the greatest inwardness. Only *the articulated sound*, the *word*, is such an inward external thing. To want to think without words, as Mesmer once tried to, is therefore clearly an absurdity ... The inexpressible is in truth only something dark, fermenting, which only achieves clarity when it is able to attain verbal expression.[41] (para. 462, Zusatz)

---

[37] See, for example, ibid., pp. 597–600. It is some measure of Hegel's perceptiveness here that even such a great modern art historian as Panofsky, who is normally anything but reluctant to find meanings and thoughts expressed in paintings, implausibly denies them to this sort of painting (E. Panofsky, *Meaning in the Visual Arts* (Chicago, University of Chicago Press, 1982), p. 32).

[38] See, for example, *Hegel's Aesthetics*, pp. 28, 626, 891–894.

[39] Ibid., pp. 899–900.

[40] Ibid., pp. 902, 932, 954. Passages such as these show that readings of Hegel's position on instrumental music which emphasize his conception of it as contentless – for example, E. Hanslick, *On the Musically Beautiful* (Indianapolis, Hackett, 1986), pp. 77, 83, and P. Moos, *Die Philosophie der Musik von Kant bis E. v. Hartmann* (Berlin, 1902), pp. 148–149 – tell only half of the story.

[41] Cf. my "Hegel and Some (Near) Contemporaries: Narrow or Broad Expressivism?" p. 173.

In short, a significant heretical side of Hegel both begins and remains strongly inclined to stay *faithful* to positions (1) and (2).

III

Now it may just possibly be the case that Hegel has ways of reconciling these apparent conflicts in his position. For example, concerning the apparent conflict between rejection of and commitment to position (1) in the *Phenomenology of Spirit*, I have argued elsewhere that this conflict is probably only apparent rather than real – due to a transition that occurs within the text between significantly different theoretical contexts which require different concepts of meaning and, accordingly, different approaches to interpretation.[42] And in his 1826 review article on von Humboldt, Hegel himself develops another potential strategy of reconciliation (one which may be compatible with that just mentioned): To recast his idea slightly in terms of a modern distinction of Frege's, he in effect suggests that interpretation in conformity with position (1) is what is needed in order to specify people's *meanings*, but that an assimilating sort of interpretation which violates position (1) is what is needed in order to specify their underlying *referents* (i.e., the features of reality which they are trying to express, however inadequately).[43] Again, one author who has noted a version of Hegel's apparently conflicting commitment to and rejection of position (2) within the *Phenomenology of Spirit* has attempted to provide a systematic reconciliation for this case too.[44]

However, I will leave this question aside here, since it is likely to be of more interest to Hegel scholars than to more general readers. Instead, I would like to consider the (prima facie) conflicts simply as such, and say something toward their adjudication.

IV

It seems to me that positions (1) and (2) are in fact basically correct, and that the prominent strand in Hegel and (under his influence) subsequent hermeneutics which attacks them is misguided.

Consider first position (1). It is not altogether easy to discern Hegel's reasons for rejecting this position in favor of interpreting viewpoints from the past in a way which assimilates them to his own concepts and

---

[42] *Hegel's Idea of a Phenomenology of Spirit*, pp. 418–419.
[43] *Rezension der Schrift "Über die unter dem Namen Bhagavad-Gita bekannte Episode des Mahabharata. Von Wilhelm von Humboldt,"* p. 184.
[44] S. Hahn, "Hegel on Saying and Showing," *Journal of Value Inquiry*, 28:2 (1994).

principles, but I would suggest that the following three considerations all play important roles for him:

Argument (a). One line of argument which seems prominent in *On the Nature of Philosophical Critique* and the *Phenomenology of Spirit* is essentially this: It turns out, Hegel believes, that when one interprets non-Hegelian views in the scrupulous manner of position (1), they all prove to be implicitly self-contradictory (indeed, at the fundamental level of their very concepts, or the very perspectives – the very "shapes of consciousness" – within which they are articulated); that only Hegel's own viewpoint is self-consistent, and that it alone proves to be justified and true. Once this has been shown, further interpretation of non-Hegelian views in the manner of position (1) consequently seems rather pointless; it now seems more fruitful to try to interpret them in a charitable manner which aims to maximize the recovery of Hegel's own standpoint from them.[45]

Argument (b). A second, closely related, line of argument is this: History, including in particular the history of expressions of meaning and thought (in art, religion, and philosophy), can ultimately be seen to have been teleological in character, to have been aiming at the achievement of the standpoint of Hegelian philosophy in the modern world, a standpoint which (in contrast to those which preceded it) is at last self-consistent, justified, and true. This implicit teleology again warrants interpreting views from the past as attempts to express the standpoint of Hegelian philosophy.

Argument (c). A further and quite different line of argument is this: As I have explained in more detail elsewhere,[46] Hegel takes the novel and radical position that mental states in general, including states of meaning in particular, are constituted by physical behavior, but in an open-ended way such that as long as a person is still alive and so can engage in further behavior he can continue to modify even his "past" mental states or states of meaning (which is why in the *Phenomenology of Spirit* Hegel writes approvingly of "Solon, who thought he could only know [someone's particular individuality] from and after the course of the whole life" [para. 315], and makes the corresponding point concerning the supra-individual absolute mind that "of the Absolute it must be said that it is essentially a *result*, that

---

45 Cf. my *Hegel's Idea of a Phenomenology of Spirit*, pp. 418–419.
46 See ibid., pp. 93–102.

only in the *end* is it what it truly is" [para. 20]). Also, as I have again explained elsewhere,[47] Hegel takes the further position that meaning is essentially *social*, that it is of its very nature constituted by the linguistic behavior not merely of an individual but of a whole community or communal tradition. Now if one puts these two positions together, they seem to imply that as long as the relevant community or communal tradition continues to exist, even the meanings of a dead individual from the past are going to be subject to modification by that community or communal tradition. So I would suggest that this is a further line of argument which inclines Hegel to a rejection of position (1) in favor of his contrary proto-Gadamerian position concerning interpretation.

Now a first point to note here is that it is by no means clear that these arguments are consistent with each other. In particular, arguments (a) and (b) seem to imply that there *is* such a thing as the sort of original meaning aimed at by the interpretive method of position (1) (the problem being merely that it always turns out to be saying something self-contradictory, unjustified, and untrue) whereas argument (c) seems to imply that there is *not*. However, since each of the arguments also faces independent problems, I will not pursue this problem of mutual inconsistency any further here.

None of the arguments seems to me compelling in the end. The plausibility of argument (a) depends on the plausibility of Hegel's attempts in his *Logic* and his *Phenomenology of Spirit* to demonstrate that all non-Hegelian concepts or all non-Hegelian "shapes of consciousness" are implicitly self-contradictory. But surely, only the most hardbitten and uncritical of Hegelians would want to claim that those attempts are successful. It seems very unlikely indeed that all non-Hegelian views (or indeed, all non-*anything* views) are afflicted with implicit inconsistency.

Argument (b) fares no better. For it is surely in the end quite implausible to suppose that it is the case, let alone that Hegel has shown it to be the case, that the whole of human history, including in particular the whole history of thought, has been teleologically directed at the attainment of Hegelian philosophy in the modern world (or indeed, at the attainment of any other modern viewpoint for that matter). Hegel's attempt to prove that it has rests on two main pillars: first, his demonstration of the standpoint of his mature *Logic* by means of the *Phenomenology of Spirit* and by means of the internal argument of the

[47] Ibid., p. 205ff.

Logic itself; and second, his demonstration in his later lecture series on art, religion, and philosophy that the viewpoints which have arisen in these several areas of culture over the course of past history can plausibly be interpreted as progressively more and more adequate expressions of that standpoint. But it would be implausible to suggest that either of these pillars stands up to critical scrutiny in the end.

Nor, I think, does argument (c) work. One way in which to see why not is to excavate one of the lines of thought which probably led Hegel to embrace his radical open-ended behaviorist conception of the mind and meaning in the first place.[48] Hegel's predecessor Herder had conceived mental states, including states of meaning, as "forces [Kräfte]," which he conceived in a realist manner as underlying conditions apt for producing certain patterns of behavior (not in an antirealist manner as simply reducible to those patterns). However, Hegel in his early *Logic, Metaphysics, and Nature Philosophy*, and then again more famously in the "Force and Understanding" chapter of the *Phenomenology of Spirit*, subjected such a realist conception of force to a critique which led him to reconceive force in antirealist terms. Implicitly retaining Herder's generic conception of mental states, including states of meaning, as forces, but now reconceiving the latter in this antirealist manner, left Hegel with his open-ended behaviorist theory.

Now the important thing to note here is that if Hegel's arguments against the realist conception of force can be satisfactorily answered (as I will not try to argue here but assume they can), then the Herderian position has plausible resources for undermining both Hegel's open-ended behaviorism and his social theory of meaning, and hence for undermining argument (c) in two ways.

First, it promises to undermine Hegel's open-ended behaviorism by providing an attractive contrary theory that mental states, including states of meaning, are *underlying conditions* apt for producing patterns of behavior, conditions which moreover may very well *occur determinately at specific times within* an individual's life.

But second, it also promises to undermine Hegel's argument for his social theory of meaning. That argument, which he develops in the *Phenomenology of Spirit*, takes the form of attempting to show that none of the various ways in which one might try to validate our commonsense intuition that meaning is something which could in principle be purely individual, and which can be achieved determinately by an individual at a particular point within his life, is defensible.[49] Herder's conception of states of meaning as realist "forces" promises to undermine

---

[48] For a more detailed treatment of this subject, see ibid., ch. 2 and p. 338 note 109.
[49] For an account of this argument, see ibid., p. 207ff.

that argument by showing how meaning *could* be a purely individual achievement, and moreover one achieved determinately at a particular point within the individual's life.[50]

Furthermore, note that the Herderian conception of mental states and states of meaning as realist "forces" has several compelling intuitive advantages over Hegel's alternative conception of them: Unlike Hegel's conception, Herder's can make sense of strong commonsense intuitions we have that people are often in mental states which happen to receive no behavioral expression at all that the fact of being in a mental state is constituted solely by something that happens at the time to which we assign it (not in addition by future behavior); that a mental state is often the cause of corresponding behavior (not merely constituted by it); that there could, in principle, very well be purely individual acts of meaning, for example if a cosmic Robinson Crusoe were to start keeping track of his goats by developing a system of chalk marks on his cave wall signifying the goats and their numbers; and that what a person meant is a fact constituted solely by what happened at the time to which we assign his having done so (not in addition by his own future behavior and that of a community or communal tradition to which he belongs).

In short, it seems to me likely that argument (c) breaks down at two key points, and moreover for reasons which one of the champions of position (1) in the previous hermeneutical tradition, namely, Herder, had essentially already supplied.

However, it may also be worth considering Gadamer's arguments for rejecting position (1), since these turn out to be significantly different from Hegel's. As far as I can see, Gadamer offers four main arguments, as follows:[51]

> Argument (a). Both in the case of the arts and in the case of linguistic texts and utterances, interpretations change over time, and these changing interpretations are internal to the meaning of the

---

[50] For a fuller statement of what is essentially the same philosophical point, see my *Wittgenstein on the Arbitrariness of Grammar* (Princeton, Princeton University Press, 2004), ch. 4, where I invoke a realist conception of *dispositions* very similar to Herder's realist conception of forces in order to defeat Wittgenstein's much more famous analogue of Hegel's argument.

[51] I do not consider to be, and therefore will not treat as, arguments a large family of Gadamerian urgings that we should assimilate interpretation (in the sense of achieving an accurate understanding of a text, utterance, or whatnot) to various other sorts of activities from which, prima facie at least, it is in fact essentially and crucially different – in particular, the re-presentation of a work of (theatrical or musical) art; legal "interpretation"; textual *explication* and *application*; conversation aimed at achieving agreement; and translation into another language.

art, text, or utterance in question, so that there is no such thing
as an original meaning independent of these changing interpretations.[52]

Argument (b). The original meaning of artistic or linguistic expressions from the past is always strictly speaking unknowable by
us due to the essential role in all understanding of a historically
specific form of "pre-understanding" or "prejudice" which one
can never entirely escape.[53]

Argument (c). The original meaning is something "dead," something no longer of any possible interest to us.[54]

Argument (d). *All* knowledge is historically relative, so interpretive
knowledge is so in particular.[55]

Now a first point to note about this whole case is that arguments (a)–
(c) seem to be inconsistent with each other: argument (a) seems to say
that there is no such thing as an "original meaning" whereas arguments
(b) and (c) seem to say that there is (but that it is unknowable and "dead");
argument (b) seems to say that it is unknowable whereas argument (c)
seems to imply that it is knowable (but "dead," of no possible interest to
us). However, Gadamer might perhaps be able to cope with this problem
by recasting these three arguments in the form: there is no such thing as
an "original meaning" . . . ; moreover, even if there were, we could not
know it . . . ; and furthermore, even if we could know it, it could be of
no possible interest to us . . . .[56] And as we will see, the arguments face
independent problems. So I will not dwell further on this problem of
mutual inconsistency, but will instead consider each of the arguments
separately.

Argument (a) seems to be implicitly incoherent: Consider the case
of texts, for example. To say that interpretations of a text change over
time is presumably to say, roughly, that the author of the text meant
something in particular, that there then arose an interpretation A which
meant something a bit different from that, that there then arose a
further interpretation B which meant something a bit different again,

---

[52] See, for example, *Truth and Method*, pp. 304, 350.

[53] See, for example, ibid., p. 218ff., 261, 269, 235–274. Also *Gesammelte Werke*, vol. 2,
p. 475; vol. 8, p. 377.

[54] See, for example, *Truth and Method*, p. 149; cf. *Gesammelte Werke*, vol. 8, p. 377
(where Gadamer alludes revealingly to Nietzsche's famous argument along similar
lines).

[55] See, for example, *Truth and Method*, pp. 175, 203ff.

[56] Cf. Gorgias's treatise *Concerning Nature or What is Not*: there is nothing; even
if there were, one could not know about it; even if one could know about it, one
could not communicate that knowledge to anyone else.

and so on. In other words, the very notion of changing interpretations seems to *presuppose* an original meaning (indeed, a whole *series* of original meanings, one belonging to the text, and then one belonging to each of its subsequent interpretations).[57] Moreover, as far as I can see, Gadamer offers no real argument for his very counterintuitive claim that subsequent (re)interpretations are internal to an author's meaning in the first place. In particular, the mere facts that (re)interpretations occur, and that authors often anticipate and even welcome this, by no means suffice to show this.

Argument (b) runs into an epistemological problem: If one is always locked into a modifying pre-understanding, then how can one possibly *know* that other perspectives which are being modified exist? (In one formulation of his position which especially prompts this sort of objection, Gadamer writes that "the discovery of the historical horizon is always already a fusion of horizons."[58]) Moreover, as I have argued elsewhere, this sort of epistemological problem eventually leads to a conceptual problem as well: a problem about whether in that case it even makes *sense* to speak of such perspectives.[59] Furthermore, Gadamer's assumption that pre-understanding is internal to understanding and that it is always insurmountably historically specific seems very questionable to begin with. One possible objection to it, which many contemporary Anglophone philosophers would be likely to find attractive, is that the notion that pre-understanding is internal to understanding violates an antipsychologistic insight concerning meaning and understanding which we owe to Frege and Wittgenstein.[60] However, I believe that one

---

[57] Gadamer's strange suggestion at one point that the interpreter's contribution always gets reabsorbed into the meaning and so vanishes (*Truth and Method*, pp. 430–431) seems to be a symptom of this incoherence in his position. What he is really trying to say here is that there both is and is not a reinterpretation involved, but he masks this contradiction from himself and his readers by casting it in the more picturesque and less transparently self-contradictory metaphorical form of a process of precipitation followed by reabsorption.

[58] *Gesammelte Werke*, vol. 2, p. 475. For a fuller development of this sort of objection against a relevantly similar position of Wittgenstein's, see my *Wittgenstein on the Arbitrariness of Grammar*, ch. 7.

[59] See ibid. The argument is complicated, so I will not go into it here.

[60] Gadamer would no doubt reject the characterization of his theory of pre-understanding as "psychologistic," on the ground that pre-understanding is rather a feature of a deeper Husserlian life-world or Heideggerian *Dasein*, or what not. Indeed, at one point he himself expresses sympathy with a *form* of antipsychologism, namely Husserl's (*Gesammelte Werke*, vol. 2, p. 197). However, it could plausibly be argued that the sort of antipsychologism which we owe to Frege and Wittgenstein conflicts not only with seeing run-of-the-mill psychological processes (e.g., having sensations or images) as internal to meaning and understanding, but

should be skeptical about this antipsychologism.[61] So it is not on *this* ground that I would question Gadamer's assumption. Instead, I would suggest that what is wrong with it is its implication that it is impossible to abstract from one's own pre-understanding and recapture the pre-understanding of a historical other. Indeed, I would suggest that Herder's conception of the essential role of *Einfühlung* in the interpretation of texts from the past already quite properly pointed toward an ability which we possess to perform just this sort of imaginative feat, and to the essential contribution which exercising this ability makes to our achievement of an exact understanding of past texts' original meanings.[62]

Argument (c) is perhaps the weakest part of Gadamer's case. Far from inevitably being "dead," or of no possible interest to us, the original meanings of texts and utterances from the past, and from contemporary "others," can be of *great* interest to us, and for *many* different reasons. One reason (which Herder and Dilthey both already properly stress) is simply that discovering such meanings satisfies our curiosity and enriches our experience. Another reason (again already important to Herder) is that such discoveries both express and promote respect and sympathy for "others." Another reason (again already dear to Herder) is that it is reasonable to hope that such discoveries will acquaint us with concepts, convictions, values, techniques, and so on which help us to improve our own in various ways. Another reason (again one already important for Herder and Dilthey, but also, as I mentioned earlier, for Hegel) is that such discoveries promise to make essential contributions toward our *self*-understanding, both by enabling us to situate our own perspective in a comparative context and by enabling us to understand how it arose. And no doubt there are further good reasons as well.

Finally, argument (d) does not seem compelling either. One problem with it lies in the well-known fact that the thesis of relativism seems to run into problems of self-contradiction in connection with the question of whether this thesis is *itself* of merely relative validity. Gadamer touches on this problem at various points, but his answers to it are naïve and unconvincing: At one point he concedes that a self-contradiction arises, but responds that this merely shows the

also with seeing Gadamerian pre-understanding as internal to meaning and understanding.

[61] For a little discussion of this matter, see my "Herder's Philosophy of Language, Interpretation, and Translation: Three Fundamental Principles," pp. 354–356.

[62] For more about this, see ibid., and also my "Herder's Importance as a Philosopher," in *Von der Logik zur Sprache*, ed. by R. Bubner and G. Hindrichs (Stuttgart: Fromann-Holzboog, 2007).

weakness of the sort of "reflection" that reveals this and objects to it![63] At another point he argues that the thesis of relativism is not a "proposition" but merely something of which one has "consciousness," so that it and its own subject matter are "not at all on the same logical level."[64] But surely the alleged fact that what is involved is merely a consciousness that relativism is true, rather than, say, an outright assertion that it is true, would not diminish either the fact or the unacceptability of the self-contradiction one whit.[65] Another problem with argument (d) is that, contrary to Gadamer's evident intention to hold that meaning's relativity makes it distinctive vis à vis other subject matters, and hence resistant to the sorts of methods which can legitimately be used in connection with them, in particular the "positivist" or objectivity-presupposing methods of the natural sciences, this argument would leave meaning *no less (if also no more) objective than anything else.*

In short, it seems to me that neither Hegel nor Gadamer has provided us with any compelling argument against position (1).

V

Let us turn now to position (2). As was mentioned earlier, in his *Aesthetics* lectures Hegel treats ancient Egyptian architecture and ancient Greek sculpture as counterexamples to this position, as expressions of meanings and thoughts which were not yet expressible by the artists in question in any other way, and in particular not in a linguistic way. However, as was also mentioned, Hegel in the very same lectures interprets other nonlinguistic arts, in particular the painting and instrumental music of the Christian era, as *conforming* to position (2), as expressing whatever meanings and thoughts they express in a way that is parasitic on a prior linguistic articulation or articulability. Now it seems to me that the former side of this whole account is implausible, but that the latter side is plausible, so that, to this extent at least, position (2) in the end appears more plausible than its rejection. Let me say something to justify each half of this assessment in turn.

Consider, to begin with, the side of Hegel's account which *conflicts* with position (2). To repeat, this side of his account mainly appeals to

---

[63] *Truth and Method*, pp. 308–309.

[64] Ibid., pp. 406–407.

[65] For a discussion of a broader range of possible relativist positions and an explanation of what is wrong with each of them, see my "Hegelian versus Kantian Interpretations of Pyrrhonism: Revolution or Reaction?" (long version forthcoming).

two cases, namely, the architecture of the ancient Egyptians and the sculpture of the ancient Greeks; in sharp contrast, his intuitions about later painting and instrumental music conform to position (2). Now it should, I suggest, immediately arouse one's suspicion here that it is the older materials, for which his knowledge of relevant linguistic, textual, cultural, and biographical context is naturally thinner, which receive the former treatment, whereas the more recent materials, for which his knowledge of such context is naturally richer, receive the latter. That is to say, it seems reasonable to suspect that whereas his assessment of the more recent materials as conforming to position (2) is evidentially well-grounded, his assessment of the ancient materials as incompatible with position (2), his denial of a linguistic or textual basis to the meanings and thoughts which they express, is merely a result of his relative ignorance of relevant evidence.

That general suspicion is, I think, borne out by closer scrutiny of his account. Consider, first, the case of ancient Egyptian architecture. It does seem beyond serious doubt that this expressed religious meanings and thoughts, as Hegel believes (though whether, as he also believes, the thoughts in question were *true* ones is of course quite another matter). But why should one take the meanings or thoughts in question to have been linguistically unexpressed and inexpressible by the Egyptians rather than linguistically expressed or expressible by them? Is Hegel's inclination to do so not simply an error resulting from the fact that in his day people did not yet have the means to identify the Egyptians' linguistic expressions of, or linguistic means for expressing, the meanings or thoughts in question because Egyptian hieroglyphics had not yet been properly deciphered, nor Egyptology yet established as a proper academic discipline?[66] In other words, Hegel seems simply to have misinterpreted the real situation that the buildings in question clearly expressed religious meanings and thoughts *but he happens not to know any Egyptian linguistic expressions of, or linguistic means for expressing, these due to his lack of relevant information* as a situation in which the buildings in question clearly expressed religious meanings and thoughts *but these were not linguistically expressed or expressible by the Egyptians.*[67]

---

[66] Champollion first deciphered Egyptian hieroglyphics in the 1820s, the decade in which Hegel delivered his *Aesthetics* lectures, but really only published the results in 1832 in his *Grammaire égyptienne* and *Dictionnaire égyptien*. Academic Egyptology really only began after Richard Lepsius's expedition of 1842.

[67] Cf. Bungay, *Beauty and Truth* (Oxford, Oxford University Press, 1984), p. 102. Bungay offers a similar diagnosis of Hegel's general inclination to see the Egyptians as intrinsically mysterious, but does not bring this general point to bear on the more specific issue with which I am concerned here.

What about Greek sculpture? *Prima facie* at least, one would surely think that the salient point to make here was one which Herder had already made forcefully and repeatedly, namely, that Greek sculpture was deeply grounded in, and expressive of, ideas from Greek poetry and myth, that is, ideas which were already *linguistically* expressible, and indeed expressed – so that the case of Greek sculpture conforms well with position (2).[68]

Hegel's contrary assessment of Greek sculpture rests on his judgment that it was the Greeks' *highest* expression of the Absolute, that it expressed something about the Absolute which no other area of Greek culture, and in particular no *linguistic* area of Greek culture, yet expressed or was able to express (at least, not as clearly). What was this something? Hegel's answer is not exactly obvious from his texts, but it seems to be that Greek sculpture already expressed *God's identity with mankind,*[69] and that in this way it already anticipated Christianity's subsequent more explicit, linguistic expression of such an identity.[70] This is an important part of the force of his remark that Greek "sculpture . . . individualizes the character of the gods into an entirely specific human form and perfects the anthropomorphism of the classical Ideal,"[71] and also of his frequent characterization of Greek sculpture as combining *universality* with *individuality* – which in essential part means: divinity with humanity.

However, it seems to me that this Hegelian interpretation of Greek sculpture again proves to be quite dubious on closer inspection. There are two main problems with it (standing in mild tension with each

---

[68] Concerning Herder's statements of this position, see my "Gods, Animals, and Artists: Some Problem Cases in Herder's Philosophy of Language," pp. 78, 91 note 72.

[69] Not merely God's qualitative *similarity* with mankind, note. In Hegel's view, *that* was something which had already been well expressed by other areas of Greek culture besides sculpture, for example, by poetry. Thus already in his early theological writings he had emphasized that traditional Greek poetry and myth had already expressed the gods' qualitative similarity with men (in contrast to at least a prominent strand of the subsequent Judeo-Christian tradition, which instead stressed God's qualitative dissimilarity with men).

[70] See, for example, *Hegel's Aesthetics,* p. 435. Strictly speaking, Hegel's position must, I think, be a little more complicated. It could be objected to the position which I have just attributed to him that even if the Greeks had not yet linguistically *expressed* such an identity, such an identity was surely at least already linguistically *expressible* by them (after all, they had the linguistic concepts *theos, anthrôpos,* and *esti*!). Hegel's response to such an objection would, I think, be that, strictly speaking, what Greek sculpture expressed was not merely the identity of God and mankind but their "absolute identity" or their "identity in difference," and that *this* is a concept which the Greeks did *not* yet possess in a linguistic form.

[71] Ibid., p. 490.

other): First, it seems vulnerable to an objection that it involves an erroneous reading-in of a meaning or thought that was not yet intended by the Greek sculptors. The Greeks' pervasive and clear expressions in their traditional literature of a sharp numerical distinction between gods and men (coincident with the qualitative distinction between divine immortality and human mortality) provide a good prima facie reason for rejecting this Hegelian interpretation of their sculpture. For example, did not Phidias make his statue of Zeus at Olympia – or even much later, Chares his statue of Helios at Rhodes (the "Colossus of Rhodes") – as huge as he famously did in important part precisely in order to accord with such a traditional conception of a sharp distinction between gods and men?

Second, someone might, though, reasonably respond to this objection on Hegel's behalf that the historical situation is not so clear-cut. In particular, such a person might reasonably point to the general exaltation of the human in comparison with the divine which occurred in fifth-century Athenian democratic culture, taking a secular form in Protagoras, and a (for present purposes, even more relevant) religious form in Aeschylus (whose Prometheus has sometimes been interpreted as really mankind itself, for example); and also to the Orphic and Pythagorean tradition which culminated in Plato's *Phaedo*, with its own very different way of effacing the division between the human and the divine (namely, by classifying the human soul as immortal and hence divine). Hegel may indeed himself have such evidence in mind, for he singles out as human embodiments of Greek sculpture's ideal both fifth-century Athenian democratic leaders, such as Pericles, Thucydides, and Xenophon, on the one hand, and Socrates and Plato, on the other.[72] However, such a response on Hegel's behalf, rather than helping him, in fact leads to serious difficulties of its own. For one thing, it is by no means clear that this evidence can overturn the anti-Hegelian interpretation of the intended significance of Greek sculpture based on traditional literature (perhaps the sculptors were more rooted in that than in this more avant-garde philosophy and literature). For another thing, and more importantly, this response is self-defeating, because the two strands of Athenian culture to which it appeals were both *linguistic* ones which *pre-existed* (or at least co-existed with) the sculpture in question. In other words, ironically enough, the very existence of such evidence for the ideas in question poses a problem for Hegel; his theory could in principle have

---

[72] See Bungay, *Beauty and Truth*, p. 113. Concerning the second of the two traditions just mentioned, note that Hegel says of all these individuals that they "stand like immortal, deathless images of the gods, beyond the reach of death and temporality."

withstood the *absence* of any independent evidence for such ideas at the time in question, since, as we saw, it is part of his position that sculpture *leads* the rest of the culture in developing them, but his theory cannot withstand the *presence* of *philosophical-literary* evidence for them, for the very linguistic nature of such evidence entails that, in superficially seeming to support the theory (by showing that the sculptors may have had the relevant ideas in mind), it in truth rather refutes the theory (by showing the theory's claim of the ideas' autonomy of language to be erroneous).[73]

In the end, therefore, as in the case of Egyptian architecture, Hegel's interpretation of Greek sculpture as incompatible with position (2) looks implausible.

In sum, the main evidence on which Hegel bases his denial of position (2) seems not in fact to support that denial. His conviction that it does so results from his mistakenly reading-*out* linguistic meanings and thoughts where they were probably in fact present (especially in the case of Egyptian architecture) and from his mistakenly reading-*in* not-yet-linguistic meanings and thoughts where they were probably in fact either simply absent or else already linguistic (especially in the case of Greek sculpture).[74]

Concerning, next, Hegel's explanation of painting and instrumental music in a manner which *conforms* to position (2): As I hinted earlier, Hegel's most considered observations on painting and instrumental music in this spirit – namely, those in which he is prepared to see these

---

[73] This problem is not, I think, significantly reduced if, following a suggestion I made in Footnote 70, one understands sculpture's message to be, for Hegel, more strictly the "identity in difference" of God and mankind. The two strands of philosophical-literary culture in question here could in fact fairly plausibly be interpreted as expressing some such conception, but in that case, once again, in thus seeming to support Hegel's theory on the one hand, they would to the same extent be undermining it on the other.

[74] A hardboiled Hegelian might, perhaps, respond to this sort of criticism that the nature of the Absolute and of its necessary self-development has been independently proved by Hegel's *Logic* and that it is therefore legitimate for Hegel to impute corresponding nonlinguistic meanings and thoughts to the historical art in question despite the absence of supporting evidence or even in the face of contrary evidence. However, such a response would not be very convincing. First, it seems quite unlikely that Hegel really proved any such thing in his *Logic* (though it would of course require a detailed examination of his *Logic* to show that he did not). Second, it is an important part of Hegel's own official methodology – on which he prides himself in comparison with Schelling, for example – that in applying the *Logic* to empirical evidence one must not, so to speak, *strongarm* the latter (see, for example, the preface to the *Phenomenology of Spirit*, and the introduction to the *Encyclopaedia*'s Philosophy of Nature).

arts as expressing meanings and thoughts, but understands the meanings and thoughts in question to be linguistic in nature – are generally plausible and perceptive. This is strikingly true of his account of Dutch genre painting, for example. Still, his refusal to see any counterexample to position (2) in these artforms requires, but fortunately also admits of, further defense.

Although Hegel himself evidently feels otherwise, painting and especially instrumental music are unusually potent sources of a temptation to deny position (2). For in contemplating these artforms, especially instrumental music, one surely often does get a powerful sense that meanings and thoughts are being expressed which it is beyond the capacity of (existing or perhaps even any) language to capture. Accordingly, theories of these artforms, especially of instrumental music, which attribute to them some sort of ineffable meaning and thought abound. Here are two examples:

> Version (a). As was mentioned earlier, the later Dilthey in his essay *Musical Understanding* treats instrumental music as a prime example of the falsehood of position (2). Specifically, he argues that while such music does indeed often merely express *linguistic* thoughts, in its highest forms it also expresses *non*linguistic ones, in particular ones about the nature of Life itself.[75]
>
> Version (b). Hanslick argues that music expresses strictly *musical* ideas.[76] And, following this lead, Stephen Bungay argues – in explicit rejection of Hegel's approach to instrumental music – that it is just obvious that there are nonlinguistic musical ideas and thinking.[77]

Despite the admitted seductiveness of such intuitions about painting and especially instrumental music, I strongly suspect that Hegel is in the end right to judge that these artforms should be explained in conformity with principle (2). Let me therefore make a few points in support of such an assessment, focusing primarily on the especially interesting case of instrumental music. (Corresponding points would apply to painting, and probably also to other nonlinguistic arts.)

The sense that instrumental music conveys meanings and thoughts which it is beyond the power of (existing or perhaps even any) language to express can indeed seem very compelling, and I do not want to suggest that it should be dismissed lightly. Nonetheless, it seems to me probable that it is illusory. (It may be salutary in this connection to remind oneself

---

[75] See *The Formation of the Historical World in the Human Sciences*, p. 245.
[76] Hanslick, *On the Musically Beautiful*, pp. 10, 28.
[77] Bungay, *Beauty and Truth*, p. 137.

of the – presumable – illusion to which we often fall victim in waking from a dream that we have entertained meanings and thoughts in the dream which are linguistically inexpressible.)

Consider, first, Dilthey's attempt to vindicate that sense. Dilthey believes that instrumental music in its higher forms expresses some sort of metaphysical or quasi-religious thought (about "Life").[78] This is a common enough conviction, and is indeed no doubt correct. But why should one take the thought in question to be linguistically inexpressible rather than – as Herder and Hegel had both already implied – linguistically expressible (and perhaps, moreover, actually derived from linguistically expressed metaphysics or religion)?[79] Admittedly, the sort of thought to which Dilthey refers here may only be rather *vaguely* expressible in language. But is there really any reason to suppose that the music expresses it any *less* vaguely?

Bungay's attempt to vindicate the sense in question is different. His claim is not that instrumental music expresses metaphysical or religious thoughts which transcend language, but rather that it expresses distinctively *musical* ideas and thoughts which do so. This claim strikes me as somewhat more plausible, but still in the end very questionable. It seems important to distinguish between two sorts of cases here. First, there are cases in which the relevant person, say a composer, possesses a linguistic or notational means of expressing the putative musical ideas or thoughts in question. In such cases, it *does* seem to me appropriate to speak of his having musical ideas and thoughts. But then, these are also cases in which he can express them *linguistically* (even musical notation being plausibly considered a part of language). Second, there are certainly in addition cases in which a person develops putative

---

[78] The characterization of "Life" as a metaphysical or quasi-religious principle is mine rather than Dilthey's own.

[79] For a discussion of the mature Herder's commitment to this sort of position concerning instrumental music's expression of metaphysical or religious thoughts, see my "Gods, Animals, and Artists: Some Problem Cases in Herder's Philosophy of Language," pp. 78–79. Concerning Hegel's commitment to such a position: (1) Hegel's implication that instrumental music sometimes expresses a metaphysical meaning is especially clear at *Hegel's Aesthetics*, p. 932, where he notes that such music sometimes develops dissonances and oppositions and their resolution in harmony and melody, that is, a self-developing structure analogous to that of the Absolute as he conceives it. (For a helpful discussion of this aspect of Hegel's account of instrumental music, see H. Heimsoeth, "Hegels Philosophie der Musik," *Hegel Studien*, 2 (1963), pp. 197–201.) (2) Given his general account of the nature of instrumental music, and in particular his conception of it as a "romantic" art founded on Christianity's message, such a metaphysical meaning must presumably in his view ultimately be language-based.

musical ideas or thoughts *without* having any corresponding linguistic or notational means for expressing them. (Think, for example, of the not uncommon phenomenon of the skilled jazz or blues musician who does not read music and is verbally inarticulate to boot.) However, is it really so clear that in such cases one should speak literally of the person's having musical *ideas and thoughts* rather than, say (an appealing alternative), of his creating/perceiving complex sound-patterns and -relationships? To my linguistic ear, at least, such a characterization would sound out of place if meant literally (though no doubt alright if only meant metaphorically). In short, it seems to me that nonlinguistic *musical* ideas and thoughts may well, once again, be a will-o'-the-wisp.

However, to turn from mere refutation to diagnosis, I suspect that there are also some deeper sources feeding the delusive temptation to suppose that instrumental music expresses linguistically inexpressible meanings and thoughts. In particular, I would suggest that this temptation arises from instrumental music's peculiar combination of a certain sort of inarticulateness with a certain sort of articulateness – namely, relative inarticulateness in expressing meanings and thoughts and relative articulateness in expressing nuances of feeling and emotion (in both cases, relative as compared to language).[80] This combination of features

---

[80] In suggesting that instrumental music expresses something about feeling or emotion which cannot be as accurately expressed by language (alone), I am in broad agreement with a tradition which includes both composers and philosophers. For example, the composer Mendelssohn says that musical feeling is indescribable because it is too precise for words (see J. W. N. Sullivan, *Beethoven: His Spiritual Development* (New York, Vintage, 1960), pp. 20–21; R. Scruton, *The Aesthetics of Music* (Oxford, Oxford University Press, 1999), p. 165, and the philosopher S. Langer articulates a similar position in several works, including *Feeling and Form* (New York, Charles Scribner and Sons, 1953), *Problems of Art* (New York, Pantheon, 1957), and *Philosophy in a New Key* (Cambridge, Cambridge University Press, 1978). The suggestion that instrumental music expresses feeling or emotion, and that it conveys nuances thereof more precisely than language (alone) can, requires some defense and qualification, however. For it is by no means always conceded that instrumental music expresses feeling or emotion at all, let alone that it does so more precisely than language – for example, Hanslick famously denies this. Perhaps the most serious objection to such a view is one which was first raised by Hanslick himself (*On the Musically Beautiful*, pp. 8–10): feelings and emotions of their very nature incorporate intentional objects, which seem beyond the reach of musical expression. Scruton (*The Aesthetics of Music*, p. 165ff.) has provided a very perceptive two-part response to this sort of objection which we can take over and build on here. First, he points out that instrumental music often *does* in fact express intentional objects (e.g., church music expresses the thought of God). Second, he notes that, despite the fact that emotions essentially include intentional objects, it is in an important sense possible to identify emotions without pinning down their intentional objects – that if, for example, one comes upon an unknown woman weeping in a park, one may be able by observing her behavior

can easily give rise to illusions that instrumental music expresses linguistically inexpressible meanings and thoughts in at least two distinct ways: First, instrumental music often expresses a composer's *linguistically expressible* meanings and thoughts but in ways which are vague, making it hard for a listener to pin down the meanings and thoughts in question with any precision (from the music). This genuine presence of definite linguistically expressible meanings and thoughts which, however, the listener finds himself unable to pin down linguistically with any precision easily gets misconstrued by him as a presence of definite meanings and thoughts which cannot be linguistically expressed.[81] Second, music often expresses and communicates more precisely than could be done by language (alone) certain nuances of feeling and emotion – that is, certain psychological states which are other than meanings and thoughts but which can easily be mistaken for them (especially given that they do *involve* them,[82] and that other meanings and thoughts are expressed in the music as well).[83]

I therefore suggest that when one thinks through the several possible forms and sources of the tempting intuition that instrumental

to identify the character of her emotion without knowing the intentional object involved (e.g., whether she is weeping over the death of a parent, the thanklessness of a child, abandonment by a husband, or what not). Third, I would add that in such cases it may also in a certain sense be possible by observing the person's behavior to identify the emotion *more precisely* than could be done from a verbal description, that the person's complex behavior in its context may convey to one the quality of the emotion in a way that could not be achieved by a mere verbal description either of the behavior and its context or of the emotion itself (though only "in a certain sense" because of course in another sense, namely that of pinning down the intentional object, the identification is ex hypothesi *less* precise). This situation suggests that, similarly, nuances of emotion may in a certain sense be expressed more precisely by instrumental music than could be achieved by language (alone) (even though, once again, in another sense – that concerned with the identification of the intentional object – they can usually only be expressed less precisely).

[81] A variant of this illusion can arise in connection with a composer's *technical* meanings and thoughts, which are capable of linguistic or notational expression by him. These will be precisely graspable by a listener who has technical expertise in music. However, a layman will again often sense their presence but find himself unable to pin them down linguistically with any precision, and so be encouraged to imagine that linguistically inexpressible meanings and thoughts are involved.

[82] Concerning this point, see Footnote 80.

[83] There may well be further sources of the delusive temptation to ascribe ineffable meanings and thoughts to music in addition. For example, Raffman somewhat plausibly diagnoses such a temptation in terms of the existence of a sort of musical grammar, which leads to a false expectation of a musical semantics due to the conjunction of grammar with semantics in the linguistic case (D. Raffman, *Language, Music, and Mind* (Cambridge, MA, MIT Press, 1993), pp. 40–41).

music expresses linguistically inexpressible meanings and thoughts in this way, the intuition in the end proves to be illusory.

As I implied earlier, analogous points hold for painting as well (and probably also for other nonlinguistic arts). For painting too sometimes expresses (vague) metaphysical or (quasi-)religious thoughts; it too involves technical "ideas" and "thoughts" which are sometimes linguistically expressible by the artist and sometimes not (e.g., ones concerning perspective or color); and it too tends to combine relative inarticulateness in the expression of meanings and thoughts with relative articulateness in the expression of nuances of feeling and emotion (the former part of which point is perhaps obvious; in connection with the latter, think for example of the nuances of feeling and emotion expressed by Rembrandt's self-portraits).

In summary, whereas Hegel's interpretation of ancient architecture and sculpture as counterexamples to position (2) in the end seems implausible, his interpretation of subsequent painting and instrumental music as conforming to position (2) in the end seems plausible. To this extent at least, position (2) in the end looks like the correct position to adopt.[84]

VI

In conclusion, then, I would suggest that Hegel deserves high praise for having championed several valid and important principles concerning the *scope and significance* of hermeneutics, but that his contributions concerning the *very nature of interpretation* itself were much more ambiguous. In this connection, he was in particular responsible for two dramatic and influential turns which occurred in the development of hermeneutics, but he was himself ambivalent about both of them, and they both arguably on reflection prove to have been mistakes (albeit important and interesting ones). Where the very nature of interpretation itself is concerned, therefore, it is in the end tempting to propose the slogan: Back to the Herder–Schleiermacher tradition, and to the heretical strand in Hegel himself which remained faithful to it!

[84] For two important qualifications of this assessment (which do not, though, overturn it), see my "Hegel and Some (Near) Contemporaries: Narrow or Broad Expressivism?" pp. 178–191.

8   Hegel's Social Philosophy

Hegel's social philosophy, as articulated in his *Philosophy of Right* (1821),[1] presents a vision of the rational social order that, despite certain obvious archaisms, is still of relevance to anyone interested in reconciling the best aspects of liberal social thought, including its concern for the rights and dignity of individuals, with the human need for deep and enduring communal attachments. Hegel's fundamental claim is that a single idea, properly understood – the idea of *freedom*[2] – provides the philosophical resources needed to ground a comprehensive account of the good society: what makes social institutions good, on Hegel's view, is that they play an indispensable role in "realizing" freedom (*PR*, §4).[3] The aim of this paper is to explain this basic thought by examining how

---

[1] A helpful guide to the text is Dudley Knowles, *Hegel and the Philosophy of Right* (London: Routledge, 2002).

[2] More precisely, it is practical freedom – freedom realized through action – that is at issue in Hegel's social philosophy. Hegel distinguishes this from speculative freedom, which is *reconciliation* that results from comprehending the world philosophically and affirming it as good.

[3] "*PR*" refers to G. W. F. Hegel, *Elements of the Philosophy of Right*, ed. by Allen W. Wood, trans. by H. B. Nisbet (Cambridge, UK: Cambridge University Press, 1991), followed by section (§) number. Hegel's remarks (*Anmerkungen*) are indicated by "A" and his additions (*Zusätze*) by "Z." '§151+Z" refers to both paragraph 151 and its addition. Other works of Hegel are cited as follows:

> *E* = *Hegel's Philosophy of Mind*, trans. by William Wallace (Oxford: Oxford University Press, 1971), which is Part III of the *Enzyklopädie der philosophischen Wissenschaften*;
>
> *EL* = Encyclopedia Logic, translated as *Hegel's Logic*, trans. by William Wallace (Oxford: Oxford University Press, 1975);
>
> *PhG* = *Phenomenology of Spirit*, trans. by A. V. Miller (Oxford: Oxford University Press, 1977);
>
> *VPR*1 = *Die Philosophie des Rechts: Die Mitschriften Wannenmann (Heidelberg 1817/18) und Homeyer (Berlin 1818/19)*, ed. by Karl-Heinz Ilting (Stuttgart: Klett-Cotta, 1983);
>
> *VPR*2 = *Philosophie des Rechts: Die Vorlesung von 1819/20 in einer Nachschrift*, ed. by Dieter Henrich (Frankfurt am Main: Suhrkamp, 1983).

Hegel understands and employs the ideal of freedom in justifying the three institutions he regards as essential to a rational social order: the nuclear family, civil society (the market-governed realm of production and exchange), and the modern constitutional state.

Yet articulating Hegel's conception of freedom is considerably more complicated than this characterization of his position suggests.[4] This is because there is not just one conception of freedom at work in his social philosophy but three: personal freedom, the freedom of moral subjectivity, and "substantial" freedom (*PR*, §§149, 257) or, as I will call it, "social" freedom. Each of these conceptions of freedom grounds one of the *Philosophy of Right*'s three major divisions: (i) personal freedom is the basis of "Abstract Right" (*PR*, §§34–104); (ii) moral freedom is the topic of "Morality" (*PR*, §§105–41); and (iii) social freedom is the concern of "Ethical Life" (*Sittlichkeit*) (*PR*, §§142–360).[5] Clearly, understanding Hegel's social philosophy depends on differentiating these three conceptions of freedom. But more is required as well. Since in the rational social order these three types of freedom are realized together – and since social freedom itself includes realizing the conditions that make the other two possible – understanding Hegel's view requires us to grasp how the three conceptions fit together to constitute a single, though complex, ideal of freedom. Hegel's social philosophy, then, can be viewed as an attempt to demonstrate the compatibility of three distinct conceptions of freedom that Hegel takes his contemporaries (and us) to regard as important. In undertaking this project, Hegel thinks of himself as articulating philosophically what history itself has already demonstrated. For it is Hegel's view that the distinctive social achievement of post-Enlightenment modernity (in Western Europe) is the creation, in basic outline, of a complexly organized yet coherent social order that allows freedom in all its forms to be fully realized. Let us begin, then, by examining the three conceptions of freedom that Hegel's social philosophy distinguishes.

THREE CONCEPTIONS OF FREEDOM

The simplest of these conceptions is personal freedom, which serves as the foundation of Hegel's theory of individual rights, the main concern of "Abstract Right." The type of freedom at issue here is the free

---

[4] A comprehensive account of Hegel's conception of freedom is provided by Alan Patten, *Hegel's Idea of Freedom* (Oxford: Oxford University Press, 1999).

[5] I expand on these and other issues concerning Hegel's conception of freedom in Frederick Neuhouser, *Foundations of Hegel's Social Theory: Actualizing Freedom* (Cambridge, MA: Harvard University Press, 2000).

(undetermined) choosing of ends. Persons are conceived of as possessing a set of given drives and desires that have the capacity to motivate them to act, but they are persons in virtue of the fact that they are not *determined* to act on the drives and desires they happen to have. Persons have the ability to reject some of their desires and to embrace others; they are able, in other words, to "step back" from their given inclinations and to decide which to satisfy and how precisely to do so (*PR*, §12). Hegel sometimes calls the will that defines personhood an "arbitrary will" [*Willkür*] (*E*, §492) in order to emphasize that a person's will is considered free simply by virtue of having chosen which ends to act upon, regardless of its reasons for having chosen as it did.

The doctrines of abstract right are arrived at by considering how the social order must be structured if personal freedom is to be systematically realized (realized by all its members). Hegel's answer is that personal freedom is realized when an individual exercises control over a determinate set of willless entities, or "things" (*PR*, §42), that constitute his *property*. Over that specific portion of the external world the person has unlimited sovereignty, including the right to be unimpeded by others in the pursuit of his own chosen ends. The purpose of abstract right, then, is to define and protect for each person an exclusive domain for action that is subject only to his own arbitrary will. Abstract right accomplishes this by ascribing to persons a set of rights guaranteeing them the liberty to do as they please with their property – their lives, their bodies, and the material things they own. Individuals realize personal freedom, then, when they inhabit a social world that secures for them a private sphere of action within which they are unhindered by others – by both other individuals and the state – from pursuing whatever ends they choose.

Moral freedom is a more complex type of freedom appropriate to what Hegel calls the "moral subject."[6] Moral subjects are free, or self-determining, not because they merely choose (arbitrarily) which among their given desires they want to take as ends for action but because they choose in accordance with principles that "come from themselves." More precisely, moral subjects set ends for themselves in accordance with their own understanding of what is (morally) good. (Kant's conception of the autonomous agent, who decides how to act by consulting what her own reason – via the categorical imperative – tells her to do, is the paradigm of a moral subject.) The self-determination associated with moral subjectivity is more complex than that ascribed to persons not only because it involves willing in accordance with normative

---

[6] Hegel often uses just the term "subject" in this context, but I use "moral subject" in order to avoid confusing this idea with other uses of "subject" in Hegel's philosophy.

principles but also because those principles are "the will's own" in the sense that the moral subject has the capacity to reflect rationally on the principles it follows and, on that basis, to affirm, reject, or revise them. Individuals realize moral freedom, then, when they subscribe to a rationally held vision of the good, determine their ends in accordance with it and successfully realize their vision of the good through their own actions.[7]

One way social institutions are implicated in the realization of moral freedom derives from the requirement that moral subjects be bound only by principles they themselves recognize as good. This implies that the rational social order must satisfy what Hegel calls the most important right of moral subjects (PR, §132), namely, that all practical dictates governing their lives, including the laws and norms of social life, be accepted and affirmed as good by the subjects whose actions they govern (E, §503A). It is not enough, however, that social members *in fact* regard their social order as good; the ideal of moral freedom also requires that their attitude be rationally defensible, that the social order they affirm be genuinely *worthy* of affirmation. A set of institutions that realizes moral freedom, then, must be able to withstand the rational scrutiny of its members. A social order that prohibits rational criticism or whose appearance of goodness could not survive such questioning might be able to win the actual assent of its members, but it would fail to satisfy the demands placed on it by the ideal of moral freedom.

In contrast to personal and moral freedom, where the emphasis is on the free individual conceived of as independent of others, social freedom consists in certain ways of belonging to and participating in the three principal social institutions of modernity (the family, civil society, and the state). The starting point for Hegel's conception of social freedom is his understanding of the freedom that (free, male) citizens enjoyed in the ancient Greek city-state. According to this understanding, citizens in ancient Greece had so deep an attachment to their polis that their membership in it constituted a central part of their identities. For the ancient Greeks, participating in the life of the polis was valuable for its own sake (not simply as a means to achieving other, egoistic ends), as well as a principal source of the goals, projects, and social roles that were central to their understanding of themselves. Hegel regards the subjective relation that Greek citizens had to their polis as a kind of freedom for two reasons. First, the fact that citizens did not regard the

---

[7] As Hegel puts it, the moral subject strives "[i] to have insight into the good, [ii] to make the good its intention, and [iii] to bring about the good through its activity" (E, §507, emphases omitted).

good of their community as distinct from their own enabled them to obey the laws that governed them – laws directed at the collective good – without experiencing the laws as external constraints on their wills. Second, the classical polis was the source of a distinctive and deep satisfaction for its members. It provided a social framework that gave meaning to their lives and served as the primary arena within which, by fulfilling their roles as citizens, they achieved their "sense of self" through the recognition of their fellow citizens. (As we will see, the form of social freedom that Hegel espouses includes two further elements: first, the institutions that individuals subjectively embrace must also objectively promote their personal and moral freedom; second, the social order *as a whole* – not just the individuals who comprise it – must realize a kind of "self-determination," insofar as it constitutes a teleologically organized, self-sustaining system.)

As these references to ancient Greece suggest, Hegel's project in the *Philosophy of Right* can be understood as an attempt to reconcile three distinct visions of freedom – personal freedom, moral freedom, and social freedom – that modernity has inherited from the past. Hegel himself endorses this reading of his project by identifying each conception of freedom with a particular historical era in which it arose and was dominant. According to this view, the idea of personal freedom comes to us from ancient Rome and is expressed in the Roman legal practice that recognized all citizens of the empire (though not slaves) as *personae*, bearers of specific personal and property rights. The idea of moral freedom, in contrast, is a product of the modern world. It appears first in the theology of the Reformation (in the view that God's word is present in the heart of all believers), but it is most clearly articulated in Kant's conception of the autonomous moral subject, who is bound only by principles that derive from his own rational will.

Implicit in this historical understanding of Hegel's project is the view that, as inheritors of this tradition, we moderns could not regard a social order that excluded any of these forms of freedom as a fully rational, satisfying world. From this perspective, then, the rational social order can be defined as one that fulfills its members' aspiration to be free in all three of these senses. Hegel's social philosophy is an attempt to show that, contrary to appearances, the three principal social institutions of modernity, working in concert, can accommodate each of these ideals. The idea of social freedom plays a central role in this argument, for in its modern form it integrates the freedom of ancient Greece with the two forms of freedom that succeed it historically, and it does so in two respects. First, socially free individuals have a subjective relation to their social order that is similar to the one Greek citizens had to theirs but that is also crucially different: in the modern world having identity-constituting attachments to one's community is made compatible with conceiving of oneself as an *individual* – that is, as a *person* with rights and interests separate from those of the community, and as a *moral subject* who is both able and entitled to pass judgment on the goodness of social practices.[8] Second, the institutions within which modern individuals achieve their particular identities also promote personal and moral freedom by bringing about the social conditions (explained below) without which those freedoms could not be realized.

There is, at the same time, a philosophically more rigorous way of defining the project of the *Philosophy of Right*. The three divisions of Hegel's text, together with the conceptions of freedom each is based on, can be understood as stages of a philosophical argument whose aim is to articulate a comprehensive, fully adequate conception of (practical) freedom. This conceptual (rather than historical) argument begins with the simplest conception of a self-determined will – the arbitrarily choosing will that characterizes persons – and demonstrates the necessity of supplementing that conception with a more complex idea of freedom (moral freedom) by showing how personal freedom by itself is incomplete. A conception of freedom is shown to be incomplete when the attempt to think a world in which it is realized reveals that such a world fails in some way fully to embody the core ideal of freedom, that of a will determined only by itself. Hegel's conceptual (or "logical") argument in the *Philosophy of Right* is obscured by the fact that it is not articulated in the straightforwardly deductive form that philosophers traditionally employ. Instead, its central claims are embedded (implicitly) in the famous "dialectical" transitions that mark the text's progression from "Abstract Right" to "Morality" to "Ethical Life."

Hegel's argument in the first of these transitions can be reconstructed as follows. As I have noted, personal freedom is realized when an individual is granted exclusive, arbitrary control over a certain portion of the world that constitutes his property. The incompleteness of this conception of freedom comes to light by considering the conditions under which personal freedom can be realized universally – that is, by every being with the capacity for free choice (which is to say, every human being). Hegel's claim is that when we attempt to think a world in which personal freedom is realized universally, we see that it cannot be the

---

[8] The compatibility of individuality and social membership is a prominent theme in Michael O. Hardimon, *Hegel's Social Philosophy: The Project of Reconciliation* (Cambridge, UK: Cambridge University Press, 1994).

only kind of freedom that the inhabitants of such a world enjoy. More precisely, personal freedom cannot be the only freedom such beings enjoy, *if the goal of complete self-determination is to be achieved.* The thought here is that a person living in a world where the personal freedom of all individuals is guaranteed could not be fully self-determined if he possessed only an arbitrarily choosing will, for there would be a respect in which his actions would have to be constrained by laws that do not themselves come from his own (merely arbitrary) will. This is because in order to realize the personal freedom of everyone, the actions of all must be subject to constraints. That is, everyone's actions must be bound by those principles – the principles of abstract right – that specify which of an individual's actions are inconsistent with the personhood of others. Thus, one of the conditions of the systematic realization of personal freedom is that individuals' actions conform to the fundamental command of abstract right: "Respect others as persons" (*PR*, §36). The rational social order will codify the principles of abstract right into a system of laws and use the threat of punishment to enforce them, but if the persons who inhabit such a world are to be fully self-determined, they must be able to grasp the rational purpose behind those laws and affirm them; that is, they must be able to will the principles that constrain their actions. But this is just to say that persons who are fully self-determined must also possess the more complex configuration of will that Hegel ascribes to the moral subject (which takes itself to be bound by moral principles that come from its own will).

What, then, are the deficiencies of moral freedom that necessitate the move to "Ethical Life" and its distinctive conception of freedom (social freedom)? Here, too, the inadequacies of moral freedom come to light by envisaging the conditions under which it can be realized in the world. The problems associated with realizing moral freedom are of two types. First, realizing moral freedom depends on something outside the individual subject's will in the sense that becoming a moral subject presupposes various social processes of character formation, or "education" [*Bildung*]. Among other things, moral subjects must be socialized to regard their actions as constrained by normative principles, to reflect on the principles that ought to guide their actions, and to willingly obey the principles they recognize as good. Second, moral subjects fall short of complete self-determination in the sense that, considered on their own – apart from the places they occupy in the basic institutions of society – moral subjects lack the resources they need to give concrete, nonarbitrary content to the idea of the good. While socially detached moral subjects may sincerely desire to realize the good, without a concrete vision of the projects and forms of life that best promote the freedom and well-being of all (the good), they cannot know what specific actions their allegiance to the good requires of them. In Hegel's words, moral subjectivity is "abstract," "empty," and "formal" (*PR*, §§134–137, 141); it fails to satisfy the criteria for a fully self-determining will because it cannot by itself give sufficient determinacy to its own governing concept.

The idea behind Hegel's doctrine of social freedom is that the remedy for both defects of moral subjectivity lies in an account of good (or rational) social institutions. Thus, for Hegel, rational social institutions are charged with the dual task of socializing their members into beings who possess the subjective capacities required to realize personal and moral freedom, and of providing a social framework that defines the particular projects that make their lives meaningful and give determinacy to their understanding of the good. Each of these tasks points to an important respect in which the systematic realization of personal and moral freedom depends on rational social institutions. That such institutions secure the conditions necessary for realizing personal and moral freedom should not, however, lead us to think that Hegel values social membership for purely instrumental reasons (merely as a means to achieving personal and moral freedom). On the contrary, if the problems posed by the first two forms of freedom are to be solved in a way that remains true to the ideal of complete self-determination, this solution must itself give rise to a new configuration of the self-determining will, one that finds expression in the idea of social freedom. In other words, the means through which rational social institutions secure the conditions of personal and moral freedom must themselves embody a kind of self-determination; more than being merely means to the realization of freedom, the rational social order must also itself, considered as a whole, *instantiate* freedom.[9]

This claim points to a distinctive and potentially misleading feature of Hegel's view: social freedom is a property that can be predicated of both the rational social order as a whole and the individual social members that compose it. Until recently, interpreters of Hegel often construed his talk of "the free whole" as evidence of the totalitarian character of his social philosophy, which was thought to subordinate the interests of individuals to some mysterious "freedom of the whole." One of the principal aims of this paper is to discredit that mistaken understanding. For in addition to being a property of the rationally organized social order itself, social freedom is a freedom that *individual*

---

[9] Hegel puts this point by saying: "In *Sittlichkeit* freedom *is*" (*VPR*1, 248).

social members realize:[10] by participating (in the right ways) in the institutions of ethical life, individuals not only secure the conditions of their personal and moral freedom, they also give reality to their own particular identities and, by affirming the laws and social norms that govern them, they see their social participation as having its source in their own wills.

Bringing together the various requirements social freedom is supposed to meet will provide us with a concise statement of its essential features: In addition to (i) securing the necessary conditions of personal and moral freedom, the rational social order will realize freedom in two further senses; (ii) individual social members will be self-determining in the sense that, because their self-conceptions are linked to the social roles they occupy, their participation in the institutions of ethical life will be not only voluntary but also an activity through which they constitute and express their identities; and, (iii) the social order itself – the ensemble of social institutions – will constitute a self-determining whole, one that is more completely self-determining (or self-sufficient) than any individual on its own can be. Thus, the actions of socially free individuals will proceed from their own wills in a dual sense: first, their social participation will be expressive of their own self-conceptions (e.g., as mother, teacher, and citizen of a particular state). Second, by acting in accordance with their self-conceptions, they will produce the totality of social conditions that make their own personal and moral freedom possible, as well as help to realize an entity – the social order itself – that is more completely self-determined than any individual.

THE DUAL STRUCTURE OF SOCIAL FREEDOM

When Hegel sets out to articulate the idea of social freedom in the *Philosophy of Right*, he characterizes ethical life as "the unity of objective... and subjective freedom" (*PR*, §258A). In another location he says something similar: "ethical life is [i] objective, real freedom that [ii] has an existence in self-consciousness befitting of freedom" (*VPR*1, 248). In the latter claim freedom appears in two guises, once as "objective, real freedom" and once as a subjective phenomenon (a "*self-consciousness* befitting of freedom"). In connecting ethical life to freedom in these two ways, Hegel is asserting two claims. First, social freedom has both an objective and a subjective component (*PR*, §§144, 146); the former exists in "the laws and institutions" of the rational social order (*PR*,

---

[10] This issue is addressed in detail in my discussion of the holistic character of social freedom; Neuhouser, pp. 38–49.

§144; *E*, §538), whereas the latter consists in the frame of mind, or "disposition," of social members. Second, the terms "objective freedom" and "subjective freedom" imply that each component of social freedom can be understood as a kind of freedom in its own right: Freedom both "has its actuality in the subjective disposition" of individuals (as subjective freedom) and is "objective and real" (as objective freedom) in the institutions of the rational social order (*VPR*1, 248).

The intuition underlying Hegel's two-part account of social freedom is captured in the following two thoughts. First, in calling the laws and institutions of ethical life "objective freedom," Hegel means to claim that there is a sense in which rational laws and institutions *objectively* embody freedom – that is, they realize freedom independently of the subjective relation social members have to them. Hence, freedom can be said to be realized (at least partially) simply in virtue of the fact that rational (i.e., freedom-promoting) laws and institutions exist and are sustained over time. One idea Hegel relies on here is that rational laws and institutions create the social conditions of individuals' personal and moral freedom. Thus, if I live in a social world that supplies the conditions and resources I need in order to exist as a person and a moral subject – if my society educates me to value my freedom, enforces a system of individual rights, makes it possible for everyone to own property, and so forth – then there is a sense in which I am free "objectively," regardless of whether I affirm, reject, or am indifferent to the institutions that in fact secure my freedom. (As we will see below, rational laws and institutions embody objective freedom in a further sense: together they constitute a social order that realizes – or approximates – the properties of a fully self-determining being.)

The second component of social freedom is expressed in the demand that objective freedom acquire "an existence in self-consciousness befitting of freedom." The idea here is that social members whose behavior conformed externally to the requirements of rational laws and institutions but who lacked the appropriate subjective relation to those laws and institutions would fall short of the ideal of freedom in an important respect. The mere fact that individuals do what rational laws and institutions require of them is not sufficient to ensure that their activity is *subjectively* free – that is, free in the sense in which actions can be said to come from one's own will or to be freely willed (as opposed to involuntary, coerced, or determined by an alien will). In the absence of subjective freedom, social members would be subject to principles (embodied in laws and institutions) that remained external to their wills. Since the social participation of such beings would be governed not by their own wills but by something external, their actions would not be, subjectively speaking, their own. If social members are to be fully self-determining, then, it is not enough that they merely conform to the principles that make them free (objectively); they must also have a conscious relation to those principles that makes their social activity subjectively free – they must in some manner *know* and *will* those principles as their own.

The Subjective Element of Social Freedom

The subjective element of social freedom consists in what Hegel calls the "subjective disposition" of social members. It can be thought of as a certain frame of mind, or conscious attitude, that individuals have with respect to the social institutions to which they belong. This subjective disposition is "befitting of freedom" in the sense that it is in virtue of it that individuals experience their social participation – their conforming to the demands of social institutions – as their own freely willed activity. It may be surprising to discover that Hegel characterizes the disposition that is supposed to make individuals subjectively free as a kind of *trust* in their social institutions (*PR*, §268; *E*, §515). Even more surprising, this trust is said to be grounded in a relation of *identity* (*PR*, §147A), or *oneness* (*PR*, §158), between individuals and their institutions in which the former perceive the latter not as "other" (*PR*, §268) or "alien" (*PR*, §147) but as undifferentiated from themselves (*PR*, §147). In trying to understand what Hegel means by such claims it is important to bear in mind that the point of his doctrine of subjective freedom is not that individuals ought to adopt an attitude of trust toward their institutions regardless of what those institutions are like. Its point, rather, is to articulate the kind of attitude individuals would have to be able to take to their social order if they were to realize the full panoply of freedoms available in the modern world. In other words, the doctrine of subjective freedom is an account of the disposition social members ought to have when the social order is functioning as it should (and *can*, in the modern world).

Hegel spells out the content of the subjective disposition appropriate to free social membership in terms of three elements: socially free individuals are conscious of their *oneness* with social institutions insofar as they regard those institutions as (i) their *purpose* (or end); (ii) their *essence*; and (iii) the *product of their own activity* (*PR*, §257).[11] The first of these elements can be thought of as a oneness of wills: socially free individuals embrace the collective ends of social institutions as their own, and they regard their activity on behalf of

---

[11] Although *PR*, §257 describes the subjective disposition involved in membership in the state, this threefold account applies as well to the disposition appropriate to ethical life in general. See the nearly identical accounts at *PR*, §152 and *E*, §514.

those ends as valuable for its own sake rather than as merely instrumental to achieving their private good. The second element refers to a oneness between social members and their institutions at the level of individuals' self-conceptions, or *practical identities*.[12] That is, social members' understanding of who they are as particular individuals is constituted by and expressed through their social membership. According to the third, socially free individuals regard themselves as one with their social institutions in that they know themselves to be the *producers* (or reproducers) of their institutions: they see their social world as sustained by and therefore dependent on their own collective activity.[13]

Hegel often characterizes the oneness of will that exists between socially free individuals and their social institutions as a unity of *particular* and *universal* wills (*VPR2*, 124). This unity obtains when individuals need pursue only their own particular ends in order for the good of the social whole (the end of the universal will) to be achieved. Hegel's point here has its origins in Adam Smith's understanding of the harmony that exists among individual and collective interests in a market economy, where "in furthering my end I further the universal, and this in turn furthers my end" (*PR*, §184Z). Yet, the harmony of interests that supposedly characterizes market-governed civil society falls short of the more perfect unity of particular and universal wills that figures most prominently in Hegel's social philosophy. Even though universal and particular wills converge in civil society, they remain "external" to one another in an important respect: in a market economy the good of the whole is realized only "behind the backs" of individual participants. That is, particular wills are in harmony with the universal will independently of any conscious relation individuals have to the good of the whole. This is not the case in the family and the state. Family members, for example, differ from members of civil society in that their wills are universal not only objectively but subjectively as well. This means that family members have a conscious understanding of what is good for their family as a whole and that they are motivated to realize that good, even when doing so conflicts with their own interests as separate individuals.

If family members and citizens consciously strive to realize the collective good of their families and states, it might be wondered in what sense their wills are particular at all. Two points are relevant here. First, particularity for Hegel is associated with the ideas of qualitative

---

[12] I borrow this term from Christine Korsgaard's discussion of the topic in *The Sources of Normativity* (Cambridge, UK: Cambridge University Press, 1996), pp. 100–107.

[13] I will say nothing further about this aspect of social members' subjective disposition since it is much easier to grasp than the other two.

determinacy and difference from others. To be a particular being is to have at least one specific quality (or "determination") that is not common to all beings of the same species. To call a human will particular, then, is to say that it has an end or interest that is not shared by all human wills and that therefore marks it as different from at least some other human wills. This is also to say that the ends of a particular will derive not from some universal feature of human beings but from the specific position an individual occupies in the world. The particular ends I embrace as a family member – to care for the particular members of my family in ways appropriate to my particular place within it – distinguish my will not only from the wills of the members of other families (my end is to care for *this* family) but also from the wills of the other members of my own family (I care for this family in accord with *my* place within it). Given this conception of particularity, it is no longer puzzling how a will can be both particular (having determinate ends that distinguish it from others) and universal (consciously directed at the collective good).

The second point relevant to understanding the particularity of social members' wills is that particular wills are attached to their ends not through abstract reason (reason that commands independently of desire) but through *inclination* (broadly construed).[14] This means that individuals have a motivation for acting on their particular ends independently of any reflection undertaken from the standpoint of a purely rational agent who abstracts from his particular circumstances, including his particular relations to others. Hegel's idea is that a particular will is always motivated, in part, by its conception of its *own* good and that its actions on behalf of the whole also provide it with (or at least promise) a kind of particular satisfaction. To say that the wills of family members are both particular and universal, then, is to say that family members are inclined to act in ways that further their family's good as they understand it *and* that they experience their action for the sake of the whole as intrinsic to their own good. In caring for my children and spouse, for example, I do good to those I love, I secure in turn their love for me, and, as we will see below, I "satisfy" myself by carrying out a social role that I identify with and through which I win recognition (as a good

---

[14] Hegel uses "inclination" (*Neigung*) to refer to natural, sensible inclinations, but he also speaks of spiritual or rational inclinations (*E*, §474A), which are not naturally given but are the results of socialization. The latter inclinations are spiritual in that they are expressions of an individual's self-conception and therefore possible only for spiritual, or self-conscious, beings. The desire to care for one's children and the desire to vote in an election are both examples of spiritual inclinations.

parent and spouse), both from my fellow family members and from the members of society at large.

Of course, to say that socially free individuals are inclined to work for the collective good does not mean that they never experience conflicting desires in situations where the requirements of their roles collide with some of their purely self-interested desires. When my child's need for attention conflicts with my desire to read my newspaper in peace, I may have to exert some effort to deny that desire in order to do what I know is best overall (including best for myself, since being a good parent is important to me). The point is that in such a case any hesitation I experience is not a struggle between inclination, on the one hand, and abstract reason, on the other, but between two "inclinations" – two kinds of particular satisfaction – one of which I regard as less central to who I am than the other.

In addition to working willingly to achieve the collective good of the institutions to which they belong, socially free individuals view those ends as their "highest," "absolute" ends (PR, §258; E, §514). This means that their participation is not only intrinsically valuable to them but also their *most highly* valued activity. Understanding this leads us to the second element of the subjective disposition associated with social freedom: the oneness between social members and their institutions with respect to their "essence," or practical identities. It is this feature of Hegel's view that explains how forsaking purely self-interested (egoistic) ends in favor of the good of the whole can be regarded not as self-sacrifice but as its opposite, namely, an activity through which social members achieve selfhood by establishing identities as particular individuals. Although Hegel acknowledges many important differences among the family, civil society, and the state, he takes these institutions to share one basic feature: each functions by fostering among its members a distinctive kind of particular identity – as family member, as member of a profession, and as citizen of a state – that makes it possible for particular wills to serve universal ends without a sacrifice of freedom. Hegel's idea here is that individuals can work freely for the collective good of a group to which they belong, insofar as doing so is also a way of giving expression to a particular identity they take to be central to who they are. This means that participation in the family, civil society, and the state can be both universally beneficial and particularly satisfying, since to act on the basis of one's identity as a family member, as the member of a profession, or as a citizen is at the same time to work for the good of the whole.

What free social members regard as their own "essence," then, is not in the first instance social institutions but the particular roles they occupy within them: members of ethical life define themselves as mothers or fathers, as farmers or teachers, as citizens of a specific country. An individual's positions within the institutions of ethical life make up his "essence" in the sense that his particular roles as parent (of these children), teacher (of this subject), and citizen (of this nation) provide him not only with his "sense of self" (*PR*, §261A) and "dignity" (*PR*, §152) but also with the projects and ends that give meaning to his life. It is important not to infer from this that Hegel denies the need for free individuals to think of themselves as abstract, universal beings as well. Both persons and moral subjects are universal in precisely this sense. The point, rather, is that at the core of social freedom are the ways in which individuals, through social participation, win identities as particular beings by achieving a kind of standing "in their own eyes and in the eyes of others" (*PR*, §207).[15] In summary, then, Hegel regards the subjective dispositions just described as essential to social freedom for two reasons: first, it is by virtue of these dispositions that social members are able to embrace the collective ends of the groups to which they belong as their own (and hence to obey willingly the demands of their institutions); second, these dispositions make social activity the source of a deep, "substantial" satisfaction for individuals, insofar as it is through such activity that they express and realize their own particular identities.

We are now in a better position to understand what Hegel means when he characterizes the subjective disposition appropriate to social freedom as trust in one's social order. As Hegel defines it, this trust consists in "the awareness that my substantial and particular interest is contained and preserved in the interest and end of an 'other' [i.e., the institutions in question]" (*PR*, §268). Trust, then, is simply the enduring confidence of social members that that their own fundamental interests are inseparably intertwined and in essential harmony with the ends of their social institutions – that, in other words, their institutions constitute a "home." It is important to note that, understood in this way, trust need not be blind or unconditional and, hence, exclusive of rational reflection. Indeed, if this were the kind of trust Hegel were advocating, he would undermine one of his own fundamental aims, namely, to make social freedom compatible with moral freedom. For, as we have seen, the latter includes the ability to submit the principles one endorses to rational scrutiny and to reject or revise them as reflection demands. Thus, a theory of *modern* ethical life insists that the trust of social

---

[15] This is true even in civil society, where professional identities imbue labor with more than instrumental significance and also serve as the basis for bonds of solidarity among members of the same profession.

members be able to survive good-faith reflection on the merits of their institutions. Moreover, if moral freedom is to be realizable for all, the rationality of the social world cannot be visible only to the few but must allow of being made transparent to the average social member. In other words, in order to realize the full range of freedoms available to them as modern subjects, social members must not only have the subjective disposition just described, they must also be able to reflect on and understand *what makes it rational* for them to have such an attitude to their social world. For Hegel, this is just to say that their trust must be compatible with understanding how, apart from their subjective attachment to it, their social world makes them, objectively speaking, free.

THE OBJECTIVE ELEMENT OF SOCIAL FREEDOM

As indicated above, Hegel's conception of social freedom is not exhausted by his account of the subjective disposition of social members. In order to ascribe social freedom to individuals it is not enough to establish merely that they *take* their social world to be a "home;" their world must also *be* a home, which means it must in fact contribute to the realization of practical freedom (in all its guises). In other words, if social freedom is to be achieved, the institutions that social members subjectively endorse must also be *worthy* of their endorsement. The doctrine of objective freedom is Hegel's answer to the question: What about the family, civil society, and the modern state makes it rational (or good) that individuals subjectively embrace those institutions and live within them? A clear understanding of Hegel's answer to this question has frequently eluded even sympathetic readers. This is partly because in the few instances in which Hegel speaks of objective freedom he fails to clarify what it means and how it functions in his theory. A further reason for confusion is that objective freedom is realized in two quite disparate (though compatible) features of a rational social order. On the one hand, Hegel considers social institutions to realize objective freedom when they constitute a self-sufficient, self-reproducing system that, taken as a whole, is "self-determining."[16] On the other hand, objective freedom is realized when institutions secure the social

---

[16] This view is apparent in the following claim: "The *rationality* of ethical life resides in the fact that it is the *system* of the determinations of the Idea. In this way ethical life is freedom, or the will that has being in and for itself as something objective" (*PR*, §145+Z). See also *PR*, §§144, 258A+Z, 261Z, 270Z; *E*, §539.

conditions necessary for their members to achieve personal and moral freedom.[17]

That Hegel relies on both of these conceptions of objective freedom is consistent with my earlier claim that his social philosophy is driven by the conceptual (or "logical") project of articulating a coherent and fully adequate conception of practical freedom. If we keep this project in mind, it becomes clear how the two versions of objective freedom distinguished here are essential to Hegel's view. First, if practical freedom is to be realized, the social order must secure the social conditions that make it possible for its members to achieve the two relatively individualistic forms of freedom with which the *Philosophy of Right* begins: personal freedom and moral freedom. But, second, if the conditions of these forms of freedom are to be secured in a manner consistent with the ideal of a self-determined will – if practical freedom is to be *completely* realized – the social order that secures them must itself be a self-determining entity, that is: a living, self-reproducing system that has the structure of what Hegel calls "the Concept."

The latter, distinctively Hegelian claim is best made sense of in terms of the ideal of teleological organization. Thus, one thing Hegel means when he says that the rational social world *is* objective freedom is that, as a whole, it exhibits the kind of intelligibility sought by a biologist examining an unfamiliar form of life or by a critic seeking to interpret a work of art. Each of these investigators attempts to understand his object by figuring out how its various parts work together to form a coherent, harmonious whole. What each seeks to find in his object is a purposive order that makes the object intelligible as a whole. Finding this order involves discovering at least two things: first, the end, or telos, of the entity as a whole; and, second, how its individual parts are determined by that end – that is, how its specific features can be explained in terms of what it requires in order to realize its essential function. Such a being represents a *self-determining* whole, not only because its specific features are determined by (derive from) nothing other than itself (its essential nature, or telos) but also because, in the case of the rational social order, that governing telos is itself freedom. More precisely, the social order that meets Hegel's criterion for a self-determining whole will exhibit four characteristics: it will be a (i) *teleologically organized*, (ii) *self-reproducing* whole that integrates (iii) *specialized, semiautonomous functions* (family, civil society, and state)

---

[17] This position is implicit in Hegel's statement that personhood and moral subjectivity "cannot exist on their own" but "must have ethical life as their bearer and foundation" (*PR*, §141Z).

into (iv) a form of organization that is *determined by the Concept* (or "derives from the single concept of the rational will") (*E*, §539).

It follows from this ideal that each sphere of a rational social order will carry out a distinct function necessary for society's material reproduction: the family furnishes society with human individuals; civil society supplies the goods required to sustain life; and the state supports and coordinates these "lower" spheres. Of course, since social life has an ethical significance, its telos includes not merely material reproduction but freedom as well. This means that it belongs to the essence of the rational social order to reproduce itself in a way that accommodates the greatest possible freedom of its members. For Hegel, then, one of the characteristics of modern ethical life that makes it rational is that its particular institutions, working in concert, are especially well-suited to achieving the two primary ends of the social order as a whole, namely, its material reproduction and the formation of conscious agents of social reproduction who are free as both persons and moral subjects.

Hegel's conception of rational organization includes a further, more obscure element that is bound up with his metaphysical doctrine of the Concept [*der Begriff*],[18] as developed in his *Logic*. "The Concept" is Hegel's term for the basic structure that reason in general must attribute to its objects if they are to satisfy its demand that the world be intelligible to it. The relevance of this metaphysical thesis lies in its claim to give a certain content to the idea of a rationally organized whole. More precisely, Hegel appeals to his account of the three essential constituents of any rationally ordered whole – the "moments" of immediate unity, difference, and mediated unity[19] – in order to determine the number and nature of the parts of the rational social order. Thus, in the context of social philosophy, Hegel's doctrine of the Concept translates into the requirement that the social world be made up of three distinct social spheres, each corresponding to one of the three moments of the Concept: the rational social order is one whose basic institutions allow the moments of immediate unity, difference, and mediated unity to attain full and compatible expression.[20]

---

[18] See especially *PR*, §144, where the "differences" that characterize *Sittlichkeit* are said to be "determined by the Concept." Similar statements can be found throughout the *Philosophy of Right*, for example, at *PR*, §§145Z, 260Z, 262, 263+Z, and 270Z.

[19] These elements can also be specified as *universality*, *particularity*, and *individuality*, but when Hegel refers to the structure of the Concept in the context of ethical life (e.g., *PR*, §§157–158, 181) he normally employs the terms I use here.

[20] This formulation is inspired by Charles Taylor's discussion of the topic in *Hegel* (Cambridge, UK: Cambridge University Press, 1975), p. 374.

In this context immediate unity, difference, and mediated unity designate the type of unity that characterizes the institution in question, as well as the kinds of relations among its members that such unity involves. The family counts as an instance of immediate unity because love is the principal bond that unites its members and makes it possible for them to have a collective will, each regarding the good of the family as his own good. Civil society represents the moment of difference because its members participate in it as independent individuals who work and trade in order to satisfy their own particular needs.[21] The state, in contrast, embodies mediated unity. Following Rousseau, Hegel conceives of the political sphere as the public realm where legislation is framed and executed in accordance with a shared conception of the society's collective good.[22] The state incorporates the "difference" of civil society because citizens enter the political sphere with diverse identities as individuals whose family ties and positions within civil society provide them with divergent particular interests. Because the moment of difference is not to be suppressed by the state but incorporated into it, the state's main task is to find a way of integrating the particular wills of citizens into a general will that frames laws that further the good of the whole. In explaining how citizens are able to assent to laws that sometimes subordinate their private interests to the good of the whole, Hegel appeals to a familiar idea: individuals can embrace the ends of the state as their own only if being joined together as a single nation, or people [Volk], provides them with a shared project, the pursuit of which is for them an end in itself and a substantial source of the value they find in their own lives. The unity that characterizes the state, Hegel insists, is not grounded in immediate feeling or any other "bond of nature" (such as blood) (VPR1, 250, 268). The state, rather, is a mediated unity because the tie that binds its citizens arises through a collective act of reason – that is, through the making of laws that are universally binding, explicitly known, and consciously endorsed through a process of public reflection on the common good (PR, §270).

---

[21] This is a simplification of Hegel's view, since civil society also includes certain groups, the corporations, in which members partially shed the perspective of independent individuals and acquire bonds of solidarity with the fellow members of their trade or estate. Yet even these bonds develop out of egoistically motivated productive activity and are therefore grounded in members' status as independent individuals who pursue private ends.

[22] For more on Hegel's conception of the state, see Eric Weil, Hegel and the State, trans. Mark A. Cohen (Baltimore: Johns Hopkins Press, 1998) and Harry Brod, Hegel's Philosophy of Politics (Boulder, CO: Westview Press, 1992).

Implicit in Hegel's view of ethical life's Conceptual structure is the claim that part of what makes the modern social world rational is that it allows its members to develop and express different, complementary identities. The idea here is that each type of identity has a distinct value for individuals and that possessing them all is essential to realizing the full range of possible modes of selfhood. To miss out on any of these forms of social membership, then, is to be deprived of one of the basic ways of being a self and hence to suffer an impoverishment of one's life (in this one respect). The reason for this is that membership in each sphere brings with it different kinds of practical projects, each possessing its own distinctive satisfactions and rewards: while family members engage in shared projects defined by the good of others to whom they are attached through love, civil society is the sphere in which individuals "pursue their own welfare in their own way, choose their own way of life, and enter into voluntary relations with others who are likewise free choosers of their own ends and activities."[23] Membership in the state is important because it provides citizens with projects and attachments that round out and enrich their otherwise merely particular lives. In contrast to the other two spheres, the state affords its members the opportunity to acquire a universal identity (one shared with all other citizens), the achievement of which most closely approximates the ideal of self-sufficient subjectivity: in the state, citizens – constituted as a single body – determine themselves in accordance with universal principles legislated by their own public reason.

Social institutions embody objective freedom in the second sense distinguished above when they secure the social conditions necessary for individuals to achieve personal and moral freedom. The most important of Hegel's claims here is that the rational social order has as its task the *Bildung* – the formation or education – of its members into agents who possess the subjective capacities required for personhood and moral subjectivity. Thus, the aim of *Bildung* is freedom, but since unformed subjects lack even the aspiration to be free, *Bildung* must take place unconsciously and involuntarily, behind the backs, so to speak, of the very subjects who undergo it. *Bildung* is necessarily involuntary for a further reason: the subjective capacities freedom depends on are typically acquired only through the severity of a disciplinary regimen,[24]

---

[23] Allen W. Wood, *Hegel's Ethical Thought* (Cambridge, UK: Cambridge University Press, 1990), p. 239.

[24] It may be helpful to recall the necessary roles played by servitude, fear, and labor in the formation of *Geist* as related in *The Phenomenology of Spirit*, 152–155.

such as is to be found in labor (the form of discipline distinctive to civil society) or in subjection to the will of a higher authority (the basis of discipline in the family).

These claims make clear why the formative functions of social institutions count as part of the doctrine of objective freedom: *Bildung* represents one way in which individuals are made to be free (here, they come to be equipped with the subjective conditions of their freedom) independently of their knowledge or consent. The fact that individuals submit to the process of formation only out of necessity makes the family and civil society especially well-suited to carrying out *Bildung*'s tasks. For individuals belong to the family and civil society not out of choice but because their neediness – both their helplessness as children and their enduring need for the means of survival – leaves them no other option. Human neediness guarantees that individuals will take part in the family and civil society, and, when rationally ordered, these institutions both alleviate that neediness and put it to work in service of freedom.

There are many respects in which the family and civil society are thought by Hegel to be instruments of *Bildung*; in the present context two examples will suffice to indicate the general thrust of his view. Of the various ways the family contributes to the *Bildung* of its members the easiest to articulate is the cultivation of moral subjectivity in the rearing of children. Here the most important aspect of family life is parental discipline. The significance of parental discipline resides less in the teaching of specific moral precepts than in providing children with a particular capacity of will that is essential to the self-determination distinctive of moral subjects. The rational end of discipline, as Hegel conceives it, is to raise children out of their "natural immediacy" (*PR*, §175), where the will is simply determined by the "drives, desires, and inclinations" nature gives to it (*PR*, §11), to a condition in which the will is no longer determined by its natural content. The subjective capacity that discipline instills in children is the ability to say no to their immediate desires and to follow instead an external, "objective" will (the dictates of the parent) that takes precedence over immediate desires and (in the case of good child rearing) exhibits a constancy that is lacking in a will determined by caprice or momentary urges. Although determining one's will in accordance with the will of a parent clearly falls short of the ideal of moral self-determination (determining one's will in accordance with one's own reasoned understanding of the good), a period of subjection to parental authority is an essential part of the formative process that must be undergone by originally immediate beings like ourselves in order to achieve that end.

The educative effects of civil society have their source in the fact that its members' productive activity takes place within a system of cooperation marked by a division of labor (PR, §187). Since no one in such a system can satisfy his needs through his labor alone, members of civil society must learn to tailor their activity so as to take into account the needs, desires, and perceptions of other individuals. In other words, labor in civil society is informed by a recognition of the subjectivity of others, including a recognition of the necessity of letting others' ends enter into the determination of one's own actions. For this reason civil society can be seen as helping to form its members into moral subjects. Although labor in civil society is not itself moral action (since it is motivated by egoistic ends), it cultivates in individuals a subjective capacity without which moral action would be impossible, namely, the ability to discern, and determine one's activity in accordance with, the ends of one's fellow beings. Beyond this, participants in the modern economy are required to take others' wills into account in a quite specific manner – that is, labor in civil society is essentially the production of *exchangeable* goods.[25] The point here is not simply that the fruits of one's labor can be exchanged after the fact for others' products but rather that from the very beginning production is determined by the intention to do so. This means that productive activity in civil society is carried out not with the aim of meeting the needs or wishes of determinate individuals but in accordance with the demands of an impersonal market. Because their interactions are mediated by a "universal" medium of exchange (money), members of civil society do not relate to one another as concrete, particular individuals but only as abstract buyers and sellers who are essentially identical to one another, insofar as all have the same rights and obligations of exchange. But this feature of civil society, in Hegel's view, fosters a kind of self-consciousness among members of civil society that is essential to the realization of personal freedom. That is, participating in civil society encourages individuals to think of themselves and others as beings who, despite their many concrete differences, are fundamentally alike. More precisely, they come to conceive of themselves and others as *persons*, who, as such, are identical to all other persons and who count as persons (as bearers of the same rights) not because of any particular qualities they possess but solely in virtue of their status as a human being: "that I am taken to be a *universal* person, identical to *all*, is a part of *Bildung*.... The human being counts

---

[25] In the *Encyclopedia* treatment of *Sittlichkeit* Hegel makes this point more explicitly than in other places; productive activity in civil society is characterized there as "the bringing forth of exchangeable goods through one's own labor" (E, §524).

as such because he is a human being, not because he is a Jew, Catholic, Protestant, German, Italian, and so forth" (PR, §209A).

SOCIAL FREEDOM AND MORAL REFLECTION

Critics of Hegel have frequently objected that the rational social order as he depicts it accords no place for the expression of the central feature of moral subjectivity that Hegel calls *conscience*: "the absolute authority of subjective self-consciousness, namely, to know what right and duty are both *within oneself* and *as proceeding from oneself*, and to recognize nothing other than what it thus knows as the good" (PR, §137A).[26] One charge interpreters have made is that the subjective disposition required by social freedom is incompatible with adopting a universal, nonparochial perspective from which one could ask whether the norms and practices of one's social order are rationally justified. The idea behind this charge is that whereas social freedom requires that one subjectively identify with one's social institutions, rational reflection presupposes just the opposite, namely, that one's attachments to social institutions be sufficiently loose to allow one to evaluate one's social order from a detached, universal perspective. This charge, however, rests on a mistaken understanding of the sense in which membership in the rational social order, for Hegel, is constitutive of individuals' identity. Hegel does not claim, as contemporary communitarians sometimes appear to, that social roles *exhaust* practical identities in the sense that individuals are nothing more than bearers of the various social roles they occupy. As we have seen, Hegel's claim that individuals find their identities in their social roles means only that social roles furnish them with the ends and projects that constitute their life-defining activity, and that a substantial part of their "sense of self" – their "worth and dignity" (PR, §152) – derives from the recognition they receive as a result of successfully fulfilling their social roles. When identity is understood in this more limited sense, there is nothing in Hegel's account of the subjective disposition of free social members that precludes distancing oneself reflectively from one's social roles in order to ask, as a moral subject, whether the social order one inhabits is rationally justifiable. On the contrary, the capacity for such reflection is a necessary part of the freedom Hegel's social philosophy is concerned with, for without it individuals would not be socially free in a manner appropriate to their

---

[26] One such critic is Ernst Tugendhat, *Self-Consciousness and Self-Determination* (Cambridge, MA: MIT Press, 1986), pp. 315–316.

status as moral subjects (who are bound only by principles that their own reason sanctions).

Yet even if we grant that Hegel's social philosophy allows room for individuals to take up a reflective, evaluative stance with respect to their social order, a further concern remains: are individuals in a position not only to reflect on but also to *criticize* the social order they inhabit? The charge that Hegel fails to make sufficient room for criticism of the existing social order comes closer to hitting its mark than the objection that social freedom is incompatible with rational reflection. There are, for example, no passages in the *Philosophy of Right* that acknowledge the importance of citizens' freedom to engage in public discourse critical of social institutions. One place we would expect to find such an acknowledgment is the discussion of the press's role in political society (*PR*, §319+A). But here Hegel ignores the function a free press could serve as a forum for rational, critical debate. Instead he appears to defend freedom of the press (in a very limited form) only because it satisfies the need of individuals "to express even their subjective opinions concerning the universal" (*PR*, §308A) and because the falsity, distortion, and derision that are likely to result from such freedom can do little damage in a well-constituted state.

Despite these deficiencies in Hegel's view, it would be wrong to conclude that social criticism can have no place in his theory. In order to see this, it is sufficient to note an obvious but frequently overlooked feature of his view, namely, that the social order the *Philosophy of Right* lauds as "actual" [*wirklich*] has never existed in precisely the form in which Hegel presents it. Despite Hegel's reputation as an apologist for the Prussian state, the institutions he endorses are obviously not identical to those of nineteenth-century Prussia. It is precisely here – in the disparity between existing institutions and those that are "actual" in Hegel's technical sense – that the possibility for social criticism is to be found. For the *Philosophy of Right*'s *idealized* account of modern social institutions provides us with the resources for seeing where existing institutions do not fully measure up to what they should be and for thinking about how they can be made to conform to their own (immanent) rational principles.

That the critical potential of Hegel's social philosophy is so often overlooked is no doubt due in part to a natural misunderstanding of his claim that the primary aim of philosophy is to reconcile human beings with the actual world. (In the case of social philosophy, reconciliation – affirming the world as hospitable to the fundamental aspirations of human subjects – is the result of comprehending how the actual social order systematically realizes practical freedom.) But it is important to recognize that reconciliation is not incompatible with social criticism directed at the reform, as opposed to the radical overhaul, of existing institutions. Criticism and reform are consistent with the spirit of Hegel's social philosophy, insofar as they aim at transforming institutions to make them conform more faithfully to the rational principles already implicit in their existent practices. This is just to say, in Hegelian jargon, that the proper object of our reconciliation is actuality [*Wirklichkeit*], not existing reality [*Realität*]. Actuality, as Hegel conceives it, is not to be identified with whatever exists; it is, instead, the *unity* of existing reality [*Existenz*] and its rational essence (*EL*, §142).[27] Applied to the social world, "actuality" refers to existing social reality as reconstructed within philosophical thought – thought that aims to clarify and bring into harmony the basic principles underlying the various existing social orders that typify Western European modernity. As such, actuality represents a purified version of existing reality that is more fully rational than any particular existent social order but that is not for that reason independent of, or out of touch with, the existing world. Thus, the normative standards Hegelian social criticism brings to bear on existing reality are actual, and not "merely ideal," in the sense that they are not externally imposed upon, but already belong to, the existing object of criticism.

We are now in a position to understand how a critical perspective on social reality is compatible with the subjective disposition that social freedom requires of individuals. These two attitudes can appear to be in direct conflict, since finding one's identity in one's social membership requires an affirmation of the existing social order that seems incompatible with criticizing it. In fact, however, no such conflict exists since, strictly speaking, the proper object of our affirmation as socially free individuals is not institutions as they presently exist but something like "our institutions as they aspire to be, almost are, and in principle could be, if only we worked hard enough to bring them better in line with their own ideals." There is nothing contradictory in thinking, for example, that a single individual can take his U.S. citizenship to constitute a substantial part of who he is (in the sense required by social freedom) and at the same time believe that in their present form, U.S. political institutions do not measure up to their own immanent ideals. What *is* required for this synthesis to be possible is that existing institutions come close enough to realizing their own ideals to be recognizable

---

[27] For a helpful discussion of Hegel's concept of *Wirklichkeit*, see Hardimon, pp. 53–63.

as genuine, albeit imperfect, embodiments of the rational social order, or as on their way to becoming such.

The sort of critique that Hegel does regard as at odds with the fullest realization of freedom is what could be called *radical* social criticism. Radical critique can take two forms: the first rejects the basic values that existing institutions embody (or seek to embody), whereas the second accepts those values but insists that the existing social order is incapable of realizing them and must therefore be replaced by new institutions. It is easy to see how adopting a radically critical stance toward existing institutions is in conflict with social freedom, since doing so is incompatible with finding one's identity within one's social roles. This alone, however, does not establish that Hegel regards radical criticism as always undesirable, for it is possible to imagine cases in which one can subjectively identify with one's social order only by, in effect, relinquishing one's status as a moral subject. For if existing institutions are fundamentally bad – if they stand in the way of, rather than promote, the realization of freedom in its various forms – then social members who affirm those institutions fail to will in accordance with (true) principles of the good. In other words, Hegel does not believe that radical social criticism is unwarranted in all historical circumstances. On the contrary, radical social critique is unwarranted only in the modern (Western) world, and this is because, for Hegel, modernity's three social institutions are, in basic outline, rational. In historical circumstances in which the latter condition does not obtain, refusing to affirm the existing social order must be regarded as a legitimate expression of moral subjectivity.[28]

---

[28] Even in these circumstances Hegel's preferred response is withdrawal from the social world rather than critique or social activism (*PR*, §138Z). This is no doubt due to his belief that fundamental historical progress is never the direct result of human planning but takes place behind the backs of human participants, via the ruse of reason.

9   Hegel's Philosophy of Religion

HEGEL'S LECTURES ON THE PHILOSOPHY OF RELIGION

Hegel lectured on the philosophy of religion for the first time in the summer semester of 1821 at the University of Berlin, lectures that he was to repeat on three occasions, in 1824, 1827, and 1831. His delay in addressing the topic of religion was not a sign of lack of interest. On the contrary, there was no topic in which he had a deeper and more abiding concern, as evidenced from his days as a theological student in Tübingen through the years in Frankfurt, Jena, and Nuremberg.[1] Upon his departure from Jena, he wrote to a friend: "I was eager to lecture on theology at a university and might well have done so after some years of continuing to lecture on philosophy."[2] However, the opportunity to do so did not present itself until after his arrival in Berlin. He was stimulated to offer his own views by the impending publication of Friedrich Schleiermacher's *Glaubenslehre*, a work with which Hegel had reason to believe he would find sharp disagreements.[3] As a philosopher, he did not lecture on theology per se but on philosophy of religion, a discipline that he took to be engaged not simply with the phenomenon of religion but with the nature and reality of the object of religion, namely, God. Since this transcendent referent had been rendered problematic by Enlightenment philosophy, history, and science, Hegel set out to develop a new philosophical theology that would reestablish the conceptual foundations of religion by offering a postmetaphysical and

---

[1] For excerpts from writings on religion prior to the philosophy of religion, see *G. W. F. Hegel: Theologian of the Spirit*, ed. by Peter C. Hodgson (Minneapolis and Edinburgh: Fortress Press and T&T Clark, 1997), chapters 1–5.

[2] Hegel to I. Niethammer, November 1807, *Briefe von und an Hegel*, ed. by J. Hoffmeister and J. Nicolin, 4 vols., 3rd ed. (Hamburg: Felix Meiner Verlag, 1969–1981), vol. 1, p. 196.

[3] See Richard Crouter, "Hegel and Schleiermacher at Berlin: A Many-Sided Debate," *Journal of the American Academy of Religion*, 48 (March 1980), pp. 19–43.

postcritical way of thinking about God.[4] At the very beginning of his lectures he said:

> God is the beginning of all things and the end of all things; [everything] starts from God and returns to God. God is the one and only object of philosophy. [Its concern is] to occupy itself with God, to apprehend everything in God, to lead everything back to God, as well as to derive everything particular from God and to justify everything only insofar as it stems from God, is sustained through its relationship with God, lives by God's radiance and has [within itself] the mind of God. Thus philosophy *is* theology, and [one's] occupation with philosophy – or rather *in* philosophy – is of itself the service of God. (1:84)[5]

This passage is from Hegel's lecture manuscript of 1821, which survives in a Berlin library. With the exception of various miscellaneous papers, it is the only writing on philosophy of religion in Hegel's own hand. The bulk of the resources is in the form of auditors' notebooks or transcriptions [*Nachschriften*] of the four series of lectures. These materials were amalgamated into an editorially constructed text by the original editors of Hegel's *Werke* in the 1830s and 1840s. Since Hegel changed the structure and details of his analysis considerably from one year to the next, the editorial amalgam introduced marked tensions and inconsistencies. The critical edition published by Walter Jaeschke in the 1980s reconstructs the 1821, 1824, and 1827 lectures as separate texts based on the best available resources.[6] The one feature of the lectures that remains constant through the years from 1821 to 1831 is their division, following an Introduction, into three main parts: the Concept of Religion, Determinate Religion, and the Consummate or Revelatory Religion. The sections of this chapter follow this division. It is not

---

[4] See Walter Jaeschke, *Reason in Religion: The Foundations of Hegel's Philosophy of Religion*, trans. by J. Michael Stewart and Peter C. Hodgson (Berkeley and Los Angeles: University of California Press, 1990), pp. 1–9.

[5] In-text references are to the translation cited in Footnote 6.

[6] *Vorlesungen über die Philosophie der Religion*, ed. by Walter Jaeschke, 3 vols. (vols. 3–5 in Hegel's *Vorlesungen: Ausgewählte Nachschriften und Manuskripte* [Hamburg: Felix Meiner Verlag, 1983–1985]). The English translation is *Lectures on the Philosophy of Religion*, 3 vols., ed. by Peter C. Hodgson, trans. by R. F. Brown, P. C. Hodgson, and J. M. Stewart with the assistance of H. S. Harris (Berkeley and Los Angeles: University of California Press, 1984–1987; reprint Oxford University Press, 2007). A one-volume edition of the lectures of 1827 is also available. The 1831 lectures cannot be reconstructed since only excerpts presently exist. For details on the texts and their editing, see the editorial introduction to volume 1 of the German and English editions. The analysis contained in this chapter is based on my monograph, *Hegel and Christian Theology: A Reading of the Lectures on the Philosophy of Religion* (Oxford: Oxford University Press, 2005). Used by permission of Oxford University Press.

possible in a brief presentation to attend to the distinctive nuances of the individual lectures.

Hegel's logic functions as a hermeneutical key for reading and interpreting experience. The *Werke* edition presented his lectures on the various topics of philosophy as part of a completed, consistent, unitary system, but we now know that Hegel lectured with an innovative spirit, unwilling ever simply to repeat what he had said before. On no subject was this truer than that of religion. Far from imposing an abstract, a priori schema on the history of religions, Hegel approaches this topic as an experimental field in which a variety of interpretative arrangements must be tried out. His evident willingness to incorporate new data and test new schemas suggests that for him speculative philosophy as a whole involves a conceptual play with the logical deep structure in order to arrive at new insights, to grasp connections, differences, types, trends, directions, to understand more fully the inexhaustible wealth of what presents itself in experience. He is not offering empirical descriptions but imaginative constructions. For this purpose the medium of oral lectures was ideally suited, and it is notable that Hegel was reluctant to constrain the fluidity of speech through publication.[7]

THE OBJECT, CONTEXT, AND METHOD OF PHILOSOPHY OF RELIGION

In the Introduction to his lectures (1:83–184), Hegel establishes that the object of the philosophy of religion is both religion and its referent, God. Thus he says that philosophy of religion has the same purpose as the natural theology of the school philosophy of the seventeenth and eighteenth centuries: knowledge of God by reason alone, as distinct from what is known of God on the basis of positive revelation (1:83), although he also argues later that no contradiction exists between reason and revelation, for what is revealed is rational, and reason itself is revelatory (3:63). The object of the philosophy of religion is the same as the object of religion, namely, "the supreme or absolute object" that exists strictly for its own sake and is radically free and unconditioned; likewise occupation with it must be free and unconditioned. Contra Schleiermacher's emphasis on the feeling of absolute dependence, religious consciousness is the "absolutely free consciousness," which enjoys its object in the state of blessedness and manifests the glory of God in such a way that everything transient and finite wafts away into eternal harmony (1:113–114).

---

[7] See the introduction by Duncan Forbes to *Lectures on the Philosophy of World History: Introduction: Reason in History*, trans. by H. B. Nisbet (Cambridge, UK: Cambridge University Press, 1975), xiii–xiv.

The object of the philosophy of religion is not just God but religion, or God and religion together. If the object were simply God, then the concept of God would be restricted "to the sterile result of an abstract essence [*Wesen*] of the understanding" (1:116) – the Enlightenment understanding of God as a "supreme being." Here God is not yet grasped as a living being, as *spirit* [*Geist*]. To think of God as *Geist* rather than as *Wesen* is to think of God as God is present in religious belief, that is, in the community of faith. "God can only be genuinely understood in the mode of his being as *spirit*, by means of which God makes himself into the counterpart of a community and brings about the activity of a community in relation to him; thus it will be evident that the doctrine of God is to be grasped and taught only as the doctrine of *religion*" (1:116–117). "God" and "religion" are relational concepts: God is God only in relation to the knowledge of and faith in God on the part of human communities, and religion is the relationship between God and consciousness.

The "modern" doctrine that humans can know nothing of God undercuts the philosophy of religion project as thus conceived. It is the distinction of our age, says Hegel, "to know an infinite mass of objects, but only of God to know nothing" (1:86–87). Ours is an essentially secular age to which the religious injunction to know God is accounted mere folly. Surely it is ironic to arrive at the conclusion through cognition itself that cognition grasps everything but the truth. This is the pressing issue of modernity to which Christian theology should fashion a convincing response. But Christian theology itself has mostly acceded to such a view; and Hegel's lectures are intended to fill the void left by theological agnosticism (1:89).

One of the characteristics of modern secularism is the opposition between religious consciousness and the rest of consciousness, a gulf that is reinforced by natural science, which constructs a finite system of the universe in which God is not needed and has no place (1:92–93, 102–103). The compartmentalization of religion and the notion of double truth (a human truth of reason and a divine truth of faith) are symptomatic of "the discord of our times" (1:107). Hegel insists that there cannot be two kinds of reason and two kinds of truth:

Human reason . . . *is* reason generally, is the divine within humanity. Spirit, insofar as it is called divine spirit, is not a spirit beyond the stars or beyond the world; for God is present, is omnipresent, and strictly *as spirit* is God present in spirit. God is a living God who is effective, active, and present in spirit. Religion is a begetting of the divine spirit, not an invention of human beings but an effect of the divine at work, of the divine productive process within humanity. (1:130)

To affirm this deep truth is the proper vocation of theology. Much of the Introduction to Hegel's lectures is given over to a critique of the theologies of his time for failing to do so: metaphysical theology, rational theology, historical theology, agnostic theology, ethicotheology, theologies of feeling, and atheistic and pantheistic theologies. Hegel's critique of the latter is of special interest in view of the irony that he himself was accused of atheism and pantheism in his own time, and continues to be so accused. Pantheism is not the absurd view that all things simply *are* God, but rather that God is the *essence* within accidents, the *universal* within the particular, the *one* within the many, and the *substance* within accidents. In the philosophical sense the world has no independent actuality, although of course empirically it exists. This is Spinoza's position, according to Hegel, and it is properly described as "acosmism," not "atheism" or "pantheism" (1:374–377). It is not God who is absorbed into the world, but the world into God. However, speculative philosophy, with its mediation of logical idea, nature, and finite spirit, consummated in God as absolute spirit in whom distinctions are preserved rather than annihilated, avoids both atheism and acosmism, and it certainly is not crude pantheism. It is more accurately described as "panentheism" – all things have their being or actuality *in* God – or as "holism." Whether Hegel allows sufficient independence to the world over against God is one of the lasting issues of debate over his thought.[8]

The method of philosophy of religion is "speculative," by contrast with the empirical and critical methods epitomized by Hume and Kant. Kant's philosophy starts with sense experience received in the form of intuition. By application of a priori categories (time, space, causality, substance), the mind constructs these intuitions into a picture of reality. We can never, Kant insists, get beyond these constructions to know reality or the world as it is in and for itself. The constructed object simply reflects mind back to itself. For Hegel there is a "getting beyond" in the form of a turn, a reversal, such that what is constructed also shows or manifests itself, gives itself on its own terms, which partly correspond to but also enrich and correct consciousness. Something new is known beyond self-knowledge; there is a spiraling ahead, and consciousness proves to be participatory and receptive as well as critical and constructive. Reality is, to be sure, a mirror of consciousness; but *consciousness is also a mirror of reality.* "Speculation" (from the Latin *speculum*, "mirror") involves a relationship of double mirroring in which a reversal in the flow of meaning occurs – from object to subject as well as from subject to object. The condition of possibility for this reversal is that

---

[8] William Desmond offers a scathing critique in this regard; see *Hegel's God: A Counterfeit Double?* (Aldershot: Ashgate Publishing, 2003).

subject and object, self and world, participate in, are moments of, of an encompassing whole, which Hegel calls variously "truth," "actuality," "the universal," "the absolute," "spirit" – or "God." In addition to a first and a second, there is a third, which overreaches the first and the second and is the relationship between them. This relationship, or whole, is not separable from its component elements but becomes actual and manifests itself, only in their double mirroring.

Hegel contends that an identity exists between the method of a science such as philosophy of religion and its content, which is nothing other than the "the self-explicating concept." This means that truth and method are ultimately one, and that scientific procedure follows from the movement of the subject matter itself. Thus, the first moment in the philosophical treatment of religion is *the concept of religion* in its abstractness and ideality; the second moment comprises the *determinate forms* of the concept, the way it actually appears in concrete religions; and the third moment is the *consummation* of the determinations of the concept as it returns to itself enriched by its instantiations. This consummation, claims Hegel, occurs in the Christian religion, while the determinate religions "constitute the stages of transition for the concept of religion on the way to its consummation" (1:109–112, 174–176). This threefold division is the one constant feature of all the lectures on the philosophy of religion. It poses an immediate problem for a contemporary reader. The return of the concept to itself seems to involve a transcendence of the historical determinacy through which the concept has emerged. If so, then it is difficult to understand how any historically determinate religion such as Christianity could simply *be* the absolute, true, and consummate religion – which nonetheless is understood to be an *existing* religion, something that must come to pass in history (1:141). Hegel's speculatively imagined consummate religion would seem more plausible and more adequate to the concept if it were to draw upon the resources of a diversity of religious traditions. The concept is formed in the matrix of history as a whole, and (as Hegel himself knew) the history of religions cannot be ordered into a linear trajectory culminating in Christianity.

THE CONCEPT OF RELIGION

Empirical and Speculative Definitions of the Concept of Religion

The first two lecture series (1821, 1824) move toward a definition of the concept of religion by distinguishing between empirical and speculative approaches (1:185–232, 257–328). The empirical approach is in vogue today, says Hegel, because it starts with immediate experience or feeling and defines religion as a modification of feeling (1:261–288). It quickly arrives at an impasse, however, for it is principally aware of the antithesis between the self as a finite, feeling, particular subject and God as the infinite, independent, universal object. How, then, is a relationship between finite and infinite possible? From the point of view of empirical observation, only two options seem plausible: either God remains what is totally other and beyond, the negation of finitude, of which one can have no cognitive knowledge; or finitude itself is what is exhaustively real and good, existing solely for itself. Finitude is related either *negatively* to God or *affirmatively* to itself; it cannot be related *affirmatively* to *God*. Finitude attempts to bridge this gulf in the form of "reflective" knowledge, which appears philosophically as "understanding" and religiously as "representation," but from this point of view the infinite remains either an incomprehensible beyond or a mere projection of the finite. The negative relationship to God is expressed in the feeling of utter dependence, as described by Schleiermacher. The affirmative relationship to the self is the basis of modern atheism, from Kant and Fichte onward. Only from the point of view of reason or thought is it possible to conceive the infinite as that which "overreaches" the finite, both encompassing and transcending it as an "affirmative infinitude" (1:288–310). Here the perspective shifts from finite consciousness to the infinite self-mediation of spirit. There is no way of passing over from the finite to the infinite unless the infinite itself constitutes the passage; but this is already the speculative insight.

"The speculative" for Hegel, as we have said, involves a relationship of double mirroring between consciousness and object and a reversal in the flow of meaning – from object to subject as well as from subject to object. Religion, speculatively defined, is not merely our consciousness of the absolute but the self-consciousness of absolute spirit, mediated in and through finite consciousness (1:314–318). Religion is both a human and a divine process; what transpires in it is not human projection but "the self-knowing of divine spirit through the mediation of finite spirit" (1:318 n. 7). Hegel expresses this idea with powerful metaphors. "To philosophical cognition, the progression [of consciousness] is a stream *flowing in opposite directions*, leading forward to the other, but at the same time working backward, so that what appears to be the *last*, founded on what precedes, appears rather to be the *first* – the foundation" (1:227 n. 115). The image of a stream flowing in opposite directions suggests a "speculative reversal": the rise of finite consciousness to the absolute is at the same time the return of absolute spirit to itself. What appears to be the result of the phenomenology of consciousness proves rather to be its presupposition. To these thoughts articulated in 1821,

Hegel adds in 1824: "Absolute truth cannot be a result; it is what is purely and simply first, unique. It is what takes up simply everything into itself – the absolute plenitude in which everything is but a moment. ... It is in this result itself that the one-sidedness is abolished: the result casts off its position as result and develops a *counterthrust,* so to speak, against this movement" (1:322). The counterthrust is another image of reversal and mirroring. It means that God is both alpha and omega. Two moments or movements together – God creating the world, and the world betaking itself back to God – make up the activity of God. This process first shows itself outside of religion, then within religion. Outside religion, there is an innocence with respect to God; within religion, it is God who is strictly the first and the last (1:323–324).

The Concept of God

The reversal and mirroring signify that the concept of religion is really the concept of God – of God as abstract being or substance, as the creator who "unlocks" godself and releases what is not God into existence, and as the consummator who brings all things back into relationship with God. The 1827 lectures start at this point – with the speculative insight into the nature of God and religion at which the 1824 lectures arrive only at the end (through a laborious but illuminating process). The concept of God focuses on three themes that correspond to the triune life of God (although the approach at this point is philosophical rather than theological): the abstract being of God,[9] the knowledge of God in the religious relationship, and the consummation of this relationship in the worship of God (1:365–449).

The *abstract being of God* corresponds to what is ordinarily meant by the word "God," namely, that being which is absolute truth and universality, from which everything proceeds and into which everything returns. This One, says Hegel, is the result of the whole of philosophy that precedes the philosophy of religion, and the latter discipline must accept it as a premise (1:367–368). While this definition of God is abstract and formal, the universal "shows itself to be something absolutely concrete, rich, and full of content" (1:368–369). The

---

[9] This section appears as such only in the 1827 lectures, although analogues to it are found in the other lectures where it is used as a vehicle to present proofs of the existence of God. These proofs constitute a specific religion's "abstract concept" or "metaphysical concept" of God, and the proofs are discussed as they appear in the determinate religions (part 2) and the consummate religion (part 3). The 1827 lectures gather all the proofs together into a lengthy subsection at the end of the section on "The Knowledge of God" in part 1.

development through which it manifests itself is not something alien to its universality but already implicit within it; from the outset it is a concrete universal. Expressed in more familiar philosophical categories deriving from Spinoza, we say that "God is the absolute substance, the only true actuality" – the substance or essence upon which everything else depends for its existence (1:369). If we cling to this declaration in its abstract form, then we seem to be guilty of Spinozism or pantheism.[10] "But the fact that God is *substance* does not exclude *subjectivity*." Indeed, substance is an attribute of God's absolute being-with-self and abiding-with-self that we call "spirit, absolute spirit." When we speak of substance, "the universal is not yet grasped as internally concrete"; only when it is so grasped is it spirit (1:370–371). God is not sheer, undifferentiated substance, not a "mere soil" out of which distinctions subsequently grow, but an "abiding unity" in which all distinctions remain enclosed: just this is the meaning of the immanent Trinity as an inexhaustible generative matrix. Thus in creating the world God does not step out of unity with godself. God remains the One, the abundant universal – "not an inert, abstract universal, but rather the absolute womb or the infinite fountainhead out of which everything emerges, into which everything returns, and in which it is eternally maintained." With these sensual, sexual images drawn from a Neoplatonic-mystical trajectory, Hegel unpacks the definition of God as universal substance. At the same time he remarks that we have this God not primarily in the mode of feeling and sensation but in the mode of *thought*. The mystical and the rational are connected for Hegel. "Thought is alone the soil for this content, is the activity of the universal – the universal in its activity and efficacy." "Animals have feelings, but only feelings. Human beings think, and they alone have religion." Thus religion has its "inmost seat" in thought, though doubtless it can also be felt, believed, imagined, and practiced (1:372–374).

These last remarks point to the second major topic considered under the concept of God, namely, the *knowledge of God*. The relationship of God and consciousness (which is what religion is all about) has two aspects: God's self-manifestation or self-communication and human comprehension or knowledge (1:380–383). Just as it is God's very nature to communicate godself, so it is humanity's very nature to know God.

---

[10] This remark leads Hegel into another discussion of and defense against pantheism (1:374–380) in terms similar to those used in the Introduction to the lectures (as summarized above). In 1827 he returns to the topic for a third time in his discussion of Buddhism in part 2 (2:572–575). He encountered the charge of pantheism directed against his own philosophy for the first time in the mid-1820s, and in the 1827 lectures he was especially concerned to refute it.

Hegel distinguishes among four basic forms of the knowledge of God: immediate knowledge, feeling, representation, and thought. *Immediate knowledge* is the immediate certainty that God *is*, and indeed that God is "this universality have being in and for itself, outside me and independent of me, not merely having being for me" (1:386). The most basic form of this certainty is *faith*, which is not placed in opposition to knowledge but is a form of knowledge (1:386–389). Faith means holding something to be true for which we lack direct empirical evidence or intellectual intuition of its necessity. Faith rests on both external authority (the testimony of others) and the inner witness of the Spirit (not only the Holy Spirit but our own spirituality). It has two basic modalities: feeling (which illumines its subjective aspect) and representation (which concerns the objective mode of its content, how it is an object of consciousness for us).

Feeling arises from sense but belongs to the realm of ideality, of subjectivity. When I say that "I feel God," I mean that God is within my being: we are not two but one, yet the one remain two, for God is not a product of feeling but exists independently of me as the ground of my being (1:268–270). While feeling is a necessary aspect of religious experience, it has severe limitations. It is indeterminate, neither good nor evil, neither true nor false; and it has no capacity for making judgments with respect to the validity of its contents. The feelings of the heart must be purified and cultivated, and this involves precisely thought. Thought "is the ejection of the content out of feeling; it is a kind of liberation" (1:391–396). Hegel delivers the coup de grâce to feeling when he remarks that "feeling is what human beings have in common with the animals; it is the animal, sensuous form." Thus if we agree with Schleiermacher, "that religion rests on th[e] feeling of dependence, then animals would have to have religion too, for they feel this dependence" (1:273, 279).[11]

Representation [*Vorstellung*] attends to the objective aspect, the content, of whatever it is that we feel or are subjectively certain of, but it does not yet penetrate this content rationally or cognitively. It relies on the understanding [*Verstand*]], which places images and sense impressions *under* categories [*ver-stehen*] and *before* the mind [*vor-stellen*] as objective, unmediated entities. Since this is how people ordinarily think, "religion is the consciousness of absolute truth in the way

---

[11] This remark about Schleiermacher ignores the latter's distinction between ordinary sense-based feeling and religious feeling as the awareness of utter or absolute dependence on God, an awareness that is the condition of possibility for all knowing and doing. As such it is closer to what Hegel calls immediate knowledge or faith. The mutual polemics between Hegel and Schleiermacher were often misdirected.

that it occurs for all human beings." Philosophy has the same content, and its task is solely that of transforming representations into concepts. The content remains the same, although philosophy is often reproached for removing the content as it separates out from it what pertains only to representation (1:396–397). This operation is supposed to be not a reduction but a transformation, yet the question remains as to how and to what extent representational images continue to reverberate in concepts. Without images, concepts become dry and abstract. Hegel's own thinking is famously replete with images, metaphors, and analogies.

Thought seeks for relationships and universality among the various contents that representation apprehends only in their determinate isolation (1:404–406). It does this by raising representational figures to conceptual ideas. A "concept" (*Begriff*) grasps- or holds-together (*be-greifen*) those elements that remain disparate in the simple placing before the mind of various sensible or nonsensible images. Conceptual thinking for the most part does not invent new terms or convert everything into the grammar of logic but makes use of materials furnished by representation. It develops arguments and hypotheses that elucidate the unity of representational features. It grasps the logical relations implicit in narrative relations. In this fashion it arrives at conviction, which is certainty in the form of thought. Thought is not a new conceptual apparatus but a way of thinking dialectically. Thus it is evident that thought continues to be fructified by the imagistic materials thrown up by representation; without representation there could be no thought, and a dialectic between representation and thought takes place.

Thought involves mediation, and the *proofs of the existence of God* are a form of mediation between consciousness and its object; they are equivalent to the third term of a syllogism, which links the other two and has the character of a proof. Moreover, the mediation contained in this knowledge is religion itself, for religion is an act of mediation: it is not simply a reference to an object but inwardly a movement, a passing over or an elevation to God. The passage is of a twofold sort: from finite to infinite being (or from finite being to the concept of God), and from subjective to objective infinitude (or from the concept of God to the being of God). The first of these passages corresponds to the cosmological and teleological proofs, the second to the ontological proof. The proofs, then, are the concrete forms that the knowledge of God assumes in the various religions (1:411–416).

Two sorts of distortion are present in the attempt to "prove" God's "existence." The first (1:417–418) is the suggestion that God can be said to "exist," for "existence" [*Dasein*] refers to determinate, finite being, whereas God's being is in no way limited. It would be better to say, "God and his being, his actuality or objectivity," and the purpose of the proofs would be to show the connection or coherence between God and being, that is, between the concept of God and the being (or actuality, objectivity) of God. The second distortion (1:419–421) is the notion that it is possible to "prove" or demonstrate God's being from finite being, for this would be to be make God a result or a consequence, dependent upon the being of the finite, whereas God is precisely the nonderivative, is "utterly actual being in and for itself." But religion remains an "elevation" to God even after this form of demonstration has been stripped away. The Kantian critique of the demonstrative form of the proofs cannot be considered to have demolished religious knowledge and activity as such. It is only that elevation to God does not properly entail a demonstration of the infinite from the finite on the basis of a self-projection of the finite.

For this reason, the cosmological and teleological proofs, while containing useful elements, are not finally valid. The only genuine proof is the ontological proof, which passes over, not from (finite) being to God, but from God to being, that is, from the concept of God to the being or reality of God (1:433–441, 3:351–358). The problem with Anselm's argument from "perfection" – a problem clearly exposed by Kant – is that it presupposes the very unity of concept (thought) and being (reality) that must be demonstrated. Hegel provides his own post-Kantian demonstration. The true concept is not a subjective idea or a fantasy of the imagination (for which being is rightly not a predicate). The true concept contains objectivity within itself. It is alive and active; it mediates itself with itself; it is the movement or process of self-objectifying by which its subjectivity is sublated – just as when human beings realize their drives or purposes what was at first only ideal becomes something real. The concept "makes itself reality and thus becomes the truth, the unity of subject and object." The most perfect concept is the most perfectly real, and God is the most perfect concept. This logical truth becomes fully manifest in the Christian religion, which is the religion of incarnation. The proof does not involve some illicit logical trick but is provided by God's involvement in world-process. God, who is utterly actual being [das Seiende], takes on worldly, determinate, existential being [Dasein]. The religious elevation to God presupposes this divine descent, which is God's self-proof.

Of course this proof will not work for those who have no concept of God, no knowledge of God, and no experience of religious elevation and divine descent. There is no way of proving a person into being religious. What is required is involvement in the practice of a religious community, its *worship of God*.[12] In the case of the knowledge of God, I am immersed in my object and know nothing of myself. But the true situation is the *relationship* between myself and this object; I must *know myself* as filled by it. What accomplishes this unity is *action*, the activity of the cultus. Cultus is "the including, within my own self, of myself with God, the knowing of myself within God and of God within me" (1:443). This is accomplished through the act of "enjoyment," "partaking," "communion," or "eucharist," which is the definitive cultic act. To describe it Hegel uses the term *Genuß*, which has at its root the physical image of eating and drinking: symbolically we ingest or assimilate the crucified God, who is really present in the sacramental elements. This action does not *bring about* the reconciliation of God and humanity by a substitutionary atonement, for example, or by sacrifices pleasing to God. Rather it presupposes reconciliation, participates in it as something already implicitly and explicitly accomplished by the grace of God (1:443–444). Hegel remarks that the preoccupation today in Protestant churches seems to be solely with subjective faith, not with participation in God through ritual practice. He distinguishes four aspects of the cultus: devotion (an engaged thinking), sacrifice (a negation of the finite by offering it up to God), sacraments (reconciliation brought into feeling), and repentance (an offering of one's heart to God). Notably no mention is made of preaching. When purity of heart is properly "cultivated," it issues in *ethical life,* which is "the most genuine cultus," but only to the extent that consciousness of God remains bound up with it (1:446). Thus social and political ethics represent an extension and realization of the religious cultus.

DETERMINATE RELIGION

Determinate Religion is by far the largest of the three parts of the philosophy of religion. Another chapter would be needed to do it even minimal justice. By the time of the 1824 lectures Hegel had become engaged with the topic of the history of religions. It clearly fascinated him, and its proper interpretation deeply challenged him toward the end of his career. This is evident from two facts: the reading he undertook in primary sources and secondary literature for this part of the lectures, and his inability to arrive at a satisfactory arrangement of the materials. Hegel had an extensive knowledge of world religions for his time, but

---

[12] This topic is discussed by Hegel not only (briefly) at the end of the Concept of Religion in the 1827 lectures (1:441–449) but also (extensively) in relation to each of the determinate religions and to the consummate religion in all of the lectures. In the Concept of Religion it is described principally in terms of Christian worship.

his sources left a great deal to be desired as far as a scientific study of religion is concerned (many were based on travel and missionary reports). He focused his attention on the original or classical expressions of the religions, for the most part not attending to their subsequent histories or contemporary living expressions, if any. He viewed the history of religions as primarily a thing of the past, with the exception of Christianity – and of Islam, which is missing from Determinate Religion and is briefly mentioned only in Part Three of the lectures as a contemporary rival of Christianity. This is one of the severest problems with Hegel's treatment, for several of the religions he discusses are certainly still alive: nature or indigenous religions, Chinese religion (Confucian and Daoist), Buddhism, Hinduism, Judaism, Zoroastrianism. The dead religions to which he devotes considerable attention are the Egyptian, Greek, and Roman religions. Hegel's view seems to be that, while religions continue to be practiced throughout the word, *Geist* has left most of them behind. Christianity alone truly lives, surrounded by fossilized forms, and it is possible that it too will become a fossil. Yet he is not sanguine about a postreligious future.

Hegel's inability to arrive at a satisfactory arrangement of the materials is indicated by the fact that his organization of Determinate Religion differed widely in each of the four lecture series. Whereas the treatment of Consummate Religion fell into place with the 1824 lectures, and of the Concept of Religion in 1827, Hegel experimented with yet another arrangement of Determinate Religion in 1831, which had as many problems as the previous arrangements. Yet all the arrangements and detailed discussions of specific religions are packed with insights. Walter Jaeschke remarks that Hegel's "treatment of the history of religion forms an experimental field in which virtually everything is tried out."[13] Thus Jaeschke suggests that what Hegel offers in Determinate Religion is less a history of religion than a typology or geography of religion.[14] To be sure, religion is fundamentally historical, but its historicality follows from the historicality of human spirit. Since there is no single history of human spirit, there cannot be a single, unified history of religion organized under an encompassing philosophical conceptuality. Hegel's claim to be able to do the latter is falsified by his actual achievement in the successive lectures, which should have made it clear that the objective of a logical construction of the history of religion cannot be attained. What Hegel gives is a typology of shapes in which spirit appears in religious history and by which it develops, but these shapes need not, indeed cannot, be linked into a unitary history directed to

---

[13] Jaeschke, *Reason in Religion*, 277.
[14] Ibid., pp. 272, 277–284.

a common goal. He is able to demonstrate the necessity of a diversity and plurality of religions, because spirit comes to itself only through movement and distinction, but not the necessity of a universal history of religion. The shapes appear as dispersed geographically in distinctive cultural trajectories rather than as linked in a temporal progression. Hegel himself was aware of this insofar as for him Christianity does not evolve from the sequence of the determinate religions (although it is of course linked to Judaism). Rather than a historical progression, what he pictures is that a break occurs and something new emerges out of crisis – a religion that corresponds fully to the concept of religion, and thus a religion in which God is known as God is in godself. This new religion seems to be released from the course of history.

THE CONSUMMATE RELIGION

Christianity as the Consummate and Revelatory Religion

The correspondence of Christianity to the concept of religion and of God is marked by the fact that its inner structural elements articulate moments in the triune life of God. These are what Hegel came to call (in the 1831 lectures) the kingdoms of the Father, the Son, and the Spirit. His understanding of this structure evolved from that of a philosophical triad to a theological trinity.[15] The triad, as described in the 1821 lectures (3:73ff), corresponds to the three branches of philosophy: the logical idea, nature, and finite spirit. Applied to Christianity's "concrete representation," it has the peculiar result of locating Christ in the third moment of the triad, while the Spirit becomes an appendage treated under the theme of "community, cultus." A modification is needed so that the second and third moments of the triad (nature, finite spirit) together comprise the second moment of the trinitarian dialectic, the creation and redemption of the world through the work of the Son; while the Spirit is brought into the Trinity as the third moment, the consummation and return of all things to God as absolute spirit.

Hegel makes such an adjustment in 1824 and thereafter when he identifies the three "elements" or "kingdoms" that make up the Christian idea of God (3:185–188, 271–274, 362–363). The first, the kingdom of the Father, concerns the idea of God in and for itself, the immanent Trinity; the second, the kingdom of the Son, encompasses the processes of differentiation, estrangement, and reconciliation whereby

---

[15] For details, see the editorial introduction to vol. 3 of the *Lectures on the Philosophy of Religion* (3:11–14), including the table that provides a comparative analysis of the structure of the Consummate Religion (3:54–55).

the world is created, falls into evil, and is redeemed; and the third, the kingdom of the Spirit, concerns the formation of the community of faith and its eschatological orientation to the perfection of all things in God. Together the three kingdoms form an inclusive Trinity (an economic Trinity that incorporates an immanent Trinity as its first moment). The inclusive Trinity articulates the complex life of God, which unfolds from self-identity through differentiation and otherness to completion and wholeness. This is the Christian metanarrative. What Hegel offers in the third part of the *Lectures on the Philosophy of Religion* is a speculative redescription of the metanarrative by means of which its mythological worldview, sequential view of space/time, and representational language are translated into a philosophical conceptuality that will protect it from the hostile demythologizations of modernity.[16]

The terms by which Hegel names the Christian religion in his speculative redescription of it are noteworthy. The two principal names, which appear in the heading of his lecture manuscript, are "consummate" [*vollendete*] and "revelatory" [*offenbare*] (3:61–63, 163–164, 249–250). The concept of religion is completed or fulfilled in Christianity as *die vollendete Religion* because at the center of this religion is the "infinite idea of the incarnation of God" in which the extremes of finite and infinite, consciousness and object, are unified: this is the "speculative midpoint" of religion (1:245; 3:125). Christianity is also *die absolute Religion* (3:165–169), and the term "absolute" forms a set with "consummate," but with distinctive nuances. "Absolute" for Hegel is not a static but a dynamic, relational concept. Absolute spirit is utterly connected with everything: it is nothing but relationality. God is absolutely free within godself, and it is precisely in this absolute freedom that God "absolves" or "releases" the other to exist as a free and independent being. "This other, released as something free and independent, is the world as such" (3:292). The world that God releases is a genuine otherness with which God has reciprocal relations, but it is not something that resides "beyond" the absolute by which the latter might be limited and rendered finite; the divine life is all-encompassing. The verb *entlassen*, "to release," is a Germanic equivalent to the Latin verb *absolvere*, "to loosen from" or "let go," from which the word "absolute" derives. Hegel's association of "release" with the the absolute" shows that the latter, for him, has just the opposite meaning than its conventional usage.

---

[16] See Emil Fackenheim, *The Religious Dimension in Hegel's Thought* (Bloomington: Indiana University Press, 1967), and Cyril O'Regan, *The Heterodox Hegel* (Albany: SUNY Press, 1994).

Hegel's other preferred name for the Christian religion is "reve-latory" [*die offenbare Religion*]. This is so because "revelatoriness" [*Offenbarkeit*] is one of the defining attributes of its God (3:63, 170). God is intrinsically revelatory, self-manifesting; God is not jealous, does not withhold or conceal godself, as Plato and Aristotle con-tended against the mystery cults. What God reveals is not so much truths or information *about* God but rather that revelatoriness and self-communication are essentially what God is. This is what it means to say that God is "spirit," for spirit is essentially a being *for* spirit, for another, a relating, revealing, self-opening, self-dirempting spirit (1:382–383, 3:250–251). Christianity is, however, more commonly spo-ken of as the "revealed" religion [*die geoffenbarte Religion*], suggest-ing that something has been disclosed through it in a historical, pos-itive, objective fashion. Hegel affirms this claim[17] but insists that in the first instance what has been *revealed* about God is simply that God is intrinsically *revelatory, manifest* (3:170–171, 252–253). What is revealed is revelatoriness, openness. Revelation has no object or con-tent other than itself. The coincidence of *offenbar* and *geoffenbart* means that for Hegel the whole debate in late Enlightenment thought over reason versus revelation was misplaced. What is revealed is pre-cisely the process in which reason and truth make themselves open and manifest.[18]

Trinity: God as Absolute Spirit

The intrinsic revelatoriness and self-communication of God are expressed for Christianity in the doctrine of the Trinity or the con-cept of God as absolute spirit. What makes spirit absolute and infinite is that all of its relationships occur within a matrix of communication and recognition. Absolute spirit incorporates the externality of finite relations, but its own relations are properly internal, which is to say that they are moments of an inwardly differentiated whole (3:186–168). In a holistic system the other is not reduced to the same, but neither are the same and the other viewed as mutually exclusive atoms. Hegel's holism seeks a middle ground between atomism and monism.

Christianity articulates the holism of absolute spirit in terms of the doctrine of the Trinity (3:77–86, 192–197, 275–290). Hegel's inclusive

---

[17] In the *Encyclopedia of the Philosophical Sciences* Hegel names Christianity *Die geoffenbarte Religion*, whereas in the *Phenomenology of Spirit* as well as the philosophy of religion lectures it is *Die offenbare Religion*.

[18] Further aspects of Christianity such as truth, freedom, and reconciliation follow from its consummate and revelatory character.

or holistic Trinity, as we have seen, incorporates the immanent and economic Trinities distinguished in Christian tradition. Classical theology accorded precedence to God's ideal self-relations, of which the world is an epiphenomenal reflection. Modern theology has prioritized the economic Trinity, God's appearance and work in the world as Son and Spirit, on the grounds that nothing can be known of God's inner life, of what God is in and for godself. Hegel will have nothing of this division, for it destroys the very heart of what God is. The elements are distinguishable but not separable. While in a discursive treatment they are unavoidably discussed in linear fashion, they are related not linearly but spirally or concentrically, with each spiral overlapping and encompassing the previous ones. The pattern is that of a trinity within a trinity, of Father within Son within Spirit.

The difficulty with the classical doctrine of the Trinity, from Hegel's perspective, is not only that it divides the two trinities but also that it is couched in representational language employing numbers and persons. As to numbers, the Trinity cannot be a matter of quantity or counting. Quantitative thinking cannot grasp how unity manifests itself in diversity and difference. Hegel suggests that "reason can employ all the *relationships* of the understanding, but only insofar as its destroys the *forms* of the understanding" (3:192). For the representational form of understanding [*Verstand*], the Trinity is a suprarational paradox, something to be accepted on the authority of faith; it is not a truth of reason itself [*Vernunft*].

As to persons, it can only be misleading to introduce the figurative, familial relationships expressed by "Father" and "Son." In truth, "all three [persons] are spirit" (3:194–195). The Trinity is a play of spiritual relationships by which God is God. "Father" is not a divine person but a symbol designating the immanent Trinity, while "Son" is a symbol designating the economic or worldly Trinity, and "Spirit" is a symbol designating the inclusive or holistic Trinity. In the 1831 lectures, this provocative statement occurs: "The abstractness of the Father is given up in the Son – this then is death. But the negation of this negation is the unity of Father and Son – love, or the Spirit" (3:370; cf. 3:324 n. 199). Hegel does not mean that the Father and the Son simply disappear into the Spirit, but rather that the Spirit is the most concrete and encompassing of the trinitarian symbols. The death of Christ signifies the death of the transcendent father-figure and of the individual savior-figure. But there can be no Spirit apart from the abstractness of the Father and the death of the Son – apart, that is, from the dialectic of identity and difference and universality and particularity.

God is to be understood not as three persons but as infinite personality or infinite subjectivity, which constitutes distinctions within itself but sublates these distinctions and achieves a richer unity. Personality is not a dead, unmoving substance but a living play of relationships formed by love and friendship. Only speculative thinking is able to grasp how distinctions are both posited and resolved, and why contradictions are present in everything living and concrete. Speculative theology comprehends the rationality of the divine mystery not only in terms of the logical paradigm that governs Hegel's system but also by introducing the analogy of ethical relationships and by describing the nature of personality. "Ethical life, love, means precisely the giving up of particularity, of particular personality, and its extension to universality – so, too, with friendship. In friendship and love I give up my abstract personality and thereby win it back as concrete personality. The truth of personality is found precisely in winning it back through this immersion, this being immersed in the other" (3:285–286). God is the utterly concrete, universal personality, accomplished in and through the totality of the divine life, not in the abstraction of purely interior relations.

Creation, Humanity, and Evil

Creation is a very important doctrine for Hegel because it describes the process by which the internal differentiation within the divine life is outwardly posited as a concrete, material reality (3:86–90, 198–201, 290–294). As we have noted, he uses the metaphor of "release" of "letting exist" [Entlassen]. The absolute freedom of God is such that God is able to release the otherness that is intrinsic to God's own being into actual, independent existence, which is the world vis-à-vis God. The other within God, the eternal Son, obtains the determinacy of other-being, becomes a historical Son. In this way, the nonserious play of love with itself (the immanent Trinity) becomes deadly serious, subject to the ruptures, conflicts, and suffering of the finite world (3:291–293). God is not thereby diminished but enlarged, for the world precisely in its otherness from God remains a moment within the divine life. God does not abandon the world but preserves and saves it, and indeed is enriched and completed by it; but this is an existential, not a logical completion. Both truths must be maintained: that God is complete apart from the world, and that God achieves completion through the world.

The world divides into the realms of nature and humanity (finite spirit). God is present and active in both realms, but only human beings are capable of knowing and relating to God. Humans, however, are riven by an internal contradiction: they belong to nature but must raise themselves from nature to spirit by the use of reason. Such an action involves a separation or cleavage brought about by the consciousness of self and other. Evil results when cleavage [*Entzweiung*] becomes alienation [*Entfremdung*] between separated elements, or when a retreat occurs back into natural immediacy with its selfishness and struggle for survival (3:92–103, 202–205, 295–300). This is Hegel's demythologized version of the biblical story of the "fall," which is also, paradoxically, a "rising" (3:101–107). What is presented here is a tragic view of human nature: the condition for the possibility of good includes also the possibility of evil. In order to rise out of the natural state and realize their spiritual potential, human beings must exercise their rational capacity, which is what makes them like God, but which also produces anxiety, alienation, and efforts at self-securing. The knowledge that makes humans also wounds them (3:205–206, 301–310). It is sometimes said that Hegel trivializes the problem of evil by connecting it too closely with knowledge and failing to recognize its absurd and irrational aspects. From Hegel's point of view what gives evil its extraordinary power is precisely its connection with knowledge. It is a distortion and perversion of what is highest in humanity, not of what is lowest, and thus it has a potency that far outstrips natural destruction as well as a capacity for self-deception that reason on its own cannot overcome. What is required is a redemption of reason – not its displacement.

Christ and Redemption

This redemption comes about through the incarnation of God in a single human being at a specific time and place. Hegel devotes considerable efforts to establishing the possibility, necessity, and actuality of such an incarnation. The *possibility* resides in the implicit unity of divine and human nature, which is given with humanity's awareness that God is its absolute truth and destiny. Divinity and humanity are not ontologically incompatible natures but belong to each other despite their present estrangement. The actualized unity of divine and human nature is Hegel's philosophical interpretation of "incarnation." The becoming-human [*Menschwerdung*] of divinity is not something that happens only once as an extrinsic miracle; rather it is a "moment in the process of the divine nature" (3:109–110, 211–212, 310–312). The *necessity* of incarnation is that the unity must appear and be accomplished in history. On the one hand, God must share in the anguish of history to become a spiritual God; and on the other hand, humans need such an appearance as a concrete sensible verification of their redemption (3:110–112, 214–215, 312–313). Finally, the *actuality* focuses on a single human being.

God is present in the concrete subjectivity of individuals, and each individual is unique. Moreover, there must be only *one* individual in whom the idea of divine-human unity appears *in a revelatorily definitive way* because several would be an abstraction and because one must stand apart from all the others in their need and ignorance (3:112–114, 145, 214, 313–314). That this individual is Jesus of Nazareth cannot be established philosophically but is given by history. The claim that Jesus is the Christ, the bearer and revealer of redemption, is a claim of faith, but Hegel believes that it can be shown to be congruent with historical fact (3:114–115, 142–149).

History shows that Jesus was an extraordinary teacher whose life conformed to what he taught about love and friendship, the revolutionary reversal of values, and the defining relationship to God (3:115–122). On this basis Hegel makes strong claims. The life of this teacher is "in conformity with" his teaching and "strictly adequate to" the idea of divine-human unity. The content of his life is simply the kingdom of God that he proclaims. "Since it is the divine idea that courses through this history, it occurs not as the history of a single individual alone, but rather it is implicitly the history of actual humanity as it constitutes itself as the existence of spirit" (3:122–124, 145). Jesus is not merely a teacher but a prophet through whom God speaks. The speech and activity of Jesus is that of a human being, yet it is at the same time "essentially the work of God – not as something suprahuman that appears in the shape of an external revelation, but rather as [God's] working in a human being, so that the divine presence is essentially identical with this human being" (3:316–321). The faith that the divine life flows in this human life is based on the witness of the Holy Spirit to individuals and to the community of faith. Hegel is clear about this: only faith can see that *God* is present in Christ; but there are reasons for this envisagement; it does not run counter to the historical witness (3:368–369). Faith is rooted in history, but no proof of God can be given from history.

The perspective from which faith sees the presence of God in Christ is a postdeath and postresurrection perspective. For Hegel the death of Christ is of great significance, for it is to be seen as the death of God, that is, as the most extreme "divestment" [*Entäußerung*] of divinity (3:124–128, 131). The "deepest anguish" of the cross (a shameful, dishonoring death) is also the highest expression of God's love for humanity. This is not to be construed as a substitutionary atonement or extrinsic sacrifice, but as the historical manifestation of the reconciliation eternally accomplished within the godhead (3:219–220). The death of Christ also represents a transition from the sensible to the spiritual presence of God in the community of faith (3:322–326). This transition is Hegel's demythologized interpretation of the resurrection, which

occurs with the rise of a new communal existence patterned on Christ
(3:131–133).

Spirit and Community

Human subjectivity, when it is transfigured by the indwelling of the
Spirit of God, becomes a communal subjectivity, an intersubjectivity
in which external distinctions and social rankings are abolished. In the
presence of God all human beings are free and equal. Their relationships
are based not on attraction or personal fulfillment but on "the infinite
love that comes from infinite anguish." The anguish, the shared suffering, creates a new kind of human fellowship in which persons find
themselves only by losing themselves for the sake of others. Love in
the fullest sense is compassion, suffering with and on behalf of others.
It is grounded in the divine compassion revealed in Christ. The Holy
Spirit is the power and reality of this love made subjectively present and
actual in the life of the community. It is "the Spirit of God, or God as
the present, actual Spirit, God dwelling in his community" (3:133–142,
331).

This is Hegel's radical vision of the Christian community. He knows
that it can exist in history only by means of institutional forms that
are inadequate to the divine content; yet without form or shape, spirit
dissipates: no *Geist* without *Gestalt*. The institutional forms of the
church follow from the twofold task of *coming* to the truth (baptism,
faith, doctrine) and *appropriating* the truth (repentance, worship, sacraments) (3:333). Hegel devotes considerable attention to these forms,
culminating in the eucharist, which, while a sensuous act of partaking,
brings about a mystical or spiritual union by appropriating the eternal sacrifice that is God. The eucharist extends into the life of the
community the self-divestment of God in Christ (3:152–154, 235–236,
337).

The community in turn has the mission of extending this pattern to
the world, of giving up its inward spirituality for the sake of the redemption of the world. Hegel describes a three-step process by which this
happens: the reality of worldly institutions (monasticism, the medieval
church, ethical life, and the state), the ideality of abstract reflection
(Enlightenment, Pietism), and the mediation of reality and ideality by
speculative philosophy (which defends religion against the attacks of
modern rationalism and preserves its truth in conceptual form). But
ironically the philosophical resolution is only partial, for philosophy
forms "an isolated order of priests" whose mission is to preserve and
interpret the truth but not to struggle for it. Thus, the *Philosophy of
Religion* lectures (at least those of 1821) end on a "discordant note,"

which reflects Hegel's ambivalent attitude toward the church and the-ology on the one hand, and post-Enlightenment culture on the other hand. He believes that religion must "take refuge" in the concept, and that the work of theology is more adequately performed by philosophy. But Hegel's own awareness of the insecure place of philosophy in the modern world is a sober warning against advancing hegemonic claims on its behalf. [19]

[19] Here a wealth of material (3:237–247, 339–347) is compressed into an inadequate summary. Hegel's own presentation is compressed and incomplete because of the approaching end of the semester. This summary does not take into account the discrepancy between the ending of the lectures in 1821 (3:158–162) and in later years.

10 Hegel and Mysticism

I. INTRODUCTION

That there is something "mystical" about Hegel's philosophy is a familiar claim. In the years following Hegel's death it was a commonplace. In an 1840 essay on Meister Eckhart, the Danish philosopher Hans Martensen remarked that Hegel (as well as Schelling) had "demanded that philosophical thought rejuvenate itself in the immediate knowledge of God and divine things found in mysticism."[1] Friedrich Theodor Vischer remarked that the Hegelian philosophy had come forth "from the school of the old mystics, especially Jakob Boehme."[2] In his 1835 work *Die christliche Gnosis*, Ferdinand Christian Bauer claimed that Hegel was a modern Gnostic, and argued for his philosophical kinship with Boehme. Wilhelm Dilthey later noted the same affinity between Hegel and the mystics. More recently, authors as different as Bertrand Russell and J. N. Findlay have claimed a "mystical element" in Hegel's thought – Russell in order to disparage Hegel, Findlay in order to elevate him.

In this chapter, I shall survey the evidence for the influence of mysticism on Hegel's writings. I shall argue that the evidence is abundant and the influence decisive. However, even if it can be established that there was such an influence, and that it was of importance, this does not mean that the Hegelian philosophy can itself be accurately described as mystical. Therefore, this issue must be addressed as well, and I shall approach it, primarily in section three, through an examination of what Hegel himself had to say about the relationship of his philosophy to mysticism.

I am actually going to put off defining precisely what is meant by mysticism until section three. In fact, I will let Hegel himself define the

---

[1] *Between Hegel and Kierkegaard: Hans L. Martensen's Philosophy of Religion*, trans. by Curtis L. Thompson and David J. Kangas (Atlanta: Scholars Press, 1997), p. 154.
[2] See Ernst Benz, *The Mystical Sources of German Romantic Philosophy*, trans. by Blair G. Reynolds and Eunice M. Paul (Allison Park: Pickwick Publications, 1983), p. 2.

253

term for us. For now, I intend to rely on my readers' intuitions about the meaning of the term. Philosophers have a sense of what counts as "mystical," a sense which amounts to an intuitive recognition of "family resemblances" between certain thinkers, claims, and styles of writing. Even in the absence of a definition, I think that this sense generally serves us quite well, and so I see no serious problem in relying on it, at least initially.

What would count as evidence for the influence of mysticism on Hegel? We would probably have to establish three things: that Hegel read widely in mysticism and showed an active interest in it, that he wrote (and wrote approvingly) about the mystics, and that his philosophy would not have taken the form it did in the absence of his encounter with mysticism. The first two points can be established with relative ease. The third point is more difficult to prove.

II. THE INFLUENCE OF MYSTICISM ON HEGEL

Perhaps the most sensible way to proceed is to move chronologically, tracing the evidence for the influence of mysticism throughout Hegel's entire life.[3]

Hegel's childhood in Stuttgart – from 1770 to 1788 – does not provide much evidence of mystic influence, but allows for some tantalizing speculations. During this time, Hegel's homeland, Württemberg, was a hotbed of interest not only in mysticism, but also in such "Hermetic" fields as alchemy. Mystical and Hermetic literature was plentiful in Württemberg, and works by Paracelsus and Boehme were widely circulated. The *Schwäbischen Magazin*, a highly influential publication in Swabian literary culture, printed alchemical and theosophical works.

Hegel's religious upbringing is thought to have been, broadly speaking, pietist. The leading Swabian exponents of pietism, J. A. Bengel (1687–1752) and F. C. Oetinger (1702–1782) were heavily influenced by the tradition of German mysticism, especially Meister Eckhart (1260–ca. 1327) and Jakob Boehme (1575–1624). This has led some scholars to speculate that from early on, Hegel may have received some influence, however indirect, from mystical sources. Franz Wiedmann writes that "Hegel's home, like that of every old, established family in Stuttgart up to the beginning of our century, was marked by Protestant Pietism. And thus Hegel was steeped in its theosophy and mysticism from

---

[3] Most of the material presented in this section is discussed much more fully in my book, *Hegel and the Hermetic Tradition* (Ithaca, NY: Cornell University Press, 2001; revised paperback edition, 2008). Readers who wish a more detailed argument for the influence of mysticism on Hegel are referred to that work.

childhood."[4] Writing of both Hegel and Schelling (who was also Swabian), Robert Schneider has emphasized their intellectual distance, starting at a very early age, from the mechanistic materialism of the Enlightenment. Their "conceptual world," he writes, was that of the "ancient categories of chemical (i.e., alchemical)-biological philosophy of nature," deriving from "Oetinger, Boehme, van Helmont, Boyle, Fludd, Paracelsus, Agrippa von Nettesheim, Telesio, and others . . . . This philosophy of nature was still alive in Württemberg during Schelling and Hegel's youth."[5]

There is no hard documentary evidence, though, for the influence of mysticism on Hegel during this period. To be sure, some of Hegel's earliest jottings do touch on issues characteristic of Württemberg Pietism. He laboriously copied out passages from religious texts, but there is nothing overtly mystical in any of it. I shall have reason, however, to return later to the question of the possible influence on Hegel of Oetinger.

Hegel's studies in the Tübingen *Stift* (1788–1793) also give precious little evidence of the contribution of mysticism to Hegel's development. At the *Stift*, Hegel studied with a faculty of rather conventional theologians and read works by Plato, Kant, Schiller, Jacobi, Hemsterhuis, Montesquieu, Rousseau, and Herder. The remarks of Hegel's instructors indicate that he had little interest at the time in metaphysics, let alone mysticism.[6]

From 1793 to 1801, Hegel was employed as a private tutor in Berne and then in Frankfurt. Hegel's biographer Karl Rosenkranz has referred to this as a "theosophical phase" in Hegel's development. His claim has proved controversial among Hegel scholars. However, it does seem that during this period Hegel began to study the works of Boehme, Eckhart, Tauler, and possibly also (if Rosenkranz is to be believed) Franz von Baader. It was Boehme who made the greatest impression on him.

Why did Hegel suddenly take up the writings of several of the greatest German mystics? That he did lends some plausibility to the thesis that there was an influence of the mystics on Hegel in his boyhood. Perhaps prior to the Berne-Frankfurt period he had never studied the

---

[4] Franz Wiedmann, *Hegel: An Illustrated Biography*, trans. by Joachim Neugroschel (New York: Pegasus, 1968), p. 14. As an adult, Hegel was critical of pietism, but his later endorsement of the work of Karl Friedrich Göschel (1784–1862), who tried to fuse Hegelianism and pietism, indicates that he was not entirely unsympathetic to it.

[5] Robert Schneider, *Schellings und Hegels schwäbische Geistessahnen* (Würzburg: Tiltsch, 1938), p. 2.

[6] Johannes Hoffmeister, *Dokumente zu Hegels Entwicklung* (Stuttgart: Fromann, 1936), p. 430.

mystics directly, but then, after a long period studying more conventional authors and subjects, he turned at last to their original texts. This is quite plausible, but it is pure speculation. We know that during this period Hegel also became involved in Masonic circles.[7] When Hegel made the move from Berne to Frankfurt, partly in order to be reunited with his close friend Hoelderlin, he sent the latter a poem titled "Eleusis," which contains Masonic imagery.[8] Various strains of Masonry existed at the time, and some were purveyors of Enlightenment rationalism and political liberalism, rather than theosophy. It is believed that Hegel (who never actually became a Mason) was involved with the Enlightenment wing of Freemasonry. Nevertheless, some Masons, particularly those in Germany, combined both liberal politics and mysticism, and it could be that one or more individuals Hegel met through these contacts encouraged his study of the mystics.[9] In any case, it is subsequent to this "theosophical phase" that Hegel begins to produce the first writings which bear his distinctive stamp.

In Jena (1801–1807) Hegel's interest in mysticism appears to have intensified. He now found himself once again in the company of Schelling, who was avidly interested in the writings of Boehme, Oetinger, and the visionary Emanuel Swedenborg (1688–1772). David Walsh writes that Jena during this period

... had become the focal point of the German Romantic movement, and many of its greatest figures were assembled there, including Tieck, Novalis, Schelling, F. Schlegel, and A.W. Schlegel. Within that company an intense center of interest was formed by their rediscovery of the German mystical tradition. For the first time the works of the great medieval and Reformation mystics were becoming widely available within their native land. The appearance of Eckhart and Boehme in particular was heralded as a liberating release from the deadness of Enlightenment rationalism. They read, too, the major eighteenth-century commentators of Boehme ... and the Swabian Pietist theologian Friedrich Christoph Oetinger, in whom they found a more contemporary application of the great mystical insights of the past.[10]

[7] See Jacques D'Hondt, *Hegel Secret: Recherches sur les sources cachées de la pensée de Hegel* (Paris: Presses Universitaires de France, 1968). See also H. S. Harris, *Hegel's Development: Toward the Sunlight (1770–1801)* (London: Oxford University Press, 1972), p. 156.

[8] See D'Hondt, pp. 227–281. See also my discussion of the poem, drawing on D'Hondt, in *Hegel and the Hermetic Tradition*, pp. 75–76.

[9] Heinrich Schneider notes that the German lodges were "teeming with magical, theosophical, mystical notions" and that much of their lore was Kabbalistic. See Schneider, *Quest for Mysteries: The Mystical Background for Literature in Eighteenth Century Germany* (Ithaca: Cornell University Press, 1947), pp. 22, 102.

[10] David Walsh, "The Historical Dialectic of Spirit: Jacob Boehme's Influence on Hegel" in *History and System: Hegel's Philosophy of History*, ed. by Robert L.

Hegel's lectures on the Philosophy of Nature at this time show an interest in Paracelsus and alchemy. More importantly, his *Lectures on the History of Philosophy* include lengthy, largely positive accounts of Giordano Bruno and Boehme. Hegel's treatment of Boehme occupies almost thirty pages in most modern editions, far exceeding the amount of text Hegel devoted to many "canonical" philosophers. Indeed, it would be easy enough to argue for the influence of mysticism on Hegel simply by confining oneself to Boehme. H. S. Harris is "inclined to believe in Boehme's influence upon Hegel from 1801 onwards."[11]

Boehme was a shoemaker in Goerlitz, in Lusatia on the borders of Bohemia, who had a mystical vision in 1600. Transfixed by a gleam of light reflected in a pewter vessel, he felt suddenly able, for a quarter of an hour, to intuit the essences or "signatures" of all things. He wrote nothing for many years, then produced *Aurora* (*Morgenröthe im Aufgang*) in 1612, his first attempt to lay out in a "piecemeal" fashion the revelation he had received all at once twelve years earlier.

Central to Boehme's thought is a conception of God as dynamic and evolving. Rejecting the idea of a transcendent God who exists outside of creation, complete and perfect, Boehme writes instead of a God who develops Himself through creation. Shockingly, Boehme claims that apart from or prior to creation God is not yet God. What moves God to unfold Himself in the world is the desire to achieve self-consciousness, and the mechanism of this process was thought by Boehme to involve conflict and opposition.[12] In a later work, Boehme wrote, "No thing can be revealed to itself without opposition."[13] Thus, God must "other" Himself in the form of the world. The process of creation, and of God's coming to self-consciousness, eventually reaches consummation with man. Boehme explains these ideas, and lays out the stages of creation,

Perkins (Albany: SUNY Press, 1984), pp. 22–23. Ernst Benz has also said that "In a certain sense one can refer to the philosophy of German Idealism as a Boehme-Renaissance, when Boehme was discovered at the same time by Schelling, Hegel, Franz von Baader, Tieck, Novalis and many others." See Benz, *Adam der Mythus vom Urmenschen* (Munich: Barth, 1955), p. 23.

[11] H. S. Harris, *Hegel's Development: Night Thoughts (Jena 1801–1806)* (London: Oxford University Press, 1983), p. 85.

[12] David Walsh states that, "At the core of his construction was Boehme's discovery that conflict and opposition were necessary to the self-revelation of God. It was an extrapolation from what is required for the self-realization of man to what is required for the self-realization of God." Walsh, "A Mythology of Reason: The Persistence of Pseudo-Science in the Modern World," in *Science, Pseudo-Science, and Utopianism in Early Modern Thought*, ed. by Stephen McKnight (Columbia: University of Missouri Press, 1992), p. 153.

[13] Jakob Boehme, *Vom Göttlicher Beschaulichkeit*, in *Sämtliche Schriften*, ed. by Will-Erich Peuckert (Stuttgart: Frommann, 1955–1961), vol. 4, chap. 1, §8.

in terms of a baffling account involving seven "source spirits" (*Quell-geister*). The identity of these spirits differs from work to work, but a sampling of some of the names he gives to them will offer an indication of the obscurity of Boehme's thinking: Sour (*Herb*), Sweet (*Süss*), Bitter (*Bitter*), Flash (*Schrack*), Heat (*Hitze*), Sound (*Ton*), Body (*Corpus*), and so forth.

In his 1805 *Lectures on the History of Philosophy*, Hegel refers to Boehme as the *philosophicus teutonicus* and pairs him with Francis Bacon as the two representatives of "Modern Philosophy in its First Statement."[14] Hegel's treatment of Boehme is long and respectful, but he ends it, as he does his account of most other philosophers, by pointing out the crucial shortcoming in Boehme's thought: "Boehme's great mind is confined in the hard knotty oak of the senses – in the gnarled concretion of the ordinary conception – and is not able to arrive at a free presentation of the idea."[15] It would be erroneous to conclude from this, however, that Hegel is simply dismissing Boehme. The length and tone of his treatment of the *philosophicus teutonicus* here and elsewhere suggest that this would be a misreading.[16] As H. S. Harris has stated, Hegel's criticism of Boehme is consistent with his "evident desire" to demonstrate that Boehme's writings (and those of Paracelsus) "contained symbolic expressions of important speculative truths."[17]

---

[14] M. J. Petry writes that "For Hegel ... the Idea of Nature involves a combination of Baconian and Boehmean attitudes to natural phenomena." Petry, introduction to *Hegel's Philosophy of Nature*, 3 vols., trans. by M. J. Petry (London: George Allen and Unwin, 1970), vol. 1, p. 114.

[15] Hegel, *Lectures on the History of Philosophy* (henceforth *LHP*), 3 vols., trans. by E. S. Haldane (London: Kegan Paul, Trench, Trübner, 1892), vol. 3, p. 195; *G. W. F. Hegels Werke* (henceforth *Werke*), 20 vols., ed. by Eva Moldenhauer und Karl Markus Michel (Frankfurt am Main: Suhrkamp, 1986), vol. 20, p. 98. *Note*: in referring to Hegel's publications which he divided into numbered paragraphs, I will refer to those paragraphs so that the reader may easily consult any edition. When referring to works, or portions of works, without paragraph numbers, reference will be to page numbers in a specific German edition, usually *Werke*. In either case, I will also cite a readily available English translation.

[16] Hegel is unambiguous in sharply rejecting Boehme's "picture thinking." For example, in an 1828 review essay Hegel – writing of Ludwig Tieck's fascination with Boehme's mysticism – states, "The equally enormous defectiveness in this mysticism becomes obvious, to be sure, only to the requirements of thought." See *Miscellaneous Writings of G. W. F. Hegel*, ed. by Jon Stewart (Evanston, IL: Northwestern University Press, 2002), p. 369; *Werke*, 11:227. Some Hegel scholars seize on such statements to try and argue that Hegel repudiates Boehme. However, what he repudiates is merely the *form* of Boehme's thought; he makes it quite clear that he admires its content or substance.

[17] Harris, *Night Thoughts*, p. 399.

In essence, Hegel's attitude toward the mysticism of Boehme and others is analogous to his attitude toward religion in general: mysticism, like religion, has the same content or the same object as philosophy, and approximates to a truth which only philosophy can fully unveil. Hence the study of mysticism, like religion, may offer the philosopher important signposts pointing the way to philosophy's goal. Hegel states that "It is the distinctive task of philosophy to transmute the *content* that is in the representation of religion into the *form* of thought; the content [itself] cannot be distinguished."[18] Hegel refers to religions as "sprouting up fortuitously, like the flowers and creations of nature, as foreshadowings, images, representations, without [our] knowing where they come from or where they are going to."[19] "Religion," he writes in the same text, "is a begetter of the divine spirit, not an invention of human beings but an effect of the divine at work, of the divine productive process within humanity."[20] Hegel distinguishes between varieties of mysticism just as he distinguishes between religions, in terms of how closely they come to the truth. For example, in the *Lectures on Aesthetics*, he contrasts Christian mysticism (in the person of Angelus Silesius) with the mysticism of the East, and, predictably, makes it clear that he regards the former as on a higher plane.[21]

In the years 1804–1805, while heavily under the influence of Boehme, Hegel had composed and then critiqued a "myth" about Lucifer. Hegel writes in this text,

God, having turned toward nature and expressed Himself in the pomp and dull repetition of its forms, became aware of His expansion... and became angry over it. Wrath [*Zorn*] is this formation, this contraction into an empty point. He finds Himself in this way, with His being poured out into the unending, restless infinity, where there is no present but an empty transcendence of limit, which always remains even as it is transcended.[22]

Hegel's use of "wrath" here is influenced by Boehme's concept of the Sour (*Sauer*), which expresses the initial moment of God's being, His will to close Himself and remain unmanifest. Hegel would later use the term *Zorn* in speaking of Boehme's philosophy in the *Lectures*,

[18] Hegel, *Lectures on the Philosophy of Religion* (henceforth *LPR*), 3 vols., ed. and trans. by Peter C. Hodgson, et al. (Berkeley: University of California Press, 1984), vol. 1, p. 333; *Vorlesungen über die Philosophie der Religion* (henceforth *VPR*), 3 vols., ed. by Walter Jaeschke (Hamburg: Felix Meiner, 1983–1987) vol. 1, p. 235.

[19] *LPR*, 1:196; *VPR*, 1:106.

[20] *LPR*, 1:130; *VPR*, 1:46.

[21] Hegel, *Aesthetics*, 2 vols., trans. by T. M. Knox (Oxford: The Clarendon Press, 1975), vol. 1, p. 371; *Werke*, 13:478.

[22] Hoffmeister, *Dokumente*, pp. 364–365.

where he identified the "first principle" of Boehme's thought as *Gott in Zorn*.[23]

In Hegel's "myth," God externalizes Himself in nature, but becomes "angry" over it and through this becomes conscious of Himself. God's wrath becomes the spirit of Lucifer, which reflects God back to Himself. Hegel critiqued his own myth as "the intuitions of barbarians" (*die Anschauungen der Barbarei*) because of its picture-thinking. The tone and language of this account are echoed in the "Revealed Religion" section of the *Phenomenology of Spirit* (1807). Walsh states correctly that this section is "from start to finish identical with the theosophic Christianity of Boehme."[24] There, Hegel writes of the "first-born Son of Light" (who is Lucifer), "who fell because he withdrew into himself or became self-centered, but that in his place another was at once created."[25]

In the winter of 1804–1805, Hegel produced a work that scholars have come to call the "divine triangle fragment." The actual text no longer exists, but Hegel's biographer Karl Rosenkranz quotes and describes it at length.[26] Rosenkranz argues that the text was heavily influenced by Boehme (and Franz von Baader) and he summarizes its content as follows:

To express the life of the idea, [Hegel] constructed a *triangle of triangles*, which he suffered *to move through one another* in such a way that each one was not only at one time extreme, and at another time *middle* generally, but also it had to go through this process internally with each of its *sides*. And then, in order to maintain the ideal plasticity of unity amid this rigidity and crudity of intuition, to maintain the fluidity of the distinctions represented as triangle and sides, he went on consistently to the further barbarity of expressing the totality as [a] *square resting* over the triangles and their process. But he seems to have got tired in the following out of his labour; at any rate he broke off at the construction of the *animal*.[27]

Hegel's first triangle ("God the Father") describes the "Godhead" closed within itself, à la Boehme's Sour-Sweet-Bitter, the primordial

[23] *LHP*, 3:192; *Werke*, 20:95.
[24] Walsh, "The Historical Dialectic of Spirit," p. 28.
[25] Hegel, *The Phenomenology of Spirit* (henceforth *PS*), trans. by A. V. Miller (Oxford: Oxford University Press, 1977), p. 468; *Phänomenologie des Geistes* (henceforth *PG*), ed. by Hans-Friedrich Wessels and Heinrich Clairmont (Hamburg: Felix Meiner, 1988), p. 504. *Note*: paragraphs are numbered in Miller's translation, but not in Hegel's original. In Miller, the paragraphs are numbered to correspond to J. N. Findlay's paragraph-by-paragraph commentary, printed as an appendix.
[26] Karl Rosenkranz, "Hegels ursprüngliches System 1798–1806," *Literarhistorisches Taschenbuch*, 2 (1844), pp. 157–164. Translated in Harris, *Night Thoughts*, pp. 184–188.
[27] *Ibid.*, p. 160 (Harris, p. 185).

trinity of conflict within God, preceding his manifestation. In the second triangle ("God the Son"), God recognizes Himself in the form of otherness. This otherness, if broken off from the whole, has the potential for evil. Therefore, it must be brought into oneness with God. Hegel states that "the Son must go right through the Earth, must overcome Evil, and in that he steps over to one side as the victor, must awaken the other, the self-cognition of God, as a new cognition that is one with God, or as the Spirit of God; whereby the middle becomes a beautiful, free, divine middle, the Universe of God."[28] A new triangle then comes into being, that of the Holy Spirit. Hegel writes that "the Earth as the self-consciousness of God is now the Spirit, yet it is also the eternal Son whom God intuits as Himself. Thus has the holy triangle of triangles closed itself. The first [triangle] is the Idea of God which is carried out in the other triangles, and returns into itself by passing through them."[29]

It is clear that in this early text, as well as in the "Lucifer myth" of the same period, Hegel is working out the broad outlines of his philosophical system, and that both his ideas and his language are heavily influenced by Boehme. Hegel's first triangle, "God the Father" is analogous to the later *Logic*, with its tripartite structure of Being-Essence-Concept. The second triangle, that of the Son or Earth, corresponds to the *Philosophy of Nature* (Mechanics-Physics-Organics). In Hegel's words, the "Idea of God" becomes "the universe of God." The Idea's *telos* is to become embodied, another element which strongly suggests the influence of Boehme (and also, as we shall see, F. C. Oetinger). In the third triangle, God intuits the Son, or Earth, as Himself, and achieves self-awareness, a moment which approximates the role played by Spirit in Hegel's mature system.

Hegel remained interested in Boehme throughout his lifetime. In 1811, a former student named Peter Gabriel van Ghert (1782–1852) sent Hegel Boehme's collected works as a gift. Hegel responded in a letter dated July 29, 1811: "Now I can study Jakob Boehme much more closely than before, since I was not myself in possession of his writings. His theosophy will always be one of the most remarkable attempts of a penetrating yet uncultivated man to comprehend the innermost essential nature of the absolute being. For Germany, he has the special interest of being really the first German philosopher."[30]

---

[28] *Ibid.*, p. 163 (Harris, pp. 187–188).

[29] *Ibid*, pp. 162–163 (Harris, 187).

[30] See *Hegel: The Letters*, trans. by Clark Butler and Christianne Seiler (Bloomington: Indiana University Press, 1984), p. 573 [henceforth, Butler]; *Briefe von und an Hegel*, 4 vols., ed. by Johannes Hoffmeister (Hamburg: Felix Meiner Verlag, 1952–1981); Hoffmeister numbers the letters; this is number 192. It should be noted that

The year 1816 was a fateful one for Hegel, for he received invitations to teach at both Heidelberg and Berlin. It was to Heidelberg he would go, for Hegel's chances in Berlin were ruined by the powerful theologian Wilhelm Martin Leberecht de Wette (1780–1849). De Wette condemned Hegel's *Logic* as an obscure "occultism" (*Geheimwissenschaft*).[31] In an 1815 letter to Jakob Friedrich Fries (1773–1843), himself no friend to Hegel, de Wette had written that "Mysticism reigns here mightily, and how deep we have sunk is shown in the thought of Hegel."[32]

Of course, in 1818 Hegel did eventually get his post in Berlin. Contrary to what one might expect, during this period, the final act of Hegel's life, his interest in mysticism seems only to have intensified. After coming to Berlin, Hegel worked hard to establish a friendship with Franz von Baader. The preface to the second edition of the *Encyclopedia of the Philosophical Sciences* (1827), includes more than one reference to Boehme, whom Hegel calls a "mighty spirit."[33] The preface also includes admiring references to Baader, who was then the foremost interpreter of Boehme. In a remarkable footnote, Hegel expresses delight that Baader agrees with some points of his philosophy, and adds "About most of what he contests – and even quite easily about everything – it would not be difficult for me to come to an understanding with him, that is to say, to show that there is, in fact, no departure from his views in it."[34] This is certainly a remarkably deferential attitude to take toward a man most academics regarded as an occultist and *Schwärmer*.

Hegel's interest seems merely to have puzzled Baader, who privately referred to the Hegelian system as a "philosophy of dust." Nevertheless, the two did establish a friendship. Baader visited Hegel in Berlin, and the two studied Meister Eckhart together. Baader reports that on reading a certain passage in Eckhart, Hegel cried *"da haben wir es ja, was wir wollen!"* ("There, indeed, we have what we want!").[35] Hegel then subsequently introduced a quotation from Eckhart into his 1824 *Lectures*

Hegel's library also came to include works by Agrippa, Bruno, and Paracelsus. The fact that Hegel did not purchase Boehme's works should not be taken as indicating a lack of interest on his part. During this time books, especially collections, were very often difficult to obtain and quite expensive, and Hegel was not a wealthy man.

[31] Wiedmann, p. 53.

[32] Gunther Nicolin, ed., *Hegel in Berichten seiner Zeitgenossen* (Hamburg: Felix Meiner, 1970), p. 117.

[33] Hegel, *The Encyclopedia Logic*, trans. by T. F. Geraets et al. (henceforth *Geraets*) (Albany: State University of New York Press, 1991), p. 15; *Werke*, 8:28–29. When Hegel's numbered paragraphs are referred to, the abbreviation *EL* will be used.

[34] *Geraets*, 15; *Werke*, 8:29.

[35] Nicolin, p. 261.

on the Philosophy of Religion: "The eye with which God sees me is the same eye by which I see Him, my eye and His eye are one and the same. In righteousness I am weighed in God and He in me. If God did not exist nor would I; if I did not exist nor would he."[36]

Baader was widely reputed to be a member of the mystical order of the Rosicrucians, which had been revived in the late eighteenth century. The Rosicrucians of Hegel's time had a reputation for alchemy and Hermetic interests of all kinds, as well as for political conservatism. In the Preface to the 1821 *Philosophy of Right*, Hegel launches an attack on political idealism and states "To recognize reason as the rose in the cross of the present and thereby to enjoy the present, this is the rational insight which reconciles us to the actual...."[37] In the 1824 *Lectures on the Philosophy of Religion*, the same metaphor occurs: "in order to pluck reason, the rose in the cross of the present, one must take up the cross itself."[38] Most commentators agree that Hegel is making a reference to the imagery of the Rosicrucians, whose symbol was a rose blooming from the center of a cross. Hegel himself makes it clear that he was referring to the Rosicrucians, in a review essay published in 1829.[39]

In the Preface, prior to the "rose in the cross" image, Hegel refers to the reason inherent in nature as *der Stein der Weisen*, or, as it is usually translated into English, "the philosopher's stone." These are equivalent metaphors in the Preface: both the rose in the cross and the philosopher's stone represent, for Hegel, reason, which he is calling upon his readers to discern in the present day. Given that the Rosicrucians were widely known as alchemists, Hegel could not have been ignorant of the connection between these two metaphors.

But why would Hegel make reference to the Rosicrucians in the *Philosophy of Right*? Some have claimed that Hegel is somehow criticizing the powerful Rosicrucian courtiers to the King of Prussia. Adriaan Peperzak, for example, interprets Hegel's remarks to be an attempt to "give the appearance of agreement with the Rosicrucians among the politicians," in the context of what actually amounts to a criticism of their ideas.[40] But Friedrich Wilhelm II, the Rosicrucian king, died in

---

36 *LPR*, 1:347–48; *Werke*, 16:209. This is actually a composite quotation, built out of lines from several of Eckhart's writings.

37 Hegel, *Philosophy of Right*, trans. by T. M. Knox (Oxford: Clarendon Press, 1952), p. 12; *Grundlinien der Philosophie des Rechts*, section 27.

38 *LPR*, 2:248 note 45.

39 "Über die Hegelsche Lehre oder absolutes Wissen und moderner Pantheismus–Über Philosophies überhaupt und Hegels Enzyklopaedie der philosophischen Wissenschaften insbesondere," (1829) in *Werke*, 11:466.

40 Adriaan Th. Peperzak, *Philosophy and Politics: A Commentary on the Preface to Hegel's Philosophy of Right* (Dordrecht: Martinus Nijhoff, 1987), p. 109. See

1797. The Rosicrucians had all been purged from the court by his successor, Friedrich Wilhelm III, the king who reigned during Hegel's time. By 1821, no one in Prussia could have gained anything by appearing to agree with the Rosicrucians – quite the reverse, in fact. It may therefore be that Hegel really does agree with the Rosicrucians, at least in some ways.

When, near the end of his life, Hegel turned to the project of revising his *Science of Logic*, Boehme was again very much on his mind. In the 1812 Doctrine of Being, Hegel had introduced the terms *Qualierung* and *Inqualierung*. He had said nothing about the source for these unusual terms, and remarked only that they came from "a philosophy which goes deep but into a turbid depth...."[41] However, in the 1832 version of the Doctrine of Being (the only section of the work Hegel completed revisions on before his death), this passage has been changed. Now the two terms (which are given as synonyms) are explicitly identified as "an expression of Jakob Boehme's."[42] Why had Hegel chosen not to name Boehme in the 1812 edition? Actually, the only reference to Boehme in Hegel's published writings up until the Berlin period is in the 1817 *Encyclopedia*, where a brief reference occurs in paragraph 472 of the *Philosophy of Spirit*. Perhaps Hegel felt it prudent not to advertise his interest in Boehme in his published writings. By the Berlin period, however, he felt secure from academic persecution, and so decided to openly acknowledge his interest in print. Hence, not only does a reference to Boehme appear in the 1832 Doctrine of Being, but also, as mentioned, in the preface to the 1827 *Encyclopedia*. This, plus the encounter with Baader, makes it exceedingly difficult for scholars to dismiss Hegel's interest in mysticism as a mere "aberration of youth."

III. "THE SPECULATIVE IS THE MYSTICAL"

The evidence that Hegel was influenced by mysticism and took it seriously until the end of his life is, in short, abundant. However, as noted

---

also Kenneth Westphal, "The Basic Context and Structure of Hegel's *Philosophy of Right*," in *The Cambridge Companion to Hegel*, ed. by Frederick C. Beiser (Cambridge, UK: Cambridge University Press, 1993), pp. 238–239. Westphal has a similar thesis, and commits the same errors.

[41] *Wissenschaft der Logik: Das Sein* (1812), ed. by Hans-Jürgen Gawoll (Hamburg: Felix Meiner, 1986), p. 82. Since A.V. Miller bases his translation on the 1832 edition, this passage is not translated in the most popular English edition of the work.

[42] Hegel, *The Science of Logic* (henceforth *SL*), trans. by A.V. Miller (London: George Allen and Unwin, 1969), p. 114; *Wissenschaft der Logik: Die Lehre vom Sein* (1832), ed. by Hans-Jürgen Gawoll (Hamburg: Felix Meiner, 1992), p. 109.

earlier, the fact that Hegel was positively influenced by mysticism does not mean that Hegel himself was a mystic or that his philosophy could be plausibly described as a mystical one. In this section, I shall be concerned precisely with whether or not one can make such claims.

Many readers who have not even bothered to explore the mystical influences on Hegel still see something "mystical" in his thought. What is it that they can be seeing? To begin with, looking at the overall structure of Hegel's philosophical system, one can see that it contains many parallels to mysticism. Of course, in order to see this one has to know what to look for. If one is ignorant of the mystical tradition, then the claim I have just now made will seem implausible.

Mysticism is usually portrayed as a path to knowledge of the divine or Absolute that begins with an initial stage of purification or initiation. This tradition, of course, goes all the way back to the cults from which mysticism takes its name: *ta musteria*, the mystery rites of Ancient Greece. The initiation at Eleusis was supposed to alter the consciousness of the initiate. It was supposed to purge one of false or misguided ways of looking at the world and then offer a glimpse of the truly real. The experience was often a difficult and traumatic one. This stage on the path to wisdom is represented in Hegel's philosophy by the *Phenomenology of Spirit*, in which, by following out the dialectic, one is raised above the level of the Understanding to the standpoint from which one may receive Absolute Knowledge.[43] And it must be noted that Hegel promises actually to have got beyond the *love* of wisdom entirely. Like the great mystical and Hermetic teachers, he claims to be imparting a finished and complete wisdom. The *Phenomenology* even references the Eleusinian mysteries, most famously in the "Bacchanalian revel" passage.[44] John Burbidge notes that the Phenomenology, "with its lengthy and arduous process of initiation, came at a time when Hegel was frequenting the company of known Masons, some of them graduates of the banned Illuminati."[45] K. J. H. Windischmann, whose review of the *Phenomenology* was one of the most important notices of Hegel's early career, took the work as an expression of Masonic themes.[46]

And what does one receive on initiation into the Hegelian mysteries? What is Absolute Knowledge? Hegel states that the subject matter of his

---

[43] H. S. Harris writes that "In [Hegel's] view we have to annihilate our own selfhood in order to enter the sphere where Philosophy herself speaks." *Night Thoughts*, p. 51.

[44] *PS*, 27; *PG*, 35. I have discussed this and Hegel's other references to Eleusis in *Hegel and the Hermetic Tradition*, pp. 130–132, 139, 148.

[45] From Burbidge's introduction to Jacques D'Hondt, *Hegel in His Time*, trans. by John Burbidge (Lewiston, NY: Broadview Press, 1988), p. xi.

[46] See his letter to Hegel dated April 27, 1810; Hoffmeister letter 155.

Science of Logic is "truth as it is without veil and in its own absolute nature. It can therefore be said that this content is the exposition of God as He is in his eternal essence before the creation of nature and a finite spirit."[47] Hegel tells us in the *Lectures on the Philosophy of Religion* that philosophy's task is to unveil God's nature "as it manifests and develops itself."[48] In the *Lectures on the History of Philosophy*, Hegel states that "The philosophers are closer to the Lord than those who live by the crumbs of the Spirit; they read, or write, the cabinet orders of God in the original; it is their duty to write them down. The philosophers are the *mystai* who have been present at the decision in the inner-most sanctuary."[49] The *Logic* presents a God as yet unmanifest; merely the "idea" of God. The notion of a process of development and actu-alization in God is perhaps the most significant point on which Hegel appears to have been influenced by Boehme. And given the centrality of this idea in Hegel's system, one could argue on this basis alone that Hegel's philosophy could not have taken shape without the influence of mysticism. Indeed, what explains Hegel's choice of the title *Logic* is the word's derivation from the Greek *logos*, a favorite topic of the Ger-man mystics, especially Eckhart. The ascent to the Absolute Idea of the Logic closely parallels the classical mystic ascent to the *Logos* or the Universal Mind.

The *Philosophy of Nature* shows how the Absolute Idea or "God before creation" is "embodied." Notoriously, Hegel employs Neopla-tonic emanation imagery to describe the transition from *Logic* to *Phi-losophy of Nature*, saying that the Idea "freely releases itself."[50] This sort of approach is to be found in Eckhart as well. In one of Eckhart's German sermons, he states that God "created the whole world perfectly and entirely within the Now," that is, outside time. The world exists in God eternally, yet flows out from God as well. "It is an amazing fact that something should flow out and yet remain within. That the word [i.e., the *Logos*] flows out and yet remains within is astonishing; that all creatures flow out and yet remain within is also astonishing."[51] The *Phi-losophy of Nature* furthers the transformation of consciousness begun in the *Phenomenology*: we come to see all of creation as a reflection of

[47] SL, 50; *Wissenschaft der Logik (1832)*, pp. 33–34.

[48] LPR, 1:117; VPR, 1:33–34.

[49] Hegel, *Geschichte der Philosophie*, ed. by Hermann Glockner, *Jubiläumsausgabe* (Stuttgart: Fromann, 1927–1940), vol. 3, p. 96.

[50] SL, 843; *Wissenschaft der Logik: Die Lehre vom Begriff (1816)*, ed. by Hans-Jürgen Gawoll (Hamburg: Felix Meiner, 1994), p. 305.

[51] *Meister Eckhart: Selected Writings*, trans. by Oliver Davies (London: Penguin Books, 1994), p. 123; *Meister Eckhart: Deutsche Predigten und Traktate*, ed. by Josef Quint (Munich: Carl Hanser Verlag, 1963), p. 356.

the *Logos*. This form of "enlightenment," in which the entire world is transfigured for the initiate, is, of course, typical of mystical paths.

Hegel's *Philosophy of Spirit* represents the "return" of nature to God through the coming into being of human consciousness. Human beings are able to rise above nature and literally complete the actualization of God in the world through speculative philosophy. This moment of "return to the source," making human life necessary for God's being, is an idea that is not to be found in the mainstream philosophical tradition, but it is frequently found in Hermeticism, a form of mysticism I shall discuss in the final section of this chapter. Some version of this claim is to be found in the Indian, Jewish, Christian, and Islamic mystics. Sometimes the claim is simply that God "desires to be known," and human beings satisfy this desire. This claim is to be found in Sufism, for example. Eckhart and others hold that God would not be God without creation, especially without human creatures. Recall the quotation Hegel employs from Eckhart: "The eye with which God sees me is the same eye by which I see Him, my eye and His eye are one and the same.... If God did not exist nor would I; if I did not exist nor would he."[52] Sometimes, as in some forms of Kabbalism, the claim is made that the religious community, in following the divine law, is charged with perfecting God's creation or realizing God in the world.

One can thus see that, in its outlines, Hegel's philosophy bears a striking resemblance to mystical thought. But simply making such comparisons cannot suffice. A comparison is only valuable if the items being compared have been interpreted correctly. Setting aside what I have said about mysticism, the statements I have made above concerning the tenets of Hegel's philosophy, while I myself would stand by them, are open to a bad infinity of scholarly objections. Furthermore, even if my interpretation of Hegel is accepted, a sceptic would still likely charge that the resemblance to mysticism is a superficial one. We must, therefore go deeper than this. Let us look at what Hegel explicitly says about mysticism. Surprisingly, Hegel makes few direct references to mysticism as such. Perhaps the most significant of these is in a *Zusatz* to the *Encyclopedia Logic*.[53]

Hegel ends the "Preliminary Conception" or *Vorbegriff* to the *Encyclopedia Logic* (the section that precedes the "Doctrine of Being"), with a section titled "More Precise Conception and Division of the Logic" (*Näherer Begriff und Einteilung der Logik*). He writes as follows: "With

---

52 *LPR*, 1:347–348; *Werke*, 16:209.
53 This passage is also quoted and very briefly discussed in *Hegel and the Hermetic Tradition*, 86. The discussion that follows is much more extensive and represents an advance on how the passage is treated in my book.

regard to its form, the *logical* has three sides: (α) *the side of abstraction* or *of the understanding*, (β) *the dialectical* or *negatively rational side*, [and] (γ) *the speculative* or *positively rational* one."[54] Hegel then devotes a subsection to each of these aspects of the logical. The third, or speculative moment, of course, corresponds to Hegel's own conception of what philosophy, properly, should be. Of this moment, Hegel says, "The *speculative* or *positively rational* apprehends the unity of the determinations in their opposition, the *affirmative* that is contained in their dissolution and in their transition."[55] In the *Zusatz* to this subsection, we find the following remarkable statement, which I shall quote at length:

> It should also be mentioned here that the meaning of the speculative is to be understood as being the same as what used in earlier times to be called "mystical" [*Mystische*], especially with regard to the religious consciousness and its content. When we speak of the "mystical" nowadays, it is taken as a rule to be synonymous with what is mysterious and incomprehensible; and, depending on the ways their culture and mentality vary in other respects, some people treat the mysterious and incomprehensible as what is authentic and genuine, whilst others regard it as belonging to the domain of superstition and deception. About this we must remark first that "the mystical" is certainly something mysterious, but only for the understanding, and then only because abstract identity is the principle of the understanding. But when it is regarded as synonymous with the speculative, the mystical is the concrete unity of just those determinations that count as true for the understanding only in their separation and opposition. So if those who recognize the mystical as what is genuine say that it is something utterly mysterious, and just leave it at that, they are only declaring that for them, too, thinking has only the significance of an abstract positing of identity, and that in order to attain the truth we must renounce thinking, or, as they frequently put it, that we must 'take reason captive.' As we have seen, however, the abstract thinking of the understanding is so far from being something firm and ultimate that it proves itself, on the contrary, to be a constant sublating of itself and an overturning into its opposite, whereas the rational as such is rational precisely because it contains both of the opposites as ideal moments within itself. Thus, everything rational can equally be called 'mystical,' but this only amounts to saying that it transcends the understanding. It does not at all imply that what is so spoken of must be considered inaccessible to thinking and incomprehensible.[56]

Hegel scholars are wary of relying upon the *Zusätze* to his work, since these were compiled from student notes. But that these words accurately reflect Hegel's ideas is confirmed by other texts. In the *Lectures on the*

[54] Geraets, 125; *EL*, §79.
[55] *Geraets*, 131; *EL*, §82.
[56] *Geraets*, 133; *EL*, §82 *Zusatz*.

Philosophy of Religion of 1824, speaking of the Eleusinian mysteries, Hegel states that "The mystical is the speculative, what lies within."[57] In the same lectures, he also states, "The Trinity is called the *mystery* of God; its content is mystical, i.e., speculative."[58] In the *Lectures* of 1827, Hegel states that "As a whole the mystical is everything speculative, or whatever is concealed from the understanding."[59] In the *Lectures on the History of Philosophy*, Hegel devotes a short section to several Scholastics whom he terms "mystics," and states, "Among them genuine philosophy is to be found – termed also mysticism."[60]

There is much to digest in these statements. To begin with the obvious, Hegel equates the mystical with the speculative. And given that "speculative" is the name of the Hegelian philosophy, he appears to be saying that his philosophy is mystical. A close reading shows that he *is* saying this, but only in a qualified sense.

The mystical, Hegel tells us, is what transcends the Understanding. In Hegel's philosophy, of course, "the Understanding" has a special, technical sense. It means, essentially, a kind of dyadic thinking that proceeds by holding certain conceptual oppositions as fixed and permanent. For example, what two concepts could be more opposed to each other than being and nothing? But, in a superb example of Hegel's conceptual sorcery, he shows us in the *Logic* how these two concepts, since they each denote nothing definite at all, are actually identical. This is the sort of thing Hegel means when he says that the Understanding proves itself "to be a constant sublating of itself and an overturning into its opposite." The sort of thinking associated with the Understanding is supremely conventional, a thinking within the square of opposition. Speculation (or Reason) stands on a higher plane, for it goes beyond the oppositional thinking of the Understanding. In the popular language used today to discuss mysticism, it "goes beyond the pairs of opposites."[61]

Hegel tells us that speculation is mysticism, just insofar as speculation, like mysticism, goes beyond the Understanding. It is also clear from Hegel's treatment of the mystics elsewhere that he regards the *content* of their thought – not just its aims – as equivalent in important

---

[57] *LPR*, 2:491; *VPR*, 2:391.
[58] *LPR*, 3:192; *VPR*, 3:125.
[59] *LPR*, 1:445; *VPR*, 1:333.
[60] *LHP*, 2:91; *Werke*, 19:584.
[61] Hegel states in the *Lectures on the History of Philosophy*, "The Understanding does not comprehend the speculative, which simply is the concrete, because it holds to differences in their separation; their contradiction is indeed contained in the mystery, which, however, is likewise the resolution of the same." *LHP*, 1:79–80; *Werke*, 18:100–101.

respects to his own. His comments on Boehme in the *Lectures on the History of Philosophy* and his use of Eckhart in the *Lectures on the Philosophy of Religion* provide evidence that Hegel regarded himself as laying bare the inner meaning of mystical statements. To take a further, small example, in the *Philosophy of Nature*, Hegel discusses the statements of Boehme and Paracelsus regarding the alchemical triad of sulphur, mercury, and salt. He states that if taken literally, such ideas are easy to refute, but says "It should not be overlooked ... that in their essence they contain and express the determinations of the Concept."[62] H. S. Harris notes that in his early lectures on the *Philosophy of Nature*, Hegel frequently insists on finding an "earlier pedigree" for his ideas in Boehme and Paracelsus.[63]

However, one must be careful not to claim too much for this apparent equation of the speculative and the mystical, for there is another element to mysticism, referred to by Hegel in the quote from the *Encyclopedia Logic*, and that is *mystery*. Speculation is mysticism insofar as it transcends the Understanding, in Hegel's sense of the term. But frequently when mystics assert that their knowledge goes "beyond the understanding," they mean that it is ineffable, or beyond the capacity of language to express, and of reason to comprehend. Hegel rejects this conclusion entirely. Further, the mystics often claim that their knowledge is ineffable because it consists in a non-rational, immediate intuition of the Absolute (the so-called mystical experience). Obviously, Hegel rejects this as well. The *Zusatz* from the *Encyclopedia Logic* has Hegel identifying himself with the mystics up to a point – but on the key issue of the ineluctability of mystery, Hegel parts company with them.[64]

If one examines the major mystical traditions, one will find three elements over and over again: (1) the treatment of the ultimate reality behind appearances as a *coincidentia oppositorum* (coincidence of opposites); (2) the claim that, in some fashion, God and man are one; and (3) the claim that ultimate reality is unknowable *in any fashion* through human concepts, because human concepts deal only with appearances. One finds this last claim in the Indian tradition in the concept of *Brahman*. It appears in the Jewish Kabbalah as *Ein-Sof*. It is to be found in

---

[62] Petry, pp. 2, 117; *Naturphilosophie*, §316.

[63] Harris, *Night Thoughts*, p. 278.

[64] However, Hegel elsewhere embraces "mystery," understood in his own, idiosyncratic manner: "Mysteries are in their nature speculative, mysterious certainly to the Understanding, but not to Reason; they are rational, just in the sense of being speculative." *LHP*, 1:79; *Werke*, 18:100.

Eckhart in his concept of *Grunt*. And the same basic idea is to be found in Sufism.

When Hegel discusses mysticism in the *Encyclopedia Logic*, he is emphasizing the *coincidentia oppositorum* as characteristic of mysticism; in other words, the idea that all difference and opposition in the world is really only apparent, and that "beyond" this all is one in God. Eckhart's thought provides us with an excellent illustration of this principle, and of just what Hegel is getting at in the *Zusatz*. For Eckhart, God is ineffable, but through paradox we may at least approach Him. Essentially, this amounts to employing the dyadic categories of the Understanding in order to show that they are inadequate for knowing God, and that we must somehow leave them behind. So, for example, Eckhart says that God is both distinct and indistinct and so, in a way, neither. Likewise God is both transcendent and immanent. Nicholas of Cusa, who was influenced by Eckhart (and was, incidentally, the first author to refer to God as *Absolutum*) takes a similar approach. He states that God is both maximum and minimum. Since being *maximum* means being everything in the greatest sense, God must also be *minimum*. We cannot reconcile these paradoxes rationally. God is an ineffable mystery lying on the other side of them.

Hegel's claim in the *Encyclopedia Logic* is that speculation, like mysticism, recognizes the necessity of transcending the categories of the Understanding, or the "opposites." However, Hegel parts company with most mystics by saying that this should not lead us to embrace "mystery." In Hegel's thought, the tension between opposites is used as a stepping stone to go beyond the Understanding to a higher level of thought from which we can know, in discursive, rational form, the actual nature of God or the Absolute. Hegel employs a logic of contradiction (dialectic) to articulate the "moments" or aspects of this God, taken as an organic whole. Instead of merely pointing to an Absolute that transcends the oppositions of the Understanding, Hegel uses these oppositions to define the Absolute itself in terms of a system of moments in which each element depends upon every other, and each is what it is only in relation to the whole.

In taking this approach, Hegel *is* parting company with much of traditional mysticism, and especially the assumption of the ultimacy of the *coincidentia oppositorum*. However, he is embracing the heterodox mysticism of Boehme and his followers, who also sought to transcend the *coincidentia oppositorum* and offer up discursive knowledge of God. Further, the conception of the divine as an organic whole unfolding or developing through conflict and contradiction is the centerpiece of Boehme's thought.

I believe that Hegel was aware of the fact that Boehme's doctrine was unique in the history of mysticism, precisely in its rejection of God as an ineffable Absolute. To be sure, Boehme does speak of God as *Ungrund*, a concept close to the Kabbalah's *Ein-Sof* (or "Infinite").[65] However, Boehme claims that in the *Ungrund* God is "not called God."[66] God develops "out" of the *Ungrund*, and is only God, to borrow some words of Hegel's, "in the whole wealth of [His] developed form."[67] In the section that follows I shall argue, through a close reading of several passages from the Preface to the *Phenomenology of Spirit*, that Hegel consciously drew upon Boehmean mysticism in framing his mature views on the nature of Absolute Knowledge. Simultaneously, I shall be arguing that he consciously opposed the Boehmean system to traditional mystical conceptions as a means of critiquing the thoughts of his contemporaries.

IV. HEGEL'S BOEHMEAN CHALLENGE TO SCHELLING

In the Preface to the *Phenomenology*, Hegel attacks a certain type of philosophy which speaks of the Absolute. He writes, "Dealing with something from the perspective of the Absolute consists merely in declaring that, although one has been speaking of it just now as something definite, yet in the Absolute, the A=A, there is nothing of the kind, for therein all is one."[68] This passage has always been taken as a criticism of Schelling, and indeed it is. In fact, it is at this point in the Preface that we may understand Hegel to be opening a covert debate with Schelling.

What must be understood about Hegel's criticism of the Schellingian Absolute, however, is that his remarks are also quite clearly a criticism of the mystical doctrine of *coincidentia oppositorum*. Schelling was drawing on that tradition, Hegel knew he was, and Hegel had studied that tradition himself.[69] Furthermore, as noted earlier, Hegel wrote the *Phenomenology* in a time and place in which there had been a great revival of interest in the works of authors like Eckhart, in whom the *coincidentia oppositorum* doctrine figures prominently. We may thus also understand Hegel to be engaging in dialogue with other contemporary intellectuals influenced by the same mystical doctrine, and, of course, with the mystics themselves.

---

[65] Most Kabbalists have treated God as *Ein-Sof*, or "infinite," meaning that God transcends the world, and all human concepts.

[66] Boehme, *Mysterium Magnum* in *Sämtliche Schriften*, ed. by Will-Erich Peuckert (Stuttgart: Frohmann, 1955–1961), vol. 7, chap. 7, §14.

[67] *PS*, 11; *PG*, 15.

[68] *PS*, 9; *PG*, 13.

[69] In the *Lectures on the Philosophy of Religion* of 1827, Hegel treats Schelling's Identity philosophy as equivalent to pantheism (*LPR*, 1:374–375; *VPR*, 1:272).

The passage from the *Phenomenology* continues as follows: "To pit this single insight, that in the Absolute everything is the same, against the full body of articulated cognition, which at least seeks and demands such fulfillment, to palm off its Absolute as the night in which, as the saying goes, all cows are black – this is cognition naively reduced to vacuity."[70] This passage has also been understood as an attack on Schelling – and Schelling himself took it that way.[71] But, again, it must be emphasized that Hegel's criticism also applies to the mystical promulgators of the *coincidentia oppositorum*, and their latter-day followers.

What kind of conception of the Absolute does Hegel want to put in place of Schelling's Eckhartian "Indifference point"? A Boehmean one. Two paragraphs later in the Preface, Hegel states that the Absolute "is the process of its own becoming, the circle that presupposes its end as its goal, having its end also as its beginning; and only by being worked out to its end, is it actual" (Miller, p. 10; *PG*, 14). Hegel accepts Schelling's conception of the Absolute as beyond the subject–object distinction, but he asserts that without an understanding of the Absolute as a system whose identity consists in its unfolding, it is a vacuous notion. A few lines later, Hegel states that the Absolute must be conceived in "the whole wealth of the developed form. Only then is it conceived and expressed as an actuality."[72]

The next paragraph provides the climax to the concealed dialogue with Schelling and his followers. Hegel writes, "The true is the whole [*Das Wahre ist das Ganze*]." Most Hegel scholars have missed the fact that this is almost a quotation from (and quite clearly an allusion to) the Swabian "speculative pietist" F. C. Oetinger. Oetinger was a follower of Boehme who exercised a great influence on the religious and intellectual life of Württemberg in the mid to late eighteenth century, and was an important influence on Schelling.

Klaus Vondung writes that, "Hermeticism was brought to Schelling's attention by Oetinger, who was an expert in all sorts of esoteric knowledge, although this connection has not been investigated satisfactorily." Vondung believes that it was Oetinger who bequeathed to both Schelling and Hegel the ideal of *pansophia*, or an all-encompassing,

---

[70] *PS*, 9; *PG*, 13.

[71] Indeed, in a letter dated May 1, 1807 Hegel tried to prepare Schelling for this criticism, by claiming that in the Preface he is attacking Schelling's *followers*: "In the Preface you will not find that I have been too hard on the shallowness that makes so much mischief with your forms in particular and degrades them into mere formalism." Butler, p. 80; Hoffmeister # 95.

[72] *PS*, 11; *PG*, 15.

total knowledge.[73] We know that Schelling's father owned Oetinger's works. Schelling's first published work was a poem written on the occasion of the death of P. M. Hahn, an important follower of Oetinger. In a letter to his father dated September 7, 1806, Schelling states that Franz von Baader has asked him if he could help him obtain Oetinger's writings. Schelling passed this request on to his friend Christian Pregizer (1751–1824), who was the founder of a pietist sect called the "Joyous Christians." Pregizer reports that when he first met Schelling in 1803, they spent almost the entire meeting discussing Boehme and Oetinger.[74] Schelling is known to have remarked to one of his students in Jena that Oetinger was "clearer" than Boehme.[75] It has also been argued that Schelling's terminology (especially in the 1809 *Freiheitschrift*) shows his familiarity with Oetinger's work.[76] Ernst Benz demonstrates, furthermore, that in his work, Schelling occasionally employed unorthodox translations of biblical passages made by Oetinger, without attributing them to him.[77]

Oetinger's first book was a commentary on Boehme (*Aufmunternde Gründe zur Lesung der Schriften Jacob Böhmens*, 1731). Indeed, his thought can be understood as an attempt to expand upon and systematize Boehme's theosophy, which he accomplished through a strong infusion of Kabbalist and alchemical elements. Oetinger describes God as "an eternal desire for self-revelation" (*eine ewige Begierde sich zu offenbaren*).[78] His philosophy depicts the stages and mechanism of God's actualization in the world. Oetinger identifies the fully realized God with *Geist* (Spirit), however he holds that *Geist* is only actual when it is embodied concretely in the world. He states "Embodiment is the goal of God's work."[79] Separated from body, *Geist* is mere ghost.

---

[73] Klaus Vondung, "Millenarianism, Hermeticism, and the Search for a Universal Science," in McKnight, pp. 132, 126.

[74] Benz, *Mystical Sources*, pp. 13–14.

[75] Paola Mayer, *Jena Romanticism and Its Appropriation of Jacob Böhme* (Montreal: McGill-Queen's University Press, 1999), p. 185.

[76] See, for instance, *Mystical Sources*, 30; Robert Schneider, p. 10. Gershom Scholem also states that he discerns Oetinger's influence in the thought of both Schelling and Hegel. See Scholem, *Kabbalah*, New York: New American Library, 1974), p. 200.

[77] Benz, *Mystical Sources*, pp. 54–56.

[78] Oetinger, *Biblisches und emblematisches Wörterbuch* (1776; reprinted, Hildesheim: Georg Olms Verlag, 1969), p. 536.

[79] *Ibid.*, p. 407. Under the influence of Oetinger, Schelling writes in *Die Weltalter* (a title he borrowed, incidentally, from Bengel): "The ultimate purpose is that everything, as much as possible, be brought to visible, material form; embodiment is, as the ancients [Alten] expressed it, the endpoint of the way of God ... who wants to reveal Himself as spatial or as temporal." Schelling, *Sämtliche Werke*,

Following Boehme, Oetinger conceives this corporealization as coming about through the conflict and opposition of forces. Chief among these are Expansion (*Ausbreitung*) and Contraction (*Stärke*), concepts he inherits from the Kabbalah and which he bequeaths to the *Naturphilosophie* of Goethe (where they appear as *diastole* and *systole*).[80]

Oetinger conceives the actualized *Geist* (or *Geistleiblichkeit*) as an organic whole (or, in his terminology, an *Intensum*) in which the whole is immanent in every part. Oetinger sought a new type of thought that would allow one to articulate such a whole. The end result, he believed, would be the *Zentrallerkenntnis* ("central knowledge"), in which one would have an insight into the whole. Oetinger conceives *Zentrallerkenntnis* as a knowledge that goes beyond the duality of subject and object, and thus his conception invites comparison to Hegel's Absolute Knowing (*das absolute Wissen*). Oetinger writes of it as follows: "The truth is a whole [*Die Wahrheit ist ein Ganzes*]; when one finally receives this total, synoptic vision of the truth, it matters not whether one begins by considering this part or that."[81] This was a rather well-known passage in Oetinger. And so when Hegel announces in the Preface to the *Phenomenology* that "Das Wahre ist das Ganze," which conveys just the same idea, with the wording only slightly altered, he knew that at least one of his readers – Schelling – would get the reference.[82]

Even if Hegel had not read Oetinger himself, it is almost certain that he knew of Schelling's interest in Oetinger and at least of the rough outlines of Oetinger's thought. It should also be mentioned that there is strong evidence that Hoelderlin too was influenced by Oetinger.[83] It seems unlikely that Hegel could have been entirely ignorant of Oetinger when his two closest friends, with whom he roomed at Tübingen, were

---

14 vols., ed. by Karl Friedrich A. Schelling (Stuttgart/Augsburg: J. G. Cotta'scher Verlag, 1856–1861), vol. 8, p. 325.

[80] See Rolf Christian Zimmerman, *Das Weltbild des jungen Goethe: Studien zur hermetischen Tradition des deutschen 18. Jahrhunderts*, 2 vols. (Munich: Fink, 1969, 1979), vol. 1, p. 187.

[81] F.C. Oetinger, *Sämtliche Schriften*, vol. 5, ed. by Karl Chr. Eberh. Ehmann (Stuttgart: Steinkopf, 1858–64), p. 45.

[82] It might be argued, of course, that there is a big difference between saying that the true or the truth is "*the* whole" and "*a* whole." But the words Oetinger writes immediately after that line (quoted above) clearly convey that he means the same thing as *the* whole. He is telling us that truth as such, what is true, is a totality.

[83] See Priscilla A. Hayden-Roy, "*A Foretaste of Heaven*": *Friedrich Hölderlin in the Context of Württemberg Pietism* (Amsterdam: Rodopi, 1994); Ulrich Gaier, *Der gesetzliche Kalkül: Hölderlins Dichtungslehre* (Tübingen: Max Niemeyer, 1962); and Walter Dierauer, *Hölderlin und der Speculative Pietismus Württembergs: Gemeinsame Anshauungshorizonte im Werk Oetingers und Hölderlins* (Zürich: Juris, 1986).

strongly influenced by him.[84] In fact, the likelihood is that Hegel was familiar with Oetinger's ideas and had probably read at least something by him. Hegel never mentions Oetinger, but then neither does Schelling, even though we know from independent sources that Oetinger was important to him. The reason for this silence is very clear. Academics and clergymen who referred to Oetinger or expressed sympathy for his ideas were generally ridiculed and even sometimes dismissed from their posts.[85] It must also be noted that Hegel doesn't refer to *Schelling* by name in the Preface either. In fact, the *Phenomenology* refers to few individuals by name. In making largely indirect reference to other thinkers, Hegel was following an older literary tradition, and, in fact, emulating Schelling.

But why would Hegel place an allusion to Oetinger in the Preface? One must understand the allusion in the context of his debate with Schelling. Hegel is giving Schelling the key to get past the dead-end of his doctrine of the Absolute as *coincidentia oppositorum*, or Indifference Point. The key is the developmental, organic conception of God to be found in a different mystical tradition, the Boehmian-Oetingerite one. Immediately after writing "The true is the whole," Hegel states: "But the whole is nothing other than the essence consummating itself through its development." The developmental, organic understanding of the nature of the Absolute was, as far as Hegel and the other idealists knew, original with Jakob Boehme and his school. The climax of the Preface's covert dialogue with Schelling involves Hegel, therefore, in criticizing Schelling by invoking the authority of Oetinger's Boehme-influenced speculative pietism.

Schelling apparently got the message. He would go on to publicly accuse Hegel (after the philosopher's death) of having lifted much of his philosophy from Boehme.[86]

---

[84] Benz writes, "Oetinger was the mediator of cabalistic ideas for the German idealistic philosophers, especially Schelling, who returned often to the Swabian theological sources, with which he had been indoctrinated in his youth during his sojourn as a theological student at the *Stift*, the seminary at Tübingen, and which he called to mind in all the decisive crises of his spiritual and philosophical development." Benz, *Mystical Sources*, p. 48.

[85] See Hayden-Roy, p. 69; Robert Schneider, p. 47.

[86] For example, in lectures given in the 1830s, Schelling remarks disdainfully, "Jakob Boehme says: divine freedom vomits itself into nature. Hegel says: divine freedom releases nature. What is one to think of this notion of releasing? This much is clear: the biggest compliment one can pay to this notion is to call it 'theosophical.'" See F. W. J. Schelling, *On The History of Modern Philosophy*, trans. by Andrew Bowie (New York: Cambridge University Press, 1994), p. 155.

That Hegel should criticize another thinker for being "insufficiently Boehmean" seems incredible, but in fact Hegel gives the same treatment to Spinoza! In the *Lectures on the History of Philosophy*, delivered two years earlier, Hegel states that Spinoza's philosophy "is only fixed substance, not yet Spirit; in it we do not confront ourselves. God is not Spirit here because He is not the triune. Substance remains rigid and petrified, without Boehme's sources [*Quellen*]. The particular determinations in the form of thought-determinations are not Bohme's source spirits which work and unfold in one another."[87]

This criticism of Spinoza is especially significant in light of the latter's influence on Schelling's "system of Identity," which Hegel is critiquing in the Preface. Schelling (and also Hoelderlin) had come under the influence of Spinoza through reading Jacobi's *Über die Lehre des Spinoza in Briefe an den Herrn Moses Mendelssohn*. In this work, Jacobi records Lessing as having said, "The orthodox concepts of the deity are no longer for me. *Hen kai pan* [one and all], I know no other." Hoelderlin adopted the phrase *hen kai pan* as his personal motto and took it, and Spinoza's philosophy, to be an expression of pantheism. Apparently, his enthusiasm was shared by Schelling and Hegel. *Hen kai pan* is actually supposed to convey the idea that all *is* one, and it is an expression of the perennial mystical conception of *coincidentia oppositorum*. In the context of a discussion of mysticism (in which he identifies Schelling's philosophy as a synthesis of Plotinus, Spinoza, Kant, and Boehme) Schopenhauer states that "The Ἐν καὶ πᾶν [*hen kai pan*] has been forever the laughingstock of fools and the everlasting meditation of the wise."[88] Schelling's Identity philosophy can be understood as a sophisticated, post-Kantian attempt to express the meaning of *hen kai pan*.

V. CONCLUSION: HEGEL'S HERMETICISM

In the preceding section, I implicitly drew a distinction between two types of mysticism. One strain of mysticism emphasizes the ineffable mystery of the *coincidentia oppositorum*, and stops there. The other strain, exemplified by Boehme, actually seeks positive knowledge of the nature of the divine, usually through some method of articulating the different "aspects" of God.

Elsewhere, I have termed the latter form of mysticism *Hermeticism*. The *Hermetica* (or *Corpus Hermeticum*) are a collection of Greek and

---

[87] *LHP*, 3:288; not present in *Werke*, see *Sämtliche Werke*, vol. 19, ed. by Hermann Glockner (Stuttgart: Fromann, 1928), p. 377.

[88] Arthur Schopenhauer, *On the Basis of Morality*, trans. by E. F. J. Payne (Providence, Rhode Island: Berghahn Books. 1995), p. 209.

Latin texts probably written in the first or second centuries A.D. The mythical author of these texts was Hermes Trismegistus (or "Thrice-Greatest Hermes"). Hermeticism is the tradition that grew up around these texts over the course of centuries. Many different influences came together to create the Hermetic tradition, until, in fact, it had drifted considerably beyond the ideas expressed in the *Hermetica*. These influences include alchemy and occultism of various kinds, Kabbalism, Lullism, and the mysticism of Eckhart and others.

Hermeticists typically reject the mysticism that stops short at "mystery," and, like Boehme and Hegel, hold that actual, discursive knowledge of the nature of God is possible, as opposed simply to an "immediate experience."[89] However, Hermeticists usually go much farther than this in declaring that God requires creation, especially the human beings who contemplate Him, in order to be truly actual.[90] As has been noted by others, Hermeticism can be seen as a positive form of Gnosticism, positive insofar as it does not denigrate creation but makes it play a central role in the being of God.[91] The ideal of the Hermeticist is to grasp the nature of God, and reality as such, in terms of an all-encompassing system of thought. Possession of this total wisdom was thought to perfect and empower the individual. In the modern period, the "Hermeticism" of certain thinkers refers not just to their endorsement of these positions, but also typically to their interest in a grab bag of loosely-related subjects, including alchemy, extrasensory perception, dowsing, Kabbalism, Masonry, Mesmerism, Rosicrucianism, Paracelcism, *prisca theologia, philosophia perennis*, "correspondences," "cosmic sympathies," and vitalism. "Hermetic" thinkers typically were interested in most of these subjects. Certainly, such thinkers as Boehme, Oetinger, and Baader can be called Hermetic, not just on this basis but

---

[89] In the *Lectures on the Philosophy of Religion*, Hegel declares that any point of view that stresses man's inability to know God is "directly opposed to the whole nature of the Christian religion, according to which we should *know* God *cognitively*, God's nature and essence, and should esteem this cognition above all else," (*LPR*, 1:88; *VPR*, 1:7).

[90] See Ernest Lee Tuveson, *The Avatars Of Thrice Great Hermes: An Approach to Romanticism* (Lewisburg, PA: Bucknell University Press, 1982), pp. 15–16, 34.

[91] Hermeticism is often confused with Gnosticism. This occurs in otherwise very valuable scholarship on Hegel. The earliest example is Baur's aforementioned *Die christliche Gnosis* (1835). For more recent scholarship, see Gerald Hanratty, "Hegel and the Gnostic Tradition: I," *Philosophical Studies* (Ireland), 30 (1984), pp. 23–48; "Hegel and the Gnostic Tradition: II," *Philosophical Studies* (Ireland), 31 (1986–1987), pp. 301–325; and Jeff Mitscherling, "The Identity of the Human and the Divine in the Logic of Speculative Philosophy" in *Hegel and the Tradition: Essays in Honor of H. S. Harris*, ed. by Michael Baur and John Russon (Toronto: University of Toronto Press, 1997), pp. 143–161.

due to their endorsement of the basic tenets of Hermeticism described above.

Recently, a number of scholars have argued for the influence of Hermeticism on such important modern philosophers as Bacon, Descartes, Spinoza, Leibniz, Newton, and Kant.[92] Through these thinkers, Hermeticism has shaped modernity as such. The Hermetic image of the *magus*, with his perfect *gnosis* and world-transforming powers, inspired modernity's project of the progressive mastery of nature and emancipation of mankind though science, technology, and social engineering.

Eric Voegelin suggests that we should count Hegel among these thinkers. Voegelin writes that he was unable to understand Hegel until he learned that "by his contemporaries Hegel was considered a gnostic thinker." Voegelin argues, however, that it would be more precise to characterize Hegel's thought as Hermetic, and he boldly asserts that Hegel "belongs to the continuous history of modern Hermeticism since the fifteenth century."[93]

I have written an entire book arguing for essentially this thesis. Specifically, I argue that Hegel's system is Hermetic in content and form, that Hegel shared in the curious collection of interests that are typical of Hermeticists, and that these parallels between Hegel and the Hermetic tradition are not accidental, because there is ample evidence that Hegel took an active interest in Hermeticism throughout his intellectual career.

So there is a "mystical" element in Hegel's thought and a mystical influence upon it. But so what? Is this a mere historical curiosity, or does it have larger implications for Hegel scholarship and for the history of ideas in general? I believe that it has important implications.

First, it should serve as a corrective to the tendency of philosophically-trained Hegel scholars to narrate Hegel's intellectual development solely in terms of his encounter with mainstream German philosophy, specifically Kant, Fichte, and Schelling. One can patch together an amazing lifelike simulacrum of Hegelian philosophy from bits and pieces of these and other academically respectable figures. But that is not how Hegel did it.

---

[92] These scholars include Frances Yates, Antoine Faivre, Richard Popkin, Allan Debus, Betty Jo Teeter Dobbs, Paul Otto Kristeller, D. P. Walker, Stephen McKnight, Allison Coudert, and Gregory R. Johnson.

[93] Eric Voegelin, "Response to Professor Altizer's 'A New History and a New but Ancient God,'" in *The Collected Works of Eric Voegelin*, vol. 12, *Published Essays, 1966–1985*, ed. by Ellis Sandoz (Baton Rouge: Louisiana State University Press, 1990), p. 297. See also Voegelin, "On Hegel: A Study in Sorcery," in Sandoz.

Second, an appreciation of the role of mystical ideas in the thought of Hegel and other modern thinkers opens new vistas, new paradigms for the history of modern philosophy and for the philosophy of history. Modernity is a project, a social and historical movement with a linear trajectory: from unreason to reason, superstition to science, domination by nature to dominion over it, mastery and slavery to universal freedom, darkness to light. The central presupposition of this project is that its driving force, reason, is self-grounding and can therefore emancipate itself from and transcend unreason, i.e., it can progress beyond the historical contingencies of its starting point. In Hegel's terms, reason determines history; history does not determine reason.

Modern historians of philosophy naturally have viewed their subject matter through the same progressive optic, as reason asserting its autonomy and progressively dispelling the darkness of superstition. But if the very idea of the autonomy and progressive unfolding of reason has deeply irrational roots, then perhaps history is better understood as Heidegger saw it, not as an intelligible progression from superstition to reason, but merely as a random and contingent succession of superstitions, the most stubborn of which are those that present themselves as most rational.[94]

---

[94] I wish to thank Frederick Beiser, Clark Butler, Tom Darby, and Cyril O'Regan for their constructive criticisms of my research. I am especially indebted to Gregory R. Johnson for his help with an earlier draft of this chapter.

11 Philosophizing about Nature: Hegel's Philosophical Project

I. INTRODUCTION

Though it was initiated by Pythagoras, expanded in Plato's *Timeaus*, comprehensively developed by Aristotle, and healthy throughout the Mediaeval, Renaissance and Modern periods well into the nineteenth century,[1] in the twentieth century among analytic and scientifically minded philosophers, "philosophy of nature" apparently vanished. Fortunately, the increasing calibre of recent research in history, methodology and philosophy of science has once again revealed fascinating issues at the intersections among the natural sciences, scientific methodology, history of science, and philosophy of science, which today – precisely because no discipline can plausibly monopolize them – are rightly designated philosophy of nature. Placing Hegel's notorious *Philosophy of Nature* within this interdisciplinary area does not yet illumine it.[2]

---

[1] See, for example, Ernst Cassirer, *Das Erkenntnisproblem in der Philosophie und Wissenschaft der neueren Zeit* (Hamburg: Meiner, 1999); Uwe Meixner and Albert Newen, *Geschichte der Naturphilosophie* (Paderborn: Mentis, 2004); Richard McKeon, *On Knowing — The Natural Sciences* (Chicago: University of Chicago Press, 1994); and David Malament, ed., *Reading Natural Philosophy: Essays in the History and Philosophy of Science and Mathematics* (Chicago: University of Chicago Press, 2002).

[2] The following editions of Hegel's works have been used:

GW: Gesammelte Werke. See Hegel, 1968.
M: Hegel's Phenomenology of Spirit. See Hegel, 1977a.
MM: Werke in Zwanzig Bänden. See Hegel, 1970a.
PhdG: Phänomenologie des Geistes. See Hegel, 1980.
WL1: Wissenschaft der Logik, vol. I, 2nd ed. See Hegel, 1984.
WL2: Wissenschaft der Logik, vol. II, 1st ed. See Hegel, 1981.
G. W. F. Hegel, 1801. *Dissertatio Philosophica de Orbitis Planetarum.* Jena, Prager. Corrigenda in Ferrini, 1995, pp. 11–16; critical edition in *GW*, 5:223–253.
–, 1808. "Philosophische Enzyklopädie für die Oberklasse" (*Texte zur philosophischen Propädeutik,* 1). MM, 4:9–69. Translated in Hegel, 1986, pp. 124–169.
–, 1810/1811. "Logik für die Mittelklasse" (*Texte zur philosophischen Propädeutik,* 7). MM, 4:162–203. Translated in Hegel, 1986, pp. 74–104.

Hegel classifies his philosophy of nature as rational physics.[3] "Rational physics" may sound quaint, outdated, and even presumptuous. However, Newton identified the genre of the *Principia* as "rational mechanics" (a proper part of rational physics),[4] and rational physics remains a serious discipline today, with professional journals and recent

–, 1968–. *Gesammelte Werke.* Rheinisch-Westfälischen Akadamie der Wissenschaften and Deutsche Forschungsgemeinschaft, ed. by H. Buchner and O. Pöggeler (Hamburg, Meiner).

–, 1970a. *Werke in Zwanzig Bänden,* ed. by E. Moldenhauer and K. M. Michel (Frankfurt: Suhrkamp).

–, 1970b. *Hegel's Philosophy of Nature.* 3 vols. (*Enzyklopädie*, vol. II.), trans. by M. J. Petry (London: George Allen and Unwin; New York: Humanities Press).

–, 1970c. *Hegel's Philosophy of Nature. (Enzyklopädie*, vol. II), trans. by A. V. Miller (Oxford: The Clarendon Press).

–, 1977a. *Hegel's Phenomenology of Spirit,* trans. by A. V. Miller (Oxford: The Clarendon Press).

–, 1977b. *Faith and Knowledge ,* trans. by W. Cerf and H. S. Harris (Albany: SUNY Press).

–, 1977c. *The Difference Between Fichte's and Schelling's System of Philosophy,* trans. by H. S. Harris and W. Cerf (Albany: SUNY Press).

–, 1980. *Phänomenologie des Geistes. GW,* 9.

–, 1981. *Wissenschaft der Logik,* vol. II, 1st ed. (1816). *GW,* 12; cited as "WL2".

–, 1984. *Wissenschaft der Logik,* vol. I, 2nd ed. (1832). *GW,* 21; cited as "WL1".

–, 1986. *The Philosophical Propaedeutic,* ed. by M. George and A. Vincent and trans by A. V. Miller (Oxford: Blackwell).

–, 1987. " Philosophical Dissertation on the Orbits of the Planets (1801) "; Preceded by the 12 Theses Defended on August 27, 1801, trans by P. Adler. *Graduate Faculty Philosophy Journal,* 12, 1, pp. 269–309.

–, 1991. *Hegel's Encyclopedia Logic,* trans. by T. Geraets, W. Suchting, and H. S. Harris (Cambridge, MA: Hackett Publishing Co).

–, 1994. *Vorlesungen über die Philosophie des Geistes. Berlin* 1827/1828, trans. by J. E. Erdmann and F. Walter and ed. by F. Hespe and B. Tuschling (Hamburg: Meiner).

–, 2000. *Vorlesung über Naturphilosophie Berlin 1823/24,* trans. by K. G. J. v. Griesheim, ed. by G. Marmasse (Frankfurt am Main: Lang).

–, 2001. *Vorlesungen über die Logik. Berlin 1831,* transcribed by Karl Hegel, ed. by U. Rameil and H.-Chr. Lucas (Hamburg: Meiner).

–, 2002. *Vorlesung über Naturphilosophie Berlin 1821/22. Nachschrift über Naturphilosophie,* ed. by G. Marmasse and T. Posch (Frankfurt am Main: Lang).

–, forthcoming a. *The Phenomenology of Spirit,* trans. by T. Pinkard (Cambridge, UK: Cambridge University Press).

–, forthcoming b. *The Science of Logic,* trans. G. Di Giovanni (Cambridge, UK: Cambridge University Press).

[3] *Enz.,* II, Introduction; *MM,* 9:10–11; Hegel, 1970c, p. 2.
[4] Newton, *The Principia: mathematical principles of natural philosophy,* ed. by I. Bernard Cohen and A. Whitman (Berkeley: University of California Press, 1999), p. 381, cf. 11.

textbooks to show for it.[5] "Rational physics" is physical theory which emphasizes the conceptual foundations and basic principles of physics and how these can be used to explain particular physical phenomena, rendering them comprehensible. This is the key aim of Hegel's *Philosophy of Nature*, because sufficient analysis of the conceptual foundations of natural sciences requires philosophical resources which complement the resources found within scientific theories and methods, which alone, he argues, are insufficient to the task. Hegel's *Philosophy of Nature* is fascinating in its own right and also sheds important light on the character of Hegel's philosophy as a whole, because as Henry Harris notes, "the Baconian applied science of this world is the solid foundation upon which Hegel's ladder of *spiritual* experience rests".[6] Indeed, Hegel's study of gravitational theory played a central role in the development of his "dialectic" from a merely destructive set of sceptical equipollence arguments directed against contemporaneous physics and astronomy to a constructive set of philosophical principles based on gravity exhibiting the essential interrelatedness of physical bodies.[7]

Though it has been easy to condemn Hegel's alleged errors – the supposed debacle regarding Bode's Law of interplanetary distances and the discovery of the asteroid, Ceres; his apparently scandalous attack on Newton's *Principia* – such criticisms generally redound upon their sources, once *Hegel's* sources have been properly identified and assessed.[8] Hegel's postgraduate instruction in physics was excellent,

---

[5] See, for example, C. W. Kilmister and J. E. Reeve, *Rational Mechanics* (London: Longmans, 1966).

[6] H. S. Harris, *Hegel's Ladder* (Cambridge, MA: Hackett, 1997), vol. 2, p. 355.

[7] Cinzia Ferrini, "On the Role of Newton's Mechanics and Philosophy of Nature in the Genesis of Hegel's Dialectic", in *Hegels Denkentwicklung in der Bonner und Frankfurter Zeit*, ed. by M. Bondelli and H. Linnweber-Lammerskitten (Paderborn: Fink, 1999), pp. 197–224; cp. *De Orbitis Planetarum, GW*, 5:247.29; Hegel, 1987, p. 295.

[8] And once corruptions in the Latin of Hegel's *Dissertatio* are corrected; see Ferrini, *Guida al 'De orbitis planetarum' di Hegel ed alle sue edizioni e traduzioni* (Bern: Haupt, 1995), and the critical edition in *GW*, 5:231–253. Regarding Bode's Law, see Wolfgang Neuser, *Hegel, Dissertatio Philosophica de Orbitis Plaentarum/ Philosophische Eroerterung ueber die Plantenbahnen* (Weinheim: Acta humaniora, 1986), pp. 50–60) and Ferrini, "Framing Hypotheses: Numbers in Nature and the Logic of Measure in the Development of Hegel's System", in *Hegel and the Philosophy of Nature*, ed. by Stephen Houlgate (Albany, NY: SUNY Press, 1998), pp. 283–310. Regarding Newton, see below, §2; Edward Halper's contribution, Chapter 12, in this volume; Ferrini, *Guida*; Paul Ziche, *Mathematische und naturwissenschaftliche Modelle in der Philosophie Schellings und Hegels* (Stuttgart: Fromann-Holzboog, 1996), pp. 133–199; and Michael J. Petry, *Hegel and Newtonianism* (Dordrecht, The Netherlands: Kluwer, 1993).

and he had sufficient background in mathematics to understand it thoroughly.[9] Michael John Petry's massive three volume edition of Hegel's *Philosophy of Nature* shows conclusively that Hegel was both broadly and deeply versed in the natural sciences of his day, as well as any nonspecialist possibly could be and far more than his vociferous critics ever were, that Hegel made very few outright errors about contemporaneous science and that those errors usually stem from credible sources.[10] Though not a professional mathematician, Hegel taught calculus and understood mathematics well enough to have informed reasons for preferring French schools of analysis, particularly LaGrange's (§267 n. 2).[11] Indeed, he was sufficiently well informed about problems in the foundations of (mathematical) analysis to critically assess Cauchy's ground-breaking "first reform" of analysis.[12] Moreover, Hegel was a rarity among philosophers, because he was also directly engaged in

---

[9] See Christoph Friedrich von Pfleiderer, *Physik. Naturlehre nach Kluegel. Nachschrift einer Tuebinger Vorlesung von 1804*, ed. by Paul Ziche (Stuttgart: Fromann-Holzboog, 1994). For discussion, see Westphal, "Force, Understanding and Ontology", *Bulletin of the Hegel Society of Great Britian* 57/58 (2008).

[10] M. J. Petry, "Introduction" to *Hegel's Philosophy of Nature* (London: George, Allen & Unwin, 1970), vol. 1, pp. 49–59. Petry's edition also indicates the original date of publication of the various passages included in Hegel's final edition (1830). A somewhat better translation is provided by Miller, *Hegel's Philosophy of Nature* (Oxford: Clarendon Press, 1970). See Buchdahl, "Hegel's Philosophy of Nature", *British Journal for the Philosophy of Science*, 23 (1972), pp. 257–266. Hegel's *Philosophy of Nature* is the second of three parts of his *Encyclopedia of Philosophical Sciences*, comprising §§245–375. This *Encyclopedia* was Hegel's lecture syllabus. It contains consecutively numbered sections, often complemented by published Remarks (*Anmerkungen*). Posthumous editions of Hegel's *Encyclopedia* have appended relevant lecture notes from students to these sections as "*Zusätze*" (additions). All otherwise unattributed section numbers refer to Hegel's *Encyclopedia*. These may be followed by "*Anm*" for Hegel's published Remarks, a "*Z*" for lecture material, or an "n" for Hegel's published footnotes. As a lecture syllabus, Hegel's *Encyclopedia* was intended for oral elaboration; his lecture notes are crucial resources. Recently, several complete sets of lecture transcripts have been found, edited, and published. The most important of these are Hegel, 2000 and Hegel, 2002. The recent English translations of Hegel's works listed above provide the pagination of *GW*; hence no page numbers are cited for these translations.

[11] The second edition of LaGrange's *Théorie des fonctiones analytiques* (1811) is now available in English translation. See J. L. La Grange, *Analytical Mechanics*. Edited and translated by A. Boissonnade and V. N. Vagliente (Dordrecht, The Netherlands: Kluwer, 1997). Hegel used the first edition, LaGrange, *Mechanique analytique*. (Paris: Desaint, 1788).

[12] See Michael Wolff, "Hegel und Cauchy. Eine Untersuchung zur Philosophie und Geschichte der Mathematik", in *Hegel und die Naturwissenschaften*, ed. by R.-P. Horstmann and M. J. Petry (Stuttgart: Klett-Cotta, 1986), pp. 197–263.

natural science, specifically geology and mineralogy.[13] Hegel simply is not the charlatan whose image still arises in connection with his philosophy of nature.

Understanding the philosophical character of Hegel's *Philosophy of Nature* requires recognizing some basic legitimate philosophical issues embedded in the development of physics from Galileo to Newton (§2). These issues illuminate the character of Hegel's analysis of philosophical issues regarding nature (§3) and the central aims and purposes of Hegel's philosophy of nature (§4).

II. GALLILEO, NEWTON AND PHILOSOPHY OF NATURE

2.1

Galileo directly disputed authority as a criterion of truth in scientific matters. He also knew that sensory evidence could not serve as this criterion; he recognized that motion is relative and that illusions and appearances can infect observation. Galileo held that mathematical formulation of laws of nature can afford demonstrations of genuine regularities in natural phenomena. This requires that mathematical formulae be fitted to careful observation, whilst the joint satisfaction of these two demands must also be rationally intelligible. The crucial methodological point is that giving mathematical expression to natural regularities guides the physical analysis and explanation of the phenomena. The factors in the mathematical formula must be plausibly interpretable as factors in the physical situation. Galileo explicitly disavowed metaphysics as a guide to determining the plausibility of those factors, at the beginning of Day 3 of his *Discourses Concerning the Two New Sciences*. This incensed Descartes and the same attitude in Newton worried Kant, though it was decisive for the development of modern science and became even more pronounced in Newton's *Principia*.[14] Newton's mathematical theory of orbital motion forged an important kind of independence of physical theory from metaphysical and physical questions about the ultimate nature of space, time or gravity: For Newton's work, it sufficed to regard gravity as a centrally

---

[13] See Cinzia Ferrini, "Reason: Certainty, Truth and Observing Nature", in *The Blackwell Guide to Hegel's Phenomenology of Spirit*, ed. by K. R. Westphal (London: Blackwell, 2009), chapter 5.

[14] Descartes to Mersenne, 11 Oct. 1638; Kant, *Metaphysical Foundations of Natural Science* (hereafter "*Foundations*"), vol. 4, pp. 472–473.

directed force, where that centre is specified only by its mass and location.[15]

The relevance of this point to Hegel can be seen by considering Gerd Buchdahl's (1980) account of how scientific theories are developed, evaluated and revised within a methodological framework comprising three broad kinds of considerations, a "probative component" regarding proper standards and techniques for collecting and assessing observational and experimental data, a "systemic component" regarding the internal unity of a theory and its integration with other scientific theories and an "explicative component" concerning the intelligibility or plausibility of the basic concepts or factors involved in a scientific theory, including heuristic principles and basic principles of explanation. In brief, Hegel's philosophy of nature is dedicated to showing that, when properly explicated, the basic concepts involved in an adequate scientific theory are mutually contrastive and interdefined in such a way that no genuine further questions about explanatory causes remain. The questions set aside by Galileo and Newton, the very questions Descartes and Kant sought to answer, are not, in the final Hegelian analysis, genuine questions at all. This point can be illustrated and further specified by considering part of Hegel's critique of Newton.

2.2

Newton sought to answer two questions: Given an orbiting body's trajectory, find the law of force, and more importantly, given a law of force, find the trajectory of an orbiting body.[16] Newton's theory involves generalizing Galileo's law of free fall to regard the deviation of an orbit from its tangent as an indicator of centrally directed force, where the extent of deviation is proportional to the square of the time. Since the motion in question is an elliptical orbit, the direction of deviation from a tangent is directed towards a focal centre, and so is not constant. Since the orbit is elliptical, the force which produces the deviation also varies with the distance from the centre (by an inverse square proportionality). These facts require incorporating time into the geometrical calculations. Newton included time by generalizing Kepler's law of areas; the time elapsed when traversing a given arc of its orbit is proportional to the area of the sector swept out by a radius from the centre point to the orbiting body. Because the direction of motion changes continuously, the geometrical calculations must be restricted to very small or nascent

---

[15] François DeGandt, ed. *Force and Geometry in Newton's Principia.* (Princeton, Princeton University Press, 1995), pp. 265–272.

[16] Ibid, p. 8.

motions. Combining these factors required sophisticated mathematical analysis which eluded Newton's predecessors, though they perceived many of the relevant physical factors.

Because one of the two central problems was to derive the law of force from a given orbit, it is significant though unsurprising that Newton's inverse square law of gravitational attraction can be derived from Kepler's orbits. Hegel contends, however, that Newton's purely mathematical demonstration of Kepler's laws is inadequate because Newton's mathematical analysis alone cannot establish the reality of Kepler's *physical* laws (§270R; see below, §2.3).[17] Yet Newton's second problem is more important and more acute: to derive a body's orbit from the law of attraction. Newton developed a bevy of ingenious geometrical techniques to solve this problem, but it ultimately is beyond those means to handle. In principle, Newton's expanded geometrical methods can only determine one point at a time, the trajectory of a body which begins motion with any initial velocity under the influence of any central force depending on distance. However, only with integral calculus can the curve of the trajectory be completely described and the geometrical species of the curve (if it has one) be determined. The problem and the solution were first demonstrated by Jean Bernoulli using integral calculus.[18]

Though I have found no reference by Hegel to Bernoulli's works, Hegel refers directly to the weaknesses of Newton's proof that the planets move in ellipses; in particular, his remarks suggest the problem of the uniqueness of the ellipse as a solution to the problem of determining the orbit on the basis of the law of force. The problem of the uniqueness of the solution was taken up from Bernoulli by subsequent analyses using integral calculus, including Francoeur's *Traité élémentair de Mécanique* (1801) to which Hegel refers in this connection (§270 *Anm.*). Hegel cites (in 1827 and 1830) Laplace's *Exposition du Systèm du Monde* (1796) to the same effect in his lectures (§270Z). Yet Hegel learned of this problem much earlier from Castel (1724), a rare work widely publicized by Montucla (1758), which Hegel likely studied when visiting the university library in Geneva from Bern and which he implicitly used both in his dissertation, *De Orbitis Planetarum*,[19] and in his *Science of*

---

[17] See Cinzia Ferrini, "On Newton's Demonstration of Kepler's Second Law in Hegel's *De Orbitis Planetarum* (1801)". *Philosophia naturalis*, 31 (1994), pp. 150–170; and Westphal, "Force, Understanding and Ontology", *Bulletin of the Hegel Society of Great Britain* (forthcoming).

[18] See DeGandt, *Force and Geometry*, pp. 248–249, 263–264.

[19] Hegel (1801, 1987); see Ferrini, "On Newton's Demonstration"; *Guida*; and "Die Bibliothek in Tschugg: Hegels Vorbereitung für seine frühe Naturphilosophie", in

Logic.[20] Castel showed that Newton's demonstration of Kepler's areal law entails the absurd conclusion that all central orbits are circular.[21] This is a crucial example of a point repeatedly emphasized by Hegel's physics instructor, Pfleiderer (1994): to determine what can, and what cannot, be accomplished using geometry and what instead requires analysis (calculus).

2.3

Newton's point-by-point calculation of an orbit illustrates Hegel's complaint about the "unspeakable metaphysics" unleashed by Newton's *Principia* (§270 *Anm.*). Newton's point-by-point calculations require dividing up a continuous motion and dividing up the various factors which constitute that motion and treating them as if they were mutually independent quantities. The point of Hegel's critique is that no sensible physical interpretation can be given to the mathematical factors involved in Newton's calculations:

The presuppositions, the course, and the results which analysis requires and provides, remain quite beside the [present] point, which concerns the *physical* value and the *physical* significance (*Bedeutung*) of those determinations and that course [of Newton's geometrical demonstration]. (§270 *Anm.*)

Hegel objects to Newton's reifying his analytical factors into apparently mutually independent realities; he contends that Newton's geometrical methods cannot but encourage this misleading tendency by carving up a continuous mutual causal interaction into fictitious discrete impulses. Indeed, this contrast illuminates Hegel's repeated stress on how "modern [mathematical] analysis" has dispensed with Newton's methods of proof (e.g., §270 *Anm.*).

2.4

Hegel's criticism of Newton's intricate geometrical methods illuminates Hegel's account of causal dispositions and causal laws. Consider three standard views of scientific laws and explanations. It is often supposed

---

Hegel in der Schweiz (1793–1796), ed. by H. Schneider and N. Waszek (Frankfurt am Main: Lang, 1997), pp. 237–259.

[20] *WL; GW*, 21:378.29–379.4; *GW*, 379.6–379.9; see Ferrini, "Il giovane Hegel critico di Newton", *Intersezioni*, 17 (1997), pp. 413–414.

[21] See Mauro Nasti deVincentis, "Gli argomenti hegeliani contro il modello newtoniano", in Ferrini, *Guida*, pp. 203–240.

that genuinely explanatory laws refer to "subobservable" theoretical entities, whose properties and interaction produce an observed macroscopic phenomenon. In sharp contrast to this, instrumentalism regards theoretical entities as mere fictions for calculating predictions and retrodictions of observable phenomena.[22] A third view is that scientific laws should be "phenomenological" in the sense that they merely describe regularities in manifest, observed phenomena. Kepler's laws are of this type. This view of natural laws is also found, for example, in the theories of Joseph Black, John Keil, W. J. M. Rankine, and Gustav Kirchhoff.[23] Among the standard options, this third view is closest to Hegel's. However, Hegel's logical *cum* philosophical explication seeks the insight or comprehension promised by explanatory laws while avoiding recourse to a potentially sceptical gap between observed phenomena and theoretical posits. The clue lies in Hegel's supposed "Aristotelianism", that is, his opposition to corpuscularism.

2.5

Corpuscular theories of matter rejected Aristotelian accounts of "natures" to account for change. According to corpuscularism, matter is discrete, inert, and consists solely of extension and impenetrability. Because matter is inert, all changes of matter must result from some nonmaterial cause, either directly or indirectly; no forces are inherent in matter. The postulation of inert matter fared ill as science developed. Newton ascribed the power of inertia to matter. Eighteenth-century physicists lost their Cartesian and corpuscular aversions to ascribing gravity as a physical force to matter and the development of chemistry, beginning with Newton himself, though especially as developed by Black, Priestly and Lavoisier, required ascribing other active forces

---

[22] *Cf.* Hume, *An Enquiry Concerning Human Understanding*, ed. by P. H. Nidditch, (New York: Oxford University Press, 1975), §VII, part I, final note (on *vis inertiae* and gravity).

[23] See Westphal, *Hegel's Epistemological Realism: A Study of the Aim and Method of Hegel's* Phenomenology of Spirit. Philosophical Studies Series in Philosophy, vol. 43, ed. by Keith Lehrer (Dordrecht, The Netherlands: Kluwer, 1989), pp. 160, 273 note 29. This third view is ascribed to Hegel by Buchdahl, "Conceptual Analysis and Scientific Theory in Hegel's *Philosophy of Nature* (with Special Reference to Hegel's *Optics*)", in *Hegel and the Sciences*, ed by R. S. Cohen and M. Wartofsky (Dordrecht, The Netherlands: Reidel, 1984), pp. 13–36 and by Brigitte Falkenberg, "How to Save the Phenomena: Meaning and Reference in Hegel's Philosophy of Nature", in Houlgate, ed., *Hegel and the Philosophy of Nature*, pp. 97–135, esp. p. 132 note 3.

to matter.[24] The alternative theory of matter was dynamic; it attributed active forces or dispositions directly to matter. First unambiguously advocated in chemistry, the dynamic theory of matter lent itself directly to Newtonian physics because it afforded a way to understand gravitational force as inherent in matter and thus removed one prop supporting mechanical explanations of gravity. The other prop was the problem of action at a distance, which is only a problem for completely mechanical conceptions of matter which in principle require contact for one body to change the motion of another body. This problem, too, is alleviated by a dynamic concept of matter.

I say that the dynamic concept of matter was first unambiguously advocated in chemistry, even though Newtonian mechanics ultimately ascribes gravitational force to matter. Throughout his life, out of deference to the Cartesian tradition he opposed and in accord with the corpuscular tradition to which he adhered, Newton insisted that "gravity" was only a mathematical, and not a physical characteristic of matter.[25] Newton was deliberately evasive in formulating his *Quaeries* in the *Opticks* in 1717. It remained for later Eighteenth century physicists to rescind their corpuscular and Cartesian qualms about the active forces of matter and to take Newton's famous *Quaery* 31 at face value. (Newton himself regarded impenetrability as a fundamental characteristic of body, while Descartes held that it derives from the primary characteristic of extension.)[26]

A central objection to Newton's theory of gravity from both the Cartesian and the corpuscular traditions was that Newton's theory of gravity appeared to reinstate discredited Aristotelian forms or active powers of matter. Newton sought to remain neutral about the causes of gravitational attraction. Yet, this official agnosticism about the nature and status of gravity ultimately compromises the natural-scientific credentials of Newton's physical system of the world because it required Newton to

---

[24] For discussion of the chemical revolution in connection with Kant, see Michael Friedman *Kant and the Exact Sciences* (Cambridge, MA: Harvard University Press, 1992), pp. 264–290.

[25] See Alexandre Koyré, "Newton and Descartes", in *Newtonian Studies* (London: Chapman & Hall, 1965), pp. 149–163 and Rupert and Marie B. Hall, "Newton's Theory of Matter", *Isis*, 51 (1960), pp. 131–144.

[26] Sir Isaac Newton, *Opticks*. (New York, Dover, 1952), pp. 389, 400; *Unpublished Scientific Papers of Isaac Newton*, ed. by R. and M. Hall (Cambridge, UK: Cambridge University Press, 1962), p. 106; and Descartes, *The Philosophical Writings of Descartes*, 3 vols., trans. by J. Cottingham, R. Stoothoff, and D. Murdoch, with A. Kenney (Cambridge, UK: Cambridge University Press, 1991), vol. 3, pp. 361, 372. On Newton's corpuscularism, see Maurice Mandelbaum, *Philosophy, Science, and Sense Perception* (Baltimore: Johns Hopkins University Press, 1964), pp. 66–88.

insert a transcendent, theological postulate into his erstwhile physical theory, namely that God set the astronomical clockwork going and occasionally intervenes to prevent the whole system from running down. As Hegel recognized in his *Dissertatio*, this postulate simply rescinds the key aim of offering an entirely natural and thus genuinely scientific explanation of natural phenomena.[27]

Hegel further recognized, however, that Newtonian physical theory in fact provides adequate grounds for ascribing gravitational attraction directly to matter; matter is "essentially heavy" in the sense that material bodies inherently tend – they gravitate – towards one another (§§262, 269).[28] Indeed, Hegel held that adequate scientific explanation provides the only possible grounds for ascribing active characteristics – causal dispositions – to material phenomena. Comprehending essential characteristics of things provides explanatory insight. This is Hegel's view beginning already in the *Phenomenology of Spirit*, which he developed there *in nuce*, expressly leaving its full development for his system of "science",[29] which came to include not only his *Science of Logic*, but also his *Encyclopaedia*, including centrally the *Philosophy of Nature*.

2.6

In "Force and Understanding" (*Phenomenology*, chapter 3) Hegel repeatedly criticizes attempts to reify aspects or moments of force into supposed distinct or independent entities. For example, he criticized the reification of "expressed" and "repressed" force (e.g., the contrast between kinetic and potential energy) or "solicited" and "soliciting" force. Kant used the term "solicitation" to refer to the effect of a moving force on a body in a given moment, which gives the moment of acceleration. Kant used this to try to prove the law of continuity (*Foundations*, 4:551–553). Hegel's point is that thinking of forces in

[27] *GW*, 5:247.12–23; Hegel, 1987, p. 294. For discussion of Newton's view, see Martin Carrier, "Isaac Newton. Prinzipien der Naturphilosophie: Raum, Kraft, Bewegung und Gott", in *Philosophen des 17. Jahrhunderts. Eine Einführung*, ed. by L. Kreimendahl (Darmstadt: Wissenschaftliche Buchgesellschaft, 1999), pp. 176–197.

[28] See Buchdahl, "Conceptual Analysis", pp. 18–25. Buchdahl, "Hegel's Philosophy of Nature", pp. 260–261, recognizes Hegel's "Aristotelianism", but never reconciles it with Hegel's alleged preference for "phenomenological" laws of nature because he doesn't quite see Hegel's enriched account of "phenomenological" laws which I highlight here. This important point is already central to Hegel's *Dissertatio* (*GW*, 5:247.29; Hegel, 1987, p. 295).

[29] *PhdG*, *GW*, 9:101.17–27/*M*,102. Natural science is also fundamental to Hegel's analysis of "The Certainty and Truth of Reason" and "Observing Nature"; see Ferrini, "The Certainty and Truth of Reason" and "Reason Observing Nature".

terms of "moments" of solicitation encourages a misleading division of a continuously effective force into a series of (quasimechanical) impulses of just the sort found in Newton's geometrical analysis of gravitational force (above, §2.4). Hegel described a set of theoretical causal laws, such as Newton's *Principia*, Book One, as a "quiet supersensible realm of law" because abstract formulations of laws of nature don't account for actual phenomena precisely because they are abstract idealizations. Accounting for actual phenomena additionally requires providing their specific parameters, their initial conditions and the theoretical links between the abstract formulae of general laws of nature and the specific versions of those laws which pertain to the specific domain in question.[30] Likewise, subsuming particular laws of phenomena under more general laws requires tremendous abstraction – from particular phenomena and their complex, fully determinate conditions.[31] Thus explaining particular phenomena requires reintroducing their specific parameters. Nevertheless, the fact that various specific phenomena can be brought under a common general law, and not merely a common mathematical function, shows that these phenomena are in fact interrelated; they are not mutually independent, self-sufficient objects or events.[32] The very concept of law-like relations, and likewise the very concept of force, requires interdefined factors into which the phenomena can be analysed.[33] Thus *"the force is constituted exactly like the law"*.[34] Hegel thus aims to show that adequate scientific explanation provides the sole and sufficient grounds for determining the essential characteristics of the objects and events in nature.[35] Why ascribe forces to material

---

[30] *PhdG*, *GW*, 9:91.31–91.37/*M*, 91. For further discussion, see Westphal, "Force, Understanding and Ontology".

[31] *PhdG*, *GW*, 9:92.10–92.19/*M*, 91.

[32] *PhdG*, *GW*, 9:92.23–92.26/*M*, 91. Pfleiderer, *Physik*, repeatedly drew his students' attention to mathematical functions exhibited in natural phenomena and their underlying causal laws, and stressed that distinct causal laws may exhibit common kinds of mathematical functions. A key error of Schelling's philosophy of nature is his persistent tendency to mistake analogies for identities, thus he disregards Pfleiderer's crucial point. This error is one object of Hegel's condemnation of relying on mere analogies, especially on the basis of intuition (*Enz.*, Introduction; *MM*, 9:9; Hegel, 1970c, p. 1; §246 *Anm.*). Schelling's apologists have yet to address Hegel's devastating rebuke. Cf. Houlgate, "Schelling's Critique of Hegel's *Science of Logic*". *Review of Metaphysics*, 53 (1999), pp. 99–128.

[33] *PhdG*, 93.7–94.28/*M*, 92–3.

[34] *PhdG*, 95.12–13/*M*, 95; original emphasis. Hegel's claim is consistent with recognizing various kinds of idealizations typically involved in stating causal laws, but these niceties cannot be discussed here.

[35] See Westphal, "*Intelligenz* and the Interpretation of Hegel's Idealism: Some Hermeneutic Pointers", *The Owl of Minerva* 39, 1–2 (2008–09), §6.

phenomena? Because so far as logical, epistemic, or metaphysical necessity may be concerned, natural phenomena could instantiate any mathematical function, or none whatsoever. Hegel realized that Kant's *Foundations* fails utterly to account for this.[36] The fact that a natural phenomenon exhibits a mathematical function indicates, as nothing else can, that something in that phenomenon is structured in accord with the relevant mathematical function exhibited in its behaviour. That "something" is the causal structure of the phenomenon, its causal disposition(s). Hegel's claim must be taken literally: the force is constituted exactly like the law.[37] Hegel's account of causation has great significance for his ontology, in general, and especially for his *Philosophy of Nature*.

2.7

Despite his penetrating critique of Newton's flawed geometrical methods, it is crucial to recognize that Hegel's central account of concepts, of *Begriffe* as internally complex, systematically integrated and instantiated conceptual structures, owes its foundation, both for its meaning and for its justification, to the Newtonian theory of universal gravitation.[38] Hegel himself insists that:

> Gravitation is the true and determinate concept of material corporeality, which is realized as idea (zur *Idee realisiert* ist). (§269)

> Universal gravitation as such must be recognized as a profound thought; it has already acquired attention and confidence, above all through its associated quantitative determination and has been vindicated by experience from the solar system right down to the phenomenon of the capillary tube .... (§269 *Anm.*)

Hegel's profound admiration for the enormous scope and integrative power of the theory of universal gravitation, expressed briefly here, is something he learned from his physics instructor Pfleiderer, who

---

[36] Westphal, "On Hegel's Early Critique of Kant's *Metaphysical Foundations of Natural Science*", in Houlgate, *Hegel and the Philosophy of Nature*, pp. 137–166. Radical empiricists such as Bas van Fraassen hold that insisting on having an "account" is already to beg the question in favor of an illicit realism about explanations and explananda. Radical empiricism of this sort, however, is an unwarranted holdover of misguided, early eighteenth-century philosophical preconceptions about science. See Westphal, 'Hegel, Realism, and Pragmatism", in *A Companion to Pragmatism*, ed. by J. Margolis and J. Shook (Oxford: Blackwell, 2006), pp. 177–183 and Andreas Hüttemann, *Idealisierungen und das Ziel der Physik. Eine Untersuchung zum Realismus, Empirismus und Konstruktivismus in der Wissenschaftstheorie* (Berlin: deGruyter, 1997).

[37] On Hegel's analysis of causality in "Force and Understanding", see Westphal, "Force, Understanding and Ontology".

[38] See Ferrini, "On the role of Newton's Mechanics".

used this lesson to explain an extremely important kind of scientific explanation. Pfleiderer's account serves as the best commentary on Hegel's own brief remark:

> Physics is concerned with the most exact knowledge of natural phenomena possible. From what we observe in nature we make certain rules according to which bodies interrelate under certain conditions. ... In the previous [example; omitted] natural laws were expressed merely as general occurrent (*eintretender*) consequences; but one also speaks of properties and capacities of bodies because it lies in the nature of our way of representing things (*unseres Vorstellens*) to regard whatever we consistently remark in something as its property or power. In this way we of course gain brevity and richness of expression, but one must not thereby mislead oneself into believing that the cause of the phenomenon has thus been found. If we say, for example, the body falls because it is heavy, no cause is thus adduced; rather, heaviness is a mere designation of the very same phenomenon. However if such a law is now found, e.g., that an unsupported body moves toward the earth until it again finds support, in that way we still don't know the phenomenon sufficiently; what matters instead are other circumstances, in this case the direction and speed of the motion and the relations among various different bodies in this regard. To inform ourselves about these requires experiments. For example, one places bodies in a space from which as much air as possible is expelled and finds that now all bodies fall with almost equal speed. The rules constructed from compiling and comparing individual phenomena are then applied again to explain other particular complex phenomena, indeed ones which often at first seem to contradict them, e.g., the swinging of the pendulum, the rising of light bodies, water spouts, suction pumps, *etc.* These latter phenomena one used to believe were explained by the so-called *horror vacui*; however this was basically no more than an ill-suited expression for the phenomenon itself. Afterwards one found that the matter could be fully explained by the pressure of air on the water, and that in this way it could be traced back to the law of gravity, of which it first seemed to make an exception. If one then wants to go further and adduce actual causes of phenomena, then one must admittedly be satisfied with probabilities and hypotheses. (Pfleiderer, 1994, 59–60; tr. *KRW*)

Pfleiderer's dismissive closing remark about "probabilities and hypotheses" pretty clearly alludes to Newton's *hypothesi non fingo*.[39] Pfleiderer's point is that mathematical description of natural regularities enables us to find common regularities underlying diverse and apparently opposed or conflicting phenomena and that this is centrally a

---

[39] About what Newton counted and rejected as mere hypotheses, see the brilliant analysis by William Harper, "Howard Stein on Isaac Newton: Beyond Hypotheses?" in *Reading Natural Philosophy*, ed. by D. B. Malament, ed. (Chicago: University of Chicago Press, 2002), pp. 71–112 and especially his *Isaac Newton's Scientific Method: Turning Data into Evidence for Universal Gravity* (New York: Oxford University Press, forthcoming).

matter of exact mathematical description combined with comprehensive classification of natural phenomena under common mathematical functions. Pfleiderer thus espoused the standard "phenomenological" account of scientific laws and explanations, which Hegel significantly refashioned when he realized that this kind of empirical evidence coupled with exact mathematical description provides the sole and sufficient basis for ascribing causal dispositions to natural phenomena (above, §2.5). Yet Hegel retained Pfleiderer's lessons about the inadequacy of the covering-law model of scientific explanation and the enormous importance of seeking scientific explanation in systematic integration, a view that has only recently be considered by analytic philosophers of science.[40] With these basic points about Hegel's view of Newtonian physics in hand, we can now consider the basic philosophical character of Hegel's *Philosophy of Nature*, before considering its central systematic aims (below, §4).[41]

III. HEGEL'S PHILOSOPHY OF NATURE: ONTOLOGY, METAPHYSICS OR SEMANTICS?

Interpretations of Hegel's *Philosophy of Nature* tend to divide into two kinds: According to some, Hegel's development or derivation of the various concepts treated in his *Philosophy of Nature* is purely conceptual and a priori, and merely draws illustrative, corrigible examples from the empirical domains of the natural sciences. Others contend that the very basis of Hegel's *Philosophy of Nature* is the entirety of natural science, so that the conceptual network developed in Hegel's *Philosophy of Nature* is as corrigible as natural science itself, which has changed radically since 1830.[42] The holistic character of Hegel's philosophy together

---

[40] For example, Friedman, "Explanation and Scientific Understanding", *Journal of Philosophy*, 71 (1974), pp. 5–19 and Margaret Morrison, *Unifying Scientific Theories: Physical Concepts and Mathematical Structures* (Cambridge, UK: Cambridge University Press, 2000).

[41] Further details of Hegel's critical reconsideration of Newton's *Principia* are discussed by Halper in Chapter 12 in this volume. For detailed discussion of Hegel's rational physics, and his acute account of the role of mathematics in it, see K. N. Ihmig, *Hegels Deutung der Gravitation* (Frankfurt am Main: Athenäum, 1989); Antonio Moretto, *Filosofia della Mathematica e della Meccanica nel Sistema Hegeliano*. Revised edition (Padova: Il Poligrafo, 2004); and D. Wandschneider, *Raum, Zeit, Relativität. Grundbestimmung der Physik in der Perspektiv der Hegelschen Naturphilosophie* (Frankfurt am Main: Klosterman, 1982).

[42] Houlgate, *Hegel and the Philosophy of Nature*, pp. xiii–xiv. For a review of recent work on Hegel's philosophy of nature, see Petry, "Hegelianism and the Natural Sciences: Some Current Developments and Interpretations", *Hegel-Studien*, 36 (2001), pp. 199–237.

with his epistemology renders suspect the dichotomy formed by these two approaches, which presumes, in effect, the supposedly exclusive and exhaustive Aristotelian distinction between "rational" and "historical" knowledge. Both kinds of knowledge adhere to a foundationalist model of justification. "Historical" knowledge (*historia*) is based squarely and solely on perception or empirical evidence; it is inevitably partial and unsystematic, or at least cannot be known to be otherwise. "Rational" knowledge [*scientia*] is the only rigorous form of knowledge, for it justifies conclusions solely by deducing them from original "first" principles. This distinction held sway throughout the Modern period, was central to Kant's epistemology and is still detectable today in the deductivist assumptions often made about empirical justification.[43] Hegel was deeply suspicious of this classical dichotomy. This is indicated by his rejection, by 1802, of distinctions in kind between both the a priori and the a posteriori and between the analytic and the synthetic.[44] Hegel's critique of Kant's Critical philosophy and his solution to the Pyrrhonian Dilemma of the Criterion reject the traditional dichotomy between *scientia* and *historia*, along with the foundationalist model of justification they embody.[45] More careful recent research suggests more sophisticated lines of interpretation of Hegel's *Philosophy of Nature* which avoid the ultimately untenable dichotomy between "rational" and "historical" knowledge.[46]

---

[43] Descartes, *Philosophical Writings*, 1:13, uses this distinction in passing in the third of his *Rules for Directing the Mind*. This distinction gives the point to Locke's claim (*Essay 1.1.2*) to use the "historical, plain method" and to Hume's (*Enquiry*, §8, para. 64.2) contrast between "inference and reasoning" *versus* "memory and senses" as sources of knowledge. Kant uses it in the same sense as Descartes in a parallel context in the *Critique of Pure Reason* (A835–837/B863–865).

[44] See *Glauben und Wissen* (*GW*, 4:335.2–6).

[45] See Westphal, 'Urteilskraft, gegenseitige Anerkennung ind rationale Rechtfertiging', in H-D Klein, ed., *Ethik als prima philosoptic?* (forthcoming).

[46] My thinking about these matters owes much, though probably not yet enough, to B. Falkenburg *Die Form der Materie. Zur Metaphysik der Natur bei Kant und Hegel.* (Frankfurt am Main: Athenäum-Hain, 1987); "How to Save the Phenomena: Meaning and Reference in Hegel's Philosophy of Nature", in Houlgate, ed., *Hegel and the Philosophy of Nature* (1998), pp. 97–135; Ferrini *Guida* and "On The Role of Newton's Mechanics"; and Houlgate, *An Introduction to Hegel: Freedom, Truth and History* (London: Blackwell, 2005), pp. 106–180, though I present a distinctive interpretation anchored in Hegel's epistemology and semantics. Houlgate's comprehensive introduction is highly recommended, especially for its detailed synopsis of Hegel's *Philosophy of Nature*. Also see Alfredo Ferrarin H*egel and Aristotle*. (Cambridge, UK: Cambridge University Press, 2001), pp. 201–233. A good background synopsis of Hegel's organicism is provided by Beiser, *Hegel* (London: Routledge, 2005), pp. 80–109. However, *pace* Beiser (p. 107), among many others, Hegel's serious and independent engagement with natural science began

Hegel insists that, while the two disciplines are distinct (§§7–9), natural science is fundamental to philosophy:

Not only must philosophy accord with the experience nature gives rise to; in its *formation* and in its *development*, philosophic science presupposes and is conditioned by empirical physics. (§246R; cf. Hegel, 2000, p. 72)

This remark, made very early in Hegel's Introduction to the *Philosophy of Nature*, concerns not only the second part of his *Encyclopaedia*. Nor does it concern only the development of spirit out of nature in part three. It also and fundamentally concerns Hegel's *Logic*. Just quoted was the second sentence of Hegel's Remark; the first sentence refers to Hegel's discussion of the relation between philosophy and the empirical sciences in the Introduction to the *Encyclopaedia* as a whole. There Hegel states directly that philosophy is stimulated by and grows out of experience, including natural-scientific experience, and that the natural sciences develop conceptual determinations in the form of generalizations, laws, and classifications which must be reconsidered philosophically (§12). Thus Hegel insists that his *Logic* cannot be properly understood apart from his *Philosophy of Nature*, nor can his philosophy of nature be understood apart from Hegel's knowledge and understanding of the methods and content of natural science. Hegel's *Logic* examines the ontological and cognitive roles of ontological categories (e.g., being, existence, quantity, essence, appearance, relation, thing, cause) and principles of logic (e.g., identity, excluded middle, noncontradiction). His *Logic* also analyses syllogism, judgment and principles of scientific explanation (force, matter, measure, cognition; mechanical, chemical, organic, and teleological functions), by using which alone we are able to know the world. Even this brief list suffices to cast grave doubt on the suggestion that Hegel's *Logic* can be a purely a priori investigation, for it involves too many quite specific concepts and principles, at least some of which obviously derive from historical science (e.g., "chemism"). Much less so, then, can Hegel's attempt in his *Encyclopaedia of Philosophical Sciences*, to show that and how these concepts and principles are specified and exhibited in nature and in human life, be purely a priori.[47]

long before his arrival in Jena; it began at least by his time in Bern. See Ferrini, "On Newton's Demonstration", and "Die Bibliothek in Tschugg: Hegels Vorbereitung für seine frühe Naturphilosophie", in *Hegel in der Schweiz (1793–1796)*, ed. by H. Schneider and N. Waszek (Frankfurt am Main: Lang), pp. 237–259.

47 Regarding Hegel's treatment of chemistry, see D. von Engelhardt, *Hegel und die Chemie. Studie zur Philosophie und Wissenschaft der Natur um 1800*. (Wiesbaden: Guido Pressler, 1976); D. von Engelhardt, "The Chemical System of Substances, Forces and Processes in Hegel's Philosophy of Nature and in the Sciences of the Time", in *Hegel and the Sciences*, ed. by R. S. Cohen and M. Wartofsky (Dordrecht,

Yet the fact that Hegel expressly avows the empirical and scientific sources of many of the key concepts and principles analysed in his *Logic* and especially in his *Philosophy of Nature* does not make his philosophical project merely empirical or merely explicative. In the remark just quoted, Hegel distinguishes sharply between the basis and development of his philosophy out of reconsideration of the natural sciences and his philosophical science proper, for which the natural sciences are not foundational. Instead, the foundation or basis of Hegel's *Philosophy of Nature* is something he calls "the necessity of the concept" (§246 *Anm.*), which philosophy elucidates in part with some of its own conceptual resources (§9). In what can this conceptual necessity consist, if it cannot be pure a priori and if many of the concepts and principles it involves derive from natural science?

Calling the relevant necessity "metaphysical" doesn't help, though it recalls Hegel's observation that metaphysics is nothing other than "the full range (*Umfang*) of universal determinations of thought (*Denkbestimmungen*); as it were, the diamond net in which we bring everything and thus first make it intelligible" (§246Z). Hegel's concern is that basic concepts and principles used in natural science are either assumed to be familiar – as Newton assumed our familiarity with space and time – or they are introduced independently of one another in ways that obscure their conceptual significance, which is a function of how each concept is both distinguished from and also integrated with other concepts in its domain and their proper ontological interpretation (§246Z). Hegel advocated moderate holism about conceptual content or meaning: concepts can only be properly defined and understood by integrating them with their proper counterparts within any specific domain, and likewise integrating specific domains under higher-order concepts or principles, while also integrating specific concepts with their instances. Hegel's moderate semantic holism rests on what may be called his "codetermination thesis".

3.1

Hegel's codetermination thesis is an important semantic and cognitive insight, which Hegel gained by reconsidering Kant's theory of cognitive judgment and what it reveals about the interdependence of categorical, hypothetical, and disjunctive judgments. Hegel regarded Kant's account of the Table of Judgments as inadequate, though extremely instructive

The Netherlands: Riedel, 1984), pp. 41–54; and John Burbidge, *Real Process: How Logic and Chemistry Combine in Hegel's Philosophy of Nature* (Toronto: University of Toronto Press, 1996).

(§171Z). Kant noted that a proper disjunctive judgment divides up the whole of a specific range ("sphere") of predicates relevant to a particular possible cognition.[48] Denying one predicate of the relevant kind of subject entails that another predicate within that range must be true of that subject. Conversely, affirming a predicate of a relevant subject is tantamount to denying of that subject the other predicates within that range. Hegel recognized that singular categorical judgments and hypothetical judgments both presuppose disjunctive judgments. Hypothetical judgments require disjunctive judgments because establishing any judgment of the form, "If A then B", requires judging that no relevant alternative to B either follows or results from A. Such conjoined hypothetical and disjunctive judgments are central to Kant's Analogies of Experience, because causal judgments are discriminatory: Identifying any one causal relation requires distinguishing it from its causally possible alternatives.[49] Hence the categorical judgments required to identify objects or events in synthetic judgments a priori about them – judgments required for us to be self-conscious – also require disjunctive judgments whereby we discriminate any one object from other objects and other kinds of objects. Because such disjunctive judgments require a grasp of the whole of the relevant range of alternatives within a class or "sphere", singular cognitive judgments about objects are possible only on the basis of (locally) holistic judgments about the relevant class of objects and predicates, that is, about the relevant alternatives. This requires (within any "sphere") a complete set of mutually exclusive categories, at least some of which are in fact instantiated. Such a set of categories differs significantly from a complete set of logically possible categories, such as the traditional "sum of all possibility", or taken as instantiated, the traditional *ens realisimum* – the topics of Kant's *Ideal of Pure Reason* (*KdrV*, A571/B599f.). (Is it logically possible that we could perceive more colours than are found in the standard spectrum of visible light? Who would "we" be if we could? What genuine sense could an answer to either question have?) Hegel's point is threefold: Hypothetical and categorical judgments are codetermined, they can be codetermined only within a complete set or "sphere" of contrasting predicates (requiring

---

[48] A73–74/B98–99. For brilliant discussion of Kant's Table of Judgments, see Michael Wolff, *Die Vollständigkeit der kantischen Urteilstafel.* (Frankfurt am Main: Klostermann, 1995); "Erwiderung auf die Einwände von Ansgar Beckermann und Ulrich Nortmann", *Zeitschrift für philosophische Forschung*, 52 (1998), pp. 435–459; and "Nachtrag zu meiner Kontrovers mit Ulrich Nortmann", *Zeischrift für philosophische Forschung*, 54 (2000), pp. 86–94.

[49] On the joint role of such judgments in Kant's Analogies, see Westphal *Kant's Transcendental Proof of Realism* (Cambridge, UK: Cambridge University Press, 2004), pp. 146–157.

disjunctive judgments) and they can be codetermined only in connection with extant things and events. This is Hegel's "Codetermination Thesis".[50]

3.2

If "semantics" is philosophical theory of conceptual content and cognitive or linguistic reference, then "metaphysics", as the study of our "diamond [conceptual] net" with which Hegel identifies his *Logic*, is fundamentally semantic. Hegel's philosophical analyses of issues in philosophy of nature exhibit great sensitivity to the ontological implications of conceptual content and to the importance of the ontological interpretation of metaphysical and scientific principles (above, §2). This may sound anachronistic, but is not: Kant's semantics are far richer and more sophisticated than has generally been recognized[51] and Hegel adopted the core points of Kant's semantics. Thus I agree with Pirmin Stekeler-Weithofer that Hegel's *Logic* is fundamentally a critical theory of meaning.[52] If this is surprising, this is only due to the pre-Kantian, Cartesian character of so much recent philosophy (and the neglect of semantics and epistemology by most of Hegel's expositors).[53] Kant was

---

[50] This way of making Hegel's point decouples it from intellectual intuition and thus suggests how Hegel could retain this view in his mature philosophy without relying on any kind of intuitionism. On Hegel's codetermination thesis and his rejection of intuitionism, see Westphal, "Kant, Hegel, and the Fate of 'the' Intuitive Intellect", in *The Reception of Kant's Critical Philosophy: Fichte, Schelling, and Hegel*, ed. by S. Sedgwick (New York: Cambridge University Press, 2000), pp. 283–305 and "*Intelligenz* and the Interpretation of Hegel's Idealism".

[51] See Robert Hanna, *Kant and the Foundations of Analytic Philosophy* (Oxford: Clarendon Press, 2001) and Westphal, *Kant's Transcendental Proof of Realism*.

[52] Pirim Stekeler-Weithofer's semantic interpretation of Hegel's *Logic* dovetails perfectly with Hegel's transcendental-pragmatic epistemology. See his *Hegels Analytische Philosophie. Die Wissenschaft der Logik als kritische Theorie der Bedeutung* (Paderborn: Schöningh, 1992). On this, see Westphal, *Hegel's Epistemology: A Philosophical Introduction to the Phenomenology of Spirit*, (Cambridge, MA, Hackett, 2003); "Hegel's Manifold Response to Scepticism in the *Phenomenology of Spirit*", *Proceedings of the Aristotelian Society*, 103 (2003), pp. 149–178; "Can Pragmatic Realists Argue Transcendentally?" in *Pragmatic Naturalism and Realism*, ed. by J. Shook (Buffalo, NY: Prometheus), pp. 151–175; and "Hegel and Realism", in *A Companion to Pragmatism*, ed. by J. Margolis and J. Shook (Oxford: Blackwell 2006), pp. 177–183. This is a strong consideration in favor of Stekeler-Weithofer's interpretation. The excellent conspectus of Hegel's *Logic* by Burbidge corroborates these points. See Burbidge, "Hegel's Logic", in *Handbook of the History of Logic* ed. by D. M. Gabbay and J. Woods (Amsterdam, Elsevier), vol. 3, pp. 131–175.

[53] The misfortune here lies in failing to appreciate that semantic and epistemological considerations can be put to sound hermeneutical use in understanding Hegel's

the first great anti-Cartesian in philosophy, and Hegel learned Kant's lessons well.[54] The *Denkbestimmungen* analysed in Hegel's *Logic* and *Philosophy of Nature* are, Hegel argues, fundamental structures of the extant world itself (*Denkbestimmungen des Seins*).[55] One of the most important *Denkbestimmungen*, Hegel argues, is "force", especially as introduced and justified by Newton. Hegel already understood the central role of natural scientific investigation, on the one hand, and conceptual and semantic analysis on the other, for determining whether and to what extent alleged *Denkbestimmungen* are indeed genuine structures of nature. Hegel's cognitive semantics is equally fundamental both to his *Logic* and to his *Philosophy of Nature*. Only by pursuing both of these investigations together can we identify *Denkbestimmungen* that are indeed basic structures of what is [*des Seins*] and in particular of nature.[56]

IV. CENTRAL SYSTEMATIC AIMS OF HEGEL'S PHILOSOPHY OF NATURE

Hegel's lead question in the *Philosophy of Nature* is simple to state, though puzzling to understand: "What is nature?"[57] Is this a philosophical question? Why? The Modern corpuscular answer, that nature is nothing but bodies in motion, only generates more questions: What bodies and what kinds of bodies? What motions and what kinds of motions? What, exactly, is ruled out – and ruled in – by the clause, "nothing but"? Yet the seventeenth-century materialist view of nature has proven amazingly durable among philosophers, even many who profess a marked interest in philosophy of science, or who proclaim that philosophy is nothing but an extension of or appendage to natural science.[58] The

---

philosophy, especially in view of his explicit epistemological and also semantic concerns.

[54] See Westphal, "Consciousness and its Transcendental Conditions: Kant's Anti-Cartesian Revolt," in *A History of Consciousness*, ed. by S. Heinämaa, V. Lähteenmäki and P. Remes (Dordrecht, The Netherlands: Springer, 2007), pp. 223–243.

[55] *Enz.*, §24Z; Hegel, (1808), §164; Hegel, (1986), p. 158.

[56] *WL*, I, *GW*, 21:11–12, Hegel, 2001, pp. 153.584–593, 155.644–659; see Westphal, *Hegel, Hume und die Identität wahrnembarer Dinge* (Frankfurt am Main: Klostermann, 1998), chapter 10, and "*Intelligenz* and the Interpretation of Hegel's Idealism," esp. §§4, 6.

[57] *Enz.*, II, Introduction; *MM*, 9:12; Hegel, 1970c, p. 3.

[58] Westphal, "Science and the Philosophers", in *Science: A Challenge to Philosophy?*, ed. by H. Koskinen, S. Pihlström, and R. Vilkko, Scandinavian University Studies in the Humanities and Social Sciences (Frankfurt am Main: Lang, 2006), vol. 27, pp. 125–152.

corpuscular answer echos throughout the narrowly reductionist conceptions of "naturalism" that is prevalent in contemporary philosophy.[59]

The mind–body problem is unknown to the Greeks and Mediaevals.[60] In a world comprising various kinds of enmattered forms, where the behaviour of each particular is a function of its Aristotelian essence or soul, and where each casts off its perceptual "species" (literally "shapes") by which we can grasp its essence, the now-obvious mind-body problem was profoundly unfamiliar. One key source of its development was the newly quantified science of nature: physics. Central to scientific investigation of natural phenomena, whether terrestrial or celestial, are the size, shape, location, motion, number, and material constitution of objects. These "primary" qualities were regarded as the only fundamental or "real" qualities of bodies. All the others qualities that make life so colourful, tasty, and delightful are thus "secondary" qualities, derivative from the effects of the primary qualities of bodies on our sensory receptors. With the mechanization of nature inevitably came the mechanization of the human body. Descartes' innovation was not the mind, it was the body as *machina*: it too is exhaustively describable in purely quantitative terms, hence it too is open to purely scientific, mechanical explanation. Thus even our sensory organs cannot themselves be qualified by the "secondary" qualities – colours, odours, tastes, or auditory tones – we experience so abundantly. This is the key shift away from Aristotelian and Mediaeval notions of the human body. Since we *do* experience such qualities, they must "be somewhere" or in-here in "something"; since we *experience* them, they must inhere in our minds. This line of reasoning gave strong impetus for regarding sensed qualities as "modes" of the mind, caused by physical objects in our surroundings and transmitted to us mechanically via our bodies and sensory physiology. From here it was but a short step, or rather a short leap to representationalist theories of perception, according to which all we are "directly" aware of are our mental representations or "ideas", which are caused by objects in our surroundings, and which (in favourable circumstances) enable us to perceive objects in our surroundings. Yet if "mind" consists solely in nonextended, active, thinking substance, and if "body" consists solely in nonthinking, inert, extended substance, how

---

[59] See the excellent discussion in Joseph Rouse, *How Scientific Practices Matter* (Chicago: University of Chicago Press, 2002).

[60] See Wallace Matson, "Why Isn't the Mind-Body Problem Ancient?" in *Mind, Matter, and Method*, ed. by P. Feyerabend and G. Maxwell (Minneapolis: University of Minnesota Press, 1966), pp. 92–102 and Peter King, "Why Isn't the Mind-Body Problem Mediaeval?" in *Forming the Mind: Conceptions of Body and Soul in Late Medieval and Early Modern Philosophy*, ed. by A. H. Lagerlund and O. Pluta, (Berlin: Springer, 2007), pp. 187–205.

can mind and body interact? If all we are directly aware of is our mental representations, how can we know anything about our surroundings? Can we determine whether we know anything about our surroundings? If Copernicus, as it were, dislodged the earth from the centre of our universe, Galileo's distinction between "primary" and "secondary" qualities ultimately dislodged us from our natural surroundings, from what had been thought and profoundly believed to be our natural home and habitat. The Cartesian predicament of modern epistemology is borne of profound alienation from nature, not only from our physical and biological environment, but also from our own physiological embodiment.

Philosophy became "Modern" with a profoundly changed world view, a view of the world to which quantitative natural science was fundamental. Yet if this modern world view dispenses with Aristotelian forms and perceptual species, one of Kant's central questions looms: How is natural-scientific, or even commonsense knowledge of the world possible?[61] Since it is actual, it must be possible – but how? Hegel's transcendental proofs of mental content externalism show *that* we have some empirical knowledge, if we're self-conscious enough even to wonder about whether we do.[62] Yet knowing that we have at least some empirical knowledge of nature around us doesn't at all tell us how extensive is our knowledge of nature, or how extensive it can be. Part of the answer to the broad question of *how* empirical knowledge is possible belongs to epistemology and cognitive psychology, which Hegel treated accordingly.[63] But general epistemology does not answer questions about the character and possibility of specifically natural-scientific knowledge. Answering these questions requires, *inter alia*, examining specific scientific concepts, principles of reasoning, methods and their actual use in observational and experimental science. Hegel examines key concepts and principles of reasoning central to natural science in his *Logic*, including causal dispositions and laws, and the core principles of mechanical, chemical and biological explanation. He re-examines these concepts and

---

[61] *KdrV*, B20, *Prolegomenon*, §§15, 23, 24.
[62] See Westphal, "Kant, Hegel, and the Transcendental Material Conditions of Possible Experience", *Bulletin of the Hegel Society of Great Britain*, 33 (1998), pp. 23–41; "On Hegel's Early Critique of Kant's *Metaphysical Foundations of Natural Science*", in Houlgate, *Hegel's Philosophy of Nature*, pp. 137–166; and "Must the Transcendental Conditions for the Possibility of Experience be Ideal?" in *Eredità Kantiane (1804–2004): questioni emergenti e problemi irrisolti*, ed. by C. Ferrini (Naples: Bibliopolis, 2004), pp. 107–126.
[63] On Hegel's cognitive psychology, see Hegel, 1994; William deVries, *Hegel's Theory of Mental Activity* (Ithaca: Cornell University Press, 1988); and Westphal, "Hegel and Realism", in *A Companion to Pragmatism*, ed. by J. Margolis and J. Shook (Oxford: Blackwell, 2006), pp. 177–183.

principles in connection with theories and examples drawn from natural science throughout his *Philosophy of Nature*.[64]

One reason for Hegel so doing is to show that the concepts and principles analysed in his *Logic* are in fact instantiated in nature and are reflected (if often only obliquely) in natural scientific knowledge (§246 *Anm.*). A second reason for his so doing is to show that the concepts, principles and forms of classification and explanation used in natural science in fact capture genuine features of nature and so are not merely conventional expressions convenient for noncognitive reasons or purposes (§§229 *Anm.*, 246Z, 367Z).[65] A third aim in his so doing is to show the great extent to which the world, nature, is knowable. Hegel undertakes this examination in order to justify his rationalist aspiration to show that all the fundamental features of the world are knowable and are knowable by us – even if philosophy only makes a limited contribution to this knowledge (§270Z).

How must we reconceive our minds and cognition in order to understand the new phenomenon of natural science and the new knowledge of nature it provides? One strategy for avoiding Descartes' dualism was to consider whether matter might not have the power, if properly configured, to think. Perhaps materialism does not require eliminating mental phenomena, even if it banishes "the mind" as a distinct kind of substance.[66] Kant deployed another strategy: Rather than asking what the mind is made of, ask what it does. What are our key cognitive functions, and how can or do they provide us genuine empirical knowledge? Kant's answers to these questions are ultimately functionalist.[67] However, Kant refused to develop his functionalist insights explicitly and insisted on a dualist account of biological phenomena.[68] Kant insistently argued that principles involving purposes of any kind can have only a heuristic, regulative role in natural science (*Critique of Judgment* §§74, 75). Schelling dispensed with Kant's Critical restrictions on the

---

[64] The centrality of scientific experiments to Hegel's philosophy of nature is established by Emmanuel Renault, *Hegel: la naturalisation de la dialectique* (Paris: Vrin, 2001), pp. 159–290.

[65] See Westphal, "*Intelligenz* and the Interpretation of Hegel's Idealism".

[66] See John Yolton, *Thinking Matter: Materialism in Eighteenth-Century Britain* (Minneapolis: University of Minnesota Press, 1983).

[67] See R. Meerbote, "Kant's Functionalism", in *Historical Foundations of Cognitive Science*, ed. by J.-C. Smith (Dordrecht, The Netherlands: Kluwer, 1990), pp. 161–187; Patricia Kitcher, "Kant's Dedicated Cognitivist System", in *Historical Foundations of Cognitive Science*, ed. by J.-C. Smith (Dordrecht, The Netherlands: Kluwer, 1990), pp. 189–206; and Andrew Brook, *Kant and the Mind* (Cambridge, UK: Cambridge University Press, 1994).

[68] Kant, *Foundations*, 4:544.7–19, *Critique of Judgment* §§61, 66, 64, 73, 80, 81.

use of teleological principles and boldly ascribed intrinsic purposes to biological organisms. His so doing gave crucial impetus to the development of biological science in the eighteenth century,[69] though Schelling can hardly be credited with any careful analysis of functionalist and teleological principles of explanation, or the basis for their legitimate (justifiable) ascription to various organisms. Hegel did so, and carefully articulated some key ways in which teleological organization involving conscious purposes requires and can only build upon the more basic level of functional organization involved in, for example, biological organisms.[70]

Hegel's analysis of the distinctions between (merely) functional and teleological principles of organization is one stage of a broad and ambitious program: Hegel sought to avoid both substance dualism and eliminative reductionism by developing a sophisticated and subtle emergentism.[71] Long derided by reductionist philosophers, emergentism has recently regained philosophical credibility among analytical philosophers both in philosophy of biology and in philosophy of mind.[72]

[69] See Robert J. Richards, *The Romantic Conception of Life. Science and Philosophy in the Age of Goethe* (Chicago: University of Chicago Press, 2002).

[70] See William DeVries, *Hegel's Theory of Mental Activity*.

[71] To say that Hegel is an emergentist is to reject strongly holistic interpretations of Hegel's views, according to which "the whole" has ontological priority over its parts and determines their characteristics, or at least, more so than vice versa. Hegel's holism is moderate because he insists, *inter alia*, that any "substance" and its "accidents" are thoroughly mutually interdependent for their existence and characteristics (Westphal, *Hegel's Epistemological Realism*, pp. 141–145; Hegel, 2003a, §§32, 34). Hegel inverts philosophical tradition by insisting that there is nothing more to any "substance" than the totality of its "accidents" (Hegel, 1810/11, §§62, 63, 68, /Hegel, 1968, pp. 87–88; *WL*, I, *GW*, 11:394.33–35; *GW*, 395.3–5; *GW*, 395.39–396.26; *Enz.*, §151), a view Hegel developed by 1805 and which he deploys both in social ontology and ontology of nature. As H. S. Harris notes, Hegel's moderate holism puts paid to "totalitarian interpretations of Hegel's philosophy." See his *Hegel's Development: Night Thoughts (Jena 1801–1806)*. (Oxford: Clarendon Press, 1983), pp. 364–365. 367–368, 370. On Hegel's approach to biology, see Engelhardt, "Die biologischen Wissenschaften in Hegels Naturphilosphie", in *Hegels Philosophie der Natur*, ed. by M. J. Petry and R. P. Horstmann, (Dordrecht, The Netherlands: Kluwer, 1986), pp. 121–137; D. Dahlstrom, "Hegel's Appropriation of Kant's Account of Teleology in Nature", in Houlgate, *Hegel and the Philosophy of Nature*, pp. 167–188; and Errol. Harris, "How Final Is Hegel's Rejection of Evolution?" in Houlgate, pp. 189–208.

[72] See Herbert Simon, "The Architecture of Complexity", *Proceedings of the American Philosophical Society*, 106 (1962, pp. 467–482; reprinted in *idem.*, *The Sciences of the Artificial* (Cambridge, MA: MIT Press, 3rd ed., 1996), pp. 183–216; Beckermann, Ansgar, Hans Flohr, and Jaegwon Kim, eds., *Emergence or Reduction? Essays on the Prospects of Nonreductive Physicalism* (Berlin: de Gruyter 1992); William Wimsatt, "The Ontology of Complex Systems", *Canadian Journal of Philosophy*, 20, supplement pp. 207–274; and William Wimsatt, "Emergence as

"Emergence" refers to properties or behaviour of a complex system that are not simple aggregative functions of the properties or behaviour of the individual parts of that system. Emergence thus highlights the importance of the organization of the parts within a complex system to enable or to produce properties or behaviours which may be "realized" (or instantiated) in various different kinds of component parts, or are "autonomous" from the dynamic properties of the individual component parts or which display regularities that are "anomalous" with respect to regularities exhibited by the system's individual component parts. Emergentism thus opposes eliminative reductionism, though not (necessarily) materialism.[73] There are various kinds and aspects of emergent behaviour of complex systems and there are complex issues about which of these kinds are exhibited in any particular case. These important questions cannot be considered here; here it suffices to note that the core principles of emergentism are philosophically legitimate and that they have regained philosophical legitimacy in large part because they are so important to understanding so many kinds of natural phenomena.

One of Hegel's aims in his *Philosophy of Nature* is to systematically order our most basic ontological and natural-scientific concepts and principles (§§246Z, 247Z, 249 & Z), beginning with the most abstract, undifferentiated and universal (space and time, §§254–257), and working through a finely grained series of steps (§249) towards the most complex, the organic life of animal species (§§367–376). The third part of Hegel's *Encyclopaedia* then continues this series of levels, no longer merely in nature, but in the human or moral sciences ("spirit", *Geist*, §§377–387), from anthropology (§388) through cognition, action and freedom at the individual level (§§445–482) and then through social, moral, political, and legal philosophy (§§483–552) – treated with much greater detail and sophistication in Hegel's *Philosophy of Right* – up to a brief sketch of '"absolute spirit" in its three forms, art, manifest religion and philosophy (§§553–577), topics treated *in extenso* in Hegel's Berlin lectures.

Why does Hegel undertake this ambitious project? Hegel's question can be put in a Kantian formula: All of these natural and social phenomena are actual. How are they possible and how is our knowledge of them possible? Hegel's philosophical contribution to answering this

Non-Aggregativity and the Biases of Reductionisms", *Foundations of Science*, 5, 3 (2000), pp. 269–297.

[73] Harris, *Night Thoughts*, pp. 238–298 contends that, by 1803/1804, Hegel's philosophy of nature became materialist and is properly characterized as a kind of neutral monism.

broad question is to identify, clarify and integrate, as accurately and thoroughly as possible, the specific concepts and principles required at each level and at each relevant sublevel, in order to understand each kind of phenomenon and its proper species. This involves identifying both the preconditions of each kind of phenomenon and identifying what is unique and new to it vis à vis preceding levels. For each basis level, Hegel seeks to determine why it alone affords the necessary basis for its emergent successor level. For each emergent level, Hegel seeks to determine what is unique in it, and through a similar analysis of a series of sublevels within that new level, how it provides the necessary basis for enabling in turn the emergence of its successor (§252Z). Hegel insists that this conceptual sequence of stages and substages does not concern the natural development (historical genesis) of ever more sophisticated organizational complexity (§249).

What kind of "necessity of the concept" (§246 & *Anm.*, cf. §249) guides this development? Hegel's phrase may appear to mean either of two things, both misleading. It may seem that the relevant necessity lies in a preordained rationalist *telos* of a completely self-developing and self-explicating system. Hegel does have some such *telos* in view, but the notion that it is in anyway preordained relies on transferring conscious purposes from their proper domain (human behaviour) to a transcendent, theistic domain which at best can be nothing but idle speculation. If there is a first rule of Hegel's metaphysics, it is: Posit no transcendent entities. The other notion stems from purely a priori interpretations of Hegel's *Logic* and *Encyclopaedia*, which require that Hegel's logic uses some special successor notion to formal-logical deduction.[74] It must be a successor notion, because formal-logical deduction does not permit inferring the more specific from the more general. Despite long favour among Hegel's expositors, I confess that I do not yet understand what any such successor notion could be, despite many attempts in the literature. Fortunately, there is another alternative.[75]

---

[74] An excellent, highly informative presentation of this kind of interpretation is Houlgate *An Introduction to Hegel: Freedom, Truth and History* (London: Blackwell, 2005), pp. 106–180. I am indebted to Stephen for many years of discussion of these and related issues, despite our divergence on this central point.

[75] Another problem with the "top down" approach, beginning with Hegel's *Logic* and examining its instantiation in nature (in *Enz.*, II), is that this approach cannot avoid the charge Hegel hurled at Schelling of "schematizing formalism". Hegel can avoid the sin of schematizing formalism only by showing, on the basis of an internal examination of natural phenomena for their own sake, that those phenomena exhibit the kinds of conceptual structures and principles articulated in Hegel's *Logic*.

Kant understood the "deduction" of a concept or principle in a legal sense, of showing that we are entitled to use it in genuine, justifiable judgments, whether cognitive or practical (*Critique of Pure Reason*, B117). Though Hegel's strategy for justifying concepts and principles in his *Philosophy of Nature* is not transcendental, it does share this general Kantian sense of "deduction" (§88). Hegel seeks to determine the extent to which and the ways in which we are justified in using various concepts and principles in genuine cognition of natural phenomena. This is built into his emergentist agenda of showing why nothing less than a certain set of concepts and principles suffices to comprehend natural phenomena of a certain level of systematic complexity and how these concepts and principles provide the necessary basis for understanding the successor level. The upper endpoint or *telos* of this series of levels is provided, not by antecedent divine preordination, but by the facts of human cognition and action, on the one hand, and their – that is, *our* – remarkable productions in the natural and social sciences and more generally in society, history, art, religion and philosophy on the other. Carefully demarcating in the *Philosophy of Nature* the natural preconditions of these human phenomena shows in broad outline how nature makes our human form of mindedness possible, both by providing for humanly minded individuals and by providing for humanly comprehensible objects of knowledge (taken as a whole, nature) and a humanly manipulable context of action (nature). This is Hegel's emergentist strategy for avoiding both (Cartesian) substance dualism and eliminative materialism.

Obviously there is a rich historical and metaphysical background to Hegel's emergentist and (moderately) holistic world view. It is important both to recognize and yet not to overestimate the significance of that background. Hegel certainly does seek to identify and defend a richly systematic orderliness in nature, and indeed in all phenomena. In this context it is important to recall Hegel's standard approach to the grand aspirations of theology. Hegel consistently argues that the theistic and metaphysical ascription of such aspirations to a transcendent creator who tends to them (God) is in every case a human projection of human needs onto the fabric of the universe. Yet unlike Feuerbach, Marx, or Freud, Hegel interprets such projections as reflecting, if figuratively, genuine and legitimate human aspirations.[76] Hegel

---

[76] Westphal, *Hegel's Epistemological Realism*, 163–164; Harris, *Hegel's Ladder*, vol. I, pp. 64, 112, 192–193, 409–410, 417–418; vol 2, pp. 125–130, 252–253, 344–346, 367, 448, 533–534, 537–540, 678, 681–682, 691, 738, 746; Franco Chiereghin, "Freedom and Thought: Stoicism, Skepticism, and Unhappy Consciousness", in *The Blackwell Guide to Hegel's Phenomenology of Spirit*, ed by. K. R. Westphal

seeks to show the ways in which and the extent to which the actual world (natural, social, and historical) in fact satisfies these aspirations, to a much greater extent than is typically appreciated.[77] This is part of Hegel's ongoing effort to overcome our modern alienation from the world, including our epistemological alienation wrought by Descartes' mechanical and eliminativist account of the body (cf. §246Z). In the present case, Hegel thinks that the pre-Modern "great chain of being" expressed, however metaphorically and inadequately, a legitimate aspiration and anticipated, however obliquely, a correct idea: Nature *does* form a systematically ordered hierarchy (§246Z) within which human beings have a particular and quite special place: Through our knowledge of the world-whole, the world-whole gains knowledge of itself. We are, as it were, the homunculi in *Geist*. In performing this role within the world-whole, we determine through a properly conceived and executed philosophy of nature – despite modern forms of alienation, including the cognitive alienation wrought by Gallileo's distinction between primary and secondary qualities and by Descartes' dualism – that nature is our proper environment, both as cognitive and as active agents.[78]

V. CONCLUSION

When considering the aims, character and merits of Hegel's *Philosophy of Nature*, it is important to consider carefully an observation by Henry Harris:

The balance of social influence has shifted so drastically between Hegel's time and ours ... from the religious to the scientific establishment, that Hegel's own contribution to this shift has itself become an obstacle to the right understanding of what he said. He wanted to swing religious consciousness into full support of

---

(Oxford: Blackwell, 2009), chapter 4; and George di Giovanni, "Religion, History, and Spirit in Hegel's *Phenomenology of Spirit*", in *The Blackwell Guide to Hegel's Phenomenology of Spirit*, chapter 11.

[77] See Westphal, "Hegel's Critique of Kant's Moral World View", *Philosophical Topics*, 19 (1991), pp. 133–176.

[78] See Westphal, "Science and the Philosophers", in *Science: A Challenge to Philosophy?*, ed. by H. Koskinen, S. Pihlström, and R. Vilkko, Scandinavian University Studies in the Humanities and Social Sciences, vol. 27 (Frankfurt am Main: Lang, 2006), pp. 125–152 (cf. forthcoming "*Intelligenz* and the Interpretation of Hegel's Idealism"). Here I contend that Hegel's epistemology provides an approach to understanding natural scientific knowledge that is far superior to those of his predecessors, including Kant, and to Hume's twentieth-century empiricist heirs.

a scientific interpretation of human life.... His own choice of language was conditioned by the Christian teaching, but also by the knowledge that the Christian doctrine of spirit was derived from Stoic sources. (Harris, 1983, p. 302)

The Stoics were, as Hegel knew, thoroughgoing materialists and naturalists. The common disregard of Hegel's philosophy of nature, especially among Anglophone Hegel scholars, leaves two central members of Hegel's philosophical system, *Logic* and *Philosophy of Spirit*, precariously imbalanced because they lack their third supporting member, *Philosophy of Nature*. This neglect inevitably generates serious misunderstandings of Hegel's philosophy, both in part and in whole. Fortunately, recent, mainly European, research has begun rectifying this neglect. Certainly Hegel's *Philosophy of Nature* has grand, if not grandiose aspirations; Hegel himself would eagerly and thoroughly revise much of it in view of subsequent developments in the natural sciences. Nevertheless, Hegel's *Philosophy of Nature* is a landmark in the philosophical assessment of nature and the natural sciences that deserves careful consideration today, for its central aims and issues, for its methods, for its staggering erudition and for its bold attempt to make philosophical sense of nature as a whole whilst appreciating its profuse diversity.[79]

[79] For helpful comments on previous drafts of this chapter, I gratefully thank Fred Beiser, Hans-Christoph Schmidt am Busch, and especially Cinzia Ferrini.

12   Hegel's Criticism of Newton

Few scientists, or philosophers, have patience for a priori science. It is widely supposed that modern science owes its progress to subjecting hypotheses to experimental tests, and that nature is simply too intricate and surprising to determine without empirical investigation. Philosophers who have tried to study issues of *substantial* scientific doctrine or theory are regarded as embarrassments, and recent philosophers of science have narrowed their vision to scientific method. Probably no philosopher is more embarrassing than Hegel because he couples a priori science with a dialectical method that purports to derive concepts from each other in ways that bear no connection with either experience or material processes.[1] Some contemporary scholars emphasize the empirical elements in his text, hoping, perhaps, to make his philosophy of nature more palatable[2] against the long tide of philosophers

---

[1] Recent interest in Hegel's Philosophy of Nature has been spurred by Michael J. Petry's three-volume translation, *Hegel's Philosophy of Nature* (London: George Allen and Unwin, 1970), along with the published proceedings of three conferences he helped organize: R.-P. Horstmann and M. J. Petry, eds., *Hegels Philosophie der Natur: Beziehungen zwischen empirisher und spekulativer Naturerkenntnis* (Stuttgart: Klett-Cotta, 1986); M. J. Petry, ed., *Hegel und die Naturwissenschaften* (Stuttgart: Frommann-Holzboog, 1987); and M. J. Petry, ed., *Hegel and Newtonianism* (Dordrecht, The Netherlands: Kluwer Academic Publishers), 1993.

[2] See, for example: J. W. Burbidge, "Real Process," in *Real Process: How Logic and Chemistry Combine in Hegel's Philosophy of Nature*, Toronto Studies in Philosophy (Toronto: University of Toronto Press, 1996) and J. W. Burbidge, "Chemism and Chemistry," *The Owl of Minerva*, 34 (Fall/Winter 2002–2003), pp. 3–17. For an assessment, see S. Houlgate, (2002–2003) "Logic and Nature in Hegel's Philosophy: A Response to John Burbidge," *The Owl of Minerva*, 34 (Fall/Winter 2002–2003), pp. 107–125, as well as the other articles in this issue of *The Owl of Minerva*. B. Falkenburg, "How to Save the Phenomena: Meaning and Reference in Hegel's Philosophy of Nature," in *Hegel and the Philosophy of Nature*, ed. by S. Houlgate, SUNY Series in Hegelian Studies (Albany: SUNY Press, 1998), pp. 130–131, claims that Hegel's philosophy of nature is not a priori because it "presupposes the concepts of phenomenological natural kinds which are suggested by physics" and aims to organize them "into an adequate phenomenological system of natural kinds."

who quickly dismiss his philosophy of nature. In my view, the current antipathy toward a priori science is misplaced: many great scientific achievements came from thinking through the implications of concepts through so-called thought experiments and other modes of nonempirical or, at least, not wholly empirical inference.[3] Be that as it may, my concern here is Hegel's account of mechanics and, in particular, his criticism of Newtonian mechanics. I argue that Hegel not only discovered a contradiction in Newton or, rather, in Newton plausibly interpreted, but proposed a solution that carried the day in its tenor if not in its substance. Whether the solution was accepted *because* of Hegel is an historical question that I cannot address here. What is interesting for us is his argument. But before we can appreciate it, we need to grasp what

T. R. Webb, "The Problem of Empirical Knowledge in Hegel's Philosophy of Nature," *Hegel Studien*, 15 (1980), p. 184, argues that Hegel's philosophy of nature is neither a priori nor a posteriori because it takes up the results of empirical research and gives them an "absolute form" by grasping them as contingent elements of a necessary whole.

One important justification for emphasizing the empirical dimension of Hegel's Philosophy of Nature is his famous declaration of the "impotence of Nature" even to comprehend, let alone deduce, the "contingent products of Nature." See G. W. F. Hegel, *Werke 9. Enzyklopädie der Philosophischen Wissenschaften im Grundrisse (1830). Zweiter Teil. Die Naturphilosophie. Mit den mündlichen Zusätzen*, ed. by E. Moldenhauer and K. M. Michel 'Frankfurt am Main: Suhrkamp, 1970', vol. 9, pp. 34–35 and G. W. F. Hegel, *Hegel's Philosophy of Nature: Being Part Two of the Encyclopaedia of the Philosophical Sciences (1830)*, trans. by A. V. Miller (Oxford: Clarendon Press, 1970), p. 23.

In my view, Hegel begins with a concept of nature that he derives from his logic (see E. Halper, "The Logic of Hegel's *Philosophy of Nature*: Nature, Space and Time," in *Hegel and the Philosophy of Nature*, ed. by S. Houlgate, SUNY Series in Hegelian Studies (Albany: SUNY Press, 1998), pp. 29–49), and he derives the subsequent categories of Nature from it dialectically. Whether his derivations succeed and whether the entirety of his Philosophy of Nature can be so derived are, of course, different questions. Results from the empirical sciences must surely have suggested to Hegel conceptual paths to explore, but that does not make his derivations a posteriori any more than measurements of the sides of right triangles would render a proof of the Pythagorean theorem a posteriori. That his categories of nature align as well as they do with empirical science supports Hegel's approach. S. Houlgate, *An Introduction to Hegel: Freedom, Truth, and History* (Malden, MA: Blackwell, 2005), p. 143, seems to thinks that some, though not all, of Hegel treatment of nature is a priori even if it was inspired by empirical evidence.

[3] Unlike most others, S. Sambursky, "Hegel's Philosophy of Nature," in *The Interaction Between Science and Philosophy*, ed. by Y. Elkana (Atlantic Highlands, NJ: Humanities Press, 1974), pp. 147, 148–149, 151, 168–169, appreciates the insights Hegel arrives at through his a priori dialectical method. He credits Hegel with recognizing the identity of space and time, rejecting absolute space and time, and the dualism of inertia and gravity, all moves that anticipate Einstein; but he rejects Hegel's method while praising his results.

is at issue and to set aside both certain misconceptions about Hegel and certain truths. At stake is not merely a specific problem in mechanics, but also philosophy's relation to and role in science. Since Hegel thinks that philosophy proceeds by finding and overcoming contradictions, his claim that Newtonian mechanics is contradictory does not imply that it is worthless, as we might suppose; but he does think, rightly I argue, that his a priori science, the Philosophy of Nature, advances empirical science.

I

The "Philosophy of Nature" is the second part of Hegel's three part system; it follows the "Logic" and is followed by the "Philosophy of Spirit."[4] It was part of the *Encyclopedia*, the summary handbook he wrote for his students. Unlike "Logic" and portions of "Philosophy of Spirit," Hegel never produced a full version of "Philosophy of Nature." Its core argument is extremely compressed. Hegel used this text as the basis for lectures that elaborated and illustrated the argument, and the text of "Philosophy of Nature" is usually published along with a synopsis of lecture notes taken by his students. Here the notes are longer and, because we have only the briefest of texts, may be more significant than student notes on other portions of the *Encyclopedia*.[5]

---

4 Since all three are parts of Hegel's *Encyclopedia*, I enclose these titles in quotes, but I also use them, without quotes, to refer more generally to portions of Hegel's system. When the reference is to a specific passage of Hegel's text, I italicize these terms because the texts are now usually published separately along with compilations of notes his students took at his lectures, "additions" (*Zusätzen*). (See my text and the next footnote.) On the other hand, references to the general subject of, for example, philosophy of nature are in lower case. Thus, "Philosophy of Nature" refers to Hegel's treatment of nature in the *Encyclopedia*; Philosophy of Nature refers more generally to this portion of his system; *Philosophy of Nature* refers to the book published under this title; and philosophy of nature refers to the general subject treated by Hegel and others.

Analogously, I usually use capital letters to refer to specific Hegelian categories and lower-case letters to indicate more general concepts or predicative usages of the categories. Thus, "Nature" refers to one of Hegel's categories and "nature" to whatever we usually mean by the physical world – neither will generally appear in quotes. It is impossible to make this distinction in German because all nouns are capitalized, and Hegel himself, in any case, seems *not* to distinguish Nature from nature or to make the analogous distinctions.

5 The critical edition contains only Hegel's own text: G. W. F. Hegel, *Gesammelte Werke, Im Auftrag der Deutschen Forschungsgemeinschaft*, vol. 20, *Enzyklopädie der philosophischen Wissenschaften im Grundrisse* (1830), ed. by W. Bonsiepen and H.-C. Lucas (Hamburg: Felix Meiner, 1992). Hence, I have cited editions that contain the compilations of student notes, "additions" (*Zusätzen*). The "Philosophy

The Philosophy of Nature is the least discussed portion of Hegel and, possibly, the most difficult. It has not had a good press: not only is it supposed to have no scientific value, but it is often said to be filled with errors that demonstrate Hegel's scientific incompetence. So far as I can tell, these alleged errors stem from readers' failure to appreciate his peculiar usage and his goal. The "Philosophy of Nature" purports to be a dialectical unfolding of the categories of nature from the most abstract, Space and Time, to the most concrete, Animal Organism. To put a complicated matter too simply, the development occurs by showing the existence of inner principles that are progressively richer. Whereas in "Mechanics," the first of the three sections of "Philosophy of Nature," Nature has no inner principle of motion, in "Physics" and "Organics," the two subsequent sections, the sources of motion are internal. It is clear that when Hegel speaks of "Physics," he has in mind the Greek term *phusis* and, in particular, Aristotle's understanding of *phusis* as an internal principle of motion (*Physics*, B.1.192b8–14). Importantly, this *internal* principle accounts for the motions characteristic of a particular natural kind as well as for its other essential attributes; thus, it is in respect of its nature that fire rises. Whereas in "Physics" Hegel confines himself to the primary substances with a limited range of motions – earth, air, fire, water, and inorganic derivatives of them that have uniform parts – in "Organics" he focuses on living beings, substances with multiple, complex parts that function together. The discussion of the former includes a treatment of chemistry, a subject that had only recently received a scientific treatment.[6] Hegel's criticism of Newton is mainly in the first part of the "Philosophy of Nature: "Mechanics."

Before turning to this, though, it is well to say something about Hegel's philosophical predecessors. Perhaps the most important is

---

of Nature" portion appears in: G. W. F. Hegel, *Werke 9. Enzyklopädie* (The other two parts of the *Encyclopedia* appear in volumes 8 and 10 of this edition.) It is rendered into English as: Hegel, G. W. F. *Hegel's Philosophy of Nature*.

Hegel numbers his paragraphs, and here I use paragraph numbers that are not further specified to indicate his paragraphs. In his text, a numbered paragraph begins with a highly condensed argument that is sometimes followed by a remark and usually supplemented with lecture notes on the paragraph. I designate his remark with an "*A*" after the paragraph number and his students' notes with a "*Z*" after the paragraph number.

[6] Kant doubts that Chemistry could ever be made scientific, I. Kant, *Philosophy of Material Nature: The Complete Texts of* Prolegomena to Any Future Metaphysics That Will be Able to Come Forward as Science *and* Metaphysical Foundations of Natural Science, trans. by J. W. Ellington (Indianapolis: Hackett, 1985), p. II.7.

Aristotle whose own science looms surprisingly large through most of the "Philosophy of Nature."[7] It is from Aristotle that Hegel must get his notion that an inner principle that unifies complex diverse parts through their common functioning is a higher principle than one that unifies simple uniform parts (the type of principle at work in "Physics"). And it must be in contrast with Aristotle's understanding of the *inner* principle of a *phusis* that Hegel conceives of "Mechanics," a realm for which there is no Aristotelian analogue, as the realm of externality and otherness. Whereas an Aristotelian *phusis* has (or is) an inner source of motion, the bodies of "Mechanics" are moved by external sources, other bodies. Whereas earth, fire, and other Aristotelian natures are distinguished by their qualities, bodies differ from one another only quantitatively, by size and position. This latter means that the science that studies bodies and their motions, mechanics, is more universal than Aristotelian physics, but also that it is, thereby, more abstract and undifferentiated. Hence, Hegel places "Mechanics" before "Physics" in his "Philosophy of Nature" even though, inasmuch as it includes modern physics, mechanics was developed much later. It is important to understand that Hegel's treatment of material bodies in motion is the precursor to his discussion of Aristotelian natures. He thinks that the former contains contradictions that are resolved in the latter.

Hegel's notions that Newtonian physics is flawed and that Aristotelian physics is superior to it astound contemporary readers. His alleged scientific incompetence is sometimes ascribed to his Aristotelianism.[8] In particular, scholars have claimed that Hegel misunderstands inertial motion as self-limiting because he models it on Aristotelian motion; the latter always comes to an end unless it is sustained by a perpetually acting cause such as an unmoved mover. Hegel has also

---

[7] For a useful, extended discussion of the Aristotelian background of the Philosophy of Nature, see A. Ferrarin, *Hegel and Aristotle*, Modern European Philosophy (New York: Cambridge University Press, 2001), pp. 210–234. Ferrarin concludes that "the case for the Aristotelianism of Hegel's Philosophy of Nature appears strong" (p. 219). This is certainly true of the last two parts of this work. However, Aristotelianism influences the first part of the work only indirectly, as I explain in my text.

[8] W. R., Shea, "Hegel's Celestial Mechanics" in *Hegels Philosophie der Natur*, pp. 34–36, accuses Hegel of equating mass with weight, as he thinks Aristotle did, in the remark to §262 and of endorsing Aristotle's distinction between celestial and terrestrial mechanics in §269Z. Ferrarin, *Hegel and Aristotle*, p. 204, repeats the latter charge, as does Houlgate, *Freedom, Truth, and History*, p. 154. Houlgate does, though, defend Hegel against Shea's charge that he does not understand inertial motion.

been charged with retaining Aristotle's distinction between terrestrial motion and celestial motion. In my view, neither charge is true, and Hegel's mechanics might provoke fewer objections if more readers understood the distinction between "Mechanics" and subsequent sections of the "Philosophy of Nature" as that between the motions that belong to bodies insofar as they are mere bodies and the motions that belong to them insofar as they are bodies of a specific type, such as, say, water, charged particles, or quarks. Hegel is arguing that abstract and general claims about bodies do not give us an adequate understanding of nature. He does so by arguing, characteristically, that the abstract and general account breaks down and collapses, as it were, into an account of "Physics." Thus, Hegel does not presuppose Aristotelian physics so much as argue for it. To appreciate his treatment of mechanics, it is important to understand where he is going. The question of the nature or essence of matter, fundamental to Aristotle yet set aside by Newton, always lurks in the background of "Mechanics" and will be the central factor in his criticism of Newton.

A key respect in which Hegel also follows Aristotle is the notion that scientific knowledge does *not* consist of discovering new facts but in drawing connections between what is already known. Aristotle claims that all scientific inquiry aims to find the middle term of a syllogism (*An. Po.*, B.2.90a5–7); this term is, paradigmatically, the essential character in respect of which the third term, an attribute, belongs to the first, a substance. All three terms would generally be known before inquiry commences, as would the syllogism's conclusion. What is new is the insight into how the terms are linked. Some scholars continue to assume that Aristotle proposes to deduce new scientific results from known premises, but his text is really quite clear that scientific inquiry seeks the middle term and, thereby, the cause of a "conclusion" that is already known. New scientific *knowledge* is not the syllogism's conclusion, but the "aha" of understanding a connection between terms that are already apparent. Likewise, Hegel's philosophy of nature does not aim to produce new scientific results but to deduce already established results by dialectical, a priori argument.[9]

---

[9] Sambursky, "Hegel's Philosophy of Nature," p. 150, holds that Hegel "rejects, lock, stock, and barrel, the Newtonian dynamics... including gravitation," and thereby anticipates Einstein's general relativity (p. 151). H. Paolucci thinks Hegel anticipated Bohr in §271Z. Paolucci's general thesis is that Hegel's criticisms of Newton anticipated those of modern physicists and that his reconstructions anticipated Einstein. See his "Hegel and the Celestial Mechanics of Newton and Einstein," in *Hegel and the Sciences*, ed. by R. S. Cohen and M. W. Wartofsky, vol. 64, Boston Studies in the Philosophy of Science (Dordrecht, The Netherlands: D. Reidel, 1984),

Another of Hegel's predecessors who is also central to the Philosophy of Nature is Kant. In the *Metaphysical Foundations of Natural Science* Kant aims to give an a priori deduction of the principles of Newtonian physics.[10] The basic assumption of his argument is that any material entity would, insofar as it is movable, need to fall under each of his four groups of categories. Thus, a body will have some *quantity* (possibly zero) of motion, it will occupy some volume of space with some *qualitative* degree of intensity, it will exert a causal force on another or exist self-subsistently, and it will be capable of being experienced as possibly, actually or necessarily moving. Kant identifies the capacity for each of these determinations as a distinct type of matter. Accordingly, there are four different types of matter. With this framework Kant argues, strikingly, for Newton's law of gravity and for his three laws of motion. He also argues for the composition of motions based on the conservation of momentum and gives his own account of Newton's bucket. If Kant is right, the bulk of Newtonian physics can be known a priori.[11]

p. 69. Thus, he sees Hegel's dialectical transformation of space into time as anticipating Riemann–Einsteinian space–time (p. 74), his doctrine of "moving place" as equivalent to the field (p. 77), and his endorsements of circular motion as anticipating the curvature of space (pp. 75, 80–81). Both Samburksy and Paolucci are right to note the interesting anticipations, but both see Hegel as engaged in the same enterprise as physicists. Relativity physics stems from the same concerns that motivate Newton, namely, to describe and predict the movements we experience. I think Hegel's "Philosophy of Nature" aims at something different.

[10] The extent to which Kant's philosophy of nature is a priori is, of course, as controversial as claims about Hegel's philosophy of nature. G. Buchdahl, "Hegel's Philosophy of Nature and the Structure of Science," in *Hegel*, ed. by M. Inwood (Oxford: Oxford University Press, 1984), p. 127, contends that both are concerned to demonstrate "intelligible possibilities" rather than a priori truths of nature. However, he acknowledges that "it is a matter of more and less," and proposes that Hegel's derivation of the law of the acceleration of falling bodies, though "not a strictly deductive account" (p. 121), is a "search for intelligibility" leading to "conceptual explication" (p. 134). His view of Hegel's indebtedness to Kant (pp. 118–127) is, accordingly, quite different from mine.

[11] Kant rejects Newton's notion of absolute space and, consequently, absolute motion. Interestingly, though, in the observation that concludes his fourth chapter, he distinguishes circular motion as actual and *true* from the merely possible rectilinear motion, and he refers to the reciprocal motions of two bodies according to Newton's third law as necessary. See Kant, *Philosophy of Material Nature*, pp. II.128–131. In the cases of circular and reciprocal motions, the motion belongs to the bodies rather than to something external. Michael Friedman creatively reconstructs the ways that Kantian principles ground some *empirical* constructions of the *Principia*. See M. Friedman, "The Metaphysical Foundations of Newtonian Science," in *Kant's Philosophy of Physical Science: Metaphysische Anfangsgründe der Naturwissenschaft 1786–1986*, ed. by R. E. Butts (Dordrecht, The Netherlands: D. Reidel), 1986, pp. 25–60.

Whereas the *Critique of Pure Reason* uses the schema of the categories to lay out the transcendental conditions for the existence of objects of intuition, the *Metaphysical Foundations of Natural Science* uses the same schema to set out the a priori conditions for the possibility of *material* objects.[12] The existence of material bodies cannot be proven a priori; it must be ascertained empirically. Hence, Kant distinguishes the a priori knowledge possible for natural science from the types of a priori knowledge found in metaphysics and mathematics: whereas the latter depend only on our faculties and the pure forms they grasp, the pure portion of natural science presupposes the existence of material bodies.[13] Even if we cannot prove that there are material bodies and, thus, that there is any nature to know, Kant argues that we can know what must hold of material bodies if they do exist and this includes, besides the Newtonian laws, that nature must be known through mathematics and that any material object must have certain mathematically described characters.

Hegel is not to be outdone. His philosophy of nature extends the scope of what can be proven a priori, and he would remove all empirical elements from the pure treatment of nature. To Kant's list of a priori scientific truths, he adds an independent proof of Kepler's laws, and, importantly, he derives scientific categories from each other through dialectical reasoning that he takes to be intrinsic to the faculty he calls "reason." These latter derivations allow Hegel to avoid Kant's concession to experience. Hegel's issue with Kant, as with Newton, is that both rely on the faculty of "understanding." This is obvious in Kant's case, for his categories are "categories of the understanding," and a central aim of the *Critique of Pure Reason* is to reject the dialectic that the faculty of reason, uncritiqued, must generate. As noted, Kant derives his four kinds of matter from his four groups of these categories. Hence, his treatment of matter is rooted in the faculty of understanding. Hegel sees a sign of Kant's reliance on this faculty in the fact that his different kinds of matter co-exist without being unified; for the faculty of reason is synthetic.[14]

---

[12] Compare the four parts of section 3, chapter 2 of *The Critique of Pure Reason*, book II, "Analytic of Principles" with the four chapters of the *Metaphysical Foundation of Natural Science*.

[13] Kant, *Philosophy of Material Nature*, p. II.9.

[14] Hegel's distinction between concepts belonging to these two faculties is elaborated in his early Jaener piece, G. W. F. Hegel, "Verhältniss des Skepticismus zur Philosophie, Darstellung seiner verschiedenen Modificationen, und Vergleichung des Neuesten mit dem Alten," in *Jenaer Kritische Schriften*, ed. by Hartmut Buchner and Otto Pöggeler, *Gesammelte Werke*, im Auftrag der Deutschen Forschungsgemeinschaft (Hamburg: Felix Meiner, 1986), pp. 197–208. The same distinction

It is very helpful to understand Kant's treatment of matter, because the same four senses of matter appear, in the same sequence, in Hegel's account. As usual, Hegel is terse and assumes some of Kant's arguments without setting them out or even indicating his source.[15] What is new is that Hegel derives them from each other and sees them, consequently, as aspects of a single concept of matter. The problem Hegel has with Kant is not just his having separate matters, but his abdicating, as it were, the explanatory function of philosophy of nature; for, insofar as these matters are distinct, there is no explanation for why all four matters belong to a single physical entity nor, indeed, is there properly a single entity. A metaphysics of the understanding can only be analytic, whereas the faculty of reason can be explanatory because it is synthetic.

II

Hegel thinks that the separation of types of matters was also a mistake Newton made.[16] It is at the root of the criticism that I want to focus on here. Hegel also criticizes Newton's optics on parallel grounds: Newton analyzes white light into lights of distinct colors that are each simple

appears in the Philosophy of Nature. In the notes on the second numbered paragraph of the *Philosophy of Nature*, §246Z, Hegel distinguishes the philosophy of nature from physics by "the kind of metaphysics used by them both" (p. 11). He criticizes the metaphysics used by physics on two grounds: (1) its Universal determination is "abstract or only formal," whereas, on the other side, (2) its Particular content stands outside the Universal and is, therefore, splintered and destroyed. There can be no doubt that he is describing a metaphysics of the understanding because its contents remain distinct from each other. In contrast, the metaphysics used by Philosophy of Nature synthesizes these components into a unity. Later on he identifies the metaphysics of empirical science as "the metaphysics of the understanding," §304Z, p. 152.

[15] Hegel does, however, discuss Kant's treatment in the *Logic*, in a lengthy remark on Attraction and Repulsion, G. W. F. Hegel, *Hegel's Science of Logic*, trans. by A. Miller, Muirhead Library of Philosophy (London: Allen & Unwin, 1969), pp. 178–184.

[16] Newton famously thought that mathematical principles could be read directly from nature without making hypotheses. In the *Science of Logic*, p. 273, Hegel objects that mathematical (quantitative) manipulations cannot prove qualitative claims about the physical world. Paolucci, "Hegel and the Celestial Mechanics of Newton and Einstein," pp. 67–68, thinks that Hegel's point is to deny that "mathematics of itself, or mathematically conducted experiments, can lead to true knowledge of the realities of Nature.

The distinction between gravitational and inertia/mass is implicit in Newton's laws: the m in the second law $F=ma$ is inertial mass; the m in the law of gravity $F = G\,Mm/r^2$ is gravitational mass, more commonly called "weight." Newton argues that a pendulum experiment shows that they are proportional. Recent measurements have shown them to be equal to a high degree. See P. M. Kluit, "Inertial and

and indecomposable, whereas Hegel claims that colored lights are each complex and transformable into different colors.[17] Here too, Newton's error lies in relying on the faculty of understanding rather than reason. My concern in this chapter, however, is confined to Hegel's criticism of Newton's notion of matter and his mechanics. The criticism requires recognizing Newton's unstated assumptions; but, that said, it is both striking and obvious – so obvious, indeed, that a reader or, at any rate, this reader feels its recognition as a blow to the head. The simplest formulation of the problem is that Newton's understanding of the character of matter in his three laws of motion is at odds with his understanding of matter in his law of gravity. In the former, matter is passive in the sense that it does not cause motion and is "only with difficulty put out of its state either of resting or moving."[18] In the latter, matter is active, causing other bodies to move toward it and accelerating itself toward other bodies. To be sure, Newton does not mention the nature of matter in his laws and without this there is no explicit contradiction. However, there is good reason to think that Newton does regard the laws as expressing fundamental characteristics of matter.

Let us consider these claims in more detail. Newton's first law, commonly called the "law of inertia," asserts that matter in motion or matter at rest would remain so unless "compelled to change its state by forces impressed," that is, unless acted upon by an outside body.[19] The implication is that matter does not move itself or interfere, positively or negatively, with any motion that it has, no matter how large or small that motion is. Likewise, setting a body in motion does not increase or diminish its matter. A body's matter is "inert" in the sense that its quantity remains unaltered by whatever motion it receives and in the sense that the body does not diminish or increase its own motion. We can appreciate this inertness by comparing it with Aristotle's understanding of matter as potential for a form.[20] His motion consists of the actualization of this potential, and motion ceases when the potential is fully actualized. Since matter is always a potential for a specific form, not only does the motion cease when the form is realized, but, except

Gravitational Mass: Newton, Hegel and Modern Physics," in *Hegel and Newtonianism*, pp. 229–230, who argues against a challenge to the equivalence of the two matters.

[17] Hegel's lengthy discussion of the *Optiks* is contained in §320A, Z.

[18] See definition 3 of I. Newton, *The Principia; Mathematical Principles of Natural Philosophy*, trans. by I. B. Cohen and A. M. Whitman (Berkeley, CA: University of California Press, 1999), p. 404.

[19] Newton, *Principia*, p. 416.

[20] *Physics*, I.9.192a27–32; 3.1.201a29–b13.

for several important cases, the potential to receive a form ceases once that form comes to be present. When the acorn realizes its potential, it becomes an actual oak and it loses the potential to become an oak. Matter is, in some sense, used up or, at least, radically altered in the course of motion.[21] Significantly, Newton's matter does not alter when it moves, nor does it affect whatever motion it receives. It follows that any motion that it has would have come to it from an outside source, and there is no obstacle to a matter's receiving any quantity of motion or to its continuing indefinitely in motion.

Likewise, Newton's second law, that matter is accelerated in accordance with the force it receives, depends on the matter's not itself interfering with a force that is imposed on it, again a mark of its passivity and inertness. The force moves the matter without altering it as matter. And the third law, that action equals reaction, asserts that when A acts on B, B acts on A with the same force in the opposite direction. This is possible if, again, the matter that is acted upon by a force from A does not alter insofar as it is matter. Indeed, it is because B is as much matter as A, that an impact of A on B is also an impact of B on A.

The ideal model for the three laws consists of rigidly hard balls that remain unchanged by impact or by motion. Measured deviations from the laws are explained either by a ball's interaction with other bodies, by

---

[21] Aristotle defines motion as the actuality of a potential *qua* potential (*Physics*, 3.1.201a10–11), and he explains that the actuality of the buildable lies in the building, "for when the house would be, the buildable no longer is" (201b11–12). L.A. Kosman, "Aristotle's Definition of Motion," *Phronesis*, 14, (1969), p. 57, speaks of the "auto-subversive" and "tragic" dimension of motion: "Its whole purpose and project is one of self-destruction." Kosman distinguishes the actuality that is the motion from the actuality that results from the motion; for example, house building from the house built.

To be sure, Aristotle argues that matter persists through change (1.7.190a13–21). So it might be tempting to insist that his matter is, to this extent, as inert as Newton's. In fact, Aristotle alternates between (a) speaking of matter as the substrate that persists through the acquisition of a form (or of its privation) and as (b) a composite that contains both this substrate and a privation (or a form) in contrast with the form (or privation) it becomes. In the latter sense, Aristotle affirms that matter does come to be and cease to be (1.9.192a25–34). An example of this latter matter is the boards and bricks that are potentially the house because they contain the privation of the form of the house. Once they receive the house form, they no longer have the potential to lose this form. Hence, this matter is altered when it loses its potential to become a house, though they now have. Furthermore, in order to claim that (a) a material substrate persists even through substantial change, Aristotle proposes that the matter is the seed (1.7.190b1–5). But the seed or the acorn does not persist as such; it is radically altered as the organism develops. Thus, again, Aristotle's matter changes as its potential is realized.

friction, or by alterations to the *internal* structure of the ball's matter – on the assumption that this structure is *itself* composed of real bodies, which do conform to the law, could we but measure them. That is to say, in much of our experience, the character of a matter *does* appear to affect the motion it has or receives; but the effects are slight, and they are plausibly explained and discounted. Such cases make clear that the Newtonian notion that matter is inert and does not affect motion is an idealization.

It is a consequence of this idealization that each material body that moves requires some external source of motion, and, consequently, the entire universe requires an external agency as the source of its initial motion: hence, Newton posits God.[22] The constant assumption is that matter alters only when an outside force is "impressed upon it."

Contrast this notion of matter as inert with the notion of matter that is implicit in the law of gravity. According to this law, every bit of matter exerts a force of attraction toward every other bit of matter. Our tendency not to float off the earth and the limited distance we can jump from it remind us of our gravitational attraction to the earth, but earth's gravity is noticeable only because it is so large. Conceptually, there is no difference between earth's gravity and the gravitational force exerted by any other body. Experimentally, gravity is measured by calculating how much a close heavy object slows down an oscillating ball. Discussing the first law, Newton alludes to the gravity of the earth as a force that could be impressed upon a body and cause it to alter its motion,[23] and due to its size, earth's gravity is apt to seem like an outside force. But this is not exactly right. Both bodies are moving toward each other because of their matter, and it is no more true that the one *attracts* the other than that each moves itself by its own nature toward the other matter even the earth's motion is imperceptible. The point is that all matter by its nature falls or, rather, propels itself toward other matter. Gravity is characteristic of all matter, and as such matter does move itself.[24]

---

[22] Newton. *Principia*, pp. 940–943.

[23] Ibid, p. 416.

[24] It has been proposed that in formulating his notion of gravitational attraction, Newton drew on his study of alchemy and was motivated by theology. According to M. J. Osler, "Mechanical Philosophy," in *Science and Religion: A Historical Introduction*, ed. by Gary B. Ferngren (Baltimore: Johns Hopkins University Press, 2003), pp. 150–151, Newton thought that "gravitation results from God's direct action on matter." (I owe this reference to Joseph Bracken.) This account absolves Newton of the contradiction Hegel ascribes to him even while it implicitly acknowledges that gravity *would* conflict with inertia were gravity (as it is generally taken) characteristic of matter. It implies, moreover, that those who reject Newton's theology are left with the contradiction.

What, then, are we to say: is matter inert, or does it move itself? Is matter independent of motion, neither altering motion nor being altered by it, or does matter rather cause a body to move itself toward other bodies and them to move toward it? In short, the nature implicitly ascribed to matter by the three laws is at odds with the nature of matter presupposed by the law of gravity.

Scientists are unlikely to be concerned because the contradiction, if there is one here, turns on the *nature* of matter and does not undermine or, indeed, even affect predictions about the motions of bodies. Let me consider predictions first and turn to the nature of matter later. In terms of the way that Newtonian physics is used, the law of gravity does not come into conflict with the other Newtonian laws. Indeed, so far from causing difficulties, the two work nicely together. We use the law of gravity to determine one vector component of a body's motion and then add vectors for the motions that the body has in other directions. The resultant is the body's overall path. That is to say, we calculate a body's motion by treating gravity and inertia as distinct and independent components. There is, to be sure, a long-standing question in Newtonian physics whether the mass in the formula of gravitational attraction is equal to the mass in the second law, that is, whether, gravitational mass is equal to inertial mass. But this is taken to be an empirical question that needs to be resolved with precise measurements, and these have supported a high degree of identity.[25] In short, not only do no empirical anomalies result from Newton's distinguishing two types of matter, but his treating them independently was one of his outstanding successes. How odd that Hegel would choose matter to launch his critique!

Hegel's discussions of Newton's laws have convinced many readers that he does not understand them and led them to conclude that his criticism stems from ignorance.[26] A number of his claims lend credibility to this charge. It is jarring to see Hegel refer to two opposing "forces" on a body in circular motion, centripetal and centrifugal forces, and to read that the one force dominates the other at different times even though the one should destroy the other. Everyone familiar with elementary physics knows that "centrifugal force" is a fiction. Water in a pail swung over one's head does not fall out because it tends to continue traveling in the same direction, at every instant the direction that is the tangent to the circular arc the pail makes. But this tendency

---

[25] See Footnote 16.

[26] "As far as Newton's mechanics are concerned, Hegel lacks the most elementary knowledge, probably on account of his lack of mathematical skill and the preponderance of his structure of notional determinations." See F. H. van Lunteren, "Hegel and Gravitation," in *Hegels Philosophie der Natur*, p. 53.

is matter's inertia, not a force. Moreover, the centripetal force that pulls the pail remains constant, as does the inertial tendency of the water in the pail, contrary to what Hegel seems to say.

But Hegel's apparent mistakes stem from odd locutions that, in turn, derive from Newton's.[27] It is, after all, Newton who speaks of the *"vis inertia,"* the *force* of inertia, and identifies it with the *"vis insita,"* the force inherent in bodies.[28] Newton explains that "a body exerts this force only during a change of state caused by another force impressed upon it, and this exercise of force is, depending on the viewpoint, both resistance and impetus: resistance insofar as the body, in order to maintain its state, strives against the impressed force, and impetus insofar as the same body... endeavors to change the state [of another body]."[29] This last part is a way of saying that the moving body that impacts another body and exerts a force over it must itself have its own inner "force" that maintains it in a state of motion and resists its being affected, in turn, by the impacted body. We no longer speak of force as an internal character of a body, but it is clear what Newton means. When one body impacts another, the first exerts a force over the second, a force that, we know from Newton's second law, will accelerate the second body. Likewise, the impacted body will, at the moment of impact, exert a force over the first body that will, in turn, accelerate or decelerate it. The second law is expressed as $F = ma$, and we often think of force as if it somehow existed abstractly. In Newton's universe, however, force can only come from gravity or a body in motion; in the latter case, it is that body's being in motion (relative to the impacted body) that allows it to exert the force. Clearly, the amount of force exerted here depends on

[27] E. J. Dijksterhuis, *The Mechanization of the World Picture*, trans. by C. Dikshoorn (Oxford: Oxford University Press, 1969), p. 466, claims that Newton does not think that rectilinear motion of a point would continue but holds the Aristotelian view that every motion requires a mover as its cause and the view that body is that cause. This claim is repeated by I. Bernard Cohen in "A Guide to Newton's *Principia*" (p. 98), in his lengthy introduction to: Newton, *Principia*, p. 98. Shea, "Hegel's Celestial Mechanics," pp. 37–39, claims that although the idea of motion as produced by some external force "led Newton to the *Principia*," Newton himself begins "with 'force' as inherent force causing a uniform motion ($F = mv$). The inherent force represented for Newton one of the universal properties of matter, not displacing extension, but standing equally beside it together with hardness and impenetrability." Hegel holds the same view, as we will see, but, oddly, Shea apparently does not think this enough to absolve Hegel of the charge of deficient understanding of Newtonian physics.

[28] See his third definition; Newton, *Principia*, pp. 96–101. Cohen claims that we must follow Newton and distinguish "internal 'force' and external forces" (p. 96).

[29] Newton, *Principia*, pp. 404–405.

how much *motion* the impacting body has. Hence, an impacting body will exert a force in proportion to its momentum or, more precisely, to the momentum it has *relative* to the impacted body. The question then arises as to how either body can exert force on the other without itself having a force to exert. Hence, it makes sense for Newton to speak of the force that is *internal* to a body and to identify this force that resists change with the force that enables the body to impose change. From all this, it follows that the force that initially belongs internally to the impacting body is exerted over the impacted body, that this force accelerates the impacted body, thereby, augmenting the impacted body's own internal force. To be sure, we now treat this situation simply as a problem of conservation of momentum and ignore force. That is fine for computations, but conceptually Newton is right. Kant also uses "force" to designate the inner state of a body,[30] and Hegel follows him.[31] Should we conclude that none of the three understood mechanics because their usage is out of tune with current usage?

Once we see that speaking of a body's inner force is simply another way to speak about its momentum, some of Hegel's other alleged mistakes are rectified as well. A body that is in an elliptical orbit travels with varying velocities, as Kepler's second law asserts. If its inner force depends on its velocity, then that force will vary with its position in orbit. Since this inner force expresses the inertia of the body, it is the so-called centrifugal force.[32] It follows that the relative values of the centripetal to centrifugal forces do vary throughout a planet's orbit, as Hegel claims. In short, Hegel is not making the egregious, elementary mistakes ascribed to him. What is central to his account of Newton is that gravity and inertia are distinct and independent factors contributing to a body's overall motion and that they must be combined to calculate the overall path of a projectile.

There is another important respect in which Hegel deviates from ordinary scientific notions, his interpretation of equations. Scientific laws

---

[30] "In mechanics, the force of a matter set in motion is regarded as present in order to impart this motion to another matter," Kant, *Philosophy of Material Nature*, p. II 95.

[31] "The magnitude of its motion is determined by these two moments: by mass and by the specific tangential motion as velocity. If this magnitude is posited as something internal, it is what we call force" (§265Z, p. 51). Shea, "Hegel's Celestial Mechanics," pp. 37–41, sees Hegel's usage as rooted in ambiguities in Newton, especially in the notion of an inner force. He thinks that Hegel's objections could have stemmed from these ambiguities, but that they represented, instead, Hegel's failure to grasp Newtonian physics.

[32] Newton, *Principia*, book III, prop. 19, pp. 822–823, uses the term "centrifugal force."

are, of course, typically stated in equations, and we use these equations to make calculations and predictions, without much reflection on what they mean. Hegel reads these laws with metaphysical literalness. Galileo's law of gravitational acceleration at the earth's surface, for example, asserts that the distances a body falls is proportional to the square of the time it falls, traditionally expressed as: $s = \frac{1}{2}gt^2$. The formula indicates that velocity of the falling body will increase in proportion to the time so that its velocity at the end of a time interval, t, will be $2s/t$, double its average velocity during the time interval, that is, s/t. Equivalently, the change in velocity, g, is constant, and Galileo's law is simply the law of uniform acceleration. Closely following Newton, Hegel explains that the law expresses an "accelerating force imparting one and the same impulse in each unit of time, and a force of inertia which perpetuates the (greater) velocity acquired in each moment of time."[33] That is to say, gravity is an *outer* force that continually augments whatever *inner* inertial force the body has already acquired. This reasoning relies on the faculty of understanding to divide the force on the body into two constituents. While Hegel acknowledges the mathematical achievement, he also claims, rightly, that so far from proving uniform acceleration, the law, rather, presupposes it. The law leaves open the question of *why* a body falls with uniform acceleration.

He proposes to answer this question with a metaphysical derivation that uses the faculty of reason to derive the law from the concept of a body. As we will see shortly, a body moves itself toward a center of gravity. In any motion, the body traverses some space in some time. But in what Hegel calls the "free motion," the motion that derives from the nature of the moving body itself, the relation between space and time depends merely on *their* natures. Hence, the problem for Hegel is to determine how these two disparate natures can be equated so that the space traversed is *equal* to the time traversed. Hegel thinks that the nature of space lies in its otherness, its having one part next to or outside of another (§254). This "self-otherness" is also a self-relation; space is self-related through its own nature. Time, on the other hand, is not self-related. Each moment of time exists independently of any other; as such, time is an instance of Hegel's logical category of "being-for-self." Hegel's reasoning is too complex to repeat here, but he argues that this latter category comes to be self-related and the result is another logical category, the one.[34] Mathematically, self-relation amounts to

[33] §267A. Hegel, *Werke 9. Enzyklopädie*, p. 75. Hegel, *Hegel's Philosophy of Nature*, p. 57. Hegel is nearly quoting Newton, *Principia*, p. 424.
[34] Hegel, *Hegel's Science of Logic*, p. 163.

being raised to the second power or being squared. Since space contains self-relation *within* itself as its very nature, space is, in itself, a kind of square. Time, on the other hand, is not self-related in itself; it is a kind of root that becomes one when it is self-related. Since a body that traverses space will also traverse time, the amount of space must be somehow equal or proportional to the amount of time. But time must be squared to be equal to space because, again, space is already intrinsically squared. Hence, the space traversed by a body is proportional to time squared.[35] So understood, Galileo's equation asserts some sort of metaphysical identity between two entities: time and space.

Whatever we make of its value, this type of reasoning is bound to raise eyebrows because it discusses what we typically think of as simply mathematical quantities in metaphysical terms, and because Hegel thinks that his metaphysical derivation is superior to mathematical derivations of the law. It seems unlikely that he could have derived the law solely from reason by thinking along these lines, and we can well ask what this type of speculation contributes to our grasp of the law. If grasping the law means making calculations, then the metaphysical derivation is unnecessary and unhelpful. However, Hegel *does* address a real question: why do time and space stand in the proportion they have in the formula? No merely mathematical derivation of the law could answer this question. Whatever our skepticism about how well Hegel succeeds in answering it, we should see that the question is worth asking. It is important, as well, to realize that a metaphysical derivation of the law does not undermine either the mathematical derivation of it through the faculty of the understanding or the grasp of its meaning that enables us to use it to make predictions. Hegel is not doing what we generally think of as science: he is not evaluating the accuracy of a law's predictions. He is doing metaphysics.

Hegel approaches Newton's laws in much the same way. His concern is neither the science nor the mathematics. What, then, is his objection? The issue is conceptual. Again, Hegel's claim is that Newton has two distinct notions of matter that are at odds with one another. According to one, matter is "inert": it does not cause motion in itself or other bodies, nor does it impede or enhance motion. According to the other,

---

[35] Buchdahl, "Hegel's Philosophy of Nature and the Structure of Science," pp. 127–134, discusses Hegel's derivation, but he sees it as more of a conceptual explication than a deduction. A better discussion of this passage appears in L. Fleishhacker, "Hegel on Mathematics and Experimental Science," in *Hegel and Newtonianism*, pp. 211–213. Houlgate, *Freedom, Truth, and History*, pp. 138–144, has a very clear and helpful discussion of Galileo's law and Hegel's derivation of it.

matter does cause motion because every body moves toward the center of gravity because of its matter. As Hegel puts it, "Gravitation directly contradicts the law of inertia: for, by the former, matter strives to get away *out of itself* to another" [and moves toward another] (§269A).[36] Inertia is matter's striving *to remain as it is*. Thus, the contradiction he ascribes to Newton lies in the incompatible *natures* that the two laws implicitly ascribe to matter.

Again, scientists are unlikely to be concerned with this conceptual contradiction. Indeed, Hegel's claims about the nature or the concept of matter would seem to represent exactly the sort of thinking that Newton aims to overcome: Hegel is objecting to Newton's not explaining how matter could be both inert and active, whereas Newton prides himself, famously, on his not "feigning hypotheses."[37] When he says this, Newton is referring specifically to his being unable to determine the cause of gravitational attraction. His law of gravity is a mathematical formula. There is no explicit contradiction between it and mathematical formulae that express the inertial laws. The nature of matter figures into the statements of neither group of laws. So there is no need to identify the inert and active characters of matter. What is to be gained by insisting that they must both stem from the same material "nature"? Indeed, is not this latter merely an empty, Scholastic notion that deflects attention away from the sort of scientific work that advances our understanding of matter and its motions and toward a metaphysical and occult discussion of causes?

So the Newtonian. His position is apparently endorsed by Kant who also recognizes distinct types of matter, as we saw. The first of his matters is that involved in inertial motion, the second that which is subject to gravity. Kant must agree with Newton that we can keep the multiple matters conceptually distinct; for he does not seek a unifying principle, nor does he ascribe any nature to the matters other than their capacity to receive determination through the qualitative or quantitative categories.

At first glance, Hegel may seem to have little to say in response. What he takes to be contradiction in Newton is just the sort of *conceptual* problem that Newton wants to shrug off. However, I think that Hegel has a good case. First, I think he is right to insist that matter must be one. The supposition to the contrary strikes me as a holdover from ancient philosophy. Aristotle takes matter to be potential, and he speaks of different kinds of matter (*Met.*, H.1.1042a25–b6) that could be present together in the same sensible substance. This is not an option for

---

[36] Hegel, *Werke* 9, *Enzyklopädie*, 83. Hegel, *Philosophy of Nature.* p. 63.
[37] Newton, *Principia*, p. 943.

Newton because he makes matter a fully realized entity. If matter exists as a body, whatever characters belong to matter must stem from its nature. Second, there is good reason to think that Newton himself was concerned with the nature of matter and that this interest has continued in contemporary science. What is his doctrine of the "inner force" (in the third definition) if not the recognition that bodies must contain some internal character that allows them to maintain their integrity as bodies by resisting forces imposed upon them and yet also to carry those forces in such a way as to pass them along to other bodies? And what is this internal character other than the nature of matter that manifests itself in the constitution of bodies.[38] It is not just Kant who is concerned with how bodies can be constituted and with the fundamental characters that belong to them. Newton claims that a stone swung in a sling "endeavors to leave the hand that is whirling it,"[39] suggesting that he thinks this behavior a property of the body. Likewise, his first law asserts, "Every body perseveres in its state of being at rest or of moving uniformly straight forward except insofar as it is compelled to change its state by forces impressed."[40] That bodies persevere in their states is presented here as a fundamental character of bodies, part of their nature. This is, I think, the answer to the question why Newton includes the first law when it seems to be a limiting case of the second: whereas the second refers to a change in motion being in proportion to an impressed force, the first law makes the claim that matter's nature is not to change its motion of its own accord.[41] This latter is a point about the *nature* of matter, and Newton gives it pride of place as the first law.

---

[38] See Bernard Cohen's discussion in Newton, *Principia*, pp. 96–98. Cohen notes that Newton refers, in a letter, to the inner force as "innate, inherent, and essential."

[39] In definition five; Newton, *Principia*, p. 405.

[40] Newton, *Principia*; p. 416. Kant, *Philosophy of Material Nature*, p. II.106, objects that "inertia does not signify a positive effort of something to maintain its state." Only living things make such an effort, but matter is entirely lifeless because it cannot "determine itself to motion or rest." That is, "matter has no absolutely internal determinations and grounds of determination" (p. II.105). Kant is clearly speaking about the nature of matter, he identifies its lack of self-determination with its inertia. (He thinks that the second law is properly the law of inertia.) Inertia in this sense is clearly at odds with the idea of gravity as a force through which matter naturally acts upon itself; indeed, it is even more clearly at odds with gravity than Newton's inertia, though Kant does not take note of it.

[41] Bernard Cohen's explanation for why the first and second laws are distinct is that the forces in the two laws are different. See Newton, *Principia*, p. 110. In the second law, force is impulsive; whereas in the first law, it is conceived as continuously acting. I am not convinced that a case in which the force is assumed to be 0 is best described as continuous force. However, insofar as it is the body's internal force that maintains it in motion (see pp. 96–97), the inertial "force" has to be

Newton is hardly unique; when scientists speak of their work, they often present themselves as trying to fathom the inner workings and essential features of matter. Philosophers tend to read such claims as declarations of enthusiasm, and we are accustomed to interpreting scientific laws as weakly existential. Most contemporary readers would, for example, take a claim like "all men are mortal" to assert that every human being, those who have lived and those yet to be born, is alive for a finite period of time. However, in other eras such a claim would typically be understood as an assertion about human physical nature. It is not only that the modality of these two interpretations is different; but the first is merely extensional and descriptive, whereas the second expresses an essential character. In the present case, I think that contemporary thinkers tend to see Newton's first law as asserting the existence of a fact about matter. By the same token, they tend to read the law of gravity as asserting another fact about matter. So understood, the two laws are consistent because the facts are independent.

So far as I can see, Newton asserts these laws as claims about the *nature* of matter. What is certain is that both Kant and Hegel read Newton's laws this way.[42] Indeed, it is not an exaggeration to say that Hegel reads *every* claim as an assertion about an essence, and that that has posed a major obstacle to contemporary readers' appreciating his thought. If, then, Newton's first law asserts that matter does not of its nature cause motion in itself nor does it either impede or enhance whatever motion it already has, and if the law of gravity implies that any material body will, by its own nature, somehow move itself toward the center of mass, then the two laws assert contradictory characters of matter and are contradictory. The contradiction lies in the nature of matter that these laws assert on the strong, essential reading of them. In these terms, moreover, Kant aims to skirt the contradiction by distinguishing two distinct matters, one of which is passive and inert, and the other active (along with two other distinct matters). Hegel rejects the distinction and insists on a single matter. He argues that the feature that enables matter to be impacted, its ability to resist an impressed force, is the very feature that is responsible for matter's gravitational attraction. (More on this shortly.) That is to say, he thinks that the "inner force" that Newton equates with inertia and sees as necessary for the

---

natural, as I think Cohen sees. In my view, the difference between the first two laws is that whereas the second asserts positively that the action of an external force will accelerate or decelerate the body, the first claims that there will be no such acceleration or deceleration in the absence of an external force. Thus, the first law is a statement about the nature of the body.

[42] See the remarks on Kant in Footnote 40.

first three laws is also the gravitational force responsible for holding the body together.

Apart from this reasoning, it is widely supposed that the matter that figures in the law of gravity *should* be the same as inertial matter because some single quantity of matter constitutes the body. It might be said that Einstein's General Relativity theory explains the identity by making gravity and inertia both functions of the curvature of space, and the curvature of space, in turn, dependent on matter. From Hegel's point of view, such a unification represents a significant advance over Newton's treatment of matter, but it is still a scientific theory and therefore relies on the faculty of understanding and, importantly, leaves open the question of what matter is. In any case, my contention here is that the idea that matter is or ought to be one and the idea that science ought to elucidate its essential features are widely accepted in science, at least as ideals. This is a metaphysical ideal with which even Newton, ever anxious to discover the nature of matter, might well have concurred.

Newton's problem is, rather, epistemic: he has not discovered what the deep causes of matter are. Moreover, since he aims to discover causes by describing motions, it is not likely that he could discover deep causes. He thinks that merely characterizing phenomena will contribute to scientific knowledge and also insulate him from the kind of criticism that Hegel brings. The root of the issue between them is not just whether matter has a nature that we can grasp that can account for both inertia and gravity, but also what we can know about nature and how we can come to know it. Newton limits the scope of physics; he settles for describing motions whose causes, he frankly admits, he does not know. Hegel insists that finding those causes is the central task of the Philosophy of Nature, but to find them he needs to grasp matter in a way that is not supported by empirical evidence. Given Newton's reluctance to acknowledge the kind of evidence Hegel has to offer or, indeed, even to acknowledge the problem, Hegel needs to show, first, that Newton himself is committed to some notion of the nature of matter and, second, that he (Hegel) can expound this nature in a way that overcomes the contradiction. That is to say, Hegel's criticism has no teeth in the face of Newton's admission of his own failure to know nature unless Hegel can show that he can resolve the contradiction in Newton's laws by properly explicating the nature of matter.

In my view, Hegel does this twice over. His richest and most far reaching resolution is contained in his paragraphs on "Absolute Mechanics," the final portion of "Mechanics." I sketch this in Section III. However, Hegel has a second, weaker but more plausible and cogent resolution that is implicit in the argument that leads up to this section. I sketch this argument in my final section. Whereas the former resolution shows

Hegel being, we might say, most Hegelian, the latter is more powerful and important for science.

III

We can now acknowledge that Hegel has found a contradiction in Newton's conception of matter, if not in his laws. The resolution that Hegel advances is dialectical. Rather than dismissing Newton's laws because they presuppose a contradiction, he uses the contradiction to arrive at an understanding of the nature of matter. Because Hegel's resolution has not been understood and because it helps to explain his critique of Newton, I sketch it, albeit briefly, in this section. I must acknowledge, however, that this discussion will not help my case for taking Hegel's a priori science seriously. His ultimate understanding of the nature of matter is simply too remote from anything that we can recognize as scientific and too internally problematic to accept, however fascinating it is when taken in its own terms.

Between Hegel's exposition of the contradiction in Newton's conception of matter and his resolution of it, there is an important intermediate step. He shows that both gravity and inertia spring from the same conception of matter, a concept held, but not acknowledged, by Newton. That is to say, before Hegel overcomes the contradiction, he embraces it. Indeed, that Newton's laws presuppose contradictory notions of matter signals, for Hegel, their essential insight into matter and their importance in the conceptual movement toward a higher grasp of it. This higher grasp is expressed in "Physics," and in the transition to it at the end of "Mechanics," Hegel lauds Kepler's laws and declares that Newton's laws are consequences of them. Kepler's laws come close to explaining motion through an inner principle, as "Physics" goes on to do. To understand what Hegel is looking for, it helps to recall the Aristotelian model. Aristotle traces nature's attributes, including its essential motions, to an inner principle. Now there is no *inner* principle of matter that accounts for Newton's three laws or for gravity, but Hegel claims that there is a principle that does account for all of Newton's mechanics. It is an *outer* principle; indeed, Hegel sometimes calls it Otherness.

That Otherness is the principle of matter is presupposed by Newtonian mechanics. Consider, first, Newton's supposition that his three laws of motion are independent of the law of gravity. The law of inertia asserts that a body will continue in its state of rest or motion unless disturbed. Were there a single body in the universe, it would continue forever at rest or in a straight line of motion. However, insofar as matter is inert and not a cause of motion, this body could neither alter its own motion nor cause itself to move. Hence, if it does move, it must have acquired its motion through a force exerted by another body. It follows that the supposition of a single body in the universe continuing in motion forever is impossible: a body that were truly by itself could have no motion because it would need another body to move it (unless its cause were nonphysical). Because bodies are inert, the causes of their motion *must* lie outside themselves. However, between the body that is moved and the body that moves it, there must be a gravitational force of attraction that would decelerate the impacted body. Practically, the gravitational force is likely to be so much less than the force of impact that it is inconsequential for calculations of motion. But theoretically, the unavoidability of gravitational attraction in any impact means that there could *never* be true inertial motion. Gravity would always work against inertia and in no case would a body in motion actually remain in motion at the same velocity in a straight line. At best, inertial motion is an approximation.

We might, perhaps, say that the fact that there is no actual inertial motion does not detract from the first law because it asserts only the *tendency* of matter to remain in motion and that this is amply confirmed by the actual motion's being the resultant of inertial and gravitational motion. But again, Hegel is not denying that Newton's techniques work. The issue is whether inertia can be *theoretically* separated from gravity, and the problem is that the inertness of matter makes another body necessary. This other body, impacting the first body, causes it to move rectilinearly but also to decelerate. Since, moreover, the second body is itself inert, its own motion must have come from still another matter, which latter also exerts a gravitational force on both it and the first body. It is possible that these impacts will be head on, but the more general case is that one body hits another at some distance from its center imparting to it a rectilinear motion at some angle. In this case, the gravitational attraction does not merely slow the second body down; it curves the second body's trajectory. The degree of curvature depends on the masses of all the bodies and their relative positions. The impacted body would not be curved if all the matter in the universe were arranged in a straight line, but this case is merely a remote and abstract possibility. In general, the motion the impacted body receives is not rectilinear, as Newton would have it, but elliptical. The degree of curvature depends on the masses of all the bodies and their center of gravity. If we say that rectilinear motion has a curvature of 0, then we can say that whenever a body receives motion it *must* be curved. If this is right, motion is essentially curvilinear, and it depends on the masses of the impacting bodies. Insofar as a material body is inert, its motion is determined by what is *other* than it.

That one body's motion is determined by another body is also a consequence of gravity. In order for one body to impact on another, each must be constituted so as to occupy a determinate volume of space. As we will see in the next section, the principle that so constitutes a body is gravity. Gravity is, first, a force that attracts the parts of a single body toward a center; but, as we will also see, this force necessarily extends beyond the boundaries of the body and attracts other matter. Any two bodies are, then, mutually attracted and move toward a center point, and by the same reasoning there must be a center of gravity for the universe toward which *all* bodies are attracted.

This seemingly ordinary Newtonian idea has, Hegel thinks, a profound consequence. If the principle that makes a body be a body also makes it move toward some point outside of itself, then for something to be a material body is for it to seek something other than itself. The nature of matter is, thus, to move away from itself and seek to be *other* than itself. To put the point more like Hegel would, the character that belongs most of all to matter, its nature, is just its *not* being what it is.[43] This nature of matter is gravity, a movement of attraction toward something else, even if matter appears not to move itself. Again, Otherness is the essence of matter: matter's *inner* nature is its motion toward a point *outside* of itself, the center of gravity of all matter. However, matter's nature is also its *lack* of its own character and consequent determination by another. That is to say, gravity and inertness both come to the same thing, matter's being essentially something other.

Of course, it sounds bizarre to speak of laws of physics as consequences of a concept, particularly when the implication of doing so is that that concept, matter, is contradictory. What Hegel is after is a conceptual derivation of mechanics from the nature of matter. His problem is that the nature of matter lies outside of matter; matter itself must depend on something else. That means that to derive mechanics from the *inner* character of matter is ultimately to derive it from something *other* and *external*. Derived from a contradictory concept, mechanics must itself be contradictory. More concretely, the problem here is that the center of gravity lies outside matter, but inasmuch as the center of gravity belongs intrinsically to matter, it is (conceptually, at least) within matter.

Such a relation exists physically in the solar system: the nature of the orbiting bodies lies in the point around which they revolve. The

---

43 See: Houlgate, *Freedom, Truth, and History*, p. 137. For more on Otherness as the essence of Nature, see E. C. Halper, "A Tale of Two Metaphysics: Alison Stone's Environmental Hegel," *Bulletin of the Hegel Society of Great Britain*, 51/52 (2005), pp. 7–10.

planets have their natures outside of themselves, but their motions toward the sun preserve them in the positions that they occupy, that is, their orbits. Hence, their being *other* is what preserves them as the *same*. From the perspective of the solar system, matter's nature is not strictly other, for the gravitational center that defines matter lies within the solar system, in the sun. Furthermore, within the solar system, the gravitational motion of the orbiting bodies is now understood to be their continuous *inertial* motions. What is fascinating here is Hegel's idea that because the nature of matter is to be other, the matter arranges itself, as it were, into a structure that manifests this otherness and that in manifesting itself as other, matter locates its principle within itself and ceases to be other. We see here the beginnings of a new type of mechanics that is based on the primacy of elliptical motion, a mechanics where the nature of matter is no longer simply otherness but an otherness that is also an inner nature. Hegel has made the transition to Physics. Ultimately, he resolves the contradiction between inertia and gravity that he imputes to Newton by moving to this higher plane.

A dialectical argument based on otherness as the inner nature of matter hardly seems scientific. However, there is a remarkably interesting proposal here: it is not rectilinear motion that is fundamental to matter, but elliptical motion, and matter naturally moves itself elliptically as manifested in the solar system. If inertial motion is an elliptical motion around a center of gravity, then gravity and inertia are no longer at odds. Hegel's question then becomes why particular planets occupy the orbits they do, a question that he acknowledges himself unable to answer. What he does emphasize is that the character of their orbits is constant. Kepler's third law declares that there is a constant proportion between the cube of a planet's semimajor axis and the period of its revolution, and this Hegel understands as a form of identity between space and time that is a kind of enrichment of the identity we saw in the law of free fall.[44] For reasons that are obscure, Hegel sees this relation as expressing the conceptual nature of gravitational attraction and, thereby, of matter, and he credits Kepler with grasping its conceptual necessity and persevering in finding empirical confirmation.[45] It is, thus, clear why Hegel prefers Kepler to Newton: it is Kepler who proposes that matter moves elliptically by its very nature, as it were, and that the solar system is

---

[44] Hegel, *Werke*, 9 *Enzyklopädie*, pp. 92–93; *Philosophy of Nature*, p. 71.
[45] Hegel, *Werke*, 9 *Enzyklopädie*, p. 96; *Philosophy of Nature*, pp. 73–74. Hegel claims that Kepler spent twenty-seven years searching for a connection between the cube of the distance and the square of the period because of his faith that reason would manifest itself in nature. The implication is that Kepler grasped the a priori necessity for the law long before he found it.

a manifestation of the nature of matter. Reasoning dialectically with Hegel, we could say that the sun, as center of gravity, must belong to the nature of the matter that it attracts. But to say this is to identify an *inner* nature of matter and thereby to undermine its otherness. With this, matter has been transformed into *phusis* and the subject for study is no longer bodies, but a solar system as a whole with its necessary internal parts and structure.

IV

Scientists do not feel comfortable with a dialectical treatment of "the nature of matter," and, anyway, identifying it as otherness seems hopelessly anthropocentric. Hegel's full solution to the contradiction in matter's nature is so far-reaching, even for a metaphysics of nature, that it obscures the positive contribution that metaphysical reflection can make to science. Hence, this section will sketch the steps in Hegel's argument, necessarily repeating some of what has been said, in order to make clear what I regard as the essential element in his solution and how a priori metaphysics of the sort practiced by Hegel can help to advance science.

1. The first thing to notice is how the category of Matter emerges from Motion and Place (§§260–261). There is a conceptual exercise here that is unfamiliar but not really difficult. Think, first, of a point that lies somewhere within uniform, infinite Space. This point should locate a position in space, and position is essential to space which, in its entirely abstract form, just is *position*. However, a single point stands in exactly the same relation to infinite space as any other point does. No point could be closer or further from the boundary of unbounded space. Hence, no single point by itself could mark out a position in space. If to be a point is to mark or to occupy a position in space, then the point's not marking out a position is a kind of failure to be what it is, a kind of conceptual destruction. On the other hand, without the point, space is entirely uniform, extending in every direction the same way; it is (abstract) position without any (concrete) position. As such, Space requires a point in order to define itself properly as position. But once it is posited, the point again destroys itself. More simply put, we cannot think the idea of Space without supposing it to contain a point that concretely defines position; but since no single point could concretely define position in infinite space, we cannot think of Space with a single point. This mental process of positing a point and destroying it is the point's coming to be and passing away, that is, the point's motion. However, the plurality of points generated in this way does succeed in marking off position, but position defined in respect of points temporally and spatially *related to*

each other, rather than, as before, in respect of a single point's relation to abstract space. On the other hand, from the perspective of the points, becoming and ceasing are events that they experience and through which they persist as relative positions in space. The collection of the points that persist in space through the process of change constitutes matter. This is Hegel's first understanding of Matter. (We explored his more proper understanding of matter in the previous section.)

2. The plurality of points that constitutes matter are united into a body. However, in order for these points to be united, they must also be different from each other. Conceptually, the gathering together of these points also presupposes their inherent distinctness (§262). As Hegel puts it, their attraction presupposes a repulsion – not only an internal repulsion of part against part that maintains their volume, but a repulsion of the collection of such parts from what becomes external to them. Hegel's term for such a self-attraction achieved through repulsion is "One," the logical category that I mentioned earlier. Thus, matter is one body with parts that are united and extended. He is speaking *conceptually* here, but his characterization also describes the *physical* reality of a matter that occupies a volume of space. Since its parts are all united into a single body, there must be an attraction; but there is also some repulsion that keeps them all from collapsing into a point.

In a remark on this argument, Hegel refers to Kant's *Metaphysical Foundations of Natural Science* (§262A). I think that he is presupposing Kant's argument. Kant is easier to understand because he is talking about physical entities rather than conceptual relations. Kant thinks that any physical object must be spatial, and that means that it will occupy some volume of space, but its degree of intensity in this space can range between 0 and 1. That is to say, matter is what fills a volume of space to some degree. The degree to which the volume is filled depends on the degree to which matter is compressed by outside forces. Since the body's matter holds together and does not dissipate, there must be some force that pulls it toward the center of the object; since the matter does not collapse into the center, there must be a counteracting repulsive force. Now we might object that this attractive force is unnecessary because the repulsive forces from surrounding bodies will suffice to prevent the body from expanding indefinitely. This will not do, Kant argues, because the surrounding matter "itself requires a compressive force in order that it be matter."[46] In other words, we cannot rely on surrounding bodies to define a body, because each of them would need its own principle of attraction before it itself could exist as a body. Since the

---

[46] Kant, *Philosophy of Material Nature*, II. chap. 2, prop. 5.

attractive force is a principle of matter, that is, since matter depends on this force, it cannot depend on (some other) matter. This attractive force that holds a body together might seem to be some sort of cohesion, but Kant rejects this supposition because even though liquids and gases have less cohesion, they do not, for that reason, necessarily occupy greater volume. What is needed is an attractive force that prevents a body from expanding indefinitely, and this Kant identifies as gravity. Now this attractive force must operate wherever the boundaries of the body exist, be the body expanded or compressed, and, again, since it is a principle of matter, it is prior to matter and cannot depend on it. Hence, the attractive force exists independently of the boundary of matter. Since, though, to put the argument rather too simply, matter does not limit it, there is nothing to prevent gravity from extending infinitely, though it will be diminished by being diffused through the volume of space.[47] In short, Kant argues that the law of gravity is a priori because gravity, together with a force of repulsion, makes material bodies possible.

What Hegel takes issue with in this account is Kant's identification of *two* distinct forces. He insists that there is rather a single contradictory principle at work: there cannot be an attraction unless there is something diverse to attract. Specifically, what makes matter have a force of attraction *is* its apartness in space, that is, its occupying space. And it is just the repulsion between the parts intrinsic to its occupying space that makes the matter of a body be attracted to its center. Thus, occupying a volume of space is at once an attraction and expansion of points.

Furthermore, for the same reason that parts of one material body are attracted to its center, the parts of two or more bodies are attracted to the center between them. Hence, the attractive force of any individual material body is directed to some unifying center point that lies *outside of itself*. Ironically, gravity, the essential feature of a matter, is a kind of *otherness* of matter. We are not, thus far, ahead scientifically, but we have seen why gravity and repulsion both belong essentially to bodies and why the force of gravity extends throughout space. Yet, since gravity and repulsion are not simply one inasmuch as the center of gravity generally falls *outside* of the matter (which occupies some volume), there remains a certain unintelligibility to matter.

3. Insofar as a body is a filled volume of space, it exists in space as well as time, but the position it occupies in space or in time does not affect its character (§263). It follows that moving through space and time, that is to say, being in motion, also does not affect it (§264). It is inert. But since it is inert, any motion it acquires must come from contact with

[47] Ibid, p. II.68.

some other body that is itself in motion. At the moment of impact, the two bodies constitute a single body that moves as one. However, the impact is only possible because the two bodies *resist* each other, and their resistance is due to the internal repulsion between the parts of each, a repulsion that exists because of their being distinct bodies, each with its own inner gravity. It is this inner gravity that constitutes a body as a body and makes it capable of acquiring inertial motion from impact. In impact, then, the two bodies become one, but also remain distinct masses (§265). Their common motion depends on their relative matters and their relative motions. The matter and the velocity of the impacting body are, thus, interchangeable insofar as each of these produces the same effect on the impacted body. The total motion of impacting and impacted bodies remains the same before and after impact because the matter remains inert and unaffected by motion. Or more scientifically, the total momentum of the system does not change.

4. Each of the colliding bodies has its own center of gravity, but inasmuch as they differ only through the quantities of their masses, the two together constitute a single body that has its own center of gravity (§266). In respect of this latter center of gravity, both bodies are in motion: before impact, each body is *falling* toward this center (§267). Inasmuch as this center of gravity is the point of attraction, the bodies are moving toward it not with the uniform inertial motion initially supposed, but with the uniform acceleration of gravitational attraction. In order that the bodies be able to impact each other, each must have its own internal gravity and repulsion. But if each has its own gravity, then together they have a common center of gravity that is attracting both. Hence, their fall toward this center is not of uniform velocity, but is the free fall of gravitational attraction. Moreover, the motion between these bodies is an essential consequence of their being material bodies in space (§268).

It follows that there can be no *pure* uniform rectilinear motion, as we saw in Section III. The impact that places one body in motion must be caused by another body to which it cannot but be attracted gravitationally; or, rather, because impact does not occur in absolute space but in respect of the relative position of another body, the appropriate frame of reference is the gravitational center toward which both bodies move.[48] But motion toward a *gravitational* center is always an acceleration toward that center. Hence, all actual motion is gravitational acceleration. Again, rectilinear motion is only theoretically possible in a universe with a single body, but such a body could never

---

[48] Ibid, pp. II.28–30.

receive the force it needs to move. In short, gravity undermines inertia (§269A).

5. For the same reasons that two balls have the same center of gravity, all material bodies ought to have, in addition to their individual centers of gravity, a collective center of gravity (§269). Then, every material body would be attracted to it, and in respect of the distance between them and it, all would be falling toward it. Falling is thus the essential motion of bodies. It is contingent insofar as a body's separation from the center is contingent, but necessary in respect of the nature of matter (§267). Moreover, this universal attraction must, again, presuppose some sort of plurality that is attracted. These bodies each have their own centers of gravity and, thus, maintain their individual identities. A body's falling toward the collective center does not undermine its identity, but the way it falls depends on its matter and motion. This attraction to the center manifests itself as motion *around* the center; in particular, as the elliptical motions of the planets around the sun. Hegel refers to this as the "free motion" of matter. His point is that matter realizes itself in a universe where matter moves in a cyclical motion wherein it returns to itself.

Newton's famous bucket experiment was supposed to show that some motions are real: He imagines a bucket with water in it suspended by a string, rotated, and then released. As the rope unwinds, the water climbs up the sides of the bucket; and Newton takes this to indicate that the rotation of the bucket is a real motion that results as an effect from an agent's act.[49] Kant also argues that circular rotary motion is actual or true.[50] Hegel agrees that the rotation of matter about a center is real, but he argues that it follows necessarily from the nature of matter. As we have seen, Hegel insists that this real motion exists in the elliptical motions of the bodies orbiting the sun; for these orbiting bodies, elliptical motion would be at once inertial and gravitational. So the solar system is a kind of synthesis between gravitational and inertial motions. Again, the reason that Hegel praises Kepler and disparages Newton is that Kepler realizes that the solar system is an expression of the nature of matter. His claim is that the planetary motions are not composite motions but fundamental and that these motions, thereby, overcome the "contradiction" in Newton's laws. Unfortunately, Hegel's argument for this last striking claim (§270) is thin, and his remarks are long.

Hegel does not know that the structure of the atom mirrors that of the solar system; he does not know that on the Bohr model the orbits

[49] Newton, *Principia*, pp. 412–413.
[50] Kant, *Philosophy of Material Nature*, pp. II.122–123, 127–130.

of electrons around the nucleus are not composite motions.[51] Nor does he know Einstein's famous contention that matter is a form of energy. He might have counted all this as evidence for his notion that rotation around a center is a fundamental character of matter. Matter does, at the subatomic level, take on a fundamental and necessary structure that is different from what either gravity or inertia by itself suggests. Importantly, this structure is intelligible and explains features of matter, even though it adds nothing to the predictions that we usually identify with science. These developments show that Hegel's approach was, at least, not misguided.

Hegel's scientific contribution is, however, different and, perhaps, deeper. The particular structure that he proposes is not as important as the principle at stake. Newton understands matter as inert. It is a body. Apart from its quantity, it has no distinguishing characteristics. One body is the same as any other as far as Newton's physics goes. What is nice about this conception of matter is that laws of bodies are completely general: particular characteristics that distinguish one body from another need not be considered. This view of matter as "neutral stuff" stands in contrast with the premodern notion of matter as "undetermined potential." On this latter view, there is no matter that stands by itself; matter is always that which is determined by something else. And matter is understood only as the potential for the specific form it can receive. Thus, wood is matter insofar as it has the potential to be fashioned into a house, even though it is also a formal determination of elements, which latter are, in turn, *its matter*. Since matter has no independent identity, ancient and medieval science could make only the broadest and emptiest claims about matter in general. Any more detailed understanding of matter would need to focus on one particular type of matter, such as the matter of dogs, the matter of plants, and so forth, and explain how such matter takes on specific functions when it receives a form. This is what Aristotle and his followers wanted science to do. In relation to this premodern view, the Newtonian 'matter as stuff' view has the big advantage of allowing general claims about matter. And such claims constitute Newtonian physics. However, the problem with this new approach to matter is that it abstracts from real differences between different kinds of things. In fact, the *mere* bodies it treats do not exist. Moreover, in abstracting all particular characteristics to arrive at a mere 'body,' we take away all that could give the body its own character. As a result, body *must* be inert. It cannot cause motion in itself or another body, and any motion it acquires does not alter it. Motion must, thus,

---

[51] Paolucci, "Hegel and the Celestial Mechanics of Newton and Einstein," p. 69, thinks he anticipated Bohr in §271Z.

exist as a kind of accidental attribute of matter. However, this conception of matter as inert body runs against the character that matter needs to have to constitute itself as a body. This latter consists of attractive and repulsive forces that allow it to occupy a volume of space, forces that, as we saw, *cause* motion. Hegel resolves this contradiction by proposing a *system* in which the center and the motions around it are inert because they are governed by attractive and repulsive forces. Although Hegel identifies it with the solar system, what is really important about this solution – far more than what it is embodied in – is the notion that matter has its own *activity*. This, I contend, is what we really learn from Hegel's solution. The notion implicit in Newtonian mechanics that matter is merely inert is incompatible with the activity that matter must have even to sustain itself as a body: matter must be active.

Hegel arrives at this conclusion through metaphysical reflection on the concept of nature. In the early twentieth century scientists also reflecting on basic scientific concepts as well as actual and possible experimental results arrived at the same conclusion. The inner dynamics of the atom constitutes one obvious example of matter's intrinsic activity. Electrons are no longer supposed to move around the nucleus as planets move around the sun; they seem rather to exist in states of excitation, as does the equally active nucleus. Einstein's identification of matter as a form of energy expresses the same idea: matter is active. This intrinsic activity of matter explains why the addition of motion, especially motion close to the speed of light, *does* affect the quantity of matter, though we need more reasoning to see why the change is what the Lorenz transformation describes. That matter, according to general relativity, does not naturally move in straight lines but somehow bends space and time with which it is intrinsically connected, and that matter exists as elementary particles or waves, each with its own motions and properties, both suggest that contemporary science has accepted key features of Hegel's view of matter.

Just how matter is active needs a different sort of investigation. This is where philosophy of nature ends and science begins. What Hegel sees is that there is an important role for philosophy of nature in uncovering problems and resolving them conceptually, as well as in making intelligible answers to "why?" questions that science does not address. Philosophy of nature does not replace science, but neither is it without implication for science. Hegel recognizes a significant problem in Newtonian physics that is not easy to resolve, and his solution, in its form if not its detail, continues to have an impact on the way we see and explore matter. At least on this issue, Hegel the armchair, a priori metaphysician beat the great empiricist who eschewed metaphysics. I rather think that he opened a path on which philosophers should not fear to tread.[52]

[52] Versions of this paper were read at a Metaphysical Society of America meeting at the University of Pittsburgh, at the University of Warwick, and at an annual meeting of the Canadian Society for the History and Philosophy of Science. Comments from these audiences helped improve the paper, and I especially thank those who kindly sent me written remarks after these presentations. I am grateful to Todd Baker for correcting an error in the physics and to David Johnson for comments on the penultimate draft.

13 The Logic of Life: Hegel's Philosophical Defense of Teleological Explanation of Living Beings

Hegel accords great philosophical importance to Kant's discussions of teleology and biology in the *Critique of the Power of Judgment*, and yet also disagrees with Kant's central conclusions there.[1] More specifically, Kant argues for a generally skeptical view of teleological explanation

---

[1] *In citing works, the following abbreviations have been used:*

HEGEL: Most writings are contained in the *Werke in zwanzig Bände*, ed. by E. Moldenhauer und K. Michel, Frankfurt: Suhrkamp, 1970–1971. The first references to these writings are by volume: page in that edition. The exception is that I cite the Encyclopedia by §§number, with "*A*" indicating Anmerkung and "*Z*" indicating the Zusatz; where helpful I also add after a "/" a citation from *Werke*. I indicate individual works using the abbreviations below. Citations from works not contained in the above edition are from the editions listed below. And I add, after a "/", page references to the translations listed below:

EL: Encyclopaedia Logic, trans. by T. F. Geraets, H. S. Harris, and W. A. Suchting (Indianapolis: Hackett Publishing Co., 1991).

PhG: Phenomenology of Spirit, trans. by by A.V. Miller (Oxford: Oxford University Press, 1977).

PN: Hegel's Philosophy of Nature, trans. by W. Wallace and A. V. Miller (New York: Oxford University Press, 1970).

PP: The Philosophical Propaedeutic, ed. by M. George and A. Vincent and trans. by A. V. Miller (Oxford: Blackwell; 1986).

VGP: Lectures on the History of Philosophy, 3 vols., trans. by E. S. Haldane and F. H. Simson (Lincoln: University of Nebraska Press, 1995).

VL: Vorlesungen über die Logik. Berlin 1831. Transcribed by Karl Hegel, ed. by U. Rameil and H.-Chr. Lucas, (Hamburg: Meiner, 2001).

VN: Vorlesung über Naturphilosophie 1821/22. Nachschr. von Boris yon Uexküll, hrsg. vyon Giles Marasse und Thomas Posch (Wien: Lang, 2002).

VPA: Aesthetics: Lectures on Fine Art, 3 vols., trans. by T. M. Knox, (Oxford: Clarendon Press, 1975).

VPN: Vorlesungen über die Philosophie der Natur: Berlin 1819/20, nachgeschr. Von Johann Rudolf Ringier, hHrsg. von Martin Bondeli und Hoo Nam Seelmann. 2002 (Hamburg: Meiner, 2002).

VPR: Lectures on the Philosophy of Religion, 3 vols., trans. by Rev. E. B. Speirs, and J. Burdon Sanderson. (New York: Humanities Press, Inc., 1974.)

WL: Hegel's Science of Logic, trans. by A. V. Miller (London: George Allen & Unwin, 1969).

of living beings; Hegel responds that Kant should instead defend such explanation – and that the defense of teleology should have led Kant to different conclusions throughout his theoretical philosophy.

To be sure, Kant's view is not entirely skeptical. Kant actually argues that we necessarily conceive of living beings in irreducibly teleological terms. But we cannot know that living beings themselves truly satisfy the implications of teleological judgment. We cannot know whether teleology truly explains anything in biological cases. And this skepticism requires Kant to carefully limit his positive claims about teleology: it is subjectively necessary we conceive of living beings in teleological terms, and this conception is legitimate when employed not as an explanation but as a heuristic aid for scientific inquiry.[2]

Hegel's response in his *Science of Logic* and *Encyclopedia* is by no means entirely critical.[3] Hegel frequently praises a distinction central to Kant's analysis of teleology – the distinction between "external" and "inner purposiveness" [*innere Zweckmäßigkeit*]. On the one hand, there is the concept of a complex system, like a pocket watch with many parts, which satisfies the implications of teleological judgment in virtue of the work of a separate or external intelligent designer. Here the parts of the system are means to the external ends or purposes [*Zwecke*] of a designer (e.g., reliable indication of the time). On the other hand, we can conceive of another way in which a system might satisfy the implications of teleological judgment – not in virtue of external design but in virtue of its own inner nature. Here the parts would be means to a system's own *inner* ends or purposes. Kant argues that the latter concept of "inner purposiveness" is logically consistent and meaningful. And that it is understandable and heuristically useful for us to conceive of real living beings in this way. Hegel finds Kant's analysis here to be of great philosophical importance – for philosophy generally and not

---

KANT: All references to Kant's writings are given by volume and page number of the Akademie edition of Kant's *Gesammelte Schriften* (Berlin: de Gruyter, 1902–). *KU: Critique of the Power of Judgment*, trans. by P. Guyer and E. Mathews (Cambridge, UK: Cambridge University Press, 2000). German text from volume 5 of *Gesammelte Schriften* for the published version of the book, and from volume 20 for the "first introduction."

[2] For example, Kant aims to justify "a heuristic principle for researching the particular laws of nature, even granted that we would want to make no use of it for explaining nature itself" (*KU*, 5:410). Kant consistently denies that he is justifying teleological *explanation*; see also *KU*, 5:360 and *KU*, 5:417.

[3] My main focus is the argument of the "Life" section in both the book version of the *Wissenschaft der Logik* (*WL*) and the first part of Hegel's *Encyclopedia* (*EL*). I will also draw from other texts, mostly limiting myself to those written after the (1807) *Phenomenology of Spirit*.

just for philosophical issues concerning life. In Hegel's terms, "with this concept of inner purposiveness, Kant has resuscitated the idea in general and especially the idea of life."[4] And Hegel will rarely pass up the chance to dismiss and even ridicule the idea of conceiving living beings or nature in terms of external purposiveness, as in an artifact; Hegel sees such claims as a distraction from the important philosophical issues, and an invitation to popular superstitions or to triviality, as in the suggestion that God "has provided cork-trees for bottle stoppers."[5]

But Hegel draws on Kant's concepts to argue against Kant's own skeptical insistence that there are philosophical barriers blocking our knowledge of natural teleology: Hegel argues that living beings do manifest true "internal purposiveness," that their structure and development is explicable in teleological terms, and that we can have objective knowledge of this natural teleology – and of its broader metaphysical implications. So Kant should not, Hegel says, have been satisfied in investigating whether the application of teleology to nature provides "mere maxims of a subjective cognition." Speaking of "the end relation," Hegel says, "on the contrary, it is the absolute truth that judges objectively and determines external objectivity absolutely" (WL, 6:444/739).

It is worth noting that subsequent developments in the biological sciences have not resolved the status of teleology in biology. To be sure, it has sometimes been popular to hold that teleological language in modern biology can be only a *façon de parler*, perhaps best replaced by a substitute like "teleonomy." But those not attending to philosophy of biology of the last thirty years or so might not realize that it is now also popular, perhaps more so, to defend teleology. There are skeptics who see these defenses as misunderstanding natural selection, or as covertly replacing rather than defending teleology. But this is to say that debate continues.[6] Some readers may well side with the skeptics, thinking that

---

[4] *EL*, §§204A; see also *EL*, §55A and *WL*, 4:440–1/737.

[5] *PN*, §§245Z, *PN*, 9:14/6. The cork example is a joke borrowed from Goethe and Schiller's *Xenia*. Hegel returns to the example frequently: *EL*, §§205Zu; VPR, 17:520; VGP, 20:23. On "superstition" and external purposiveness see *VGP*, 20:88/3:186.

[6] L. Wright's, *Teleological Explanations: An Etiological Analysis of Goals and Functions* (Berkeley: University of California Press, 1976) and R. G. Millikan's *Language, Thought and other Biological Categories* (Cambridge, MA: MIT Press, 1993), have led to many defenses of teleology within the philosophy of biology. See, for example, K. Neander's, "The Teleological Notion of Function," *Australasian Journal of Philosophy*, 69 (1991), p. 454. Neander comments: "today it is generally accepted" that "the biological notion of a 'proper function' is both teleological and scientifically respectable". And see J. Lennox's short summary of the debate from Plato and Aristotle, through Darwin, and from behaviorism to current defenses of teleology, "Teleology," in *Keywords in Evolutionary Biology*, ed. by Evelyn Fox Keller and Elisabeth Lloyd (Cambridge, MA: MIT Press, 1992). For criticism of the new

any defense of teleology must be somehow scientifically obsolete. It would be fair enough to seek to defend that claim in the contemporary debate, where it would be controversial. But we must not simply assume this claim and then view Hegel through that lens. If we did that, then we will seek to understand him as defending teleology specifically by providing alternatives to contemporary science – perhaps an alternative to the theory of natural selection, or a proposed explanation of the origin of all life. To be sure, by looking in the right places one can find claims in Hegel which conflict with scientific theories we now know to be true. But we must not make assumptions about what role, if any, these claims play in Hegel's argument against Kant in defense of natural teleology.

Instead of looking through the lens of contemporary biology and assumptions about its philosophical implications, we should simply seek to understand Kant and Hegel's philosophical arguments in their own terms. We can then try to understand whether and how those arguments – though scientifically uninformed by our standards – might really bear on the underlying philosophical issues of continuing importance and interest. That, in any case, is what I seek to do here. I think that both Kant and Hegel provide compelling arguments whose real philosophical force is easy to miss. So I do not aim here to decide the issue between them, but to uncover and explain the arguments. I begin with a brief look at Kant's case for his skeptical conclusions, and then consider at greater length Hegel's response and the conclusions it aims to support. I close with a brief discussion of the importance of this topic within Hegel's broader metaphysics.

I. KANT'S ANALYSIS

To begin, we must distinguish two of the endeavors Kant pursues in the *Critique of the Power of Judgment* (hereafter *KU*). Kant seeks to analyze the concept of a complex system which would satisfy the implications of teleological judgment by nature or in virtue of "inner purposiveness," rather than in virtue of the work of an external designer. He seeks to analyze the concept of a *Naturzweck* [natural end or purpose]. Another goal of Kant's is to determine what sorts of reasons we might have,

defenses of teleology, see Robert Cummins, "Functional Analysis," *Journal of Philosophy*, 72 (1975), pp. 741–765 and "Neo-teleology'" in *Functions: New Essays on the Philosophy of Psychology and Biology*, ed. by R. Cummins, M. Perlman, and A. R. Ariew (Oxford: Oxford University Press, 2002), pp. 157–173 and Elliot Sober, "Natural Selection and Distributive Explanation: A Reply to Neander," *British Journal for the Philosophy of Science*, 46 (1995), pp. 384–397.

if any, to conceive of actual living beings as teleological systems by nature.[7]

Kant's analysis consists of two requirements governing the relations, in a complex system, between the parts and the whole. The first condition specifies the conditions under which a complex system will satisfy the implications of teleological judgment, or will be a *Zweck* [end or purpose]. And Kant argues that this will be so only where the parts are means to an overall end realized in the whole. To begin with, this requires that the parts and their organization are such that all this jointly benefits the whole. But it is crucial that mere benefit is not sufficient for teleology. For something might have beneficial consequences for something else merely by coincidence.[8] So Kant's first requirement requires that the presence of jointly beneficial parts is not merely coincidental; such parts must be present because of the way in which they are beneficial in relation to an overall end or purpose realized in the whole. In Kant's terms, "for a thing as a natural purpose [*Naturzweck*] it is requisite, first, that its parts (as far as their existence and their form are concerned) are possible only through their relation to the whole" (*KU*, 5:373).

When it comes to actual living beings, the question raised by the first requirement is not "do the parts and their organization contribute in complex ways to the survival of the whole?" It is empirically obvious that they do. But the important question concerns explanation, namely: Are such beneficial parts present in a living being specifically for the sake of this benefit, or because of an end or *Zweck*?

When it comes to artifacts, we have an obvious reason to answer in the affirmative. For example, are the parts of a watch present specifically because of purposes, or because of the way each contributes to the

---

[7] P. McLaughlin carefully distinguishes Kant's two endeavors here. See his *Kant's Critique of Teleology in Biological Explanation* (Lewiston: Edwin Mellen Press, 1990), pp. 46–47. See also A. Wood, *Kant's Ethical Thought* (Cambridge, UK: Cambridge University Press, 1999), p. 219. I take this to rule out the idea that "*Naturzweck*" is Kant's "expression for biological organisms." See C. Zumbach, *The Transcendent Science. Kant's Conception of Biological* Methodology (The Hague: Nijhoff, 1984), p. 19; J. D. MacFarland, *Kant's Concept of* Teleology (Edinburg: Edinburg University Press, 1970), p. 102; and W. deVries, "The Dialectic of Teleology," *Philosophical Topics*, 19 (1991), pp. 51–53. We must distinguish the concept of a *Naturzweck* from the empirical concepts such as *living being* and *organism* in order to make sense of Kant's denial of the possibility of knowledge that living beings are *Naturzwecke*.

[8] To take Kant's example, a receding sea might benefit a forest growing on the shore; this need not mean that the sea recedes *for the sake of* the forest, or *because* of any benefit or any end or purpose at all. Note Kant's own emphasis of the "because" (*darum* and *weil*) in discussing this issue. In Kant's terms, such "relative purposiveness" "justifies no absolute teleological judgments" (*KU*, 5:369).

further end of the whole reliably indicating the time? Yes; a designer has selected each part for that very reason. In virtue of the designer's work, such cases satisfy the explanatory implications of teleological judgment – the structure of the whole, and how that structure came about, can be explained by ends or purposes.

Kant wants to argue that there is, at least in principle, room for another kind of "in virtue of" here, another way in which the explanatory implications could be satisfied. There is room for a meaningful concept of a system that is teleological (is a "*Zweck*" or end or purpose) not in virtue of external design but by nature, or in virtue of "inner purposiveness."[9] This is the concept of a *Naturzweck*. To complete his analysis of this concept, Kant needs a second requirement which will exclude the merely "external purposiveness" of artifacts, leaving only "inner purposiveness." The intuition behind Kant's strategy is clear enough: the parts of artifacts are means to an end only insofar as the overall structure or organization has been imposed; a *Naturzweck*, by contrast, would have to "self-organizing" (*KU*, 5:374). Kant seeks to formulate this as a requirement, like the first, governing part–whole relations. Framed in this way, it would have to require that the structure or organization of the whole is determined not by something else but by the parts themselves. But for a part to contribute to the determination of the structure would be to contribute toward determining what other kinds of parts are present and their arrangement. So for a *Naturzweck*, it is required "second, that its parts be combined into a whole by being reciprocally the cause and effect of their form" (*KU*, 5:373).

II. NATURAL TELEOLOGY IS "PROBLEMATIC"

With respect to this concept of a *Naturzweck*, Kant seeks to argue for a complex and balanced conclusion: On the one hand, the concept is logically consistent, and conceiving living beings in these terms is heuristically useful. On the other hand, we can never know that anything real actually satisfies that concept.

Kant will argue against the possibility of knowledge by applying what we now often call the 'backwards causation problem' to his own requirement that the existence and form of the parts of a teleological system

---

[9] Clearly, then, Kant does not use teleological notions – for example, the term "*Zweck*," sometimes translated as "purpose" – so that they are supposed *merely by definition* to require external intelligent design. He is interested neither in ordinary usage nor in stipulating here but in the philosophical question of whether parts can be present *for the sake of* a whole, or *because* of an end, without this being due to external intelligent design.

must depend on their relation to the whole.[10] A part of a system can have beneficial consequences for the whole only once it is already present along with the other parts. So these beneficial consequences cannot have any influence over the process, entirely prior in time, by which the part originally came to be present – this would be akin to something reaching back in time and causing its own cause. In Kant's terms, "it is entirely contrary to the nature of physical-mechanical causes that the whole should be the cause of the possibility of the causality of the parts" (*KU*, 20:236). The only exception would be if the system originates in a prior concept of the whole – a concept dictating the ways in which each part is to contribute along with the others. So Kant's first condition – the parts depend on their relations to the whole – can only be met where there is "a concept or an idea that must determine a priori everything that is to be contained in it" (*KU*, 5:373).

Interpreters of both Kant and Hegel sometimes miss the strength of Kant's argument here. Some see Kant as worried about how an end or telos could be an efficient cause, and reply that we should instead entirely distinguish teleology from explanation in terms of efficient causes, so that we can then say that both legitimately and independently explain, perhaps insofar as each addresses distinct explanatory interests or practices of our own.[11] As far as I can see, this line of thought does not address the considerations introduced by Kant. True, different kinds of explanation might explain in context of different interests or practices.

---

[10] See also Kant's consideration of the house example: in the order of "real causes," an end or purpose (*Zweck*) cannot precede and thereby influence its own causes, so it can do so only as "ideal," or as first represented (*KU*, 5:372). MacFarland, *Kant's Concept of Teleology*, stresses the backwards causation problem (1970, p. 106), but the argument is stronger than he recognizes there. See also R. Zuckert, "Purposiveness Time and Unity: A Reading of the *Critique of Judgment*" (Chicago: Ph.D. dissertation, 2000), ch. 2 and Guyer, "Organisms and the Unity of Science,"in *Kant and the Sciences*, ed. by Eric Watkins (Oxford: Oxford University Press, 2001), p. 265.

[11] The first steps of this response are suggested in deVries's account of Hegel's response to Kant: The problem with Kant's "model" – on which teleology requires prior representation of a concept – is that it "reduces final causation to the form of efficient causation." See his "Dialectic of Teleology," p. 56. By contrast, "the ancients saw no problem about the status of teleological judgments or explanations. Final causes were one of the four Aristotelian "becauses," so questions about teleology were always in order in the Aristotelian system" (p. 52) – and Hegel follows them (p. 54). I argue that Kant's argument is not so easily dismissed, so that Hegel requires (and seeks in Aristotle) a line of argument which addresses Kant's argument more directly. Contrast also Zumbach's claim that Kant can be read as *defending* a kind of teleological explanation, and that Kant does not put the point this way because of his narrow conceptions of *causality* and *explanation*. See his *Transcendent Science*, pp. 95–97, 123.

On the face of it, however, explanation is also constrained by what is really going on in the world. If X plays no role in determining or influencing Y, then no appeal to X can legitimately explain Y, no matter what your interests and practices might be. For example, if the movements of the stars which make up the constellation Sagittarius have no real influence on my current mood, then it is simply a mistake for anyone to explain the later by appeal to the former.[12] But it is hard to comprehend how any kind of determining or influencing (whether we think of this as causal or otherwise) could operate backwards in time. So it certainly seems legitimate for Kant to worry about how an end or a *Zweck* realized in a whole system could possibly play any real role in determining or influencing the entirely prior process by which the structure first came to be present in that system.

Other interpreters worry that Kant here seeks to defend teleological explanation of living beings in a scientifically outdated manner.[13] But, first, the point does not directly concern actual living beings. It is a conceptual point about the very idea of a teleological system (a *Zweck*). And, second, the point is meant as reason to doubt that we can know living beings to be teleological systems. In this case, we can have no knowledge of any originating concept – Kant denies us knowledge of anything like a designer of nature.[14] The argument is similar to the common contemporary claim that a teleological system can only be an artifact – now generally offered as a reason why teleology can have no place in biology at all.[15]

---

[12] When it comes to Hegel's view, compare his limited praise of Bacon's *skepticism* about teleology: Bacon at least helps to counteract the sort of "superstition" which "makes two sensuous things which have no relation operate on one another" (*VGP*, 20:88/3:186). So where an end has no real relation to a process, it would be merely superstitious to apply teleology. Garrett makes this general point in considering early modern considerations of teleology more generally: "a teleological explanation is one that explains a state of affairs by indicating a likely or presumptive consequence (causal, logical, or conventional) of it that is implicated in the state's origin or etiology. . . . No proposed teleological explanation, no matter how appealing or compelling, can be correct unless it cites an actual example of teleology." See his "Teleology in Spinoza and Early Modern Rationalism," in *New Essays on the Rationalists*, ed. by J. Gennaro and C. Huenemann (Oxford: Oxford University Press, 1999), p. 310.

[13] See MacFarland, *Kant's Critique of Teleology*, p. 106.

[14] We cannot have knowledge of "an (intelligent) world cause that acts according to purposes" (*KU*, 5:389; see also *KU*, 5:400 and *KU*, 5:410) Compare especially Descartes' response to Gassendi's first objection to the fourth meditation.

[15] For example, Cummins argues that any notion of function which purports to explain the presence of the parts of a complex system will apply only to artifacts: "it seems to me that the question, 'why is *x* there?' can be answered by specifying

But what is so interesting and so difficult to grasp here is that Kant's further case also differs crucially from such contemporary skepticism about natural teleology. Kant does not argue that teleological judgment implies that a system is an artifact. He carefully aims to preserve as logically consistent the concept of a system that satisfies teleological judgment, but not in virtue of its being an artifact.

More specifically, Kant argues as follows: A teleological system requires an originating concept. If the purposiveness is to be inner, then the structure of the whole is due to the parts. Putting these requirements together, the parts would have to determine the structure in a manner guided by a concept. But the parts of the real complex systems of which we have empirical knowledge, such as living beings, are ultimately matter. And matter cannot represent concepts or intend to act in accordance with them: "no intention in the strict sense of the term can be attributed to any lifeless matter."[16] So Kant's two requirements have incompatible implications about the origin of a system when applied to a material system: to say that the structure of an exclusively material system is due specifically and entirely to its own parts – to say that it has an origin in "a mechanical kind of generation" – is to deny that any end or purpose [Zweck] plays any role in bringing about or originating that structure.[17] This is why Kant says that "one kind of explanation excludes the other" (KU, 5:412). So, to know that an apparently teleological material system manifests true inner purposiveness would be to know that it was never really a teleological system at all.

But none of this shows that a real Naturzweck is logically impossible. For it is not a logical truth that everything must be such that we can comprehend it and know it. More specifically, problems about backwards causation would not apply to anything nonspatiotemporal. So we cannot rule out on logical grounds the possibility that there is a nonspatiotemporal "supersensible real ground of nature" or a "thing in

---

x's function only if x is or is part of an artifact." See his "Functional Analysis," p. 746.

[16] KU, 5:383. This claim about matter has a surprisingly strong status in Kant. For the concept of matter is supposed to be somehow *empirical* and yet also *a priori*. See especially M. Friedman, "Matter and Motion in the Metaphysical Foundations and the First Critique: The Empirical Concept of Matter and the Categories," in Watkins, *Kant and the Sciences*, pp. 53–69. See also *KU*, 5:394, *Lectures on Metaphysics*, 29:275, and *Metaphysical Foundations of Natural Science*, 4:544.

[17] More specifically, "if we consider a material whole, as far as its form is concerned, as a product of the parts and of their forces and their capacity to combine by themselves ... we represent a mechanical kind of generation. But from this there arises no concept of a whole as a *Zweck*" (KU, 5:408). The problem here concerns origins; Kant himself refers to "the whole difficulty surrounding the question about the initial generation of a thing that contains purposes in itself" (KU, 5:420).

itself (which is not an appearance) as substratum" which could – unlike matter in space and time – somehow self-organize itself from within, in accordance with a concept, without anything like external design. We cannot comprehend how such self-organization might be possible, but we can conceive of a higher form of intellect – an "intellectual intuition" or an "intuitive understanding" – which might.[18] And this higher intellect might be in a position to say two very different things about real living beings: (i) as material systems in space and time, they are "in accordance with mechanical laws"; and yet (ii) as somehow determined or conditioned by a "supersensible real ground" they are "in accordance with teleological laws" (*KU*, 5:409). We can have neither comprehension here, nor any reason to assert knowledge of any of this. Still, the concept of something that is a teleological system by nature rather than by design is logically consistent. And the possibility that living beings might be such systems "can be conceived without contradiction but cannot be comprehended" (*KU*, 5:371).

In this way Kant opens up the space for positive claims about other uses – aside from the assertion of knowledge or explanation – for the concept of a *Naturzweck*. First, living beings suggest self-organization in various ways: their parts mutually compensate for one another, they incorporate matter in order to grow, and they generate new living beings by reproduction (*KU*, 5:371-2). For this and other reasons, Kant will hold that our experience "exhibits" but nonetheless cannot "prove" the existence of real *Naturzwecke* (*KU*, 20:234). Second, Kant will argue that thinking of living beings in such teleological terms provides us with an indispensable heuristic aid, and that we would have no hope of gaining any scientific understanding of living beings without this aid; Kant even argues that we must for simliar reasons judge nature itself as if it were a *Naturzweck*.[19]

---

[18] More specifically, our merely "discursive" understanding is dependent on sensibility, and the forms of all our sensible intuition are space and time. The further knowledge would require an "understanding which is not discursive but intuitive because it goes from the synthetically universal (of the intuition of a whole as such) to the particular, that is, from the whole to the parts" (*KU*, 5:406) Note that, strictly speaking, what is logically possible is that there might be a system which satisfies the implications of teleological judgment *in virtue of its own inner nature*. But if we take "nature" to mean *empirical* reality in space and time, or *material* reality, then Kant has *not* preserved even the logical possibility of an entirely "natural" end or purpose.

[19] With regard to living beings, see Kant's famous denial of the possibility of a Newton for a blade of grass. Note that Kant carefully makes this claim relative to what it is possible for "humans" to "grasp," while leaving *open* the possibility that living beings really originate in "mere mechanism" (*KU*, 5:400). With regard to nature as a whole, see the arguments of the published and unpublished introductions.

But what is most important for our purposes is Kant's skeptical conclusion: we cannot comprehend how both requirements could be jointly met, so we cannot have knowledge that living beings are true *Naturzwecke*, or knowledge that teleology truly explains the structure and development of living beings. In Kant's terms, the concept of a *Naturzweck* is "problematic": when employing it "one does not know whether one is judging about something or nothing" (*KU*, 5:397).[20]

III. HEGEL'S AIMS

It is worth briefly clarifying Hegel's aims by contrasting some readily apparent routes by which one might seek to challenge Kant's skeptical conclusion. To begin with, Hegel is under no illusions that one can defend teleology in response to Kant merely by pointing out that it is a distinct and different form of explanation – whether different from mechanism, efficient causality, and so forth. Teleology and mechanism cannot be shown to be mutually "indifferent" and equally valid simply by noting that they differ: "if mechanism and purposiveness stand opposed to one another, they cannot for that very reason be taken as indifferent concepts, each of which is correct on its own account, possessing as much validity as they other." Nor does an "equal validity" of both follow "because we have them both" (*WL*, 6:437/735). At issue, then, is not whether we have an interest in explaining living beings in teleological terms, but whether such explanation can be valid. And Hegel recognizes that, at least from the point of view of a philosophical outlook like Kant's, the possibility of real inner purposiveness is "an incomprehensible mystery" (*WL*,6:473/763). Hegel wants to show that natural teleology is not problematic, and not incomprehensible – not on account of an incompatibility with mechanism, nor for any other reason. But Hegel recognizes the need for an argument that addresses Kant's specific concerns.

Some contemporary readers might be attracted to the idea that the notion of "function" of use in biology carries no implications about origins at all, and so none that could generate any mystery by conflicting with mechanism. But this kind of contemporary approach aims to get rid of teleological notions (and is vulnerable to attacks by contemporary defenses of teleology). To say that something has a "function" in a sense with no implications about origins – for example, to say that it is part of "teleonomic" system – does not imply that its existence and

---

[20] I stress the importance of this conclusion in my more detailed reading of Kant's argument in "The Inexplicability of Kant's Naturzweck: Kant on Teleology, Explanation and Biology," *Archiv fur Geschichte der Philosophie*, 87 (2005), pp. 270–311.

form is really explained by an end, [*Zweck*], or telos. Kant, by contrast, defends the importance of a concept that does involve teleology in this sense [*Naturzweck*], and Hegel aims to go even further by defending the possibility of knowledge that this concept applies to natural beings.[21]

One might obviously directly refute Kant's case by arguing that matter itself, rather than being constrained or governed by necessary laws, is actually capable of representing concepts and acting in accordance with them. But we will see that this is not Hegel's strategy. Hegel elsewhere takes issue with some of Kant's claims about matter, but he does not defend such panpsychism.[22]

So Hegel's basic goal is to show, without arguing that matter can act intentionally, that we can comprehend the possibility of a *Naturzweck*. Hegel will try to meet this goal by showing, first, that we can comprehend how a living being might satisfy the implications of teleological judgment without thinking of it as the product of an agent representing a concept. And, second, that we can know this purposiveness to be truly inner without knowing anything about the capacities of the underlying constituent matter. And so the inability of matter to represent concepts and act in accordance will no longer prevent our comprehending the possibility that living beings might really be teleological systems in virtue of their own nature.

IV. THE ANALYSIS OF LIFE

Hegel argues this in the *Science of Logic* by means of an analysis of a concept of life. It can be difficult to understand what the point of

---

[21] It is crucial that Kant's strategy is *not* similar to contemporary attempts to replace teleology, for example, with "teleonomy," contra C. Warnke "Naturmechanismus und Naturzweck: Bemerkungen zu Kants Organismus-Begriff," *Deutsche Zeitschrift für Philosophie*, 40 (1992), pp. 42–52, and Düsing 'Naturteleologie und Metaphysik bei Kant und Hegel' in *Hegel und die Kritik der Urteilskraft*, ed. by H.-F. Fulda and R.-P. Horstmann (Stuttgart: Frommann-Holzboog, 1990), p. 142. In contemporary terms, a truly *teleological* notion of "function" would have to be an "etiological" notion – one which carries implications about the factors which determine or cause the presence of the parts of a complex system; the point tends to be agreed by those who defend *and* those who criticize the scientific status of such teleological notions. Those who defend teleology argue that nonteleological notions of function, without implications about origins, can be ascribed too broadly (on the basis of any capacity of interest to us, rather than just those for the sake of which a part itself is really present) and yet also not broadly enough (they cannot apply to a part which fails to fulfill its function.)

[22] For Hegel's complaints about Kant on matter and mechanics, see *WL*, 5:200ff./178ff, and *PN*, §§262An. See also Beiser's denial that Hegel's defense of teleology is pansychist, *Hegel* (London: Routledge, 2005), pp. 101–102.

the analysis is. It is not an attempt to give an a priori logical deduction of the features real living beings must have.[23] Nor is it a direct replacement for or competitor to Kant's analysis of the concept of a *Naturzweck*. Nor is Hegel seeking merely to reflect on our conceptual scheme in order to analyze our ordinary concept of life or living being. The analysis must be understood as a theoretical tool, or in terms of what Hegel seeks to do with it – in terms of how he will use it to argue that we can comprehend the possibility of a system with true inner purposiveness. But the best way to follow Hegel is initially to set aside questions about how the larger argument functions, and attend first just to the content of the analysis, or the content of Hegel's concept of life.

Hegel's analysis, and the crux of his philosophical response to Kant on teleology and biology, is found in a section called "Life" in both versions of the Logic. The analysis also provides the structure for Hegel's discussions of plant and animal biology in the Philosophy of Nature and elsewhere. In all of Hegel's treatments, the analysis has three requirements.

The first requirement mirrors Kant's analysis in terms of the relations between part and whole: "all the members are reciprocally momentary means as well as momentary ends."[24] Hegel puts the point more directly elsewhere: "the organs are the means of life, and these very means, the organs themselves, are also the element in which life realizes and maintains itself . . . this is self-preservation."[25]

But Hegel's concept of life also demands that a complex system itself requires some kind of assimilation from the outside environment in order to grow and preserve itself. In Hegel's terms: "in and through this process against an inorganic nature, it maintains itself, develops itself and objectifies itself" (*EL*, §219). Alternatively, it must be engaged in a "struggle with the outer world" (*PN*, §365Z).

Third, Hegel's concept of life also requires that individuals must be mortal, and must aim for the reproduction (e.g., sexual reproduction) by which a species endures.[26] So anything satisfying Hegel's concept must also pursue self-preservation in an additional sense: it must aim to

---

[23] For example, "it is quite improper" to try to "deduce" the "contingent products of nature" (*PN*, §§250).

[24] *EL*, §§216. See Kant's similar formulation at *KU*, 5:375, to which Hegel refers at *EL*, §§57. In Hegel, see also *WL*, 2:420/766–767; *PN*, §§352; *PN*, §356.

[25] Similarly, "the one exists only through the other and for the other, and all the members and component parts of men are simply means for the self-preservation of the individual which is here the end" (*VPR*, 17:503/330).

[26] On mortality specifically, see *EL*, §221, *WL*, 6:486/774, *PN*, §§375f., *VL*, 213, and *VPN*, 184.

reproduce itself – it "produces itself as another individual of the same species" (PP, 4:32/142). And survival of the species requires that self-preservation in this latter sense dominates: "the end of the animal in itself as an individual is its own self-preservation; but its true end in itself is the species."[27] In Hegel's terms, the third requirement demands the "process of the *Gattung*" [genus, kind or species] or the *Gattungsprozess*.[28] (Hegel's term *Gattung* – usually translated as "genus" – can seem to suggest the idea that there is a perfect hierarchical classification system defined by clear necessary and sufficient conditions for different categories; Hegel's analysis does not require that claim, and he elsewhere denies it.[29] The requirements of the analysis alone fix the meaning of *Gattung* here: it refers to a general kind within which individuals reproduce, generating more individuals of the same kind. I will generally use "species" to refer to this idea.)[30]

Hegel's three requirements are interrelated in several ways. For example, the first governs internal structure. But combining this with the second and third requirements will generate additional demands on structure: if the parts are to be mutually beneficial, then they will have to be organized in a manner that realizes the capacities, or makes possible the activities, required for assimilation and reproduction.[31] It makes sense, then, for Hegel to say elsewhere that life requires a "system of activities which is actualized into a system of organs through which those activities proceed" so that "in this way the living thing is articulated purposefully; all its members serve only as means to the one end of self-preservation" (VPA, 13:193/1:145).

Finally, note that the structure of Hegel's analysis of the concept of life differs greatly from Kant's analysis of the concept of a *Naturzweck*. Kant's analysis itself consists entirely of two requirements governing

---

[27] VGP, 20:87; VGP, 3:185. Also on the way in which the end of preservation of the species trumps preservation of the individual, see EL, §§221 and WL, 6:484/773–774.

[28] For example, WL, 6:486/774; EL §221; PN §367ff; VL, 213.

[29] Biology does not allow "an independent, rational system of organization" (PN, §§370) Life "in its differentiating process does not actually posses any rational ordering and arrangement of parts, and is not an immanently grounded system of shapes" (PhG, 178–179, 224–225). See also VN, 199. And "naturally there are also animals which are intermediate forms" (PN, §368Z).

[30] "Species" is the best translation, for example, where Hegel refers to the propagation of the "species" or "*die Fortpflanzung der Gattung*" (PN, §§365Z/9:492). I will continue to *also* use "kind" and *Gattung* because it is important that Hegel uses the same term for natural kinds, as in chemical kinds: for example, "the universal essence, the real kind (*Gattung*) of the particular object" (WL, 6:430/728).

[31] On these capacities, see EL, §218Z; PN, §344Z, §§354–358).

specifically part-whole relations within a complex system.[32] He recognizes assimilation and reproduction. But he argues that the general philosophical problem concerning natural teleology is independent of these specific ways in which our experience of real living beings happens to suggest the self-organization of a *Naturzweck*. Hegel's analysis of life is more complex: It also demands a specific relationship between the whole and the outside environment and between the whole and other wholes of the same general kind or species. In itself, simplicity would be a philosophical advantage – unless Hegel can show that these additional features are relevant to, and in fact resolve, Kant's general philosophical problem concerning natural teleology.

V. COMPREHENDING THE ORIGIN OF A NATURZWECK

This being Hegel, it is too much to hope for an immediately and easily transparent statement of how the argument of the "Life" section in the Logic is supposed to work. But I think we can see the answer clearly enough by considering how Hegel's analysis specifically relates to Kant's argument, and then working our way toward progressively better understandings of Hegel's initially opaque terminology. To begin with, it is the origin or genesis of a *Naturzweck* – we cannot comprehend how any origin could satisfy both of Kant's requirements. And Hegel's analysis of life does conspicuously address the topic of origins: the analysis requires reproduction, or "the generation of individuality" (*WL*, 6:486/774). The first question is, then, why should it be possible for a complex system to satisfy the implications of teleological judgment in virtue of this kind of origin, without requiring an originating representation of the whole?

To begin with, Hegel's analysis adds a distinction between something particular and something general or universal – between individuals and their general species or kind. Distinct individuals – parent(s) and offspring – are (though in many ways different) identical in one respect: they are the same in species or kind (*Gattung*). So there is a sense in which, in reproducing, an individual produces not something else but rather "produces itself as another individual of the same species" (*PP*, 4:32/142). Furthermore, the general structure of the offspring will generally be identical and determined by the parent(s); for example, "through the male and female natures, there emerges a determination of the entire structure" (*PN*, §365Z, 9:459/377). And now we can see

---

[32] "All determinations of the concept of natural purpose that Kant introduces have to do with the relation of part and whole." See McLaughlin, "Kant's Critique of Teleology," p. 50.

how the general structure of a new organism precedes its development –
not in the form or an intelligent designer's representation, but in the
structure shared by the parent(s) and previous generations of the same
species.

How does this help with teleology? Consider the question in terms of
parts and whole, following Kant's analysis. Take as an example a tiger –
I will call him Hobbes – and his claws. On Kant's account, the problem
is this: how can the beneficial consequences of Hobbes's claws, once
present in Hobbes, have any influence over the process, entirely prior in
time, by which these very claws first came to be present in Hobbes? That
is indeed problematic. But Hegel's analysis reconceives the problem. If
different individuals are the same in structure, then they will have the
same general kinds of parts or features – or "members," in the Hegelian
terms we will come to below. The general kinds of parts of living beings –
for example, claws, heart, lungs – have beneficial consequences for
wholes of the species generally. For example, "the teeth, claws, and
the like . . . it is through these that the animal establishes and preserves
itself as an independent existence" (*PN*, §368A). Kant's problem will
now look very different; the question is now: how can the beneficial
consequences of a general kind of part possibly have influence over how
a new instance of that same general kind of part came to exist within
this new individual? This is no longer so problematic. Hobbes's claws
will be a benefit to him. And, crucially, this is no coincidence: this
general feature or "member" contributes to assimilation and so to the
survival of tigers generally; and this general benefit has already helped to
make possible the survival of previous tigers, and so also the production
of Hobbes and his claws. More generally, a new individual and its new
parts are possible only insofar as parts of that general kind are beneficial
in relation to wholes of the same general kind. So the new individual
meets Kant's demand that, in a teleological system the "parts (as far as
their existence and their form are concerned) are possible only through
their relation to the whole" (*KU*, 5:373). And we can comprehend in this
way how a complex system might be throughout all its parts, "means
and the instrument of the end" (*WL*, 6:476/766). Or, more specifically,
might be such that "all its members serve only as means to the one end
of self-preservation" (*VPA*, 13:193/1:145).

Some may feel that true teleology is somehow eliminated or reduced
in an account of this sort. To be sure, intelligent design (as with artifacts)
is missing; but it is clearly Hegel's goal to show that Kant's analysis of
teleology can be met without this, or without external purposiveness.
More generally, Hegel specifically seeks to do without the requirement
for an originating representation (whether this is supposed to be on

the part of a separate designer, or whether matter itself is imagined to represent a goal and organize itself in accordance).[33]

And this is no defense of teleological explanation of the historical development of a species. But the *Logic* analysis of "life" makes no special requirements about how or even whether a biological species originates or develops in time at all. It does not rule in or out any stand on this topic. By not mentioning any of this, it treats the topic as an empirical matter not relevant to the resolution of the general philosophical problem concerning how teleology might explain the structure and development of a complex system such as an individual organism.[34] (Of course, Hegel elsewhere insists that "spirit" (*Geist*), or sometimes "self-consciousness," does develop progressively over time; but this is a distinct topic.)

One might certainly worry that the account sketched so far cannot render comprehensible genuine self-organization or true inner purposiveness. For Hegel's account does nothing to explain how we could get from mere matter alone to an organized living being, capable of assimilation and reproduction. But this is not itself the precise problem at issue between Kant and Hegel. To begin with, Kant does not hold that we cannot have knowledge of the existence of anything which we cannot explain in terms of matter and its laws; Kant allows knowledge of the existence of living beings which assimilate and reproduce, even though he thinks we lack such explanatory insight here.[35] Kant's problem is focused more directly on the concept of a *Naturzweck*. For the inner purposiveness of a *Naturzweck*, the structure of the whole would have to be due to the parts. This is why Kant sees questions about matter as relevant: to know that the structure of a material system is due to its parts we would have to know how its structure can and does emerge entirely from the law-governed behavior of the underlying matter. But to know this would be to know that this system does not have the kind of origin required for a teleological system at all.

One way to challenge Kant's conclusion here would be to offer an explanation of how matter alone might generate a genuinely

---

[33] And this leads Hegel to limited praise of the most famous *critics* of natural teleology: with the Stoics, "all external, teleological superstition is taken under their protection and justified," and Epicurianism (though wrong about natural teleology) at least "proceeds towards the liberation of men from this superstition" (*VGP*, 19:267/2:248). Hegel also compares the way in which Bacon's criticisms of natural teleology at least help to counter modern superstitions (*VGP*, 20:87/3:185).

[34] Compare: Kant's analysis treats the phenomena of assimilation and reproduction as real but irrelevant to the general problem concerning the concept of a *Naturzweck*. This is obviously not to say that Kant denies the reality of those phenomena.

[35] See, for example, the famous blade of grass claim is at *KU*, 5:400.

teleological system. If we think that this is Hegel's way, then we will try to understand him as responding to Kant on grounds of some scientific theory of epigenesis, or vital forces, or something of the like. But the "Life" section of the Logic proposes nothing of the sort. Instead, Hegel argues that whether or not the structure of the whole depends on the parts, in the sense required for inner purposiveness, need not have anything at all to do directly with the capacities specific to the lowest-level underlying constituent stuff or matter. The key here is again the connection between the particular and the general or universal, so that parent(s) and offspring are the same in species and in structure. The general idea is just that a new individual is self-organizing insofar as its structure is due to its own nature, in the sense of its species [*Gattung*]. To see the point, consider again the general kinds of parts or "members" present in parent(s) and offspring. It is the contribution of such parts in previous generations which makes possible the generation of a new individual with the same structure. So the structure of the new organism is not determined by something else or something other – the structure of the whole is due to the parts, in the sense of the general kinds of parts present within it.[36] In Hegel's terms (to which I will return below) living beings satisfy the requirements of inner purposiveness not in virtue of the relation between the whole and the mutually external material "parts" in space, but in virtue of the relation between the whole and the general kinds of parts or "members" (*WL*, 6:476/766). In this way, Hegel's analysis suggests that the specific nature of the lowest-level underlying material is irrelevant to the general question of whether or not something manifests true inner purposiveness.

Strictly speaking, it remains for Hegel to argue in the *Philosophy of Nature* that our empirical knowledge of plant and animal biology fits the analysis of life. But the main point here will be uncontroversial – after all, there are living beings, and they do assimilate and reproduce. The philosophical heavy lifting comes in the *Logic* argument for a conceptual conclusion: the concept of something that is a teleological system by nature or by virtue of inner purposiveness is not problematic; if we know something to satisfy Hegel's analysis, then we know it to be a *Naturzweck*.

---

[36] Or consider Kant's official formulation – the demand that the "parts be combined into a whole by being reciprocally the cause and effect of their form" (*KU*, 5:373). Take the tiger for example: one feature (like the claws) contributes toward making possible the generation of a new tiger with many different features (like lungs, legs, etc.); all those other features also contribute toward making possible the generation of a new tiger with claws. So the claws as a general feature of tigers contributes to causing all the parts of our new tiger; and the other general features of tigers also contribute to causing the claws in our new tiger.

VI. IMMEDIACY, THE CONCEPT, AND ARISTOTLE'S INFLUENCE

I turn now to consider some of the distinctive ways in which Hegel presents his case and his conclusions. To begin with, we must attend to the way in which Hegel presents the three parts of the "Life" section of the Logic not as an articulation of three merely stipulated requirements of a concept of life, but as three steps of a unified course of argument. To do so, we must follow his use of the term "immediate" there. Initially, Hegel's analysis governs only part-whole relations or "the process of the living being inside itself" (*EL*, §217). Here Hegel is arguing that an analysis governing only part-whole relations within a system, such as Kant's, would indeed make the genesis or origin of inner purposiveness into a mystery. In Hegel's terms, there can be here no mediation through which we could either comprehend this possibility; the first step concerns only a "first, immediate individuality" (*WL*, 6:437/764). Or, at this point, an assertion that there is something that is a teleological system by nature could only be an immediate "presupposition" which is impossible to make good. But this begins to change once we move toward Hegel's analysis of what he calls "the universal concept of life." So once Hegel concludes his second step, and begins to introduce the third, he looks back on the first step and says that "the living individual, at first disengaged from the universal concept of life, is a presupposition that is not as yet authenticated by the living individual itself." But now, given Hegel's account, "its genesis, which was an act of presupposing, now becomes its production" (*WL*, 6:484/772–773). The conclusion of the argument is this: only by focusing on assimilation and reproduction can we comprehend the possibility of the origin of something that would be a teleological system by nature. In Hegel's terms, the significance of the third requirement and the completed analysis is that "the living individual, which was at first presupposed as immediate, is now seen to be mediated and generated" (*EL*, §221).

And we cannot understand Hegel's presentation of his conclusions about teleology and biology without attending to his use of the term "the concept" [*der Begriff*]. Hegel argues that there can be a teleological system without need of an originating representation the whole. So Hegel naturally seems to be challenging Kant's claim that there can be a teleological system only where there is an originating concept of the whole. But part of the reason that Hegel accords such broad philosophical significance to the topic of teleology and biology is that he sees his argument differently here. Hegel takes himself to be accepting Kant's demand for an originating concept, while showing that this demand can be met by something unlike a "concept" in any ordinary sense of that term. It can be met by what Hegel calls "the concept" [*der Begriff*]. More specifically, in biological cases "the concept" is the kind or species [*Gattung*]. It makes sense to use the term "concept" here insofar as the *Gattung* is something general or universal – insofar as there are multiple instances of one and the same kind. But "the concept" in this sense is in no way dependent on its being represented by an agent. Nor is it dependent on its somehow containing representations of necessary and sufficient conditions of its application, or (as in Kant's account of concepts) containing "marks." Individuals of a given kind distinguish themselves from everything else in their struggle to survive: "the animal establishes and preserves itself as an independent existence, that is, distinguishes itself from others" (*PN*, §368A). And such individuals bind themselves together as instances of one and the same general kind by relations of reproduction, so that the "product" of this process is "the realized species (*Gattung*), which has posited itself identical with the concept (*der Begriff*)" (*WL*, 6:486/774). Clearly the *Gattung* here is not a "concept" in any ordinary sense, or any sense in which one might say that it is "only a concept" of ours; it is rather what Hegel sometimes calls an "objective concept."[37]

The general question at issue here is this: Are concepts of the different biological species only abstractions of ours, or are the species themselves independently real and explanatorily important features of the world? This is still debated in today's extremely complex disputes about the nature of a biological species, so we must not assume without further investigation that Hegel's answer is scientifically obsolete.[38]

[37] On "only a concept," see, for example, *WL*, 6:258/587. On "objective concept," see, for example, *WL*, 6:271/597.

[38] On the contemporary debate, see especially E. Sober, "Evolution, Population Thinking, and Essentialism," *Philosophy of Science*, 47 (1980), pp. 350–383. He takes issue with Mayr's claim that "only the individuals of which the population are composed have reality" (pp. 351–352). Sober also points out that neither temporal changes nor diversity of individuals nor vague boundaries suffice to refute "essentialism" – though Sober thinks that there is something else wrong with that view. But issues concerning "essentialism" are complicated, in part because there is no agreement about what that view involves. And the issues concerning the biological species are complex, in part because it is also popular to hold that a species is an *individual*. But this does not necessarily rule out something like Millikan's treatment of biological species as "real kinds" as opposed to "nominal kinds." See R. G. Millikan, "Historical Kinds and the Special Sciences,"*Philosophical Studies*, 95 (1999) pp. 45–65. Finally, contemporary defenses of teleology generally require treating the general *traits* of a general *species* as real and explanatorily important features of the world; for example, Millikan's definition of function refers to "traits having been causally efficacious." See "White Queen Psychology and Other Essays for Alice," (Cambridge, MA: MIT Press, 1993), p. 41.

Furthermore, Hegel's defense of natural teleology does not rest on the mere assumption of a sweeping metaphysical claim – such as the claim that there is a perfectly knowable "absolute" of some kind, or that reality must somehow be completely transparent to or identical with thinking, and so forth.[39] On the contrary, further consideration of Kant's analysis of inner purposiveness is so important because it is supposed to provide philosophical support for Hegel's metaphysics. To begin with, attention to self-preservation and reproduction is supposed to demonstrate something about "the concept," or show us a philosophically interesting way in which something general or universal – a species or kind [Gattung] – can have an effective impact within the world without being represented.

And it is easy to see that Hegel's general claim about "the concept" is indeed essential to his defense of natural teleology. The basic ideas are these: the structure of a new individual is prior in time, not in a representation but in the general species or "the concept"; and the new organism is not the product of something entirely other or external because it is determined by this general nature, species, or "concept" shared with previous generations. Hegel puts the point directly: "since the concept [der Begriff] is immanent in it, the purposiveness of the living being is to be grasped as inner" (WL, 6:476/766). Similarly, a philosophical view like Kant's must see the possibility of real inner purposiveness as an "incomprehensible mystery" specifically "because it does not grasp the concept, and the concept as the substance of life."[40]

Hegel's presentation is also influenced by his view that his basic ideas are present in Aristotle.[41] First of all, on Hegel's account, Aristotle recognizes and resolves the backwards causation problem. It is at least easy to see how one could read Aristotle in this way. Aristotle says that final, formal, and efficient causes can be "one and the same" in natural cases. How can the efficient cause which begins a process of

---

[39] At least when it comes to the topic of inner purposiveness, Hegel's criticism of Kant does not fail to be "immanent" by requiring some such assumption. Contrast K. Düsing, "Das Problem der Subjektivität in Hegels Logik," Hegel-Studien. Beiheft 15 (Bonn: Meiner, 1976), p. 119 and P. Guyer, "Thought and Being: Hegel's Critique of Kant's Theoretical Philosophy", in The Cambridge Companion to Hegel, ed. by Frederick Beiser (Cambridge, UK: Cambridge University Press, 1993).

[40] Or, more specifically still, because such views treat concepts as representations – as "the formal concept" (WL, 6:472–473/763), or what Hegel elsewhere calls "the subjective or formal concept" (EL, §§162).

[41] Kant's advance in conceptualizing inner purposiveness is really supposed to be a "resuscitation" of Aristotle's insights (EL, §§204A), better developed by Aristotle insofar as they are free of Kant's limitation of teleology to a merely subjective status (VGP, 19:177/160).

development be the same as the form of the developed organism which is the end of that process? Because the same form was already present in the parents: "That from which the change originates is the same in form as these. Thus a man gives birth to a man."[42] Note Hegel's gloss on this point from his lectures on Aristotle:

That which is produced is as such in the ground, that is, it is an end (*Zweck*), kind (*Gattung*) in itself, it is by the same token prior, before it becomes actual, as potentiality. Man generates men; what the product is, is also the producer. (*VGP*, 19:176)

And Hegel follows the view he sees in Aristotle: Hegel insists that, when considering teleology, "we must not merely think of the form of the end as it is in us, in conscious beings." We must distinguish the manifestation of "the end" in living beings, where "beginning and end are alike. Self-preservation is a continual production by which nothing new, but always the old, arises" (*VGP*, 18:384/1:333).

As this last passage suggests, Hegel also sees Aristotle as connecting natural teleology closely with the end of self-preservation. Hegel uses as an example the development of a seed "directed solely to self-preservation." This, Hegel says, is Aristotle's "concept of the end as immanent" (*PN*, §245Z/9:14/6). Again, it is not hard to see what Hegel is thinking of in Aristotle. Aristotle identifies (in some sense needing interpretation) "soul" with the characteristic activities for which something is organized. For example, "if the eye were an animal, sight would be its soul."[43] Hegel praises Aristotle for treating "the soul" not "as a thing" but rather in terms of "activity"; but the similarities and differences here are complex and in need of separate discussion.[44] What is important for us is Aristotle's claim that specifically the "nutritive soul" is that "in virtue of which all are said to have life." And the activities of the nutritive soul are assimilation and also self-preservation in the sense of reproduction: "the acts in which it manifests itself are reproduction and the use of food."[45] Furthermore, Aristotle appeals to the natural

[42] *Physics*, 2.7, 198a. Contrast deVries' account of Hegel: "the ancients saw no problem about the status of teleological judgments or explanations. Final causes were one of the four Aristotelian 'becauses,' so questions about teleology were always in order in the Aristotelian system." See his "The Dialectic of Teleology," *Philosophical Topics*, 19 (1991), pp. 51–70.

[43] *De Anima*, 2.1 412b.

[44] *VGP*, 19:199; *VGP2*:181. For more on Hegel on "the soul" and Aristotle's influence here, see especially deVries, *Hegel's Theory of Mental* Activity (Ithaca: Cornell University Press, 1988) and M. Wolff, *Das Koerper-Seele-Problem: Kommentar zu Hegel, Enzyklopadie (1830)*, §389. (Frankfurt: Klosertmann, 1992).

[45] *De Anima*, 415a.

end of self-preservation, common to all life, in explaining more specific biological capacities. For example, he explains in these terms why self-moving beings have the capacity of sensation: "Every body capable of forward movement would, if unendowed with sensation, perish and fail to reach its end, which is the aim of nature; for how could it obtain nutriment?"[46]

Hegel's basic approach to natural teleology combines this last idea with the idea that parent and offspring are the same in form. To elaborate on Aristotle's last example: Why does an individual self-moving animal have the power of sensation? Because the power of sensation is required by the natural or immanent end (or telos) of self-preservation. If this general kind of animal did not have the power of sensation, then it could not assimilate and survive. In that case, previous generations would not have reproduced. So only insofar as sensation allows self-preservation can there come to be a new individual of the same kind with the same power.[47]

VII. TELEOLOGY AND MECHANISM

Hegel also seeks to follow Aristotle in another respect. Hegel sees Aristotle as defending natural teleology while also holding that matter is governed by necessity, or that "necessity" is also present or active "in natural things." Hegel praises Aristotle's philosophy of nature for defending "two determinations: the conception of end and the conception of necessity" (*VGP*, 19:173/2:156).

To be sure, Hegel does not hold that living beings can be explained in two different ways; they can only be explained in teleological terms. The basic reason is that a living being has by its own nature an intrinsic end or purpose. And it has parts or "members" which are themselves means to the intrinsic end. Neither matter nor chemical substances fit the analysis of life, and neither have intrinsic ends in this sense. So the nature of living beings and their "members" is neither mechanical nor chemical. To be a living being or the "member" of a living being, then, is not

---

[46] *De Anima*, 434a–b. I am borrowing this passage, and this way of making the case for the importance of self-preservation in Aristotle, from Richardson (unpublished, p. 71).

[47] I make no argument as to whether this combination of ideas really is already present in Aristotle. Recent philosophical defenses of elements of Aristotle's account of natural teleology see this combination as present in Aristotle himself. See, for example, Lennox, "Teleology," p. 327; D. J. Furley, 'What kind of cause is Aristotle's final cause?' in *Rationality in Greek Thought* ed. by M. Frede and G. Striker (Oxford: Oxford University Press, 1996), p. 73, and also Richardson's comments on this kind of reading (unpublished, 104f.).

to have a certain material or chemical composition; it rather involves having an intrinsic end. In Hegel's terms, the living being as such does not have, strictly speaking, mutually external "parts" in space; it has "members" present because they are means to an end: "the objectivity of the living being is the organism; it is the means and instrument of the end... in respect of its externality the organism is a manifold, not of parts but of members."[48] And such "members" "are what they are only by and in relation to their unity" – only insofar as they are means to the end of the whole.[49]

This is not to deny the applicability of lower-level forms of mechanical and chemical explanation within the spatiotemporal bounds of a living being. So long as we have no teleological ends or purposes in view, what we explain by this means will not itself be living being as such – nor will it be the "member" of a living beings as such. So Hegel says of the living being that "the mechanical or chemical relationship does not attach to it." He adds, however, that "as externality it is indeed capable of such relationships, but to that extent it is not a living being." Hegel then puts the point in terms of two distinct ways we can "take" or "grasp" an object under investigation: "When the living thing is taken (genommen) as a whole consisting of parts, or as anything operated on by mechanical or chemical causes... it is taken (genommen) as a dead thing." But we can also "grasp" (fassen) it as "living being" in terms of a "purposiveness" that is genuinely "inner" (WL, 2:419/766).

Hegel's favorite example is the process by which assimilated external elements make their way into the blood – afterward, these elements have taken on the intrinsic end of the whole, or become something which is whatever it is only in relation to the whole. This transition cannot be understood in terms of necessitating causes (WL, 6:228/562). But Hegel does not deny that we can apply mechanistic and chemical explanation within the blood stream; what he denies is that this can ever explain blood as such: "blood which has been analyzed into these constituents is no longer living blood" (PN, §365Z; see also EL, §219Z). For to be blood is not to have a certain chemical constitution, but to be a means to mediate ends and thereby to the intrinsic end of self-preservation (e.g. we might say that it is to be a means to the end of distributing oxygen throughout the body, and thereby to self-preservation). More broadly, we can explain the behavior of the substances and reactions found along the way of the broader process of assimilation in "inorganic" terms, in which case their interconnection or organization will be "superfluous." But this does not conflict with the claim that all of these things are

[48] WL, 6:476/766. See also VL, pp. 210–211.
[49] EL, §§216Z; see also WL, 2:419–420/766; PN §350Z.

present, in this particular arrangement, all for the sake of an end: "but still the course of organic being in itself occurs for its own sake, in order to be movement and thus actuality" (*PN*, §365Z/9:485).

Some may worry that the applicability of lower-level explanations to all matter should exclude the possibility of teleological explanation of anything. This topic is important, but I will not pursue it further here. For unlike Kant's worries arising from the backwards causation problem, such exclusion problems do not specifically concern the problem of teleology without design. If exclusion is a problem, then it will also threaten design. If exclusion is a problem, then it will threaten all higher-level teleological explanation of our actions in terms of our representations of ends or goals.[50]

Finally, Hegel's stance on the compatibility of teleology and mechanism has important consequences concerning how we understand his claims about "the concept" [*der Begriff*]. For example, Hegel claims that the goal-directed development of a seed into a plant reveals clearly the reality and explanatory import of "the concept": The seed is "visible evidence to ordinary perception of what the concept is." And the seed is "the entire living being in the inner form of the concept" (*WL*, 6:486/774). But we must not take this to mean that "the concept" is supposed to be like an additional thing bumping up against the other elements here. Nor that "the concept" is a kind of additional force – perhaps a kind of vital force – somehow overpowering gravity or other forces at work here. Nor is anything else, like "the soul," supposed to play the role of such a special thing or force. The point is rather, first,

---

[50] That is, the presence of a prior representation of an end prevents the backwards causation problem from applying to consideration of purposive action. But this will not make any difference if exclusion is a problem: if lower-level explanations can explain the movements of our physical bodies in terms which make no appeal to the representation of an end *as such* (even if some of the physical states involved happen to be token-identical with mental representations of ends), then this can seem to threaten to exclude teleological explanation appealing to the representation of an end *as such*. The possible vulnerability of functionalism and anomalous monism to such problems has been a huge topic of recent discussion (e.g., in J. Heil and A. Mele *Mental Causation* (Oxford: Clarendon Press, 1993). The connections between teleology applied to biology and teleological explanation of action in terms of mental representations has played an important role recently as well – for example, in both L. Wright, *Teleological Explanations: An Etiological Analysis of Goals and Functions*. (Berkeley: University of California Press, 1976) and R. G. Milliken *Language, Thought and Other Biological Categories* (Cambridge, MA: MIT Press, 1984). The connection is important for Kant's purposes, insofar as he compares the problem of *Naturzwecke* to the problem of freedom: in both cases the idea of the supersensible allows a "possibility which cannot of course be understood, although the objection that there is an alleged contradiction in it can be adequately refuted" (*KU*, 5:195).

that whatever is going on with the lower-level stuff, all of it is present specifically on account of the way in which it contributes to the end of the development of a mature organism capable of self-preservation and reproduction. And, second, the end of the process of development can explain that very process specifically insofar as there is an explanatory role here for something general – for the species or kind [*Gattung*] or "the concept" [*der Begriff*] in this sense: each stage of development occurs here as it does specifically because of the general species, and more specifically because of the way in which this general kind of stage has consequences which benefit the end of the development of organisms of the same general kind or species.

VIII. A KANTIAN REJOINDER AND A CONTEMPORARY COMPARISON

How might Kant or a Kantian rebut Hegel's argument? Kant refers at one point to "the whole difficulty surrounding the question about the initial generation of a thing that contains purposes in itself" (*KU*, 5:420). This certainly suggests a line of attack. Hegel argues that the structure and development of a living being can be explained in teleological terms in virtue of its place in the larger process of reproduction within a species. A Kantian might well respond as follows: This approach just shifts the philosophical difficulties away from the origin of the individual living being to rest on the question of the initial generation of the species. If there is an origin in a concept, then whatever follows is only external design. If not, then the results will not include any teleological systems.[51]

Granted, if the demand here is for an explanation of how one might get from mere matter alone to complex living beings and the different species we know today, then Hegel is indeed in no position to explain. True, one can find relevant comments in the Philosophy of Nature. Some of them are false – for example, Hegel denies the possibility of the different species emerging from a common ancestor. And Hegel continues from here to a claim that is simply inconclusive: "even if the

---

[51] Compare Kant's own argument against the proposal that nature might "initially bear creatures of less purposive form, which in turn bear others that are formed more suitably," eventually producing the living beings we know from our experience. The possibility of a real *Naturzweck* is not *explained* thereby; rather, we have "merely put off the explanation." In other words, *if* we are to take the creatures generated by such a process to be genuine ends or *Zwecke*, then we would have to find at the beginning of the process "an organization purposively aimed at all these creatures, for otherwise the possibility the purposive form of the products of the animal and vegetable kingdoms cannot be conceived at all" (*KU*, 5:419–420).

earth was once in a state where it had no living things but only the chemical process, and so on, yet the moment the lightning of life strikes into matter, at once there is present a determinate, complete creature" (*PN*, §339Z/9:349/284). Neither the hypothetical nor the comparison to a lightening strike suggests any positive explanation of anything. Perhaps this is one of those cases in which, as Hegel says elsewhere, "there is plenty that cannot be comprehended yet" (*PN*, §268Z).

But why should any of this have anything to do with Hegel's rejoinder to Kant in "Life" from the Logic? Hegel does not there undertake to explain how to get from matter to living beings. He provides an explanation, in response to Kant's specific problem, of how a complex system (e.g., an organism) produced by reproduction might satisfy the requirements of inner purposiveness. As noted in Section 5), satisfaction of these requirements (on Hegel's account) simply has nothing to do with the lowest-level underlying matter. In Hegel's terms, living beings satisfy the analysis of inner purposiveness not in virtue of the relation between the whole and the mutually external material "parts" in space, but in virtue of the relation between the whole and the "members" (*WL*, 6:476/766). If this argument works, then it is only important that there are assimilating and reproducing organisms – and who could doubt this?

A contemporary Kantian might want to force the issue by insisting on a thought experiment: Imagine that some heap of matter were, by incredible coincidence (perhaps literally involving a lightning strike), to rearrange itself into a simple one-celled organism. This would not be a teleological system, no matter how effectively its parts might benefit the whole; ex hypothesi, the parts are present not because of an end or purpose but merely by coincidence. So if this organism reproduces and assimilates, then it would satisfy Hegel's analysis without being a truly teleological system. Such a thought experiment is entirely alien to Hegel's procedure. But if a contemporary Kantian were to insist on the experiment, then a contemporary Hegelian could respond: An individual of a future generation is a teleological system. For it exists on account of the general species or "concept" it shares with previous generations. Or, it exists only insofar as its parts are "members" – insofar as these kinds of parts are a benefit in relation to this kind of whole. So it will be a teleological system by Kant's own standard: "its parts (as far as their existence and their form are concerned) are possible only through their relation to the whole" (*KU*, 5:373).[52]

---

[52] Perhaps a contemporary Kantian would propose as well that we might create by *design* a reproducing creature. We could give the same response: The first creature will be a means only to *our external* end. But – as above – the parts of *future* generations will *also* be present on account of the intrinsic end of self-preservation.

Recall as well that Hegel is not defending teleological explanation of the historical development of the species. On my view, Hegel actually denies the possibility of such explanation of biological species. (He does of course say that "spirit" (*Geist*), or sometimes "self-consciousness," does make progress through history.)[53] But my point here is that change through historical development is a separate topic. Obviously, contemporary biology is vastly superior to everything Hegel says or knows about when it comes to scientific explanation of the changes over time in a biological species. But if Hegel's argument in the "Life" section of the *Logic* works at all, then none of this will matter to the resolution of Kant's specific problem concerning teleological explanation of the structure and development of a living being.

Finally, it is interesting to compare the most popular contemporary defenses of teleological explanation in biology. These differ immensely from Hegel's, for they defend natural teleology by drawing on the theory of natural selection; so they hold that the status of teleological explanation of the structure and development of individual organisms depends on the nature of the process by which a species itself historically develops. And critics attack precisely here, arguing that the theory of natural selection, properly understood, can do nothing to support such teleological explanation.[54] It seems to me worth considering whether there

---

Note here that Kant's concept of a *Naturzweck* aims to articulate the conditions under which something would satisfy the implications of teleological judgment in virtue of inner purposiveness. That need not itself rule out the possibility that this same something might *also* be designed. Finally, Kant himself might actually have something like this in mind. After all, he argues that we have reason to believe (though lack knowledge) that there is an "author of the world" who creates nature for the sake of a "highest good" (*KU*, 5:450). So when we are conceiving of a living being as a *Naturzweck* with an inner end or purpose, it seems were are also to consider it as designed by the for the sake of another purpose. Of course, Kant denies the possibility of *knowledge* of any of this.

[53] Hegel contrasts a biological species with the kind of which all thinking beings are instances, which he calls *Geist*: "The world of *Geist* and the world of nature continue to have this distinction, that the latter moves only in a recurring cycle, while the former certainly also makes progress" (*EL*, §§234Z). Alternatively, "the fate (*Schicksal*) of the living being is in general the *Gattung*, which manifests itself through the perishableness of the living individuals." And this means that there is no reason (teleological or otherwise) which necessitates a broader course of development: "what befalls them is a contingency" (*WL*, 6:421/720). Hegel there contrasts the "fate" of "self-consciousness." See also *VPN*, 184–185. Furthermore, a species can go extinct, without a purpose or an end explaining why (*VGP*, 19:175/2:158; and *PN*, §§339Z/280). This is one example of Hegel's general point that "even the species (*Gattungen*) are completely subject to the changes of the external, universal life of Nature" (*PN*, §§368A).

[54] For defenses, see Millikan, *Language, Thought and Other Biological Categories* and *White Queen Psychology* and Neander, "Teleological Notion." For criticisms,

is room for another approach, one that would be impervious to such attacks. In particular, we might consider looking to Hegel for inspiration, and trying to articulate a defense of teleological explanation in biology which requires only the struggle for survival and reproduction of structure, thus neither conflicting with natural selection, nor requiring support from any particular interpretation of natural selection at all.[55]

IX. THE BROADER PHILOSOPHICAL SIGNIFICANCE

The interpretation of the general themes of Hegel's philosophy as a whole is, of course, an enormous undertaking in its own right. But it is worth briefly noting some of the broader implications of Hegel's defense of natural teleology.

To begin with, Hegel's defense of the possibility of our having knowledge of natural teleology is connected to a much broader contrast between Kant and Hegel. Especially when it comes to explanatory knowledge of nature, Kant has a much more restrictive understanding of our epistemic limits. Kant does argue in the *Metaphysical Foundations of Natural Science* that we can have a special kind of a priori insight into the universal laws governing matter specifically. But elsewhere, as in the *KU*, Kant portrays our pursuit of explanatory knowledge of natural laws and kinds in terms of the idea that we can only make progress toward a goal that cannot in principle be achieved by a finite intellect such as our own.[56] By contrast, Hegel sees Kant as overly beholden to empiricist ideas about in principle limitations on what sorts of objects of knowledge are accessible to us (*EL*, §50). So Hegel is more

---

see Sober, "Natural Selection and Distributive Explanation"and Cummins, and "Neo-Teleology."

[55] See Buller's case that contemporary philosophy of biology has largely failed to clearly distinguish this kind of approach from those which require a section-history. He defends an approach of the former kind: "A current 'token' of a trait *T* in an organism *O* has the function of producing an effect of type *E* just in case past tokens of *T* contributed to the fitness of *O*'s ancestors by producing *E*, and thereby causally contributed to the reproduction of *T*s in *O*'s lineage" (1998, p. 507). See D. J. Buller, "Etiological Theories of Function: A Geographical Survey," *Biology and Philosophy* 13 (1998), pp. 505–527. esp. p. 507. J. Richardson in "Aristotle's Teleologies," carefully distinguishes this kind of view, and considers the possible evidence for interpreting Aristotle as holding it, but he finds philosophical disadvantages insofar as the view cannot provide "explanation of why *just these* species exist" (p. 107); I would ask: why shouldn't it be better for a philosophical defense of natural teleology to leave *that* question to empirical science?

[56] See the unpublished and published introductions to the *KU*, and the "Appendix to the Transcendental Dialectic" in the first *Critique*.

optimistic about the prospects for our achieving explanatory knowledge generally of "universal determinations" such as natural laws and kinds (*Gattungen*), and about our doing so in cases (e.g., biology) well beyond the laws of matter.[57] My own view is that both approaches here have their philosophical costs and benefits throughout theoretical philosophy; an attempt at a final weighing of these would be a huge undertaking.

Furthermore, one reason Hegel takes teleology and biology specifically to be of such broad importance is that he wants to argue that biological phenomena are more completely intelligible or explicable than matter and other natural phenomena.[58] This is, in part, what Hegel means by saying that "the highest level to which nature attains is life" (*PN*, §248A). And we can at least anticipate the general outlines of Hegel's argument here. Lower-level phenomena can be explained in terms of universal laws (e.g., gravity) and general natural kinds (e.g., chemical kinds).[59] But here there can be no further explanation of the connection between the particular and the universal, or of how the universal governs the particular. The point is not that there is a more complete explanation of, for example, gravity, to which we lack access; rather, mechanistic phenomena themselves are only incompletely intelligible or explicable.[60] In biological cases, by contrast, there is explanation to be had concerning the relations between the particular or concrete and the universal or general. For example, reproduction by individuals explains the how the general kind [*Gattung*] is realized and effective in the world;

---

[57] For example, "The empirical sciences do not stop at the perception of single instances of appearance; but through thinking they have prepared the material for philosophy by finding universal determinations, kinds, and laws" (*EL*, §12A).

[58] Also on Hegel's case for the superior intelligibility of teleology, see Forster *Hegel's Idea of a Phenomenology of Spirit* (Chicago: University of Chicago Press, 1998), p. 64f, and my own "Hegel's Critique of Pure Mechanism and the Philosophical Appeal of the Logic Project," in *European Journal of Philosophy*, 12 (2004), pp. 38–74.

[59] See, for example, Hegel on chemical kinds: "the universal essence, the real kind (*Gattung*) of the particular object" (*WL*, 6:430/728).

[60] Hegel argues against the idea that our difficulties here are at root epistemological. He sees this as inevitably suggesting a version of the idea that either forces or universals are unknowable and absolutely fundamental *things*, residing in a kind of immaterial higher *realm* inaccessible to us; and he thinks that problems concerning the interaction between realms would make things *less* intelligible or explicable rather than more so. See, for example, Hegel on Plato in the *Lectures on the History of Philosophy*, and the "Force and the Understanding" in the *Phenomenology*.

and the kind reciprocally explains how new individuals have the capacities required to survive and reproduce. Here Hegel will argue that the concrete and the universal are two sides of one system, which he calls "concrete universality." This is why Hegel takes biology to be relevant in a book about logic. For example, a judgment "S is P" will be of very different significance depending on whether we have an ordinary case (e.g., "the sun is hot") or whether we are dealing with a case of "concrete universality" (e.g., "Hobbes is a tiger"). In the latter kind of case,

> Subject and predicate correspond to each other and have the same content, and this content is itself the posited *concrete universality*; it contains, namely, the two moments, the objective universal or the *kind* (*Gattung*), and the *individualized* universal. Here, therefore, we have the universal which is *itself* and continues itself through *its opposite* and is a universal only as *unity* with this opposite.[61]

Obviously, all this raises more questions than it resolves. I think that the most important and general questions concern how Hegel's claims about the greater intelligibility of biological phenomena are supposed to fit into an overall metaphysical account of what truly or absolutely exists.

One easily accessible approach to this question would be to read Hegel, and perhaps some of his post-Kantian contemporaries as well, as defending a view that I will call "organic monism." The basic idea is that (following Spinoza) everything real must be "in" one single "substance"; but that substance is an organism. Or, more precisely, that substance must manifest the inner purposiveness of a *Naturzweck*: its structure and development over time are explicable in terms of an intrinsic end.

But I think that this approach to Hegel's metaphysics faces interpretive difficulties when it comes to Hegel's actual defense of natural teleology against Kant. As McTaggart notes in his commentary, Hegel's analysis in the "Life" section of the *Logic* cannot possibly apply to "the universe," or the whole of everything, or "substance" in the above sense (1910, p. 275). For substance could not depend on or have need

---

[61] WL, 6:349/662. Hegel is speaking of concrete universality in general here, not of biology in particular. But biological examples certainly help to illuminate the point. See also Hegel's connection between the concrete universal and Kant's analysis of inner purposiveness (WL, 6:443/739). On this issue, see M. Thompson, "The Representation of Life," in *Virtues and Reasons: Phillipa Foot and Moral Theory*, ed. by R. Hursthouse, G. Lawrence, W. Quinn (Oxford: Oxford University Press, 1995), pp. 247–296.

of assimilation from an outside environment – it will have no out-side, and nothing with which it could be said to struggle. And sub-stance could not be said to be mortal and to reproduce new individ-uals of the same kind – for all individuals would have to be "in" the same single substance itself. Furthermore, insofar as Hegel's analysis cannot possibly apply to the universe as a whole, Hegel's argument in "Life" does not even attempt to defend (against Kant) the idea that we could possibly know the universe to be a *Naturzweck* – nor even the idea that we could comprehend how the universe could possibly be a *Naturzweck*.

I see two possible basic reactions here. One is to say (with McTaggart) that Hegel advocates "organic monism," and sees Kant's analysis of inner purposiveness as crucial for that reason, but that Hegel does not defend organic monism where he specifically responds to Kant's worries about the inner purposiveness of living beings. My own preference is for the alternative: to hold that the *Logic* and the *Encyclopedia* offer philosophical arguments in favor of a different metaphysical account of reality – one that contrasts with "organic monism".[62]

There can be no question of explaining and defending here any par-ticular alternative approach to the whole of Hegel's metaphysics. But the broad issues at stake might at least be clarified by contrasting a brief sketch.[63] One could read Hegel not as defending "organic monism," but as arguing that the whole of reality is structured into different "levels" or *Stufen*.[64] Mechanistic phenomena form the lowest level, and bio-logical phenomena form a much higher level. Furthermore, the higher levels are more completely intelligible than the lower levels. This is not to say that everything is an organism or part of an organism. So when we explain, for example, the rotation of planets in terms of the neces-sary laws governing matter, we are not making a mistake or accepting a merely subjective appearance of something that is in truth or most

---

[62] My own sense is that Kant is right to hold that comprehending how the universe could be a *Naturzweck*, and having knowledge of this, would require a higher form of intellect – something along the lines of Kant's descriptions of "intellectual intuition" and "intuitive understanding." And although there are some complex issues here concerning Hegel's early work and his development, in the *Logic* and the *Encyclopedia* Hegel lays a tremendous amount of stress on his criticisms of appeals by his contemporaries to "intellectual intuition" and other forms of supposedly "immediate knowledge" (*WL*, 5:65/67; *EL*, §61–§78). So my view is that these criticisms provide Hegel with good reason to prefer something else to organic monism. But this case would require much more defense.

[63] Yet another alternative would be the one attributed to Hegel by R.-P. Horstmann *Ontologie und Relationen* (Koenigstein: Athenaum, 1984), p. 70ff.

[64] On Hegel on "levels" or *Stufen* specifically of nature, see the opening sections of the *Philosophy of Nature* and deVries, *Hegel's Theory of Mental Activity*, ch. 3.

fundamentally an organic or teleological phenomenon. Rather, mechanistic phenomena are perfectly real but only imperfectly intelligible. Living beings are more completely intelligible. And, ultimately, the only thing that is perfectly intelligible is us – or, more precisely, the general kind or *Gattung* whose instances are thinking and self-conscious beings. Hegel calls this kind *Geist* [mind or spirit]. In Hegel's terms, there is a standard of complete intelligibility – "the idea." And although everything is intelligible to some degree, most everything falls far short of the standard. The standard of "the idea" is met to some degree by living beings, and completely only by *Geist*.[65] On this view, insofar as reality itself is organized or structured, it is comparable to an organism in this respect.[66] But it is crucial that reality as a whole would not have a structure because it is really an organism, organic, or a *Naturzweck*. The point would be precisely the opposite: reality has a differentiated structure insofar as there are many different kinds or levels of phenomena which differ in real and important ways from biological phenomena and from one another.[67] In summary, then, there are ways of interpreting Hegel's metaphysical ambitions, and the importance of his defense of natural teleology, without reading him as an "organic monist" at all.

My topic here has not been Hegel's broader metaphysics, however, but his response to Kant concerning the status of teleological explanation of the structure and development of living beings. I have tried to show that Kant provides a forceful argument in support of his skeptical conclusion – his denial of the possibility of our having knowledge that teleology truly explains the structure and development of a living being. And I have tried to show that Hegel recognizes this argument and meets

---

[65] "Life" is the first subsection under the heading "The Idea" in the *Logic*. But Hegel argues, as he puts it, that the "truly absolute concept" is the "idea of infinite mind" (*WL*, 6:279/605). Also, Hegel famously says "substance is essentially subject" (*PhG*, 3:28/14). On the current reading, this will mean that there *is* something completely or ideally intelligible, something which meets Spinoza's definition of substance: it "is in itself, and is conceived through itself" (*Ethics*, 1D3). But Hegel argues "God or substance" in this sense cannot be everything or a whole of everything; it can only be *Geist*. We ourselves are both living beings and also *geistig* beings; see especially *VPN*, 184–185.

[66] On this organization see, for example, *PN*, §§246. Similarly, Hegel compares the earth to an organism, while emphasizing that it is not really alive (*PN*, §§339 and *Zusatz*).

[67] K. H. Ilting stresses a similar claim in discussing the broader importance of Hegel's account of life: "Hegel beabsichtigt nicht etwa, in allen Gestaltungen der Natur und des Geistes nur immer wieder dieselbe logische Struktur aufzuweisen." See "Hegels Philosophie des Organischen," in *Hegel und die Naturwissenschaften*, ed. by M. J. Petry (Stuttgart: Frommann-Holzboog, 1987), p. 367.

it with an argument of his own in defense of teleological explanation in biology. It would of course be very difficult to attempt any sort of final or definitive weighing of the philosophical advantages and disadvantages of each view of teleology and biology – let alone the costs and benefits of the broader approaches to theoretical philosophy with which each view is closely connected. But we can at least see that, when it comes to the topic of teleology and biology, Kant and Hegel provide arguments that bear on underlying philosophical issues of continuing interest and importance.[68]

---

[68] For helpful comments on this material, and other assistance, I would like to thank: Michael Della Rocca, Michael Forster, Dean Moyar, David McNeill, Robert Pippin, Candace Vogler, and Rachel Zuckert. As usual, any errors are my own.

14 Hegel and Aesthetics: The Practice and "Pastness" of Art

Hegel's achievements as a philosopher of art have been both widely recognized and endlessly disputed. His position as the "father of art history" (Gombrich) has been confirmed Oedipally, by a succession of figures in that profession who have criticized Hegel's alleged tendencies to (among other things) progressivism, essentialism and historical determinism.[1] While he is regarded by many (Henrich, Danto, T. J. Clark) as a philosophical forerunner of theoretical discourse on modernism in art, his own (in)famous remarks about the "end of art" are often cited against him as evidence of an inability to imagine the development of just such later movements.[2] He is rightly regarded as having pushed forward the independent status of art in its own right, yet this independence is frequently held to be vitiated by the demands of his own philosophical system.[3]

---

[1] E. H. Gombrich, "The Father of Art History," in *Tributes: Interpreters of Our Cultural Tradition* (Ithaca, NY: Cornell University Press, 1984), pp. 51–69 and *In Search of Cultural History* (Oxford: Clarendon Press, 1977). For a helpful discussion of the issues of historicity in Hegelian aesthetics raised by Gombrich and others, see Martin Donougho, "Hegel on the Historicity of Art," *Encyclopedia of Aesthetics* (Oxford: Oxford University Press, 1998): vol. 2, pp. 365–368.

[2] Of course, many of those who see Hegel's claims about romantic and postromantic art as proleptic of the later movements of modernism suggest, as Henrich does, "the prospect of disengaging Hegel's theory of art from his own short-term predictions for the art of the mid-nineteenth century" (Dieter Henrich, "Art and Philosophy of Art Today: Reflections with Reference to Hegel," trans. by David Henry Wilson et al., in *New Perspectives in German Literary Criticism: A Collection of Essays*, ed. by Richard E. Amacher and Victor Lange (Princeton: Princeton University Press, 1979), pp. 107–133, a translation of Henrich's original essay in *Poetik und Hermeneutik*, vol. 2 (Munich: Wilhelm Fink, 1966), pp. 11–33, 524–533. ed. by R. Koselleck and W. D. Stempel (Munich: 1972)). See also Alain Besançon, *The Forbidden Image: an intellectual history of iconoclasm* (Chicago: University of Chicago Press, 1994), p. 224.

[3] On this point, see especially Dieter Henrich, "Art and Philosophy of Art Today: Reflections with Reference to Hegel," pp. 112–116.

The difficulty of assessing Hegel's achievements in aesthetics has led to a number of attempts to rescue some version of an Hegelian aesthetics by going beyond what the presumably "official" account itself offers. In what follows, I want to examine what resources might lie within Hegel's aesthetics for a view of the *practice* of art, something I hope will shed light not only on some of the famous systematic difficulties in Hegel's aesthetics but also on questions such as the endlessly interpreted "end of art" thesis. I will begin with a brief look at the developmental and systematic significance of aesthetics for Hegel, turn to his explicit consideration of the role of artistic practice within the text of the *Lectures on Aesthetics* and then take up the question of the "pastness" of art and its relation to Hegel's own aesthetic ideals.

I. DEVELOPMENT, SIGNIFICANCE, AND SYSTEMATIC PLACE OF HEGEL'S AESTHETICS; STRUCTURAL APORIAI AND THE "END OF ART" THESIS

Development and Significance

Emerging from a period in which post-Kantian idealists and romantics all gave vigorous new energy to the question of art and its relation to philosophy, Hegel's aesthetics represented a determinate stance of its own – one which developed certain tendencies inherent in both Kantian and romantic aesthetics but which stoutly rejected others, yet without reverting to a classical (precritical, preromantic) perspective.[4] Most crucially, what becomes articulated within this distinctively Hegelian aesthetic stance is a new position with respect to art's *autonomy*, not only in relation to its freedom from nature but also in terms of its relation to philosophy.[5]

---

[4] For the break with the precritical, pre-Romantic tradition, cf. Stephen Bungay's conclusion (based on a remark by Hegel's student Rötscher) that two attitudes to art common in the eighteenth century could be said to have disappeared with Hegel and his generation: "nobody any longer demanded that art have a moral effect and be edifying or instructive; and nobody demanded that it imitate nature" (S. Bungay, *Beauty and Truth: A Study of Hegel's Aesthetics* (Oxford: Oxford University Press, 1984), p. 188).

[5] Hegel links these two issues – the *autonomy* of art but its underlying *connection* to philosophy (as well as religion) – in the first pages of the *Lectures on Aesthetics*: "what *we* want to consider is art which is *free* alike in its end and its means.... Now, in this freedom alone is fine art truly art, and it only fulfils its supreme task when it has placed itself in the same sphere as religion and philosophy...." (Hegel, *Aesthetics: Lectures on Fine Art*, trans. by T. M. Knox (Oxford: Oxford University Press, 1975), vol. I, p. 7; *G. W. F. Hegel: Werke, Vorlesungen über die Aesthetik*, vol. 13, ed. by Eva Moldenhauer and Karl Markus Michel (Frankfurt: Suhrkamp,

What is distinctive about Hegel's view of art's autonomy can be seen first in his centering of art within the realm of *Geist* or Spirit, whose characteristic – in contrast with nature – is an ability to *maintain* or *be itself* (Hegel refers regularly to autonomy in this sense as *Beisichselbstsein*, literally "being-by-itself") in its engagement with an other.[6] Art is more particularly, however, a mode within *Absolute* Spirit, the realm in which Spirit is no longer finite (as are the moments of Objective and Subjective Spirit) but infinite in its self-knowledge. And, finally, although religion and philosophy are higher modes of Absolute Spirit which arise respectively in turn from art, Hegel is careful to make clear why art is an articulated moment of Absolute Spirit which cannot be merely reduced to those higher modes.[7] Hegel thus departs, on the one hand, from Kant in articulating a notion of beauty as decisively related to works of *art* rather than natural phenomena but avoids, on the other hand, a Romantic valorization of art *over* philosophy.[8]

Hegel's view of art is differently construed at different times in his development, but during none of those phases can it be said to have been a marginal issue for him. Of particular concern from Hegel's earliest phase was the "religion of beauty" that characterized ancient Greece – an ideal first invoked in a comparative way against certain trends in Christianity and later. With the historical inflection his philosophical project picked up in the years preceding the *Phenomenology of Spirit*,

1970), vol. XIII, pp. 20–21. Further references by volume and page number to these two volumes are to *Aesthetics* and *Vorlesungen*, respectively.)

[6] The notion of *Beisischselbstsein* as central to Hegel's account of the autonomy that is present in the realm of Spirit can be seen, for example, in his *History of Philosophy* discussion of the importance of the state's capacity to make and follow its own laws (*Lectures on the History of Philosophy: Introduction*, trans. by H. B. Nisbet (Cambridge, UK: Cambridge University Press, 1975), p. 97; *Die Vernunft in der Geschichte*, ed. by J. Hoffmeister (Hamburg: Meiner, 1966), p. 115) as well as in his *Philosophy of Right* discussion of the concrete will, where freedom is described as the ability to "will something determinate, yet to be with oneself [*bei sich*] in this determinacy" (*PR*, 7A).

[7] Thus, while Hegel sees an important continuity between speculative philosophy and poetry in that both produce works which have through their content "perfect self-identity" as well as an "articulated development" in which the parts have the "appearance of independent freedom," he nonetheless differentiates between the two modes (see *Aesthetics*, II:984, *Vorlesungen*, XV:254–255, a passage discussed in Part II of this chapter).

[8] As Jean-Marie Schaeffer has argued, however, this does not mean that Hegel simply reverted to a preromantic view of art in its relation to philosophy: for Hegel, as for the Romantics, art has a decisive *speculative* significance (J.-M. Schaeffer, *Art of the Modern Age: Philosophy of Art from Kant to Heidegger*, trans. by Steven Rendall (Princeton: Princeton University Press, 2000), p. 135).

Hegel saw this religion as an unrecoverable past moment in the larger narrative of the West's cultural and philosophical self-awareness, which he later comes to speak of in terms of "Spirit."[9]

The *Lectures on Aesthetics*, which date from Hegel's later Heidelberg (1816–18) and Berlin (1818–1831) periods, are not among the writings which Hegel published himself. Hegel gave five series of lectures on the topic – one at Heidelberg in 1818 and four at the University of Berlin (in 1820–1821, 1823, 1826, and 1828–1829). Hegel's student H. G. Hotho compiled Hegel's manuscripts and student notes (taken by Hotho and others) from the last three versions of the lecture series into what are now known as the *Lectures*.[10]

Systematic Place of Aesthetics; Aporiai

In Hegel's mature system, as reflected in the ultimate shape of his lectures, art, religion, and philosophy are the three moments in which Absolute Spirit comprehends itself. Within this triad, art is distinctive because it requires an *immediate and sensual shape* for expression (in, for example, a sculptor's stone); religion, by comparison, is characterized as a form of representational consciousness [*das vorstellende Bewusstsein*] and philosophy a form of free thought itself [*das freie Denken*].[11] These three modes share the same *content*, but grasp it in different ways. Art is thus on Hegel's view "one way of bringing to our minds and expressing the *Divine*, the deepest interests of mankind, and the most comprehensive truths of the spirit [*das Göttliche, die*

---

[9] The most aesthetically charged text associated with Hegel in his earliest period is no doubt the so-called *Oldest Systematic Program of German Idealism* (a text written in his hand, but whose authorship has been variously claimed for Schelling and Hölderlin as well). The development of Hegel's early concern with the Greek "religion of beauty" can be seen in the fragments he wrote during his Frankfurt period (1797–1800) collected under the title, "The Spirit of Christianity and its Fate." For important continuities between the aesthetics of Hegel's emerging system at Jena and the ultimate lectures at Heidelberg and Berlin, see Otto Pöggeler, "Die Entstehung von Hegels Ästhetik in Jena," in *Hegel in Jena: Die Entwicklung des Systems und die Zusammenarbeit mit Schelling*, ed. by D. Henrich and K. Düsing, *Hegel-Studien Beiheft*, 20 (Bonn: Bouvier, 1980).

[10] Editions of the 1820–1821, 1823, and 1826 versions of the lectures have been published separately: *G. W. F. Hegel: Philosophie der Kunst oder Ästhetik (1826)*, ed. by A. Gethmann-Siefert and B. Collenberg-Plotnikov (Munich: Wilhelm Fink, 2003); *G. W. F. Hegel: Vorlesungen über die Philosophie der Kunst. Berlin 1823. Nachgeschrieben von Heinrich Gustav Hotho*, ed. by A. Gethmann-Siefert (Hamburg: Meiner, 1998); and *Vorlesung über Ästhetik: Berlin 1820/1*, ed. by Helmut Schneider (Frankfurt: Peter Lang, 1995).

[11] *Aesthetics*, I:101; *Vorlesungen* XIII:139.

tiefsten Interessen des Menschen, die umfassendsten Wahrheiten des Geistes]."[12]

The distinctive focus of art as this first mode of absolute spirit centers around a notion of beauty in terms of the *ideal,* which Hegel understands in terms of the relation between content (the Idea) and form (its configuration [*Gestalt*] as a concrete reality). The potential adequate and inadequate relationships between form and content are what shape Hegel's differentiation of the "forms of art" – the symbolic, classical, and romantic. When form and content are adequate to one another, as in Hegel's account of classical sculpture, the work of art's significance and form of expression are at one: it is "not a meaning *of* this or that but what means [*Bedeutende*] itself and therefore intimates [or 'interprets,' *Deutende*] itself."[13] More concretely, we might say that the classical sculpture of an anthropomorphic god represents or reveals the human body in its ideal shape.

By comparison, the symbolic and romantic art forms are ones in which content and form fall apart. In the symbolic form, which Hegel links to preclassical art in Egypt and Asiatic religions, the as-yet undetermined idea is still in a "search" of its true portrayal: a stone idol may represent the divine but does not *embody* it in the sense of the classical form. The romantic form is defined against the "pinnacle" of connection between content and form which the classical has achieved: here the defect, Hegel says, "is just art itself and the restrictedness of the sphere of art."[14]

In addition to these *forms* of art – what Hegel came to associate with the *particular* in aesthetics – Hegel also develops a differentiation of *individual arts* themselves. Drawing on an existing notion of a system of five arts,[15] Hegel sketches their relation in terms of an increasing arc of abstraction: from architecture to sculpture to painting, music, and poetry.

A number of famous problems arise in considering both the relation between the series of art-forms and the series of specific arts on the one hand, and the relation of the various forms and arts among themselves on the other hand. The relation between the art forms and the specific arts, according to Hotho's text, is determined by an underlying tripartite division: universal (ideal of the beautiful), particular (art-forms) and

---

[12] *Aesthetics,* I:7; *Vorlesungen,* XIII:21.

[13] *Aesthetics,* I:427; *Vorlesungen,* XIV:13.

[14] *Aesthetics,* I:79; *Vorlesungen,* XIII:111.

[15] On Hegel's sources here, see Paul Oskar Kristeller, "The Modern System of the Arts," *Journal of the History of Ideas,* 12 (1951), pp. 496–527 and 13 (1952), pp. 17–46.

individual (specific arts). Yet Hegel himself in the 1823 lectures appears only to have had a two-part division, according to which the art-forms are *universal* and the specific arts *particular*.[16] Adding to this formal difficulty is an apparent diversity of ways Hegel actually *applies* his scheme for point-to-point comparisons. The official version would seem to be that there are specific arts which correlate most closely with an art-form (architecture for the symbolic, sculpture for the classical, and painting and music for the romantic), but nonetheless each specific art can appear under the guise of the other forms as well (thus there are symbolic, classical, and romantic forms of architecture and the other arts as well). But there are clear difficulties in making this work: as Bungay and Schaeffer, among others, have noted, architecture has its paradigmatic form in the Greek temple (a classical, not a symbolic moment), while only romantic painting and music (and not classical or symbolic forms of these arts) seem to come up for much discussion in the lectures. Moreover, Hegel clearly thinks some point-to-point connections are more intimate than others: thus architecture can in fact be divided by means of its symbolic/classical/romantic forms, but sculpture is too closely wedded to the classical ideal to permit such a development. While various attempts have been made to work out a more speculatively coherent systematic scheme relating both the two series and likewise Hegel's apparent solution of the difficulty for point-to-point comparisons, it may be that what is at issue here are inherent *aporiai*, given the elements Hegel wished to incorporate in his aesthetics and his own apparent indecisiveness about how philosophically to organize them. Schaeffer's point that it is part of Hegel's originality and depth to have tried at all to link these two sets – one stemming from the Romantic influences in his inheritance and the other, more broadly, from an Aristotelian conception of the specific arts themselves – is suggestive here.

As mentioned, there are further problems about the internal relations within each set, as well. Perhaps most discussed is the relation among the art-forms, and how the classical can be regarded as achieving the fullness of *beauty* while the romantic is nonetheless a higher *form of art*. Hegel seems particularly concerned to point this difference up in the course of the *Aesthetics*, as he does, for example, at the beginning of his discussion of the romantic arts:

[C]lassical art became a conceptually adequate representation of the Ideal, the consummation of the realm of beauty. Nothing can be or become more beautiful.

---

[16] *G. W. F. Hegel: Vorlesungen über die Philosophie der Kunst. Berlin 1823. Nachgeschrieben von Heinrich Gustav Hotho*, ed. by Annemarie Gethmann-Siefert (Hamburg: Meiner, 1998), pp. v–xiv.

Yet there is something higher than the beautiful appearance of spirit in its immediate sensuous shape, even if this shape be created by spirit as adequate to itself.[17]

The shape which Spirit moves on to is a shape which is not bound by the external solidity of sculpture but one which is instead more reconcilable with the internality of Spirit's ultimate progress. Art turns, in other words, to the romantic realm of (two-dimensional) painting and (nondimensional) music – and ultimately to that of poetry, which rests on the inwardness of the imagination.

In some ways, the move to the romantic is reminiscent of the falling-apart of form and matter which characterized the symbolic form of art, but this transition is different in that here the guiding force is not internal to art but governed by the larger demands of Spirit: "if the perfect content has been perfectly revealed in artistic shapes, then the more far-seeing spirit rejects this objective manifestation and turns back into its inner self."[18] The "more far-seeing spirit" is one which, in fact, is ultimately dissatisfied with the realm of art and looks instead to the higher realms – because less tied to specific *Darstellungen* of artistic shaping – characteristic of religion and philosophy.

Art in its classical prime, so Hegel seems to want to say, is the highest revelation of what is divine – Homer and Hesiod "gave the Greeks their gods" – but "the form of art has ceased to be the supreme need of the spirit."[19] Now the "unity of divine and human nature" that is so essential to classical art is "raised from an *immediate* to a *known* unity."[20] In religious terms, this means that Christianity now "brings God before our imagination as spirit," and thus retreats to a spiritual inwardness; in philosophical terms, this means that thought and reflection rather than artistic presentation become most crucial to the cultural activities of the modern age.

The "End" of Art

With these claims, a host of questions about the status of art in the postclassical world arises. If not art but religion and philosophy are now the modes in which the "supreme need of the spirit" are to be addressed, has art in fact reached an end? Hegel's remarks at this point in the text of the *Lectures* would appear to cut in two ways. There is his famous statement of what would appear to be art's inevitable pastness: "No

---

[17] *Aesthetics*, I:517; *Vorlesungen* XIV:127–128.
[18] *Aesthetics*, I:103; *Vorlesungen* XIII:142.
[19] *Aesthetics*, I:103; *Vorlesungen* XIII:142.
[20] *Aesthetics*, I:80; *Vorlesungen* XIII:112.

matter how excellent we find the statues of the Greek gods, no matter how we see God the Father, Christ, and Mary so estimably and perfectly portrayed: it is no help; we bow the knee no longer." But his remark is prefaced with a qualification: "We may well hope that art will always rise higher and come to perfection."[21]

How are these comments to be understood? The discussion of the "end" of art in Hegel has produced a long literature, indeed, of overlapping and not always consistent interpretations.[22] At the same time, there have been attempts to discount from Hegel's comments about the art world of his own day and to look instead to resources within his account of the romantic and postromantic in art which might be helpful in claiming some of the territory of movements like modernism for an Hegelian approach.

Dieter Henrich, in a famous early essay, noted basic tendencies in Hegelian aesthetics which he found helpful for a consideration of modernism – the renunciation of artistic utopia, a stress on an artist's reflectiveness and capacity to take up any content, and the partial (not fully self-transparent) character of the most recent art – but sketched a critical revision of Hegel's project which incorporated a wider range for the reflectedness of the work of art itself than he thought Hegel allowed.[23] The modernist work of art, which takes itself for a theme – Henrich cites Cubism – thus requires, on his view, an extension of the Hegelian notion of reflection.

---

[21] *Aesthetics*, I:103; *Vorlesungen* XIII:142.

[22] Stephen Bungay (*Beauty and Truth: A Study of Hegel's Aesthetics*, pp. 71–88) and Martin Donougho ("Art and History: Hegel on the End, the Beginning and the Future of Art," in *Hegel and The Arts*, ed. by Stephen Houlgate [Evanston: Northwestern University Press, 2007], pp. 179–215) suggest ways in which the various interpretations of the thesis may be distinguished and related. See also Stephen Houlgate, "Hegel and the 'End' of Art," *The Owl of Minerva* 29, 1 (Fall 1997), pp. 1–22; Fred L. Rush, Jr., "Hegel's Conception of the End of Art," *Encyclopedia of Aesthetics* (Oxford: Oxford University Press, 1998), vol. 2., pp. 368–371; Karsten Harries, "Hegel on the Future of Art," *Review of Metaphysics*, 27 (1973–1974), pp. 677–696; and Willi Oelmüller, "Hegels Satz vom Ende der Kunst," *Philosophische Jahrbuch*, 73 (1965), pp. 75–94. For a wider recent (not merely Hegelian) consideration of issues in modern and "postmodern" art, see Donald Kuspit, *The End of Art* (Cambridge, UK: Cambridge University Press, 2004).

[23] D. Henrich, "Art and Philosophy of Today: Reflections with Reference to Hegel." For Henrich's more recent views, see *Versuch über Kunst und Leben: Subjektivität – Weltverstehen – Kunst* (Munich: Hansler, 2001). A thoughtful criticism of the earlier Henrich essay can be found in M. Donougho, "Art and History: Hegel on the End, the Beginning and the Future of Art," which questions the underlying notion of "reflection" relevant for Henrich's assessment of Hegel.

More recently, Robert Pippin has suggested that the elements of abstraction and reflexivity in Hegel's philosophy of art remain decisive terms for any aesthetics of modernism and modernity. The "end of art" thesis does not spell the end of art but rather the "end of a way of art's mattering": "human beings require, less and less, sensible, representative imagery in order to understand themselves (with respect to the highest issue – for Hegel their being free subjects)."[24] The relevant phenomena here, for Pippin, are not aesthetic formlessness or preoccupation with "pure" form that is empty of content, but rather artistic works which have their own form *as* content, as Proust's novel may be said to be *about* novel writing or certain experiments in painting are *about* painting itself. From the perspective of *this* sort of concern with form, "modernism after Hegel would then look something like what Hegel prophesied after romantic art: 'the self-transcendence of art but within its own sphere and in the form of art itself.'"[25]

Taking these suggestions about an Hegelian interpretation of modernism in art, I will explore in the following sections two issues which would be central to any extension of Hegel's aesthetics – his account of artistic practice and the "pastness" of the ideal around which the *Aesthetics* is supposedly situated. Much recent stress has (rightly) been placed on the experience of modernism in the visual arts,[26] and an extended "Hegelian" account of these phenomena might well pick up where such accounts have left off. I will be focusing instead in what follows on another art which Hegel appears to have thought gave a philosopher of his premodernist generation perhaps its best window onto the concerns of self-transcendent, postromantic art: the drama.

II. HEGEL ON ARTISTIC PRACTICE

In seeking what light Hegel might shed on later forms of art where the "self-transcendence of art" becomes explicitly a concern, it might make sense to begin with Hegel's own account of what it is that artists *do*. Underlying many points of discussion in the *Aesthetics* is an account of artistic practice which has surprising resonances with Hegel's understanding of artistic content and philosophical reflection. I will turn in this section to four issues: (1) art as an activity which makes explicit an implicit content, (2) the relation of this activity of making-explicit to

---

[24] Robert Pippin, "What Was Abstract Art? (From the Point of View of Hegel)," *Critical Inquiry*, 29 (Autumn 2002), p. 3.

[25] Pippin, "What Was Abstract Art?" p. 23.

[26] See, among others, T. J. Clark, *Farewell to an Idea: Episodes from a History of Modernism* (New Haven, CT: Yale University Press, 1999), especially chapter 6.

the more reflective activity of philosophy, (3) what this account of art and its relationship to reflection suggests about the Hegelian possibilities inherent in postromantic art, and (4) what general conclusions can thus be drawn from artistic practice for understanding the "pastness" of art in Hegel's sense.

Art as Making-Explicit an Implicit Content

Early in the *Aesthetics* Hegel claims that "art's vocation is to *unveil* [*enthüllen*] *the truth* in the form of sensuous artistic configuration...."[27] While Hegel does not say much about what is involved in such *unveiling* – and *Enthüllung* is by far a less-discussed Hegelian term of art than, for example, *Darstellung* [presentation] – it is clear that artistic transformation in Hegel's sense involves the making *explicit* of something which is *implicit* – in art's early phases, a unity which only the artist can reveal to his viewers. And, at these early stages, there is seemingly more for art to draw on: "[a]rt in its beginnings still leaves over something mysterious, a secret foreboding and a longing," Hegel says.[28]

Implicitness appears to be important to Hegel's account of artistic practice in two ways – first in the unrevealed that art finds *before* its transforming activity and second (as in this last quotation) in the "something mysterious" that is left *behind* it. Each mode is challenged by reflectiveness – the first especially by the potential replacement of the artistic grasp of the absolute in the more reflective activity of philosophy, and the second by the mining-out of the mysterious from within art's activity itself.

Art and Philosophy

Given the shared content of these two realms of absolute spirit, Hegel must give an account of their relation. Although he does not make it clear until his discussion of the art of poetry, the correlation Hegel draws is between two modes of making-explicit:

[T]he work of art differentiates the fundamental topic that has been selected as its center by developing its particular features, and to these it imparts the appearance of independent freedom; and this it must do because these particulars are

---

[27] *Aesthetics*, I:55; *Vorlesungen*, XIII:83. (Only the word "truth" is italicized in Knox's translation.) See also Hegel's remark that it's at Absolute Spirit that we see an "unveiling of what the world of appearance is in its true nature" (*Aesthetics*, I:93; *Vorlesungen*, XIII:130).

[28] *Aesthetics* I:103; *Vorlesungen* XIII:142.

nothing but that topic itself in the form of its actually corresponding realization. This may therefore remind us of the procedure of speculative thinking
which likewise must develop the particular, out of the primarily undifferentiated universal, up to independence.... By means of this mode of treatment,
speculative philosophy likewise produces works which, like poetical ones in this
respect, have through their content itself perfect self-identity and articulated
development.[29]

In comparing these two modes of apprehending unity – the artistic and
the speculative – Hegel makes clear that a chief difference is the greater
explicitness of philosophy:

poetry, on the other hand, does not get so far as such a deliberate exposition:
the harmonizing unity must indeed be completely present in every poetical
work and be active in every part of it as the animating soul of the whole, but
this presence is never expressly emphasized by art; on the contrary, *it remains
something innner and implicit*, just as the soul is directly living in all the members of the organism but without depriving them of their appearance of existing
independently.[30]

In saying that the unifying activity of the artist remains something
inner and implicit, Hegel clearly does not mean that the artist is not
also a reflective or thinking individual. "It is... an absurdity to suppose that poems like the Homeric came to the poet in sleep. Without
circumspection, discrimination and criticism the artist cannot master
any subject-matter which he is to configure, and it is silly to believe
that the genuine artist does not know what he is doing."[31]

Even the artist of the classical period requires reflection in his activity, but the pervasive culture of *modern* reflectivity raises new questions
entirely about what the artist does.

"It is not, as might be supposed, merely that the practicing artist
himself is infected by the loud voice of reflection all around him and
by the opinions and judgments on art that have become customary
everywhere, so that he is misled into introducing more thoughts into
his work; the point is that our whole spiritual culture is of such a kind
that he himself stands within the world of reflection and its relations,
and could not by any act of will and decision abstract himself from
it."[32]

[29] *Aesthetics*, II:984, *Vorlesungen* XV:254–255.
[30] *Aesthetics*, II:984–985; *Vorlesungen* XV:255.
[31] *Aesthetics*, I:283; *Vorlesungen* XIII:365.
[32] *Aesthetics* I:10–11; *Vorlesungen* XIII:25.

Reflection and Postromantic Art

What sort of artistic practice is then possible in such a reflective modern world? Although Hegel can be quite derisive about the work of his artistic contemporaries, there are nonetheless passages where he suggests what modern artistic practice might draw on especially. Henrich's attention, for example, was drawn to the following analogy in the discussion of postromantic art:

In our day, in the case of almost all peoples, criticism, the cultivation of reflection, and, in our German case, freedom of thought have mastered the artists too, and have made them, so to say, a *tabula rasa* in respect of the material and the form of their productions, after the necessary particular stages of the romantic art-form have been traversed. Bondage to a particular subject-matter and a mode of portrayal suitable for this material alone are for artists today something past, and art therefore has become a free instrument which the artist can wield in proportion to his subjective skill in relation to any material of whatever kind. The artist thus stands above specific consecrated forms and configurations and moves freeely on his own account.... Therefore the artist's attitude to his topic is on the whole much the same as the dramatist's who brings on the scene and delineates different characters who are strange to him.[33]

Hegel's appeal to *drama* at this point in the *Aesthetics* – at the end of the division on the romantic form of art and the series of art-forms as a whole – is interesting. Lacking contemporary examples from the visual arts (such as Cubism) in which the artistic "self-transcendence" characteristic of modernism is present, Hegel turns instead to an example from the art which for him is supposedly most fully capable of producing perfect embodiments of beauty – and which is described at the end of the *following* division of the *Aesthetics* (the conclusion of the discussion of the specific arts themselves) as the art in which "*the whole man* presents, by *re*producing it, the work of art produced by man (*der ganze Mensch das vom Menschen produzierte Kunstwerk reproduzierend darstellt*)."[34]

---

[33] *Aesthetics* I:605. In the 1823 lectures, Hegel appears to have extended the dramatic analogy into a further remark about the universalization of the breadth of drama itself: "The artist is, as it were, a dramatist who has alien shapes make their appearance, embeds his genius in them, makes them organic though they remain alien also. This, then, is the modern situation in sum – [an] abstract facility, without ties to the material. Dramatic art, e.g., in recent times scans all ages and peoples. With that art is completed. It is no longer intimate [*in Innigkeit*] with the material, which remains all the same to it." G. W. F. Hegel: *Vorlesungen über die Philosophie der Kunst. Berlin 1823. Nachgeschrieben von Heinrich Gustav Hotho,* ed. by Annemarie Gethmann-Siefert (Hamburg: Meiner, 1998), p. 204. (I quote here from Martin Donougho's translation of the lecture series; I am grateful to him for sharing the manuscript with me.)

[34] *Aesthetics* II:627; *Vorlesungen* XIV:262. (Italicizations in the translation are mine.)

Hegel thus appears to turn to drama not only as the highest embodiment of beauty – representing and represented by the "whole man" – but also as an art in which postromantic artistic self-transcendence *as* an exploration of the human might be most visible (thus Hegel's famous appeal here to the *Humanus* which is the "new holy of holies" – the artist acquiring here his subject matter in himself, to which nothing human can be alien).[35]

There is here in Hegel's presentation of the possibilities inherent in the art of the dramatist a curious duality which goes directly to the issue of art's function and the issue of its "pastness." On the one hand, as Hegel likes to present it, the great Greek figures are in the first instance *artists of themselves*, and so Pericles, Phidias, Plato, and "Sophocles above all" are "all of them out-and-out artists by nature, ideal artists shaping themselves, individuals of a single cast, works of art standing there like immortal and deathless images of the gods."[36] In this sense, the actors who step out on stage mentioned in the quotation above are indeed only *re*producing the work of some dramatist, and every notable Greek is himself a dramatist. On the other hand, the appeal to the art of the dramatist in the quotation about postromantic art suggests the side of potential alienation within the artist's ability. Drama, in other words, is at once an art that opens up the fullest possibilites within the supposed Hegelian ideal of Greek plasticity and beauty but at the same time an art that (as Hegel himself categorizes it) belongs fully to the *romantic*.

Artistic Practice and Pastness

Hegel's double appeal in the preceding passages to an art which is put under the heading of "romantic" arts but which is for him also deeply associated with the classical ideal suggests some questions about art's pastness that will be taken up in the following section. We can draw already, however, some conclusions about pastness and Hegelian art from the consideration of artistic practice.

The movement involved in artistic practice – of making the implicit explicit – suggests a sort of one-way retrospectivity or pastness to the activity. What has been "unveiled" by the transformation of the artist no longer remains unclear or unseen; as his discussion of romantic and postromantic art suggests, Hegel clearly holds that art may reach the point at which no further "mystery" is available for artistic activity.

---

[35] For commentary on this passage as a whole, see Martin Donougho, "Remarks on 'Humanus heisst der Heilige,'" *Hegel-Studien*, 17 (1982): pp. 214–225.

[36] *Aesthetics*, II:719; *Vorlesungen* XIV:374.

How should the "pastness" of art, then, be viewed? I will turn in the final section to some suggestions about this question which differ from a number of the usual construals involved in the "end of art" thesis already under discussion.

III. HEGEL AND THE "PASTNESS" OF ART

Hegel is frequently read as simply *having* or endorsing a classical ideal of perfect correlation between artistic form and matter, but one might raise a question about the place of this ideal in Hegel's aesthetic scheme. Martin Donougho, for example, has questioned whether it is right to assume, as so many commentators on the *Aesthetics* have, that Hegel is some form of (neo)classicist.[37] I want to suggest here that the preceding account of artistic practice – that art always involves a making-explicit which requires a retrospective view – gives some further reasons to follow such a line of questioning.

As Donougho suggests, it is certainly an odd fact that Hegel's prophecy about the "end" of art coincides at once with the emergence of bold new claims about art's sovereignty and the "museumization" (for want of a better word) of works of past art – the collecting and staging that characterized the new museum and concert-hall culture of Hegel's time. One might say a good deal in this connection by examining the relation between Schinkel's new art museum on the Spree and Hegel's aesthetics, but I will turn instead in this context – partially with an eye to the Hegelian appeal we have seen to the dramatist's representational abilities – to another example from the drama.[38]

One way of placing the pastness of the ideal of Hegel's aesthetic system into some perspective might be to consider, then, his idealization of Greek drama in the light of Hellmut Flashar's important dramaturgical observation that the first production of a Greek tragedy on a German stage without additions, textual revisions or inclusion of other sorts of (musical, dance, or operatic) performance occurred ten years after Hegel's death.[39] The performances of Greek tragedy which Hegel

---

[37] Donougho, "Art and History: Hegel on the End, the Beginning and the Future of Art," p. 185.

[38] On Hegel and the cultural life of Berlin, see Otto Pöggeler, ed., *Hegel in Berlin: Preussische Kulturpolitik und idealistische Ästhetik: Zum 150. Todestag des Philosophen* (Berlin: Staatsbibliothek Preusisscher Kulturbesitz, 1981) and Otto Pöggeler and Annemarie Gethmann-Siefert, eds. *Kunsterfahrung und Kulturpolitik im Berlin Hegels* (Bonn: Bouvier, 1983).

[39] The famous 1841 production of Sophocles' *Antigone* was first presented in Potsdam and afterward in Berlin. Hellmut Flashar, *Inszenierung der Antike: Das griechische Drama auf der Bühne der Neuzeit 1585–1990* (Munich: Beck, 1991), p. 60.

himself saw (in Berlin, Paris, and elsewhere) tended to be actually *operatic* performances of the tragic material.[40]

Hegel himself discusses this issue in the lectures in terms of the stageability of Greek dramas as such. In the 1826 lectures, he expressed the following paradox: "Greek dramas are not produced, yet we find this infinite satisfaction in them...."[41] This paradox – that classical drama is both "unproducible" and at the same time appealing to modern audiences – suggests that, on Hegel's view, there is always a dialectical perspective from which the "classical" ideal of adequate embodiment of form – the realm of the blissful gods of Greece – is in tension with the "romantic" ability of the artist to reconstrue or "stage" a work with a different sense of that past.

Viewed from this perspective, Hegel's "ideal" conception of classical art should be seen not as a privileged moment of transparency against which romantic art simply falls short (the stance one might associate with a neoclassical aesthetic which builds from a presumably immediate focus on a specific moment within art's past – Phidian sculpture, or another facet of fifth-century Athenian art, for example). Rather, the Hegelian ideal of classical art should be viewed in the light of an ongoing engagement with past works which takes into account, with an eye over its shoulder, the very practices of staging (for a particular setting) or collecting (with an eye to a particular audience) that mediate an audience's encounter with the past. In this light, Hegel himself may be seen as a figure much more self-conscious of his role within the contemporaneous construals and reconstruals of the romantic and postromantic in art and culture.

What such a shift in Hegel's aesthetic stance might say for the relationship between art and *philosophy* is another question which can only be addressed briefly here. Art, as Schaeffer has suggested, *is philosophy's past.*[42] That Hegel thinks this is at least partially true gains some confirmation by his procedure both in the *Phenomenology of Spirit* and in the *Aesthetics.* In the *Phenomenology*, Hegel presented a gallery of narratives in which a philosophical narrative emerges from the

---

[40] For a discussion of Hegel's treatment of the importance of this form, see Annemarie Gethmann-Siefert, "Das 'moderne' Gesamtkunstwerk: Die Oper," in *Phänomen versus System: Zum Verhältnis von philosophischer Systematik und Kunsturteil in Hegels Berliner Vorlesungen über Ästhetik oder Philosophie der Kunst* (Bonn: Bouvier, 1992).

[41] *"Griechische Dramen werden nicht angeführt, doch finden wir diese unendliche Befriedigung in ihnen..."* Quoted in Flashar, *Inszenierung der Antike*, p. 61.

[42] Jean-Marie Schaeffer, *Art of the Modern Age: Philosophy of Art from Kant to Heidegger*, p. 137.

narrative of "religion in the form of art."[43] While the *Aesthetics* may be less concerned with the *narrative* relation between these two activities, it is nonetheless clear, especially from a consideration of the passages in the preceding section, that part of Hegel's central philosophical task there is to account for two modes of apprehending a unity which itself tends toward greater explicitness.

---

[43] For an account of Hegel's approach to the relationship between art and philosophy in the *PhG*, see my *Hegel, Literature and the Problem of Agency* (Cambridge, UK: Cambridge University Press, 2001), especially chapter 1.

15 The Absence of Aesthetics in Hegel's Aesthetics

> "Presentness is grace."
> Michael Fried, *Art and Objecthood*[1]

I

A central topic of modern aesthetics after Kant is the problem of aesthetic judgment. The question concerns the proper understanding of logical form of such judgments (such as "this is beautiful") and their possible objectivity. But Hegel does not offer, anywhere in his discussions of fine art, a recognizable theory of aesthetic judgment.[2] He does not even work out a well defined account of aesthetic experience.[3] This

---

[1] Michael Fried, "Art and Objecthood", in *Art and Objecthood: Essays and Reviews* (Chicago: University of Chicago Press, 1998), p. 168.

[2] The following editions and abbreviations have been used:

HS: G.W.F. Hegel, "Hamanns Schriften" in *Berliner Schriften*, ed. by J. Hoffmeister (Berlin: Felix Meiner, XXXX) 1956

E: G.W.F. Hegel, *Enzyklopädie der philosophischen Wissenschaften*, vol. 6 of *Hauptwerke in sechs Bänden* (Hamburg: Felix Meiner, 1992).

FK: G.W.F. Hegel, *Faith and Knowledge*, trans. by Walter Cerf and H. S. Harris (Albany: SUNY Press, 1977).

GW: G.W.F. Hegel, *Glauben und Wissen*, vol. IV of *Gesammelte Werke* (Hamburg: Felix Meiner, 1968).

JA: G.W.F. Hegel, *Sämtliche Werke. Jubiliäumausgabe in zwanzig Bänden*, ed. by H. Glockner (Stuttgart-Bad Cannstatt: Frommann, 1965–1968).

LFA: G.W.F. Hegel, *Aesthetics: Lectures on Fine Arts*, 2 vols., trans. T. M. Knox (Oxford: Clarendon Press, 1975).

PhG: G.W.F. Hegel, *Die Phänomenologie des Geistes*, vol. 2, *Hauptwerke in sechs Bänden* (Hamburg: Felix Meiner, 1992).

PhS: G.W.F. Hegel, *Hegel's Phenomenology of Spirit*, trans. by A.V. Miller (Oxford: Oxford University Press, 1977).

VA: G.W.F. Hegel, *Vorlesungen über die Ästhetik*, Bd. 13, 14, 15 in *JA*.

[3] There are really only two *loci classici* for Hegel's theory of art (besides the theoretical commitments implied by Hegel's use of literature in works such as the *Phenomenology of Spirit* [see R. Pippin (forthcoming_a) and aside from marginal

divergence from much modern aesthetic theory is largely due to the complexity of the concept of art itself as Hegel invokes it. For Hegel's treatment is famously historical; the account of the nature of art is narrative rather than analytic.[4] And he arrives at a most paradoxical conclusion as a result of this narrative: much of what we consider post-classical art (what Hegel calls "romantic" art)[5] is treated as art in the process of "transcending itself as art," somehow "against itself as art," and as much a manifestation of the "limitations" and increasingly dissatisfied "life" of the practice of the production and appreciation of art as it is a part of a continuous tradition. (The even deeper paradox is that romantic art is all of this *as art.*") In less dramatic terms, Hegel denies the autonomy of the aesthetic, or at least its complete autonomy, and this denial is the basis of the claim that art must be considered as a

essays like his "Hamanns Schriften," Hegel (*HS*).) There are paragraphs in sections §556 to §564 in the Absolute Spirit section of the *Encyclopedia*, and the four lecture courses on fine art (1821, 1823, 1826, and 1828/1829.) In 1835 (and then in a second edition in 1842) one of Hegel's students, H. G. Hotho, working from Hegel's own notes (which are now lost) and student transcriptions, compiled an edition based on (apparently) the last three of these lecture series. This was published in the Moldenhauer–Michel edition and was the basis for Knox's Oxford English translation. Hotho's edition has been vigorously challenged for more than twenty-five years by Annemarie Gethmann-Siefert, the editor of the critical edition of the lectures. (She is putting out essentially the student notes for all of the lecture series independently and has long claimed that what people treat as Hegel's aesthetics is actually Hotho's aesthetics.) See A. Gethmann-Siefert "H. G. Hotho," *Hegel-Studien, Beiheft*, 22 (1983), p. 237 and "Ästhetik oder Philosophie der Kunst: Die Nachschriften und Zeugnisse zu Hegels Berliner Vorlesungen," *Hegel-Studien*, p. 26. While there are some indications that the Hotho version may here or there include some of Hotho's enthusiasms for various art objects (See Lydia Goehr, "The Ode to Joy: Music and Musicality in Tragic Culture," *International Yearbook of German Idealism*, IV (2006), pp. 83–86 on Hegel's tastes in music and similar claims by Gethmann-Siefert in A. Gethmann-Siefert, (1992) "Das 'moderne' Gesamtkunstwerk: Die Oper," in *Phänomen vs. System: zum Verhältnis von philosophischer Systematik und Kunsturteil in Hegels Berliner Vorlesungen über Ästhetik oder Philosophie der Kunst*, ed. by A. Gethmann-Siefert (Bonn: Bouvier, 1992) p. 197ff.) and that he may have edited Hegel as he interpreted Hegel (how could it be otherwise?), I have never seen evidence to the effect that the Hotho version is seriously unreliable or is some kind of fraud, at least with respect to the basic issues treated here. There is one serious issue, but it seems to me unresolvable. See Footnote 7.

4 Officially, it is both narrative, in the lectures, and systematic, in the *Encyclopedia*. In the latter, though, sections §561 and §562 make it clear that the account there depends on the historical distinction among *symbolic*, *classical*, and *romantic*. For the systematic meaning of those divisions, see Terry Pinkard, "Symbolic, Classical and Romantic Art," in *Hegel and the Arts*, ed. by Stephen Houlgate (Evanston: Northwestern University Press, 2007), pp. 3–28.

5 It should be stressed that Hegel is only interested in a theory of *great* art and is not terribly interested in the strictly ontological question of art "just as art."

social institution linked to the development of the norms and values of a society as a whole, and that it is best understood in terms of its similarities with religion and philosophy and not as autonomous.

Hegel's approach remains quite controversial.[6] Someone who denies the autonomy of art seems on the verge of making art a means to something else or the manifestation of a deeper reality: a sign of the contradictions of capitalist society, a formalist refusal of the culture industry, a site of negative resistance to spreading "identity thinking" and so forth. Such approaches often explain away art, rather than render it more intelligible as art. But the fact that Hegel largely ignores the question of the logical peculiarities of aesthetic judgments and their possible validity also highlights two potential advantages of his approach. First it opens up the possibility of addressing the question of the meaning of radical normative change in art making and art appreciating. (If the conceptual content of "the aesthetic" *can* change, and radically so, then there is no obvious way to isolate logically "the" nature of aesthetic judgment and aesthetic experience. All of *that* changes too.) And Hegel's approach might put us in a position to understand the significance of by far the greatest revolution in art history – modernism.

More specifically, what I want to show is that Hegel's account of art has to be understood as relying on two of his most interesting and challenging claims: his understanding of the relation between thought and sensibility in experience, and his understanding of what he calls the "inner- outer" relationship in his theory of agency. In both cases a strict duality is rejected, especially in his account of agency, where the model of inner states causing external bodily action is denied. The bearing of these claims on his account of art might help frame the issue of art after Hegel.

II

Since Hegel's full position – his claim that art is the sensible appearance or "showing" [*Schein*] of "the Idea"[7] – is not as well known as many

---

[6] One of the main interpretive controversies: does Hegel mean that art is wholly dispensable, in favor of a fully reflective philosophical account ("of the Absolute"), or is it overcome only as the *primary* mode of human self-knowledge, a position it held basically just once, in fifth century Athens? My own view is that the evidence is dispositive: that he meant the latter. For an account in accord with such a verdict, an account of the "nontranscendent" view of the achievement of absolute spirit, see Nuzzo (2006), p. 303.

[7] This phrase, "das sinnliche Scheinen der Idee," raises the most serious issue about Hotho's reliability, as noted above. It does not appear in the extant student transcripts, only in Hotho's edition. See A. Gethmann-Siefert, *Einführung in Hegels Ästhetik* (Munich: Wilhelm Fink, 2005) p. 241ff.

other major positions in the philosophy of art, I want to start with summary sketch of what I understand to be Hegel's theory of fine art. This will have to be quite breathless, and we will quickly see that no such summary is possible without also involving an interpretation of Hegel's most ambitious general philosophical position, so I will have to say something about that in Section III. Then we can return to the questions posed above. There are four points that we need on the table.

1. One of the things that distinguishes Hegel from many modern philosophers of art is his focus on the centrality of *aesthetic content* in his account of successful and especially great art. Contrary to post-Kantian formalism in philosophical aesthetics and criticism, for Hegel inadequate understanding of content (of the "Idea") = bad art. "Works of art are all the more excellent in expressing true beauty, the deeper is the inner truth of their content and thought." (*LFA*, 74, *VA*, 105)[8] The great enemy is indeterminacy, mere gestures at the beyond, or worshipful awe at the unsayable. Hence Hegel's hostility toward the sublime as regressive.

What does he mean by content? He is given to saying that the reason art should be understood as belonging together with religion and philosophy is that the content of all of these "bring to consciousness and express the Divine" (*LFA*, 7; *VA*, 21).[9] But when he first introduces such a claim in the Introduction, he follows it with a number of appositives and qualifications that strip it of much traditional religious association and so must have left his original auditors somewhat confused. He writes of artistic content as the Divine, *das Göttliche*, (and not God) and his appositives are, the Divine, that is, "the deepest interests of mankind," and "the most comprehensive truths of spirit." (*LFA*, 7; *VA*, 21) Art is said to share with religion and philosophy the attempt to express what is simply called "the highest" (*das Höchste*). This could be taken to mean the obvious: simply that in all great art issues of the utmost gravity and importance are at stake: justice versus vengeance; the competing claims of city, religion, and family; the gods; human perfection; what it is to live well with blind fate and moral luck; and death – perhaps even the "meaning of Being." But we know from Hegel's other works that for him the highest value or aspiration is freedom, that freedom is a form of rational agency, the actualization of reason,[10] that such

---

[8] Cf. *Encyclopedia* §562A.

[9] See also: "...the Divine is the absolute subject matter of art." (*LFA*, 607; *VA*, 237) Note too that Hegel immediately says that the Divine "...had to objectify itself, and therefore proceed out of itself into the secular content of subjective personality." (Ibid., my emphasis.)

[10] Poetry is, for example, even said to be "reason individualized" [das individualisierte Vernünftige] *LFA*, 977; *VA*, 245. The link between freedom and reason as Hegel

responsiveness to reason is constitutive of all intelligibility, and that he treats all other prior expressions of "the highest" as incomplete manifestations of such freedom. This is a considerably more ambitious claim than "important matters are at stake."

He frequently claims in the lectures that the "need" for art springs from a need of human subjects to be able to "externalize themselves" in the public world and so to be able to recognize themselves in the world and in objects and in the other humans which confront any subject. (This need for externalization [*Entäußerung*] Luther's translation for the biblical *kenosis*, in any actual exercise of freedom will play a crucial role in all aspects of the theory, as we will see.)[11] Now Hegel adds that in art (as well as religion and philosophy) this externalization and self-recognition concerns "the highest things." Again, he roughly means some sort of self-knowledge about the nature and "actuality" of freedom. Such a highest truth is regularly said to be "the idea," which, in his remarks on Solger, he calls simply and somewhat unhelpfully "infinite absolute negativity," the Idea's activity "in negating itself as infinite and universal as to become finitude and particularity." For the moment, it is safe to say that if Hegel is expressing a religious view, then he is a member of a Christian sect with only one member. (All of which is not yet even to mention the flabbergasting claim in §560 of the *Encyclopedia*: "The work of art is just as much the work of free will, and the artist is the master of God [*Meister des Gottes*].)"

2. The relation between the issue of beauty and the norms relevant to fine art is not one that Hegel states with any clarity. In Hotho's edition, he first announces the subject matter as the "realm of the beautiful" but then immediately says that, more particularly [*näher*], the subject is art, and then adds that he means *die schöne Kunst*, the phrase regularly translated as "fine" art, as if in testimony to the *kalos k'agathos* issue from antiquity. Officially, Hegel's position is that the beauty of nature is not a proper or significant subject for reflection (nature is "spiritless" [*geistlos*] and by and large natural beauty simply doesn't matter), and that fine or beautiful art reached its culmination in Greek antiquity. Greek architecture, sculpture, and literature amount to the culmination and perfection of what art is qua art, that is, beautiful. Somewhat inconsistently, he will also refer to the task of making the spiritual, inner realm

understands it is not a Kantian one, and it does not just involve the exercise of an individual faculty. See R. Pippin, *Hegel's Practical Philosophy: Rational Agency as Ethical Life* (forthcoming, Cambridge University Press).

[11] In Hegel's unusual theology, both the account of creation in the Hebrew bible and the Christian doctrine of Incarnation are "images" of the "logical" necessity of such *Entäußerung*.

of romantic art *beautiful* ("the spiritual beauty of the absolute inner life as inherently infinite spiritual subjectivity"), although he also refers to such beauty as "something subordinate" [*etwas Untergeordnetes*] and notes that romantic art must aspire to something more "substantial" than this, the realm of the "willing and self-knowing spirit" [which he does not refer to as beautiful]. (*LFA*, 518; *VA*, 129) Here is a summary claim of his official position:

> Therefore the world-view of the Greeks is precisely the milieu [*Mitte*] in which beauty begins its true life and builds its serene kingdom; the milieu [*Mitte*] of free vitality which is not only there naturally and immediately but is generated by spiritual vision and transfigured by art; the milieu [*Mitte*] of a development of reflection and at the same time of that absence of reflection that neither isolates the individual nor can bring back to positive unity and reconciliation his negativity, grief, and misfortune. (*LFA*, 437; *VA*, II, 26)

Art after the beautiful (which Hegel calls "romantic" art) is not more beautiful but, Hegel often says, simply "*better*," "more excellent" [*vortrefflicher*] even if not better art.[12] He goes on to remark that what is lacking or defective in classical art is just what is lacking in art itself (*LFA*, 79; *VA*, 111) and he suggests frequently that this defect consists in the very assumption constitutive of art itself: that the "ideal" (the true nature of reality) *can* have an adequate sensible form. Romantic art then must be art in which the limitation of art as a vehicle of self-knowledge is itself expressed and in some way transcended, not present merely as a *failure*, a negative limitation or nostalgic longing or a sublime mystery. His puzzling formula is: "In this way romantic art is the self-transcendence of art within its own sphere and in the form of art itself" (*LFA*, 80; *VA*, 112). Naturally such a claim raises the question: what *is* art once it has become its own self-transcendence? Hegel has a number of answers, ranging from philosophy to religion to displays of virtuosity to a memorializing art or an art of remembrance alone, but I believe his position itself at least allows us at least to suggest a possible answer: European modernism.

Actually – in testimony to the fact that any summary of anything in Hegel has to be multiply qualified – for all this philhellinism, Hegel also points out that the limitations of the beautiful as an aesthetic ideal were already dramatically, vividly present in Greek drama, in tragedy.[13] It is

---

[12] Beauty itself is mostly defined in terms of Hegel's systematic project and it does sound "classical," a familiar criticism of Hegel. " . . . the beautiful thing in its existence makes its own Concept appear as realized and displays in itself subjective unity and life." (*LFA*, 114; *VA*, 155.)

[13] It is actually Schiller, not Hegel, who simply idealizes the beauty of all Greek art (cf. "Hymnen an die Nacht"), and Hegel seems to accept Novalis's critique of

already true in tragedy that "art now transcends itself, in that it forsakes the element of a reconciled embodiment of spirit in sensuous form and passes over from the poetry of the imagination to the prose of thought." (*LFA*, 89; *VA*, 123) The impossibility of the sort of reconciliation and harmony necessary for the beautiful to function as an ideal, and the emphasis on the prosaic nature of bourgeois modernity will play large roles in Hegel's treatment of late romanticism and so for his views of art in modernity. There is a passage in the Preface to the *Phenomenology* that summarizes this point dramatically.

Death, if that is what we want to call this non-actuality, is of all things the most dreadful, and to hold fast to what is dead requires the greatest strength. *Lacking strength, Beauty hates the Understanding* for asking of her what it cannot do. But the life of Spirit is not the life that shrinks from death and keeps itself untouched by devastation, but rather the life that endures it and maintains itself in it. It wins its truth only when, in utter dismemberment, it finds itself. (§32, 18–19)[14]

3. The two key notions in Hegel's account of beauty and fine art are the notions of *Schein* or appearing, showing, or often simply a visual "shining," and variations on liveliness, life and enliven, *Lebendigkeit, beleben, Leben,* and so forth "The beautiful is characterized as the pure appearance of the Idea to sense." (*E*, 111) In terms of his frequent Ur-image: " ... the outer must harmonize with an inner which is harmonious in itself, and just on that account, can reveal itself as itself in the outer." (*E*, 155) The manifestation (or shining) of the Idea in sensuous material, however, is not anything like a cognitive awareness, and Hegel's attempt to explain why it is the closest he ever gets to an account of distinctly aesthetic experience.[15] Rather than cognitive awareness, fine art is said to awaken in us an emotional and spirited responsiveness to everything which has a place in human spirit (Hegel quotes Terence's "*Nihil humani* ... " principle.) Here is his summary claim.

such beauty-worship, both among the Greeks (that they "aestheticized" suffering and death, could make no place for "the negative" in human life) and of German philhellenism.

[14] So Hegel would never go as far as Barnett Newman's "The impulse of modern art was to destroy beauty." See Newman, "The Sublime is Now." *The Tiger's Eye,* vol. VI, p. 51; quoted in Alexander Nehamas, *Only a Promise of Happiness: The Place of Beauty in a World of Art* (Princeton: Princeton University Press, 2007), p. 13. Nothing needs to be destroyed. The time for the beautiful as an ideal of high art has simply passed.

[15] It isn't straightforwardly such a theory because what counts as this enlivened responsiveness also changes.

[Art's] aim therefore is supposed to consist in awakening [wecken] and vivifying [*beleben*] our slumbering feelings, inclinations, and passions of every kind, in filling the heart, in forcing the human being, whether educated or not, to go through the whole gamut of feelings which the human heart in its inmost and secret recesses can bear, experience and produce, through what can move and stir the human breast in its depth and manifold possibilities and aspects, and to deliver to feeling and contemplation for its enjoyment whatever spirit possesses of the essential and lofty in its thinking and in the Idea. . . . (LFA, 46; VA, 70)

Such claims can sound very much like romantic boilerplate unless we realize that Hegel believes that it is quite possible for the various "highest" norms governing acceptable and authoritative knowledge claims or practical, ethical, and political life actually to "go dead" in a certain way, to function in a matter of fact way in constraining claims of authority and kinds of conduct, but to do so, as he says, "positively," merely as an "external" lifeless authority.[16] In such a context, this somewhat Schillerean concern with this enlivening function has its own objective social conditions for successful realization. Indeed this ability, central to art's function, to help sustain (by expressing) the "life" of the highest norms (when they can be so successfully affirmed) is said to be essential to the authority of such norms themselves. Here is a well-known passage from the Jena *Phenomenology of Spirit* about this issue:

The manner of study in ancient times differed from that of the modern age in that the former was the proper and complete formation of the natural consciousness. Putting itself to the test at every point of its existence, and philosophizing about everything it came across, it made itself into a universality that was active through and through. In modern times, however, the individual finds the abstract form ready-made; the effort to grasp and appropriate it is more the direct driving-forth of what is within and the truncated generation of the universal than it is the emergence of the latter from the concrete variety of existence. Hence the task nowadays consists not so much in purging the individual of an immediate, sensuous mode of apprehension, and making him into a substance that is an object of thought and that thinks, but rather in just the opposite, in freeing

---

[16] In Hegel's development, this concern with the "life" of norms, rules, principles, and ideals, or rather the life and death of such norms, has to count as his most prominent concern, beginning early with his account of love in the Christian community, developing into a general view of "life," and culminating in the mature theory of *Geist* or "spirit." This *Liebe–Leben–Geist* trajectory was first proposed by Dilthey, *Die Jugendgeschichte Hegels*, in *Gesammelte Schriften* Bd. 4 (Goettingen: Vandenhoeck & Ruprecht, 1990) in 1905 and reappears in such commentators as H. S. Harris, *Hegel's Development: Toward the Sunlight 1770–1801* (Oxford: Oxford University Press, 1971) and Dieter Henrich, *Hegel im Kontext* (Frankfurt: Suhrkamp, 1971).

determinate thoughts from their fixity so as to give actuality to the universal, and impart to it spiritual life. (§33, 19–20)[17]

It would not be too much of an exaggeration to say that Hegel's philosophy of art is not a theory of representation or expression, not a classical theory of mimesis or a post-Christian theory of creation (genius)[18] but of "enlivening," once we notice too that such enlivening is a crucial element in the conditions for the possibility of any norm's grip on those bound to it, and that this grip can loosen and fail, thus requiring something different from art. (That is, such an externalization can be said to help "*bring*" such norms and principles and values "*to* life," not merely to express their life. The sensible showing of the Idea is not an attempt to provide an example or a paradigmatic instance but, as Hegel puts it, to "realize or actualize the universal itself."[19] I will try to make use in a minute of Hegel's account of agency and the realization of an intention to try to make this clearer.) In sum, we learn something about the "life" of such values when we see them externalized in art objects, and we learn this in a way unique to art.

4. Aside from these gestures at "quickening" or enlivening, Hegel does not have a particularly rich or detailed theory of aesthetic experience. Most of the time, he speaks rather dryly of a "*Kunstbetrachtung*," a way of considering art, and he seems to agree with Schlegel that the critic should now understand himself not as judge, as avatar of

---

[17] The same language appears in the *Lectures on Fine Art*. Note especially that in the list of modern oppositions he includes the contrast between "the dead, inherently empty concept, and the full concreteness of life" (*LFA*, 53–54; *VA*, 80; cf. also *LFA*, 1006; *VA*, 282) Since one would presumably want to understand something in its proper life, not dead, or empty, this implies paradoxically a higher more adequate status for art when compared with philosophy. See R. Pippin, "The Status of Literature" for a discussion of this issue.

[18] Of course, Hegel being Hegel, it is also possible to say that for him art is also *all* of these alternatives, but that they all can be shown to be incomplete manifestations of the full notion of art as enlivening appearing, that such incomplete manifestations are themselves tied to an incomplete (not erroneous) self-understanding of freedom.

[19] This highlights a peculiarity in Hegel's treatment of art, made much of by Henrich. The "*Ende*" or end of art is not treated as a *Vollendung* or completion or fullest realization of possibilities, as is, one could argue, Hegel's treatment of the modern representative state, or Lutheranism or Hegelian systematic idealism. Art's ending is much more, in Henrich's terms, a *Zerfall*, a kind of decay; as if art's possibilities are exhausted, as if "the life had gone out of them," one might put it. Even within the art history lectures the "end" of symbolic and classical art are forms of transition; but this is not true for the end of romantic art. See Henrich, "Zerfall und Zukunft: Hegels Theoreme ueber das Ende der Kunst," in *Fixpunkte: Abhandlungen und Essays zur Theorie der Kunst* (Frankfurt: Suhrkamp, 2003) pp. 82–83, and p. 96.

exemplary taste, but as interpreter. (What "enlivening" inspires is what we now call criticism, not appreciation.) Hegel distances himself from any belief in what he calls the "mere subjectivity" and "affectivity" of the artistic response and speaks instead of the attempt to "plunge the depths of a work" and to go ever "deeper" into it [*das Kunstwerk zu versenken und zu vertiefen*]. (*VA*, 54) He also says that the "contemplation [*Betrachtung*] of beauty is of a liberal kind [*liberaler Art*]; it leaves objects alone as being inherently free and infinite." (*E*, 114) This introduces the problem of the autonomy of the aesthetic dimension, and also introduces the relation between these lectures and, let us say, his basic position.[20]

III

I have begun by suggesting that the first thing we should understand about Hegel's view is that there is an "absence of aesthetics" in Hegel's treatment of the beautiful and fine art. That is, as is already quite apparent, he is interested in a wide variety of issues that do not have much to do with what became the philosophical issues of aesthetics in the eighteenth century after Baumgarten's use of that term established a kind of philosophic subdiscipline.[21] I don't mean to suggest that Hegel failed to appreciate that the primary modality in the experience of the beautiful and of fine art is sensible. He makes this point in his own way many times. But primary modality does not for Hegel mean independent modality, and that is the beginning of the Hegelian story that will ultimately associate art with religion and philosophy and which will provide the basis for his claim about the essential historicity of art. His clearest statement occurs in the Introduction:

Of course the work of art presents itself to sensuous apprehension. It is there for sensuous feeling, external or internal, for sensuous intuition and ideas, just as nature is ... But nevertheless the work of art, as a sensuous object, is not merely for sensuous apprehension; its standing is of such a kind that, though sensuous, it is essentially at the same time for spiritual apprehension; spirit is meant to be affected by it and to find some satisfaction in it. (*LFA*, 35; *VA*, 57)

---

[20] See the discussion in Bubner, "Is There a Hegelian Theory of Aesthetic Experience?" in *The Innovations of Idealism*, trans. by Nick Walker (Cambridge, UK: Cambridge University Press, 2003), pp. 216–230. Bubner makes use of what Hegel has to say about symbolic art to work his way toward the "traces" of a theory of aesthetic experience in Hegel. Much of what he says about such an experience is quite suggestive for the category of modernist art.

[21] For a useful, brief summary of the Baumgarten–Hegel history, see A. Nuzzo, "Hegel's Aesthetics as a Theory of Absolute Spirit," *International Yearbook of German Idealism*, IV (2006), pp. 293–295.

Later Hegel formulates his own version of Kant's disinterestedness claim, insisting that an art work does not exist for the satisfaction of any desire but "for the contemplative side of spirit alone," and that it is "meant to satisfy purely spiritual existence." (*LFA*, 36–37; *VA*, 58)

But again, adding to the complexity, by "for the contemplative side" Hegel does not mean "for contemplation." There *is* supposed to be something distinctively aesthetic about the *Schein* of some ideal, even if such an experience is not autonomous or a realm of experience wholly unto itself. At one point Hegel simply proposes that art be understood as making "every one of its productions into a thousand-eyed Argus," that art makes every human action, event, speech, and tone of voice "into an eye, in which the free soul is revealed in its inner infinity." (*LFA*, 154; *VA*, 203) This suggests that the treatment of some action or speech in an art work, however sensibly apprehended, invites in a unique way interrogation at a more sustained, reflective and involving – "lively" – level, suggesting that like the eye and the human soul, the art work becomes both the vehicle of sight, that by which we see, and that into which the soul, the human meaning or significance of the action or speech, can be seen.[22]

To be sure, neither Kant's nor Schiller's aesthetics, the greatest influences on Hegel, were sensualist or empiricist, but Kant's claim about the relevance of purposiveness to aesthetic experience and Schiller's interest in the relevance of our moral vocation are not what Hegel has in mind. For, in making this point, Hegel is making his usual and most repeated point, familiar since the *Differenzschrift* and *Glauben und Wissen*.[23] It is the point that I want to say is central to Hegel's critique of the putative independence of aesthetic experience, although admittedly, one that is *very* hard to restate properly. It is that the distinguishability of concept and intuition in experience – which Hegel is happy to concede – is not equivalent to and does not entail the separability of concept and intuition as *independent* contributors to experience.[24] Contrary to some

---

[22] Cf. "Car je ne le regarde pas comme on regarde une chose, je ne le fixe pas en son lieu, mon regard erre en lui comme dans les nimbres de l'Etre, je vois selon ou avec lui plutôt qu je ne le vois." See Merleau-Ponty, "*L'Oeil et l'Esprit*" (Paris: Gallimand, 1964), p. 23. In many respects, *L'Oeil et l'Esprit* is a powerful restatement of many Hegelian themes. The critique of Cartesian optics is much like Hegel's rejection of a "two-stage" process of perception, as is what Merleau-Ponty calls "un mystère de passivité" in perception, passive but not wholly receptive (p. 52). An important difference: Hegel stresses more the social dimension of artistic meaning.

[23] *GW*, 343; *BK*, 92. See also *GW*, 327; *BK*, 69–70.

[24] I. Kant, *Kritik der reinen Vernunft* A51/B75. Kant's claims about the strict distinction between these two "sources," even as he emphasized in his own way Hegel's dialectical point about their necessarily intertwined, even inseparable role

criticisms of this position, there is no reason to think that Hegel is collapsing or eliminating the distinction between the sensual or passive and
the conceptual (or active) elements in knowledge. His position is much
more complicated than that. There is no reason to think he is collapsing
the two, any more than there is any reason to think that someone claiming that "X cannot be representationally significant except as Y'ed" can
be assumed to be claiming "There are no X's; there is only Y'ing," or
even that to be claiming "*X's not playing **all by itself** a representationally significant role* means it *plays **no** role whatsoever*, has no function
within knowledge claims."[25]

More broadly, Hegel's denial of a scheme-content distinction means
that for him the question of how discursive thought informs sensibility
in our acquiring perceptual knowledge is of the same logical form as the
question of how thought or inner intention informs or is manifest *in*
bodily action.[26] In neither case is there a "two-stage" process, neither
the conceptualization of independently acquired sensory material, nor
an inner intention functioning as distinct cause, initiating a subsequent
bodily movement as one might kick a ball to start it rolling. It is, in
that sense, his Ur-question. Hegel's attempt to state properly the implications of this claim – sensibility is the *primary* aesthetic modality but
not an *independent* one, just as concept and intuition are *distinguishable* even if not *separable*, just as intention is not *reducible* to bodily
motions, even while not an independent *cause* of such motion – is an
attempt that surfaces on nearly every page of his work, early and late.[27]

in knowledge, was the basis of his critique of the entire prior philosophical tradition, elements of which, he famously claimed, either "sensualized all concepts of
the understanding" or "intellectualized" appearances (A271/B327).

[25] For Hegel as for the Tractarian Wittgenstein, thought does not "stop short" of the
world; a way of thinking about an object [a *Sinn*] is not an intermediary entity
between us and the referents of thought; it is a way of seeing the world. There is
still plenty of substantive content and empirical guidedness in experience on such
a picture. The claim is only, again, that thought's relation to such objects cannot be
secured or even intuitively pinned down, *by the deliverances of sensibility alone.*
The broadest way to restate the point is simply that the domain of the normative –
in this case what ought to be claimed – is autonomous. Principles constraining
what we ought to believe, what could count as a possible object of experience or
what one ought to do are wholly independent of claims about how the mind works
or what people generally do or what the received world determines us to think.
Fichte appreciated this point in the deepest way and built his whole philosophy
around it.

[26] The aesthetic formulation of the point: " ... art consists precisely in the connection, the affinity and the concrete interpenetration [*dem konkreten Ineinander*] of
meaning [*Bedeutung*] and form [*Form*]." *LFA*, 763–764; *VA*, 299)

[27] Cf. McDowell's apt formulation in *Mind and World* (Cambridge, MA: Harvard
University Press, 1994), pp. 89–90: "Similarly intentions without overt activity are

The master image in almost all these discussions is one we have already seen and it is also not easily accessible: that the right way to understand the "inner–outer" relation at work in all such cases is as a speculative inner–outer "identity." This is a frequent enough summary image that we should expect it to inform his treatment of fine art and that is indeed what we find. (One of his more accessible formulations: "The universal need for art . . . is man's rational need to lift the inner and outer world into his spiritual consciousness as an *object* in which he recognizes *his own self.*" (*LFA*, 31; *VA*, 52, my emphasis) The relation between the artist and her product (inner to outer) and the art object and human receptivity (outer to inner) is supposed to involve such an "identity," with the latter often expressed as spirit (both producer and appreciator) "finding itself" in the art object. The crucial discussions of the end of symbolic art (in the epigram) and of classical art (in Roman satire) are couched in terms of some unresolved and ultimately unbearable distorted self-understanding of this inner–outer relation. The rather grand and considerably less accessible but canonical formulation from the *Encyclopedia* (the formulation that, somewhat unfortunately, guides everything in the Fine Art lectures): "Hence what is only something inner, is also thereby external, and what is only external is also only something inner." (*EL*, §140)

And it is clear often that Hegel makes a great deal of his version of this interdependence in his account of art. "In this way," he claims about art, "the sensuous aspect of art is spiritualized [*vergeistert*], since spirit appears in art as made sensuous. [*versinnlicht*]" The art work is said "to want sensible presence" [sinnliche Gegenwart]

. . . which indeed should remain sensuous, but liberated from the scaffolding of its purely material nature. Thus the sensuous aspect of a work of art, in comparison with the immediate existence of things in nature, is elevated to a pure appearance, and the work of art stands in the middle between immediate sensuousness and ideal thought. It is not yet pure thought, but, despite its sensuousness is no longer a purely material existent either . . . the sensuous in the work of art is itself something ideal. (*LFA*, 38; *VA*, 60)

And,

Art by means of its representations, while remaining within the sensuous sphere, liberates man at the same time from the power of sensuousness . . . art lifts (man)

idle; movements of limbs without concepts are mere happenings, not expressions of agency."

with gentle hands out of and above imprisonment in nature . . . " (*LFA*, 49; *VA*, 74)[28]

Again, a conventional view of what Hegel urges as a successor to "aesthetics" is an institutional or social theory of art objects (understood by some Hegel commentators to mean that whatever some community, say the art market, determines to be the norm for art and good art, *is* thereby art and good art, that some such norm comes to be an inseparable element in aesthetic experience itself).[29] This is what many understand to be the import of the idealist claim about the mediated, nonindependent status of the aesthetic dimension. The mediation is supposed by such commentators to be "socialy normative," in the "inverted-Hegelian" way that Marx would come to consider the primary mediating or meaning-making function in modern societies, including aesthetic meaning, to be "the commodity form." There is something right about this characterization of Hegel's position, but at the very least Hegel also thinks that the transition to modern, romantic art (and beyond) can be said to make some sort of clear, compelling sense (not at all like a change in fashion or a purely contingent sequence) and at most he undoubtedly wants to understand this transition as progressive in some way, that such art reflects some truth about norm, meaning and human activity "better" than earlier art, even if not, as he often says, better "as art". (It is at this point that Hegel obviously parts company with the "anything goes" version of the social-institutional theory of art.) At any rate, like the left-Hegelian or Marxist interpretation, Hegel's approach completely alters the sense of the question of "by what right" one would claim that a single work is better or better art or art at all. That question cannot be answered as a question about art alone, certainly when framed about

---

[28] It should be noted that Hegel thinks that in his aesthetics Kant came much closer to realizing the nature of the true relation between immediacy and mediation, in general, than anywhere else. He notes that Kant realized that the material element of art – sense, feeling, emotion, inclination – is not "subsumed under universal categories of the understanding, and dominated by the concept of freedom in its abstract universality, but is so bound up with the universal that it is inwardly and absolutely adequate to it. Therefore *thought is incarnate in the beauty of art*, and the material is not determined by thought externally, but exists freely on its own account – in that the natural, sensuous, the heart, etc., have in themselves proportion, purpose, and harmony; and intuition and feeling are elevated to spiritual universality, just as thought not only renounces its hostility to nature but is enlivened thereby." (*LFA*, 60: *VA*, 88; my emphasis) Hegel then goes on to make his usual criticism of Kant for construing this as having only a "subjective" meaning, rather than about "what is absolutely true and actual." (Ibid.)

[29] For a survey of the recent (post-1970) history of the institutional theory of art, see D. Graves, "The Institutional Theory of Art: A Survey," *Philosophia*, XXXV (1997), pp. 51–67.

a particular work, and can only be approached if framed in terms of a general theory of a collective attempt at self-knowledge and productive activity. The skeptic's worry that any categorization of or evaluation of art might express idiosyncratic personal preferences already starts off far too far downstream for it to have any interest or bite. If such a question arises, it arises "inside" the practice of the production and appreciation of art as a social self-regulating activity, and can be addressed according to the norms of that practice. The "theorist" has no special authority about any such question.

Of course, all such qualifications on the supposed autonomy of the aesthetic cannot be so formulated that such considerations obscure the distinctness of the *aesthetic* manifestation of the idea. This is a dialectical tightrope that appears frequently throughout Hegel's "system." (The fact that moral considerations only get a grip within and as dependent on a distinct and substantive form of ethical life – that they are not matters of pure practical reason – does not mean that Hegel is out to deny the authority or distinctness of moral considerations, any more than his position on the inseparability of concept and intuition means to deny the possibility of empirical knowledge.) Simply put, the Idea's sensible living appearance is a vital, but not fully articulated manifestation. The "ethical harmony" of Greek spirit is sensible and, in Hegel's sense, alive, in Greek architecture, but not in the way in which it becomes an object of reflection in Greek philosophy, and eventually in Hegel's account in the *Phenomenology*. The painful internal tensions and incompatibilities of that ethical world are directly sensible in Greek tragedy, but not in the more self-conscious (and hence "freer") way such tensions are manifest in Socrates' challenges in the Platonic dialogues.

The second implication is a thoroughly historicized account of such institutional or social settings, given that Hegel treats conceptual norms as necessarily variable in time.[30] His case for the historicity of such norms is complicated but the basic idea is that the denial of a scheme-content distinction means that traditionally empiricist or transcendental strategies for establishing the normative authority of norms for thought or action are not available. Thought does not exogenously shape

---

[30] This latter is often said to be Hegel's major contribution to not just the philosophical but the academic and scholarly study of art, that, largely thanks to Hegel, the problem of art's intelligibility or meaning should be raised and pursued within "art history" departments. Gombrich famously called Hegel "the father of art history" (although Hegel should not be blamed for anything Gombrich said about art history or art). See E. Gombrich, "Hegel und die Kunstgeschichte," *Neue Rundschau*, 88 (1977), pp. 202–219.

the material of thought and is not simply shaped by it; practical reason does not legislate to our material impulses, or merely devise strategies for their efficient satisfaction. Conceptual and normative change, an inevitable result of simple human finitude, must then be accounted for "internally," brought about by the finitude and incompleteness of some attempt to regulate what we allow each other to say and do, again within a general account of how we go about allowing or forbidding each other's claims and actions.[31]

IV

So Hegel's philosophy of art is dependent first of all on a theory of spirit, on some account of collective, norm-governed human mindedness and an account of the kind of finitude or lack of which explains the production of art works and the legislation of norms for their production and evaluation. We simply need to know how social norms work in order to know how artistic norms work. This theory of such a need and such production is itself doubly dependent. It is first dependent on what Hegel keeps referring to as the "logic" of the inner–outer relation central to properly understanding spirit and its products. The distinct feature of this logic is its contrary-to-common-sense denial of a strict *separation* or "two-stage" view. So in writing about the *production* of art (Greek art, in this case), Hegel writes about their ideas and doctrines [*Vorstellungen* und *Lehren*],

And it was not as if these were already there (vorhanden), in advance of poetry, in an abstract mode of consciousness as general religious propositions and categories of thought, and then later were only clothed in imagery by artists and given an external adornment in poetry; on the contrary the mode of artistic production was such that what fermented in these poets they could work out (herauszuarbeiten) only in the form of art and poetry. (LFA, 102; VA, 141; my emphasis)

And, with respect to the *reception* of the work:

But the self (das Ich) in relation to the object likewise ceases to be the abstraction of both noticing, sensuously *perceiving, and observing . . . In this [beautiful]*

---

[31] So for Hegel the question of the status of the beautiful is not simply a matter of dispute for aesthetic theory, as in, say the dispute between A. Danto, *The Abuse of Beauty* (Chicago: Open Court, 2003), p. 58, who regards the "discovery" that art could be great art without being beautiful an achievement of modern art, or the contrary defense of the beautiful in Nehamas's recent book, *Only a Promise of Happiness*. Rather there was a time when an art work *did* need to be beautiful to be great, but that time has passed. This is not the result of one age having a bad theory or a good theory.

object the self becomes [es wird] concrete in itself since it makes explicit the unity of Concept and reality, the unification in their concreteness, of the aspects hitherto separated, and therefore abstract, in the self and its object. (*LFA*, 114; *VA*, 155)[32]

And this way of talking about inner and outer – that the artist's ideas do not exist "before" but that it is only *as* "worked out" in the art production that they become determinate ideas, and that the subject "becomes" concretely the subject it is *in* aesthetic appreciation – are essential to this discussion. The claims go to the heart of the issue of how Hegel is denying the autonomy of the aesthetic, even while he is not thereby rendering art merely illustrative of or sensible instances of "the Idea," a community's most important norms. (There cannot be any conceptual content to such ideals, there is no "actuality" for such ideals, except *as* worked out (*"herausgearbeitet"* is his term) in artistic production and reception, as well as worked out in other "externalizations" like religion and political life.)

It is also a notion given free and paradoxical reign in Hegel's account of agency, where it does most of its important work, and that introduces the second dependency. As in: "Ethical self-consciousness now learns *from its deed* the developed nature of what it actually did..." (*PhG*, 235) or, "an individual cannot know what he is until he has made himself a reality through action" (*PhG*, 401).[33] In the same way, Hegel is trying to say that we do not, cannot, know who we are, what we are up to, until we have found some way to externalize some version of this knowledge or activity, in art among other enterprises, and (to speak highly metaphorically) have found a way to contest *with each other* and settle on some authoritative view.

In this respect (and this is Hegel's most ambitious claim) art-making is not an incidental or contingent or merely illustrative *expression* of an already achieved self-knowledge, any more than action is the result

---

[32] Cf. also: "In itself, that is to say, the individual in his essential nature is the totality, not the inner alone, but equally the realization of this inner through and in the outer." (*LFA*, 96; *VA*, 133.)

[33] "We are accustomed to say of human beings that everything depends on their essence [*Wesen*] and not on their deeds and conduct. Now in this lies the correct thought that what a human being does should be considered not in its immediacy, but only as mediated through his inwardness [*Inneres*] and as a manifestation of that inwardness. But with that thought we must not overlook the point that the essence and also the inward only prove themselves [*sich bewähren*] as such by stepping forth into appearance. On the other hand, the appeal which human beings make to inwardness as an essence distinct from the content of their deeds often has the intention of validating their mere subjectivity and in this way of escaping what is valid in and for itself." (EL, §112A)

of or expression of a distinct inner intention.[34] Art *is* an achieved form of self-knowledge; knowledge we would not, could not have, except for this realization; just as antecedent formulations of intention can be mere fantasies of commitment, realized or "tested," become what they truly are, only "in the deed." For better or worse, this is the claim we have to understand in order to understand Hegel's theory of art.[35]

Moreover, Hegel treats being an agent (a subject to whom deeds can be imputed) in a way that manifests that second dependency in his philosophy of art. This is because being a subject or an agent is not treated by Hegel as an ontological or strictly philosophical category but as an achieved social status such as, let us say, being a citizen or being a professor, a product or result of mutually recognitive attitudes. This means just what it seems to: different historical communities establish this status in different ways, and there is no truth-maker or fact of the matter they are getting wrong or more and more right. Likewise, art objects are not manifestations of natural kinds. No one discovered the form of opera, lying around hidden. The status, art object of a kind, is an assigned, historically achieved socially authoritative status, and to understand the art of an age we have to understand the ethical and cultural world within which its reception would make sense, posses some authority,[36] and so could "circulate."[37]

---

[34] As conceded several times, it is difficult to find the right formulation for what Hegel is getting at here, but the interpretive consequences of getting it wrong involve quite a serious departure from Hegel, as in de Man's misguided insistence on a psychological "interior thought" externalized in some material. See Paul de Man, "Sign and Symbol in Hegel's Aesthetics" *Critical Inquiry* 8 (1981), pp. 761–775. I agree with Raymond Geuss that de Man also misconstrues what Hegel means by "symbolic" and what he means by saying that "art is for us a thing of the past." See R. Geuss, "A Response to Paul de Man," *Critical Inquiry*, 10 (1983), 375–382 and de Man's reply "'Reply to Raymond Geuss," *Critical Inquiry*, 10 (1983), 383–390.

[35] This is a sketchy summary, but it should be obvious that many questions could be raised about any of these points. Couldn't it be the case, for example, that some art work brought to a suitably "lively" expression/realization some highest ideal, invited interrogation and appreciation in a way tied to the continuing vitality of that norm and so forth, but was still bad art? Hegel's answer is "No," but it would take an independent discussion to defend such a claim.

[36] "The form of romantic art" is said by Hegel to require both an account of "a new vision of the world [*Weltanschauung*]" as well as a "new artistic form." (*LFA*, 516; *VA*, 127)

[37] These two dependencies are linked for Hegel, although that is a book length topic. They are linked because what Hegel understands as the relevant "outer" in the account of *Geist* and its norms is a social, public world, and the dependence of a deed or art product for its sense on that world is a dependence on a mutable, internally "self-negating," restlessly dissatisfied world.

And finally, Hegel wants there to be clear parallels between all these instances of the inner–outer dialectic so prominent in his discussions. That is, the way an action, a bodily movement, can be said to embody a subject's intention and so bear a certain determinate meaning is not as a result of a prior, determinate subjective cause. The intention unfolds *in* the action over time, responsive as much to what is unfolding over time as "true" to an original formulation; it becomes the intention it is only as the deed unfolds. (In the clearest case of what Hegel is talking about, one can be surprised, given what one was willing to do, by what one's commitments "turned out to be," despite how they were formulated ex ante.) But this external dimension of what is only provisionally inner, the actual bodily action, is also dependent on the meaning-making practices in a community at a time; there is no privileged "ownership" of the meaning of the deed by the subject. This publicly authoritative act-description is also not something simply imposed or arbitrarily stipulated "by others." A large network of such practices must be in place and functioning authoritatively for such an ascription to be possible. (And this process can begin to fall apart, as in Hegel's accounts of tragedy.)

In point of fact, Hegel is suggesting more than parallels. He seems to want us to consider the production of art *as a form of agency*, that we should understand the "work" as we understand the bodily movements of an action.[38] In this sense, while there might have been a time (a heroic age) when the right ethical and aesthetic norm for an action might have been the beautiful, it might now be true that the appropriate norm is something like genuineness (more on this in a moment).[39]

Likewise, he wants to say, an art work bears meaning not as the product or result of the artist's intention. What the artist turned out to have intended is available (even to her) only in the work, as "actualized" or "externalized." And such a determinate meaning is itself also dependent on the authoritative social norms at a time, meaning-making practices of criticism, evaluation, categorization, and so forth that, as in the case of action, can begin to break down, or generate incompatible commitments, as at the end of classical or the end of romantic art.[40]

---

[38] In the *Phenomenology of Spirit*, Hegel frequently calls a person's deed her "*Werk*." *PhG*, 178–179; *PhS*, 194.

[39] Cf. Cavell, "A Matter of Meaning It," in *Must We Mean What we Say?* (Cambridge, MA: Harvard University Press, 1969) on "the possibility of fraudulence" as "characteristic of the modern." p. 220, and apropos of the earlier remarks here about raising the question of the point of actions as of the same logical kind as raising the question of the "point" of a painting, cf. his remarks on p. 225ff.

[40] Hegel's position on the meaning of actions is not an "expressivist" one, as that would be understood in the context of, say, Herder or Charles Taylor. (He certainly

V

So what about our age? In the simplest terms, the claim is that the art of modernity (which, for Hegel, in his own time (but *not* for all future time), was late romanticism, primarily lyric poetry) must ultimately also become "an art which transcends itself as art," eschews as nostalgic, not possibly genuine, *both* the beautiful as ideal, as a vehicle for the externalization and recognition of our highest values, as well as, in what Hegel calls the "end of romantic art," the reliance on inwardness, authenticity, purity of heart and the heightened importance of subjectivity in the romantic view of the world. (Persons and buildings and nature can still obviously *be* beautiful; the point is that such manifestations of both natural and artistic beauty have lost their significance. Such beauty doesn't *matter* as it once did.) Such an art will incorporate, in a way necessarily different from beautiful art, the absence of the possibility of reconciliation and harmony and the inspiration typical of classical art (purchased in such art at the price of too weak, incomplete or repressed an acknowledgement of human subjectivity, understood as self-determining not merely responsive to or determined by nature) as well as the romantic posture for Hegel prototypical of modernity. Here is how he describes the postclassical or romantic art enterprise we are in the process of "transcending":

... spirit is pushed back into itself out of its own reconciliation in the corporeal into a reconciliation of itself with itself. The simply solid totality of the Ideal is dissolved, and it falls apart into the double totality of (a) subjective being in itself and (b) the external appearance, in order to enable spirit to reach through this disunity [*Trennung*] a deeper reconciliation with its own element of inwardness. (*LFA*, 518; *VA*, II, 128)

does not believe that art is the "go-cart of spirit," as in Danto, *Abuse of Beauty*, p. 94.) This is because Hegel believes that this whole process of externalization is also a component of a more inclusive social practice, the giving of and asking for reasons under the pressure of possible social conflict. Such externalizations, in other words, count as a kind of proffer to others made when one's actions or products affect what others would otherwise be able to do (or virtually all actions). This is a very long story, but Hegel conceives of such practical rationality as a "social practice" or he conceives of it "pragmatically" or he has a "historicized" view of what counts as the appeal to reasons. The point is that he understands practical reason as a kind of interchange of attempts at justification among persons each of whose actions affects what others would otherwise be able to do, and all of this for a community at a time, and so, in a way that changes. He even considers the production of art as a collective attempt at mutual intelligibility and justification in a way that is a component of such a rationalizing practice. In this context, following that line of thought here would again be a book length digression, at least.

Hegel is no proponent of such dualism, but he regards this posture (the loss of beauty as an ideal, we might say) as necessary in the self-education of spirit. To use Hegel's narrative metaphors, having discovered that human beings do not have a fixed, purposive "place" in nature, no natural home (that nature is disenchanted), spirit abandons its attempt to "see itself" or "find itself" in nature or in corporeal externality at all, ceases to look "there" for purpose and natural law, and begins the attempt to see itself in its own *products*, to find a way to see its culture, work-world, politics, laws, and religion as "its own," not the contingent concatenation of events which merely happen to it and are arbitrarily produced or are imposed by necessity. Romantic art is then both psychologically sensuous and reflective, expressive of how an experience, another person, a world, seems, or feels, "for the subject" as the most important and privileged dimension of experience, and reflectively trying to make some sense that it *should* feel that way "inwardly."

VI

Hegel understands the aspiration to the beautiful in classical art to be intelligible only as part of a very broad and ambitious human aspiration to understand and properly locate all aspects of human being in a way continuous with the natural or nonhuman world. He also claims that this promise could not be fulfilled, and that the experience of suffering and death in Greek tragedy already started to reveal such a division or alienation from the given natural world.[41] Romantic art is the record of such placelessness and a record of the experience of both the need for the externalization of inner experience, and of the inadequacy of any external corporeal form to bear such a meaning.

But this withdrawn stance inevitably leads to the view of all externality, corporeality, the public social world, as having "the character of being indifferent and vulgar" (E, §562) and such elevation of an inward purity of heart amounts to a kind of pathology in Hegel's many treatments of romantic art and romanticism, what he calls in the *Phenomenology* the "law of the heart," the "frenzy of self-conceit," the "beautiful soul" and so on. It is not possible here to explore why he thinks of these implications as pathologies, or why he thinks that their being pathologies counts both towards explaining why they cannot be sustained and why they ought not to be, why they are "irrational" in his sense. But it is at this point that Hegel interprets this limitation of romantic art as a kind of final revelation of the limitation of art itself,

---

[41] "We cannot say that the Greeks interpreted death in its essential meaning." (*LFA*, 522; *VA*, 134)

as if, very crudely expressed, the alternatives come down to: inscrutable and mysterious "outer" (e.g., Egyptian art); inner fully expressed in and at home in the natural outer (classical sculpture); or the inner struggling to find expression in the outer but never doing so (romantic art). Given this sense of the alternatives, Hegel starts suggesting that a reconciliation of inner and outer can properly occur only in the religious community and finally in philosophical self-knowledge.[42] The only forms of art he allows as "postromantic" are greatly diminished in ambition and importance – a new form of modern comedy, "objective humor,"[43] with a sacralized *Humanus* at its center.

But the broad categories that emerge from Hegel's developmental account seem uniquely suited to a form of art after the beautiful and freed from the romantic polarity of inner purity and the "vulgarity" of merely contingent external barriers to the realization of the inner.[44] In other contexts, such as modern ethical life, or religion, Hegel certainly accepts that highly developed, reflective forms of mindedness can come to be embodied in habits and ongoing daily practices that seem to be counterparts to the sensible, material embodiments required by art. At least, there is nothing in his systematic project to lead one to expect that *alone* among all the projects of human spirit, indeed uniquely among

---

[42] Cf. *E*, §563: "Beautiful art, like the religion peculiar to it, has its future in true religion."

[43] Hegel was quite fond of Laurence Sterne, and quite peeved about romantic or "subjective" irony. But his model for objective humor is very strange, Goethe's *West-östlichen Divan*. Henrich's attempt to make some sense out of this choice is heroic. (2003a):

[44] First, it is thus true that on the surface Hegel seems to take the "inevitability of the collapse of classical standards of beauty within art" as "evidence that art must be superseded by philosophy." See Guyer, "Freedom of Imagination: From Beauty to Expression," in *International Yearbook of German Idealism*, IV (2006), p. 324; but that is too rapid a leap, not just for a commentator, but, so it would seem at least, for Hegel. The moments of romantic inwardness generate the same sort of unworldliness in the philosophy of objective spirit, but reconciliation and reintegration occur there in *Sittlichkeit*, not in a leap to religion or philosophy. Second, the existence of romantic art for two thousand years certainly demonstrates that there can be "nonbeautiful" forms of art, so the exclusive disjunction on the basis of which the claim just quoted depends cannot be right. And finally, since what is at stake in all art concerns sensible manifestations and understandings of freedom, and since Hegel's theory is a nonalienation theory of freedom with a subjective and objective side, a theory in which inner must become outer just in order to be determinately inner, I think we have to say that Hegel's failure to imagine a postromantic form of art (an outer form for a postromantic understanding of freedom) is just that, a failure of imagination, not a systematic or necessary exclusion. See Henrich, "Zerfall und Zukunft" p. 100, and §8, "Synthesis statt Zerfall," pp. 100–106.

the manifestations of Absolute Spirit, the production of art should suffer such a loss of vitality and significance, rather than find a mode of embodiment appropriate to Hegel's theory of the modern world.

Unfortunately, to imagine what Hegel did not seem able to imagine would require a great deal more detail about his theory of Western modernization, and – even more difficult – some comprehensive view of visual, musical, and literary modernism. There is little consensus about either issue, but I would hope the trajectory of Hegel's account is at least suggestive. It is possible, for example, to see the modernist novels of James, Proust, Joyce, Woolf, Musil et al. as presenting a historically distinct representation of human subjectivity, in unprecedented relations of social dependence and independence not capturable by even the greatest "realist" novels and so requiring a distinct aesthetic form, with shifting, unstable and highly provisional points of view and constant experimentation with authorial authority and narrative coherence. Both such an *"Idee"* in Hegel's sense and its sensible form, its *"Schein,"* seem to me consistent with and indeed a kind of implication of Hegel's historical account, especially of social subjectivity. Both embody as art what Hegel's modern "ideal," a free life, requires and implies.[45]

It is also possible to imagine a modern form of *Kunstbetrachtung* unconcerned with mere distinctions in taste and committed instead to an always historically inflected interpretation, and so to "depth" of interpretation as a value, and a theory of aesthetic appreciation oriented not from beauty and pleasure[46] but from the question of the concrete meaning of freedom under conditions different from those imagined by Hegel. I am not much of a fan of Adorno on modern music, but I can see and sympathize with what he is trying to do; likewise Beckett and Benjamin on Proust, Greenberg on abstraction, Clark on Manet, Fried on Courbet, or Manet on Menzel can all be counted as "Hegelian" interpretations of modernist moments.

What exactly it would be to be moved and gripped by such a compelling postromantic art in conditions of nearly hyperreflexivity and self-consciousness is another question. And it is a very difficult one. Hegel apparently believed something analogous to what Bernard Williams meant when he claimed that "reflection kills ethical knowledge"; in this case that a culture of reflection makes the near-immediacy

---

[45] For a defense of this claim, see R. Pippin, *Henry James and Modern Moral Life* (Cambridge, UK: Cambridge University Press, 2000) and "On Becoming Who One is (and Failing): Proust's Problematic Selves," in *The Persistence of Subjectivity: On the Kantian Aftermath* (Cambridge, UK: Cambridge University Press, 2005).

[46] These are Kantian terms but I do not mean to imply that there is not a great deal of Hegel's theory already in Kant, as with the issue of *Belebung*. See §49 in the *KU*.

of (and so a kind of honesty in) aesthetic encounters hard to imagine. This is not a situation at all improved by the liberation of art from its role in politics or religion. Ironically the autonomy of art in modernity makes this problem worse, not better. Greek architecture and church music can be said to be interwoven into the fabric of daily life in a way that allowed for a more directly sensible, that is genuinely aesthetic, encounter. Now art is experienced as "*art*," a categorization that creates so many more complex expectations and prohibitions that any direct sensible presence of the work is hard to imagine.[47] It is possible to see such radical moves as Impressionism all the way to Pollock's drip paintings, Caro's abstract steel sculptures, Stella's experiments with eccentric polygons and shaped canvases and the like as attempts to break through such reflected mediation and re-establish art as sensuous, medium-specific, credible, and "present" under these altered conditions.[48]

In fact, an art work false to these conditions, one that appears as the simple translation of an idea or plan into an external object, or one that addresses what is clearly assumed to be a fixed social convention, one that denies the provisionality and tenuousness of any claim to authority or even meaning, is an art object that fails in the attempt to be art, is kitsch or a consumer item or propaganda or didactic or – worst of all (and most prevalent) – *an example of a theory*. Worst of all because such objects are *false*, playing the role of art rather than being art (exactly what Hegel was worried about), and so the new aesthetic standard in postromantic art built on such Hegelian grounds is genuineness, the capacity to compel conviction at all under these conditions, to invite interpretation and reflection in the right way. Likewise, one might say that under such conditions an *agent* could be said to act falsely, violating the norms of agency even while relying on them, pretending to a false independence, or subjecting himself to a excessive dependence on social standards.[49] (Failing such a test in art leaves us with mere "objecthood,"

---

[47] This is captured well in Thomas Struth's museum photographs, which render the problem sensible and aesthetic, even while attending to the absence of an aesthetic sensibility in the photograph's beholders.

[48] Again, admittedly, all of this means drawing inferences from Hegel's lectures that are different from the ones he apparently drew. But Hegel himself provides the material for such inferences. I have tried to flesh out such a claim with respect to one form of modernism, abstraction, in R. Pippin, "What was Abstract Art? (From the Point of View of Hegel)," *Critical Inquiry*, XXIX (2002).

[49] I discuss this issue at greater length in "Authenticity in Painting: Remarks on Michael Fried's Art History," in *Critical Inquiry*, XXXI (2005).

an exemplary failure when embraced as such and as art, as in literalism, minimalism, and so forth.)[50]

It would take a great deal of work to get us from these very vague speculations to the claim that all these comprise the postromantic artistic self-understanding and even implied "world view" of Wagner or Cézanne or Beckett or Proust or Miró, let alone all of them. I have only wanted to suggest why Hegel does not regard the beautiful as a credible aesthetic ideal any longer, why he transforms the problem of aesthetic judgment and why, in good Hegelian fashion, these absences can suggest something about a positive notion of a reflexive and experimental art after both the beautiful and romantic inwardness.

[50] The debt here to Michael Fried's *Art and Objecthood* is, I will assume, obvious here, in the discussion throughout this chapter. See M. Fried, *Art and Objecthood*, pp. 148–172.

Bibliography

LOGIC

Bencivenga, Ermanno. *Hegel's Dialectical Logic*. New York: Oxford University Press, 2000.

Burbidge, John. *The Logic of Hegel's Logic: An Introduction*. Peterborough, Ontario: Broadview Press, 2006.

Butler, Clark. *Hegel's Logic: Between Dialectic and History*. Evanston, IL: Northwestern University Press, 1996.

Carlson, David. *A Commentary to Hegel's Science of Logic*. New York: Palgrave Macmillan, 2007.

Cirulli, Franco. *Hegel's Critique of Essence: A Reading of the Wesenslogik*. New York: Routledge, 2006.

Grier, Phillip. *Identity and Difference: Studies in Hegel's Logic, Philosophy of Spirit and Politics*. Albany: SUNY Press, 2007.

Hartnack, Justus. *An Introduction to Hegel's Logic*. Indianapolis: Hackett, 1998.

Hoffmeyer, John. *The Advent of Freedom: The Presence of the Future in Hegel's Logic*. Rutherford, NJ: Fairleigh Dickinson Univerity Press, 1994.

Houlgate, Stephen. *The Opening of Hegel's Logic: From Being to Infinity*. West Lafayette, IN: Purdue University Press, 2006.

Rinaldi, Giacomo. *A History and Interpretation of the Logic of Hegel*. Lewiston, NJ: E. Mellen Press, 1992.

PHENOMENOLOGY OF SPIRIT

Browning, Gary. *Hegel's* Phenomenology of Spirit: *A Re-Appraisal*. Dordrecht, The Netherlands: Kluwer, 1997.

Denker, Alfred, and Vater, Michael, eds. *Hegel's* Phenomenology of Spirit: *New Critical Essays*. Amherst, NY: Humanity Books, 2003.

Forster, Michael. *Hegel's Idea of a Phenomenology of Spirit*. Chicago: University of Chicago Press, 1998.

Harris, H. S. *Hegel's Ladder*. 2 vols. Indianapolis: Hackett, 1997.

———. *Hegel: Phenomenology and System*. Indianapolis: Hackett, 1995.

Kalkavage, Peter. *The Logic of Desire: An Introduction to Hegel's Phenomenology of Spirit*. Philadelphia: Paul Dry Books, 2007.

Lauer, Quentin. *A Reading of Hegel's* Phenomenology of Spirit. 2nd ed. New York: Fordham, University Press, 1993.

Pinkard, Terry. *Hegel's Phenomenology: The Sociality of Reason*. Cambridge, UK: Cambridge University Press, 1994.

Rockmore, Tom. *Cognition: An Introdution to Hegel's* Phenomenology of Spirit. Berkeley: University of California Press, 1997.

Russon, John. *The Self and its Body in Hegel's* Phenomenology of Spirit. Toronto: University of Toronto Press, 1997.

———. *Reading Hegel's Phenomenology*. Bloomington, IN: Indiana University Press, 2004.

Simpson, Peter. *Hegel's Transcendental Induction*. Albany: SUNY Press, 1998.

Stewart, Jon. *The Unity of Hegel's* Phenomenology of Spirit. Evanston, IL: Northwestern University Press, 2000.

———. ed. *The Phenomenology of Spirit Reader*. Albany: SUNY Press, 1998.

Stern, Robert. *Hegel and the* Phenomenology of Spirit. London: Routledge, 2002.

Verene, Donald. *Hegel's Absolute: An Introduction to the Reading of the* Phenomenology of Spirit. Albany: SUNY Press, 2007.

Westphal, Kenneth. *Hegel's Epistemology: A Philosophical Introduction to the* Phenomenology of Spirit. Indianapolis: Hackett, 2003.

SOCIAL AND POLITICAL PHILOSOPHY

Brod, Harry. *Hegel's Philosophy of Politics*. Boulder, CO: Westview Press, 1992.

Brooks, Thom. *Hegel's Political Philosophy: A Systematic Reading of the* Philosophy of Right. Edinburgh: Edinburgh University Press, 2007.

Browning, Gary. *Hegel and the History of Political Philosophy*. New York: St. Martin's Press, 1999.

Burns, Tony. *Natural Law and Political Ideology in the Philosophy of Hegel*. Brookfield VT: Avebury, 1996.

Collins, Ardis, ed. *Hegel and the Modern World*. Albany: SUNY Press, 1995.

Cornell, Drucilla, and Rosenfeld, Michel, eds. *Hegel and Legal Theory*. London: Routledge, 1991.

Cristi, Renato. *Hegel on Freedom and Authority*. Cardiff: University of Wales Press, 2005.

Dallmayr, Fred. *Hegel: Modernity and Politics*. Newbury Park, CA: Sage Publications, 1993.

Franco, Paul. *Hegel's Philosophy of Freedom*. New Haven, CT: Yale University Press, 1999.

Gauthier, Jeffrey. *Hegel and Feminist Social Criticism*. Albany: SUNY Press, 1997.

Geiger, Ido. *The Founding Act of Ethical Life: Hegel's Critique of Kant's Moral and Political Philosophy*. Palo Alto, CA: Stanford University Press, 2007.

Goldstein, Joshua. *Hegel's Idea of the Good Life*. Dordrecht: Springer, 2005.

Hardimon, Michael. *Hegel's Social Philosophy: The Project of Reconciliation*. Cambridge, UK: Cambridge University Press, 1994.

Hoffheimer, Michael. *Edward Gans and the Hegelian Philosophy of Law*. Dordrecht, The Netherlands: Kluwer, 1995.

Hutchings, Kimberly. *Hegel and Feminist Philosophy*. Malden, MA: Blackwell, 2003.

James, David. *Hegel's Philosophy of Right: Subjectivity and Ethical Life*. London: Continuum, 2007.

Knowles, Dudley. *Hegel and the Philosophy of Right*. London: Routledge, 2002.

Lasurdo, Domenico. *Hegel and the Freedom of Moderns.* Durham, NC: Duke University Press, 2004.

Lewis, Thomas. *Freedom and Tradition in Hegel.* Notre Dame, IN: University of Notre Dame Press, 2005.

Mills, Patricia. *Feminist Interpretations of G. W. F. Hegel.* University Park, PA: Penn State Press, 1996.

Neuhouser, Frederick. *Foundations of Hegel's Social Theory.* Cambridge, MA: Harvard University Press, 2000.

Patten, Alan, *Hegel's Idea of Freedom.* Oxford: Oxford University Press, 1999.

Peperzak, Adriann. *Modern Freedom: Hegel's Legal, Moral and Political Philosophy.* Dordrecht, The Netherlands: Kluwer, 2001.

Pippin, Robert. *Hegel on Ethics and Politics.* Cambridge, UK: Cambridge University Press, 2004.

Quante, Michael. *Hegel's Concept of Action.* Cambridge, UK: Cambridge University Press, 2004.

Redding, Paul. *Hegel's Hermeneutics.* Ithaca, NY: Cornell University Press, 1996.

Rose, David. *Hegel's Philosophy of Right: A Reader's Guide.* London: Continuum, 2007.

Salter, Michael. *Hegel and Law.* Burlington, VT: Ashgate, 2003.

Shanks, Andrew. *Hegel's Political Theology.* Cambridge, UK: Cambridge University Press, 1991.

Tunick, Mark. *Hegel's Political Philosophy.* Princeton: Princeton University Press, 1992.

Weil, Eric. *Hegel and the State.* Translated by Mark Cohen. Baltimore: Johns Hopkins Press, 1998.

Williams Robert. *Recognition: Fichte and Hegel on the Other.* Albany: SUN, 1992.

——. *Hegel's Ethics of Recognition.* Berkeley: University of California Press, 1997.

——. ed. *Beyond Liberalism and Communitarianism.* Albany: SUNY Press, 2001.

PHILOSOPHY OF HISTORY

Gallagher, Shaun. *Hegel, History and Interpretation.* Albany: SUNY Press, 1997.

Hyppolite, Jean. *Introduction to Hegel's* Philosophy of History. Gainsville: University of Florida Press, 1996.

MacCarney, Joe. *Hegel on History.* London: Routledge, 2000.

Walker, John. *History, Spirit and Experience: Hegel's Conception of the Historical Task of Philosophy in His Age.* Frankfurt: Lang, 1995.

PHILOSOPHY OF NATURE

Houlgate, Stephen, ed. *Hegel and the* Philosophy of Nature. Albany: SUNY Press, 1998.

Petry, Michael. *Hegel and Newtonianism.* Dordrecht, The Netherlands: Kluwer, 1993.

Stone, Allison. *Petrified Intelligence: Nature in Hegel's Philosophy.* Albany: SUNY Press, 2005.

AESTHETICS

Bates, Jennifer. *Hegel's Theory of the Imagination*. Albany: SUNY Press, 2004.

Houlgate, Stephen, ed. *Hegel and the Arts*. Evanston, IL: Northwestern University Press, 2007.

Maker, William, ed. *Hegel and Aesthetics*. Albany; SUNY Press, 2000.

Speight, Allen. *Hegel, Literature and the Problem of Agency*. Cambridge, UK: Cambridge University Press, 2001.

PSYCHOLOGY

Berthold-Bond, Daniel. *Hegel's Theory of Madness*. Albany: SUNY Press, 1995.

Carlson, David. *Hegel's Theory of the Subject*. New York: Palgrave Macmillan, 2005.

Forbes, Kipling. *Hegel on Want and Desire*. Wakrfield, NH: Longwood Academic, 1991.

Murray, Patrick. *Hegel's Philosophy of Mind and Will*. Lewiston, NY: E. Mellin Press, 1991.

Olson, Alan. *Hegel and the Spirit*. Princeton: Princeton University Press, 1992.

RELIGION

Burbidge, John. *Hegel on Logic and Religion*. Albany: SUNY Press, 1992.

Calton, Patricia Marie *Hegel's Metaphysics of God*. Burlington, VT: Ashgate, 2001.

Crites, Stephen. *Dialectic and Gospel in the Development of Hegel's Thinking*. University Park, PA: The Pennsylvania State University Press, 1998.

Desmond, William. *Hegel's God: A Counterfeit Double?* Burlington, VT: Ashgate, 2003.

Hodgson, Peter C. *Hegel and Chirstian Theology: A Reading of the Lectures on the Philosophy of Religion*. Oxford: Oxford University Press, 2005.

Jaeschke, Walter. *Reason in Religion: The Foundation of Hegel's Philosophy of Religion*. Berkeley: University of California Press, 1998.

Kolb, David, ed. *New Perspectives on Hegel's Philosophy of Religion*. Albany: SUNY Press, 1992.

Magee, Glenn. *Hegel and the Hermetic Tradition*. Ithaca, NY: Cornell University Press, 2001.

Merklinger, Philip. *Philosophy, Theology and Hegel's Berlin Philosophy of Religion, 1821–1829*. Albany: SUNY Press, 1993.

O'Regan, Cyril. *The Heterodox Hegel*. Albany: SUNY Press, 1994.

Walker, John, ed. *Thought and Faith in the Philosophy of Hegel*. Dordrecht, The Netherlands: Kluwer, 1991.

Index

Absolute, 60, 265, 266, 272, 273
Aesthetics: end of art, 379–81; Hegel's lectures on, 381, 384, 392; and post-romantic art, 389–90; and romantic art, 379, 392, 395, 399, 407; systematic place of, 379–81
Ameriks, Karl, 135, 136, 140, 149, 150
Analytic philosophy, 1, 3
Aristotle, 314, 315, 316, 328, 332, 364, 365–6
Art autonomy of, 380, 395–6, 410; content of, 397; and drama, 389; forms of, 382, 386; pastness of, 391–393; romantic concept of, 379, 392, 395, 399, 407

Baader, Franz von, 262, 263
Beiser, Frederick, 62–63
Being, 95–97, 128–9
Boehme, Jakob, 253, 254, 257–8, 261, 264, 274
Brandom, Robert, 4
Buchdahl, Gerd, 286
Bungay, Stephen, 199, 200
Burbidge, John, 111

Cartesianism, 97, 99, 141, 290
Categories, 112–14, 119. See also logic
Christianity, 235, 244–5, 246–8, 249–51
Concept, 99, 123, 138, 220–1, 307, 362–4,
Cousin, Victor, 43–44, 45

Descartes, René, 96, 285, 286. See also Cartesianism
Desire, 97, 99–104
Dewey, John, 74
D'Hondt, Jacques, 13
Dialectic, 106–8, 129–30

Diez, Carl Immanuel, 20–1
Dilthey, Wilhelm, 174–5, 177, 180, 200, 253

Eckhart, Meister, 262, 266, 272, 278
Evil, 248–9
Engelhardt, Dietrich, 12

Falkenberg, Brigitte, 12
Fichte, Johann Gottlieb: on derivation of categories, 116–117; on desire, 97–98; on ego, 98, 116; foundationalism of, 10; idealism of, 99, 116; influence on Hegel, 26, 96, 97, 102, 104; alleged nihilism of, 63–64, 66, 70, 72; on practical reason, 98; on recognition, 104; his 1794 *Wissenschaftslehre*, 67, 69, 70, 102
Freedom: concepts of, 205–212; duality of, 212–214; and moral reflection, 226–9; objective nature of, 219–226; role in Hegel's philosophy, 205; subjective nature of, 214–219
Forster, Michael, 54–55, 57
Foundationalism, 11, 56
Freedom: concepts of, 205–212; duality of, 212–214; and moral reflection, 226–9; objective nature of, 219–226; role in Hegel's philosophy, 205; subjective nature of, 214–219
Fogelin, Robert, 59
Fries, Jakob, Friedrich, 39, 41, 57, 262

Gadmaer, Hans-Georg, 111, 174, 175, 177–8, 180, 190–1, 193, 194
Galileo, Galilei, 285, 286, 326, 327
Gans, Eduard, 44–45
God, 5, 145, 232–5, 237–42, 260, 266–7, 322

Gravitation, 293–4, 326, 331, 333–4, 339, 340

Haering, Theodor, 81, 82
Haym, Rudolf, 81, 82
Harris, Henry, 109, 258, 270, 309
Hartmann, Klaus, 4
Heidegger, Martin, 109, 126
Hegel, Georg, Wilhelm Friedrich: family background, 16–17; in Bamberg, 30–31; in Berlin, 38–51; Berne, 22–25, 255; in Frankfurt, 25–27; in Jena, 27–29; influence of Lessing upon, 18; influence of Kant upon, 23, 31, 115–117, 317–319, 330, 337–8; influence of mysticism upon, 254–64; marriage of, 34–35; and mathematics, 284; in Nuremberg, 31–36; illegitimate son of, 29, 36, 39; university years of, 19–22, 255; and Württemberg, 15–16, 32
Henrich, Dieter, 10, 111, 385
Herder, Johann Gottfried, 190, 200, 255
Hermeneutics, Hegelian: definition of, 135–6; influence of, 174–6; and language, 177, 181–6, 194–203; and meaning, 176, 186–94; relation to pre-Hegelian, 176–181
Hobbes, Thomas, 359
Holism, 152, 155–6, 234
Hölderlin, Friedrich, 19, 21, 24, 26, 48, 50, 51
Humboldt, Wilhelm von, 186
Hyppolite, Jean, 111, 119

Idealism, Hegelian: as anti-realism, 146–9; definition of, 135–6; Kantian interpretation of, 136–146; as mentalism, 146–9; metaphysics of, 150–161; non-metaphysical interpretation of, 135–146; as conceptual realism, 161–173
Idea, 131–133, 169–173. See also concept

Jacobi, Friedrich Heinrich, 21, 56, 64–69, 70, 162
Jaeschke, Walter, 231, 243

Kant, Immanuel: on Antinomies, 79–80; on appearances, 95; on categories, 115–116; critique of metaphysics, 137,

345, 347–353; his idealism, 136–42, 168; influence on Hegel, 23, 31, 115–117; on method, 55; on nature, 317–319, 330, 337–8; on systematicity, 76–77; on teleology, 304, 345, 347–53
Karlsbad Decrees, 39–40
Kimmerle, Heinz, 12
Konstellationsforschung, 10
Kojève, Alexandre, 75, 109

Logic: and categories, 112–114; and metaphysics, 117–124; method of, 124–8; and phenomenology, 122–3. See also *Science of Logic*

Matter, 317, 319, 320–1, 322–3, 324–5, 329, 330, 334, 336, 341–2
Marx, Karl, 1, 50, 109, 407
MacTaggart, John, 374, 375
Mechanics, 312, 313, 314, 315, 331
Mechanism, 67, 134, 366–9
Metaphysics, 3, 5, 117–124, 136–46, 336, 342
Monism, 65–69
Mysticism: and *coincidentia oppositorum*, 272–3, 277; and hermeticism, 277–80; influence on Hegel, 254–64; and content of Hegel's philosophy, 264–72

Naturalism, 52, 55, 58
Naturphilosophie: and non-metaphysical interpretation of Hegel, 5; its metaphysics, 336, 342; as part of Hegel's systen, 2, 5, 6, 313–314; its rejection of distinction between pure and empirical knowledge, 296, 313; its reputation, 281–5, 311; and teleology, 304, 372; *terra incognita* of Hegel's studies, 11–12
Naturrecht, 13–14
Newton, Issac, 285, 287, 288, 289, 291, 292, 312, 314, 320, 322, 323, 324, 325, 327, 329, 330, 332, 340
Nietzsche, Friedrich, 176
Nihilism, 53, 62–69, 69–73
Notion. See Concept

Oetinger, Friedrich Carl, 254, 256, 273–6

Pantheism, 234

Peperzak, Adriaan, 263
Pfleiderer, Christoph Friedrich von, 293–5
Phenomenology of Spirit: and aesthetics, 400–1; composition of, 29, 41; and 'force and understanding', 189, 291–3; as fragment, 91–93; alleged incoherence of, 74–6, 83–9; and interpretation, 179, 186, 187, 188, 189; role of recognition in, 109–110; publication of, 84; religion chapter of, 91–2, 178–9, 181, 265; and *Science of Logic*, 122–3, 125; and skepticism, 58, 144; systematic structure of, 74–76, 83–89; title problem of, 82
Philosophy of Nature. See *Naturphilosophie*
Philosophy of Right: major divisions of, 205; on ethical life, 210–212; and natural law, 13; reputation of, 41–42; popularity of, 1–2; on abstract right, 205–210. See also freedom, *Naturrecht*
Pinkard, Terry, 117, 124
Pippin, Robert, 4, 117–8, 124, 130, 136–42, 386
Pöggler, Otto, 83
Positivism, 1, 3, 11

Reid, Thomas, 54
Reinhold, Karl Leonhard, 10
Reason, 58, 88
Religion: definitions of, 235–7; lectures on, 230–2; method of, 232–5;
positivity of, 24, 182; philosophy of, 232–7. See also God, Christianity, Spirit
Rosenkranz, Karl, 255, 260
Rosenzweig, Franz, 13
Russell, Bertrand, 253

Savigny, Friedrich Carl, 13, 57
Schiller, Friedrich, 404
Schelling, Friedrich Wilhelm Joseph, 10, 11, 19, 24, 26, 39, 50, 51, 69, 77, 272, 274, 277, 305
Schleiermacher, Friedrich, 40, 42, 176, 230, 232, 236
Schulze, Gottlob Ernst, 53–58
Science of Logic: on life, 355–8, 370; on meaning, 300; its method, 124–128; relation to philosophy of nautre, 297; its reputation, 111. See also logic
Self-awareness, 97–98, 107, 175
Skepticism: Agrippan, 59, 62, 64, 69; ancient, 52, 58–62; modern, 53–58; 53–62 ; Platonic, 59, 61–62; and Pyrrhonian, 60
Spinoza, Baruch de, 21, 53, 65, 66–69, 277, 374
Spirit, 148, 274, 380, 384, 409, 413, 416
Swedenborg, Emanuel, 256

Taylor, Charles, 2–3
Thibaut, Friedrich, 13, 36

Voegelin, Eric, 279
Vondung, Klaus, 273

OTHER BOOKS IN THE SERIES (*continued from page iii*)

HEGEL   *Edited by* FREDERICK BEISER
HEIDEGGER 2nd edition   *Edited by* CHARLES GUIGNON
HOBBES   *Edited by* TOM SORELL
HOBBES' LEVIATHAN   *Edited by* CYNTHIA SPRINGBORG
HUME, 2nd edition   *Edited by* DAVID FATE NORTON *and*
   JACQUELINE TAYLOR
HUSSERL   *Edited by* BARRY SMITH *and* DAVID WOODRUFF
   SMITH
WILLIAM JAMES   *Edited by* RUTH ANNA PUTNAM
KANT   *Edited by* PAUL GUYER
KANT AND MODERN PHILOSOPHY   *Edited by* PAUL
   GUYER
KEYNES   ROGER E. BACKHOUSE *and* BRADLEY W. BATEMAN
KIERKEGAARD   *Edited by* ALASTAIR HANNAY *and* GORDON
   DANIEL MARINO
LEIBNIZ   *Edited by* NICHOLAS JOLLEY
LEVINAS   *Edited by* SIMON CRITCHLEY *and* ROBERT
   BERNASCONI
LOCKE   *Edited by* VERE CHAPPELL
LOCKE'S 'ESSAY CONCERNING HUMAN
   UNDERSTANDING'   *Edited by* LEX NEWMAN
LOGICAL EMPIRICISM   *Edited by* ALAN RICHARDSON *and*
   THOMAS UEBEL
MAIMONIDES   *Edited by* KENNETH SEESKIN
MALEBRANCHE   *Edited by* STEVEN NADLER
MARX   *Edited by* TERRELL CARVER
MEDIEVAL JEWISH PHILOSOPHY   *Edited by* DANIEL H.
   FRANK *and* OLIVER LEAMAN
MEDIEVAL PHILOSOPHY   *Edited by* A. S. MCGRADE
MERLEAU-PONTY   *Edited by* TAYLOR CARMAN *and* MARK B.
   N. HANSEN
MILL   *Edited by* JOHN SKORUPSKI
MONTAIGNE   *Edited by* ULLRICH LANGER
NEWTON   *Edited by* I. BERNARD COHEN *and* GEORGE E.
   SMITH
NIETZSCHE   *Edited by* BERND MAGNUS *and* KATHLEEN
   HIGGINS
OCKHAM   *Edited by* PAUL VINCENT SPADE
PASCAL   *Edited by* NICHOLAS HAMMOND
PEIRCE   *Edited by* CHERYL MISAK

PHILOSOPHY OF BIOLOGY   *Edited by* DAVID L. HULL *and*
  MICHAEL RUSE
PLATO   *Edited by* RICHARD KRAUT
PLATO'S REPUBLIC   *Edited by* G. R. F. FERRARI
PLOTINUS   *Edited by* LLOYD P. GERSON
QUINE   *Edited by* ROGER F. GIBSON JR.
RAWLS   *Edited by* SAMUEL FREEMAN
THOMAS REID   *Edited by* TERENCE CUNEO *and* RENÉ
  VAN WOUDENBERG
RENAISSANCE PHILOSOPHY   *Edited by* JAMES HANKINS
ROUSSEAU   *Edited by* PATRICK RILEY
BERTRAND RUSSELL   *Edited by* NICHOLAS GRIFFIN
SARTRE   *Edited by* CHRISTINA HOWELLS
SCHOPENHAUER   *Edited by* CHRISTOPHER JANAWAY
THE SCOTTISH ENLIGHTENMENT   *Edited by* ALEXANDER
  BROADIE
ADAM SMITH   *Edited by* KNUD HAAKONSSEN
SPINOZA   *Edited by* DON GARRETT
THE STOICS   *Edited by* BRAD INWOOD
TOCQUEVILLE   *Edited by* CHERYL B. WELCH
WITTGENSTEIN   *Edited by* HANS SLUGA *and* DAVID STERN